F

Constitutional Government in America

Constitutional Government in America

Essays and Proceedings from Southwestern
University Law Review's First West Coast
Conference on Constitutional Law

edited by

RONALD K. L. COLLINS

Carolina Academic Press / Durham, North Carolina

Carolina Academic Press
P.O. Box 8795, Forest Hills Station
Durham, North Carolina 27707

To
Robert Maynard Hutchins
philosopher, educator, humanitarian
and friend of the Constitution

Contents

Acknowledgements

On September 17, 1977 there convened in Los Angeles, California perhaps the most notable assemblage of American constitutionalists ever united under one roof. Some fifty-seven participants from across the Nation filed into the respective lecture halls to present their views to room capacity audiences. When the Conference had finally concluded, it was the general consensus of all present that this had been a memorable and inspiring constitutional celebration.

The success of the Conference was the product of the combined efforts of many people, both living and dead, who devoted over one year of their labor to its actualization. Among those whose contributions merit special mention are:

Robert Maynard Hutchins' obliging assistance brought to fruition an intellectual harvest that nourished all. Dr. Hutchins was slated to give the Keynote Address at the Conference as he had early along pledged, "if I can." To those of us who knew him, his meaning was clear. On May 14, 1977, Dr. Hutchins died, thereby entrusting to us one of his final contributions to the Republic. To the memory of Dr. Hutchins this book is respectfully dedicated.

Thomas F. Hanley III served as Conference Director and without him neither the event nor this book would have been possible. Mr. Hanley is one of those indispensable parties who brought to these projects just that measure of effort and foresight that assured success.

Paul W. Wildman, President of Southwestern University, dared to devote his insight, time and resources to a project from which less courageous men shunned away. As President Wildman's record reveals, his prudence and prevision once again brought honor upon his efforts.

Paul W. Grace and Aaron L. Patton gave generously and thoughtfully of their time and were always there to fill in any of the gaps.

Cathy Kuslo and Kathy Thompson typed almost endless stacks of manuscripts, letters, notices and memoranda without either fail or complaint. Special thanks go out to these fine and able women for services rendered above and well beyond the call of their duties.

"Buster" Sussman on several occasions not only cleared the way but also "covered" it as only an experienced journalist could.

Cathy D. Younger and Robert G. Unger helped in the initial planning of the Conference three years ago.

The Editors and Staff of the *Southwestern University Law Review* (1976-77, 1977-78) donated countless hours in addition to their assigned duties.

The Administration, Faculty, Staff—including the telephone operators—and Student Body of Southwestern University all supported the "Main Currents in Constitutional Law" program both energetically and selflessly.

The Family and Friends of the editor gave of themselves in a manner that can only command his most sincere appreciation.

Finally, the name of the late Judge J. Braxton Craven, Jr. of the United States Court of Appeals for the Fourth Circuit is entered into this record with the deepest of regrets that he was unable to participate in the event that he in no small way made possible.

RKLC

Introduction

This book is the outcome of a 1977 Conference sponsored by Southwestern University[1] commemorating the one-hundred-and-ninetieth anniversary of the Federal Constitution. The papers and proceedings presented here are a record of the opinions, insights, differences and hopes of the Conference participants. As such, these contributions represent something of a constitutional almanac of many of the pressing legal issues of the time, how the contributors viewed those issues, and how they addressed them with an eye to the past, present and future. Like the Constitution itself, the breadth of these issues is vast, though not so vast as to be beyond the principled and working guidelines and limitations set forth in the great Charter. What follows is an account, by many of the most influential students of the Constitution, of the varied aspects of constitutional government in America[2] circa 1977.

A note on how to read this book: It will prove helpful to anyone reading what follows to bear in mind the particular objective of each contributor. In other words, the objective of the authors of the extended essays presented herein is not the same as that of the contributors who presented their views in more colloquial or capsulized form. This book is the product of many diverse efforts. If in reading the respective articles the reader approaches each contribution on its own terms, then, one is sure to find this collection of essays more rewarding and less disappointing than other *festschrift*-type writings.

Any undertaking of this kind is not without its shortcomings. This book is no exception. It is not unfair to ask, for example, if so many issues were addressed, how is it that some important ones were left out?[3] Unfortunately, it was impossible at the time that this enterprise was organized and with the practical limitations imposed upon it to *then* discover both the person and article needed to fill in the few gaps.

Furthermore, it may be asked that if the contents of this volume were prepared in 1977, how is it that they can remain topical (or even valid) in 1979? While it is partially true that new constitutional developments render the study of the subject matter somewhat akin to the study of Heraclitus' sun, the problem is not insurmountable. Precautions have been taken. For the most part, this problem was addressed by the efforts of the respective contributors who were asked to speak to those central principles pertinent to their subject. Thus, for example, while the articles in Part VII were authored prior to the Supreme Court's decision in *University of California Regents v. Bakke,*[4] nevertheless, the discussion of the core constitutional principles remains germane to the fundamental issues. Where, by comparison, new developments have so *substantially* altered the analysis of a particular issue, appropriate revisions and additions have been made.[5] This book does not purport to be as current as the latest supplements to the major constitutional law treatises[6] or hornbooks.[7] Rather, as stated previously, it offers the reader an opportunity to view the world of American constitutionalism through the various lenses of some of the most eminent constitutional personages—a view, that is, of that world on the occasion of the one-hundred-and-ninetieth anniversary of the Federal Constitution.

People of heterogeneous backgrounds have contributed a variety of articles to this book. Included among the contributions of the law professor are those of the historian, political scientist, journalist, lawgiver and judge. Included also are the contributions of the constitutional litigator, offering what one contributor called a view from "the trenches." This assortment of articles is intended to expose the reader to a diverse collection of viewpoints too seldom found in constitutional law literature—it presents, in part, what might be called a view from the "other side."[8]

This book is unorthodox in yet other respects. Contrary to the increasingly acceptable practice, this volume's contents are the sole product of each contributor. That is, there have been no substantial "rewrites" by some editor. Each contribution is exactly what is purports to be: reflections on a given subject *by* the person credited.

One final caveat: Several of the contributions that follow were slightly edited transcriptions of speeches delivered at the 1977 Conference.[9] As such, they cannot, and do not, claim to be as definitive and polished as a researched and refined manuscript. Yet, in this regard, the reader may find it useful to recall what Socrates said in Plato's *Apology*: "[W]hat you will hear will be spoken at random in the words that I happen upon."[10] Of course, Socrates did likewise admit that he had spent a "whole life in preparing" for what he was to say.[11] Though the analogy is admittedly exaggerated, it does serve to remind us of the particular background and knowledge behind the remarks of the person speaking. This reminder is especially appropriate when reading the exchange in Part XIII between Messrs. Wyzanski, Strong, Commager and Lerner. So as not to leave *any* doubt, the remarks of those four gentlemen were altogether extemporaneous. On the evening of September 17, 1977, and after a long day of speech and debate, Judge Charles Wyzanski kindly agreed to address a select audience of constitutionalists on the topic of judicial review. With equally short notice, Professors Frank Strong, Henry Steele Commager, and Max Lerner agreed to offer their responses to Judge Wyzanski's remarks. Though the rhetorical eloquence of the speakers cannot be captured on the printed page, their thoughts are recorded here for the benefit of all students of American constitutionalism.

*   *   *   *   *

It is fitting in closing this introduction and in commencing this book to reflect upon the words of one of the greatest of American constitutionalists, Abraham Lincoln, who in 1861 declared: "Our popular government has often been called an experiment. Two points in it, our people have already settled—the successful *establishing*, and the successful *administering* of it. One still remains—its successful *maintenance*. . . ."[12] That is the challenge of the future; that is the duty of all our people; and above all, it is with that frame of mind that we must persevere if we are to continue to enjoy the blessings of constitutional government in America.

Ronald K. L. Collins
July 4, 1979

Notes

1. The Southwestern University program, "Main Currents in Constitutional Law," has continued, on a smaller scale, at the Law School on a yearly basis. Thus, under the chairmanship of the editor, the 1978 lecture was delivered by the Honorable A. Leon Higginbotham, Jr., of the United States Court of Appeals for the Third Circuit and was entitled "Race and the Early Constitutional Law." (*See generally* A. L. HIGGINBOTHAM, IN THE MATTER OF COLOR (1978)). The program is scheduled to continue under the direction of the *Southwestern University Law Review* and faculty.

2. This book draws its title from and the introduction accepts as its starting point the definition of constitutional government presented in Woodrow Wilson's *Constitutional Government in the United States* 23-24, 56-57, 192, 195 (1908). An important guiding maxim in this regard is that "[c]onstitutional government— that is, government under law—is possible only in a society capable of tolerance and moderation." Karst, *Probing the {California} High Court: Perilous Illumination,* L. A. Times, Jul. 1, 1979, § 6 (opinion), at 1, col. 4. For two thought-provoking writings on the role of judicial moderation, *see* A. COX, THE ROLE OF THE SUPREME COURT IN AMERICAN GOVERNMENT 99-118 (1976); Schrock & Welsh, *Reconsidering the Constitutional Common Law,* 91 HARV. L. REV. 1117, 1126-45, 1171-76 (1978).

3. Thus for example, it is lamentable, to say the least, that despite repeated efforts it proved impossible to secure an article addressing the topic of the proposed Equal Rights Amendment. Several illuminating discussions of the proposed Twenty-Seventh Amendment to the Constitution are presented in Ginsburg, *Gender in the Supreme Court: The 1973 & 1974 Terms,* 1975 SUP. CT. REV. 1; Elsen, Coogan & Ginsburg, *Men, Women and the Constitution: The Equal Rights Amendment,* 10 COLUM. J. L. & SOC. PROB. 77 (1973); Brown, Emerson, Falk & Freedman, *The Equal Rights Amendment: A Constitutional Basis for Equal Rights for Women,* 80 YALE L. J. 871 (1971); Comment, *The Equal Rights Amendment and Article V: A Framework for Analysis of the Extension and Rescission Issues,* 127 U. PA. L. REV. 494 (1978).

4. 438 U.S. 265 (1978). For some informative post-*Bakke* appraisals of these issues, *see* J. H. WILKINSON, FROM BROWN TO BAKKE: THE SUPREME COURT AND SCHOOL INTEGRATION, 1954-78 (1979); *A Symposium: Regents of the University of California v. Bakke,* 67 CAL. L. REV. 1-263 (1979); Tribe, *Perspectives on Bakke: Equal Protection, Procedural Fairness, or Structural Justice?,* 92 HARV. L. REV. 864 (1979); Dworkin, *The Bakke Decision: Did It Decide Anything?,* 25 N.Y. Rev. of Books 20 (Aug. 17, 1978).

5. By consulting the notes to the various essays the reader can readily detect which ones have been updated.

6. See e.g. L. TRIBE, AMERICAN CONSTITUTIONAL LAW (1978).

7. See e.g. J. NOWAK, R. ROTUNDA & J. YOUNG, CONSTITUTIONAL LAW (1978); see also C. H. PRITCHETT, THE AMERICAN CONSTITUTION (1977).

8. An interesting and worthwhile collection of just such viewpoints on American law in general is presented in AMERICAN LAW: THE THIRD CENTURY (B. Schwartz ed. 1976).

9. The following authors' contributions were slightly edited versions of speeches delivered at the 1977 Conference: Jesse H. Choper, Henry Steele Commager, Nathaniel R. Jones, William Kunstler, Max Lerner (judicial review exchange), John H. F. Shattuck, Frank R. Strong, Alan F. Westin and Chrles E. Wyzanski, Jr.

10. T. WEST, PLATO'S APOLOGY OF SOCRATES 21 (1979) (footnote omitted).

11. 4 XENOPHON, *Socrates' Defense to the Jury* at 643 (O. J. Todd trans. 1923) (Loeb Classical Library edition).

12. 4 THE COLLECTED WORKS OF ABRAHAM LINCOLN 439 (R. Basler ed. 1953) (footnotes omitted & emphasis in original); *see also* H. JAFFA, HOW TO THINK ABOUT THE AMERICAN REVOLUTION 45-48, 75-140 (1978); G. ANASTAPLO, THE CONSTITUTIONALIST 274 (1971); *consider finally* 4 THE COLLECTED WORKS OF ABRAHAM LINCOLN 262-71.

Constitutional Government in America

Toward A Metatheory Of Free Speech

By Laurence H. Tribe*

One of my favorite cartoons shows a tall ship, apparently the Mayflower, with two Pilgrims leaning pensively over the side. They scan the distant horizon, and one says to the other: "Religious freedom is my immediate goal, . . . but my long-range plan is to go into real estate."

I'm fond of the Pilgrim's wisecrack because it so nicely portrays the basic duality of constitutional law and history. After all, our development under the Constitution has been informed by two dramatically different sets of concerns: the first, involving intensely human and humane aspirations of personality, conscience, and freedom; the second, involving vastly more mundane and seemingly mechanical matters like geography, territorial boundaries, and institutional arrangements.

Most theories of constitutional law slight the complex relation between these two strands in our constitutional development. Conventional accounts generally do not adequately trace the complicated course these strands have followed—intertwining, diverging from, and merging with each other in different periods. In my recently published treatise, *American Constitutional Law*,[1] I sought to illuminate this course by describing the permutations it has undergone, and by identifying the seven basic models which I believe have represented the major alternatives for constitutional argument and decision in American law from the early 1800's to the present. These models are: (1) Separated and Divided Powers;[2] (2) Implied Limitations;[3] (3) Settled Expectations;[4] (4) Governmental Regularity;[5] (5) Preferred Rights;[6] (6) Equal Protection;[7] and (7) Structural Justice.[8] Although frequently overlapping, each model tends to dominate an era and then to weaken its grip on constitutional thought.[9]

I do not pretend to have succeeded, through these models, in comprehending the basic duality within constitutional law and history—although I believe they are a start. Perhaps one cannot hope fully to synthesize these strands in our constitutional development without first following each into its myriad filigrees, and only then drawing back to reexamine the whole. At least it seems clear that, when the thread of any given doctrine has been unraveled, it helps to stand aside from the doctrine as history has stitched it together in order to consider what the doctrine *should* look like in a more nearly ideal form.

In particular, it seems worth reconsidering the perennial question of what an American theory of free speech should look like. Rather than add one more theory to the existing collection, I think it would be useful to reflect briefly on what features we should expect of a satisfying theory of free speech, what criteria it should meet—in short, to sketch a metatheory of free speech.

Now, I am aware that this is a bit like trying to describe what a unicorn would have to eat or how its ribcage would have to be put together, if such a thing as a unicorn were to

*Professor of Law, Harvard University. David H. Remes, a third-year student at Harvard Law School, assisted in the preparation of this Article.

1

exist: the task is intriguing, but it is rendered somewhat problematic by the fact that unicorns—like wholly satisfying free speech theories—evidently do not exist. Still, it shouldn't be impossible to speculate on the necessary characteristics of something that many of us are trying in our own varied ways to construct. So I shall attempt here to depict the anatomy of that most elusive of constitutional beasts—a satisfactory free speech theory.

Having set myself this rather abstract task, I must remove myself to a still more distant level of abstraction if I am to describe what a metatheory of free speech should look like—to state, in effect, my *meta*-metatheory for this occasion. In my view, a metatheory in this field—and perhaps in any field of constitutional law—must include elements in at least four dimensions. *First*, it must describe the *premises* on which a free speech theory ought to draw; it must address what sorts of premises are admissible. *Second*, it must take a position on the *structure* a free speech theory ought to possess; it must describe what sort of architecture a free speech theory may employ. *Third*, the metatheory must identify a set of acceptable *methods*; it must express a view on the modes of argument and analysis a free speech theory should be allowed to invoke. And *fourth*, the metatheory must specify some *boundaries* of *content* and *substance*; it must set the perimeters of the thinkable within which any free speech theory must fit. If these four dimensions are somewhat vague, I can only hope they will take on clearer meaning as I attempt to elucidate them one by one in the following pages.

I.

First, the matter of premises. It should be clear that no satisfactory theory of free speech can presuppose or guarantee the permanent existence of any particular social system. For example, a free speech theory must permit evolution from a society built on the ideals of liberal individualism to a society aspiring to more communitarian visions—just as it must permit evolution from communitarianism to individualism.[10] It is of course possible, and indeed it may be common, to disregard the dangers of excessive parochialism and to design theories slanted toward favored conceptions of society; and surely *some* less than universal social vision must underlie *any* theory of law. But any free speech theory too narrowly conceived must either admit of its own self-destruction, as the evolution triggered by speech itself undermines the social forms the theory presupposes; or it must contain boundaries of a highly troublesome sort: boundaries that proscribe as beyond the pale communicative acts that threaten to transform society beyond the limits of its starting premises.[11]

As a corollary of this criterion of breadth, it follows that a theory of free speech should not be too confined by the assumptions of any particular form of economic life. To offer an illustration at the most obvious level, if unfettered competition among commodities does not in fact assure that the "good" products will sell while the "bad" gather dust on the shelves,[12] we may reasonably wonder why "free trade in ideas"[13] should be expected to assure the emergence of truth.[14] But to demand such assurances would itself be too parochial; if free speech has intrinsic value, that value may well be obscured to the vanishing point in the instrumentalist scheme of free speech represented by the "marketplace of ideas" metaphor, and may not be available to justify protecting expression that serves no demonstrable "purpose" analogous to the discovery of "truth." Any theory built exclusively on the assumptions of capitalism—or of any other economic system—must therefore be rejected as too narrow.

It is this circumstance, I think, that makes it so appealing to resist the current broadening of free speech protections to include commercial speech.[15] Some of those who rightly decline to ground free speech theory in the capitalist vision of society are naturally tempted to argue that detergent advertisements or drug price information disseminated for profit are not entitled to first amendment protection.[16] This temptation, however appealing, seems to me fatally flawed. For a limit on the criterion of *breadth* to which a free speech theory must be held is the criterion of *reality*. One who believes that it would be desirable to break down the capitalist structure of profit and exploitation cannot pretend, in the course of constructing a theory of free speech, that the structure has already been broken down. Thus it seems misguided to deny protection to commercial speech in the name of an egalitarian economic vision if the actual effect would be to deprive an exploited class of information needed to resist still further exploitation.[17] However ignoble one may think the profit motive of the penicillin-seller, it would be perverse to subject the impoverished penicillin-buyer to price-gouging in a market that severely limits drug price advertising.[18]

More generally, a theorist who aspires to a less coercive form of social and economic life than ours must avoid the mistake of wishing coercion out of existence in designing a body of first amendment theory. Paradoxically, the voice of the exploiter may have to be heard before the transformation to a less coercive society may occur.

II.

Second, I turn to the question of structure. The parts of a free speech theory must be related to the whole not solely as means are related to ends, but as elements of a composition are related to the total work. Infinite regress can be avoided only if harmony and appositeness, in addition to mere efficacy, provide the organizing principles of the theory's structure. To say that speech is valued because it facilitates self-government,[19] for example, is simply to push the inquiry a step back: why, after all, is self-government to be valued? Instrumental arguments invite such regress and promise to run out of replies before the inquisitive thirst is quenched. Only forthright claims of intrinsic value—claims rooted in an explicit vision of the necessary elements of the good—can avoid the endless chase of means after ends.[20] To posit that expression is an element of the human may be controversial, but this at least moves discussion to the limits of language more directly than is possible with instrumental claims.[21]

A second structural requirement is that the theory be reasonably self-contained. Not only must each substantive component of the theory be intrinsically justified, each intrinsic justification must ultimately apply throughout the theory and must compel respect in every case. Fatal to the coherence and persuasive force of any theory is dependence on a *deus ex machina*: the experience that, when adherents of a theory paint themselves into a corner, windows miraculously appear in the walls permitting their escape. If each substantive component of the theory has its own specially tailored justification, of course, this problem disappears—but only at the cost of reducing the theory to a hodge-podge of *ad hoc* claims, without unity or analytic power.

Credibility also suffers when the same justification (whether instrumental or intrinsic) is advanced for each substantive component of the theory—but with dramatically differing degrees of plausibility. To insist, for example, that speech matters as a means to the end of representative government, and then be forced to justify music and sculpture as only more remote contributions to intelligent political choice,[22] is to deprive the theory's premises of binding force and thereby render its structure essentially boundless. The fact that Gödel showed all finite but nontrivial logical structures to be inherently open-ended[23] need not deter constitutional theorists: they may strive for unity and completeness without having to devise axioms that fit the finite, definitive set philosophers would demand of mathematicians.

Closely related to the requirement that the theory be self-contained is the requirement that it avoid artifice. How the empty speech-conduct distinction[24] could have survived as long as it did in a world without extrasensory communication remains a mystery to me.[25] For that matter, I have yet to reconcile myself to the durability of the Orwellian ploy of reading obscenity out of the sphere of protected expression by simply "defining" it as a form of nonspeech.[26] To a degree, such distinctions may be accidental by-products of the case-by-case development of free speech theory by the Supreme Court over several decades. Nevertheless, to the extent that a theory appears to *require* such phony props, one is entitled to suspect that it lacks a cohesive foundation and an integrated structure.[27]

III.

Third, turning to method, the two basic requirements I would posit are *consistency* and *richness*. Credibility suffers no less when the form of one's argument shifts with the winds of rhetorical convenience than when the propositions of one's theory are guided largely by *ad hoc* justifications. It will not do to patch a theory together from historical arguments when something in the debates of the 1790's serves one's ends, textual arguments when an analysis of plain meaning seems to point in the desired direction, structural arguments when considerations of system design seem just right, and functional arguments when there is a ready link between the desired conclusion and an innocuous premise about underlying purposes. Some hierarchy must be established among forms of constitutional demonstration, and some principles established to govern the choice of forms in identifiable contexts.

Yet if such consistency is purchased at the price of shallowness, the theory that it embodies will be worth little. For example, to say that the common-sense meaning of "abridge" is to govern all disputed issues regarding the alleged abridgment of free speech is to obtain a seeming consistency only by sacrificing vital richness of theory. No simple index of such richness is available, but at least two criteria might reasonably be applied. First, the theory must have ways of connecting historical argument to doctrinal development: methods that do not consider the dialectical interplay between history and vision cannot suffice. And second, the theory must embody ways of linking substantive propositions to structural rules: methods that have little to say about the connection between what the government does and how the government does it fall distinctly short. In particular, any adequate free speech theory must distinguish among the different kinds of "encounters" between government and the speaker for the purpose of identifying the appropriate scope of judicial review in first amendment cases. I would defend the view, for example, that in an "encounter of the first kind," where a government regulation is aimed at the communicative impact of an act, the regulation should be held unconstitutional unless government shows that the message being suppressed would cause imminent harm that further dialogue could not avoid;[28] and that in an "encounter of the second kind," where a government regulation is aimed at the noncommunicative impact of an act, the regulation should be upheld as constitutional—even as applied to expressive conduct—so long as it does not, on balance, unduly constrict the flow of information and ideas.[29]

The distinct advantage of the foregoing style of analysis is that it can fit substantive propositions to structural rules without subjecting them to a Procrustean bed of dogmatic preconception. A free speech theory embodying such analytic richness can thus resist the snare of many fruitless controversies. In the example above, for instance, the theory offers a principled resolution of the dispute between those who claim the first amendment is "absolute" in its protection, and those who claim it always requires case-by-case "balancing" of competing interests of government.

IV.

Fourth, and finally, I turn to the boundaries of content and substance. No free speech theory can be satisfactory if it posits the existence of certain unacceptable ideas, just as no satisfactory theory of free speech can be expected to guarantee the existence of any particular social system.[30] Nor can an acceptable free speech theory demand that government be an ideological eunuch; the theory must be subtle enough to distinguish government as *censor* from government as *speaker*,[31] and discerning enough to distinguish the government voice that merely *adds* to public debate from the government voice that *monopolizes* it. The theory must also justify protecting the dissemination of "fact" along with the dissemination of "opinion"—it cannot be limited, as some theories have been, to expression calculated to change values.[32]

Most important, a satisfactory theory of free speech must prove adequate to the challenge of the affirmative state. It cannot evade the need for positive governmental action in some cases to secure meaningful opportunities for speech,[33] and it must confront the paradox that governmental action to facilitate the expression of any idea may depend on coerced contributions from citizens who not only reject the idea but find it deeply offensive.[34]

This sketch of the criteria for a satisfactory free speech theory is doubtless incomplete, but its elements seem to me necessary even if they are insufficient. Even more clearly, it seems to me vital that theory-builders throughout constitutional law, and throughout law generally, pay more attention to what an acceptable theory must contain. How else will we be able to know the unicorn when we finally see it?

Notes

1. L. TRIBE, AMERICAN CONSTITUTIONAL LAW (Foundation Press, Mineola, N.Y. 1978) [hereinafter cited as TREATISE].

2. TREATISE, §§2.1-6.33.

3. *Id.*, §§8.1-8.7.

4. *Id.*, §§9.1-9.7.

5. *Id.*, §§10.1-10.19.

6. *Id.*, §§11.1-15.21.

7. *Id.*, §§16.1-16.57.

8. *Id.*, §§17.1-17.3.

9. *See* TREATISE, *supra* note 1, §§1.1, 17.1-17.3. I suggest in §17.1 that we are now witnessing the emergence of the Model of Structural Justice, which seeks to achieve such ends as human freedom not through any *one* characteristic structure of choice, but through that *combination* of structures that seems best suited to those ends *in a particular context. See also* Tribe, *Structural Due Process,* 10 HARV. C.R.-C.L.L. REV. 269 (1975); Tribe, *The Emerging Reconnection of Individual Rights and Institutional Design: Federalism, Bureaucracy, and Due Process of Lawmaking,* 10 CREIGHTON L. REV. 433 (1977).

10. For an account of these two world views and their corresponding social systems, see R. UNGER, KNOWLEDGE AND POLITICS (1975).

11. *See* text part IV, *infra.* Some paradoxes of structures of limited liberty are discussed in O. KIRCHHEIMER, POLITICAL JUSTICE 170-72 (1961).

12. *See* R. WOLFF, THE POVERTY OF LIBERALISM 11-12 (1968). Accepting the analogy between the market of goods and the market of ideas, some commentators have called for a more consistent approach to government regulation of the two "markets." *See, e.g.,* R. Coase, *The Market for Goods and the Market for Ideas,* 64 2 AM. ECON. REV. 384 (1974). Other commentators, rejecting the analogy, have taken the opposite view; *see, e.g.,* J. MILTON, AREOPAGITICA, A SPEECH FOR THE LIBERTY OF UNLICENSED PRINTING 29 (1959) ("Truth

and understanding are not such wares as to be monopolised [sic] and traded on by tickets and statutes and standards. We must not think to make a staple commodity of all the knowledge in the land, to mark and license it like our broadcloth and our woolpacks.").

13. Abrams v. United States, 250 U.S. 616, 630 (1919) (Holmes, J., dissenting).

14. A useful critique of the "marketplace of ideas" model is set forth in Baker, *The Scope of First Amendment Freedom of Speech,* appearing *infra.*

15. *See* TREATISE, *supra* note 1, § 12.15.

16. *See, e.g.,* Baker, *Commercial Speech: A Problem in the Theory of Freedom,* 62 IOWA L. REV. 1 (1976).

17. Of course, this is not to say that in our society commercial information is an adequate antidote to exploitation. Plainly, government regulation of false or misleading price and product advertising is desirable, and can be defended on several grounds consistent with the first amendment. *See, e.g.,* Virginia State Bd. of Pharmacy v. Virginia Citizens Consumer Council, 425 U.S. 748, 771-72 n.24 (1976); *id.* at 777-79 (Stewart, J., concurring); Bates v. Arizona State Bar, 433 U.S. 350, 383-84 (1977). But saying that commerical speech may be regulated more readily than other forms of speech is altogether different from saying that it is entitled to no first amendment protection at all. *See* TREATISE, *supra* note 1, § 12.15 at 655-56.

18. *Virginia Bd. of Pharmacy,* 425 U.S. at 763.

19. *See generally* A. MEIKLEJOHN, FREE SPEECH AND ITS RELATION TO SELF-GOVERNMENT (1948); A. MEIKLEJOHN, POLITICAL FREEDOM (1960). For an early anticipation of Meiklejohn, see Stromberg v. California, 283 U.S. 359, 369 (1931).

20. For an examination of instrumentalism, *see* Tribe, *Technology Assessment and the Fourth Discontinuity: The Limits of Instrumental Rationality,* 46 S. CAL. L. REV. 617 (1973).

21. Illustrations of the inevitable instrumentalist march toward intrinsic values come readily to mind. For example, theorists defending free speech as crucial to the polity are inclined to respond to the "why" by arguing that political participation is valuable in part because it enhances personal growth and self-realization, *see, e.g.,* J. S. MILL, CONSIDERATIONS ON REPRESENTATIVE GOVERNMENT 203 (1882). But if that is so, why do not those values themselves explain much of our commitment to freedom of speech without the intermediate step of the Meiklejohn thesis? And do they not explain it in terms broad enough to encompass the full sweep of expressional activity with far less strain?

22. *See* A. Meiklejohn, *The First Amendment is an Absolute,* 1961 SUP. CT. REV. 248, 263.

23. *See* E. NAGEL & J. NEWMAN, GÖDEL'S PROOF (1958).

24. *See, e.g.,* Cox v. Louisiana, 379 U.S. 559 (1965) (Cox II); *see also* TREATISE, *supra* note 1, § 12.7.

25. The distinction may be taken at most as shorthand for an inquiry into the aim of a challenged government regulation. *See* TREATISE, *supra* note 1, §§ 12.2, 12.3, 12.5, 12.6.

26. *See, e.g.,* Roth v. United States, 354 U.S. 476, 483 (1957). Although it might be possible to reconile first amendment premises as well as norms of even-handed treatment with "time, place, and manner" regulations of sexually explicit materials, Young v. American Mini Theatres, 427 U.S. 50, 60, 62, 63, 70-71 (1976), the attempt to single out some images or roles for complete suppression seems utterly incompatible with the first amendment notion that awareness can never be deemed harmful in itself. See *generally* TREATISE, *supra* note 1, §§ 12.16, 12.18, 12.19.

27. Strictly speaking, this anti-artifice requirement might be better treated as methodological than as structural, but because the presence of such problematic methods points to an underlying weakness in structure, I include the criterion here.

28. *See* TREATISE, *supra* note 1, §§ 12.2, 12.8-12.18.

29. *Id.,* §§ 12.20-12.22.

30. *See* text at note 10 *supra.*

31. *See* TREATISE, *supra* note 1, §§ 12.4; T. EMERSON, THE SYSTEM OF FREEDOM OF EXPRESSION 697-716 (1970).

32. *See, e.g.,* Scanlon, *A Theory of Freedom of Expression,* 1 PHIL. & PUB. AFF. 204 (1972).

33. *See* Red Lion Broadcasting Co. v. FCC, 395 U.S. 367 (1969). Jerome Barron did not understate the issue when he wrote that *Red Lion* repudiated the dogma that "censorhip could be called freedom of the press if it [is] done by private hands and not by government." FREEDOM OF THE PRESS FOR WHOM? THE RIGHT OF ACCESS TO THE MEDIA 143 (1973). However, the repudiation of this dogma has been less than thoroughgoing, *see, e.g.,* Miami Herald Publishing Co. v. Tornillo, 418 U.S. 241 (1974), and in any event carries perils of its own. *See* TREATISE, *supra* note 1, § 12.22.

34. Few people now question the government's right to finance public education from the public fisc, much less its right to provide public services to private institutions of all sorts. There is little apparent difference between coerced public contribution in these cases and in those where the government would seek to facilitate access of disadvantaged groups to media through public funding. It matters little to the taxpayer whether the voice of sin and corruption he or she is forced to support belongs to the government or to a private speaker. It is

worth noting that the majority in Abood v. Detroit Bd. of Educ., 431 U.S. 209 (1977), did not accept the proposition that a nonmember's first amendment rights were infringed by being compelled to contribute to any union activities to which the nonmember objected, whether or not related to the union's collective bargaining activities. Similarly, the majority in Wooley v. Maynard, 430 U.S. 705 (1977), tacitly accepted Justice Rehnquist's assertion that citizens of New Hampshire could be compelled through their taxes to pay for the cost of erecting and maintaining billboards proclaiming "Live Free or Die," even if they could not be compelled to display that proclamation on their license plates. But the problems posed by letting government do with carrots what it cannot do with sticks must be the subject of a further essay.

Defamatory Non-Media Speech And First Amendment Methodology

BY STEVEN SHIFFRIN[*]

INTRODUCTION

In the course of his eloquent commentary[1] upon *New York Times Co. v. Sullivan,*[2] the late Professor Kalven enthused that the Court had written "an opinion that may prove to be the best and most important it has ever produced in the realm of freedom of speech."[3] This excitement was generated not by the Court's rather narrow holding[4] but rather by the hope that *Sullivan* would serve as the opening wedge to dislodge the clear and present danger test,[5] to dismantle the "two-level"[6] approach to first amendment analysis (reflected in cases such as *Chaplinsky,*[7] *Beauharnais,*[8] and *Roth*[9]), and instead to rest free speech theory on the idea that the first amendment is centrally concerned with the protection of speech relating to self-government.[10] From that premise, Kalven thought the inclination to protect all speech in the "public domain"[11] would prove to be "overwhelming."[12]

Professor Kalven's hopes have not been realized. It is now clear that a variant of the clear and present danger test is solidly entrenched in a portion of the Court's first amendment theory[13] and that the two-level approach to first amendment analysis is alive and well.[14] Moreover, recent commentary by Justice Stewart[15] and the Court's opinion in *Gertz v. Robert Welch, Inc.*[16] suggest that *Sullivan* may be regarded as having nothing to do with free speech theory. Rather it may be described as a free press case and its principles are to be applied (at least insofar as the scope of first amendment protection is concerned)[17] whether or not the communication is considered to be of public interest or relevant to self-government.[18] Such developments make it appropriate to consider whether media communications should be accorded a greater level of protection than non-media communications, whether defamatory speech unrelated to public issues ("non-public" or "private" speech) is or should be protected under the first amendment, and whether there is a central meaning of the first amendment under prevailing Supreme Court doctrine. These comments should suffice to introduce the three major themes of this paper: First, media communications should be afforded no greater protection than non-media communications; second, defamatory non-public speech has been undervalued in first amendment theory; and third, the attempt to identify a category of speech deemed to be centrally protected under the first amendment is ill advised. Thus, first amendment methodology is explainable not in terms of self-government or absolutism (nor in terms of definitional or ad hoc balancing); instead first amendment methodology is rooted in general balancing principles which sometimes counsel ad hoc approaches and other times dictate rules of general application. Before addressing these contentions directly, it is necessary to discuss Professor Kalven's hopes, Justice Stewart's perspective, and some of the Court's observations with respect to these issues.

[*]Acting Professor of Law, UCLA. In addition to expressing appreciation for the useful assistance of the editors of the UCLA Law Review, I owe thanks to Ronald Collins, Richard Helmholz, Kenneth Karst, Robert Myers, Melville Nimmer, Gary Schwartz, and Murray Schwartz. Each of them read a draft of this article and offered helpful and often important suggestions. Particularly helpful were the comments of those who do not agree with many of the positions here taken. One of the special pleasures of writing upon and discussing controversial subjects is the experience of robust and wide-open, but friendly debate.

9

I

A. Kalven's Scenario

Professor Kalven's fondest hope was that the *Sullivan* decision would prompt the Court to adopt the theory of free speech advocated by Alexander Meiklejohn.[19] Professor Meiklejohn's theory proceeds from the hypothesis that "the principle of the freedom of speech . . . is a deduction from the basic American agreement that public issues shall be decided by universal suffrage."[20] The notion is that the Constitution's commitment to freedom of speech is nothing more than a reflection of our commitment to self-government.[21] Under this approach speech relevant to self-government is absolutely protected under the first amendment;[22] speech not relevant to self-government is beyond its scope[23] and said to be fair game for government regulation so long as due process requirements are respected.[24]

The attractiveness of a politically based interpretation of the first amendment is easily understood, and its pull has drawn favorable commentary from a diverse group of respected commentators[25] as well as from several members of the Court.[26] As a strategy of communications protection, it offers the pragmatic prospect of preventing the government from intruding into areas where its potential for bias is particularly acute.[27] As a theory of interpretation, it offers the legalistic neatness of permitting the conclusion that the absolute terms of the first amendment protect absolutely that speech within its scope.[28] It confines the area within which the judiciary may impose subjectively derived values.[29] And, finally, it offers a grand and romantic appeal by conjoining first amendment theory with the basic theory of American government.[30]

Equally understandable were Professor Kalven's high hopes for the *Sullivan* precedent. In ringing terms, *Sullivan* announced that the first amendment represented our "profound national commitment to the principle that debate on *public* issues should be uninhibited, robust, and wide-open . . .,"[31] and that the "central meaning of the First Amendment"[32] is that prosecutions for libel on government have no "'place in the American system of jurisprudence.'"[33] These conceptions were reinforced by the concurring opinion of Justice Goldberg who argued that although public speech should be absolutely protected,[34] "purely private defamation"[35] is not protected under the first amendment because it has "little to do with the political ends of a self-governing society."[36] To be sure, in holding that knowing or reckless falsehoods concerning public officials were not protected under the first amendment,[37] *Sullivan* did not go as far as Meiklejohn.[38] But with that narrow exception,[39] *Sullivan* offered the prospect of extension well beyond its holding that a public official suing for libel would have to demonstrate knowing or reckless falsity before damages could constitutionally be imposed.

To a large extent that prospect has been realized. In subsequent decisions, the Court has held that *Sullivan* applies to relatively low level public officials,[40] to public figures,[41] and to criminal libel actions.[42] Moreover, the *Sullivan* ruling has been applied by analogy in a variety of other contexts,[43] including false light privacy actions,[44] and the so-called malice exception has been narrowly construed.[45] Finally, the high point of the Kalven scenario was realized when a plurality of the Court in *Rosenbloom v. Metromedia, Inc.*[46] (with the lower courts following suit)[47] opined that before a plaintiff could collect damages in a defamation action with respect to a communication of "general or public interest," the plaintiff would have to show knowing or reckless falsity whether or not a public official or public figure was involved.[48] Thus Kalven's supposition that "the invitation to follow a dialectic progression from public official to governmental policy to public policy to matters in the public domain, like art, seems . . . overwhelming"[49] appeared to be especially apt. But, as shall be discussed later,[50] the ongoing rush to extend the *Sullivan* holding highlighted the basic weakness of the Meiklejohn theory—the dialectic progression once started has no principled stopping place, at least no stopping place consistent with common sense conceptions of the first amendment.

B. Justice Stewart's Position

Just when it appeared that Meiklejohn's theory of freedom of speech was well along the road toward judicial acceptance, Justice Stewart dropped a first amendment bombshell. In his seminal 1974 lecture at the Sesquicentennial Convocation of the Yale Law School, he stated that neither *Sullivan* nor any of its progeny had ever suggested that the "constitutional theory of free *speech* gives an *individual* any immunity from liability for libel or slander."[51] Instead, he maintained that *Sullivan* is a free press case exclusively.[52] The conflict between Justice Stewart and Professor Kalven could not be more pronounced. What Kalven regarded as the best and most important opinion in the realm of freedom of speech[53] is described by Justice Stewart as having nothing to do with freedom of speech.[54]

Although Justice Stewart's reading of *Sullivan* can be reconciled with the factual result of the case, it cannot be harmonized with either the language or rationale of the decision. At first glance it is even difficult to square Justice Stewart's position with the facts. The defendants the Court held entitled to first amendment protection included not only the New York Times Co., but also four Alabama clergymen who had not been employed by the press in any capacity.[55] The names of these clergymen (and other individuals not named as defendants)[56] had been appended by way of endorsement to a political advertisement[57] which was found to be defamatory.[58] Apparently Justice Stewart's view is that the Court reversed the judgment as to the clergymen because they, by publishing in the press, were entitled to receive whatever protections were provided to the press. They were, for purposes of the decision, the press. If the *Sullivan* rule is to be regarded as a press decision exclusively, it makes sense to give the press term at least this expansive a sweep.[59] If the goal is to prevent the states from discouraging the publication of non-malicious (in the *Sullivan* sense) defamatory statements about public officials, that goal can hardly be accomplished by imposing damages against the sources of the statements.[60]

But if Justice Stewart's position does not contradict the result, it surely does violence to the language and underlying philosophy of *New York Times Co. v. Sullivan*. The opinion explicitly states that its holding is based on both the speech and press provisions of the first amendment: "[W]e sustain the contentions of all the petitioners under the First Amendment's guarantees of freedom of speech and of the press as applied to the States by the Fourteenth Amendment. . . ."[61] Indeed, the opinion refers throughout to the "freedom of speech and press."[62]

Even more important, however, the rationale of the opinion is rooted in a fundamental respect for the right of the people, not merely the press, to criticize the government. After noting that *Barr v. Matteo*[63] holds that federal officials are absolutely immune from defamation judgments rendered with respect to statements made by them "within the outer perimeter"[64] of their duties,[65] the Court stated that

> [a]nalogous considerations support the privilege for the citizen-critic of government. It is as much his duty to criticize as it is the official's duty to administer. . . . As Madison said . . . "the censorial power is in the people over the Government, and not in the Government over the people."[66]

If the Court intended *Sullivan* to be read as a free press case exclusively, it picked a strange way to state its holding and a peculiar method to justify it. Indeed, far from holding that the clergymen citizen-critics derive immunity from the fact that they have for limited purposes become members of the press,[67] it appears that the press has derived immunity either from the fact that it can be considered a part of the class of citizen-critics[68] or that citizen-critics need a press to acquire information relevant to their decision making.[69] The clarity of the free speech underpinnings of *Sullivan* must lead us to inquire into the circumstances which have led Justice Stewart to so radical a departure from recently settled, but nonetheless basic, principles of first amendment law. What is the case for transforming *Sullivan*'s ringing endorsement of democracy into a muted approval of what might as well be called "mediaocracy"?

C. Gertz and Firestone: Hints from the Court

Only hints are provided in *Gertz v. Robert Welch, Inc.*,[70] but the indications are that the case for mediaocracy is intertwined with the case for a politically based interpretation of the first amendment. *Gertz* was decided a few months before Justice Stewart's speech[71] and it contains the Court's first[72] implication that the application of the *Sullivan* rule might depend on the media status of the defendant. *Gertz* constituted the Court's second attempt to determine the applicability of the *Sullivan* principles to a defamation case involving a plaintiff who was neither a public official nor a public figure. As previously mentioned, in the Court's first brush with the issue,[73] *Rosenbloom v. Metromedia, Inc.*,[74] a three justice plurality took the position that a private plaintiff would have to meet the *Sullivan* test in order to recover damages so long as the publication involved a matter of "public or general concern."[75] The underlying spirit of the plurality was crisply stated:

> We honor the commitment to robust debate on public issues, which is embodied in the First Amendment, by extending constitutional protection to all discussion and communication involving matters of public or general concern, without regard to whether the persons involved are famous or anonymous.[76]

Thus the *Rosenbloom* plurality stated that the first amendment protects speech involving matters of public or general concern but suggested that it might exclude speech outside those categories.[77]

Gertz rejected the *Rosenbloom* plurality view by refusing to make the applicability of *Sullivan* turn on whether a particular communication was considered by judges to be of "general or public interest"[78] or whether it was considered to provide information "relevant to self-government."[79] The "general or public interest" test was assailed first because it was thought to balance inadequately the competing interests of preserving reputational interests and safeguarding the press.[80] If a communication of "general or public interest" defamed a private plaintiff, to require a *Sullivan* showing was thought to safeguard reputational interests inadequately in view of the fact that public plaintiffs were deemed to have greater access than private plaintiffs to reply in the media[81] and that public persons were deemed to have invited public attention and comment.[82] On the other hand, if a communication were judicially characterized as without "general or public interest," to permit a recovery without a showing of fault by the press and without a demonstration of actual damage was thought to involve inadequate protection for the first amendment interest in a free press.[83] Finally, the Court "doubt[ed] the wisdom"[84] of committing to the "conscience of judges"[85] the task of determining on an ad hoc basis which statements address issues of "public or general interest" and which do not.[86]

Accordingly, the Court held that a *Sullivan* showing would be required of a public official or public figure before damages could be imposed, but that (whether or not the communication was deemed to be of "general or public interest") a private plaintiff could recover "actual"[87] (but not presumed or punitive)[88] damages only upon a showing of "fault,"[89] at least in those cases where the substance of the statement made "substantial danger to reputation apparent."[90]

At first glance, it appears that the Court has rejected the Meiklejohn interpretation of the first amendment. The Meiklejohn view of the first amendment requires the conclusion that communications not relevant to public issues be unprotected by the first amendment.[91] Yet *Gertz* plainly states that communications which are deemed to have nothing to do with self-government and which do not relate to public issues fall within the ambit of first amendment protection,[92] *i.e.*, defamation damages cannot be imposed in the absence of a showing of fault whether or not public issues are involved.

The *Gertz* rationale is qualified, however, by the Court's opinion in *Time, Inc. v. Firestone*.[93] There the Court reaffirmed the rejection of the public or general interest test as a means of determining the scope of first amendment protection,[94] but reintroduced a variant of the test for determining the level of protection (*i.e.*, malice versus fault) accorded to the defendant.[95] *Gertz* had stated that "commonly, those classed as public figures have thrust themselves to the forefront of particular *public* controversies in order to influence the resolution of the issues involved."[96] In *Firestone*, the Court elevated this description to a definition and held that a divorce proceeding involving one of the wealthiest families in America and containing testimony concerning the extra-marital sexual activities of the parties did not involve the sort of "public controversy" referred to in *Gertz*.[97]

Thus the Court which in *Gertz* doubted the wisdom of forcing judges to determine on an ad hoc basis what is and is not of "general or public interest" was prefectly willing in *Firestone* to produce a public figure test which forces judges on an ad hoc basis to determine what is or is not a "public controversy"—all of this without so much as a casual attempt to define "public controversy."[98] Perhaps the Court divines a distinction of constitutional dimension between the terms "public or general interest" and "public controversy." At least there is a distinction of practical importance. The *Firestone* decision apparently does not mean that the presence of a "public controversy" is sufficient to trigger a malice requirement. In addition, the plaintiff must have thrust himself to the forefront of the matter and attempted thereby to have influenced its outcome. It is one thing to make subjective determinations as to the newsworthy[99] character of a communication in some cases affect the level of protection afforded to it. It is quite another to make such ad hoc determinations affect the fact of protection *vel non* in all cases. The *Gertz* and *Firestone* defendants are assured that defamatory communications are entitled to *some* level of first amendment protection whether or not judges deem their communications to be "public" in character. Thus, by holding that determinations concerning the public character of the communication affect the level but not the scope of protection, the Court has assumed the burden of making the kind of difficult ad hoc decisions that it had shunned in *Gertz*, but at least has mitigated the impact of such decisions.

Whether or not the *Firestone* "public controversy" term is to be defined in the same manner as the "public or general interest" phrase (albeit in a discrete context with different consequences), the demise of the Meiklejohn doctrine (which assumes that private or non-public speech is outside the scope of the first and amendment) *seems* apparent. After *Gertz* and *Firestone*, a communication held not to be relevant to public issues is nonetheless held to be entitled to a level of first amendment protection.

On the other hand, the *Gertz-Firestone* doctrine appears to preserve the core of Meiklejohn's approach in this sense—at least in those cases where the plaintiff has attempted to influence the outcome of a controversy by means of public communication,[100] the extent to which the communication bears upon public issues determines the level of constitutional protection enjoyed by the defendant. Thus, at least in some contexts, speech on public issues is deemed to be entitled to greater first amendment protection than speech which is not.[101]

Moreover it is possible to read *Gertz* in a way which would permit the conclusion that although the Meiklejohn test has been rejected, a politically based interpretation of the first amendment has not. A clue is provided by the Court's attempt to limit its holding to a limited class of defendants interchangeably described at various points to include newspapers, and broadcasters,[102] the press and broadcast media,[103] publishers and broadcasters,[104] the media,[105] the news media,[106] the communications media,[107] and the press.[108] This apparent attempt to distinguish between media and non-media defendants is entirely unexplained.[109] One possible explanation of the Court's strategy may be traced to the influence of Meiklejohn. It may be that the Court has refused to adopt the Meiklejohn "public issues" test not because it believes that private speech (*i.e.*, speech unrelated to public issues) is as important as public speech but rather because it doubts its ability to distinguish unerringly between the two. The Court's reluctance to make the *scope* of first amendment protection turn upon ad hoc second guess distinctions between public and private speech is not difficult to appreciate. The judgment, however, that judges are unable to draw a bright line between public and private speech does not require the conclusion that there is no difference between the two. Indeed, the fact that the Court is willing to let the public character of the speech affect in some cases the level of protection afforded (despite its view that ad hoc line-drawing is tenuous and difficult) demonstrates that the Court appreciates the difference.[110] Instead, the Court's rejection of the public or general interest test, insofar as the scope of media protection is covered, may rather signal the belief that the inability to distinguish precisely between private and public speech requires that some private speech be afforded a level of constitutional protection so that public speech be not unnecessarily chilled.

If this be the Court's rationale for doubting the wisdom of committing to judges the task of making delicate distinctions with such absolute consequences, the distinction between media and non-media defendants at least becomes comprehensible. Surely the vast majority of defamatory statements by publishers and broadcasters involve matters of general or public interest. On the other hand, putting aside comments about public officials and public figures, the vast majority of defamatory comments by non-media defendants presumably do not.

Thus, by placing all defamatory media speech within the scope of the first amendment, the Court may believe it has protected relatively little non-public speech. On the other hand, the Court may fear that if *Gertz* were extended to non-media speech, the result would be to protect much speech having nothing to do with public issues, while safeguarding relatively little that does. In the non-media context, the Court may feel that some public speech must go unprotected lest too much non-public speech be unnecessarily safeguarded. Consistent with this approach, the Court could extend constitutional protection in the non-media context to any defamatory speech about public officials or public figures (on the premise that the speech was relevant to public issues) but could withhold such protection when a non-public person was the object of a defamatory statement.

So understood, *Gertz* implies that debate on public issues will be sufficiently robust and wide-open for first amendment purposes if defamatory non-media speech is constitutionalized only to the extent that it involves public persons. On this premise, *Gertz's* commitment to a politically based interpretation of the first amendment is qualified by its reluctance to afford unnecessary protection to speech not relevant to public issues.

On the other hand, *Gertz's* media dictum may reflect something entirely different. It may respect Justice Stewart's view that the media itself is constitutionally special.[111] Under this view, neither *Sullivan* nor *Gertz* would protect defamatory non-media speech. Thus all defamatory non-media speech, even that discussing public officials, would be beyond the scope of the first amendment. Ironically, even this perspective is rooted in a politically centered construction of the first amendment. To flesh out that perspective, we must turn from the Court to the commentators.

II

A. Media v. Non-media Speakers: Relative Importance

Although *Gertz* does not discuss the case for a preferred media position, the case has been made.[112] Justice Stewart contends that the primary purpose of the press clause is to insure that there will be "organized, expert scrutiny of government."[113] From this premise he asserts that media speakers should enjoy greater protection from defamation suits than non-media speakers.[114] Professor Nimmer spells out the case in greater detail.[115] He argues that "the informing and opinion-shaping function of the press is unquestioned. Most would agree that generally speech via the press is much more significant as a contribution to the democratic dialogue that is speech through non-media channels."[116] He argues in the case of non-media speakers that although some functions of free expression are involved—specifically individual self-fulfillment[117] and cathartic release[118]—the democratic dialogue function is relatively unimportant.[119] He contends that in the case of weighing the value of non-media expression against reputation, "[t]he balance *might* shift in favor of reputation if the democratic dialogue press interest is removed, as would be the case in non-media defamatory speech."[120] Still another writer puts it this way: "By comparison, the role of non-media speakers in the broad dissemination of information is relatively insignificant. This does not mean that what non-media speakers have to say is of less importance, but rather that their impact on the general information market will usually not be as great."[121] Or as Professor Nimmer puts it, "we do not know with any precision the impact of mass media communications, but we do know logically, if not statistically, that a communication to five million people is likely to affect public opinion (or the democratic dialogue) more profoundly than speech addressed to a single individual"[122]

But the issue is not whether a communication addressed to five million individuals is more likely to influence public opinion than a communication addressed to one. The issue, if influence is to be the test, is whether the communication to five million people is more influential than the communications of the five million people who discuss that communication[123] at breakfast tables, at work, in taxicabs, in bars, in universities, and elsewhere. One need not minimize the importance of the mass media[124] (particularly its importance as a broad disseminator of new ideas)[125] in order to recognize that the private daily communications of millions of individuals profoundly affect public opinion.[126] Indeed the communications literature clearly supports the conclusion that media influence is mediated by the recipients of the communications.[127] That is, the recipients of mass communications play a critical role in the dissemination and interpretation of information provided by the media, and those non-media recipients are vitally important in affecting the formation of political attitudes and beliefs.[128] In addition, the evidence is persuasive that political attitudes and beliefs are formed not merely by media communications but by prior experience,[129] by communications in family groups,[130] work groups,[131] social groups,[132] and peer groups in general.[133] If the media were deterred from publishing defamatory comments,[134] there is no question that the democratic dialogue would suffer. But there should equally be no questioning the fact that if millions of individuals were deterred from making such statements outside the media, the democratic dialogue would similarly suffer. Simultaneously, and perhaps even more importantly, the free speech values of individual self-expression and cathartic release would be seriously undercut. To the extent that the media should not be censored, therefore, neither should the "citizen-critic." Indeed, it is at least arguable that the values of individual self-expression and cathartic release apply with greater force in the non-media context than in the media context.[135] To that extent, the case for non-media protection is even stronger than the case for media protection.

There is, however, a more telling factor which superficially appears to support preferred treatment for the media. It could well be that media speakers are more likely to be deterred by defamation law from making defamatory comments than are non-media speakers. Media speakers are comparatively more likely to be aware of the libel laws (*i.e.*, have continuing access to legal advice), comparatively more likely to have financial resources sufficient to make them attractive defamation defendants, and comparatively more likely to cause the kind of damage which would encourage law suits in response.[136] Thus, it is least arguable that defamation law is more likely to chill media communications than non-media communications and that the damaging impact of defamation laws on first amendment values in the media context is correspondingly more acute.

On the other hand, it is also arguable that those non-media defendants with the financial resources to make a civil action against them supportable, who might also cause sufficient damage to make a civil action against them attractive, are also armed with sufficient knowledge of the consequences to give them pause before making defamatory statements. With respect to those with little resources causing little damage, the nature of the legal standards governing liability makes little difference. Establishing a case against a defendant when substantial damages are not involved or when a judgment is not collectible is not the kind of exercise with which many plaintiffs (or attorneys) desire to be associated. Insofar as non-media defendants are involved, those most likely to become the targets of defamation suits are those who are most likely to be deterred by the prospect of recoveries against them. Thus, the argument that media defendants are more likely to be chilled than non-media defendants, while not without force,[137] is not as imposing a consideration as might initially be supposed.

Assuming *arguendo* that the comparative chilling effect is greater with respect to media defendants than non-media defendants, it is not at all clear that first amendment consequences should be automatically triggered. The idea that first amendment protections should be consciously divided out in more generous doses to those with knowledge, wealth, and capacity to cause damage[138] is indefensible. Particularly disquieting is the idea that those with greater capacity to cause damage should be afforded special protection. Such a perspective would not only bespeak a disrespect for the interest in reputation, but it would also reflect an indifference to the growing public concern with the "vast accumulations"[139] of power in the "modern media empires."[140] Indeed, it would be ironic if the premises of Alexander Meiklejohn which were rooted in a respect for democratic decision making would ever be employed to service an elitist institutional result, *i.e.*, some citizens (those associated with the press) being more free to discuss politics than other citizen-critics (the people). It would be anomalous, for example, if non-media speakers could be penalized for repeating statements made by the media[141] while the media would be immune. The possibility that such results would breed contempt for the democratic process is one which should give considerable pause before principles of "mediaocracy" are grafted on to the first amendment.

Affording non-media defendants less first amendment protection than media defendants would deter non-media contributions to the democratic dialogue (and thus would weaken the media's contribution),[142] would favor those with greater capacity to cause damage and with greater ability to compensate for that damage (by spreading the risk),[143] would require difficult determinations as to which communications would and would not merit the label "press" or "media,"[144] would strain basic principles of first amendment equality, and would diminish respect for the democratic process.

B. Political Speech

Sullivan standards should be required of public officials or public figures whether or not the defendant fits into the media category. Justice Stewart to the contrary, the idea that citizen-critics should be free to criticize the actions of those in the public eye is one which should not be ignored. On the other hand, *Gertz* implies that at least when no public person plaintiff is involved, media defendants will be accorded constitutional protection and non-media defendants will not. The Court is unwilling to permit the rigors of the common law to impact on speech likely to be of general or public interest (media speech) but is apparently willing to tolerate the rigors of the common law with respect to speech unlikely to relate to issues of public importance (non-media speech not involving public persons) and is apparently unwilling to attempt on a general basis to determine which speech relates to issues of public importance and which does not.[145]

Although the Court's unwillingness to distinguish between public and non-public speech is defensible, the underlying assumption that defamatory non-public speech is unworthy of some degree of constitutional protection deserves to be questioned.[146] As initially set forth, the Meiklejohn theory of the first amendment protects too little; as modified, it protects too much. Initially, Meiklejohn declared that the first amendment applied "only to speech which bears, directly or indirectly, upon issues with which voters have to deal—only, therefore, to the consideration of matters of public interest."[147] So considered, the theory was capable of being interpreted to preclude first amendment protection for most literary, philosophical, and scientific writing.[148] Simply put, if a first amendment theory designed to provide absolute protection for political speech can do so only by excluding protection for Shakespeare, Aristotle, and Einstein, something is seriously amiss.[149]

In later writings, Meiklejohn sought to plug this hole by asserting that philosophy, science, art, and literature were areas from which the voter derived "knowledge, intelligence, sensitivity to human values: the capacity for sane and objective judgment which, so far as possible, a ballot should express."[150] But the idea that literature's claim to first amendment protection depends upon its relevance to political life simply does not ring true.[151] The notion that the classics of literature cannot be suppressed solely because of their relevance to voter decision making bears all the earmarks of pure fiction. Indeed, if the classics of literature are all to be characterized as political speech, it is hard to see how any speech could be called non-political.[152] Specifically, in making decisions voters are called upon to make evaluations of the character of candidates for political office.[153] As a practical matter, assessments of human personality by most voters are rarely based on sensitivity to human values derived from literature,[154] but are surely based in large part upon experiences with others in private life and on values formed through communications about other individuals in private life.[155] The impact of private speech on individuals' assessments of human personality and politicians surely dwarfs the impact made by art, literature, or science. If art and literature are protectable on the theory that they have political impact, private speech is protectable *a fortiori*. In short, once the door is opened, it becomes difficult to close. Either a politically based theory excludes speech such as literature which virtually everyone[156] (including the "founding fathers")[157] agrees is deserving of protection, or, by making adjustments to include such speech, it makes it impossible to justify a stopping point. In the absence of a stopping point, the Meiklejohn position simply unravels. Beginning with the proposition that political speech must be absolutely protected and moving to the proposition that all speech has political relevance yields the necessary conclusion that all speech must be absolutely protected. The distinction between public and private speech, so carefully developed, thus evaporates in the absence of a defensible stopping point.

C. Non-Political Defamatory Speech

Literature's claim to first amendment protection need not depend upon its relevance to voter decision making. Protection for literature advances marketplace values and values of self-expression entirely independent of any political relevance. Similarly private defamatory speech (*i.e.*, speech deemed to be unrelated to matters of general or public interest) should be entitled to some degree of constitutional protection whether or not it has political relevance.

Ordinarily considerable deference to conclusions derived from the common law process is appropriate, but the common law affords demonstrably insufficient protection for private defamation[158] and the considerations that have guided its development bear little relevance for modern times. Indeed, the judgment is virtually unanimous that, as Prosser puts it, "[t]here is a great deal of the common law of defamation which makes no sense."[159] The law of defamation makes sense, if at all, only when one understands that history, not logic, has controlled its development.[160] The common law of defamation is that a defamatory statement is presumed to be false, presumed to be malicious, and (with significant exceptions) presumed to have caused damage.[161] One branch of that law, the modern law of libel, owes its lineage to the Star Chamber whose hostility to principles of freedom of speech need not be detailed. The provisions affording strict liability to defamatory utterances were developed (in addition to protecting the government from criticism) as a means of providing an alternative to duelling. Although the desire to preserve public order is one value worthy of consideration in forming a law of defamation, it is in modern times hardly the only value[162] and surely nowhere near as pressing today as it was in sixteenth century England.

The modern law of slander as an action for damages owes its lineage to the English common law courts.[163] Slander involving criminal accusations, occupational insults, assertions of loathsome disease, and claims of unchastity for women[164] were deemed to be actionable without proof of special damage. Other defamatory statements were not considered to be per se damaging, but instead necessitated proof of "special" damage. These categories were developed not by an assessment of the needs of the substantive law, but by historical accident. The law developed by a process of accommodating the jurisdiction of the common law courts with that of the ecclesiastical courts. The common law courts had jurisdiction over crime—hence accusations of crime were first claimed as proper subjects of common law jurisdiction—and over the propriety of confinement[165] for loathsome disease— hence accusations of loathsome disease were thought to be a proper area of common law power. Occupational slander was said to involve the temporal and not the spiritual. Finally, slander causing special damage was similarly said to involve the temporal sufficiently that spiritual jurisdiction could be foreclosed.

With the decline of the ecclesiastical courts, the opportunity for reevaluation of the law of slander might have been seized. But the common law courts were flooded with slander cases, and the judges realized that by narrowly construing the categories from which damages were presumed and by creating strict standards of special damage, the propensity to bring slander cases could be mitigated. Thus, the law of slander with its indefensible[166] categories and requirements of pecuniary damage was maintained and nurtured. It need hardly be said that a body of law created out of consideration for now forgotten doctrines of judicial jurisdiction and maintained because of seventeenth century necessities of judicial administration deserves little deference as a guidepost to the appropriate accomodation between the values of freedom of speech and protection of reputation.

Individuals are told by the common law (subject to ambiguous and limited[167] "privilege"[168] exceptions) that if they make a statement critical of another which turns out to be wrong, they are liable even if the statement were honestly made and even if the statement were made with substantial support.[169] Moreover, individuals are warned by this law that if they tell someone that someone else has made a disparaging statement about another, they will be liable if the defamatory statement turns out to be wrong.[170] The message of the common law is clear: Do not make statements which are critical of others; do not tell others that individuals have committed crimes or that individuals are incompetent in their occupations; and do not inform individuals that others have made such statements.

If individuals in society did not to be informed about those with whom they interact, those rules might be appropriate. But individuals functioning in an interdependent society need to be informed about those with whom they interact (even when information comes from non-family members or from those without other special relationships).[171] They need this information at least as much as they need to know of the character of public officials and public figures and at least as much as they need to know of the facts underlying the writing of the latest Broadway play.[172] *Gertz* recognizes that the United States is an increasingly interdependent society where individuals need the opportunity to critically examine the reputation of others. There is no basis for suggesting that this need is of greater constitutional importance when the subject is of "general" interest.

This is not to say that reputations need not be protected in modern law. It is to say that reputations should not be overprotected. If negligence[173] is an appropriate standard to govern media statements about non-public persons, it is an appropriate standard to regulate statements by non-media speakers. Indeed, given the greater capacity of the media to cause damage and the capacity of most[174] media defendants to spread the risk, it can be argued (though in the final analysis not persuasively)[175] that media defendants should be held to a higher standard of care than non-media defendants. Whether negligence or some more protective standard should be employed in the media and non-media contexts will not be pursued here. Suffice it to say that strict liability is patently insufficient and that the supposition that only defamatory statements relating to matters of public interest are of sufficient importance to generate constitutional protection is indefensible.

III. First Amendment Methodology

A. The Problem

If politics is the wrong starting place for first amendment analysis, it is natural to ask what starting place is right. If the first amendment prohibits government from imposing sanctions with respect to some speech on public issues (but not all such speech) and with respect to some speech not related to public issues (but not all such speech), it is appropriate to inquire into the methodology which the Court uses to conclude that some speech can be abridged and other speech cannot. Kalven thought that a theory identifying political speech as centrally protected would provide the Court with a methodology which could support a comprehensible and comprehensive first amendment theory.[176] In the absence of such an approach, Kalven argued that the Court's general approach to first amendment questions was in disrepair.[177] The central focus of Kalven's concern was the Court's now-you-see-it-now-you-don't use of the clear and present danger test.[178] In some contexts, the Court would hold that speech was protected unless it presented a clear and present danger of a substantive evil with which government was legitimately concerned.[179] In other situations, the Court held that speech was beneath first amendment protection (because it lacked social utility) and that no necessity to involve the clear and present danger test was thereby implicated.[180] Kalven's major indictment of this two-level approach was that the Court had failed to delineate with any precision standards for determining which speech was socially useful and which speech was not.[181] Instead the Court had relied on the historical point that categories of speech such as libel and obscenity had long been regarded as worthless[182] and, therefore, had presumed their lack of worth.[183] If the Court had adopted a public speech approach, the clear and present danger test and the special logic of the two-level approach (designed to avoid that test) would have died together.[184]

Kalven's hopes, however, were doomed from the outset,[185] for *Sullivan* itself resorted to the special logic of the two-level theory.[186] Calculated falsehoods about public officials were deemed to be outside the scope of first amendment protection.[187] They were, as Justice Brennan was later to point out, deemed to be without social value.[188] Indeed, not only did *Sullivan* maintain a two-level analysis, *Sullivan* and now *Gertz* make it clear that in the Kalven sense[189] the Court has adopted a three-level approach to first amendment analysis. That is: (1) some speech is protected provided it does not present a clear and present danger of a substantive evil; (2) some speech is excluded from first amendment protection even if it does not present a clear and present danger; and (3) some speech is protected even if it does present a clear and present danger of a substantive evil with which government is legitimately concerned.

To illustrate the three-level approach, it is, of course, necessary to consult three lines of cases. First, in the context of advocacy of criminal conduct[190] (and in other areas)[191] the Court holds that such speech is protected unless it presents what amounts to a clear and present danger.[192] Second, in the context of obscenity, the Court holds in part that such speech (although it refuses to apply the label "speech") can be prohibited because it has "a tendency to exert a corrupting and debasing impact leading to antisocial behavior"[193]— surely a far cry from clear and present danger.

Third, although *Gertz* does not use the words "clear and present danger," it clearly recognizes that false defamatory speech presents a clear and present danger of a substantive evil with which government is legitimately concerned.[194] That is, *Gertz* reaffirms that the states have a legitimate interest in safeguarding reputation and that false defamatory speech unfairly threatens that interest. Indeed, it specifically holds that plaintiffs can recover damages for loss of reputation (as well as other damages)[195] arising from the publication of knowing or reckless falsehoods and in some cases merely negligent falsehoods. Moreover, *Gertz* candidly admits that false defamatory utterances create a "clear and present danger" (although again it does not use the phrase) of harm to the legitimate reputation of defamed individuals[196] even in circumstances where there are opportunities to reply. There is special first amendment significance in this concession, and we shall return to the point later. Meanwhile, it is crucial to understand that despite *Gertz's* recognition that false defamatory speech presents a clear and present danger to reputation (a substantive evil with which government can be legitimately concerned), it holds that some false defamatory speech creating such danger (non-malicious attacks on public persons and non-negligent attacks on non-public persons) in entitled to strategic first amendment protection nonetheless.

These three lines of cases, then, demand comparison. Cases such as *Brandenburg v. Ohio*[197] (advocacy of criminal action) demonstrate that the clear and present danger doctrine is not dead. Cases such as *Paris Adult Theatre I v. Slaton*[198] (obscenity) demonstrate that the absence of a clear and present danger provides no guarantee of first amendment protection, and *Gertz* (not to mention *Sullivan*)[199] demonstrates that the presence of a clear and present danger provides no guarantee that the state can abridge the speech involved. Moreover, as previously discussed, *Gertz* (not to mention *Brandenburg*) teaches us that some speech on public issues is not protected and some speech which does not relate to public issues is protected. Obviously neither Holmes nor Meiklejohn has won. First amendment adjudication cannot be explained in terms of clear and present danger nor in terms of any distinction between public and non-public speech. Moreover, the task of explaining first amendment methodology is complicated by the Court's historic unwillingness to explain why it is that clear and present danger principles are sometimes trotted out and sometimes left in the stable.[200]

B. Reconciliation

If the Court should ever attempt to put these cases side by side, it would have to admit that it employs an elaborate general balancing technique[201] to determine whether speech shall enjoy first amendment protection. There is nothing new or particularly scandalous about this. This has been the Court's approach all along. What is disquieting is the Court's failure to make its methodology public and its consequent failure to elaborate with any precision the factors it has identified as crucial in formulating conclusions as to the scope and level of protection afforded to various categories of speech.

Gertz is a refreshing departure from the norm, for it makes clear (at least in the defamation area) that the Court is balancing, and, even more important, *Gertz* lays out in some detail which interests are being balanced with what weights and why.

Gertz announces that reputation is being balanced against free press values,[202] and that the extent to which the defamed individual has invited comment and the extent to which channels of response are available to the defamed individual are factors to be considered in striking the balance. The Court maintains that to protect reputation absolutely would wreak significant damage to the structure of communications—that the media would be deterred from transmitting socially useful information, *i.e., true* defamatory speech.[203] Thus, even though defamatory communications threaten to undermine the reputations of individuals, such consequences are outweighed by the detrimental impact on first amendment values that would be effected by blanket imposition of common law libel principles. Clear and present danger is rejected as a standard because in the defamation context its use would unacceptably compromise first amendment values.

On the other hand, in *Brandenburg v. Ohio,* the Court has ruled that a variant of the clear and present danger test safeguards the relevant values in another context. In *Brandenburg,* the Court reapproached the question of the standards which should govern when an individual attempts to persuade others to the use of force or to other violations of the criminal laws. The Court held that such speech is protected unless it is "directed to inciting or producing imminent lawless action and is likely to incite or produce such action."[204]

To be sure, the *Brandenburg* test is not clear and present danger pure and simple; it is clear and present danger plus. Not only must the speech be likely to create imminent lawless action, it must be directed to that end,[205] and (though this is much less clear)[206] the language itself must explicitly call for the action. This latter requirement is apparently considered necessary lest majoritarian sentiments be employed to circumscribe unpopular speech.[207] By contrast, speech is protected in *Gertz* even if reputation is endangered with intent to bring about the danger and even if the defamatory language explicitly urges that others should think less of the defamed individual.

Seemingly a number of factors account for the use of the less protective standard in *Brandenburg.* The use of the clear and present danger test appears primarily influenced by an assessment of the worth of the speech being abridged. Advocacy of law violation is not the type of speech which one would at first glance expect a Court to support.[208] Indeed the application of the clear and present danger test is demonstrative that the marketplace of ideas concept is not the motivating animus.[209] The marketplace concept has often been described as the principal function of the first amendment.[210] As the Court explained in *Red Lion Broadcasting Co. v. FCC*,[211] "[i]t is the purpose of the First Amendment to preserve an uninhibited marketplace of ideas in which truth will ultimately prevail. . . ."[212] But in the context of advocacy of criminal law violations, the Court is not willing to rely on the marketplace. The advocacy of criminal law violations is protected unless it becomes effective advocacy; if it becomes effective, criminal sanctions can be imposed. Quite clearly, the Court has ruled that advocacy of criminal violations is a bad idea and that if the marketplace is responsive, the marketplace is wrong.

On the other hand, other limited marketplace values are respected. Although the Court is unwilling to attach value to the idea that violence should be employed, there is marketplace value in knowing that some members of the body politic are so concerned about particular government practices that violence is considered as an alternative, and there is marketplace value in knowing the premises which lead them to such conclusions.

Moreover, other important first amendment values are implicated. There is cathartic value in having speakers who might otherwise become dangerous release their tensions through verbal violence rather than physical violence.[213] Moreover there are pragmatic lessons at work, *i.e.*, that unnecessary government repression of such speech is likely to foster political instability. As Justice Brandeis put it, "fear breeds repression; . . . repression breeds hate; . . . hate menaces stable government."[214]

The importance of each of these first amendment functions is considered to be so substantial that the Court is willing to risk the possibilities of arbitrary administration that ad hoc assessments of danger necessarily invite. Particularized assessments of danger are thus considered preferable to a general rule excluding advocacy of law violation from first amendment protection. On the other hand, the potential for a chilling effect on such communications, necessarily fostered by the vagaries of individualized fact finding, is not considered dispositive because the values of public order and protection of lives and property are considered to outweigh the freedom to express ideas of limited marketplace and cathartic value.

It is perhaps instructive to recognize that the line of cases from *Schenck* to *Brandenburg* has usually involved a political component in that either the overthrow of the government or interference with military action was the alleged object of the advocacy. It is likely that this socio-political component (with its attendant first amendment values) has influenced both the rhetoric of the opinions and the substance of the test developed. How different it might be if the factual context were to involve advocacy of murder in a non-socio-political context. One suspects that little rhetoric about the marketplace of ideas or other first amendment values would be employed and that the serious and explicit advocacy of murder in a concrete way would suffice to divorce the speech from first amendment protection even in the absence of a specific showing of likelihood. The Court might well be persuaded that the State could not "reasonably be required to measure the danger from every such utterance in the nice balance of a jeweler's scale."[215] The distinction illustrates the point that the use of the clear and present danger test has been arrived at only after a balancing of factors such as the nature of the evil and the necessity for the regulation against the impact that the specific speech abridgment portends for first amendment values.

Similarly in the obscenity context, the Court's determination as to the scope of first amendment protection hinges on an assessment of the evils with which the state is concerned, the extent to which regulation of the speech is necessary to further the state's interests, and the impact of such abridgment or first amendment values. Central to the Court's weighing process in the obscenity context is the judgment that excessively (a subjective determination) candid descriptions of sexual activity are of low value in the first amendment hierarchy. The Court has concluded that obscene utterances are "no essential part of any exposition of ideas, and are of such slight social value as a step to truth that any benefit that may be derived from them is clearly outweighed by the social interest in order and morality."[216] Because of the low value placed upon this class of utterances, the Court is willing to accept legislative judgments that anti-social behavior is threatened even in circumstances when the danger is neither clear nor present.

The extent to which the Court's determination depends upon an evaluation of the speech involved is dramatized by the nature of the interests which the Court finds legitimate. The Court stresses that the very existence of obscenity "intrudes upon us all."[217] that it impinges on the privacy of others. This is nothing more than a recognition that obscenity is offensive to many, presumably most, in society. The same, for example, might be said of socialist speech; however, if "offensiveness" were the test, majority rule would replace the first amendment. In other contexts, the Court has recognized that the propensity of particular speech to evoke strong negative reactions (at least in the absence of speech which is likely to cause uncontrollable violence in response[218] or in the absence of speech thrust upon unwilling listeners)[219] is an inappropriate basis for abridgment.[220] The fact that safeguarding against "offensiveness" is considered to be a legitimate interest in the obscenity context is an indication of how little the Court thinks of the speech involved.

Contributing to the low value placed on obscene communications is the implicit determination that the cathartic function of the first amendment and the fear that repression will breed social disorder are considerations less acute in the obscenity context than in the advocacy of violence context. And the marketplace concept is avoided by the subjective judgment that ideas which do matter are not involved. Indeed the Court goes so far as to suggest that "ideas" are not involved.[221] Here again, the potential of a chilling effect is implicated—those who would "steer clear of the danger zone" may be deterred from publishing material which would otherwise be protected. But this possibility is weighed against the dangers sought to be minimized by the state[222] and against the "fact" (also subjectively determined) that the state could not accomplish its objective by less intrusive means.[223] The chilling effect is thus regarded as insubstantial.[224]

C. Court Limits On The Marketplace Model

There is an outright hostility to the marketplace model in *Brandenburg,* in the obscenity cases, and in *Gertz* that deserves attention. In such cases, the Court approves the legislative judgment that some ideas should not be in the marketplace. But the marketplace theory is based on the assumption that it is safer to leave determination of value and truth to the marketplace than to permit government impositions of necessarily subjective determinations of truth or falsehood. It would be an error to suggest, however, that the marketplace model does not influence first amendment decisionmaking. Rather part of the task for the Court in first amendment methodology is to determine when the marketplace model is appropriate and when it is not, *i.e.,* when it is permissible for governmentally imposed determinations of truth or falsity to substitute for the judgment of the marketplace.[225]

Indeed, *Gertz,* a case which protects defamatory speech in order to protect the marketplace of ideas, is a prime example of the Court's struggle to determine when the marketplace theory should be qualified. From *Sullivan* to *Gertz,* the Court has explained that it is vital that the press not be deterred from putting defamatory ideas in the marketplace. Yet it is equally important in this context to recognize that in certain respects the Court has substantially modified the marketplace approach. In *Rosenbloom,* Justice Brennan had declared that even when prominent public figures are involved, "[i]t is the rare case when the denial overtakes the original charge."[226] This analysis was accepted by the *Gertz* majority: "Of course, an opportunity for rebuttal seldom suffices to undo [the] harm of defamatory false-hood. Indeed, the law of defamation is rooted in our experience that the truth rarely catches up with a lie."[227]

The acceptance of this philosophy, quietly introduced in footnote nine, has seemingly left the first amendment in a peculiar spot. *Gertz* holds that the first amendment offers some protection for defamatory utterances presumably so that our Constitution can continue "to preserve an uninhibited marketplace of ideas in which truth will ultimately prevail. . . ."[228] And yet the Court recognizes that "an opportunity for rebuttal seldom suffices to undo [the] harm of defamatory falsehood,"[229] *i.e.,* truth does not emerge in the marketplace of ideas. Is the Court trapped in an obvious contradiction?

Perhaps *Gertz* should be read to say this: We recognize that by affording constitutional protection for defamation some false beliefs will prevail in the marketplace of ideas, but if we fail to provide constitutional protection, too many important ideas will never get into the marketplace. On balance, a level of constitutional protection for defamation advances the societal interest in learning the truth.

This is not the marketplace theory as traditionally conceived, and it is not the perspective of the first amendment depicted in *Sullivan.* As traditionally conceived, the marketplace theory presumed that truth would ultimately prevail in the marketplace, that false statements could not withstand competition.[230] *Gertz* rejects that assumption, but offers speech protection despite its belief that some falsehoods will ultimately prevail. *Sullivan* stated the broad (indeed overbroad) view that "constitutional protection does not turn upon 'the *truth,* popularity, or social utility of the ideas and beliefs which are offered.'"[231] And in *Garrison v. Louisiana* the Court proclaimed that "honest utterance, *even if inaccurate,* may further the fruitful exercise of the right of free speech."[232]

In a sweeping (albeit not unprecedented)[233] foray, however, *Gertz* has turned the traditional constitutional perspective upside down by announcing that, "[t]here is no con-stitutional value in false statements of fact"[234] and that "the erroneous statement of fact is not worthy of constitutional protection."[235]

This is dangerous doctrine. It begins with the presumption that false speech is unpro-tected and looks to determine if other factors are present which necessitate protection nonetheless. This begs the basic first amendment question: When can government percep-tions of truth or falsity be imposed upon the individual? Moreover, it demeans the interests of self-expression and cathartic release. In the final analysis, however, the *Gertz* formulation may make no difference. By recognizing that some false speech must be protected in order to prevent true speech from being driven out of the marketplace, *Gertz* arrives at the same results which would be reached if it were assumed that speech is protected whether true or false unless other important interests predominate.

Nonetheless, starting points can influence decisions, and *Gertz's* departure is to be regretted. Nor is anything of substance salvaged by *Gertz's* companion pronouncement that "[u]nder the First Amendment there is no such thing as a false idea."[236] This statement will undoubtedly send commentators, litigants, and the lower courts scurrying to make the unmakeable distinction between facts and ideas[237] on the one hand, and will set the same parties to wondering how to classify obscene statements in the *Gertz* lexicon. They are ordinarily not false statements of fact, and we are told that they are not ideas. Even if we know them when we see them, we will not know what to call them.

Presumably all the Court intended to accomplish by its fact-idea dichotomy was to assure that damages could not be imposed for the publication of generalized critical opinions about individuals.[238] In the case of non-public persons, it is not at all clear that such a doctrine invariably strikes the appropriate balance between reputation and speech. But if any advance is registered by elevating this libel-based distinction to a favored spot in the general first amendment hierarchy, it is indeed subtle. It is hard to determine how such a doctrine can possibly assist the Court in balancing the relevent interests in first amendment cases.

D. Balancing

It should be clear at this point that no single principle underlies first amendment methodology. Occasionally the Court will broadly proclaim, as it did in *Police Department v. Mosley* that, "above all else, the First Amendment means that government has no power to restrict expression because of its message, its ideas, its subject matter, or its content."[239] But any assessment of the legal regulation of communication must begin with the recognition that government does have power to restrict expression because of its content. There is no gainsaying the fact that perjury, blackmail, fighting words, defamation, advocacy of criminal law violations, obscenity, fraud, commercially deceptive advertisements are instances of expression. They are subject to sanction because their content[240] poses dangers to interests of societal concern. Indeed, a principal task of first amendment adjudication is to determine when content can be abridged.[241] That task necessitates a determination of: (1) the nature of the interest sought to be furthered by the state; (2) the extent to which the state must abridge the particular speech in order to further that interest; (3) the extent to which the abridgment will further the state interest; and (4) the impact of that abridgment on free speech values; *i.e.*, (a) the extent to which the content involved can make a contribution to the marketplace of ideas; (b) the extent to which government intervention can be tailored to prevent the arbitrary imposition of subjective values; (c) the extent to which the speech is necessary to further values of self-expression or cathartic release; and (d) the extent to which governmental abridgments can avoid substantial chilling effects on protected speech. An explication of the role which each of these factors has played in first amendment decisions will not be made here. To some extent, such analysis is not even possible because the Court has failed to reveal the extent to which a balancing of the free speech interest against the state interest has influenced the outcome.[242] Nonetheless, there are signs that the Court will pay more attention to the variety of factors involved. For this, we have *Sullivan* to thank.

Although *Sullivan* did not presage the collapse of the two-level system of first amendment methodology, it has forced the Court to reconsider the reasons why speech is and is not protected. By ruling that first amendment protection cannot be foreclosed by mere labels and by refusing to let the vagaries of history stifle first amendment development, *Sullivan*, as Kalven hoped, has made it impossible for the Court to categorically preclude speech from protection by reference to the shibboleth that it has always been that way. Thus it is no accident that the underpinnings of the commercial speech exclusion have finally been subjected to searching inquiry,[243] and the scope of that exclusion drastically confined. Indeed, the commercial speech exception is no longer so described. Commercial speech is now entitled to first amendment protection albeit to a lesser degree than political speech.[244] For example, commercially deceptive communications are considered to be entirely unprotected by the first amendment[245] even though politically deceptive communications are afforded strategic protection.[246] This distinction is based on the judgment that commercial advertising is more easily verifiable by its disseminator[247] and less likely to be chilled by regulation.[248]

As the Court put it in the *Virginia Pharmacy* case, "the greater objectivity and hardiness of commercial speech . . . may make it less necessary to tolerate inaccurate statements for fear of silencing the speaker."[249] There are echoes of *Gertz* here,[250] specifically its statement that false statements of fact are unprotected. Again, however regrettable the *Gertz* language may be, the phrasing or starting point need not and should not dictate or influence the conclusion. It analytically should make little difference that false statements of fact initially are considered unprotected so long as the impact of governmental abridgments on free speech values are carefully considered and so long as the initial consideration does not operate as a presumption. Nor should it make any difference that the result is ultimately described as an exclusion or as a rule. It makes little difference whether the speech abridged is finally described as never having been within the first amendment's protection or having been initially within its protection but in the final analysis balanced out *if* (and the if is crucial) it is understood that the process employed to determine the rule or the exclusion must include a balancing of the relevant values with appropriate respect for the first amendment functions involved. On the other hand, the *Gertz* false statements of fact doctrine hardly seems to foster respect for relevant first amendment functions. A judiciary aware that it is balancing protected speech out of the first amendment is far more likely to give speech the protection it deserves.

In any event, whatever the merits of the Court's general judgments about the objectivity[251] and hardiness[252] of commercial speech, however incomplete the Courts' abbreviated discussion may have been, and however disquieting the *Gertz* gloss may be, the Court is obviously committed to the justification of first amendment exclusions by more than historical reference. Indeed the Court in *Bigelow v. Virginia* recognized that "regardless of the particular label asserted by the State . . . a court may not escape the task of assessing the First Amendment interest at stake and *weighing* it against the public interest allegedly served by the regulation."[253] Language such as this must serve as the point of departure for first amendment decision making, not the sweeping broadside of *Mosley*. In short, any attempt to locate the central meaning of the first amendment is bound to be unavailing.

E. Absolutist Approaches

First amendment methodology is thus grounded in a paradox. Government must be restrained from imposing its views of truth by outlawing contrary communications. But the government itself makes the determination as to when this principle is to be abandoned.

The statement of the paradox exposes the obvious danger. If the state may abridge speech when it feels it is desirable to do so, the first amendment is reduced to nothing more than an admonition.[254] Some, notably Justice Black, have argued that the solution to the difficulty is to abolish the paradox by prohibiting the abridgment of any speech at all.[255] This absolutist approach to first amendment analysis is not without value. It emphasizes fidelity to the language of the first amendment and drastically confines the possibilities of subjective imposition of values by the government. To be sure, not all first amendment questions with respect to content regulation are automatically answered by this approach. It is still necessary to distinguish speech (which may not be abridged) from conduct (which may). But even though some important gray areas remain, it must be conceded that the "no law" approach provides easy answers to difficult questions and would do much to insure that the government could not silence the unpopular. Although the absolutist approach has value, it comes at too great a cost. It seemingly requires the conclusion that prejury, blackmail, knowing defamatory falsehoods, advocacy of murder and the like be absolutely protected. Some would rectify this disability by tinkering with the line between speech or "expression" and conduct.

Professor Emerson, for example, maintains that " '[a]ction' can be controlled, subject to other constitutional requirements but not by controlling expression."[256] He insists that "expression must be protected against government curtailment at all points, even where the results of expression may appear to be in conflict with other social interests that the government is charged with safeguarding."[257] These principles, however, are quickly breached.

Professor Emerson proceeds to delineate numerous areas in which action can be controlled by regulating expression and in which expression may be abridged because of its results. For example, he would permit the abridgment of speech involving "instructions" as to criminal action (on the ground that it has gone beyond persuasion to conduct),[258] solicitation to criminal action when the communication is "close, direct, effective, and instantaneous in its impact" (on the ground that it has become part of the action),[259] "obscene" communications "forced" upon persons against their will (on the ground that the harm is "direct, immediate, and not controllable by regulating subsequent action" and that it is like a physical assault and therefore classifiable as action),[260] defamation causing injury to a person's feelings (on the ground that the harm is "direct and instantaneous, and not remediable by longer range social processes that can prevent subsequent damage"),[261] and communications that invade the inner core of the personality by depicting matters of a wholly personal and intimate nature (on the ground that constitutionally protected areas of privacy "block out the rules governing the system of free expression").[262]

These permissible abridgments, purportedly based on distinctions between expression and action, bear a familiar ring. Most are based on a revitalization of clear and present danger principles, albeit in more stringent speech protective terms. These distinctions, on close scrutiny, do not turn on the question of whether expression is being regulated, but rather with the question of whether the results of the expression are sufficiently direct and harmful. Solicitation is expression; it is permissibly abridged in Emerson's scheme, because (despite protestations to the contrary) the "results of the expression may appear to be in conflict with other interests the government is charged with safeguarding."[263] Other abridgments approved by Professor Emerson are more obvious instances of balancing. Professor Emerson would permit some privacy actions abridging speech revealing embarassing details of an individuals' life, not because such speech is not expression, but rather because the interests in privacy are believed to outweigh rights of expression in limited contexts.[264]

When as thoughtful a scholar as Professor Emerson slips into doctrines he denounces (*e.g.,* clear and present danger[265] and balancing),[266] there are grounds to conclude that a distinction between expression and action is not a workable basis upon which to base a general theory.

Nonetheless the approach is instructive in that it suggests that a major principle in the hierarchy of first amendment values is that rules should be formulated on a sufficiently general basis that discretion to impose ad hoc arbitrary judgments be narrowly confined. Emerson would promote this principle by focusing on the line between expression and action; others would promote this principle by focusing on the concept of definition.

Professors Frantz[267] and Nimmer,[268] for example, would have the Court focus on the definition of "freedom of speech." Categories of speech would be either included or excluded from first amendment protection depending on how the various values are weighed, but once included the speech would be absolutely protected. It is necessary to understand that the term "definition" is used in a special sense. In *Gertz,* for example, the problem is to determine the level of abstraction at which definitions are required. If, for example, the question is defined to be whether defamation is included or excluded from the phrase "freedom of speech," the whole structure of *Gertz* must topple. It would not be possible to distinguish between the scope of the first amendment and the level of protection it affords. Instead, *Gertz,* in the lexicon of definitional balancing, "defines" at a lower level of abstraction. Negligent defamation of non-public persons is not "freedom of speech," but negligent, non-malicious defamation of public persons is. These "definitions" clearly necessitate individualized ad hoc judgments. The definition of public official may be relatively[269] free of gray areas, but the definition of public figures is disturbingly opaque and difficult to apply, particularly after *Firestone.* In addition, the concept of negligence is notoriously vague in the press context. This does not demonstrate that the definitions are wrong. It does demonstrate that the requirement of "definition" provides no assurance of freedom from subjective ad hoc determinations because the content of the definition can require value-laden applications. Examples could be multiplied. Obscenity is *defined* out of the "freedom of speech" rubric, but subjective ad hoc determinations are obviously required to apply the Court's definition.[270] *Brandenburg* similarly defines what is and is not protected, but the content of the definition requires individualized fact finding with the danger of arbitrariness that such discretion necessarily implicates. The concept of definition, therefore, also does not appear to afford any realistic restraints against judicial imposition of values on an ad hoc basis.

There are important lessons to be learned from the definitional balancers, however. It is of prime importance in first amendment methodology that rules be formulated with an eye to reducing the opportunities for subjective imposition of values on an ad hoc basis. This principle, however, cannot be absolute. For example in the context of advocacy of violence, an absolute exclusion from first amendment protection would undermine other important first amendment values; absolute protection of such speech would endanger important state interests; a middle ground with its attendant dangers of arbitrary administration appears to be the safest course when all of the functions of the first amendment are considered.

CONCLUSION

It is fashionable to assert that no first amendment theory can explain the Supreme Court's treatment of free speech questions.[271] The burden of this article has been to demonstrate that such criticism is erroneous. Failures of articulation by the Court do not demonstrate the absence of guiding methodology. The unwillingness of the Court to give exclusive emphasis to a particular value (*e.g.*, self-expression) or a single vision (*e.g.*, the marketplace analogy) or a single test (*e.g.*, clear and present danger) or a single principle (*e.g.*, expression versus action or public speech versus private speech) does not expose theoretical failure. Indeed the wisdom of first amendment jurisprudence is its recognition that the interests promoted by the first amendment are numerous and that government abridgments of speech impact on those interests in different ways. The definitional balancers understand this. The weakness of definitional balancing is its assumption that when regulation of content is involved, ad hoc balancing is always wrong.[272] Instead, the Court has pursued a general balancing approach which leaves the Court the option to decide when an accommodation of values requires general rules and when specific factual contexts necessitate ad hoc decision making. Thus, the Court will sometimes use a clear and present danger test and sometimes not; it will sometimes formulate general rules and sometimes not. This does not demonstrate confusion. Instead it reveals that different mixtures of values require different rules in different contexts.

Thus, the decision as to whether *Gertz*'s protections should be extended to non-media speech requires no revolution in methodology. It requires a weighing of the values served by the common law (*e.g.*, advancement of reputation, privacy, and preservation of order) against the values served by the first amendment (*e.g.*, furtherance of self-expression, cathartic values, and the rights of listeners to acquire information) and an appreciation of the difficulties of applying alternative standards (*e.g.*, whether fault can be defined with sufficient precision in the non-media context to avoid unacceptable chilling effects or unacceptably arbitrary decision making). The accommodation of those interests may produce a rejection of strict liability and a substitution of some level of first amendment protection for the non-media speaker (*e.g.*, fault, gross negligence, or *New York Times* malice). But whatever the results and however the outcome is phrased, the decision will be arrived at by the methodology of general balancing.

There is danger in this methodology, of course. But the potential for abuse does not justify the conclusion that the first amendment is an empty slogan. There are mitigating factors which lead to restraint. Federalism, separation of powers, the existence of an independent judiciary, the propensity to create rules of general application, and a tradition of respect for the functions of the first amendment are powerful restraints. But no one would suggest they guarantee the absence of abuse. The Court, for example, has recently gone so far as to suggest that even truthful press accounts relating to a criminal trial may be subjected to a prior restraint if the "gravity of the 'evil,' discounted by its improbability, justifies such invasion of free speech as is necessary to avoid the danger."[273] The reemployment of the *Dennis*[274] standard is sufficient reminder of the ill uses to which a balancing formula can be put. Moreover the various opinions in *Young v. American Mini Theatres*[275] and *Lehman v. City of Shaker Heights*[276] are grim evidence that we need not look back very far to recognize that a balancing approach can produce exotic opinions[277] and arbitrary results.[278] Unless we are to hold that blackmail, perjury, fraud, the advocacy of murder and the like are to be constitutionally protected, however, we appear committed to the notion that the first amendment is not an absolute and that exceptions to the scope of first amendment protection must be derived by an accommodation of values. Any first amendment theory can be manipulated to achieve unacceptable results. Strategic protection for first amendment values, however, cannot be achieved through artificial methodologies or exaggerated exaltation of individual principles. The best protection for first amendment freedoms depends not on sonorous slogans[279] but on the judiciary's wise appreciation of the valuable functions the first amendment is designed to promote.

Professor Kalven's hope that *Sullivan* would send the Court down the Meiklejohnian path has only been partially fulfilled. But his expectation that *Sullivan* would impel the Court to a reconsideration of general first amendment doctrine may yet be realized. *Sullivan* presented the opening wedge to dislodge historical reference and cavalier dictum as the starting points for first amendment doctrine. It has forced the Court to articulate the factors which lead it to adopt different tests in different contexts. In that sense, the *Sullivan* opinion may yet prove to be "the best and most important . . . ever produced in the realm of freedom of speech."[280]

Notes

1. Kalven, *The New York Times Case: A Note on "The Central Meaning of the First Amendment,"* 1964 Sup. Ct. Rev. 191.
2. 376 U.S. 254 (1964).
3. Kalven, *supra* note 1, at 194.
4. The constitutional guarantees require, we think, a federal rule that prohibits a public official from recovering damages for a defamatory falsehood relating to his official conduct unless he proves that the statement was made with "actual malice"—that is, with knowledge that it was false or with reckless disregard of whether it was false or not. 376 U.S. at 279-80. The Court also held on the facts that the evidence was insufficient to establish either malice on the part of the defendants or that the statements were made "of and concerning" the plaintiff. *Id.* at 288.
5. Kalven, *supra* note 1, at 213-14.
6. *Id.* at 217-18. The two-level approach assumes that some speech is beneath first amendment protection and that other speech is protected albeit subject to a clear and present danger limitation.
7. Chaplinsky v. New Hampshire, 315 U.S. 568 (1942) (fighting words beneath first amendment protection).
8. Beauharnais v. Illinois, 343 U.S. 250 (1952) (group libel beneath first amendment protection).
9. Roth v. United States, 354 U.S. 476 (1957) (obscenity beneath first amendment protection).

10. Kalven, *supra* note 1, at 208-09.

11. *Id.* at 221. All speech in the public domain or all speech of general or public interest can be equated with all speech relevant to self-government only by defining the term "relevant" so broadly that it can no longer serve as a term of limitation. *See* text accompanying notes 147-57 infra.

12. Kalven, *supra* note 1, at 221.

13. *See* Hess v. Indiana, 414 U.S. 105 (1973); Brandenburg v. Ohio, 395 U.S. 444 (1969).

14. *See* Paris Adult Theatre I v. Slaton, 413 U.S. 49 (1973).

15. Stewart, *"Or of the Press,"* 26 HASTINGS L.J. 631 (1975).

16. 418 U.S. 323 (1974).

17. The scope of first amendment protection is to be distinguished from the level of first amendment protection. Questions of scope determine whether a particular type of speech is entitled to any first amendment protection. Under *Gertz,* defamatory media speech is protected, but the level of first amendment protection decreases from malice to some showing of fault when non-public persons are the objects of attack. *Id.* at 347. For a discussion of the distinction between the level and scope of protection, see generally Kalven. *The Reasonable Man And The First Amendment: Hill, Butts, and Walker,* 1967 SUP. CT. REV. 267.

18. 418 U.S. at 345-47.

19. Kalven, *supra* note 1, at 221.

20. A. MEIKLEJOHN, POLITICAL FREEDOM 27 (1960).

21. *Id.* at 20-27.

22. *Id.* at 37.

23. *Id.* at 79.

24. *Id.*

25. *See, e.g.,* G. ANASTAPLO, THE CONSTITUTIONALIST (1971); BeVier, *The First Amendment and Political Speech: An Inquiry into the Substance and Limits of Principle,* 30 STAN. L. REV. 299 (1978); BlF, *The First Amendment and Privacy: The Supreme Court Justice and the Philosopher,* 28 RUTGERS CAMDEN L. REV. 41 (1974); Bork, *Neutral Principles and Some First Amendment Problems,* 47 IND. L.J. 1 (1971); Kalven, note 1 *supra,* Meiklejohn, *Public Speech and the First Amendment,* 55 GEO. L.J. 234 (1966); Comment, *Freedom to Hear: A Political Justification of the First Amendment,* 46 WASH. L. REV. 311 (1971). The diversity of views offered by these commentators dramatize the extent to which a politically based approach can lead to radically different degrees of speech protection depending in large part on how the term political is defined.

26. Brennan, *The Supreme Court and the Meiklejohn Interpretation of the First Amendment,* 79 HARV. L. REV. 1 (1965). For a discussion of the influence of Meiklejohn's views on the Court with particular emphasis on Justices Brennan and Douglas, see Bloustein, *supra* note 25, at 72-77.

27. A. MEIKLEJOHN, *supra* note 20, at 20, 27. This principle may justify greater governmental intrusions with respect to commercial speech and non-public speech than would be tolerable in the political realm.

28. *Id.* at 20.

29. Bork, note 25 *supra.*

30. *See* Garrison v. Louisiana, 379 U.S. 64, 74-75 (1974). On the other hand, there is nothing grand or romantic about supposing that art and literature are protected under the first amendment only to the extent that they have political relevance. Nor is it accurate to suppose that the Founding Fathers had so narrow a perspective. *See* note 157 *infra.*

31. 376 U.S. at 270 (emphasis added).

32. *Id.* at 273.

33. *Id.* at 291-92 (quoting City of Chicago v. Tribune Co., 307 Ill. 595, 601, 139 N.E. 86, 88 (1923).

34. 376 U.S. at 298.

35. *Id.* at 301.

36. *Id.*

37. *Id.* at 279-80.

38. A. MEIKLEJOHN, *supra* note 20, at 20. Thus the protection for defamatory public speech under *Sullivan* is not absolute. On the other hand, Kalven was apparently prepared to accept the malice exception, at least insofar as caculated falsehoods are concerned. *See* Kalven, *supra* note 17, at 294-95, 304-05. Thus in fundamental philosophy, Kalven was a definitional or general balancer, not a follower of Meiklejohn. *But cf.* Kalven & Steffen, *The Bar Admission Cases: An Unfinished Debate Between Justice Harlan and Justice Black,* 21 LAW IN TRANSITION 155 (1961) (renouncing balancing in favor of Justice Black's view at least as "a matter of rhetoric"). Indeed despite Kalven's appreciation of Meiklejohn's perspective, he, without calling attention to the fact, rejected both of Meiklejohn's major principles. Kalven believed that political expression was not absolutely immune from government abridgment, and he believed that the scope of the first amendment was not confined to political expression. Kalven, *Metaphysics of the Law of Obscenity.* 1960 SUP. CT. REV. 1, 16 [hereinafter cited as *Law of Obscenity*].

39. However narrow the exception might be, its existence demonstrated that the two-level approach to first amendment analysis was not abandoned by the *Sullivan* opinion.

40. Rosenblatt v. Baer, 383 U.S. 75 (1966) (supervisor of a ski resort).

41. Curtis Publishing Co. v. Butts, 388 U.S. 130 (1967).

42. Garrison v. Louisiana, 379 U.S. 64 (1964).

43. Pickering v. Board of Educ., 391 U.S. 563 (1968) (dismissal of teacher for criticizing school board); Linn v. United Plant Guard Workers Local 114, 383 U.S. 53 (1966) (federal labor law). *Linn* was reaffirmed (and extended beyond the NLRA to federal employment) in Old Dominion Branch 496, Nat'l Ass'n of Letter Carriers v. Austin, 418 U.S. 264 (1974). Professor Christie has suggested that *Old Dominion* is properly read for the idea that despite *Gertz* certain areas of public interest will require the application of *Sullivan* standards as a constitutional requirement even if the plaintiff is not a public person. Christie, *Injury to Reputation and the Constitution: Confusion Amid Conflicting Approaches,* 75 MICH. L. REV. 43, 50-51, 57 n. 38, 59, 62 (1976). *Old Dominion,* however, was explicitly decided under the federal labor laws without any occasion to decide first amendment arguments. 418 U.S. at 283 n. 15. Nothing in *Gertz* or Time, Inc. v. Firestone, 424 U.S. 448 (1976), indicates the slightest tendency to create special categories of subject matter triggering *Sullivan* standards. Indeed, if anything, *Firestone* suggests that the only significance of categories of subject matter is that *Sullivan* standards may not be constitutionally required when subject matter is not of the quality to permit a controversy to be called a "public" one for purposes of defining a public figure. *See* text accompanying notes 93-101 *infra.*

44. Time, Inc. v. Hill, 385 U.S. 374 (1967). *Hill* applied the *Sullivan* test to false light privacy cases when the content of the material in question involved "matters of public interest." *Id.* at 387-88. In Cantrell v. Forest City Publishing Co., 419 U.S. 245, 250-51 (1974), the Court left open the question of whether *Hill* has survived *Gertz. Gertz* refused to determine what is or is not of general or public interest in the defamation context and held that reputational interests would be inadequately served if a non-public person had to meet *Sullivan* malice standards in the defamation context even if the matter were of public interest. Thus, different standards are required of the same class of plaintiffs, *e.g.,* malice of a false light privacy plaintiff, fault of a defamation plaintiff. It does not inexorably follow that *Hill* is undermined by *Gertz.* First the Court has been willing to distinguish matters of general interest from matters not of general interest in other contexts. Time, Inc. v. Firestone, 424 U.S. 448 (1976). *See* text accompanying notes 93-101 *infra. Cf.* Miller v. California, 413 U.S. 15 (1973) (Court willing to determine what is of serious literary, artistic, political or scientific interest) and Cox Broadcasting v. Cohn, 420 U.S. 469, 491 (1975) (Court leaves open question of whether disclosure of embarrassing facts tort is constitutional). Second, the Court could refuse to distinguish between newsworthy and non-newsworthy items in a false light privacy context and still maintain a malice standard, since the question of whether the Court should distinguish between newsworthy and non-newsworthy speech is different from the question of the level of protection which should be afforded to the defendant.

As to the different levels of proof required by private plaintiffs, the Court might say as it suggested in *Hill* that since the state interest in reputation is greater than the included interest in avoiding false light invasions of privacy, a lesser showing may be permitted for plaintiffs seeking redress for invasion of the greater interest. 385 U.S. at 391. *But cf.* Time, Inc. v. Firestone, 424 U.S. 448 (1976) (*Gertz* standards applicable in defamation case even if no damage to reputation shown). *Compare* Zacchini v. Scripps-Howard Broadcasting Co., 433 U.S. 562, 573 (1977) (maintaining that the interest in permitting recovery for placing the plaintiff in a false light is that of reputation) *with* Gertz v. Robert Welch, Inc., 418 U.S. at 335 n. 6 (contending that the statute in *Hill* permitted damages for harm caused by exposure to public attention not for factual inaccuracies) *and* Note, *Defamation, Privacy and the First Amendment,* 1976 DUKE L.J. 1016 (criticizing *Firestone's* failure to require damage to reputation).

Presumably the most significant distinction is that in *Gertz,* unlike Hill, the substance of the statement warned the editor that substantial danger to an individual's interest was implicated. As the Court observed in *Hill,* "negligence would be a most elusive standard . . . when the content of the speech itself affords no warning of prospective harm to another through falsity." 385 U.S. at 389. And *Gertz* specifically has left open the question of which standards should apply in the defamation context when the content of the statement does not by itself warn the editor of the danger. On the other hand, *if* the defendant has actual knowledge of those facts which make the danger apparent, should a different standard apply merely because the content of the statement does not signal the danger? The real question is what the standard should be when neither the content of the statement nor other known facts manifest the danger.

45. St. Amant v. Thompson, 390 U.S. 727, 731 (1968) ("There must be sufficient evidence to permit the conclusion that the defendant in fact entertained serious doubts as to the truth of his publication.")

46. 403 U.S. 29 (1971).

47. *See* sources cited in note 99 *infra.*

48. 403 U.S. at 44. Significantly, however, even the *Rosenbloom* plurality was unwilling to subscribe to a literal following of Meiklejohn's views. The plurality noted that the first amendment's concern with "public

issues" was not confined to "matters bearing broadly on issues of responsible government." *Id.* at 42. Meiklejohn would have protected speech on public issues by contending that such speech necessarily related to issues of responsible government. His conception of and definition of political speech was broader than the plurality's. The difference between the plurality and Meiklejohn, however, is nevertheless fundamental. The plurality's position is that the scope of the first amendment is not confined to political expression. By expanding the scope beyond that proposed by Meiklejohn, resort to balancing of some type becomes almost inevitable.

49. Kalven, *supra* note 1, at 221.

50. *See* text accompanying notes 147-57 *infra*.

51. Stewart, *supra* note 15, at 635 (emphasis in original).

52. *Id.* at 633-35.

53. Kalven, *supra* note 1, at 194.

54. Stewart, *supra* note 15, at 635.

55. 376 U.S. at 256-57.

56. *Id.*

57. *Id.* at 257.

58. *Id.* at 262-63.

59. *But see* Note, *First Amendment Protection Against Libel Actions: Distinguishing Media and Non-Media Defendants,* 47 S. CAL. L. REV. 902 (1974) [hereinafter cited as *First Amendment Protection*].

60. *But cf.* Branzburg v. Hayes, 408 U.S. 664 (1972) (reporter required to disclose sources of material in grand jury context).

61. 376 U.S. at 264 n. 4.

62. *Id.* at 264, 265, 268.

63. 360 U.S. 564 (1959).

64. 376 U.S. at 282.

65. *Id.*

66. *Id.*

67. The line drawing can be difficult. If a person holds a press conference and the material is not published, does the press clause apply? If the material is published, does the protection extend only to the published version or to the oral conference as well? Are non-media republications after media publication covered by the press clause? *Compare* note 72 *infra with* note 174 *infra*.

68. But notice that corporations are not citizens, at least for purposes of the privileges and immunities clauses of the Constitution. Grosjean v. American Press Co., 297 U.S. 233, 244 (1936). If freedom of speech or press is dependent upon the right to vote as Meiklejohn suggests, *see* text accompanying notes 19-24 *supra*, one is led to the frivolous conclusion that corporations such as the New York Times Co. have no first amendment rights inasmuch as corporations typically cannot vote. *But see* Salyer Land Co. v. Tulare Lake Basin Water Storage Dist., 410 U.S. 719 (1973). For an excellent discussion of corporate voting rights, see Comment, *Public Officials Represent Acres, Not People,* 7 LOY. L.A.L. REV. 227, 262-66 (1974). Indeed this weakness in Meiklejohn's theory is made apparent by his specific contention that the privileges and immunities clause applies the first amendment to the states, not the due process clause, A. MEIKLEJOHN, *supra* note 20, at 53, a contention made necessary because of his bifurcated approach to speech protection. *See* text accompanying notes 19-24 *supra*. He regrets that the "clause in question protects 'citizens' rather than 'persons,'" and, hence, resident aliens are not provided for." A. MEIKLEJOHN, *supra* note 20, at 53. Meiklejohn's solution to this "difficulty" is that "[t]he essential point is not that the alien [and impliedly the New York Times Co.] has a right to speak but that we citizens have a right to hear him." *Id.* Nonetheless, it surely is surprising to learn that the New York Times Co. has no right to freedom of expression but only a right to raise the rights of others. Little did one realize the burden that third party standing rules have shouldered all these years. It could be that Meiklejohn would not apply his principles to the press clause. The same difficulties, however, would apply to non-press corporations.

69. Potential recipients of communications have standing to contest abridgment of speakers' rights. Virginia State Bd. of Pharmacy v. Virginia Citizens Consumer Council, Inc., 425 U.S. 748 (1976); Kleindienst v. Mandel, 408 U.S. 753 (1972). Presumably a speaker also has standing to assert the rights of his potential audience. *Cf.* Eisenstadt v. Baird, 405 U.S. 438 (1972) (distributor of contraceptives permitted to assert rights of recipients of the distribution).

70. 418 U.S. 323 (1974).

71. *Gertz* was decided on June 25, 1974. *Id.* at 323. Justice Stewart's speech was delivered on November 2, 1974. Stewart, *supra* note 15, at 631.

72. In each of the cases, however, the defendant has either been a media enterprise or a person who has published or broadcast in an instrumentality covered by the press clause. Professor Hill has suggested that Henry v. Collins, 380 U.S. 356 (1965), is an instance in which the *Sullivan* rule has been applied with "no media involvement whatever. . . ." Hill, *Defamation and Privacy,* 76 COLUM. L. REV. 1205, 1224 n. 91 (1976). There

the lower court failed to give a *Sullivan* instruction with respect to several communications. Two were telephone statements to reporters for publication which followed in five newspapers. Henry v. Collins, 253 Miss. 34, 42-44, 158 So. 2d 28, 30-31 (1963). One was a letter written the same day to a deputy sheriff containing the same defamatory statements. *Id.* at 42, 158 So. 2d at 30. The Supreme Court apparently required *Sullivan* standards to be applied to each of the communications. If only media defendants are to be protected, could Henry be tried under different standards for the letter than for the telephone statements (essential to the publications process) and the newspaper publications? Would a rule permitting a defendant to issue statements to the world through the media (and thus to public officials) but not directly to public officials make such sense? If the statement to the sheriff is protected because of the companion media involvement, would defamers be encouraged to rush into print to protect themselves? *See* Davis v. Schuchat, 510 F. 2d 731, 734 n. 3 (D.C. Cir. 1975) (expressing fear of such a possibility). Are not these difficulties avoided if no distinctions are made on the basis of media involvement?

    73. The issue might have been reached in Linn v. United Plant Guard Workers Local 114, 383 U.S. 53 (1966). There an assistant general manager of Pinkerton's National Detective Agency, Inc. filed a defamation suit for statements made in leaflets distributed during a union organizing campaign. The Court adopted *Sullivan* standards "by analogy" as a matter of federal labor policy "rather than under constitutional compulsion." *Id.* at 65. Inasmuch as federal labor law mandated *Sullivan* standards, there was no necessity to determine what constitutional requirements might have been required in the absence of statutory requirements. *Accord.* Old Dominion Branch No. 496, Nat's Ass'n of Letter Carriers v. Austin, 418 U.S. 264, 283 n. 15. Since *Old Dominion* and *Gertz* were decided on the same day and since *Old Dominion* reaffirms *Linn* (*id.* at 282-83), it is clear that *Linn* survives *Gertz*.

    74. 403 U.S. 29 (1971).

    75. *Id.* at 44.

    76. *Id.* at 43-44.

    77. *See id.* at 43-44 & n. 12.

    78. 418 U.S. at 346.

    79. *Id.*

    80. *Id.*

    81. *Id.* at 344.

    82. *Id.* at 344-45.

    83. *Id.* at 346.

    84. *Id.*

    85. *Id.*

    86. *Id.*

    87. *Id.* at 349. The Court did not address the question of nominal damages or whether a plaintiff could constitutionally clear his or her reputation via a declaratory judgment action without having to show fault or malice on the part of the defendant. *See generally* RESTATEMENT (SECOND) OF TORTS, Special Note On Alternative Remedies to Damages at 295-96 (Tent. Draft No. 20, 1974). Special verdicts can assist in this area except where the defendant can prevail on the fault question via summary judgment. The Court also did not discuss the constitutionality of awarding attorney's fees to prevailing plaintiffs in such actions and perforce did not discuss whether the constitutionality of such an award might depend upon a showing of fault or malice.

    88. 418 U.S. at 349.

    89. The language of the opinion strongly implied that "fault" was equated with negligence. "[P]unitive damages are wholly irrelevant to the state interest that justifies a negligence standard for private defamation actions." *Id.* at 350. *But see* Cox Broadcasting Corp. v. Cohn, 420 U.S. 469 (1975) (dictum implying that liability could be imposed for truthful statements presumably where malicious in the common law sense, thus suggesting that truth accompanied by malice equals fault). The lower courts have interpreted *Gertz* to mean that the defendant has to have been negligent in failing to recognize that the defamatory statement was false. *See, e.g.,* Cahill v. Hawaiian Paradise Park Corp., 56 Haw. 522, 543 P. 2d 1356 (1975); Troman v. Wood, 62 Ill. 2d 184, 340 N.E. 2d 292 (1975); Gobin v. Globe Publishing Co., 216 Kan. 223, 531 P. 2d 76 (1975).

    90. 418 U.S. at 348 (quoting Curtis Publishing Co. v. Butts, 388 U.S. 130, 155 (1967). This qualification may be significant in the libel per quod and false light privacy contexts. *See* note 44 *supra.*

    91. *See* text accompanying notes 19-24 *supra.*

    92. 418 U.S. at 346.

    93. 424 U.S. 448 (1976).

    94. *Id.* at 454.

    95. *Id.* at 454-55.

    96. 418 U.S. at 345 (emphasis added).

    97. 424 U.S. at 454.

98. The most the Court would do was to state that the interest of the public in a matter would not suffice to make the controversy public. *Id.*

99. The experience in applying the general or public interest test in the lower courts has been that almost every media report has been found to be newsworthy or of public interest. Eaton. *The American Law of Defamation through* Gertz v. Robert Welch, Inc. *and Beyond: An Analytical Primer,* 61 VA. L. REV. 1349, 1398 (1975); Robertson, *Defamation and the First Amendment: In Praise of* Gertz v. Robert Welch, Inc., 54 TEXAS L. REV. 199, 206-07 (1976); Comment, *The Expanding Constitutional Protection for the News Media from Liability for Defamation: Predictability and the New Synthesis,* 70 MICH. L. REV. 1547, 1560-61 n. 94 (1972). It could be that since less now hinges on the determination and since *Firestone* exhibits a restrictive approach (albeit undefined), the lower courts will tighten up. For the view that the question should hinge on whether the statements are relevant to self-government (with a narrow, indeed crabbed, view of what constitutes relevance), see Bloustein, note 25 *supra.*

100. The *Firestone* majority found it significant that the press conferences held by the plaintiff were not designed to influence the outcome of the controversy. 424 U.S. at 454-55 n. 3.

101. Arguably the very distinction between public persons and non-public persons suggests a bias in favor of public issues. But the proffered justification for the distinction in *Gertz* is put in terms of media access and voluntary assumption of risk. It is the content of the test for public figure which reveals the Court's continuing concern for the substantive character of the issues involved.

102. 418 U.S. at 322, 340.

103. *Id.* at 343, 348.

104. *Id.* at 340, 341, 343, 346, 347, 348, 350. Although the term "publishers" is a term of art in defamation law ordinarily embracing all statements (whether by media or non-media speakers) to third persons, it is clear from the framework of the opinion that the term is not used in the common law sense.

105. *Id.* at 340, 342.

106. *Id.* at 341.

107. *Id.* at 341, 345.

108. *Id.* at 342.

109. The speech of Justice Stewart now makes it apparent that the Court's constant use of media language was not inadvertent. The Court clouds the question, however, by referring to the freedoms of speech and press throughout the opinion. 418 U.S. at 325, 341, 342, 349. It apparently views the press as enjoying rights of speech. "[T]he prospect of civil liability for injurious falsehood might dissuade a timorous press from the effective exercise of First Amendment freedom*s." Id.* at 341 (emphasis added). This is not unusual. "The Court has generally viewed the freedom of the press as little more than a particularized form of freedom of speech. . . ." Note, *The Right of the Press to Gather Information,* 71 COLUM. L. REV. 838 (1971). Presumably if the Court wished to explain *Gertz's* "speech" references in a future case excluding non-media speakers from *Gertz* protections, it would now have to argue that the speech clause favors some defendants over others, an even more difficult task than attempting to argue that the press clause is to be distinguished from the speech clause in the defamation context.

The failure of the Court to discuss the media-non-media distinction could be an instance of judicial reluctance to discuss an issue not properly before it or it could reflect a division of views better suppressed than aired by greater fragmentation of opinions in a case already marked by multiple expressions of views. Justice Stewart's failure to cite *Gertz* in his speech despite its obvious relevance suggests either that it was written more than five months prior to its delivery or that an agreement not to cite *Gertz* for the distinction was reached and that the Justice feels bound by the agreement even in non-judicial publications. The decision not to cite Red Lion Braodcasting Co. v. FCC, 395 U.S. 367 (1969), in Miami Herald Publishing Co. v. Tornillo, 418 U.S. 241 (1974), is a striking example of the Court's desire to avoid fragmentation on an issue not before it. This omission has prevented the Court from reaching (or perhaps discovering) the ultimate doctrinal underpinnings of its approach to the first amendment.

110. *See* note 101 *supra.*

111. If this be the appropriate perspective, *Gertz* becomes especially difficult to justify. The notion of separation of press from government, *i.e.,* of an independent press is compromised in the extreme when the government at the instance of a defamed individual is permitted to judge not only the truth or falsity of press communications but also the reasonableness of the editorial process and the extent to which the communications involve issues of public controversy. There surely can be no pretense of a "high wall" between press and government.

112. Nimmer, *Is Freedom of the Press a Redundancy: What Does it Add to Freedom of Speech?,* 26 HASTING L.J. 639 (1975); Robertson, note 99 *supra;* Stewart, note 15 *supra, First Amendment Protection,* note 59 *supra. But see* Hill, note 72 *supra;* Lange, *The Speech and Press Clauses,* 23 UCLA L. REV. 77 (1975); Van Alstyne, *Comment: The*

Hazards to the Press of Claiming a "Preferred Position," 28 HASTINGS L.J. 761 (1977); Note, 88 HARV. L. REV. 139, 148, 152 (1974).

113. Stewart, *supra* note 15, at 634. This is also the emphasis of Robertson, *supra* note 99, at 218-20. Ultimately Justice Stewart's and Professor Robertson's views reduce to Professor Nimmer's idea that the press has a unique role to play in the political process.

114. Stewart, *supra* note 15, at 635.

115. Nimmer, *supra* note 112, at 647-50.

116. *Id.* at 653. *Robertson, supra* note 99, at 218-20, argues that the press plays a unique role in terms of checks and balances in the political process particularly for those power wielders who are not accountable in the election process. The argument fails to recognize the extent to which media influence is dependent upon robust non-media speech. *See* text accompanying notes 124-28 *infra*.

117. Nimmer, *supra* note 112, at 653. See also, T. EMERSON, THE SYSTEM OF FREEDOM OF EXPRESSION 6 (1970) [hereinafter cited as EMERSON]; Baker, *Commercial Speech: A Problem in the Theory of Freedom,* 62 IOWA L. REV. 1 (1976). The latter article argues that individual self-expression and participation is the exclusive justification for the first amendment. *But see* Symposium, *The First Amendment and the Right to Know,* 1976 WASH. U.L.Q. 1. Professor Baker's stimulating views deserve a careful response, but one cannot be made here.

118. Nimmer, *supra* note 112, at 653. *See also* EMERSON, *supra* note 117, at 7.

119. Nimmer, *supra* note 112, at 653.

120. *Id.* at 655 (emphasis added). Thus, Nimmer's point is not to argue conclusively that media speakers should be afforded greater protection, but rather that the interest in protecting the press is distinct and that any rules should be formulated only after taking such differences into account.

121. *First Amendment Protection, supra* note 59, at 925.

122. Nimmer, *Speech and Press: A Brief Reply,* 23 UCLA L. REV. 120, 121-22 (1975).

123. Of course, non-media discussions of politics are not confined to subjects discussed in the media. Even if they were, however, the case for greater media protection would not be enhanced. The power of the media as a check on government is dependent on non-media repetitions. Moreover, non-media discussions of media communications also lead to new ideas which in turn are reproduced in the media. Media-non-media interaction thus serves to check government power and to check media excesses. Even if values of self-expression and cathartic release were not of first amendment importance, even if non-media expressions were valued solely by their importance in preserving media power, non-media expression would have to be regarded as having profound first amendment significance.

124. This appears to be the approach taken by Lange, *supra* note 112, at 103. (citing Lange, *The Role of the Access Doctrine in the Regulation of the Mass Media: A Critical Review and Assessment,* 52 N.C.L. REV. 1, 18-21 (1973) (discussing the fact that social scientists have yet to demonstrate that the media is as powerful as commonly perceived). The failure of social scientists to demonstrate the power of the media may say more about the limitations of social science methodology than it does about the media.

125. *See, e.g.,* Klapper, *What We Know About the Effects of Mass Communication: The Brink of Hope,* in COMMUNICATIONS AND PUBLIC OPINION 362, 371 (R. Carlson ed. 1975).

The fact that the press broadly disseminates ideas is sufficient constitutional foundation for the common government practice of permitting the press greater access to newsworthy scenes than is otherwise made available to the general public. The fact that the government is permitted to make such distinctions, however, need not yield the conclusion that it is required to do so. *See* Pell v. Procunier, 417 U.S. 817 (1974).

Moreover no part of this argument undercuts the importance of access to the media in order to have an idea disseminated in the marketplace. Instead, the suggestion is that the power of the media is dependent on non-media communicators. Thus to the extent it is considered important that the media serve as a check on government power, the power of the check depends upon keeping non-media speech "robust and wide-open." At the same time this qualification should not be interpreted to suggest that access to the media is the only way to achieve a hearing for an idea or that the media is so powerful that its ideas are mechanically adopted by the populace.

The media need not be all important or all powerful to support a need for access. At the same time, to show the existence of a need for media access does not necessarily demonstrate that a system of access should be considered constitutional. The Court, of course, has invalidated state-mandated access to newspapers, Miami Herald Publishing Co. v. Tornillo, 418 U.S. 241 (1974), and has suppressed any hopes of expanded access in broadcasting, at least in the absence of additional FCC regulation. *See* CBS v. Democratic Nat'l Comm., 412 U.S. 94 (1973).

126. *See, e.g.,* R. MCGEE, SOCIOLOGY: AN INTRODUCTION 176-79 (1977); Brooks, *The Self and Political Role,* in SYMBOLIC INTERACTION 39 (J. Manis & B. Meltzer ed. 1972).

127. *See, e.g.,* M. BURGOON, APPROACHING SPEECH COMMUNICATION 295-97 (1974); Avery, *Communca-*

tion and the Media, in MESSAGES: A READER IN HUMAN COMMUNICATION 279, 289-91 (J. Civikly ed. 2d ed. 1977).

128. *See* sources cited in note 127 *supra.*

129. *See, e.g.,* Klapper, *The Social Effects of Mass Communication,* in THE SCIENCE OF HUMAN COMMUNI-CATION 65, 66-69 (W. Schramm ed. 1963) [hereinafter cited as HUMAN COMMUNICATION].

130. *See, e.g.,* Davies, *Psychological Characteristics of Beatle Mania,* in SOCIOLOGY: THEORIES IN CONFLICT 231, 232 (R. Denisoff ed. 1972).

131. *See, e.g.,* L. WESTON, THE STUDY OF SOCIETY 311 (1977); Lazarsfeld & Menzel, *Mass Media and Personal Influence,* in HUMAN COMMUNICATION, *supra* note 129, at 94, 103.

132. *See* sources cited in note 126 *supra.*

133. *See* sources cited in note 126 *supra.*

134. It bears emphasis that a defamatory comment is no less defamatory when it is true.

135. *Compare* Nimmer, *supra* note 112, at 654 *and* Nimmer, note 122 *supra,* at 121-22 *with* Lange, *supra* note 112, at 103-04.

136. *See* note 140 *infra.*

137. To the extent that the law cannot deter defamatory non-media comments, there is a basis for argument that it operates so selectively as to be unfair. If people commonly criticize others, there is a basis for arguing that compensation should be afforded only in aggravated cases.

138. Indeed such a view would appear to flatly contradict fundamental first amendment precepts. *See generally* Karst, *Equality as a Central Principle in the First Amendment,* 43 U. CHI. L. REV. 20 (1975).

139. Miami Herald Publishing Co. v. Tornillo, 418 U.S. 241, 250 (1974).

140. *Id.* This factor exposes the weakness of another argument used to support preferred treatment for the media in the defamation context. The argument is that generally public statements via the media may be countered with more speech, but the fact of non-media communication may not be known until too late. Nimmer, *supra* note 112, at 656. In the print media, of course, there is no right of access. More important even if some access were provided (one hopes the Miami Herald's treatment of Tornillo is atypical), the assumption that an opportunity to reply would suffice to undo the harm is questionable. Gertz v. Robert Welch, Inc., 418 U.S. at 344 n. 9. Undoing the damage of a communication addressed to millions is simply more difficult than mitigating the efforts of communications addressed to a few. Indeed the opportunity to reply in a face to face situation (as is typical in the non-media context) with the opportunity to respond to negative feedback or questions appears far more likely to minimize the harm than a situation which demands resorting to the necessarily impersonal media channels. In short, if capacity to cause damage is the test, media defendants deserve less protection, not more.

141. The common law standards is strict liability. Repetition of media statements is not privileged. RESTATEMENT (SECOND) OF TORTS § 578, Comment b (Tent. Draft No. 20, 1974).

142. *See* text accompanying notes 122-128 *supra.*

143. But *see* note 174 *infra.*

144. *See* notes 67, 72 *supra;* note 174 *infra.* It is possible that relevant differences might require such definitions in other constitutional contexts. Nonetheless, any definition would produce some vagueness and the toleration of vagueness in one context need not dictate its toleration in other contexts. Moreover, in the defamation context, it would be necessary to decide not only who the members of the press are but also to decide which communications addressed to them were so associated with the editorial process as to deserve press protection. The latter question would not even have to be addressed in a prison access context, for example, and is presumably controlled by different principles in a reporter's privilege context.

145. *But see* note 44 *supra;* text accompanying notes 98-101 *supra.*

146. *Butt see* note 158 *infra.*

147. A. MEIKLEJOHN, *supra* note 20, at 79.

148. Indeed the theory was so interpreted the year after Meiklejohn's first discussion of his theory appeared. Chafee, Book Review, 62 HARV. L. REV. 891, 896 (1949). The criticisms contained in Chafee's review (largely repeated here) have never been effectively answered.

149. *Id.* at 896. The fact that a theory premised on absolute and exclusive protection for political speech is unworkable does not mean that distinctions between political or ideological speech and commercial speech, for example, are necessarily unworkable. This article does not propose to analyze the first amendment relationships among, or relative first amendment values of, political speech, commercial speech, literature, private speech, etc. It is important, however, that such an analysis be made. A recent student comment puts it well: "[P]rac-tically speaking assigning a single weight to all types of speech means that the wider the area of coverage, the lower the level of protection." Comment, *Public Figures, Private Figures and Pubic Interest,* 30 STAN. L. REV. 157, 181 (1977). *But cf.* Karst, note 138 *supra* (arguing that the making of distinctions between kinds of speech in the absence of compelling reasons violates fundamental first amendment principles of equality).

150. Meiklejohn. *The First Amendment is an Absolute,* 1961 SUP. CT. REV. 245, 256.

151. On this point Kalven parted with Meiklejohn. *Law of Obscenity, supra* note 38, at 16 (citing Chafee, *supra* note 148, at 897).

152. Chafee, *supra* note 148, at 900.

153. This is, of course, not the exclusive basis for voter decision making, but that it is a significant variable is a proposition few would deny. *See generally* M. BURGOON, APPROACHING SPEECH COMMUNICATION 25-54 (1974); J. MCCROSKEY & L. WHEELESS, INTRODUCTION TO HUMAN COMMUNICATION 350 (1976); D. NIMMO & R. SAVAGE, CANDIDATES AND THEIR IMAGES (1976) [hereinafter cited as NIMMO & SAVAGE]; Anderson & Clevenger, *A Summary of Experimental Research in Ethos,* 30 SPEECH MONOGRAPHS 59 (1973).

154. *See* NIMMO & SAVAGE note 153 *supra.*

155. *See, e.g.,* T. CLEVENGER, AUDIENCE ANALYSIS (1971); G. MILLER & M. BURGOON, NEW TECHNIQUES OF PERSUASION (1973); P. ZIMBARDO & E. EBBESEN, INFLUENCING ATTITUDES AND CHANGING BEHAVIOR (1970).

156. There are exceptions. G. ANASTAPLO, note 25 *supra.* Bork, note 25 *supra.* Professor BeVier argues that literature is protected only if it contains "at least arguably, implicit political messages." BeVier, *supra* note 25, at 357. Presumably on this theory literature would be protected in some places but not in others and messages non-political at some times would become political at other times. At least the Court's responsibility to assess the political seriousness of obscene material is confined to patently offensive and prurient matter. The Court's position has been emphatically stated: "[O]ur cases have never suggested that expression about philosophical, social, artistic, economic, literary, or ethical matters . . . is not entitled to full First Amendment protection." Abood v. Detroit Bd. of Educ., 97 S. Ct. 1782, 1797 (1977).

157. The best evidence of this intent is the address of the Continental Congress in 1774 to the people of Quebec in which it is stated that the purpose of freedom of press is "besides the advancement of truth, science, morality, and arts in general, in its diffusion of liberal sentiment of the administration of Government, its ready communication of thoughts between subjects, and its consequential promotion of union among them, whereby oppressive officers are shamed or intimidated, into more honorable and just modes of conducting affairs." G. ANASTAPLO, *supra* note 25, at 537 n. 100 (quoting 1 J. OF THE CONTINENTAL CONGRESS, 1774-1789, at 108 (1904). Anastaplo, who argues that except for prior restraints, *id.* at 537 n. 100, the founding fathers intended to confine the first amendment protections to political speech, *id.* at 123, has his greatest difficulty with this passage. He submits that even this letter "puts the emphasis on the 'political'" which, of course, does nothing to support the view that the first amendment is exclusively political insofar as subsequent restraints are concerned. He further suggests that perhaps the letter means that art is advanced because of the general political freedoms, a suggestion which overlooks the use of the word "besides." Finally, he suggests that art is advanced by its protection from prior restraints. This is better, but it points up the principal weakness in this historical argument: It is one thing to show that the founding fathers focused on political speech; it is quite another to show that they intended political speech to be protected exclusively. Nor is it surprising that expressions of animosity to the regulation of literature did not dominate the scene. Attempts to censor literature on obscenity grounds, for example, did not become significant until the nineteenth century. *Law of Obscenity, supra* note 38, at 2.

158. The argument here is confined to defamation. It should be noticed, however, that the Court has developed doctrines that protect speech wholly unrelated to matters of general or public interest. The "fighting words" cases have normally involved matters of general or public interest (assuming the character of an individual policeman is such a matter), but the constitutional limitation on the states' ability to limit such expression does not depend upon its subject matter. Moreover, the Court has applied the first amendment in the context of labor disputes independent of whether or not they are considered to be of general or public interest. NLRB v. Gissel Packing Co., 395 U.S. 575, 617 (1969). Indeed the Court in discussing such cases has recognized that "[i]n some circumstances speech of an entirely private and economic character enjoys the protection of the First Amendment." Virginia State Bd. of Pharmacy v. Virginia Citizens Consumer Council, Inc., 425 U.S. 748, 763 n. 17 (1976). Finally, it should be observed that the touchstone of the two-level approach has been whether truth was advanced by the communication, not whether the communication was of political, general or public interest. *See, e.g.,* Chaplinsky v. New Hampshire, 315 U.S. 568 (1942). This is not to suggest that speech on public issues is not accorded a high place in the first amendment hierarchy by the Court. *See* text accompanying notes 93-110 *supra. See also* Young v. American Mini Theatres, Inc., 427 U.S. 50, 61 (1976) (plurality); Bond v. Floyd, 385 U.S. 116, 136 (1966).

159. W. PROSSER, THE LAW OF TORTS 739 (4th ed. 1971) [hereinafter cited as PROSSER].

160. The historical antecedents to the law of libel and slander briefly summarized here have been frequently recounted. *See, e.g.,* 5 W. HOLDSWORTH, A. HISTORY OF ENGLISH LAW 205-12 (2d ed. 1922); T. PLUCKNETT, A CONCISE HISTORY OF THE COMMON LAW 454-72 (4th ed. 1948) [hereinafter cited as PLUCKNETT]; 1 T. STREET, THE FOUNDATIONS OF LEGAL LIABILITY 273-95 (1906); Carr, *The English Law of Defamation, Pts. 1 &*

2. 18 L.Q. REV. 255, 388 (1902); Donnelly, *History of Defamation,* 1949 WIS. L. REV. 99; Lovell, *The "Reception" of Defamation by the Common Law,* 15 VAND. L. REV. 1051 (1962); Veeder, *The History of the Law of Defamation,* in 3 SELECT ESSAYS IN ANGLO-AMERICAN LEGAL HISTORY 446 (1909). The brief summary of defamation history which follows relies upon the sources cited in this note. Each of them recounts the same basic material, but Plucknett's is perhaps the most helpful account.

161. Kalven, *supra* note 1, at 196-97.

162. Obviously reputation is the primary value of concern today; nonetheless the value of preserving order should not be entirely discounted. The cathartic value of lawsuits is important, and the need for a forum to clear one's name (even if the defendant published without malice or negligence) can be justified in part on that principle. *See* note 87 *supra.* If one focuses on the desirability of affording an individual a forum to clear his name, the absurdity of making special damages an element of liability (via libel per quod or failure to meet the slander categories) becomes apparent.

163. The ecclesiastical courts had punished slander but had not tendered a damage remedy.

164. The unchastity for women category was added by statute with the passage of the Slander of Women Act in 1891.

165. This explanation, however, is not entirely satisfactory. It serves to explain the treatment of accusations of leprosy but may be less helpful in explaining the treatment afforded to accusations of syphilis, Veeder, *supra* note 160, at 461 n. 3, and smallpox, Donnelly, *supra* note 160, at 111-12.

166. The point is not so much that categories were created but that they became frozen, *i.e.,* no other categories could be added. *See, e.g.,* PROSSER, *supra* note 159, at 760-61. Moreover, the categories themselves were narrowly interpreted in a way that discouraged actions. *See, e.g.,* PLUCKNETT, *supra* note 160, at 465-66; F. POLLOCK, LAW OF TORTS 180-81 (15th ed. 1951); PROSSER, *supra* note 159, at 754-60. Finally, it is virtually unanimous that the distinctions between libel and slander are historical accidents. *See, e.g.,* sources cited in note 160 *supra.* As to the special damage requirement, see *e.g.,* Eldredge, *The Spurious Rule of Libel Per Quod,* 79 HARV. L. REV. 733, 755-56 (1966).

167. Most conspicuous in this respect is the confinement of the protection of interests of a third person to situations in which a request is made for information or, in the absence of a request, a family or other special relationship. Even a request for information may not be dispositive. Indeed, "[t]he mere desire to 'serve' a friend, or the public generally, is not enough." F. HARPER & F. JAMES. THE LAW OF TORTS 446 (1956) [hereinafter cited as HARPER & JAMES]. As Prosser states, "It has proved, however, unusually difficult to draw any line as to what is improper." PROSSER, *supra* note 159, at 788. Note that the effect of constitutional protection would not be to protect defamation absolutely but rather (if *Gertz* standards were applied) to safeguard statements non-negligently made. If *Gertz* were not applied, would it not be "anomolous . . . to deny the same measure of protection as is accorded to the press for its own publication of trivia"? Hill, *supra* note 72, at 1227.

168. *See, e.g.,* RESTATEMENT (SECOND) OF TORTS §§ 583-612 (Tent. Draft No. 20, 1974); HARPER & JAMES, *supra* note 167, at 419-63 (1956); PROSSER, *supra* note 159, at 776-96.

169. *See, e.g.,* RESTATEMENT (SECOND) OF TORTS § 580B, Comment b at 26-27 (Tent. Draft No. 21, 1975); Kalven, *supra* note 1, at 196. It is arguable that the common law slander case holdings are consistent with a negigence theory on the presumption that the facts in such cases involved conduct which was at least negligent. That question will not be explored here. The assumption herein is that the traditional perception of the common law has been correct.

170. *See, e.g.,* Kalven, *supra* note 1, at 196.

171. *See* note 167 *supra.*

172. *See* note 44 *supra.* The Court recognized in *Virginia Pharmacy* that commercial speech which was not itself of general or public interest could be so considered because of the importance that decisions regarding the value of products be made efficiently. Virginia State Bd. of Pharmacy v. Virginia Citizens Consumer Council, Inc., 425 U.S. 748, 765 (1976). To the extent that it is necessary to press speech into a general or public interest category, the same macrocosmic judgment can be made with respect to the importance of people having access to information about those with whom they interact.

173. *See* note 89 *supra.* The question of how the conditional privilege should be affected by an extension of *Gertz* to non-media defendants will not be explored here. *See* RESTATEMENT (SECOND) OF TORTS, Special Note at 46-48 (Tent. Draft No. 21, 1975).

174. The difficulty, of course, is that the press clause embraces everyone from the leafleteers with access to a mimeograph machine to the vast communication conglomerates. For example, if Professor Nimmer's suggestion that press publications be equated with the term publications in the copyright sense were accepted, *see* Nimmer, *supra* note 112, at 652, the press would include many who could not fairly be said to have the capacity to spread the risk. For a perceptive treatment of the difficulties of defining the media term, see Lange, *supra* note 112, at 99-107. For a persuasive argument that the capacity to spread the risk does not preclude self-censorship, see Anderson, *Libel and Press Self-Censorship,* 52 TEX. L. REV. 422 (1975).

175. *See* note 174 *supra*.

176. Kalven, *supra.* note 1, at 208, 221.

177. *Law of Obscenity,* note 38 *supra*.

178. *Id.* at 9-16.

179. *Id.*

180. *Id.*

181. *Id.* at 12.

182. *Id.* at 9.

183. *Id.* The same attack (but much more detailed) in the obscenity context against the *Roth* opinion has been made by the most articulate spokesman for the view that obscenity should not be afforded constitutional protection. H. CLOR, OBSCENITY AND PUBLIC MORALITY (1969). One of the special failures of Paris Adult Theatre I v. Slaton, 413 U.S. 49 (1973), is that it does not cite the work which contains the best defense of its position.

184. Kalven, *supra* note 1, at 218.

185. For an early recognition that *Sullivan* did not presage the abandonment of clear and present danger concepts, see Karst, *The First Amendment and Harry Kalven: An Appreciative Comment on the Advantages of Thinking Small,* 13 UCLA L. REV. 1, 8-9 (1965).

186. *See* note 39 *supra*.

187. *See* note 4 *supra*.

188. Garrison v. Louisiana, 379 U.S. 64, 75 (1964); Brennan, *supra* note 26, at 18-19 ("The underpinning of that qualification is the 'redeeming social value' test.").

189. *See* text accompanying notes 179-80 *supra*. It is not here suggested that the Court thinks in these terms or that first amendment analysis is best advanced or described in tripartite terminology.

190. *See, e.g.,* Brandenburg v. Ohio, 395 U.S. 444 (1969).

191. *See, e.g.,* Wood v. Georgia, 370 U.S. 375 (1962) (criminal contempt for publications critical of courts and judges). Moreover, the fighting words cases have apparently settled into a clear and present danger mold. *See* Gooding v. Wilson, 405 U.S. 518 (1972); Karst, *supra* note 138, at 31. Presumably a knowledge, if not an intent, requirement is also necessary. The difficult question is identifying the nature of the danger which is sufficient to divorce the speech from first amendment protection. In Lucas v. Arkansas, 423 U.S. 807 (1975), merely by dismissing a case for want of a substantial federal question, the Court held (if Hicks v. Miranda, 422 U.S. 332 (1975), is to be taken seriously) that a statute which sanctions language calculated *to arouse to anger* or to cause a breach of the peace or assault is not overbroad. *See* Lucas v. State, 257 Ark. 726, 727, 520 S.W. 2d 224, 225 (1975). The Court's enigmatic action must surely trouble those who have thought that Terminiello v. City of Chicago, 337 U.S. 1, 4 (1949), expressed basic first amendment law: "[A] function of free speech under our system of government is to invite dispute. It may indeed best serve its high purpose when it induces a condition of unrest, creates dissatisfaction with conditions as they are, or even stirs people to anger."

192. *Brandenburg* does not use the term but includes the concept. *See* notes 204-06 & accompanying text *infra*. The new language may be designed to avoid the insensitive applications of the test in decisions such as Debs v. United States, 249 U.S. 211 (1919).

193. Paris Adult Theatre I v. Slaton, 413 U.S. 49 (1973).

194. 418 U.S. at 341-43, 344 n. 9.

195. Indeed *Firestone* holds that plaintiffs may recover actual damages without a showing of harm to reputation. *See* note 44 *supra*.

196. 418 U.S. at 342-43, 344 n. 9.

197. 395 U.S. 444 (1969).

198. 413 U.S. 49 (1973).

199. It could be argued that *Sullivan* presumes that public officials, given their access to the media, can rebut false charges and always preserve their reputations, but such a reading is hard to sustain. *See* 376 U.S. at 272-73.

200. Thus, Justice Brennan in discussing the Court's first amendment theory suggested implicitly that it had none. Instead it had a number of different tests which it used in different contexts. Brennan, *supra* note 26, at 11. Thus, Professor Emerson complains that:

> The outstanding fact about the First Amendment today is that the Supreme Court has never developed any comprehensive theory of what that constitutional guarantee means and how it should be applied in concrete cases. At various times the Court has employed the bad tendency test, the clear and present danger test, an incitement test, and different forms of the ad hoc balancing test.

EMERSON, *supra* note 117, at 15.

201. Thus the Court after balancing the relevant factors will somtimes formulate rules of general applica-

tion in specific contexts. *See* Gertz v. Robert Welch, Inc., 418 U.S. at 343 (rejecting ad hoc balancing in the defamation context as unpredictable). In other circumstances, the Court will decide that ad hoc balancing is necessary. This does not mean the Court is bereft of theory. It rather suggests that the Court has been unwilling to place one value invariably above others and further suggests that the set of values involved in free speech cases is sufficiently complex that different factual situations necessitate the formulation of different standards and different approaches.

202. *Id.* at 340-43.

203. *Id.* at 339-42. Thus the Court recognizes that truthful defamatory speech is valuable. Note that defamatory speech can be true or false. RESTATEMENT (SECOND) OF TORTS § 559 (Tent. Draft No. 20, 1974).

204. 395 U.S. at 447.

205. In the early cases, Holmes & Brandeis were apparently willing to *substitute* intent for a showing of danger. Abrams v. United States, 250 U.S. 616, 627-28 (1919) (Holmes & Brandeis, JJ., dissenting) ("[T]he United States constitutionally may punish speech that produces or is intended to produce a clear and imminent danger. . . . It is only the present danger of immediate evil or an intent to bring it about that warrants Congress in setting a limit to the expression of opinion. . . ."); Whitney v. California, 274 U.S. 357, 373 (1927) (Brandeis & Holmes, JJ., concurring) ("That the necessity which is essential to a valid restriction does not exist unless speech would produce, or is intended to produce, a clear and imminent danger of some substantive evil which the State constitutionally may seek to prevent has been settled.") In *Schenck,* at least a showing of danger was necessary and apparently both intent *and* danger were required. Schenck v. United States, 249 U.S. 47, 52 (1919). *Accord,* Debs v. United States, 249 U.S. 211, 215 (1919). If there were any doubt, *Brandenburg* settles that both danger and intent are required. An individual may not be criminally sanctioned for speech which creates a danger that is not intended. Query whether an intent requirement exists in a hostile audience context. In any event, the intent requirement is not a very helpful protection in this context because intent may easily be inferred from the creation of danger. *See* Schenck v. United States, 249 U.S. at 51. This is especially the case if *Brandenburg* adopts an incitement standard. *See* note 206 *infra.* For the contention that an intent requirement is irrelevant to first amendment analysis, see Linde, *"Clear and Present Danger" Reexamined: Dissonance in the Brandenburg Concerto,* 22 STAN. L. REV. 1163, 1169 n. 26 (1970) (contending that intent is always irrelevant because when abridgements take non-criminal forms no one cares whether the material sought to be contained is intended to cause the damage alleged). But merely because an intent requirement need not be required for injunctive purposes does not render it always irrelevant for first amendment purposes. A speaker may be willing to run a risk of having an injunction issued but unwilling to face the risk of criminal sanction, thus producing a chilling effect. *See* Smith v. California, 361 U.S. 147 (1959); Kingsley Books, Inc. v. Brown, 354 U.S. 436 (1957).

206. Several leading commentators assume that *Brandenburg* adopts an incitement requirement, *i.e.,* the words themselves must explicitly call for action. EMERSON, *supra* note 117, at 157; Gunther. *Learned Hand and the Origins of Modern First Amendment Doctrine: Some Fragments of History,* 27 STAN L. REV., 719, 754 (1975); Linde, *supra* note 205, at 1185; Comment, Brandenburg v. Ohio: *A Speech Test for All Seasons?,* 43 U. CHI. L. REV. 151, 159-60 (1975). The conclusion is apparently based on this line from *Brandenburg.* "Neither the indictment nor the trial judge's instructions to the jury in any way refined the statute's bald definition of the crime in terms of mere advocacy, not distinguished from incitement to imminent lawless action." 395 U.S. at 448-49. *See also id.* at 449 n. 4. The difficulty with attaching significance to this ambiguous statement is that the term "incitement" is used in the alternative in the Court's statement of its test. Thus, advocacy of imminent lawless action is protected unless it is directed to inciting *or* producing imminent lawless action and is likely to incite *or* produce imminent lawless action. Thus, even assuming that the use of the word incitement refers to express use of language, as opposed to the nature of results (an interpretation which is strained in light of the Court's wording of the test), incitement is not necessary to divorce the speech from first amendment protection. It is enough that the speech is directed to producing imminent lawless action and is likely to produce such action. This is not to say that it would not be wise for the Court to adopt such an incitement requirement. Cases such as *Schenck* and *Debs* (particularly *Debs*) illustrate the extent to which inflamed factfinders can lightly infer danger even without language calling for illegal action. Nonetheless *Brandenburg* is at best unclear as to whether the requirement has been adopted. Nor does Hess v. Indiana, 414 U.S. 105 (1973), resolve the difficulty. *But see* Comment, *supra,* at 160-62. In *Hess,* the Court looked at the circumstances and the language to find that the speaker did not intend to produce imminent lawless action and that his speech was not likely to produce such action. 414 U.S. at 108-09. Indeed the language of the Court in Hess, if it points in any direction, strongly suggests that the words merely must be intended to produce such action rather than explicitly calling for it: "[S]ince there was no evidence, *or* rational inference from the import of the language, that his words were intended to produce, and likely to produce, imminent disorder, those words could not be punished by the State on the ground that they had a 'tendency to lead to violence.'" *Id.* at 109 (emphasis added).

Finally it is unclear as to whether Yates v. United Staes, 354 U.S. 298 (1957), survives *Brandenburg*. Specifically, how does the *Brandenburg* test apply to conspiracy charges? Does not persuading a person to perform imminent overt acts in furtherance of a conspiracy to overthrow the government at some unspecified future time amount to persuading one to imminent lawless action? If not, what does the Court mean when it approvingly cites Noto v. United States, 367 U.S. 290, 297-98 (1961), for the proposition that preparing a group for violent action and "steeling" it toward such action is not protected? If the Court intended to overrule *Yates* and *Noto*, would it do so cryptically and without analysis in a per curiam opinion while approvingly citing both cases?

207. *Cf.* Masses Publishing Co. v. Patten, 244 F. 535 (S.D.N.Y.), *rev'd*, 246 F. 24 (2d Cir. 1917) (adopting incitement standard to limit discretion). *See also* Gunther, note 206 supra.

208. For a stimulating argument that advocacy of law violation must be permitted because citizens in some circumstances have the right to disobey the state and that autonomous individuals must be afforded information to be able to arrive at an independent judgment, see Scanlon, *A Theory of Freedom of Expression*, I PHILOSOPHY & PUB. AFF. 204 (1972). The argument, however, surely is unpersuasive with respect to garden variety solicitations of murder.

209. This is not the conventional view, but it seems dispositive that the test is applied whether or not there has already been time to answer the arguments given. Suppose a debate in which after full opportunity for discussion of opposing views the audience was persuaded to go kill someone and did. Would the speaker be immune from criminal sanctions?

210. *See, e.g.,* Red Lion Broadcasting Co. v. FCC, 395 U.S. 367 (1969); Mills v. Alabama, 384 U.S. 214 (1966); New York Times Co. v. Sullivan, 376 U.S. 255 (1964); Associated Press v. United States, 326 U.S. 1 (1945). Occasionally the Court has mentioned other values. *See* Police Dep't v. Mosley, 408 U.S. 92, 96 (1972); CBS v. Democratic Nat'l Comm. 412 U.S. 94, 192-94 (1973) (Brennan, J., dissenting).

211. 395 U.S. 367 (1969).

212. *Id.* at 390. *But see* Baker, *supra* note 117, at 5-6.

213. *See* sources cited in note 118 *supra*.

214. Whitney v. California, 274 U.S. 357, 375 (1927) (Brandeis & Holmes, JJ., concurring).

215. Gitlow v. New York, 268 U.S. 652, 669 (1925).

216. Paris Adult Theatre I v. Slaton, 413 U.S. at 61 n. 12 (quoting Roth v. United States, 354 U.S. at 485 (quoting Chaplinsky v. New Hampshire, 315 U.S. at 572).

217. Paris Adult Threate I v. Slaton, 413 U.S. at 59.

218. *See* note 191 *supra*.

219. Rowan v. United States Post Office Dep't, 397 U.S. 728 (1970). *But see* Erznoznik v. City of Jacksonville, 422 U.S. 205 (1975); Cohen v. California, 403 U.S. 15 (1971).

220. Erznoznik v. City of Jacksonville, 422 U.S. at 209-10.

221. *See* text accompanying note 216 *supra*. This argument proves too much. It produces no basis for distinguishing imaginative literature not describing sexual conduct. *See Law of Obscenity*, note 38 *supra*.

222. To the extent one accepts the aesthetic sensibilities interest (*i.e.*, avoiding offensiveness) obscenity presents a clear and present danger. The extent to which balancing is required in a vagueness determination is well explained by Justice Brennan's dissent in *Paris Adult Theatre*.

223. It was on this principle that the Court in Miller v. California, 413 U.S. 15 (1973), abandoned the prevailing obscenity test to provide a less difficult burden for prosecutors.

224. Again the importance of the speech plays a role as the plurality admitted in Young v. American Mini Theates, Inc., 427 U.S. 50, 61 (1976).

225. Of course, marketplace considerations may go beyond determining truth or falsity. The permissible scope of the antitrust laws, the copyright laws, the securities laws, and acts designed to protect government secrets can be limited by the first amendment particularly insofar as they inappropriately limit the access of ideas to the communications market.

226. 403 U.S. at 46.

227. 418 U.S. at 344 n. 9.

228. Red Lion Broadcasting Co. v. FCC, 395 U.S. 367, 390 (1969).

229. 418 U.S. at 344 n. 9.

230. Dennis v. United States, 341 U.S. 494, 584 (1951) (Douglas, J., dissenting); J. MILTON, AREOPAGITICA 58 (Jebb ed. 1918). A more restrained marketplace conception is that the marketplace is the best testing ground for truth, although truth will not always prevail. Notice that even this weaker (but more sensible) version of the marketplace theory is still further weakened by *Gertz*. If footnote nine of *Gertz* is accepted, we are reduced to the proposition that in truth's best testing ground, truth can rarely catch up with a lie. It is perhaps instructive to observe that *Gertz's* distrust of the marketplace notion is matched by the legal system's rules of evidence. Although many rules of evidence are designed to avoid the presentation of irrelevant time-consuming

material, the legal system routinely keeps some prejudicial evidence from jurors, not because it is irrelevant and time consuming, but because the system endorses the view that truth will emerge in the marketplace only if censorship is employed. The point is not that the legal system is wrong, but that our commitment to the marketplace analogy is by no means unqualified and that an important first amendment inquiry is to determine the circumstances in which government intervention is preferable to an unfettered intellectual marketplace. That inquiry, of course, must also give weight to other first amendment values such as self-expression.

231. 376 U.S. at 271 (quoting NAACP v. Button, 371 U.S. 415, 445 (1963) (emphasis added).

232. 379 U.S. at 75 (emphasis added).

233. Passing comments to the effect that false communications do not serve first amendment ends were made in Time, Inc. v. Pape, 401 U.S. 279, 292 (1971), and St. Amant v. Thompson, 390 U.S. 727, 732 (1968). Unlike *Gertz,* neither urged the principle as a starting place for first amendment analysis.

234. 418 U.S. at 340.

235. *Id.* Contrast the *Sullivan* view as taken from Mill: "Even a false statement may be deemed to make a valuable contribution to public debate, since it brings about 'the clearer perception and livelier impression of truth, produced by its collision with error.'" 376 U.S. at 279 n. 19. On the significance of *Sullivan*'s treatment of falsity, see Kalven, *supra* note 1, at 210-13.

236. 418 U.S. at 339.

237. *See, e.g.,* Titus, *Statment of Fact Versus Statement of Opinion—A Spurious Dispute in Fair Comment,* 15 VAND. L. REV. 1203 (1962).

238. For an application of the distinction in the labor context by analogy, see Old Dominion Branch 496, Nat'l Ass'n of Letter Carriers v. Austin, 418 U.S. at 283-87. It is perhaps instructive to note that Justice Powell, the author of the opinion which sets the distinction in constitutional concrete, disagrees with the Court's application of the distinction.

239. 408 U.S. at 95.

240. In each case it is what is said that provides the basis for the imposition of sanctions. Some use the term *content* in a special sense, *i.e.,* the government cannot outlaw particular ideas. The term *content* is not here used in that special way.

241. First amendment considerations, of course, also require the Court to determine the limits which may be placed on the time, place, and manner of expression.

242. Vagueness cases are perhaps typical. The Court often finds cases vague or not vague without express recognition of the extent to which such considerations are implicated. Again Justice Brennan's dissenting opinion in *Paris Adult Theatre* is refreshing in that it explicitly identifies the relevant factors in the obscenity context. The dissenting conservative judges in the fighting words cases have long been arguing for a balancing test in the overbreadth context. The Court in the fighting words cases has clearly balanced but in the opposite direction, straining to find overbreadth while reluctant to identify the real motivating factors. To put it kindly, the result is that the Court's approach to the question of when parties have standing to raise a facial attack on vagueness grounds and when they have standing to raise a facial attack on overbreadth grounds is in a state of general confusion. On vagueness, *compare* Coates v. City of Cincinnati, 402 U.S. 611 (1971) *with* Broadrick v. Oklahoma, 413 U.S. 601 (1973), Parker v. Levy, 417 U.S. 733 (1974) *and* Young v. American Mini Theatres, Inc., 427 U.S. 50 (1976). On overbreadth, *compare* Broadrick, v. Oklahoma, 413 U.S. 601 (1973) *with* Erznoznik v. City of Jacksonville, 422 U.S. 205 (1975) *and* Doran v. Salem Inn, Inc., 422 U.S. 922 (1975). For a recent but flawed attempt to delineate relevant factors in the commercial speech context, see Bates v. State Bar of Arizona, 97 S. Ct. 2691, 2707-08 (1977). *See* notes 252-52 infra. At some point, the Court will not only decide which test or tests it wishes to apply in this area, but will become more explicit about the relevant factors. One suspects that the fighting words cases have been an important stumbling block to clarity. There, disguised (but arguably right-minded) decisions on the merits are apparently viewed as more palatable than ringing approbations of the right to curse your local policeman.

243. *See, e.g.,* Bates v. State Bar of Arizona, 97 S. Ct. 2691 (1977); Virginia State Bd. of Pharmacy v. Virginia Citizens Consumer Council, Inc., 425 U.S. 748 (1976).

244. Bates v. State Bar of Arizona, 97 S. Ct. at 2708-09; Virginia State Bd. of Pharmacy v. Virginia Citizens Consumer Council, Inc., 425 U.S. at 771 n. 24.

245. Bates v. State Bar of Arizona, 97 S. Ct. at 2708-09; Virginia State Bd. of Pharmacy v. Virginia Citizens Consumer Council, Inc., 425 U.S. at 711 n. 24. False speech in the Court's lexicon starts outside the first amendment and also does not get balanced in. True, but misleading, speech presumably starts inside, but is balanced out.

246. Bates v. State Bar of Arizona, 97 S. Ct. at 2708-09; Virginia State Bd. of Pharmacy v. Virginia Citizens Consumer Council, Inc., 425 U.S. at 711 n. 24.

247. Virginia State Bd. of Pharmacy v. Virginia Citizens Consumer Council, Inc., 425 U.S. at 711 n. 24.

248. *Id.*

249. *Id.*

250. Indeed the Court, citing *Gertz,* also states that "[u]ntruthful speech, commercial or otherwise, has never been protected for its own sake." *Id.* at 771. The Court also cites Konigsberg v. State Bar of California, 366 U.S. 36, 49 & n. 10 (1961) for that proposition; however *Konigsberg* merely lists various exceptions to first amendment protection; it does not discuss the relationship of false speech to first amendment values.

251. The assumption that knowledge about products is to some unspecified degree (always? unusually?) verifiable by its disseminator is questionable. Consider, for example, the massive number of studies concerning one illegal product, marijuana, and the degree of debate about its effects. It would appear that manufactures may often be unsure about the effects of their products, and it well could be that in numerous circumstance scientists in universities know more about the products' effects than the disseminators. The result of the Court's assumption about the disseminator's ability to verify, of course, is to protect non-disseminator's statements about products while not protecting the same statements by disseminators. There may be good grounds for making such a distinction, but it is doubtful that the comparative ability to verify should be the relevant focus.

252. The assumption that because disseminators have dollars at stake they will continue advertising is beside the point. The question is whether they will be chilled from making statements about their products which are controversial or which could be contested. Clearly the inclination of the manufacturer will be to stay out of litigation and to opt instead for mindless jingles and the like.

253. 421 U.S. at 826 (emphasis added).

254. Dennis v. United States, 341 U.S. 494, 580 (1951) (Black, J., dissenting).

255. *See, e.g.,* Konigsberg v. State Bar of California, 366 U.S. 36, 60-71 (1971) (Black, J., dissenting); Barenblatt v. United States, 360 U.S. 109, 140-44 (1959) (Black, J., dissenting); Dennis v. United States, 341 U.S. 494, 580 (1951) (Black, J., dissenting); American Communications Ass'n v. Douds, 339 U.S. 382, 445-53 (1950) (Black, J., dissenting). On the other hand, it is at least arguable that Justice Black's rhetoric of absolutism ultimately reduces to a form of definitional balancing. Black, *Mr. Justice Black, the Supreme Court, and the Bill of Rights,* 222 HARPER'S MAGAZINE 63, 68 (1961).

256. EMERSON, *supra* note 117, at 17.

257. *Id.* at 17.

258. *Id.* at 75.

259. *Id.* at 404.

260. *Id.* at 496.

261. *Id.* at 543.

262. *Id.* at 562.

263. *See* text accompanying note 257 *supra.*

264. *But see* EMERSON, *supra* note 117, at 549.

265. *See, e.g., id.* at 74-75.

266. *See, e.g., id.* at 718.

267. Frantz, *The First Amendment in the Balance,* 71 YALE L.J. 1424 (1962).

268. Nimmer, *The Rights to Speak from* Times *to* Time: *First Amendment Theory Applied to Libel and Misapplied to Privacy,* 56 CALIF. L.REV. 935 (1968).

269. *See* Rosenblatt v. Baer, 383 U.S. 75 (1966).

270. Miller v. California, 413 U.S. 15 (1973).

271. *See* note 200 *supra.*

272. Alternatively, definitional balancers could concede that ad hoc balancing might be appropriate in particular contexts (*e.g.,* reporter's privilege cases), but argue that the first amendment risks inherent in affording courts the authority to decide when ad hoc balancing will or will not be used are too great. If definitional balancing offered realistic constraints on judicial decision making, this argument would have force.

273. Nebraska Press Ass'n v. Stuart, 427 U.S. 539, 562 (1976) (quoting United States v. Dennis, 183 F. 2d 201, 212 (2d Cir. 1950), *aff'd,* 341 U.S. 494 (1951).

274. Dennis v. United States, 342 U.S. 494 (1951). On the particular theoretical difficulties with the use of the test in the *Nebraska* case, see Barnett, *The Puzzle of Prior Restraint,* 29 STAN. L. REV. 539 (1977).

275. 427 U.S. 50 (1976).

276. 418 U.S. 298 (1974).

277. As to *Young,* see Friedman, *Zoning "Adult" Movies: The Potential Impact of Young v. American Mini Theaters,* 28 HASTINGS L.J. 1293 (1977). *But see* Clor, *Public Morality and Free Expression: The Judicial Search for Principles of Reconcilation,* 28 HASTINGS L.J. 1305 (1977).

278. As to *Lehman,* see Karst, *supra* note 138, at 35.

279. *See* Dennis v. United States, 341 U.S. 494, 519 (1951) (Frankfurter, J., concurring). Nothing here, of course, supports Justice Frankfurter's theory of the degree of deference which should be afforded to legislative judgments.

280. Kalven, *supra* note 1, at 194.

Scope of the First Amendment
Freedom of Speech
BY C. EDWIN BAKER*

This paper develops three theories of the scope of speech protected by the first amendment: two different marketplace of ideas theories, which I will call the *classic model* and the *market failure model,* and a third, the *liberty model.* The classic model depends on implausible assumptions for its coherence. The market failure model is unworkable, dangerous, and inconsistent with a reasonable interpretation of the purpose of the first amendment. Although the court consistently has used and proclaimed the classic theory and though most modern reformist proposals recommend a market failure model, the liberty model provides the most coherent theory of the first amendment. Adoption of this theory, which delineates a realm of individual liberty roughly corresponding to noncoercive, nonviolent action, would have major, salutary implications for judicial elaboration of the first amendment.

The classic marketplace of ideas model argues that truth (or the best perspectives or solutions) can be discovered through robust debate, free from governmental interference. Defending this theory in *On Liberty,*[1] John Stuart Mill argued that three situations are possible: 1) if heretical opinion contains the truth, and if we silence it, we lose the chance of exchanging truth for error; 2) if received and contesting opinions each hold part of the truth, their clash in open discussion provides the best means to discover the truth in each; 3) even if the heretical view is wholly false and the orthodoxy contains the whole truth, the received truth, unless debated and challenged, will be held in the manner of prejudice or dead dogma, its meaning may be forgotten or enfeebled, and it will be inefficacious for good.[2] Moreover, without free speech, totally false heretical opinions which could not survive open discussion will not disappear; instead, driven underground, these opinions will smolder, their fallacies protected from exposure and opposition.[3] In this model, the value of free speech lies not in the liberty interests of individual speakers but in the societal benefits derived from unimpeded discussion.[4] This social gain is so great, and any loss from allowing speech is so small, that society should tolerate no restraint on the verbal search for truth.

Just as real world conditions prevent the laissez-faire economic market—praised as a social means to facilitate optimal allocation and production of goods—from achieving the socially desired results, critics of the classic marketplace of ideas theory point to factors that prevent it from successfully facilitating the discovery of truth or generating proper social perspectives and decisions.[5] Because of monopoly control of the media, lack of access of disfavored or impoverished groups, techniques of behavior manipulation, irrational response to propaganda, and the nonexistence of value-free, objective truth, the marketplace of ideas fails to achieve the desired results. Therefore, the advocates of the market failure model conclude that objective social realities require state intervention in the speech arena, just as in the economic arena in order to correct for these market failures;[6] only then will freedom of speech promote socially desirable perspectives and decisions.

*Assistant Professor of Law, University of Oregon. Thomas I. Emerson, Ernestine Magagna Baker, and Falcon O. Baker encouraged and aided me in writing earlier versions of this paper. Margaret Jane Radin, Jennifer Friesen, Paula Wilk and the editors of the UCLA Law Review have made helpful comments on recent drafts. The help of those and other teachers is much appreciated.

The liberty model holds that the free speech clause protects not a marketplace but rather an arena of individual liberty from certain types of governmental restrictions. Speech is protected not as a means to a collective good but because of the value of speech conduct to the individual. The liberty theory justifies protection because of the way the protected conduct fosters individual self-realization and self-determination without improperly interfering with the legitimate claims of others. Of course, the liberty theory must specify what conduct is protected. After investigating the nature of speech—its uses and the manner in which it typically affects the world—and after reviewing generally accepted notions of the values of first amendment protected activities, I argue that the constitutional protection of free speech bars certain governmental restrictions on noncoercive, nonviolent, substantively valued conduct, including nonverbal conduct. In this liberty interpretation, first amendment protections of speech, assembly, and religion are merely different markers illustrating or bounding a single realm of liberty of self-expression and self-determination. Although any one of these three concepts illuminates this realm, the concept of protected speech most clearly delineates its scope.[7] Finally, the broadened scope of protection required by the liberty theory cures the major inadequacies of the marketplace of ideas as a model for finding or creating societal "truth," thereby providing protection for a progressive process of change.

I will proceed by developing and evaluating each of these theories in turn.

I. The Classic Marketplace of Ideas Theory

A. The Theory

According to classic theory, truth is discovered through its competition with falsehood for acceptance. This result depends on certain crucial assumptions. First, truth must be "objective" or "discoverable." Truth is able to outshine falsity in debate or discussion only if truth is there to be seen. If, instead, truth were subjective, chosen or created, an adequate theory must explain why the competition among various viewpoints leads to the "best choice" or why protecting this competition provides a proper or legitimate process of choice or creation. Second, people must possess the capacity correctly to perceive truth or reality. One can distinguish two aspects of this rationality assumption. First, people's social location must not control the manner in which they perceive or understand the world. If perceptions are social creations and if people's social experiences are radically different, then mere discussion would be inadequate for discovering what truth or which perspectives are correct or best; one could not hope that employing reason in discussion would provide an unbiased insight into reality. Instead, perceptions of truth would vary, and dominance of one perception over another would depend on arbitrary circumstances and power relations among social groups. Second, people's rational faculties must enable them to sort through the form and frequency of message presentation in order to evaluate the core notions. Otherwise, the marketplace of ideas would only promote acceptance of those perspectives which were adequately packaged and promoted.

The premise that this marketplace of ideas uniformly promotes human interests implies that cultural pluralism will be progressively diminished and that no intractable conflict of values exists in society. Intractable value conflicts and permanent or progressive diversity would imply either a lack of uniform, stable content of truth or the insufficiency of truth as a basis for human action; the usefulness of the robust debate could not then be assumed but would depend on whether it operated to advance or obstruct the interests of the group whose values one adopts. Nevertheless, given the theory's assumptions about the objective nature of truth, the rational capabilities of humans, and the unity of the real aims of people, limiting the marketplace of ideas necessarily undermines the discovery and recognition of truth and impedes wise, well-founded decision making. Given the theory's assumptions, the presentation of conflicting arguments and insights aids people in discovering the truth in each position.[8]

B. Judicial Adoption

The Supreme Court steadfastly relies upon a marketplace of ideas theory in determining what speech is protected.[9] Marketplace imagery (competition of ideas, the value of robust debate) pervades Court opinions and provides justification for their first amendment "tests." Brief review of three prominent tests can illustrate this judicial reliance on the theory.

Holmes and Brandeis grounded the clear and present danger test[10] on the classic marketplace model: "[T]he ultimate good desired is better reached by free trade in ideas—that the best test of truth is the power of thought to get itself accepted in the competition of the market . . ."[11] and "freedom to think as you will and to speak as you think are means indispendsable to the discovery and spread of political truth."[12] Holmes' and Brandeis' language suggests the model's three assumptions concerning the nature of truth, human rationality, and society; and the logic of their test parallels the implications of the classic marketplace of ideas model. The danger must be "clear," as Brandeis indicated, in order to prevent suppression on the basis of irrational fear, like the fear of witches exhibited by men when they burned women.[13] And it must be "present"—because if "there is opportunity for full discussion" or "if there be time to expose through discussion the falsehood and fallacies, . . . the remedy to be applied is more speech."[14] If the danger is not "present," the gravity of the evil and the probability of its occurrence[15] must be irrelevant because, given the faith in reason and discussion, the evil must be accepted as best if people choose it after hearing both sides: "If in the long run the beliefs expressed in proletarian dictatorship are destined to be accepted . . . the only meaning of free speech is that they should be given their chance and have their way."[16] In other words, protection must be given *as long as* the market place continues to operate. "Harms" resulting from speech cannot justify suppression as long as the harm results from people being convinced by the robust debate. (If the "right" side failed to participate, they, not those spreading evil counsel, are at fault; in this situation, governmental restriction must not be allowed.)

In fact, the development of the clear and present danger test by Holmes and Brandeis merely repeats the conclusion of the classic formulation of the marketplace of ideas theory. John Stuart Mill had already noted that:

> [E]ven opinions lose their immunity when the circumstances in which they are expressed are such as to constitute their expression a positive investigation to some mischievous act. An opinion that corn dealers are starvers of the poor . . . ought to be unmolested when simply circulated through the press, but may justly incur punishment when delivered orally to an excited mob assembled before the house of a corn dealer, or when handed about among the same mob in the form of a placard.[17]

In *Roth v. United States,*[18] Mr. Justice Brennan denied obscenity constitutional protection precisely because obscenity does not contribute to the marketplace of ideas. And although many liberals quarrel with this factual perception, it is crucial for the Court's conclusion that obscenity is "utterly without redeeming social importance." "All *ideas* having even the slightest redeeming social importance . . . have full protection . . . ."[19] In regulating speech, the government must be neutral towards different ideas. Content discrimination amounts to forbidden censorship that is avoided only if all communications containing messages or conveying ideas are protected.[20] The allegedly obscene communication meets the redeeming social importance criterion and is thereby protected if, but only if, the publication participates in the marketplace of ideas. "The protection given speech and press was fashioned to assure unfettered interchange of ideas for the bringing about of political and social changes desired by the people."[21] "[T]he First Amendment's basic guarantee is of freedom to advocate ideas, including unorthodox ideas, controversial ideas, even ideas hateful to the prevailing climate of opinion."[22]

In rejecting two obvious objections to its analysis, the Court further highlights its reliance on the marketplace theory. First, Mr. Justice Douglas asks:

> When the Court today speaks of "social value," does it mean a "value" to the majority? Why is not a minority "value" cognizable? The masochistic group is one; the deviant group is another . . . . [I]f the communication is of value to the masochistic community or to others of the deviant community, how can it be said to be "utterly without redeeming social importance"? "Redeeming" to whom? "Importance" to whom?[23]

Douglas finds "social value" not in the contribution advocacy of masochism makes to the pursuit of truth in the marketplace of ideas, but in the contribution the material makes to "the needs of this group."[24] Douglas could have further argued that people's willingness to pay money for the material proves that it has some value to them — any obscenity which sells has "social value." The Court must employ the marketplace theory to avoid Douglas' constitutional conclusion without rejecting his factual observation. The Court can conclude that the willingness to pay only indicates the value of obscenity for the entertainment "needs of the group," but that only the literature's *advocacy* of a way of life and not it use *within* a way of life, only its presentation of an argument, even if ineloquent, for a set of ideas and not merely its manifestation of certain ideas, is relevant to the literature's contribution to or its redeeming value in the marketplace of ideas. Because of this focus on the marketplace of ideas, "to equate the free and robust exchange of ideas and political debate with commercial exploitation of obscene material demeans the grand conception of the First Amendment . . . ."[25] And, despite liberal protests, most would agree with the Court's assessment that obscenity does not contribute to the marketplace of ideas.[26]

Second, the Court often says that speech is protected because of its role in "bringing about political and social change." Yet a major argument for banning obscenity is that it contributes to social change.[27] Some think that obscenity leads to criminal conduct, and most would agree that its use can, and does, affect the moral or cultural tone of the community. The Court's reliance on the marketplace model explains its refusal to protect obscenity despite its contribution to bringing about social change. In the marketplace theory, speech must bring about change by the (at least partly) rational process of convincing people of ideas or opinions, not by its use in disapproved entertainment practices.

In *Paris Adult Theatre I v. Slaton,* Mr. Justice Brennan correctly objects that the Burger Court's altered standard ("serious literary, artistic, political, or scientific value") "jeopardize[s] the analytic underpinnings of the entire scheme."[28] The jeopardy results because now the government through the courts must evaluate the worth of the speech, the importance, and the "seriousness" of the ideas; in the earlier approach, the government, in theory, was required to be agnostic. Nevertheless, the new majority, although it explicitly rejects Mill's argument for liberty in general,[29] repeatedly reaffirms its allegiance to "the free and robust change of ideas," "the unfettered interchange of ideas,"[30] the prohibition of state "control of reason and the intellect," and the protection of the "communication of ideas."[31] The Court still relies upon the marketplace theory although, by its implicit balancing, the Court avoids the analytic consequences of fully accepting the theory.

The Court's basic constitutional analysis of defamation invokes Mill's marketplace of ideas theory to justify its conclusion. At least in the case of defamation of public officials, the first amendment gives absolute protection to the speaker unless the false, defamatory statement is made "with knowledge that it was false or with reckless disregard of whether it was false or not."[32] The Court explained that the first amendment "was fashioned to assure unfettered interchange of ideas," and emphasized the Constitutional faith "in the power of reason as applied through public debate."[33] In *New York Times v. Sullivan,* the Court quotes Mill for the practical point that erroneous statements are inevitably made, even in good faith, during discussions;[34] and, therefore, the erroneous statements must be protected to provide the breathing space needed by the marketplace of ideas. The Court also cites Mill's argument that falsehoods can serve a useful function by bringing about "the clear perception and livelier impression of truth, produced by its collision with error."[35] Still, the marketplace logic does not require that all defamation be protected. The Court can justify the *New York Times* rule that limits protection to those who are concerned about the truth of their statements on the ground that only these people are engaged in any search for truth or "any exposition of ideas." The first amendment protects speech totally, but only if the speech stems from honest participation in the marketplace of information and ideas.[36]

In recent cases in which the Court often undertakes explicit legislative-like balancing, the Court has developed a not-yet-complete complex of rules to cover speech injuries to non-public figures.[37] Despite abandoning the strict requirements of marketplace logic, the Court continues to emphasize the marketplace theory in order to explain the role and value of speech. For example, in *Gertz v. Robert Welch, Inc.,*[38] Mr. Justice Powell opens his discussion of the first amendment by noting that we depend for the correction of pernicious opinions "on the competition of other ideas."[39] A "false statement of fact," which Powell distinguishes from ideas, has "no constitutional value," because it does not "materially advanc[e] society's interest in 'uninhibited, robust, and wide-open' debate on public issues"; still, false statements of fact are sometimes protected because they are "inevitable in free debate."[40] Thus, although the Court does not extend the *New York Times* degree of protection, it retains *New York Times'* reliance on the classic marketplace of ideas theory of speech.

The logic of these "tests" illustrates the judicial adoption of the classic marketplace of ideas model. Other examples could be given. Marketplace notions are not the only strains to be heard in the chorus of Court pronouncements on the first amendment. Some Court opinions suggest the "liberty theory." And individual justices clearly adopt the liberty theory in some situations. Nevertheless, the marketplace theory dominates; and its rejection would have major implications for first amendment interpretation.

C. Failure of Assumptions

The assumptions on which the classic marketplace of ideas theory rests are almost universally rejected today. Because of this failure of assumptions, the hope that the marketplace leads to truth, or even to the best or most desirable decision, becomes implausible. First, truth is not objective. Even in the sciences, the presumed sanctuary of objectively verifiable truth, often only those values to which the scientists personally give allegiance provide criteria for judging between competing theories.[41] Criteria for choice of paradigms include the theory's ability to provide answers to currently pressing questions, its usefulness in suggesting further applications or new investigatable problems, and its simplicity or aesthetic appeal. The moderns appear unwilling to believe in Platonic forms or intelligble essences. Instead, knowledge depends on how people's interests, needs, and experiences lead them to slice and categorize an expanding mass of sense data. In fact, the greater diversity and conflict in people's social interests, needs, and experiences may explain why social life has a greater number of, and more constant conflict among, competing paradigms than is usually the case within a "science." And even if "rational" debate can play some role in advancing understanding within a given pardigm, discussion appears insufficient by itself to evaluate different paradigms. This failure of discussion results, in part, precisely because the value oriented criteria—interests, desires, or aesthetics—which guide the development of perceptions, appear ungrounded, incapable of objective demonstration.[42] However, one premise of my latter constructive argument will be that one must assume the value of the free development of people's humanity;[43] and that this value provides an intitial basis from which something can be said about differing paradigms and even more can be said about the desirable features of a structure of paradigm conflict and about the process of developing or creating knowledge. One could also, but I will not here, argue that this value of free development of people's humanity has been progressively unfolding in human history.[44]

The adequacy of the marketplace of ideas must be reconsidered if one rejects the assumption of objective truth and assumes that people's perspectives and understanding are chosen or created rather than "discovered." First, the contribution of the marketplace in discovering truth or reaching "better" choices would depend, in part, on the respective role of discussion and analysis as contrasted with experience in determining what perspectives we adopt. Unless reason operating in discussion can control or dominate the perspectives resulting from experience, progress in understanding would depend on the content of people's experiences and their everyday practices as much as on discussion. But if experience contributes, then restrictions on experience-generating conduct are as likely as restrictions on robust debate to stunt the progressive development of understanding; and no principle would explain why the marketplace of ideas is more deserving of constitutional protection than is expressive, experience-producing conduct. These same observations answer what at first seems a less ambitious defense of free speech: Protecting free speech insures that the individual will have more information and, thus, be able to make a more informed choice. The problem with this defense is that the individual is as likely to find needed information in experiences as in speech. Again, no objection is made to protecting verbal interchange; rather, the objection is that protection of verbal interchange is inadequate to promote the functions or values which justify protection of this realm of liberty.

Second, if truth or understanding are created or chosen, an evaluation of the market-place must consider whether the values of different people or groups are furthered by the choice or creation of the same truth or understanding. If a unity of interest exists, the differential contribution of various people or groups to the creation of understanding and perspectives may be unimportant. However, if groups have divergent interests concerning the choice of perspectives, one can presume that the marketplace of ideas (and other activities which might be protected) leads to the "best" or "proper" or "progressive" understanding only if the marketplace favors those groups who should be favored or "properly" distributes influence among various people or groups such that optimal compromises are reached. For example, Herbert Marcuse concluded that in the present historical circumstances the marketplace of ideas would work properly only if the rich and powerful were completely excluded and access were limited to progressive, leftist elements;[45] others argue for more or less equal access for all groups to the market place.[46]

This observation about the consequences of rejecting the assumption of "objective truth" leads directly to an evaluation of the other assumptions of the model. The first aspect of rationality required by the marketplace model, that people can use reason to comprehend a set reality, is undermined once one rejects the assumption of objective truth, for no set reality exists for people to understand. The sociology of knowledge provides a more precise basis for a critique of this rationality assumption. People's perspectives and understanding are greatly influenced, if not determined, by their experiences and their interests, both of which reflect their location in a specific, historical socio-economic structure.[47] Two implications of the sociology of knowledge should be relatively uncontroversial. First, dialogue cannot completely eliminate conflicts and divergences between people's perspectives as long as the social structure is such that people have very different experiences and conflicting interests. More specifically, social change—changes in the family, social, economic, or political order—not the marketplace of ideas, will have the greater impact on these divergent notions of "truth." Second, and in consequence of the first comment, not only will robust discussion be insufficient for advancing understanding (since it is at best one determinant of understanding), but also, if one continues to hope for a process of progressive development of understanding (the classic model's search for truth), the process of development will depend on the existence of a realm in which new experiences and interests can become actualities; thus, progress requires protection of some realm of conduct and of everyday activity beyond mere discussion.

The classic model also requires that people be able to use their rational capacities to eliminate distortion caused by the form and frequency of message presentation and to find the core of relevant information or argument. This assumption cannot be accepted. Emotional or "irrational" appeals have great impact; "subconscious" repressions, phobias, or desires influence people's assimilation of messages; and, most obviously, stimulus-response mechanisms and selective attention and retention processes influence understanding or perspectives. In fact, these psychological processes partially explain at the level of the individual what the sociology of knowledge observes at the level of the group. One is rewarded for adopting perspectives that further one's interests. Since interests vary with social position, the perspectives that are reinforced will also vary. These differential rewards explain *why* the sociology of knowledge finds that people maintain perspectives which promote one's interest even when presented with contrary information or alternative perspectives. The psychological technique of selective attention and retention, as well as the insights of cognitive dissonance and balance theories, suggest *how* people preserve these perspectives.

These psychological insights, extensively relied upon in practice by advertisers and propagandists,[48] eviscerate the faith in the ability of the marketplace of ideas to lead to the "best" truths or understandings. Even if one assumes that some understandings are best, one has no reason to expect these to be discovered in the marketplace of ideas. Instead, the understandings resulting from the robust debate will depend on the form and quantity of inputs, on the mechanisms by which people process these inputs, and on people's interests and experiences. Without the dominance of a rationality that can evaluate the merit of positions, people's processing of inputs cannot, in itself, be expected to lead to the best perspectives.[49] Given this diminished confidence in people's ability to *process* inputs, faith in the marketplace requires acceptance of one of two assumptions about the inputs into the robust debate. One must assume either that the quality of the resulting perspectives will not depend upon the source of input or that whatever input opportunities that happen to exist are fair or, at least, acceptable. Neither alternative can be maintained: First, as the sociology of knowledge shows, people will favor divergent perspectives and, therefore, it *does make a difference who has opportunities* to exercise influence; second, no one has seriously suggested that the existing distribution of access opportunities, which surely are most available to the rich and powerful, is fair or is apportioned in accordance with the contribution each group can make to a "best" understanding of the world.

Furthermore, apart from the purported function of the marketplace of ideas as a means to provide for the best understanding, the theory cannot be defended on the grounds that it

provides a "fair" or otherwise justifiable process for regulating the struggle between opposing groups.[50] The incredible inequalities of opportunity to use the marketplace cause a
fairness defense to fail.[51] The marketplace of ideas appears improperly biased in favor of
presently dominant groups, both because these groups have greater access to the marketplace
and because these dominant groups may legally restrict the opportunities for dissident
groups to develop patterns of conduct in which new ideas would appear plausible.[52]

Of course, unless processes or perspectives can be evaluated as better or worse, criticisms of the marketplace of ideas would seem pointless. Many people—maybe, in their
everyday lives, most people—believe such evaluations can be made and defended. Many,
including myself, would assert that these evaluations can be made on the basis of a fundamental long range unity of human interests. However, this belief neither necessarily nor
even normally leads to acceptance of a marketplace of ideas as an adequate process for moving
toward these better "understandings." For example, Roberto Unger, who maintains faith in
some sort of long term basic unity of humanity and who also presents a vibrant defense of
speculative thought, specifically argues that discussion itself is insufficient for reaching this
better understanding; instead, improved understanding *depends* on political action and social
change.[53] Thus, if, as the classic marketplace model asserts, the first amendment protects a
process for achieving improved understandings, then first amendment protection must
extend to aspects of human actions other than mere discussion.

Given that the assumptions underlying the classic marketplace of ideas theory are so
clearly incorrect, one wonders why the theory has had such popularity and so many advocates. One answer might be that its popularity is primarily limited to writers, academics and
other intellectuals who have a professional interest in supporting faith in rationality, rational
discussion or debate, and the intellectual pursuit of knowledge.[54] Although the classic
statements of faith by people such as Brandeis caution against too quickly dismissing the
theory as an ideological construct, one constantly wonders whose interests this marketplace
promotes. Since so much modern communication takes place through mass communication
media, an insight into the social role of the marketplace theory of speech may be gained by
considering how the constitutionally protected mass communication media influence
people's attitudes or behavior.

Two relatively clear results of modern social science research are: 1) that "the most
common effect of mass communication is to reinforce its audience's pre-existing interests,
attitudes, and behavior";[55] and 2) that "the media appear to be extremely effective in
creating new opinions," possibly because "the audiences have no existing opinions to be
guarded by the conscious or subconscious play of selective exposure, selective retention, or
selective perception."[56] Only in changing people's existing conceptions—the normal goal of
the critics of the status quo—does the media falter.[57] If the mass media primarily either
reinforce already held views or create views where people had no prior opinion, then those
who previously held the views that are reinforced, those who hold the new views created by
the media, and those who wanted these views reinforced or created, are likely to conclude
that the marketplace is working. This includes almost everyone except critics of the status
quo. Since media are inherently least effective in changing existing perspectives, this bias in
favor of the status quo would result even if every one had equal input. Nevertheless, equal
input does not exist. The bias in favor of the status quo is magnified because the three main
sources of media views are: the mass audience which must be willing to buy (or, at least,
receive) the communication; the present power elites, who usually own or manage the media;
and the dominant economic groups, whose advertisements largely finance the media. These
overlapping groups seldom radically oppose status quo perspectives.[58] In fact, these groups
usually want either to reinforce existing attitudes or, occasionally, to stimulate new views,
such as desires for new products that business is marketing. Thus, for most elements in

society, the market is doubly determined to appear successful: 1) "natural" participation counts—those groups who most frequently participate in the marketplace find that it "correctly" advances their interests or views; and 2) the process works—the marketplace validates those views that generally appear to be correct; that is, it reinforces currently dominant views. These observations support the conclusion that the marketplace of ideas theory is merely an ideological construct—the unregulated marketplace of ideas promotes the dominant group's interests and reflects its experiences of reality. The workings of the marketplace confirm the dominant group's self-serving belief that in the marketplace of ideas "the best ideas for the society will find the most takers."[59]

Dissenters must be expected to perceive the situation differently. Their views are least likely to be presented by the media and, when presented, are least likely to have an effect on society. Two reactions are plausible. If dissidents place faith in the individual and emphasize the value of individual expression or choice, they may be unwilling to reject the marketplace of ideas, which claims to affirm this faith. Instead, these dissidents would conclude that market failures exist and that the functioning of the market needs to be improved—possibly by government intervention.[60] Alternatively, if the dissenters view the government as an instrument of the dominant groups and perceive existing values as products of conscious or unconscious manipulations of these dominant groups, then they would postulate false consciousness and, at least under current historical conditions, would place little confidence in the power of mere speech or the workings of any marketplace of ideas.[61]

II. THE MARKET FAILURE MODEL

Society has found that the invisible hand does not always produce the results desired in the marketplace of goods; various forms of market failures require state intervention to achieve efficient allocations or desired distributions. Critics of the classic marketplace of ideas theory, relying either on the failure of the assumptions described in Part I or specifically on failures of the economic market (such as monopolization of communication channels or difficulties of organizing interest groups), have advocated various forms of governmental intervention to improve market functioning. The specific solutions proposed relate to the particular problem or market failure identified—identifications which have varied considerably among the critics.

A. The Reform Proposals

To clarify the content of the market failure model(s) I will outline the major reform positions, analyze the assumptions justifying each, and give a few examples of specific reform proposals. Reformers generally take one of four positions: 1) that economic market failures be corrected to the extent possible without restricting anyone's speech freedom; 2) that all viewpoints be guaranteed adequate, but not necessarily equal, access to the market; 3) that all viewpoints have equal access to the marketplace of ideas (*e.g.,* equal time for each candidate); or 4) that all individuals have equal access. (I should note that implementing many proposals suggested by the first two positions would be compatible with, but not necessarily required by, the liberty theory of the first amendment advanced in Part III.)

The first view—that economic market failures require government intervention—is based on the observation the inefficient resource allocations to speech activities may be caused by monopolization or by the difficulty which racial, sexual, or ethnic groups, consumers, the poor, or environmentalists, and other large, unorganized groups have, due to organization costs and freeloading, in achieving efficient levels of advocacy. Often, critics of this form of market failure propose invigorated enforcement of anti-trust laws or subsidies for advocacy by various difficult-to-organize groups.[62] However, these proposals, motivated by economic efficiency concerns, do not require or imply any particular theory of free speech; thus, they are outside the scope of the present paper. Moreover, these reform proposals raise no first amendment issues unless the economic corrective measures involve placing restrictions on activities protected within some first amendment theory.

The assumptions which require guaranteeing adequate, but not equal, presentation of all (serious?) viewpoints are very similar to those of the classic model. In fact, in *On Liberty,* Mill recommended that we search for devices to assure the forceful presentation of viewpoints that, without our positive efforts, would not be adequately presented.[63] Like the classic model, this approach must assume that reason dominates. Only if people use reason to analyze disputes will their conclusions not be controlled by the form and frequency of inputs. This approach assumes that people will use their intellect to find the core of insight, if any, in each message. It merely notes the absence of meaningful access opportunities for certain positions and advocates that these views be guaranteed adequate access to the marketplace.[64] Of course, the practical problem with this position as a constitutional standard rather than as a legislative policy is the difficulty of determining what amounts to an adequate or meaningful presentation opportunity.

This conclusion that an adequate presentation of each view is the constitutional goal points to an interesting fact about, and possibly an objection to, both this market failure theory and the classic market model. Given that some expression of a viewpoint suffices to assure its proper evaluation, a restraint on the speech of some individuals would not obstruct the search for truth as long as others forcefully express the views of those individuals. Unless persuaded by rule utilitarian objections—for example, that it would be costly to prevent or correct predictable misapplications of the power to restrict or censor individuals—government restraints on individuals, as long as the individual's message were adequately presented by others, would be unobjectionable. Despite marketplace rhetoric, a theorist's objection to such restraints often reveals an underlying concern with individual liberty that supersedes the theorist's concern for the workings of the market place.[65]

Equal access for all viewpoints is a quite unusual interpretation of a properly functioning marketplace of ideas. It makes sense, however, if truth (or a best or correct solution) exists but if people's rational faculties are too feeble to avoid or neutralize distortions caused by propagandists' use of quantity or packaging techniques. In other words, this model relies upon the classic model's truth assumption but rejects the second aspect of its rationality assumption, that people are able to sort through the form and frequency of message presentation to evaluate the core notions.[66] Equalizing the presentation opportunities for each potentially true or best viewpoint (in contrast to equalizing the opportunity for each speaker) enables each position to use quantity and packaging to neutralize the other's use. Provision for equal funding of all political candidates attempts, at least in the context of political campaigns, to accomplish that goal. (Or, if passing some threshold level of support provides evidence that a candidate is potentially the best choice, that is, the one who would win if presentation opportunities were equalized, then the state should assure equal resources to those candidates who meet this threshold requirement.[67])

Equal access for all individuals is the most logical version of the market failure theory. Each of the faulty assumptions of the classic model is replaced with a new one. First, truth is chosen or created, not made. Second, reason exists but normally does not control or dominate people's response to debate. Instead, people normally cannot divorce their understanding from their experiences in a particular social location; moreover, people respond to packaging, quantity, and context aspects of messages. Third, societal choices must fairly respond to people's different needs and groups' conflicting interests, whether or not the conflict is permanent. Given these assumptions, success in "rational" debate does not provide criteria for judging the merit of particular proposals or perspectives—at least, unless the debate is "fair." Cut adrift from the logic which explained how the marketplace of ideas advances truth, and instead assuming that truth is chosen, at least in part, on the basis of inputs into the marketplace, the democratic notion provides a solution: The marketplace works if and only if all people are equally able to participate in making or influencing the choice. Moreover, providing each person a roughly equal opportunity to generate equal quantities of carefully packaged messages increases the role of reason; the equalization neutralizes the advantage which packaging presently gives to well-financed perspectives. At first, the failure of the classic model's assumptions appeared to make faith in the market place of ideas incoherent. However, once one concludes that the purpose of the market is to provide legitimate scope for differing, often conflicting, interests rather than to promote the discovery of objective truth, and once one accepts a democratic notion that equal individual influence gives legitimate scope for differing interests, then the marketplace of ideas seems perfectly coherent as long as people have equal opportunities (*e.g.,* equal resources) for participating.

Reliance on this equality standard rather than the existing wealth (market) criterion for determining individual opportunities is not the norm in our basically capitalistic society. The area where we most commonly claim to adopt the equality standard is in the political sphere—"one person, one vote." Thus, the equality standard for individual input will seem most appropriate for speech which relates to what are perceived as political decisions, *i.e.,* collective decisions which will affect the rights as well as the values of the members of the collective.[68] For example, this could explain why the Court has concluded that wealth should not affect one's ability to vote (participate politically) even though generally wealth is, unless the political system concludes otherwise, assumed to be the proper criterion for allocating other goods.[69]

To achieve equality of opportunity for individual input requires either a combination of subsidies and expenditure restrictions or a method of making speech a free good, *i.e.,* making any amount of communication the speaker desires costless to the speaker. Some campaign reform proposals, for example, giving everyone an equal amount of government money to spend on election campaigns, can be interpreted as a *partial* move toward such an egalitarian system.[70]

B. Evaluation

Some criticisms apply only to specific versions of the market failure theory. For example, the second market failure theory, requiring adequate access for all viewpoints, or the third, requiring equal access for all viewpoints, rely respectively on the classic model's rationality or its truth assumptions. Thus, each of the reformulations is subject to the criticisms of the specific assumption of the classic model upon which it relies. Here, I intend first to develop criticisms which apply to all versions (possibly with differing force). Then, I will note serious practical difficulties with guaranteeing equal access for all individuals. This equal access argument merits special attention since, by reversing each of the classic model's assumptions, it apparently escapes all the theoretical criticisms directed against the classic model.

The most fundamental objection to the market failure theories applies when they require interference with the speech freedom of some people. This objection starkly poses the question whether equalizing "real opportunities" to speak justifies restricting speech or certain other forms of personal liberty. Since this objection is not so much a criticism of the logic of the equal access arguments as a claim that other values are more basic, the force of the objection will depend on the appeal of the liberty model—and, therefore, evaluation of this objection must be postponed until the liberty model is examined. However, several preliminary observations deserve attention.

If, as I have argued,[71] the same ethical principle requires collective concern both for individual liberty and for an egalitarian distribution of resources, these two values, equality and liberty, interpreted in light of this ethical principle, will not be incompatible. Government respect for, and treatment of, individuals as equals is necessary in order to morally justify legal obligation.[72] Respect for individuals as equals requires a concern for people's liberty (for restrictions on liberty disrespect a person's autonomy as a moral agent) and for people's opportunities (which implies a concern with the distribution of opportunities, with equality). However, both conceptually and in our constitutional system, the two values, liberty and equality, do different work.[73] The first amendment provides the best constitutional base for delineating a protected realm of liberty. Other constitutional texts, particularly the equal protection clause, provide the best basis for recognizing equality claims. For example, respecting people as equals, although consistent with considerable economic inequality, may require that certain "merit goods" be provided up to a certain level.[74] Thus, if "merit goods" properly include some opportunity to communicate one's views to a large audience, the fourteenth amendment's equal protection clause, not some market failure version of the first amendment, provides the proper constitutional base for the argument. And, fortunately, this basis avoids the serious practical difficulties, identified below, which make application of the market failure model objectionable.[75]

The correction of market failures requires criteria to guide the state in its intervention. If provision of *adequate* access is the goal, the lack of criteria for "adequacy" undermines the legitimacy of government regulation. For the government to determine what access is adequate involves the government implicitly judging what is the correct resolution of the marketplace debates—or, more bluntly, allows the government to define truth. If a purpose of the first amendment is to protect unpopular ideas that may eventually triumph over the majority's established dogma, then allowing the government to determine adequacy of access stands the first amendment on its head. (In other versions, where equality of input provides the criterion, the parallel problem will be defining equality.)

Harlan's concurrence in *United States v. O'Brien*,[76] the draft card burning case, illustrates the problem of determining adequacy of access. Harlan apparently agreed that a constitutional right to have one's view adequately presented to the public might justify violating an otherwise valid law, if the violation were necessary in order to present one's view.[77] Presumably, Harlan and O'Brien disagreed precisely over whether other "adequate" opportunities for presenting O'Brien's view were available. No criteria exist for making this determination. And the differing determinations by Harlan and O'Brien illustrate the danger of using makeshift criteria. Judges (as arms of the state), particularly given that judges are drawn almost exclusively from the dominant classes in society, will normally find that the dissidents have had adequate opportunity and that they have lost in the debate because their position is unpersuasive. In other words, state determination of adequacy will usually favor the status quo.[78]

O'Brien's defiance indicates an additional problem created by the market failure approach. Recognizing individual rights which focus on achieving results (particularly imprecisely defined results such as having society reach the best or "proper" decision) converts the right into a guaranteed adequate means to an end. This instrumentalist conception of fundamental rights inherently tends toward justifying violent or otherwise objectionable conduct. Dissenters, like O'Brien, who firmly believe reason confirms their views, are told by marketplace theory that a *properly functioning marketplace* of ideas would lead people to accept correct beliefs, their beliefs, *e.g.*, to reject the war. Under the market failure analysis, since the war continues, and given that they firmly believe their views are correct, these dissenters must conclude that the state has violated their constitutional right to a properly functioning market. Then, either because violation of this important right, until corrected, ends the legitimacy of their obligation to obey the laws of the state or because, as Harlan suggested, they have a right to take the steps required to vindicate their right, the dissenters are justified in breaking rules to do what is necessary to achieve the acceptance in the marketplace of ideas to which they are constitutionally entitled. Law breaking or violence, however, cannot be expected to stop here. Important disputes usually produce at least two sides which are firmly convinced that they are right. Thus, any success on one side will appear to the other side to justify their making an even more forceful response, thereby providing the logic for an escalating use of increasingly extreme, possibly violent, means. These normally illegal activities appear necessary to correct for the denial of one's right to a properly functioning marketplace of ideas.[79]

The argument for equality of individual access provides an apparently clear criterion for proper market functioning. But the clarity of the criterion is deceptive. Here, I will only note some key problems. For example, one cannot easily identify communication activities. Virtually all activities undertaken in a context where another will be aware of the activity communicate something; and requiring equality of resources for all publicly performed activities, an *extreme* egalitarian requirement, greatly aggravates all the problems noted below. But let us assume that communication activities can be identified. To equalize the amount that both rich and poor can speak, the state could employ a combination of subsidies and legal restrictions or could make speech a free good, costless for everyone. Either approach raises numerous problems. First, the restrictions in the subsidy-restriction approach impose an objectionable restraint on liberty. Second, this subsidy-restriction approach *unequally* burdens the speech of the rich if only the rich must pay for their speech. Third, the intensity of people's desire to speak or communicate (at different levels of communication) varies; it is not apparent that allowing two people to do the same thing, when their desire to do it differs, actually treats them equally. Moreover, whether one utilizes the subsidies or a universally "free good" approach, the resulting equality involves an inefficient use of resources, *e.g.*, those subsidized who are relatively uninterested in speech activities would have rather used these resources for other purposes.[80] Even theorists as egalitarian as John Rawls would object if the inefficiency were so great that the worst-off group would prefer less equality.[81] Fourth, if one justification for the first amendment lies in its contribution to the proper formulation of community values and improved collective decision making, guaranteeing equality of access will be objectionable. Both the subsidy restriction and the free good approach promote expression of weakly held viewpoints as compared to strongly held viewpoints, thereby preventing the marketplace of ideas from accurately reflecting the collective values or perspectives of the community.

Finally, it is unclear why the sought after equality should refer to opportunities for input as opposed to opportunities for influence.[82] If truth is chosen or created and if people diverge in their conclusions about what should be created, equality would apparently require that each be able to exercise equal influence. Since the same expenditure of money enables different people to exercise different degrees of influence, an equality of influence standard would require that the "naturally" influential be allowed even less resources for communication purposes than the non-influential. This is a curious constitutional standard. Most people would assume that it is desirable, not objectionable, to allow people with wisdom and experience to exercise greater noncoercive influence and to allow some specialization in being opinion leaders or information spreaders. In fact, if the marketplace of ideas is not to further merely random changes, those attuned to the needs for change must exercise greater influence.

In summary, all the market failure theories should be rejected as first amendment doctrine and, particularly, should be rejected as justifications for restricting liberty. Arguments for providing either "adequate" or equal access for all viewpoints rely on assumptions rejected in the earlier analysis of the classic marketplace model; moreover, they generate serious practical problems. Only equality of individual opportunities for communication relies on plausible assumptions. The most important objection to this equality standard is that it improperly subordinates liberty. Moreover, this equality standard is unworkable as it cannot be coherently defined; and, on any definition, it requires tremendous scope of state intervention. This equality standard is also objectionable as it leads to very inefficient use of resources and to serious distortions in the representation of community values or perspectives. Finally, according to the analysis in Part I, even if implemented, a "properly functioning" market of ideas will favor the status quo[83] because an equality standard that is tied to speech provides inadequate protection for dissenting perspectives to develop.

III. The Liberty Model

My thesis is that the first amendment protects a broad realm of nonviolent, noncoercive activity. The method for determining the scope of protection proceeds, first, by determining the purposes or values served by protected speech. These values, however, are also served by violent and coercive activities. Thus, I conclude that constitutional protection of speech is justified not merely because of the values served by speech but because freedom of speech serves these values in a particular, humanly acceptable manner, *e.g.,* nonviolently and noncoercively. Describing these methods is the second step of the analysis. Finally, I argue in Part IV, that when nonverbal conduct advances the same values in a relevantly similar manner, the nonverbal conduct should be viewed as speech and should receive protection.[84]

A. First Amendment Values or Purposes

In the marketplace theories, a single value—discovery of truth or reaching the "best" societal or individual decision—justified and defined the scope of protection. This focus is too limited. Professor Emerson, probably the most thoughtful and influential first amendment scholar, finds first amendment freedom essential for four values: 1) individual self-fulfillment, 2) advancement of knowledge and discovery of truth, 3) participation in decision making by all members of the society (which "embraces the right to participate in the building of the whole culture"), and 4) achievement of a "more adaptable and hence stable community."[85]

Emerson's list is acceptable. However, it is informative to see that the first value, self-fulfillment, and the third, participation in change, are key values and to understand why conduct promoting these two values ought to receive constitutional protection.

The values of self-fulfillment and participation in change impose somewhat different requirements on a satisfactory theory. The emphasis on "self" in self-fulfillment requires the theory to delineate a realm of liberty for self-determined processes of self-realization. The participation in change value requires the theory to specify and protect activities essential to a democratic, participatory process of change. Emerson's other two values are derivative. Given that truth is chosen or created, not discovered, advancement of knowledge and discovery of truth are merely aspects of participation in change.[86] Also, one apparently achieves a "more flexible and thereby more stable community" by providing for individual self-fulfillment and participation in change. Thus, henceforth, I will refer to individual self-fulfillment and participation in change as the key first amendment values.

Why should these two values receive constitutional protection? I will briefly summarize an answer I have advanced elsewhere.[87] Obligation exists only in relationships of respect. To justify legal obligation, the community must respect individuals as equal, rational and autonomous moral beings. For the community legitimately to expect individuals to respect collective decisions, *i.e.*, legal rules, the community must respect the dignity and equal worth of its members. One can elaborate this core truth of social contract doctrines in order to explain both the propriety of and proper limits on utilitarian polices.[88] And determining the proper limits on utilitarian policies is crucial for identifying constitutional rights because having constitutional protection means that the right prevails over preference maximization policies. The justification for welfare maximization policies is that, in decision making, the state should weight each person's concerns *equally,* thereby respecting the equal worth of each. This required respect for people's equal worth also explains the major limit on adopting welfare maximization policies, *i.e.*, the state's policy must respect people's integrity as rational, equal, autonomous moral beings, it must respect people as ends and not just as means. This requires that people's choices, their definition and development of *themselves,* must be respected—otherwise they become mere objects for manipulation or means for realizing someone else's ideals or desires. This respect for defining, developing or expressing one's self is precisely Emerson's value of self-realization. Moreover, since group decisions significantly influence both one's identity and one's opportunities, respecting people's autonomy as well as people's equal worth requires that people be allowed an equal right to participate in the process of group decision making—which is precisely Emerson's other key value, participation in collective decision making. Without trying to further develop this justification for the centrality of these two values, below I will merely rely on the widely accepted conclusion that *individual self-fulfillment and participation in change are fundamental purposes of the first amendment.* If, however, one accepts the justification offered here, it would help explain why utilitarian balancing does not justify limiting first amendment rights.

B. Uses of Speech

An exploration of the uses of speech will clarify both *how* and *when* speech contributes to the key values of the first amendment. A complete elaboration of the uses of speech is impossible. But in surveying the uses of speech one must take care not to adopt a too narrow or misguided vision. A very insightful article by Professor Scanlon illustrates the problems resulting from too narrow a vision. Scanlon not only argued "that all protected acts will be 'acts of expression,'" which he defines as "any act that is intended by its agent to communicate to one or more persons some proposition or attitude," but also that "almost everyone would agree" with this conclusion.[89] He is, I think, very wrong in his limitation of the category of properly protected acts although he is, possibly, correct that most would agree to his error.

Scanlon's ready acceptance of a marketplace of ideas theory, as evidenced by his emphasis on the intended communication of propositions or attitudes, illustrates the dominance of this model in our thinking. But his categorization of protected acts of expression is inadequate in three respects. First, it excludes many uses of speech. People continually speak or write without intending any person to hear their speech or see their writing. Moreover, people's "solitary" uses of speech—to record by keeping a diary, to organize by outlining or cataloguing, to understand by problem solving, to amuse or relax by singing or making up a story, to perform a duty by praying, or to order one's behavior by writing oneself a note—contribute to self-fulfillment and often to individual or social change. And, although this fact should not be relevant for determining the scope of the first amendment, the government sometimes attempts to control or regulate these solitary uses of speech—for example, if, as in Orwell's *1984*,[90] the government believes the speech is an aspect of, or contributes to, resistance to the government, or if society considers the speech to be anti-social or immoral,[91] or if the government fears the speech might lead to new knowledge or capabilities, like nuclear weapon or genetic research, that the government wants to control or suppress.

Second, many uses of speech—for example, story telling where the purpose of the story telling is to entertain rather than to promote insight—are best described as the speaker intending to do something.[92] Attempting to force such uses of speech into the category of communicating propositions or attitudes is strained. "The paradox disappears only if we make a radical break with the idea that language always functions in one way, always serves the same purpose: to convey thoughts—which may be about houses, pains, good and evil, or anything else you please."[93]

Third, Scanlon duplicates the marketplace model's emphasis on *content*. The speech is protected if, and because, it contains *propositions* or *attitudes* revelant to public debate. Instead, the first amendment values of *self*-fulfillment and *popular participation* in change emphasize the *source* of the speech in the self, and make the choice of the speech by the self the crucial factor in justifying protection.

In describing an alternative to Scanlon's categorization, Wittgenstein's warning should be kept in mind. He writes:

> But how many kinds of sentence are there? Say assertion, question, and command?—There are *countless* kinds: *countless different kinds of use of what we call* "symbols," "words," "sentences." And this multiplicity is not something fixed, given once for all; but new types of language, *new language-games*, as we may say, *come into existence*, and others become obsolete and get forgotten . . . . Here the term "language-game" is meant to bring into prominence the fact that *the speaking of language is part of an activity, or of a form of life* . . . .[94]

Given this warning, one should realize that the task must be to find characterizations of language uses or forms of life that provide insight into the scope of first amendment protection, not to develop a comprehensive catalogue. Two categories of use, self-expressive and creative, cut across the communicative, noncommunicative dichotomy and closely correlate with the key first amendment values of self-fulfillment and participation in change.

To engage voluntarily in a speech act is to engage in self-definition or expression. A Vietnam war protestor may explain that when she chants "Stop This War Now" at a demonstration, she does so without any expectation that her speech will affect the continuance of war or even that it will communicate anything to people in power; rather, she participates and chants in order to *define* herself publicly in opposition to the war. This war protestor provides a dramatic illustration of the importance of this self-expressive use of speech, independent of any effective communication to others, for self-fulfillment or self-realization. Generally, any indvidually chosen, meaningful conduct, whether public or private, expresses and further defines the actor's nature and contributes to the actor's self-realization.

Speech is not merely communicative but also creative. The Bible reports: "And God *said,* 'Let there be light;' and there was light."[95] For six days God spoke and named things and by these means created the world. Hannah Arendt reports that, to the ancient Greeks,

> [T]hought was secondary to speech, but speech and action were considered coeval and coequal, of the same rank and the same kind; and . . . finding the right words at the right moment, *quite apart from the information or communication they may convey,* is action. Only sheer violence is mute, and for this reason violence alone can never be great.[96]

And, for Arendt, "to act . . . means to take an initiative, to begin."[97] Through speech and action new worlds are created—"new" because action, which "may proceed from nowhere," "acts upon beings who are capable of their own actions," and thus "action and reaction among men never move in a closed circle . . . ."[98] The practice of the poet parallels Arendt's description of the Greek emphasis on the creative use of speech. A poem, which "should not mean [b]ut be,"[99] requires no project but instead a "flicker of the soul."[100] Gaston Bachelard describes the poetic image as "a new being in our language, expressing us by making us what it expresses . . . . Here expression creates being . . . . Through this creativeness the imagining consciousness proves to be, very simply but very purely, an origin."[101]

More mundane practices may provide more convincing evidence of the creative use of language. For example, the creative use of language is particularly prominent in: 1) making up new rules for a game or practice, as well as the language embodying the new rules; 2) coining a word, forming a new verbal image; 3) writing a poem or a play; 4) verbally formulating an analysis in order to "discover" new relationships or possibilities, or a dialogue through which *both* participants gain insights which *neither* possessed before; 5) "creating" or planning a new strategy; 6) persuading another of something; 7) teaching or developing new capabilities in another. The creative aspect, the new aspect of the world which results, varies in these examples. But in each case either the speaker or the listener or both possess something new—new images, new capacities, new opportunities, new amusements —which did not exist before and which were created by people's speech activity. Often the new creation will influence behavior. And in each case the creation has changed the social world, the world of meanings, opportunities, and restraints, in which people live.

Self-expressive and creative uses of speech *more fully and uniformly* promote the two key first amendment values, self-fulfillment and participation in both societal decision making and culture building, than does speech which communicates propositions and attitudes. First, *solitary uses* of speech contribute to self-fulfillment. Also, people's private analysis of their own character or of how to accomplish some goal, or people's practice of singing or of creating or viewing obscenity for private entertainment or relaxation, are all private speech activities which, by changing or defining people, change or modify the culture. Second, *communications* not intended to communicate propositions or attitudes of the speaker—such as story telling intended merely to entertain the listener, or singing intended merely to show the accomplishments of the singer, or group singing or a verbal ritual possibly intended to develop group solidarity—may both contribute to self-fulfillment and affect the culture. Third, self-expressive and creative uses properly exclude some uses that do not promote the key first amendment values but that would be included in Scanlon's market place definition. At first, the broad category of self-expressive acts might appear to include all speech acts. Nevertheless, to the extent that speech is involuntary, is not chosen by the speaker, the speech act does not involve the *self*-realization or *self*-fulfillment of the speaker. Focusing on the self-expressive uses of speech directs the inquiry toward the responsible source, not the content, of the speech. Thus, as I have argued elsewhere, if in modern America commercial advertising does not reflect anyone's voluntary or personal choice, this commerical speech should not be constitutionally protected.[102]

D. How Speech Operates

The first amendment could not possibly protect all the manifold activities, some of which involve violence or coercion, that further self-fulfillment or contribute to change. The logic of constitutionally protecting speech relates to the common sense perceptions both of the importance of speech for realizing certain values and of the method by which speech advances those values. In fact, in Part IV, I will argue that the first amendment protects non-verbal, creative and self-expressive activities when they advance first amendment values in a manner relevantly similar to speech.[103] Here, the central problem is to determine what *methods* or *manner* of using speech deserve constitutional protection.

Speech, unlike other behavior, is seldom thought of as physically violent or destructive[104]—the shrill voice breaking a glass is an aberrant example not typical of our normal notions of speech use. Similarly, using high decibel levels of sound to physically interefere with another's activities belies, rather than exemplifies, our characteristic image of speech; few urge constitutional protection for sheer noise used to disrupt a meeting.[105] Speech may harm others; but normally, speech differs from most other harm-producing conduct in the way it causes the harm. Both the amiable interchange which leads to replacing old with new friendships (consider the tort of alienation of affection) and the destructive interchange well illustrated in Edward Albee's *Who's Afraid of Virginia Woolf* create an effect by influencing the mind—the perceptions, feelings, beliefs or understandings—of the listener (or the speaker).

Law is typically used to prohibit certain harmful actions. But if the Constitution limits the government's power to restrict people's liberty, then either some harms or some methods of causing harms must not suffice to justify legal restrictions on behavior. This conclusion cannot be controversial. Under existing doctrine, harms caused by speech normally do not justify a restriction on speech, while harms that result from invading another's area of decision authority (*e.g.,* destruction of another's property or coercing another's behavior) normally justify outlawing the invading conduct. The theoretical justification for this doctrine, as well as the explication of its scope, depends upon showing that principle of respecting the equality and autonomy of individuals, which justifies limiting the collective's decision-making authority,[106] requires that people have the right to cause harms by certain means (speech caused harms) but not by others. This can be done. The key aspect distinguishing harms caused by protected speech acts from most other methods of causing harms is that speech harms occur only to the extent people "mentally" adopt perceptions or attitudes. Two factors deserve emphasis. First, the speech act does not interfere with another's legitimate decision authority, assuming that the other has no right to decide what the speaker should say or believe. This assumption is a necessary consequence of our respecting people's autonomy. Second, outlawing acts of the speaker in order to protect people from harms that result because the listener adopts certain perceptions or attitudes disrespects the responsibility and freedom of the listener. Both of these observations follow from our typical concept of the person which identifies a person, at least in part, with the person's perceptions and feelings; we hold a person responsible for actions that are based on the opinions or perceptions the person accepts. In fact, respecting the listener's integrity as an individual normally requires holding the listener responsible for her conduct unless she has been coerced or forced into the activity.

This explanation for protecting speech suggests the uses which do not merit protection. (Of course, one must be very careful not to find exceptions too easily—one must guard against the easy conclusion of those in authority that a particular "harmful" use of speech must fit into an exception.) The reasons why speech is protected do not apply if the speaker *coerces* the other or *physically interferes* with the other's rights. Respect for individual autonomy hardly requires protection of speech when the listener is coerced—"when [the listener] does something because of threats, the will of [the threatener] is operating or predominant."[107]

Thus, in order to determine what speech can be banned, one must be able to identify coercive speech.[108] Presumably, a major reason for a preferred status for freedom of speech is that speech behavior is normally noncoercive; instead, it depends for its power on increasing the speaker's own awareness or on the voluntary acceptance of listeners. Nevertheless, some speech may be coercive; the problem is that people sometimes invoke a carelessly formulated notion of coercion to justify regulation of behavior, or speech, of which they do not approve. A digression on the concept of coercion and of threats, an important subclass of coercive acts that must be distinguished from offers or warnings, will clarify the proper limits on protection of speech acts. A person coercively influences another if 1) she changes the other's options such that the other is worse off than he would be if he had the options that he had a moral (or legitimate) right to expect (*e.g.*, hijacking, threatened treason, or perjury) or 2) she employs means that she had no right to use for changing the threatened person's options (*e.g.*, blackmail).[109] An alternative formulation that I have rejected would use the "normal or expected course of events" or "options to which one has a legal right" rather than "options that one has a moral or legitimate right to expect" as the benchmark for determining whether the person has been made worse off. Three considerations indicate why normalcy or legality provide inappropriate benchmarks. First, particularly when used as a critical principle, for example, in evaluating a legal or social order, coercion refers to improper interferences with another's choices. If the normal conditions are morally objectionable, then one's (for example, the slave owner's) reliance on this state of affairs in influencing another's (the slave's) behavior can be coercive. Second, normality is not crucial if one has a right to change the normal order; for example, although in some contexts membership will involve continuing obligations, typically a member of a voluntary associaton is not being coercive when she states that she will change the existing situation (by dropping out of the association) unless certain conditions are met. Similarly, if the landlord normally has allowed the tenant to stay without paying rent, to demand that the tenant start paying is not coercive unless other special facts show that the tenant had a right to stay without paying or that the landlord did not have a right to demand rent. Third, reliance on law to specify the benchmark for when acts are coercive can be circular. Suppose Joe tells the Senator that he will continue his protests until the Senator supports the Equal Rights Amendment. To conclude that Joe has coerced the Senator because a law gives the Senator a right to be free from the protests is circular if Joe's protests can be legitimately outlawed only if the protests are coercive. If only coercive aspects of the speech can justify making the speech illegal, the speech's illegality cannot support the view that it is coercive. The prohibition cannot itself justify the prohibition. Clearly only an independent ethical defense of the legitimacy of the legal rule would suffice to show that its violation is coercive.

The reason for the special status of speech rights will clarify why speech is normally not coercive. Society can choose to create many different types of property rights, that is, can choose different ways to allocate decision-making authority. However, respect for the integrity and autonomy of the individual usually requires giving each person at least veto power over the use of her own body and, similarly, over her own speech. This respect implies that people should be viewed as responsible for and given maximal liberty in choosing how to use their bodies and minds to develop and express themselves and should be given an equal right to try to influence the nature of their collective worlds. Such respect is belied unless each person has a right to decide upon and employ speech—and possibly other non-coercive conduct—for realizing her substantive values and visions. The key ethical postulate is that respect for individual integrity and autonomy requires the recognition that a person has the right to use speech to develop herself or to influence or interact with others. Granted this ethical postulate, and since the concept of coercion only has a place within some such ethical order, the use of speech (normally) ought not be viewed as coercive. These observations can be illustrated by seeing how they counter two arguments for regulating supposedly coercive speech.

First, often threats of certain acts—to throw a rock through another's window—are coercive only because the law happened to give the threatened person a particular right, the right to have others not to throw, intentionally and without permission, a rock through the window. Here, the particulars of the law determine whether an act is coercive and subject to prohibition. The parallel argument is that if the law gives a person a right to be free of certain speech, such as speech that undermines one's reputation, the other person illegally injures or coerces the person by making or threatening to make that speech. The circularity of this argument as a reason to outlaw the speech has already been noted. The key failure of the parallelism is that one's authority over windows in not a crucial aspect of one's integrity and autonomy as a person and, therefore, should be allocated or specified on the basis of collective, legal, choice while the authority to decide upon one's speech and to use speech to affect the world must be allocated to the speaker; these allocations are central to a respect for one's autonomy and integrity as a person.

Second, often one concludes that acts that result from and perpetuate an unjust order—for example, unconscionable contracts—are coercive, and, therefore, should be forbidden or can be voided. The parallel argument is that speech that arguably strengthens or embodies the structure or values of that unjust order can properly be regulated or prohibited. Radicals, for instance, might argue that existing inequalities justify stifling the speech of the rich; or possibly, that these inequalities justify expenditure limits on political speech. The parallelism is false. The type reference made to a just order when considering what rights can (or should) exist in the present social order differs in two cases. The unconscionable contract involves an instrumentally valued exchange that depends on the involvement of a person who, in a just social order, would be unwilling to enter into the agreement. (This fact is the basis for claiming the contract is unconscionable.) Since, in a just order, one would have no legitimate expectation of being able to find another with whom to enter into the agreement, one has no legitimate expectation of being able to form the agreement. Therefore, legally prohibiting the agreement does not disrespect the vendor's "rights," the vendor's autonomy. In contrast, in a just social order the law must respect one's choice of speech content. No reference to legitimate expectations, to a just order, can justify restricting one's present opportunities to speak. Since the law can eliminate this contract opportunity but not the speech opportunity without disrespecting people's autonomy, the contract but not the speech may be coercive. In other words, prohibiting the speech sacrifices the individual's autonomy in order to correct an evil for which the legal order (*e.g.*, property laws), not the individual right sacrificed, is responsible. Here, not the speech, but the restriction on the speech would be coercive.

Nevertheless, these observations do not preclude finding some speech to be coercive and, therefore, subject to prohibition. Both the concept of coercion and the rationale for protecting speech draw from the same ethical requirement that the integrity and autonomy of the individual moral agent must be respected. Coercive acts typically disregard the ethical principle that, in interactions with others, one must respect the other's autonomy and integrity as a person. When trying to influence another person, one must not disregard that person's will or the integrity of the other person's mental processes. The type of speech that manifestly disregards the other's will or the integrity of the other's mental processes is not protected. Thus, the political morality summed up by the first amendment requires protection for speech that manifests or contributes to the speaker's values or visions—speech which furthers the two key first amendment values of self-fulfillment and participation in change—as long as the speech does not involve violence to or coercion of another.[110] This leaves three types of speech properly subject to positive law control: 1) speech involved in an actual or attempted taking or physical injury to another's person or property; 2) speech designed to disrespect and distort the integrity of another's mental processes; 3) speech not chosen by the speaker and which, therefore, cannot be attributed to the speaker's manifestation of her substantive values.[111]

This abstract formulation must be tested in the context of concrete issues. The theory should explain why speech activities such as fraud,[112] perjury, blackmail, espionage, and treason are unprotected. Here, for illustrative purposes, I will focus on only two: 1) blackmail, because of its similarity to a presumably protected activity, whistle blowing (public exposure of other's misdeeds); and 2) espionage, because of its relation to frequently raised first amendment issues.

Consider two situations: First, Jane says to Dick, "I will tell the public what you did (or are about to do) unless you give me $1,000." Second, Lisa says to David, "I will tell the public (or the police) if you proceed." Both statements involved the speaker "warning" the listener that he will be harmed by public exposure unless he modifies his planned course of action. Moreover, in both cases the speaker may have a right to expose the other; she may have a right to "ruin" the other by informing the public that he is a robber, rapist, or Republican.

The purpose of the "threat" as well as the latter public exposure, if it occurs, differs crucially in the two cases. In the blackmail situation, Jane attempts to make Dick a puppet of her will, while in the whistle blowing situation, Lisa does nothing more than attempt to make David bear responsibility for his act. In the first case, what Jane wants of Dick is unrelated to the facts that she might expose while, in the second situation, Lisa's precise concern is with the act that she might expose. In the first, the speaker attempts to transfer decision-making control to herself while, in the second, the speaker does not try to prevent the other from making his decision but merely forces him to take responsibility, an imposition that respects rather than subverts the other's integrity and autonomy. Since whistle blowing, but not blackmailing, involves using speech directly to make the world correspond to the speaker's substantive values rather than merely to increase the speaker's wealth (or area of decision-making domination) and does so without disrespecting the listener's integrity, it is not coercive; therefore, the first amendment should protect Lisa's speech acts. In contrast, blackmail disrespects the other's autonomy. And although Dick has no right to prevent the public exposure of the information, respecting Jane's integrity does not require that she be given an opportunity to subvert Dick's will; the state can protect people's autonomy by forbidding blackmail, a coercive use of speech.

The above example further illustrates the difference between a liberty theory of the first amendment and most marketplace theories. Marketplace theories typically focus on the content of the speech or on the effect of the speech on the social world. And in both whistle blowing and blackmailing, the content of the speech and its effect either on the person exposed or on the public could be the same. In each case, the speech could equally well serve the public's interest in or need for information. In contrast, the liberty model of the first amendment focuses on *the nature of the speaker's acts,* the purpose or method of having an effect on the world. To use a traditional example, the nature or purpose of the act is quite different when a person trips over, as opposed to when he kicks, a child. To conclude that the manner of acting is crucially different in these two cases does not require looking at the motives of the actors (although they may provide evidence as to which act was done) nor is the determination undermined by the fact that certain of the effects are the same. (The focus on "content" in the speech context resembles a focus on the physical act in the kicking or tripping case.) If the first amendment protects people's choices related to self-fulfillment and involvement in social, political, or cultural change, it must normally be agnostic in respect to content or effect. Instead, the identification of the coercive or noncoercive nature of the act, which one learns from context, is crucial for determining whether the first amendment protects the act.

The agnosticism in respect to content must also apply to evaluation of motives. The motive of both the blackmailer and whistle blower may be to achieve personal gain by her expected influence on another's behavior. In both cases, the speaker may have either "good" or "bad," public-spirited or selfish motives. However, the first amendment protection of liberty means that, within the context of protected manners of acting, people can choose and attempt to advance their own ends. Whether a person acts coercively depends on the nature of the act; in characterizing the act, an analysis of purpose, not one of motive, is often relevant. In contrast to the concept of motive which applies exclusively to human actions, the concept of purpose is in addition applicable to laws and objects. The term "purpose" refers to the intended ends or results of particular actions or to the contemplated uses or effects of particular artifacts. When describing human conduct, purpose relates to intended effects while motive relates to the reasons for desiring those effects. Clearly, our ability to determine purpose depends on our common understanding of the conventional context. We attribute a purpose to an act on the basis of our common understanding of what consequences people think will follow. Given the distinctions we make and the practices we engage in, specific features of the context allow us to distinguish the purpose of forcing a person to take responsibility for her act—which does not disrespect the person's integrity—and the purpose of subordinating the other's will to one's own. And we normally recognize the purpose without any reference to the speaker's motives. Although knowledge of motives can be a contextual factor useful in determining purpose, it is a distinct concept and our awareness of motives will often be nonessential or even irrelevant for identifying a purpose.[113] Thus, if the first amendment protects a manner of acting, the nature or purpose of the act will be crucial, but normally the state may not justify regulation on the basis of content, effect, or motive.

Espionage—at least secret transmission to a foreign nation of information which relates to the security of this nation—presents, for me, a difficult issue. The speaker uses speech (or writing) to change the world in a desired fashion. Creative uses of speech are usually protected. Moreover, the effect of espionage may be the same as publishing classified, previously secret, information in a newspaper.[114] The enemy may find the published information as useful as the information secretly delivered to its agents. And normally one's choice of audience, or its size, should not affect one's first amendment rights. Speech directed toward a large audience, no audience, or a carefully selected, exclusive audience may equally contribute to one's self-fulfillment or participation in change.

Emerson takes as a key reason for denying protection that "espionage [takes] place in the context of action"; that espionage usually "consists in conveying information concerning military secrets and would fall within the system of military operations" and always "involves aiding a foreign country." Therefore, he concludes, even if espionage is "expression," it "is not that form of domestic, civilian expression that is embraced within the system of freedom of expression."[115] I think Emerson is basically correct, but clarity requires an explanation of why the first amendment does not protect foreign-oriented, military-related expression.

An analogy will clarify the picture. Normally, the first amendment should protect publishing the layout and security system of a bank even though the publisher knows that a bank robber might use this information in a robbery attempt. Alternatively, in the context of carrying out a bank robbery, an individual's role might be to inform her associates about the bank's security and layout; this individual would be participating in an activity that used illegal force to invade and steal another's property. And, if a robbery or an attempted robbery resulted, the person who *participated* by contributing information would not be constitutionally protected.

Significant aspects of the relations between nations involve, unfortunately, both the actual and threatened use of violent force. First amendment liberty does not protect a person's knowing attempt to aid another person, or country, in the application of violent force. Engaging in espionage resembles supplying plans to fellow bank robbers. Neither the effect, which might also result from a newspaper article, nor even the motive, is crucial. Espionage is not protected only because, and only to the extent that, one's country can reasonably conclude that information gathered through espionage increases the coercive power of another country and because the purpose of the espionage activity is to have that effect. The first amendment extends protection until one's speech becomes merely one's method of involvement in a coercive or violent project.[116]

Although my focus in this and other sections has been on the speaker, communciations are also used for many diverse purposes by the listener. Without analyzing these uses, I merely assume for now that the broad categories of listener uses will resemble speaker's uses and will be protected to the same extent. Nevertheless, since each first amendment theory will have a characteristic justification for and interpretation of listener's rights, a brief digression on these interpretations may help clarify my analysis.

In the classic marketplace model, the listener's right is a correlate of the speaker's; the government must not interfere with communications between a willing speaker and willing listener. This conclusion, which correspondeds to the case law holdings,[117] is also implied by the liberty theory. However, the classic market model, which gives protection so that people will have the information they need for thoughtful pursuit of truth or for intelligent decision making, easily collapses into a market failure version that would recognize affirmative claims to get "needed" information that otherwise would not be readily available. In the market failure version, listeners would have an independent right to know, which presumably could be asserted against an unwilling speaker, against the government, or against a government restraint of an unprotected speaker.[118] This market failure analysis will raise problems that are similar to those described earlier, problems that include court balancing and conflicts with liberty.

On the liberty theory, the purpose of the first amendment is not to guarantee adequate information. The liberty theory does, however, protect noncoercive methods of getting information. The listener uses speech for self-realization or change purposes and these uses provide the basis of the listener's constitutional right. But the listener does not have a general claim for societal (information) allocations—*e.g.*, for the wealth that comes if one has unencumbered access to any desired information.[119] To grant first amendment protection to an otherwise unprotected speaker is no more constitutionally justified as an aspect of the listener's liberty than are other claims of the listener for greater wealth allocations. The listener has a right to demand that the government not prohibit the listener from receiving or using information. Restrictions on the listener's receipt or use of information must be defended as not really interfering with the listener's self-realizing activities (beyond the fact that the limitation may have a wealth allocation effect) or justified by some special characteristic of the listener—for example, one could ask whether children or prisoners or soldiers have diminished constitutional rights. Thus, the constitutional analysis of any restriction must be in terms of who is restricted—the speaker or the listener. Both parties have separate constitutional claims. Only if the restricted party does not have a constitutional claim is the government restriction permissible. Press reporting of criminal trials provides an obvious context to apply the analysis. The press, as listener, may have no access right to restricted information. However, if the press "hears," the government cannot prohibit the speaker's use (the press's publication) of the restricted information.[120] Likewise, if commercial speech were unprotected, the government could prohibit the druggist from publishing but, as Rehnquist pointed out, could not and did not prohibit the consumer from hearing or receiving price information; for example, the consumer could recieve the information as a result of reporting by newspapers or consumer guides.[121] The speaker and listener have separate, although normally overlapping, liberty claims and the constitutional analysis of the restriction must always focus on the claim of the party who is restricted.

This focus on each participant's liberty interest and on the values of self-fulfillment and participation in cultural change alters, and sometimes simplifies, the analysis of some traditional first amendment issues. As noted earlier, the marketplace theories do not provide a convincing justification for protecting obscenity. Pornography has more to do with ribald entertainment than with robust debate. Nevertheless, pornographic communications, or even pornographic materials produced and pursued by a solitary individual, contribute to building the culture. Materials that most people view as pornographic, as Douglas pointed out, play an important role in some people's self-fulfillment and self-expression. Thus, even if obscene publications do not contribute to the marketplace of ideas, they promote these key first amendment values. Therefore, the first amendment should protect the listener's or reader's interest in obscenity.[122]

Complicated problems remain. However, the general approach to determining what and why speech is protected should be clear. And, one should find several striking differences in the practical applications of this "liberty" theory, as contrasted to the "marketplace of ideas" theories. Speech is protected because, without disrespecting the autonomy of other persons, it promotes both the speaker's self-fulfillment and the speaker's ability to participate in change. This leads to the conclusion that, "[a]s long as speech represents the freely-chosen expression of the speaker while depending for its power on the free acceptance of the listener," and is not used in the context of a violent or coercive activity, "freedom of speech represents a charter of liberty for noncoercive action."[123] Now, I consider when the first amendment protects nonverbal actions.

IV. PROTECTION OF ACTION

If one concludes that the first amendment does not protect all speech, the literalist argument that all speech and *only* speech is protected loses force. Nevertheless, no accepted criteria exist to evaluate claims of first amendment protection for nonverbal conduct. I think, however, that a persuasive argument for protection of a particular type of conduct could be made by showing that: 1) the experience conduct furthers key first amendment values; 2) protection of this type of conduct is essential for an adequate realization of these values; 3) this conduct and protected verbal conduct promote first amendment values in a relevantly similar manner; and 4) principled lines can identify which conduct should be protected in what ways. My discussion will attempt to meet these four requirements.

A. *The Inadequate Expression-Action Dichotomy*

Professor Emerson's approach to delineating the scope of protection relies on a fundamental distinction between "expression" and "action,"[124] a categorization which "must be guided by consideration of whether the conduct partakes of the essential qualities of expression or action, that is, whether expression or action is the dominant element."[125] Emerson explains how to make a determination of essential qualities: "The concept of expression *must be* related to the fundamental purposes of the system [of freedom of expression] and the dynamics of its operation."[126] If protection of such "expression" meets the four criteria I have suggested, and if "expression" can be successfully identified, my inquiry can come to an end.

Unfortunately, neither identifying protected "expression" by determining the conduct's contribution to the purposes of the system nor by using common sense to distinguish between expression and action works. Clearly, the four central values of the first amendment found by Emerson, or the two key ones, self-fulfillment and participation in change, can be, and frequently are, furthered by many types of conduct—including violent, coercive action or other conduct generally thought properly subject to collective control. Thus, in themselves, these values cannot define or delineate spheres of protected expression and unprotected action.

The common sense distinction, relying on the essential qualities of expression and action, operates less to divide the world of behavior than to indicate the perspective of the person doing the dividing. If the distinction is between "expressing" and "doing," most conduct falls into both categories. Most consciously undertaken *actions* are at least self-expressive; and many—a political assassination, a hairstyle, a knife placed behind another's back—can be primarily intended to communicate something to others. Contrarily, people routinely use verbal conduct to do something—to write a poem, to command the troops, to test the student, to create a mood, to threaten an enemy, to make a promise.[127] In considering behavior, an observer can choose to focus on either what is done (other than expressing) or what is expressed. The choice of focus will be subjective: Either culture or personal idiosyncrasy, but not logical analysis, will determine the choice.[128] One might "give comfort" to a friend or to an enemy (of the state). If expression, but not action, is constitutionally protected, the determination of which element dominates in acts that "give comfort to an enemy" will likely depend on whether one believes the acts should be protected, not on the essential nature of the acts.

Not only does neither technique of distinguishing expression and action work, but since both verbal and nonverbal conduct advances first amendment values, the purpose of the distinction is unclear. Moreover, only an extremely crabbed reading of other clauses of the first amendment will be consistent with implementing an expression-action dichotomy. If religion plays a significant role in one's life, its *free exercise* normally will require doing or abstaining from certain conduct. And people typically assemble and associate to multiply their power in order to do something.[129] Nevertheless, even if his "expression-action" dichotomy is not very helpful, Emerson consistently makes very perceptive analyses of concrete situations; and these analyses frequently appear to make a different distinction: whether or not the conduct is, or is intended to be, coercive or physically injurious to another. All Emerson's examples of unprotected conduct, "action," involve coercion or injury to or physical interference with another or damage to physical property. These acts cause harm in a manner quite different from the way protected conduct causes harm. In the case of protected conduct, the supposed harm results from the assimilation of messages by an independent agent, the listener, and from the acts of that independent agent.

In the case of meetings and assemblies, Emerson says:

> [A]ll nonverbal [as well as verbal] conduct that is an integral part of assembly would normally be considered "expression". . . . On the other hand, the use of physical force or violence, against person or property, would be considered "action". . . . Disruption of a

meeting by moving about or making noise must also be counted as "action."[130]

This example illustrates that both speaking (if one includes chanting and yelling) and active conduct can be either "expression" or "action." The nonverbal conduct that Emerson would protect may well consist of doing things. The unprotected disruption of the meeting may further some people's self-fulfillment or may promote change. Neither the abstract character of the behavior nor the key first amendment values guide Emerson's categorization. Apparently, the essential distinction is solely that "action" involves coercive or physically interfering conduct.

Expressive political protests sometimes involve acts of physical obstruction like lying down in front of troop trains, blocking traffic in a city, or pouring blood over files. Emerson argues that these must be considered "action" and that to characterize them as "expression" would destroy the distinction between "expression" and "action."[131] Neither the physical activity nor the motives of the actor distinguish these "action" cases from draft card burning, which Emerson characterizes as expression. Rather, Emerson classifies the first examples of civil disobedience "action" because the "[c]ivil disobedience attempts to achieve results through a kind of *coercion or pressure*. . . ."[132] However, burning a draft card, unlike failing to carry a draft card,[133] does not involve coercing or directly injuring or physically obstructing any person or government activity. This fact apparently explains why Emerson concludes that the expression element clearly predominates in draft card burning.[134]

Emerson finds "a fundamental difference between most labor picketing and most nonlabor picketing."[135] He points out that the "labor picket line is . . . not so much a rational appeal to persuasion as a signal for the application of immediate and enormous economic leverage, based upon an already prepared position."[136] Labor and nonlabor picketing may involve the same physical acts, but the context is dramatically different. Typically, nonlabor picketing is "directed much more to the general public than to their own members" and "is a call to reason, not the application of *economic coercion,* and as as such must be classified as expression."[137] Although these distinctions deserve more careful analysis, clearly Emerson's approach is to determine whether and how the conduct is coercive. "How" appears relevant. If nonlabor picketing changes the public's opinion, the public may bring pressure on someone to change her behavior. Even if the public pressure is very forceful, the first amendment clearly protects the speech and conduct that induces this public response.[138] This interpretation of Emerson's examples suggests a surprisingly broad scope of protection. Emerson's examples indicate that the relevant question is *how the conduct advances the key first amendment values;* the conduct that advances the actor's values should be protected unless it is "coercive" or physically injurious or intended to be improperly obstructionist. But a principled description of this distinction between protected and unprotected conduct must be developed.

B. Interference with the Rights of Others

The logic of Emerson's examples suggests John Stuart Mill's conclusions concerning liberty in general (as opposed to Mill's special defense of freedom of speech). Mill argued:

> [T]he sole end for which mankind are warranted, individually or collectively, in interfer-
> ing with the liberty of action of any of their number is self-protection . . . . [T]he only
> purpose for which power can be rightfully exercised over any member of a civilized
> community, against his will, is to prevent *harm to others* . . . . The only part of the
> conduct of anyone for which he is amenable to society is that which *concerns others.*[139]

Unfortunately, the lack of criteria for determining when a person's behavior "harms" others or when a person's manner of acting "concerns others" prevents Mill's formulation from indicating when liberty should be protected. If "feeling harmed" or having one's interactions with others unfavorably "affected" count as criteria for "harm" or for being properly "concerned," then any action, no matter how privately undertaken, can be of concern to others, can harm others. Given that both one's public and private activities influence, develop, or "change" one's personality or capacities or inclinations, and since one's personality and capacities affect one's interactions with others, both one's private and public activities may cause frustration of others' desires (*i.e.,* may "harm" them). Even one's private yoga exercises or obscenity readings contribute to the culture and affect interpersonal relations in ways that may lessen some people's opportunities to realize their desires. Thus, harm to others cannot be our touchstone. In order to preserve any area of liberty one must show that either certain harms or certain ways of causing harms cannot justify certain restrictions on liberty.

Just as neither law nor custom adequately defined the benchmark from which coercive threats could be identified, they do not provide an adequate guide to distinguish "improperly harming" from "permissibly offending" another. Law and convention are inadequate guides precisely because they provide no critical principle, sought by both Mill and Emerson, that can indicate limits on the proper use of law and can delineate a proper realm of protected liberty. In order to construct such a critical principle, two distinctions need development.[140]

Rules can directly prevent a person from fulfilling her desires in either of two ways.[141] First, some rules restrict a person's liberty by giving to another the opportunity or decision authority one wants for oneself. I will call these *allocation rules.* Second, other rules deny a certain decision authority or opportunity to all people. I will call these rules *general prohibitions.*

The liberty value embodied in the first amendment places few restrictions on the state's power to choose among allocation rules: The state can decide to give property or opportunities to one person rather than another and can determine the content of property, tort, or contract rules. The two main first amendment constraints on state choice of allocation rules are: 1) the state only rarely and in limited circumstances can give one person an original right to decide what another person must do or say or not say;[142] 2) sometimes the state may be obliged to respect some neutrality criteria[143] or guarantee some minimum level of opportunity in making allocations that promote private parties' opportunity or ability to express themselves. (Note, however, that the guarantee of some minimum level of opportunity, like most constraints placed on the state's choice among allocation rules, may be best derived from the fourteenth amendment notion that the state must treat and respect people as equals.[144])

General prohibitions do not allocate decision-making authority but deny authority to all individuals as individuals. General prohibitions say: "No one (or everyone) shall do X" — *e.g.,* read pornography, pollute the air, commit suicide, fix prices, create a fire hazard. A rule relating to intentional taking of life is an allocation rule if one can give another permission to take one's life but is a general prohibition if one cannot give another such permission. Forbidding theft is an allocation rule to the extent that the owner can permit the action by making a gift of the taken object.

Allocation rules either allow one to undertake the act or, to the extent that the activity involves another person or resources allocated to another, allocation rules allow one to undertake the act if one receives cooperation or authorization from another. Allocation rules can grant decision-making authority on numerous bases: to the person strong enough to undertake the act, on a first-come-first-serve basis, to the person with the greatest need, or as an exclusive right to make a large set of decisions relating to some object. Two people cannot simultaneously engage in mutually exclusive uses of space or objects. This natural possibility of conflict—a problem that is engendered by the inherent limit on available resources (scarcity)—creates the necessity of allocation rules or practices to determine where authority resides; *formally,* such allocation rules involve the *minimum possible limit* on individual liberty.[145]

General prohibitions restrict liberty in a different and frequently more objectionable manner than do allocation rules. By excluding everyone from making certain decisions, they limit individual choice more than do allocation rules. General prohibitions let the majority directly control minorities; in contrast, allocation rules allow both the majority and minority to use their resources in ways they desire. Allocaton rules define the context for both egotistic projects and interpersonal cooperation while general prohibitions unnecessarily restrict individual and cooperative initiatives. General prohibitions that prevent people from engaging in substantively valued behavior unnecessarily restrict people's opportunity to engage in fulfilling activities. Moreover, by completely denying the opportunity to engage in certain activities in which new logics or perspectives or values could gain coherence, general prohibitions drastically limit the possibility of popular participation in change. For these reasons, I will conclude that many general prohibitions violate the first amendment. To reach this conclusion, I must first distinguish between two ways of valuing behavior. Then, I will describe the first amendment restriction on the use of general prohibitions and defend this limit against various objections, particularly "efficiency" or utility maximization arguments. Finally, I will note how this conclusion clarifies the structure of traditional first amendment arguments.[146]

An actor may or may not positively value a specific aspect of her behavior that others find offensive. Presumably, the person who chooses to read pornography, unless she happens to be a Supreme Court Justice,[147] values this "polluting" activity. (The term "polluting" will be used to refer to any activity that others find offensive and that they would prefer to exclude from the community.) Contrarily, owners of a steel plant or of an automobile that emits exhaust pollutants normally do not value polluting the air per se. Polluting the air is an undesired consequence, a subsidiary result, of their preferred behavior.

These two examples, pornography and air pollution, illustrate how the polluter can value a polluting activity either *substantively* or *instrumentally.* Since prohibiting the activity forecloses the possibility of anyone undertaking it, if the activity is substantively valued, the prohibition wholly prevents a specific form of self-fulfillment or self-realization. Contrarily, if the polluting activity is only instrumentally valued, prohibiting the pollution operates the same as an allocation rule. That is, the prohibition may affect an individual's wealth or the cost of a desired form of fulfillment, but the prohibition does not prevent one who has sufficient resources (or has the assistance of others who have rights to the needed resources) from undertaking the desired activity.

I am using "instrumentally" in a broader sense than seemed necessary in an earlier article, *Counting Preferences in Collective Choice Situations.*[148] Here, I use "instrumental" to refer to the value of distinguishable aspects of one's behavior as a means, even if this means for achieving one's aims is unrelated to the reaction of others. The auto owner can distinguish emitting pollutants and driving the car. Obviously, the aspects of the behavior that will be "distinguished" is culturally relative, dependent on how people perceive their world. In most cases, except where the actor substantively values publicity, acting in a manner that others can or will observe (*e.g.,* advocacy oriented speech), the aspects of the behavior that the actor substantively values will be distinct from the pollution aspects, but *despite* being distinguishable, if the only feasible way to engage in the substantively valued behavior is to engage also in the "polluting" behavior, a prohibition on the instrumentally valued aspects (the polluting aspects) may amount to a general prohibition on the substantively valued behavior. I tentatively conclude that in this situation equal respect for the autonomy and integrity of each individual permits the community to charge the "polluting" actor the cost (the negative value) of the pollution except that the community must not count as a cost the negatively valued aspects that the actor substantively values.

This principle will be difficult to apply in concrete contexts and will inevitably be reduced to various rule-of-thumb approximations. Sometimes, however, the application of the principle will be simple. In the context of sexual behavior between consenting adults, there will be few "pollutants" other than those aspects of the behavior that the participants specifically value; hence, neither general prohibitions nor charges are permitted. In the auto pollution situation, the rule of thumb must be that few people substantively value air pollutants. Then, if other feasible technologies exist, prohibiting the pollution only increases the "cost" of driving—an instrumental burden typical of many imposed by allocation rules. If no feasible alternative exists (the cost is infinity), the cost of these nonsubstantively valued, polluting aspects of the behavior can be charged to the auto owner. However, the substantively valued aspects cannot be viewed as a cost because that would violate the required respect for the individual chooser's autonomy.[149] A further example may help illustrate the importance of the substantive, instrumental distinction.

A rule prohibiting certain types of families from living together would prevent these families from realizing the substantive value they find in this family life.[150] In contrast, requirements that housing have a certain floor space per occupant, have adequate parking area, adequate fire protection services, etc., usually only impose added costs, impose instrumental burdens, on realizing substantive values relating to living arrangements.[151] Of course, even if this distinction between prohibiting realization of substantive values and imposing instrumental burdens is clear, its application may be difficult. Although a large group (a fraternity, a retirement community, etc.) may substantively value living together, their desire normally does not require living together at a particular place. And a geographic division of areas that only allows fraternities in certain areas might increase total community satisfaction while, at worst, only making it somewhat more expensive for particular groups to realize their values.[152] In this case, *assuming* housing opportunities for all groups are actually made available by the jurisdiction responsible for zoning, geographic limits on living arrangements would only instrumentally burden individuals—unless people not only substantively valued living together but also substantively valued living in a particular house or community or type of community, *e.g.,* an integrated community. If they substantively valued the specific location, the geographical exclusion would thwart the group's substantive values.[153] (Concern for such substantive values could provide a partial explanation for pre-existing use exemptions or for prohibitions on legally enforced racial segregation.[154]) No matter how one resolves these complexities, the distinction should be clear: The implications of a general prohibition differ when it relates to a substantively, as opposed to instrumentally, valued aspect of one's behavior.

I conclude that if a general prohibition limits instrumentally valued behavior, it operates like an allocation rule permissibly used to implement the community's substantive and distributional objectives. Also, if a few people, by engaging in a substantively valued polluting activity, could nullify the consequences of the choice of many people not to engage in such an activity, a general prohibition may be appropriate as a means to prevent domination.[155] Generally, however, *when a general prohibition applies to substantively valued behavior, it is an unconstitutional abridgement of freedom of speech or expression.* This conclusion is based on the following two observations: 1) substantively valued conduct is inherently expressive and clearly contributes to the two key first amendment values of self-fulfillment and participation in change; 2) general prohibitions forbid behavior that promotes first amendment values in the same manner as protected speech—*i.e.*, in a noncoercive manner. In fact, the evils of general prohibitions and coercive acts correspond. Like coercive acts, imposition of general prohibitions enables those who favor the rule to make use of others (if the rule requires specified conduct) or to avoid the bother of others (if it forbids specified activities) and, thereby, to treat others as means. General prohibitions also unnecessarily restrict individual liberty, and thereby, like coercive acts, disrespect individual autonomy. In contrast to the corresponding evils of coercion and general prohibitions is the way that the notions of coercion and allocation rules intertwine. By defining and then forbidding invasions of a person's realm of decision-making authority, allocation rules provide the necessary context in which an act can be coercive; indeed, allocation rules are required by the grammar of coercion.

Like unconstitutional restrictions on verbal conduct, general prohibitions restrict expressive conduct that operates noncoercively to advance self-fulfillment and popular participation in change. But before accepting the conclusion that general prohibitions of substantively valued conduct are unconstitutional abridgements of first amendment rights, one must be convinced that the justifications typically offered for general prohibitions are unpersuasive—an issue to which I now turn.

Justifications for general prohibitions normally take one of three forms. General prohibitions are valuable because they: 1) define and help form a community; 2) result from a valuable group process of choice; 3) promote efficiency or welfare maximization. Although the first two are sometimes collapsed into the efficiency argument, they merit special attention because neither focuses on the *results* furthered by general prohibitions (results being the typical focus of efficiency arguments), but instead argue that people substantively value either the general prohibitions themselves or the process of generating them.

General prohibitions (or general requirements) sometimes help form or define a community valued by its members. A religious community may partially define itself by rules that prohibit smoking, drinking, working on certain days, or fighting in unjust wars or by rules that require praying or wearing certain clothes. A political association may require that all members do or believe certain things. The mores of a community may obligate a person to love one's brother or sister, or parents, or spouse, or neighbor. Moreover, the nature of the relationships among members of a particular community or family may be incompatible with even the most direct beneficiary of certain obligations having authority either to demand or to excuse compliance. One may be obligated to help or love one's sister even in times when she tells you that you need not do so. Or one may have a duty to follow the association's political line without anyone having the authority to excuse you. In other words, sometimes the obligations defining a family or voluntary association take the form of general prohibitions or requirements rather than allocation rules.

The clear importance of these definitions of community and of relationships must be recognized. Nevertheless, their value as well as legitimacy may relate to their origin in individuals' *voluntarily* adopted practices or *voluntarily* chosen allegiance to the group defined by these rules. By contrast, state-enforced obedience to rules that are valued precisely because of how they define both individuals and the community involve the state in attempting partially to define who a person is; such a practice clearly indicates disrespect for individual autonomy.[156] Since these self-defining obligations can and often do exist within the voluntary practices of people, state enforcement with the consequent disrespect for people's autonomy requires a justification beyond the mere observation that most people value these rules. The justification could be that state enforcement promotes efficiency, *i.e.*, that enforcement satisfies more desires, either due to a marginal reduction of deviation from the popularly favored practices or due to the symbol of state enforcement, than it thwarts. This efficiency argument will be evaluated below.[157]

Second, people may value the group process of formulating rules. Positive value may inhere in the process of identifying and understanding issues, in resolving or compromising conflicts, and, finally, in expressing group unity through group decisions. Moreover, the group process may improve the quality of the resulting decisions. However, the obvious importance of these process values does not provide an unambiguous justification for government decision making in respect to general prohibitions. Group decision making concerning general prohibitions or requirements, such as what books shall be read, may be a valuable exercise for a study group but not for a state. Only in the case of voluntary groups or relationships is the process a *noncoercive* method of individual or group self-definition. Social pluralism may require the existence of opportunities for voluntary associations to create general prohibitions or requirements;[158] but this pluralism could be coercively destroyed if the state could create general prohibitions or requirements.[159] And, of course, the principle of disallowing majority-imposed general prohibitions that outlaw some people's self-defining activities does not interfere with realizing whatever process value exists in the activity of choosing allocation rules and public programs, both of which involve the community determining what type of community will exist. Nevertheless, some positive process value may exist in community decision making concerning general prohibitions, and this value would contribute to utilitarian arguments for allowing such rules. Thus, these utilitarian or efficiency arguments must now be considered.

The efficiency argument notes that people who substantively desire to act in a manner others find offensive often would agree to abandon the offensive behavior and accept a restraint on their liberty if paid an amount that those offended would be willing to pay. For example, those opposed to air or pornographic pollution might be willing to pay the polluters an amount that the polluters would be willing to accept for ceasing their pollution. However, difficulties and expenses in negotiating and carrying out the transactions prevent them from occurring. In this situation, a general prohibition, although burdening some, may increase the general level of preference satisfaction, *i.e.,* may correct for the market failure and be efficient.

Three responses persuasively undermine the efficiency justification for general prohibitions. First, the dangers (or inefficiencies) of the predictable abuse by the majority of a power to adopt general prohibitions may significantly outweigh any efficiency gains that result from their use. And additional cost, the dissatisfaction generated among those who believe, and often *properly* believe, that the majority is imposing its values and increasing its own well-being by improperly restricting the liberty of minorities, reinforces this rule utilitarian conclusion.[160] Of course, this argument loses force if those who are restricted are adequately compensated (an unlikely event in the case of most general prohibitions). Also, this argument would not apply if those restricted favor the restriction and had engaged in the restricted conduct only in order to maximize their situation given their assumption that others would also engage in the behavior (that is, if the general prohibition is designed to avoid the typical prisoner's dilemma problem). Moreover, this rule utilitarian argument may only require care and circumspection in adopting general prohibitions.[161] Hence, this rule utilitarian analysis provides only weak support for a comprehensive constitutional ban on general prohibitions of substantively valued conduct; instead, because it does not reject but only reinterprets the efficiency approach, it seems to suggest that balancing is appropriate in constitutional analysis.

Second, efficiency does not justify general prohibitions if such prohibitions violate people's rights.[162] To avoid circularity, however, one must establish that general prohibitions do violate rights; and, here, I can only sketch the argument for that view. A number of considerations provide at least a minimal argument. First, unlike allocation rules which necessarily exist and merely influence people's values and their opportunities to pursue their values, state-enforced general prohibitions of substantively valued behavior entirely prevent some people from acting in accord with their values. Second, unlike allocation rules, general prohibitions are adopted precisely in order to prevent people from living by those values. If, as argued earlier, state action must respect individual autonomy, general prohibitions of substantively valued behavior are objectionable because they violate this required respect. The majority employ general prohibitions to control and determine who other people can be. Third, these general prohibitions thwart people's self-expression and people's personal and social creativity; they directly impinge on realizing these two central values of the first amendment. Finally, although the distribution of wealth is not a central concern of the first amendment, freedom from general prohibitions provides a minimum guarantee of some "wealth" to each individual. If general prohibitions (or requirements) are permitted, except for the limitation inherent in the requirement that the rules be general in form, people could be stripped of virtually all wealth (*i.e.,* authority to make desired decisions about one's own or another's conduct) except for the value of one's political rights (*i.e.,* the right to participate in choosing general prohibitions); thus, permitting general prohibitions allows one's wealth to become even more dependent on whether one agrees with the majority.

Third, efficiency or welfare maximization may be a particularly incoherent justification for general prohibitions of substantively valued conduct. Certain activities that decrease the satisfaction of existing preferences may help create a better society where people will have "better" preferences than exist at present. Efficiency calculations must presuppose, but cannot justify, some particular, usually existing, tastes or desires as the ones to be satisfied.[163] Until some set of preferences is assumed, efficiency has no evaluative criteria. But if change is to be subject to human choice, if human self-determination is possible, then a central issue is determining what preferences are best. Thus, since efficiency analysis cannot justify its reliance on any set of preferences, it has no criteria with which to guide the choice. No intrinsic quality of *existing* tastes justifies their fulfillment always being the dominant concern. In fact, to paraphrase Mill's faith in people as progressive beings,[164] the merit of change must be evaluated not in terms of whether it fulfills existing tastes but in terms of whether it improves the type of people we are. And, as Professor Tribe has argued, the major choices facing us as a people are those that will determine who and what we will be.[165] If human integrity and responsibility require that people be free to decide (or participate in deciding) what or who they will be, then, when evaluating the process of change, it is a logical mistake to evaluate choices in terms of how well they satisfy existing preferences; rather, one must either evaluate change in terms of the legitimacy of the *process* or evaluate the political and ethical *content* of the change. This second type of evaluation corresponds to many people's practice of subjecting their attitudes and activities to ethical or political criticism. As for the legitimacy of the process, the irrelevance of an efficiency analysis that takes as given the key issue in dispute could explain why many intuitively conclude that the first amendment should (absolutely?) protect a process of change from limitations justified by mere utilitarian calculations (*i.e.,* balancing). This logical irrelevance of efficiency arguments for justifying general prohibitions should not be surprising if one accepts my earlier argument that the state is justified in adopting utility maximization as state policy only when necessary to carry out the state's obligation to treat all members as deserving equal respect as autonomous moral beings. Efficiency arguments must be irrelevant until the liberty rights of autonomous beings, particularly the right of self-determination, are assured protection.

One added argument suggests why general prohibitions are objectionable. The idea that we need, and sometimes have had, progressive change, suggests that the legal structuring of the process of change ought to protect those elements which could be progressive, and which, without protection, would be restricted. Identifying progressive elements is, of course, difficult. However, two factors indicate that barring general prohibitions of substantively valued conduct increases the chances of protecting progressive elements. Since a key aspect of general prohibitions is to suppress value realization that is contrary to majority or status quo values, one would expect popular support for precisely those general prohibitions that attempt to suppress those progressive practices which conflict with current regressive orientations. More important, our ethical and political judgments and concepts typically reflect presently shared values and logic. Theorists such as Roberto Unger argue that the confidence we should have in our judgments depends on the extent to which these shared values are formed under circumstances of non-domination.[166] Since general prohibitions characteristically involve dominating minorities on the basis of current majority interests and values, they undermine the legitimacy of the very values they promote. Contrarily, by banning general prohibitions of substantively valued conduct, we decrease majority domination and increase the legitimacy of relying on the shared judgments that do exist. By allowing minorities to live their values even when the present majority finds the behavior offensive, society protects an important process for peaceful change of tastes and values while decreasing the conditions of domination.

These criticims of efficiency justifications for general prohibitions complete the argument for barring the state from enforcing general prohibition of substantively valued expressive conduct. The above criticisms highlight many aspects of conventional first amendment analysis. Typical attempts to justify laws prohibiting specific expressive activity rely on: 1) predictions that the activity will lead to future violation of allocation rules—*e.g.*, the speech creates a clear and present danger to lawlessness, pornography leads to sex crimes; 2) predictions that the activity will lead to future violations of allocation rules—*e.g.*, the speech creates a clear and present danger to lawlessness, pornography leads to sex crimes; 2) relations—*e.g.*, public sales or use of obscenity and public use of vulgar language undermines the desired moral tone of the community; 3) disapproval of the values or attitudes expressed by the activity—*e.g.*, flag burning, wearing long hair, draft card burning, representing unpatriotic attitudes.

Well developed defenses of free speech meet each claim. First, the classic objection to the bad tendency test for restricting speech is that the state can forbid the violation of the allocation rule but cannot prohibit the speech using a general prohibition. This objection parallels criminal law and due process notions which, except in exceptional circumstances, are offended by taking away a person's liberty because of what a person might do in the future. Of course, like preventive detention, speech restrictions based on the bad tendency test may maximize preference satisfaction. The classic response relies on the same objections to efficiency as were developed above. It argues either that the bad tendency test will be abused or, like laws prohibiting obscenity or marijuana, cannot be effectively enforced and, thus, will not be efficient in practice; or more fundamentally, that speech restrictions based on the bad tendency test, even if efficient, violate individual rights that society must recognize.

Similarly, classic first amendment analyses reject the other two "efficiency" arguments for restricting people's noncoercive activities: Either the expressive activities will have a socially undesirable influence on people's personality and their behavior or the expression is itself offensive to the majority. These arguments are rejected on the ground that the majority must respect individuals' choices about their own values and not force them to falsify their values. This position is, of course, a straightforward application of the principle that the state must respect people's integrity and autonomy. Again, classic first amendment arguments repeat our objection to efficiency justifications for general prohibitions.

C. The Market Place of Ideas Revisited

One should not too quickly dismiss an analysis which has dominated informed opinion as completely as has the marketplace of ideas theory. I criticized the marketplace of ideas as a method of discovering truth or arriving at the "best" perceptions or values because its effectiveness for achieving these goals seemed dependent on several invalid assumptions. Here, my inquiry considers how protecting a broader range of expressive conduct, how forbidding general prohibitions of substantively valued conduct, blunts the criticism of the classic marketplace of ideas model. If interpreting the first amendment to include this broad protection of nonverbal conduct cures the defects of the marketplace theory, this fact would buttress the defense of this broad interpretation.

Protecting substantively valued conduct from abridgement by general prohibitions makes the hope that people will be able to make the "best" choices more plausible for at least four reasons. First, the classic model assumes that truth is discovered or found. To the extent that reality is created, the theory must be concerned with questions of who and how. Equality of opportunity to create reality provides a possible standard. However, since all conduct, not merely speech, contributes to this creation process, equality of opportunity would require a regime of *strict equality* of all resources *and skills*—a regime as unnecessary as it is inconceivable. Lack of sufficient "wealth" is only one cause of the limits on people's opportunities. In addition, general prohibitions can be used by the majority to entirely suppress opportunities for certain choices. This use of majority power can be more oppressive, more totally limiting, and is usually less justified than are limits on opportunities due to inequality of resource distribution (at least, if the inequality is not too great or if a minimum level of opportunity is guaranteed). Clearly, barring state imposed prohibitions of substantively valued conduct greatly increases opportunities of minorities to develop new realities (this notion replaces objective truth). This broadened liberty eliminates a major method by which the choice process is often limited to prevent peaceful challenges to the existing orthodoxies. Thus, such a ban seems *necessary,* whether or not sufficient, to expand people's opportunities for creating new realities.

Second, the ban on general prohibitions makes the process of creating realities much more democratic. Many people may not have the resources, the skills, or the interest to participate in a rational or political search for the best societal decisions. Most people do have an interest in their own life and their relations with others; also, most have sufficient skill (and, in the liberty model, they also have the right) to pursue their own visions and values. Only by disallowing general prohibitions can everyone, by their choice of activities, participate in the debate and in building the culture.

Third, the liberty to live one's values provides for the possibility that at present, or always, pluralism best meets human needs and goals. Moreover, by allowing this pluralism, change can occur by people living, and finding others to join in living, a set of values. Thus, peaceful, gradual change will have space and opportunity to develop.

Fourth, protecting greater liberty of action breaches the status quo bias of the marketplace of ideas. Mass communications apparently are more effective in reinforcing the status quo than in stimulating criticism. Moreover, face-to-face verbal communication and existing forms of reason typically reflect people's experience of the existing order. Even if various economic or social groups experience the existing order from radically different perspectives and evaluate it differently, that existing order dominates people's logic and perceptions when considering alternatives. By discounting preferences of the majority for limiting conduct, the first amendment protects the possibility of developing new loci of experience which potentially can falsify the existing, dominant perspectives. Moreover, this method of change requires neither violence nor the approval of the dominant societal groups. Just as in the classic market model, the power of new perspectives depends on its voluntary acceptance by people; however, protection of new, nonverbal practices allows people to make a new perspective available in a form where its logic might be coherent, thereby overcoming the status quo bias of mere verbal debate.

This revised theory replaces both the doubtful assumptions of the classic marketplace of ideas theory and its hope for a basically rational discovery of timeless truth with a defense of the legitimacy of a social process of choice. The legitimacy must be defended on at least one of two grounds: Either all people have a right to participate in the individual and social processes of *self*-determination or a "better" individual and collective expression of humanity results from this social process because of the increased opportunity of each freely to participate. Either ground justifies protecting people's liberty to engage in substantively valued conduct. Moreover, both imply that eliminating or weakening existing structures of domination that influence or distort people's choices[167] improves the process of developing and expressing values. This concern with reducing domination was the one merit of the market failure version of first amendment theory. Unfortunately, that theory's focus on equality of *speech* opportunities—usually, equality of access to channels of mass communication—belies the fact that only general economic equality would suffice to validate the approach. Because of this theoretical confusion, the market failure theorists fail to realize that providing considerable equality of access to communication channels may be less central to dismantling the existing structures of domination than banning existing restrictions, general prohibitions, on liberty. This confusion illustrates the market failure theory's basic problem; it merges the concepts of equality and liberty which provide separate, although crucial, guidance for describing a just social order.

In addition to highlighting these mistakes of the market failure or equal access theory, the liberty approach avoids the problems which engulf that theory. The liberty model avoids offering the false hope that dissenting positions, even without a real basis in experience, can be shown to be best; instead, it provides for a more realistic method of change from "the bottom up." The liberty model, which protects noncoercive uses of speech and forbids enforcement of general prohibitions on substantively valued behavior, provides clearer, less subjective criteria for proper government action than the market failure model provides. Also, because it guarantees a realm of liberty rather than a properly functioning market, one can correct for perceived infringements of the guarantee by violating the "improper restriction" on liberty rather than taking the possibly violent action needed to get "proper results."

By protecting substantively valued conduct from abridgement by general prohibitions, the liberty model provides for a process of public decision making and a search for, or creation of, truth that avoids the problems and improper assumptions of both the market models. Thus, the liberty model better promotes the key value that justified the classic marketplace of ideas theory of freedom of speech: the value of furthering the search for truth or best premises, a value that, due to a failure of assumptions, the classic theory could not adequately serve. These observations provide convincing support for this liberty theory.

V. ASSEMBLY, ASSOCIATION, AND FREE EXERCISE OF RELIGION

The argument has been that the first amendment protection of freedom of speech should be interpreted to protect other expressive conduct that serves, in a similar manner, the same central purposes or functions as does verbal conduct. This method of interpretation, although it goes beyond one common reading of speech as referring only to verbal behavior, remains faithful to the constitutional text. Any textual interpretation requires a theory that explains why those particular words are used. The theory developed herein emphasizes that "speech" is chosen because it is a particularly good embodiment of a concern for expressive, nonviolent, noncoercive conduct that promotes self-realization and self-determination. This understanding of why the constitutional text uses the word "speech" guides the proper elaboration of what verbal and nonverbal conduct should be protected.

The other clauses of the first amendment, particularly the freedom to peaceably assemble and the right to the free exercise of religion, can be read either to bolster the broad liberty interpretation of speech or as alternative grounds for protecting this realm of liberty. One useful way of viewing these clauses is to see them as separate markers or strands of a single, but hard to verbalize, concept of the realm of individual freedom needed for individual self-development and democratic control of the common community. Under this view, if one completely grasped the meaning of any of the clauses, one would come close to grasping the comprehensive conception of the protected realm of liberty. However, each clause does have a different emphasis: Assembly emphasizes plurality and action; religion emphasizes conscience. Still, the Court may be right to think that speech is the most comprehensive of the various clauses, although the Court is wrong to subsume the other clauses in a crabbed, marketplace view of speech. In this section, I claim that not only does a reasonable interpretation of the assembly and free exercise clauses support recognizing the breadth of the realm of liberty argued for herein, but also that the liberty theory clarifies the meaning of these clauses and solves difficult problems in their elaboration. Nevertheless, these clauses will be only briefly reviewed here.

A. Assembly

A typical Court treatment of assemblies, including parades, pickets, or rallies, is to analyze them as speech plus.[168] Apparently the Court's theory is that the function of assemblies is to aid in the propagation of speech or ideas. This, however, is a limited function of subsidiary constitutional importance and, therefore, the conduct aspects of assemblies are subject to regulation.[169] Nevertheless, the constitutional language that specifies "the right of the people peaceably to assemble" hardly suggests that their central purpose of the assembly must be speech. It certainly does not suggest that their purpose must be to disseminate or debate ideas. If one takes any cue from the textual language, an alternative theory would seem appropriate. People combine, assemble to do things; they assemble for a wide variety of purposes: for celebrations, for entertainment, for work, for generating or expressing power. Many of these purposes, although important for people's lives and although peaceable, fit poorly under any marketplace of ideas rubric. Of course, assemblies can be destructive and violate other's rights. The obviousness of this fact suggests why the authors of the constitutional text, who did not bother to write that only freedom of "noncoercive speech" must not be abridged, specifically restricted the protection of assemblies to "peaceable assemblies." One cannot reasonably narrow the constitutional protection of assemblies to protection merely of an adjunct to speech or some marketplace of ideas. The logic of a broader, more adequate, theory can be discussed in conjunction with the theory of associations.

B. Associations[170]

Although an independent first amendment right of association has been recognized[171] the basis of this right is seldom articulated. Worse, when the Court tries to explain the scope of the right of association, it consistently sees it as derivative of the right of speech. Associations are protected as an instrument used to communicate in the marketplace of ideas.[172] This doctrinal sleight of hand severely limits the scope of the freedom of association.[173] And this narrowness has led at least one thoughtful commentator to argue for a nontextual, independent, constitutional right of association.[174] Despite this current fad of finding nontextual, nonconstitutional bases for constitutional decision making,[175] a better tack would be to recognize the first amendment right of assembly as the logical basis of the right of association.[176] This basis does provide for an expansive interpretation of the right.[177] In essence *an association is merely an assembly dispersed over time and space.* The key aspect of both is that they are combinations, not mere aggregations, of people; and as combinations, they are a source of power. Both form relations between people that enable the group to do things—often to do things beyond merely reasoning together. People come together in assemblies or associations in order to pursue or fulfill their goals.

Clearly, the core first amendment values of self-fulfillment and popular participation in change are furthered not only by associations and assemblies designed to participate in the robust debate about truth or values or policies, but also by all associations and assemblies that people use to express, develop or implement their substantive values. As Justice Douglas pointed out in *Griswold v. Connecticut,*[178] many aspects of self-fulfillment require associations and the participation of more than one person.

Two interrelated aspects of assemblies and associations increase people's ability to participate in societal development and change. First, the interactions and relationships among people within these combinations provide the basis from which new logics, perceptions and values can grow and develop. Second, associations and assemblies generate the power needed to accomplish group goals.[179] This power-creating aspect of assemblies and associations requires close examination.

The importance of the right of association, and possibly a reason for the underdevelopment of implementing legal doctrine, derives from the fact that "[p]ower springs up whenever people get together and act in concert."[180] Often, power is incorrectly equated with violence or with the ability to employ violence.[181] This view is illustrated by the slogan that "power grows out of the barrel of a gun."[182] Because of this confused equation of power and violence, power must be distinguished from violence before one can offer a plausible interpretation of the first amendment as protecting people's right to create power.

Violence typically depends on implements, a fact which suggests the instrumental character of violence. In contrast, power is the strength and the capacity of people acting together to achieve their aims.[183] Power always involves an element of consent; it depends, at least in part, either on voluntary conformance to role positions or on accepted relationships among members of a group. Although power and violence are often found together, in these situations power will prevail since any coherent use of violence depends on the cooperative organization of the group; as long as the group exists, the violence of one person can be overpowered. Violence can be used to destroy power but not to create power. In contrast, power, people acting in concert, can be used to establish something new. Hannah Arendt uses these distinctions to show that the totalitarianism of Nazi Germany depended on a complete atomization or privatization of people's lives. Hitler used violence to destroy all dependable relations among people. This total destruction of power, destruction of the power existing in association, left only violence as a means of control, a means that had to be constantly exercised to prevent associations and opposition power from developing.[184]

Once the distinction between power and violence is clear, the contribution of associations or assemblies as the embodiment of people's power to the first amendment values of self-fulfillment or participation in change should be obvious. Also, this power-creating aspect of voluntary associations may explain the fear of developing constitutional doctrine that would allow people's combinations to go unregulated. Early defenders of free speech, operating within the marketplace theory, were wary of the power aspects of association. William Godwin concluded "though association . . . must be granted to be an instrument of a very dangerous nature, . . . unreserved communication . . ., especially among persons who have already awakened to the pursuit of truth, is of unquestionable advantage."[185] More recently, in his criticism of the other Justices' analysis of a Smith Act prosecution solely in terms of speech, Justice Jackson emphasized the power aspect of association and viewed it as justifying regulation.[186] In concluding that "there is no constitutional right to 'gang up' on the government,"[187] thereby rejecting any significant theory of freedom of assembly or association, Jackson explained:

> [A] combination of persons to commit a wrong, either as an ends or as a means to an end, is so much more dangerous [than an individual acting alone], because of its *increased power* to do wrong, because it is more difficult to guard against and prevent the evil designs of a group of persons than of a single person . . . .[188]

Once one rejects Jackson's premise that associations to create power are not protected by the first amendment and instead recognizes that the rights of assembly and association must mean that people have the constitutional right to join together to create the power needed to realize their aims, first amendment protection moves beyond a marketplace of ideas foundation. Constitutional law must develop tools to protect associations from various forms of governmental abridgements.

One possible direction of doctrinal development will be noted here. The constitutional right to join together to create power suggests that the combination, like speech, cannot itself be prohibited. Of course, just as one can find examples of verbal behavior that are not protected, some associations—agreements to monopolize, for example—may likewise be unprotected.[189] Given, however, that the criminal law already forbids particular activities that violate others' rights as well as aiding abetting or attempting to commit crimes, the only additional evil sought to be proscribed by the law of conspiracy is the association itself. As Jackson argued, the association is defined as a separate offense because the association itself is dangerous. But just as speech recommending crime, in contrast to the acts carrying out the crime, should not be punished,[190] a reasonable interpretation of people's right to join together would suggest that the conspiracy, as opposed to the actual crime, should not be punished. Of course, this distinction between what is and is not protected merely repeats the earlier distinction between general prohibitions and allocation rules. To construe the conspiracy as the crime, except in those few cases where the association itself is "coercive,"[191] amounts to a general prohibition on people's substantively valued behavior, and should not be permitted. Thus, the implication of this analysis of freedom of association duplicates the earlier conclusion about the proper scope of freedom of speech.

C. Free Exercise of Religion

The Supreme Court first considered, and improperly rejected, free exercise of religion claims in the context of the government's prosecution (and persecution) of Mormons for practicing polygamy.[192] The polygamy cases illustrate the Court's dominant approach to the free exercise clause, an approach summed up by Justice Roberts for a unanimous Court: "[T]he Amendment embraces two concepts, freedom to believe and freedom to act. The first is absolute but, in the nature of things, the second cannot be. Conduct remains subject to regulation for the protection of society."[193]

To deny conduct any protection clearly would gut the meaning of *"free exercise."* Religions demand more than holding beliefs; typically religions require the faithful to forbear or perform certain acts and to manifest certain values or principles in their conduct. In the recent conscientious objector cases, the Court recognized the conscience, ethics, or systems of value have taken the place of religion in the lives of many Americans.[194] Certainly, the free exercise of conscience, possibly the original[195] and certainly the most intelligible[196] meaning for the free exercise clause, involves people *acting* in accord with their concept of right and wrong. An adequate theory of the free exercise clause must be able to identify the actions and beliefs protected from governmental prohibition or burden.

The Court could protect conduct either by formulating a line distinguishing protected from unprotected conduct or by ad hoc "balancing" of religious claims against other societal interests. All the objections to balancing speech claims apply equally to balancing of free exercise claims. For example, if the Court decides not merely to defer to the legislature, one should expect its biases to control the balancing. The decision will embody the Court's present view of the societal importance of the particular interference with free exercise rights. It will also reflect the Court's biases for or against the particular religious group making the free exercise claim and the other groups who might have indistinguishable claims. *Wisconsin v. Yoder*[197] illustrates this tendency. There the Court emphasized that it would reach a different, nonprotective, result if the right not to attend school were claimed by a newly formed group trying to live and develop a better style of life.[198] Although this limitation might merely represent the Court's specification of its concept of religion for free exercise purposes,[199] I think, instead, it was a necessary concomitant of the Court's focused balancing. The limitation improperly allowed the Court's judgment to turn on its sympathy for the Amish, sympathy that was manifest in its emphasis on the desirable qualities of the Amish life style, particularly those aspects that allayed fears related to maintaining social control: The Amish did not commit crimes or go on welfare.[200] One wonders whether an unconscious belief that the Amish's deviation from the law posed no real threat to the values or practices of mainstream America influenced the Court's evaluation.

So far, the preferable approach of line drawing has been notably unsuccessful. Some Court decisions apparently distinguish active from passive conduct. The Court partially grounded the distinction between working on Sunday and not working on Saturday in that the first involved "overt acts" while the second "constitutes no conduct . . . of a kind within the reach of state legislation."[201] The Court has frequently rejected free exercise claims to engage in active conduct,[202] and, although the Court rejected the "passive" right not to fight in a war,[203] it has upheld other claims to refrain from action.[204]

The passive-active distinction might provide an expedient compromise position given that few positive commands of major Western religions require violations of existing state law and given that the modern state usually is more interested in preventing active disruptive conduct that offends or violates people's rights or challenges the status quo than it is in requiring conduct. Nevertheless, the distinction is misguided. It certainly does not embody a principled distinction between the importance or significance of a person's various religious or conscientious beliefs and practices. Most would concede that the first amendment protects some activities required by religions, for example, religious rituals that involve drinking small quantities of wine or eating bread. But protection of ritual is insufficient. Religion, as well as conscience, calls on people not merely to hold certain beliefs but also to act in accord with religious or ethical mandates.[205] It is irrational to deny protection to all conscientiously required practices merely because some free exercise claims—for example, conscientiously motivated kidnapping[206]—are unacceptable. From the perspective of the demands of religion or of conscience and from the perspective of the free exercise claimant, action and inaction are not intrinsically different.

Not only would using general prohibitions to ban active conduct negate reasonable free exercise claims of individuals, but also such regulations would enable the state to annul a major societal value of the constitutional guarantee. To protect religious freedom or freedom of conscience while prohibiting religious establishment amounts to a constitutional decision to protect people's right to maintain a pluralistic society.[207] This constitutional protection of pluralism in life styles is unacceptably shallow if it only protects groups in their differing inactions. Both moral and cultural pluralism require opportunities for different patterns of *active* conduct.

Some alternative to the passive-active distinction must be found. Justice Douglas suggested the line of criminal conduct.[208] Unfortunately, since the problem is to find limits on the state's authority to make acts criminal, Douglas' suggestion does not provide a solution unless one can establish definite limits to the scope of criminal law. Douglas' suggested limits—inherently "innocent" acts that "intrinsically are wholesome and not antisocial" cannot be prohibited[209]—are too vague and too much a matter of majority definition. Douglas argued that work, unlike polygamy, is not immoral;[210] but, of course, many Christians consider *Sunday* work immoral and, as Justice Murphy has pointed out, historically polygamy is the most common form of marriage and is firmly based on social and ethical principles subscribed to by many groups.[211]

A better solution would be to interpret the free exercise clause as protecting people's substantively valued conduct from general prohibitions or from governmental decisions to penalize the valued conduct.[212] Under this interpretation, kidnapping, ritualistic assassination or torture and all other forms of active conduct that clearly ought to be subject to government control can be prohibited because they all involve violations of allocation rules. Because acting as required by conscience or religion is a form of self-expression or an attempt at self-realization it should not be surprising that this solution corresponds to the limits on government implied by the liberty interpretation of the free speech clause. Similarly, the free exercise clause's protection of pluralism in life styles parallels the speech clause's protection of expressive conduct involved in culture building and the process of change. Athough the first amendment protection of speech, assembly and association, and religion and conscience describes a unified realm of liberty, this interpretation suggests that the free exercise clause should be read as emphasizing that a crucial aspect of this realm of constitutional liberty is the protection of conscience or substantively valued conduct. The free exercise clause thus supplements the role of the speech clause, which emphasizes the noncoercive and nonviolent character of expressive conduct as necessary prerequisites for first amendment protection.

CONCLUSION

Concluding that freedom of speech requires protecting self-chosen, nonverbal conduct from certain forms of government abridgement involves a considerable revision of first amendment theory. However, this conclusion appears to be the only principled interpretation of the first amendment once one demonstrates the inadequacy of both the classic marketplace of ideas theory and the market failure theory.

The argument for this liberty theory of freedom of speech involved, first, a review of the basic functions or values of the first amendment. The two key values were individual self-fulfillment and individual participation in public decision making. These values did not provide a coherent distinction between "expression," which Professor Emerson argued is protected, and "action," which he argued is not. Instead, the category of protected speech was better described as "noncoercive" expressive conduct. Neither the key first amendment values nor the noncoercive method by which clearly protected verbal conduct advances these values suggested any constitutionally relevant difference between verbal conduct and non-coercive, nonviolent, and expressive nonverbal conduct. This implies that both should be protected.

The state's authority to make allocation rules or decisions, limited mainly by equal protection notions and a required respect for people's autonomy, was assumed. However, a second category of laws, general prohibitions of subtantively valued conduct, restricted conduct that, although typically not coercive of others, did advance first amendment functions in practically the same way as verbal conduct does. Thus, these general prohibitions appeared to be unconstitutional abridgements of expressive conduct. Finally, this extended scope of protection remedied the main inadequacies of the classic marketplace of ideas model for social decision making.

It seems only appropriate to note, in conclusion, a difficult problem that an adequate first amendment theory must resolve. In the modern welfare state, as Charles Reich pointed out over a decade ago,[213] how the government decides to allocate its wealth can greatly influence people's substantively valued behavior. As the country becomes increasingly socialized, the opportunity for the government unnecessarily to limit individual freedom by imposing conditions on the receipt of needed government "gratuities" increase. A method is sorely needed for determining when government-imposed conditions on the receipt of government allocations are proper means to advance the collective notion of the good and when, like general prohibitions, they are improper restraints on people's exercise of first amendment rights. This problem must be left for another paper.

Notes

1. J.S. MILL, ON LIBERTY (1956) [hereinafter cited as ON LIBERTY]. Mill's argument was made in a long chapter, *Of the Liberty of Thought and Discussion, id.* at 19–67, which he intended to serve as an example of his defense of liberty in general. In fact, his argument for liberty in general rests on different assumptions and is not subject to the criticisms I will make of his defense of liberty of thought and discussion.

2. *Id.* at 64. *See also* New York Times v. Sullivan, 376 U.S. 254, 279 n. 19 (1964); ON LIBERTY, *supra* note 1, at 33–36, 41–43.

3. ON LIBERTY, *supra* note 1, at 41; *see* Dennis v. United States, 341 U.S. 494, 584 (1951) (Douglas J., dissenting).

4. Were an opinion a personal possession of no value except to the owner, if to be obstructed in the enjoyment of it were simply a private injury, it would make some difference whether the injury was inflicted only on a few persons or on many. But the peculiar evil of silencing the expression of an opinion is that is robbing the human race, posterity as well as the existing generation—those who dissent from the opinion still more than those who hold it.

ON LIBERTY, *supra* note 1, at 21. For the same view, see Z. CHAFEE, FREE SPEECH IN THE UNITED STATES 33–35 1964); A. MEIKLEJOHN, POLITICAL FREEDOM 26–27 (1965).

5. The analogy between the perceived need to correct for failures in the economic market and the idea market is, I think, more than accidental. Most advocates of the market failure model of the first amendment would probably also advocate considerable government regulation of the economy; typically, this group sees the government as facilitating compromises among individuals and groups having competing desires and as administering programs technically designed to achieve pre-ordained objectives. In contrast, "conservatives" advocating decreases in government regulation recommend that the "liberals" should have the same faith in economic markets as they do in the unregulated market place of ideas. *See* Coase, *Advertising and Free Speech*, 6 J. LEGAL STUD. 1 (1977); Coase, *The Market for Goods and the Market for Ideas*, 64 AM. ECON. REV.: PAPERS & PROC. 384 (1974); Director, *The Parity of the Economic Market Place*, 7 J.L. & ECON. 1 (1964). Elsewhere, I have argued that the analogy should be rejected. *See* Baker, *Ideology of the Economic Analysis of Law*, 5 PHILOSOPHY &

PUB. AFF. 3 (1975) [hereinafter cited as *Economic Analysis*]; Baker, *Commercial Speech: A Problem in the Theory of Freedom*, 62 IOWA L. REV. 1 (1976) [hereinafter cited as *Commercial Speech*].

6. *See, e.g.,* Barron, *Access—The Only Choice for the Media?*, 48 TEX. L. REV. 766 (1970); Barron, *Access to the Press—A New First Amendment Right*, 80 HARV. L. REV. 1641 (1967). *See also* Columbia Broadcasting Sys. v. Democratic Nat'l Comm., 412 U.S. 94, 170–204 (1973) (Brennan & Marshall, JJ., dissenting).

7. Some readers may object to my extending the concept of speech to cover some nonverbal conduct. This objection is, I believe, adequately met by the arguments that nonverbal conduct *with the same uses* as constitutionally protected verbal conduct should be treated as speech. *See* notes 42–68 & accompanying text *infra*. Even if this conclusion is rejected, the recommended scope of protection would be justified on the basis of a proper interpretation of the free exercise and freedom of assembly clauses. The analysis in this article is an important step in developing a proper interpretation of these clauses because 1) it develops a criticism of the marketplace of ideas paradigm that currently improperly dominates the interpretation of the free exercise of religion and freedom of assembly clauses and 2) it suggests an alternative paradigm for and resolves certain difficulties in interpreting these clauses. *See* Part V *infra*.

8. These three assumptions are all explicit in ON LIBERTY, note 1 *supra*. First, truth is objective; this assumption is clearly suggested by the language Mill uses to describe truth: persons "rediscover" truth, *id.* at 36; "give truth a chance of reaching us," *id.* at 26. Second, human rationality is necessary. The "doctrine is meant to apply only to human beings in the *maturity of their faculties.*" *Id.* at 13 (emphasis added). *See also id.* at 25. Finally, a decrease in pluralism and an absence of intractable value conflicts is expected and applauded by Mill. In agreement with the "best of men," he concludes that "no belief which is contrary to truth can be really useful," *id.* at 28; and that "the well-being of mankind may almost be measured by the number and gravity of truths which have reached the point of being uncontested." *Id.* at 53. *See also* J.S. MILL, UTILITARIANISM 40–48 (1957). A person "still needs to be conscious that his real aim and theirs do not conflict." *Id.* at 43.

9. The Court usually cites either its earlier opinions or people, such as Jefferson, who may have influenced the drafters of the first amendment. However, Mill is occasionally cited. *See* Columbia Broadcasting Sys. v. Democratic Nat'l Comm., 412 U.S. 94, 189 n.25 (1973) (Brennan & Marshall, JJ., dissenting); Furman v. Georgia, 408 U.S. 238, 467 (1972) (Rehnquist, J., dissenting); Red Lion Broadcasting Co. v. F.C.C., 398 U.S. 367, 392 n.18 (1969); New York Times v. Sullivan, 376 U.S. 254, 272 n.13, 279 n.19 (1964); Poe v. Ullman, 367 U.S. 497, 514–15 (1961) (Douglas J., dissenting); Barenblatt v. United States, 360 U.S. 109, 151 n.22 (1959) (Black & Douglas, JJ., and Warren, C.J., dissenting). *See also* Paris Adult Theatre I v. Slaton, 413 U.S. 49, 68 n.14 (1973) (rejecting Mill's argument for liberty in general).

I refer to Mill to exemplify the marketplace theory because he provides its best formulation.

10. Speech is not constitutionally protected when there is (or, in the case of attempts, when the speaker intends that there be) "a clear and present danger that [the speech] will bring about the substantive evils that Congress has a right to prevent." Schenk v. United States, 249 U.S. 47, 52 (1919).

11. Abrams v. United States, 250 U.S. 616, 630 (1919) (Holmes & Brandeis, JJ., dissenting).

12. Whitney v. California, 274 U.S. 357, 375 (1927) (Brandeis & Holmes, JJ., concurring), *overruled,* Brandenburg v. Ohio, 395 U.S. 444 (1968).

13. *Id.* at 376.

14. *Id.* at 377.

15. Learned Hand's test, "whether the gravity of the 'evil', discounted by its improbability, justifies such invasion of free speech as is necessary to avoid the danger," was adopted in Dennis v. United States, 341 U.S. 494, 510 (1951). The test, implicitly for the majority and explicitly in Frankfurter's concurrence, involves a "balancing" approach to determine the protection to be given speech. This judicial adoption of a legislative type balancing approach has been properly criticized. *See, e.g.,* T. EMERSON, TOWARD A GENERAL THEORY OF THE FIRST AMENDMENT 53–56 (1966) [hereinafter cited as GENERAL THEORY]; Frantz, *The First Amendment in the Balance,* 71 YALE L.J. 1424 (1962). However, balancing itself involves no theory of what or why speech is protected. In fact, the Court made clear in *Dennis* that they continued to rely on the marketplace of ideas as the central concept of the first amendment. 341 U.S. at 503, 545–46, 549–50, 553.

16. Gitlow v. New York, 268 U.S. 652, 673 (1925) (Holmes & Brandeis, JJ., dissenting).

17. ON LIBERTY, *supra* note 1, at 67–68. *See also id.* at 117 (if there is no time to warn another of danger then one can temporarily stop the other from crossing the unsafe bridge).

18. 354 U.S. 476 (1957). *See also* Memoirs v. Massachusetts, 383 U.S. 413 (1966).

19. 354 U.S. at 484 (emphasis added).

20. *See, e.g.,* Chicago Police Dep't v. Mosley, 408 U.S. 92 (1972). Licensing and other time, place and manner restrictions traditionally have been upheld only if they do not permit the government to discriminate among communications. Shuttlesworth v. Birmingham, 394 U.S. 147 (1969); Cox v. Louisiana, 379 U.S. 536 (1965); Cox v. New Hampshire, 312 U.S. 569 (1941). The current Court may be abandoning its rejection of content discrimination. *See* Young v. American Mini Theatres, 427 U.S. 50 (1976); Lehman v. Shaker Heights,

418 U.S. 298 (1974). For an analysis of this development, see Goldman, *A Doctrine of Worthier Speech:* Young v. American Mini Theatres, 21 ST. LOUIS L.J. 281 (1977).

Within the liberty theory developed below, some content based time, place and manner restrictions may be acceptable. Since different uses of speech serve different values, a permissible restriction would be one that did not impede people's use of speech to further that value. Thus, content restrictions on "advocacy" speech would never be allowed; but where speech is used essentially for entertainment purposes and where the speaker only wants to reach those who desire receipt of the speech, content restrictions that do not significantly limit the availability of the speech may be an acceptable method of promoting community values. *Compare* Paris Adult Theatre I v. Slaton, 413 U.S. 49, 112–13 (Brennan, Stewart & Marshall, JJ., dissenting) (1973) (suggesting that unconsenting adults can be protected from obscenity) *with* Cohen v. California, 403 U.S. 15, 21 (1971) (in context of political or "advocacy" speech, state cannot protect unconsenting viewers). The different treatment does not relate to any lesser value of entertainment speech but to whether the government did, or had a purpose to, abridge the speech.

21. Roth v. United States, 354 U.S. at 484.

22. Kingsley Int'l Pictures Corp. v. Regents of New York, 360 U.S. 684, 688–89 (1959).

23. Ginzburg v. United States, 383 U.S. 463, 489–90 (1966) (Douglas, J., dissenting).

24. *Id.* at 489.

25. Miller v. California, 413 U.S. 15, 34 (1973).

26. The Court emphasized this factor when it concluded that the method of advertising the publication, pandering, provided evidence that it was designed for the pleasure, not the opinion, market. Ginzburg v. United States, 383 U.S. at 474–75.

27. The state interest lies in protecting the "community environment, the tone of commerce . . . and, possibly, the public safety itself." Paris Adult Theatre I v. Slaton, 413 U.S. 49, 58 (1972). *See also id.* at 63–64.

28. *Id.* at 96 (Brennan, Stewart & Marshall, JJ., dissenting).

29. *Id.* at 68 n.14. However, Mill's argument for liberty in general rests on entirely different premises than does his argument for freedom of speech.

30. Miller v. California, 413 U.S. at 34.

31. Paris Adult Theatre I v. Slaton, 413 U.S. at 67.

32. New York Times v. Sullivan, 376 U.S. 254, 280 (1964).

33. *Id.* at 269, 270 (quoting from Justice Brandeis's concurring opinions in *Roth* and *Whitney*).

34. *Id.* at 272 n.13.

35. *Id.* at 279 n.19.

36. Note that one could reject the Court's approach without rejecting the marketplace model. For example, Goldberg with Douglas concurring, argued that the Court's analysis "is not responsive to the real issue presented by this case, which is whether that freedom speech which all agree is constitutionally protected can be effectively safeguarded by a rule allowing the imposition of liability upon a jury's evaluation of the speaker's state of mind." 376 U.S. at 300. This danger of the majority's approach is illustrated by its compatibility with the argument that communists should not be protected because they are not interested in truth. *See* Dennis v. United States, 341 U.S. 494 (1951). Following Goldberg, Emerson emphasizes the need to consider the system context. GENERAL THEORY, *supra* note 15, at 16–46, Emerson notes: "Most of our efforts in the past have been seriously defective through failure to take into consideration the realistic context in which such limitations are administered." *Id.* at 16.

37. Gertz v. Robert Welch, Inc., 418 U.S. 323, 348–50 (1974). One reason the Court gave for differentiating between public and private parties is their differential access to the media. *Id.* at 344. This explanation partially relies on the market failure model. *See* Part II *infra.*

38. 418 U.S. 323 (1974).

39. *Id.* at 340.

40. *Id.* (citations omitted).

41. *See* T. KUHN, THE STRUCTURE OF SCIENTIFIC REVOLUTION (2nd ed. 1970); M. POLYANI, PERSONAL KNOWLEDGE (1964).

42. For both a description of the modern view of knowledge and a discussion of the problems with it, see R. UNGER, KNOWLEDGE AND POLITICS (1975).

43. This assumption serves in my argument the same function served by Mill's assumption that nothing contrary to truth can really be useful. *See* ON LIBERTY, *supra* note 1, at 28.

44. *See* R. UNGER, *supra* note 42, at 146–47, 234, 243–45, 248. *But see id.* at 230–31.

45. R. WOLFF, B. MOORE, JR., H. MARCUSE, A CRITQUE OF PURE TOLERANCE 109–111 (1968).

46. *See* Part II *infra.*

47. *See, e.g.,* P. BERGER & T. LUCKMAN, THE SOCIAL CONSTRUCTION OF REALITY (1967); K. MANNHEIM, IDEOLOGY AND UTOPIA (1954); C. MILLS, POWER, POLITICS, AND PEOPLE (1967). *See also* P. WINCH,

THE IDEA OF SOCIAL SCIENCE AND ITS RELATION TO PHILOSOPHY (1958). This entire field, of course, owes a tremendous debt to the writings of Karl Marx.

48. The propagandist aware of the findings of the behavioral sciences no longer has as much confidence as his counterparts from the late eighteenth to the early twentieth century had in the ability of rational arguments or even of catchy slogans to influence human behavior. The evolution of psychoanalysis, clinical psychology, and experimental research on communication has made it clear that reactors' responses are affected not only by the immediate input of symbols but also (and often more powerfully) by three other sets of forces: (1) the stored residues of, and associations to, previous inputs of related symbols, which often give the reactor a predisposition and capacity to ignore or to rationalize away the current flow of symbols; (2) economic inducements . . . and coercive inducements . . . and (3) the coercive structures and processes in the surrounding social systems . . . .

12 INT'L ENCYCLOPEDIA OF THE SOC. SCI. *Propaganda,* at 585 (1968) [hereinafter cited as *Propaganda*].

49. A defense of the market model might suggest that, although not all people reason rationally all the time, progress results because some people are sometimes sufficiently insightful to reach an improved understanding and their gains are carried forward. However, the last step, how people demonstrate their new insights to others, is not explained. Two explanations seem plausible. First, historical developments may make others desirous or in need of the new insights or perspectives. *See* T. KUHN, note 41 *supra;* Wallace, *Revitalization Movements,* 58 AM. ANTHROPOLOGIST 264 (1956). Second, if the new insights are put into practice, they may provide modes of interaction which people will find more appealing or useful than dominant practices and, therefore, people would convert. Note that both explanations crucially depend not merely on the intellectual persuasiveness of the new viewpoints but on the appeal of the implementation of the insights. This suggests that faith in the marketplace might be reasserted, but only if dissenting or minority groups are free to implement their perspectives. *See* Part IV-C *infra.*

50. On the notion of pure procedural justice, see J. RAWLS, A THEORY OF JUSTICE 84–87 (1971).

51. *See* Part II *infra. See also,* Baker, *Counting Preferences in Collective Choice Situations,* 25 UCLA L. Rev. 381 (1978).

52. The power of dominant groups to legally restrict opportunities to practice alternatives, thereby developing alternative perceptions or knowledge can occur in two ways: 1) through legal prohibitions of certain behavior, *see* Part IV *infra;* or 2) through legal control of economic resources enabling them to limit work experience, *see* Gintis, *Consumer Behavior and the Concept of Sovereignty: Explanations of Social Decay,* 62 AM. ECON. REV.: PAPERS & PROC. SUPP. 267, 271 (1972).

53. R. UNGER, *supra* note 42, at 103, 242–44, 253, 255.

54. *See* Coase, note 5 *supra;* Director, *supra* note 5, at 6.

55. 3 INT'L ENCYCLOPEDIA OF THE SOC. SCI. *Communications, Mass,* at 82 (1968).

56. *Id.* at 85.

57. Jaffe, *The Editorial Responsibility of the Broadcaster: Reflections on Fairness and Access,* 85 HARV. L. REV. 768, 769–70 (1972). Each of the conclusions in the text concerning the effects of the mass media are supported by Professor Jaffe's brief survey of communications theory.

58. Conflict could potentially arise between a class conscious mass audience and power elites or dominant economic groups. In case of conflict, the second groups appear in control. The most the mass audience can hope for may be the set of communications they most prefer that are also consistent with the interests of the power elite. At present the mass audience appears to demand little that is inconsistent with status quo relations. As noted, preferences reflect patterns of social interaction. As long as dominant groups control the character and content of social experience—for example, the demeaning, hierarchical nature of the work experience or the exchange nature of both economic and personal value—a congruence of mass desires and status quo promises can be expected. This congruence may be ruptured, however, if the system has important dysfunctional characteristics. *See, e.g.,* J. HABERMAS, LEGITIMATION CRISIS (1975); C. REICH, GREENING OF AMERICA (1970). In addition constitutional protection of opportunities for people to develop alternative patterns of interaction might provide a basis for change in the mass audience's perspectives.

59. In *Propaganda, supra* note 48, at 587, the author, who explained how people are not rational but are controlled by other factors, still hoped that the marketplace would work:

> By definition, a healthily functioning democracy is a polity in which opposition to propaganda is habitually expressed primarily through peaceful counterpropaganda. It is assumed that a variety of propagandists will compete vigorously in "the marketplace of ideas," and it is hoped that the ideas best for society will find the most takers in the long run.

One wonders if this faith is sustained precisely because the marketplace aids in preserving the existing order.

60. *See* Part II *infra.*

61. *See* R. WOLFF, B. MOORE, JR., H. MARCUSE, note 45 *supra.*

62. *See, e.g.,* B. OWEN, ECONOMICS AND FREEDOM OF EXPRESSION (1975) (arguing for structural reform including anti-trust enforcement); Cooper, *The Tax Treatment of Business Grassroots Lobbying: Defining and Attain-*

ing the Public Policy Objectives, 68 COLUM. L. REV. 801, 841–59 (1968) (suggesting method of using tax laws as incentives for political speech of private groups, particularly relatively poor groups).

63. ON LIBERTY, *supra* note 1, at 46.

64. In Red Lion Broadcasting Co. v. FCC, 395 U.S. 367 (1969), the Court upheld the "fairness doctrine," which was considered to be a method of assuring that the most important views would be aired on the electronic media. In various cases the Court has suggested that it would assure that effective channels of communication exist for all positions. Linmark Assoc., Inc. v. Township of Willingboro, 413 U.S. 85, 93 (1977) (one of two grounds for decision); Columbia Broadcasting Sys. v. Democratic Nat'l Comm., 412 U.S. 94, 193–96 (1973) (Brennan, & Marshall, JJ., dissenting); United States v. O'Brien, 391 U.S. 367, 388–89 (1968) (Harlan, J., concurring); Kovacs v. Cooper, 336 U.S. 77, 102–03 (1949) (Black, J., dissenting). *See also* Columbia Broadcasting Sys. v. Democratic Nat'l Comm., 412 U.S. at 122 (opinion of Court) (where the Court, quoting Meiklejohn, suggests that assuring an effective forum for all viewpoints is constitutionally crucial: "'[W]hat is essential is not that everyone shall speak, but that everything worth saying shall be said.'").

65. The Court has struck down restraints that would prohibit some people from speaking as much as they desire even though the position of those people may already be adequately expressed in the market place. Buckley v. Valeo, 424 U.S. 1 (1976). It has also struck down laws and rejected proposals to assure some access to print or broadcast media as being contrary to, or at least not required by, the first amendment. Miami Herald Publishing Co. v. Tornillo, 418 U.S. 241 (1974); Columbia Broadcasting Sys. v. Democratic Nat'l Comm., 412 U.S. 94 (1973). *But cf.* Red Lion Broadcasting Co. v. FCC, 395 U.S. 367 (1969) (upholding "fairness doctrine," requiring each side of public issues to be given equal presentation by the media). These decisions are inconsistent with the market failure model, and although the Court continued to invoke marketplace language, *see, e.g.,* Miami Herald Publishing Co. v. Tornillo, 418 U.S. at 529 (White, J., concurring), the decisions are best explained by a liberty theory. *See Commercial Speech, supra* note 5, at 41–42 n.144.

66. This model develops difficulties if an information overload, too much "noise," decreases people's ability or willingness to assimilate messages. If even a minimal presentation of all viewpoints would produce dysfunctional levels of "noise," instead of guaranteeing presentation opportunities for all viewpoints, one might hope that the messages most often presented will be closer to truth than those not presented; or one could impose limits on how much a given message could be presented in the hope of reducing "noise" distortion. *But cf.* Buckley v. Valeo, 424 U.S. 1 (1976) (invalidating expenditure limits).

67. Federal Election Campaign Act of 1971, 2 U.S.C. §§ 431–456 (1976); 47 U.S.C. §§ 801–805 (Supp. II 1972), *as amended by* Pub. L. No. 93–443, 88 Stat. 1263 (1974).

68. *See Economic Analysis, supra* note 5, at 32–41.

69. Harper v. Virginia Bd. of Elections, 383 U.S. 663 (1966) (striking down poll tax). *See also* Lubin v. Panish, 415 U.S. 709 (1974); Bullock v. Carter, 405 U.S. 134 (1972); *see generally* Baker, *Utility and Rights: Two Justifications for State Action Increasing Equality,* 84 YALE L.J. 39 (1974); Michelman, *On Protecting the Poor Through the Fourteenth Amendment,* 83 HARV. L. REV. 7 (1969).

70. For example, this is accomplished by giving people full credit against their taxes for political expenditures (contributions) up to a certain level and, for people who do not pay taxes, by directly giving them rebates for political expenditures. Absent this second procedure, the law should succumb to an equal protection attack.

71. Baker, note 51 *supra;* Baker, note 69 *supra.*

72. R. DWORKIN, TAKING RIGHTS SERIOUSLY, 150–205 (1977); Baker, *supra* note 69, at 48–55.

73. Baker, note 51 *supra.*

74. Michelman, note 69 *supra. See* San Antonio Independent School Dist. v. Rodriguez, 411 U.S. 1, 23–24, 25 n.60, 36–37 (1973).

75. *See* text accompanying notes 76–82 *infra.* These comments are not a defense of a fourteenth amendment right to a minimum opportunity to communicate. Instead, I suggest that if an argument is made to require governmental action assuring everyone such a minimum opportunity, the analysis ought to be based on the fourteenth amendment notion that individuals be respected as equals rather than on a first amendment marketplace of ideas theory (or on the first amendment notion that persons be respected as autonomous individuals).

76. 391 U.S. 367 (1968).

77. This "passage does not foreclose consideration of First Amendment claims . . . [where a regulation] has the effect of entirely preventing a 'speaker' from reaching a significant audience with whom he could not otherwise lawfully communicate." 391 U.S. at 388–89 (Harlan, J., concurring).

78. Interestingly, the clearest example of the Court relying on this adequacy of access argument involved a situation where those excluded were not political dissidents but were presumably quite middle class. Linmark Assoc., Inc. v. Township of Willingboro, 431 U.S. 85, 93 (1977) (one—the weakest—ground for invalidating a ban on "For Sale" signs on homes was that the homeowners did not have "satisfactory" alternative means of communication). The civil rights protest cases might appear to contradict the generalization in the text.

However, when these cases favored the dissidents, the Court usually relied either on discriminatory enforcement (content discrimination) or on statutory vagueness or overbreadth grounds to set aside the convictions—not adequacy of access arguments. Unless the Court fully adopts the perspective of the dissidents, these faults are more easily seen and are more easily corrected by judicial decrees than is the inadequacy of access opportunities. These two factors suggest why the Court did not employ inadequacy of access arguments.

79. The situation was much calmer in the classic theory that assumed that the marketplace would not fail (unless *because* of government censorship) and, therefore, the government had no need to guarantee a properly functioning market. Thus, in the classic model, "when men have realized that time has upset many fighting faiths, they may come to believe even more than they believe the very foundations of their own conduct that the ultimate good desired is better reached by free trade in ideas—that the best test of truth is the power of the thought to get itself accepted in the competition of the market. . . ." Abrams v. United States, 250 U.S. 616, 630 (1919) (Holmes & Brandeis, JJ., dissenting).

80. Each of the above faults are suggested by Winter, *Poverty, Economic Equality, and the Equal Protection Clause,* 1972 SUP. CT. REV. 41. Certain faults in Winter's analysis, *see, e.g.,* Baker, *supra* note 69, at 44 n. 17, are less likely to apply if the subsidy is constitutionally required rather than legislatively chosen and if the subsidy attempts to achieve rather than absolute equality a minimal level of "merit good" availability rather than absolute equality.

81. J. RAWLS, *supra* note 50, at 302–03.

82. The Court noted that this "inequality" of equality of opportunity is a serious problem. Buckley v. Valeo, 421 U.S. 1, 56–57 (1976).

83. *See* text accompanying notes 54–61 *supra.*

84. *See* notes 124–41 & accompanying text *infra.*

85. T. EMERSON, THE SYSTEM OF FREEDOM OF EXPRESSION 6–7 (1971) [hereinafter cited as FREEDOM OF EXPRESSION]; GENERAL THEORY, *supra* note 15, at 3–15.

86. Since *democratic participation* in change focuses on the individual's freedom to participate, if the speech is not chosen by anyone, if it is not a manifestation of the speaker's values, even though the speech may cause change or advance knowledge, it does not serve this liberty value and is not protected. *See Commercial Speech,* note 5 *supra.*

87. Baker, *supra* note 51, at 413–15.

88. *See* R. DWORKIN, note 72 *supra;* J. RAWLS, note 50 *supra;* Baker, note 69 *supra.*

89. Scanlon, *A Theory of Freedom of Expression,* 1 PHILOSOPHY & PUB. AFF. 204, 206–07 (1972). Most thoughtful commentators agree with Scanlon's categorization. *See, e.g.,* L. TRIBE, AMERICAN CONSTITUTIONAL LAW 601, 605 (1978); Nimmer, *The Meaning of Symbolic Speech Under the First Amendment,* 21 UCLA L. REV. 29, 36 (1973).

90. G. ORWELL, 1984 (1948).

91. *Cf.* Stanley v. Georgia, 394 U.S. 557 (1969) (statute banning private possession of obscene material held unconstitutional. According to some, the Court only protected the pornography to the extent that no communication between people, at least people outside the home, was involved. United States v. Thirty-Seven Photographs, 402 U.S. 363, 382 (1971) (Black & Douglas, JJ., dissenting). Compare praying in a state that wants to promote atheism.

92. Compare Karl Marx's report that in ancient India the "poet . . . in some communities replaces the silversmith, in others the school master." K. MARX, CAPITAL 357–58 (1967).

93. L. WITTGENSTEIN, PHILOSOPHICAL INVESTIGATIONS § 304 (3d ed. 1958).

94. *Id.* at § 23 (emphasis added). After listing various uses, Wittgenstein continues: "It is interesting to compare the multiplicity of the tools in language and of the ways they are used, the multiplicity of kinds of word and sentence, with what logicians have said about the structure of language." *Id.*

95. *Genesis* 1:3 (emphasis added). *See also Psalms* 33:9 ("For he spoke, and it came to be."); *Hebrews* 11:3 ("By faith we understand that the world was created by the word of God."). Richardson explains that to the Hebrew mind: "Thought, word, and deed are not three separate processes or acts but are organic elements of the same single process, an act of volition." A THEOLOGICAL WORD BOOK OF THE BIBLE 232 (A. Richardson ed. 1950).

96. H. ARENDT, THE HUMAN CONDITION 25–26 (1958) (emphasis added).

97. *Id.* at 177. *See also id.* at 175–81.

98. *Id.* at 190.

99. A. MACLEISH, POEMS, 1924–1933, 123 (1933).

100. G. BACHELARD, THE POETICS OF SPACE XVIII (1969).

101. *Id.* at XIX–XX. Compare Pierre-Jean Jouve's statement that "[T]here is no poetry without absolute creation." *Quoted in id.* at XXVIII.

102. *Commercial Speech,* note 5, *supra.* My argument is that the market dictates the content of commercial speech and, therefore, even if the speech happens to correspond to the speaker's values, the content is determined by the structure of the market and is not chosen by the speaker. While not rejecting their prior commercial decisions, Justices White, Marshall and Brennan adopted the reasoning of this Article in concluding that a corporation's political speech can be regulated. First Nat'l Bank v. Bellotti, 98 S. Ct. 1407, 1430–39 (1978) (White, Marshall & Brennan, JJ., dissenting).

Criticism of this argument focuses on other situations where "external" pressures appear to control people's speech; for example, some politicians have told me that the political speech of candidates does not represent the candidates' views but is "dictated" by the need of getting elected. Numerous distinctions make this analogy unacceptable. First, for many, if not most, political actors' political activity is not primarily and, more importantly, is not necessarily determined by the need to maximize either electoral support or economic profit. That is, the political realm resembles the "household" in being an arena where expenditures are made to promote one's substantive values. *Commercial Speech, supra* note 5, at 12–14 (employing Max Weber's distinction of the "household" from the profit-oriented business enterprise). Thus, no structure requires that the speaker choose increased chances of election (which is not even an option for minor parties) over increased advocacy of their values. Second, unlike the economic sphere where efficiently fulfilling wealth-backed desires is considered the most praiseworthy aspect of the enterprise's activity, many politicians and most defenders of the political process argue that, here, it is highly praiseworthy to truthfully and forcefully state, explain, and advocate one's own visions or understanding of the public good. In fact, such speech and advocacy may be an essential element in "good" political leadership. I realize this may be less true in the type of interest group politics that many pluralist political scientists presently defend than in a political realm where the main activity is to participate in choosing and defining values. *See* C. MACPHERSON, THE LIFE AND TIMES OF LIBERAL DEMOCRACY 77–115 (1977). However, the fact that some politicians partially conform to external pressures or are psychologically controlled by the combination of their desire to be elected and their assumptions concerning what speech will promote their election merely indicates one concept of self-interest that some political actors may adopt in choosing their speech; however, other choices are possible. My argument is that other choices are not permitted for economic enterprises operating in a profit-controlled competitive market. The above distinctions, I think, explain both the importance and the fact of greater freedom in the political realm than in the market realm.

103. *See* Part IV *infra.*

104. Compare "sticks and stones may break my bones but names will never hurt me."

105. *See* FREEDOM OF EXPRESSION, *supra* note 85, at 338.

106. *See* text accomanying notes 87–88 *supra.*

107. Nozick, *Coercion,* in PHILOSOPHY, SCIENCE, AND METHOD 440, 459 (S. Morgenbesser, P. Suppes & M. White eds. 1969).

108. In developing this description of threats, I am influenced by Nozick, note 107 *supra.* I deviate from Nozick in two important (and, probably, in other less important) respects. For reasons noted in the text, I think the benchmark position cannot be the "normal and expected course of events" but must be the events or options which the person has a moral or legitimate right to expect. (Of course, often the normal course of events contributes to what one has a right to expect.) Second, because in blackmail the threatener may have a right or duty to give information to others (*e.g.,* the police), Nozick viewed the blackmailer's statement that she would accept payment in return for making the disclosure to be an offer. *Id.* at 447. In consequence of looking not only at the opportunities to which the threatened person has a rightful expectation but also to the rights of the threatener, I conclude this involves a threat. *See* text accompanying note 112 *infra.*

109. The key problem in this second category is finding the theoretical limits on the extent to which the state can restrict the threatener's "rights."

110. If one distinguishes the more positive, conventional rights—rights that typically control the instrumental aspects of one's acts—from those rights that are essential for one's autonomy, it seems autonomy rights must supersede (others') conventional rights. However, one's autonomy rights cannot override another's autonomy. In this second area, respect for one's autonomy, for one's speech rights, does not bar legal control of one's speech. Speech that invades another's area of autonomy is coercive and can be regulated. Note, however, that reputation, which depends on the precise form of the social order and the attitudes of other people, is clearly conventional or instrumental, not an autonomy right.

111. *See* text accompanying note 102 *supra.*

112. *Cf.* United States v. Ballard, 322 U.S. 78 (1944). The defendants were charged with obtaining money by false representations. Although the Court held the Constitution prevented conviction for making *false* religious claims—*i.e.,* the truth of the religious claims could not be submitted to a jury—it did not decide whether the defendants could be convicted for making religious claims which they believed to be false. In dissent, Justices Stone, Roberts and Frankfurter concluded the defendants could be and were properly convicted

for making representations which they did not believe. *Id.* at 89–90. Note that although the effect on the listener would be the same whether or not the speakers believed their statements, the purpose or nature of the speaker's act would be different. In that context, to make false representations knowingly would be the type of speech that I have argued above to be coercive, hence unprotected.

113. I must leave for another time a discussion of the confusion, in which I think the Court has been embroiled, resulting from its failure to distinguish and explain the respective relevance of motive and purpose, particularly in its analysis of equal protection and first amendment issues.

114. New York Times Co. v. United States, 403 U.S. 713 (1971).

115. FREEDOM OF EXPRESSION, *supra* note 85, at 58–59.

116. Still, one might adopt Emerson's approach and deny protection to espionage because it falls in the "system of military operation," not "the system of freedom of expression," and merely rely on the argument in the text as a justification for the distinction. I do not wish to argue the point here. But note that Emerson's approach would allow greater restrictions, for example, where the espionage agent's acts are too far removed from any actual, attempted, or foreseen use of violence to justify prohibiting or punishing the speech act under my argument. However, if courts are going to allow this behavior to be sanctioned, Emerson's categorization might promote greater purity in overall doctrine, an important achievement.

117. In protecting the privacy of involuntary listeners, the government cannot regulate in a way that would prevent the speaker from communicating with willing listeners or burden the listener's receipt of desired communications. Erznoznik v. City of Jacksonville, 422 U.S. 205 (1975); Cohen v. California, 403 U.S. 15 (1971); Lamont v. Postmaster Gen., 381 U.S. 301 (1965); Saia v. New York, 334 U.S. 558 (1948); Martin v. City of Struthers, 319 U.S. 141 (1943). However, some content-neutral time, place, and manner regulations may be acceptable. Kovacs v. Cooper, 336 U.S. 77 (1949). And restraints that only prevent communications directed to unwilling listeners will be upheld. Rowan v. Post Office Dep't, 397 U.S. 728 (1970); Martin v. City of Struthers, 319 U.S. 141, 147–48 (1943) (dicta) (state can punish those who call on a home "in defiance of the previously expressed will of the occupant"). *See Commercial Speech, supra* note 5, at 8.

118. These cases are often cited to support an independent right to know: Virginia State Bd. of Pharmacy v. Virginia Citizens Consumer Council, Inc., 425 U.S. 748 (1976) (suit by consumers invalidated prohibition of pharmacist advertising drugs); Red Lion Broadcasting Co. v. FCC, 395 U.S. 367 (1969) (upheld fairness doctrine); and Lamont v. Postmaster Gen., 381 U.S. 301 (1965) (struck down regulation burdening receipt of communist political propaganda mailed from abroad). *See* L. TRIBE, *supra* note 89, at 675–76, 676 nn. 7 & 8. Nevertheless, under *Virginia Board of Pharmacy,* once the Court concludes commercial speech is protected, presumably the pharmacist's speech is protected. *See* Bates v. State Bar of Arizona, 432 U.S. 350 (1977). In *Red Lion,* the permissibility of the government's regulation of broadcast media as a partial common carrier (or partial public forum), not a right to know, was the basis of the decision. *See* Columbia Broadcasting Sys. v. Democratic Nat'l Comm., 412 U.S. 94 (1973); *Commercial Speech, supra* note 5, at 41–42 & n. 144. As for *Lamont,* it seems strange that the first amendment, which limits government power rather than giving individual rights, would permit the government to abridge the freedom of speech of foreigners. Clearly a willing speaker (with liberty interests) and a willing listener existed; moreover, unlike in Kleindienst v. Mandel, 408 U.S. 753 (1972), the legal burden was placed directly on listeners whose liberty interests were unquestionably involved. *See* text accompanying note 121 *infra.*

119. Of course, increased access to information is normally a desirable societal policy. The general allocation effects of policies increasing access to governmental and corporate controlled information may be to increase the egalitarian and democratic nature of society. *See* Baker, *Posner's Privacy Mystery and the Failure of Economic Analysis of Law,* 12 GA. L. REV. 475 (1978).

120. Nebraska Press Ass'n v. Stuart, 427 U.S. 539 (1976). *See* New York Times Co. v. United States, 403 U.S. 713 (1971). Of course, the argument in the text may have skipped a step. If the listener used illegal means to obtain the information, does that justify a limit on the listener's use of the information? Although the courts have not unambiguously answered this question, protecting the person's rights as a speaker would require that the state be permitted, but only permitted, to punish the illegal acts involved in obtaining the information, not its latter use. *See* Nebraska Press Ass'n v. Stuart, 427 U.S. at 598 (Brennan, Stewart & Marshall, JJ., concurring) (concluding that an injunction restraining publication would not be justified no matter how the information was obtained).

121. Virginia State Bd. of Pharmacy v. Virginia Citizens Consumer Council, Inc., 425 U.S. at 781–82 (Rehnquist, J., dissenting).

122. In Stanley v. Georgia, 394 U.S. 557 (1969), the Court apparently recognized the importance of the liberty interest of the reader. *Cf.* L. TRIBE, *supra* note 89, at 676–77 (interpreting *American Mini Theatres* as involving only the lesser right of the listener if the commercial speaker had no personal first amendment claim). *But see* United States v. 12 200-Foot Reels of Film, 413 U.S. 123 (1973). As I have noted elsewhere, it may be difficult to determine whether the commercial publisher and distributor, the more typical defendant in an

obscenity prosecution, manifests a liberty interest or a market-enforced profit motive. However, the first amendment protects one particular industry—the press—from regulations relating to its product on a fourth estate theory and on the basis of the conclusion that generally its product, print or speech, contributes importantly to its recipients' liberty while not itself being coercively or violently destructive. (Speech can, of course, destroy, but it destroys through the listener's choices respecting and responding to the message.) *Commercial Speech, supra* note 5, at 30–32. Thus, the liberty interest of the reader and the special constitutional status of the press combine to protect both parties in the distribution or communication of obscenity.

123. *Commercial Speech, supra* note 5, at 7 (emphasis deleted).

124. This distinction between "expression" and "action" provides "the central idea . . . of freedom of expression;" that system "cannot exist effectively on any other foundation, and a decision to maintain such a system necessarily implies acceptance of this proposition." FREEDOM OF EXPRESSION, *supra* note 85, at 17.

125. *Id.* at 18.

126. *Id.* (emphasis added).

127. *See* J. AUSTIN, HOW TO DO THINGS WITH WORDS (1962).

128. Or the choice might be "logical" if logic is seen as conventional. *See* C. MILLS, *supra* note ,47, at 427–29. Mills quotes Ernest Nagel who said "the principles of logic are . . . conventional without being arbitrary . . . ." Mills then suggests that "laws of proof may be merely the conventional abstract rules governing what are accepted as valid conversational extensions." *Id.* at 428. In a separate essay Mills argues that "motives are the terms with which interpretation of conduct *by social actors* proceeds." *Id.* at 440 (emphasis original). Presumably, whether the motive was to do something or was to express something depends on the social context and on the needs of the interpreter.

129. The size of a demonstration hardly affects the logic of a demonstrator's views. Rather, the existence and size of the assembly are important because they suggest the power and willingness of people to promote the position. Likewise, consider the way a group boycott both expresses ideas and exercises powers. *See Commercial Speech, supra* note 5, at 54–56.

130. FREEDOM OF EXPRESSION, *supra* note 85, at 293.

131. *Id.* at 89.

132. *Id.* (emphasis added). Of course, those using coercion or pressure may believe that their acts will induce change by causing people to change their opinions; in fact, they may only want to stimulate discussion, *e.g.*, "raise consciousness," in these "action" cases.

133. Failing to carry a draft card presumably "interferes" or "obstructs" the working of the selective service system and apparently is classified as an "action" by Emerson. *Id.* at 86–87.

134. *Id.* at 84.

135. *Id.* at 445. This difference does not rely on Emerson's exclusion of commercial activities from the scope of the system of freedom of expression. *Id.* at 19–20, 447.

136. *Id.* at 445.

137. *Id.* (emphasis added).

138. *See* Organization for a Better Austin v. Keefe, 402 U.S. 415 (1971).

139. ON LIBERTY, *supra* note 1, at 13 (emphasis addded).

140. This and the following paragraphs are based on Baker, note 51 *supra*.

141. The distinction in the text refers to how rules limit a person's authority to make a decision. In addition, the content of the rules will affect and reflect people's values; and by changing the costs and benefits of different activities, the rules will encourage or discourage different forms of social relations. Any evaluation of specific rules or systems of rules should consider these effects. However, these effects of the content of rules are not important for the present analysis.

142. *Cf.* New York Times v. Sullivan, 376 U.S. 254 (1964) (invalidating state libel law that gave a person authority to control—or sanction—certain speech of others). Constitutional requirements in various clauses, including the first amendment, the due process clause and the involuntary servitude clause, may limit the way government can allocate decision-making authority concerning a person's body. The government cannot give another, *e.g.*, a husband or parent, the right to prohibit or require a woman to have an abortion. *See* Planned Parenthood of Cent. Mo. v. Danforth, 428 U.S. 52 (1976). Possibly more is required. The concept of a person as someone whose dignity, integrity, and autonomy are respected generally requires that the person have decision authority over the purposes for which his or her body is used. One arguably has a right not to be required to use one's body over a long period of time to aid and support another, even though it is readily conceded that one may be required to forego claims to physical or economic resources needed to benefit another. This conclusion, of course, supports the second of two arguments commonly invoked to support the claimed right not to be prohibited from having an abortion. The two arguments are: 1) a fetus is not a person, an issue which has no clear resolution; and 2) one cannot be forced involuntarily to use one's body to support the existence of another. *See* Thompson, *A Defense of Abortion*, 1 PHILOSOPHY & PUB. AFF. 47 (1971).

143. Time, place, and manner regulations become obvious cases of prohibited censorship when they are not neutral in respect to content. *See, e.g.,* Police Dep't v. Mosley, 408 U.S. 92 (1972). However, the issue is more complicated if the regulation, neutral on its face and applied according to its terms, will necessarily limit some groups or some points of view more than others. *See, e.g.,* Kovacs v. Cooper, 336 U.S. 77, 102–03 (1949) (Black, Douglas & Rutledge, JJ., dissenting) (total ban on sound truck disadvantages poor and favors the views of those who own the dominant forms of media communication). In such cases of "facially neutral" regulation of time, place, and manner, "[w]hen a statute deals with conduct containing elements of both expression and action, the First Amendment issue turns in part upon the question whether the legislation is directed at the expression or action . . . ." FREEDOM OF EXPRESSION, *supra* note 85, at 85 (objecting to the Court's failure to do this in *O'Brien*). Invalidation only on evidence of a conscious desire to limit the expression of certain viewpoints provides insufficient protection if the first amendment requires the government to be careful not to restrict people's freedom of speech. This broader requirement explains the relevance of least restrictive means tests in the area of time, place, and manner regulations. The argument is that the failure to adopt a reasonable, but less restrictive, regulation is objective evidence of a purpose to ignore the first amendment mandate that the government be concerned with people's freedom of speech. On this reasoning, *Kovacs,* which involved a complete ban on sound trucks, was decided incorrectly.

144. *But cf.* Karst, *Equality as a Central Principle in the First Amendment,* 43 U. CHI. L. REV. 20 (1975) (finding equality as a central value of the first amendment).

145. Since allocation of authority seems a logically necessary limit on individual liberty, I conclude that such allocation rules are *formally* the minimum limit on liberty. Put differently, allocation rules are a necessary part of the framework in which liberty can exist. If one had criteria or theory to distinguish the "amount of liberty" which possession of a specific decision-making authority gives different people, then different arrangements of allocation rules would provide different amounts of limits on liberty. For example, does control of a dollar's worth of food give a different amount of "liberty" to different people? Note, "liberty" here means relevant opportunity for self-realization, for self-determination, or for participation in group determination. This suggests liberty is a substantive matter—*i.e.,* liberty involves a person's opportunity to do or develop in the way she desires or in the way that most fully manifests or develops her potential. (Compare the popular distinction between positive and negative liberty.) Possibly, a specific combination of allocation rules and general prohibitions would be more successful in allowing everyone (or most people) to do or develop than would be possible with only allocation rules. I will argue that *sometimes* such a combination of allocation rules and general prohibitions, *e.g.,* of instrumentally valued behaviors, will be justified as proper means of promoting substantive liberty. *See* text accompanying notes 148–55 *infra.*

146. Note that rules governing transfer of rights, or rules prohibiting alienation, are allocation rules in that they merely determine who has the decision-making authority. In discussing the notion of an "inalienable right of life," Professor Feinberg apparently prefers the interpretation of the right that he attributes to our "founding fathers." In effect, Feinberg suggests the inalienable right to life means that one cannot transfer the right to decide to take one's life to another, rather than that there is a "general prohibition" on ending one's own life. Life is alienable but the right to life is not. This rejection of the general prohibition mirrors the conclusions of this paper. However, Feinberg does not determine whether the right to decide to take one's life should be inalienable or non-transferable, that is, he does not decide what allocation rule is best. Feinberg, *Voluntary Euthanasia and the Inalienable Right to Life,* 7 PHILOSOPHY & PUB. AFF. 93 (1978). Although this alienation (transferability) question should be analyzed in terms of what best indicates a respect for the autonomy and integrity, of humans, in general, as Shelley v. Kraemer, 334 U.S. 1 (1948) graphically illustrates, alienation rules raise allocation issues that involve both equality and liberty values.

147. "I can imagine no more distasteful, useless, and time-consuming task . . . ." United States v. Thirty-Seven Photographs, 402 U.S. 363, 380 (1971) (Black & Douglas, JJ., dissenting).

148. Baker, *supra* note 51, at 393–96.

149. *See id.*

150. *See* Moore v. City of East Cleveland, 431 U.S. 494 (1977) (invalidating a zoning ordinance which prohibited such living arrangements). *But cf.* Village of Belle Terre v. Boraas, 416 U.S. 1 (1974) (upholding zoning ordinance prohibiting certain types of living arrangements).

151. Village of Euclid v. Ambler Realty Co., 272 U.S. 365 (1926).

152. *See* Mishan, *Pareto Optimality and the Law,* 19 OXFORD ECON. PAP. 255 (1967). *See also* Young v. American Mini Theatres, 427 U.S. 50 (1976) (upholding zoning ordinance regulating location of "adult" theatres). In *American Mini Theatres,* the regulation did not thwart or even greatly burden people in fulfilling their substantive desire to see adult films. *Id.* at 71–72, n.35. The case can be read to say that content restrictions in time, place, and manner regulations may be permissible *if* they do not limit the realization of the substantively valued aspects of the restricted activity. Thus, such a content based restriction would never justify limiting advocacy or propaganda but are proper in *American Mini Theatres.*

153. On this analysis, nudity could normally be prohibited in most public areas on the assumption that the substantive expressive value of nudity does not require exposure to those who find public nudity offensive. However, when nudity is a form of expression, intended to confront the public and communicate a message, the argument for banning nudity from the public arena is weak. *But see* L. TRIBE, *supra* note 89, at 680–81 (1978).

154. When substantive values of two groups are involved, normally the proper solution is to maximize realization of substantive values in choosing allocation rules. But, as will be further argued below, promoting welfare maximization normally would not justify general prohibitions, which would be required if one were to favor those wanting over those opposing separation (segregation). Moreover, if maximizing realization of substantive values involves the state distinguishing between people on the basis of their inherent qualities and, then, limiting their liberty on this basis, the state's rule may violate the constitutional requirement that the state treat people as equals. *See* Baker, note 51 *supra*.

155. *See* Baker, note 51 *supra* (the determinative-additive distinction).

156. *See, e.g.*, Wooley v. Maynard, 430 U.S. 705 (1977); Wisconsin v. Yoder, 406 U.S. 205 (1972); West Virginia State Bd. of Educ. v. Barnette, 319 U.S. 624 (1943).

157. *See* text accompanying notes 160–166 *infra*.

158. *See* Part V *infra*.

159. *See, e.g.*, Wisconsin v. Yoder, 406 U.S. 205 (1972). This case illustrates both the importance for social pluralism of the ability of voluntary groups to create general prohibitions or requirements and the possibility of the government using such prohibitions or requirements to destroy pluralism.

160. The arguments in this paragraph closely parallel some developed in Michelman, *Property, Utility and Fairness: Comment on the Ethical Foundations of "Just Compensation" Law*, 80 HARV. L. REV. 1165 (1967). The "takings" Michelman discussed primarily involved *resource allocations*, not liberty of action. And according to the analysis here, resource allocations are more legitimately subject to revision by majority decision.

161. Note that this rule utilitarian argument could be leveled against general prohibitions of both substantively and instrumentally valued behavior, although both abuses of the power and dissatisfaction caused by the abuses may be greater in respect to restrictions on substantively valued behavior. Carried to an extreme, this rule utilitarian argument could be applied to most cases of government decision making. *See* J. BUCHANAN, THE LIMITS OF LIBERTY (1975).

162. *See* text accompanying notes 87–88 *supra;* R. DWORKIN, note 72 *supra; Economic Analysis, supra* note 5, at 32–41.

163. In fact, efficiency analysis must rely on both some assumed set of tastes and on some distribution of resources—and both assumptions bias the results of the calculations. *See* Baker, note 119 *supra; Economic Analysis*, note 5 *supra;* Tribe, *Technology Assessment and the Fourth Discontinuity: The Limits of Instrumental Rationality*, 46 SO. CAL. L. REV. 617, 635–41 (1973).

164. ON LIBERTY, *supra* note 1, at 14.

165. Tribe, *supra* note 163, at 640.

166. R. UNGER, *supra* note 42, at 242–45. "[T]he spiral of domination and community progresses through constant experiments in association. Unless emergent groups are free to develop and are not disadvantaged in relation to existing ones, there is the danger that a partial vision of the good will be petrified and the spiral arrested." *Id.* at 287.

167. *Cf. Commercial Speech*, note 5 *supra* (where I argue that the market structure coerces or "dictates" the choice of speech messages by economic enterprises and, therefore, enterprise speech undermines the process of democratic decision making). Generally, a more thorough analysis of the influence of various power structures on people's expression is needed.

168. For a discussion and criticism of the Court's approach, see FREEDOM OF EXPRESSION, *supra* note 85, at 292–98. Kalven popularized and then criticized the "speech plus" characterization of the Court's analysis. Kalven, *The Concept of the Public Forum: Cox v. Louisiana*, 1965 SUP. CT. REV. 1, 21–25.

169. *See, e.g.*, Cox v. Louisiana, 379 U.S. 536, 555 (1965) ("We emphatically reject the notion . . . that the First and Fourteenth Amendments afford the same kind of freedom to those who would communicate ideas by conduct such as patrolling, marching, and picketing on streets and highways, as these amendments afford to those who communicate by pure speech."); International Brotherhood of Teamsters v. Vogt, 354 U.S. 284 (1957). *But cf.* Brown v. Louisiana, 383 U.S. 131 (1966) (where Justice Fortas argued that "these rights are not confined to verbal expression [but] embrace appropriate types of action which certainly include the right in a peaceable and orderly manner to protest by silent and reproachful presence, in a place where the protestant has every right to be, the unconstitutional segregation of public facilities." *Id.* at 141–42 (footnotes omitted.)).

170. This discussion builds on remarks made in *Commercial Speech, supra* note 5, at 54–56.

171. *See, e.g.*, NAACP v. Alabama *ex rel.* Patterson, 357 U.S. 449 (1958).

172. *See, e.g.*, Bates v. City of Little Rock, 361 U.S. 516, 523 (1960) ("And it is now beyond dispute that freedom of association for the purpose of advancing ideas and airing grievances is protected . . ."). *See generally*

Raggi, *An Independent Right to Freedom of Association,* 12 HARV. C.R.-C.L. L. REV. 1, 2–11 (1977). This same reduction of the right to assemble or associate to an appendage of the right of expression is evident in Note, *Political Boycott Activity and the First Amendment,* 91 HARV. L. REV. 659 (1978). This Note persuasively argues that some bans on some picketing—*e.g.,* to promote boycotts for political reasons—involve a state purpose to suppress expression in order to prevent conduct that may result from the expression and, therefore, that these bans violate the free speech provision. It assumes that although perusading another independently to refuse to deal is constitutionally protected, associating or commencing to refuse to deal is not protected. *Id.* at 683–91. The greater power of concerted activity is obvious, but if assembly and association protect people's right to generate and apply power, the argument must show why this particular application of associational power can be banned, why it is coercive. For an attempt to analyze the problem in this way, see FREEDOM OF EXPRESSION, *supra* note 85, at 445–48.

    173. *See* Runyon v. McCrary, 427 U.S. 160, 175–76 (1976).

    174. *See* Raggi, note 172 *supra.*

    175. *See, e.g.,* Grey, *Do We Have an Unwritten Constitution?,* 27 STAN. L. REV. (1975).

    176. Apparently the Court, certainly Justices Black and Douglas, recognized this basis of the right of association in Bates v. City of Little Rock, 361 U.S. 516, 522–23 (opinion of the Court), 528 (Black & Douglas, JJ., concurring) (1960). In concurrence, Black and Douglas stated that "freedom of assembly or includes of course freedom of association." *Id.* at 528 (Black & Douglas, JJ., concurring).

    177. Raggi argued that freedom of speech and the right to petition could not support an adequately broad right of association. On this point, as long as speech is tied to a marketplace of ideas or advocacy model, she is clearly correct. However, she ignored the obvious first amendment basis of the right: the freedom of assembly.

    178. 381 U.S. 479, 486 (1965).

    179. *See* McBride, *Voluntary Association: The Basis of an Ideal Model and the "Democratic" Failure,* in 11 NOMOS: VOLUNTARY ASSOCIATIONS 202, 214, 229–30 (J. Pennock & J. Chapman eds. 1969). McBride emphasizes the fact that voluntary associations can increase individual responsibility and the "member's role in the achievement of social change."

    180. H. ARENDT, ON VIOLENCE 52 (1969); *See also id.* at 44. This paragraph and the next follow Arendt's reasoning.

    181. *See* C. MILLS, THE POWER ELITE 171 (1956): "All politics is a struggle for power; the ultimate kind of power is violence." For a modern representative of this Hobbesian view in the legal community, see Leff, *Injury, Ignorance and Spite—the Dynamics of Coercive Collection,* 80 YALE L.J. 1, 8 (1970): "Behind every final judgment procured in any court in this country, stands, ultimately, the United States Army . . . ." H.L.A. Hart's recognition of the internal aspect of rules—that is, their existence in the forms of interaction or relations among people—parallels the distinction between power and violence, and his criticism of John Austin's equation of law and coercive threats amounts to a criticism of Austin for failing to see this distinction. H.L.A. HART, THE CONCEPT OF LAW (1961). Law also illustrates that power and violence are often found together and how, when this occurs, power is always in the dominant position. Consent, at least of the officials of the system, is necessary for law to operate.

    182. *Honky Tonk Women,* in WEATHERMEN 313, 314 (H. Jacobs ed. 1970); *National War Council, id.* 337, 337. *See also* Ashley, Ayers, Dohrn, Jacobs, Jones, Long, Machtinger, Meller, Robbins, Rudd & Tappis, *You Don't Need a Weatherman to Know Which Way the Wind Blows, id.* 51, 85; *Inside the Weather Machine, id.* 321, 326.

    183. Arendt distinguishes strength from power in that strength is a capacity of the single individual while power is a capacity of the group. H. ARENDT, *supra* note 180, at 44.

    184. H. ARENDT, ORIGINS OF TOTALITARIANISM (2d ed. 1958).

    185. W. GODWIN, ENQUIRY CONCERNING POLITICAL JUSTICE 40–41 (abr. ed. 1971).

    186. Dennis v. United States, 341 U.S. 494, 570–77 (1951) (Jackson, J., concurring).

    187. *Id.* at 577.

    188. *Id.* at 573–74 (citation omitted) (emphasis added).

    189. I would argue that these are unprotected for the same reasons that commercial speech should be unprotected. *See Commercial Speech,* note 5 *supra.*

    190. *See, e.g.,* Brandenburg v. Ohio, 395 U.S. 444 (1969).

    191. "Coercive" includes situations in which the associations "determine" certain aspects of society such that choices of others, not members of the association, are made irrelevant. *See* Baker, note 51 *supra.* Although the application of the above limitation may be difficult and controversial, the possibility of associations exhibiting these coercive features can always be avoided if membership on an equal basis is available and if civil liberties of members are protected. However, it may be that the only constitutional basis on which the government can require the presence of either of these features of an association is if, in their absence, the association would be coercive. *See, e.g.,* Abood v. Detroit Bd. of Educ., 431 U.S. 209 (1977); Shelley v. Kraemer, 334 U.S. 1 (1948). *But see* Runyon v. McCrary, 427 U.S. 160 (1976).

    192. Reynolds v. United States, 98 U.S. 145 (1878). *See generally* Linford, *The Mormans and the Law: The*

Polygamy Cases, 9 UTAH L. REV. 308, 543 (1964–1965) (describing the vigor and violence of the United States government's attempt to destroy the Morman Church and its deviant life style).

193. Cantwell v. Connecticut, 310 U.S. 296, 303–04 (1940) (citations to polygamy omitted).

194. Of course, these cases involved an interpretation of statutory references to religion and not an interpretation of the constitutional meaning of religion. *See, e.g.,* United States v. Seeger, 380 U.S. 163 (1965).

195. One of the three parts of Madison's proposal, which became the first amendment, read: "The civil rights of none shall be abridged on account of religious belief or worship, nor shall any national religion be established, *nor shall the full and equal rights of conscience be in any manner, or on any pretext, infringed."* 1 ANNALS OF CONG. 451 (Gates ed. 1834) (emphasis added), *quoted* in N.Y. Times v. United States, 403 U.S. 713, 716 n.2 (1971) (Black & Douglas, JJ., concurring). Freeman argues that Congress intended the religion section of the first amendment to have the same meaning as it did when adopted by the House on August 24, 1789: "Congress shall make no law establishing religion or prohibiting the free exercise thereof, nor shall the rights of conscience be infringed." Freeman, *A Remonstrance for Conscience,* 106 U. PA. L. REV. 806, 812 (1958).

196. *See, e.g.,* Gillette v. United States, 401 U.S. 437, 465–66 (1971) (Douglas, J., dissenting).

197. 406 U.S. 205 (1972).

198. *Id.* at 235. The Court even noted that "few other religious groups or sects could make [the convincing showing made by the Amish]." *Id.* at 236.

199. *But see* text accompanying notes 194–96 *supra.* Although the point needs more elaborate development, it seems clear that the meaning of "religion" differs in the establishment and free exercise clauses. Both the historical concern and court cases emphasize, in the case of the establishment clause, the impermissibility of aid to religious sects or sponsorship of recognizably religious beliefs tied to traditional religious sects or groups. In free exercise situations, both history and court cases emphasize the individual's claims of conscience. That is, establishment relates to the sect and traditional religion, free exercise relates to the individual and conscience. Two paradoxes, otherwise unresolvable, are avoided by this interpretation. First, claims based on the free exercise and establishment clauses will not conflict. *See* Welsh v. United States, 398 U.S. 333, 344–67 (1970) (Harlan, J., concurring). Second, the legitimacy of the government using its resources to promote ethical or social values is not undermined. The establishment clause is avoided because the government action is not tied to traditional sects while the free exercise clause only requires that the government not "coerce" individuals to adopt these values.

200. 406 U.S. at 222. *But see id.* at 247 n.5 (Douglas, J., dissenting in part).

201. Sherbert v. Verner, 374 U.S. 398, 403 (1963). Three judges, Harlan, and White in dissent, *id.* at 421, and Stewart in concurrence, *id.* at 417–18, clearly reject the distinction. *See* note 212 *infra.*

202. Braunfeld v. Brown, 366 U.S. 599 (1961); Chatwin v. United States, 326 U.S. 455 (1946); Prince v. Massachusetts, 321 U.S. 158 (1944); Reynolds v. United States, 98 U.S. 145 (1878).

203. United States v. Seeger, 380 U.S. 163 (1965). Lower courts have typically rejected religious claims for exemption from public regulations whether or not the claimed exemption would involve passive or active conduct. *See* N. DORSEN, P. BENDER & R. NEUBORNE, 1 EMERSON, HABER & DORSEN'S POLITICAL AND CIVIL RIGHTS IN THE UNITED STATES 1257–64 (4th ed. 1976).

204. *See, e.g.,* Wisconsin v. Yoder, 406 U.S. 205 (1972); Sherbert v. Verner, 374 U.S. 398 (1963).

205. *See, e.g.,* Murdock v. Pennsylvania, 319 U.S. 105 (1943) (distributing religious pamphlets); Rex v. Singh, 39 A.I.R. 53 (Allahabad H.C. 1952) (carrying a sword). One's religion may require engaging in polygamy, wearing certain clothing, avoiding public exhibition of certain parts of the body, as well as many other acts not normally prohibited by law.

206. *See* Chatwin v. United States, 326 U.S. 455 (1946). Murphy, for a unanimous court, stated that "bona fide religious beliefs cannot absolve one from liability under the Federal Kidnapping Act." *Id.* at 460.

207. Compare the speech parallel. Once one abandons the idea of objective truth, one finds that expression is important for self-improvement, not because it aids society in reaching universal agreement, but because it contributes to creating the possibly different environments best suited to different people's self-fulfillment. *See, e.g.,* Ginzberg v. United States, 383 U.S. 463, 489–91 (1966) (Douglas, J., dissenting).

208. McGowan v. Maryland, 366 U.S. 420, 575 (1961) (Douglas, J., dissenting).

209. *Id.*

210. *Id.* at 574–75. *See* Cleveland v. United States, 329 U.S. 14 (1946). *But see* Wisconsin v. Yoder, 406 U.S. 205, 247 (1972) (Douglas, J., dissenting in part) (indicating a hope that *Reynolds* will be overruled).

211. Cleveland v. United States, 329 U.S. 14, 26 (1946) (Murphy, J., dissenting).

212. This approach would reconcile the generally thought unreconcilable decisions in Braunfeld v. Brown, 366 U.S. 599 (1961) (upholding prohibition on Sunday operation by certain businesses) and Sherbert v. Verner, 374 U.S. 398 (1963) (requiring the state to pay unemployment to a person who lost her job because she refused to work on Saturday). First, the state's general prohibition on certain businesses operating on Sunday decreased the instrumental value of the business for the Jewish merchant—the merchant would not be able to make as

much money (possibly not enough to stay in business) as he otherwise would—but did not prohibit substantively valued behavior. It also must be shown that denial of unemployment benefits, but not forced Sunday closure, given the governmental programs involved, ought to be viewed as a penalty on the substantively valued activity rather than a resource allocation to promote proper state programs. *See* Sherbert v. Verner, 374 U.S. at 401–02 n.4. This argument can be made, although to be complete it would require a theory of unconstitutional conditions. Second, even if substantively valued, operating a business on Sunday could be prohibited. To the extent that opening on Sunday gives the merchant a significant economic advantage, if this practice is allowed, the market may force (or at least encourage) others to adopt this business practice, thereby forcing other people either to join the religion or to leave that realm of economic life to people of the given religion. In such a situation government regulation is appropriate. *See id.* at 409; *Commercial Speech*, note 5 *supra*.

213. Reich, *The New Property*, 73 YALE L.J. 733 (1964).

Elitism, The Masses And The Idea Of Self-Government: Ambivalence About The "Central Meaning Of The First Amendment"

By Lee C. Bollinger*

Of all the First Amendment cases involving the press, certainly the most widely acclaimed, both for its result and the sweep of its reasoning, has been *New York Times Co. v. Sullivan*.[1] Viewed even from the narrowest perspective, the decision was rightly hailed as a major breakthrough for press freedom. By imposing constitutional limits on the reach of state libel laws, the Supreme Court resolved a critically important issue touching the interests of the mass media. But the significance of the decision was widely perceived as transcending the particular issue addressed in the case; nothing less was involved, it was reported, than a virtual reordering of our thinking about the concepts of freedom of speech and press. In defining the constitutional strictures on state libel laws, the Court began from the premise that the Sedition Act of 1798 was unconstitutional, as so declared by "the court of history,"[2] and in doing so it opened a new chapter in First Amendment jurisprudence. The Court was teaching us, in short, the "central meaning of the First Amendment."[3]

Harry Kalven, of course, made that phrase from the *New York Times* case famous. His remarkable article appearing in the 1964 *Supreme Court Review* was one of those rare pieces of legal scholarship that adds content and definition to a decision while purporting to "interpret" it.[4] Kalven was the first to say why the *New York Times* opinion "may prove to be the best and most important [the Court] has ever produced in the realm of freedom of speech."[5] What was at stake, he said, was more than a mere shift in rhetoric; we were being offered a new vision. The Court appeared to have abandoned the clear and present danger and balancing tests and the two-level theory of speech; in their stead we would find a new analytical framework, one which emphasized the primacy of citizen participation in political affairs and the concomitant need for an expansive view of the range of protected expression. All of this was not, Kalven went on to say, a newly arrived at theory of freedom of speech or the press. It was, in fact, a near perfect reflection of the thesis which Alexander Meiklejohn had forcefully articulated in the late 1940's.[6]

That Meiklejohn's ideas had now prevailed, or would prevail given the inexorable tendencies of the *New York Times'* logic, was a view not held by Kalven alone. Meiklejohn himself found the decision an "occasion for dancing in the streets,"[7] Kalven and Justice Brennan, the author of the Court's opinion in *New York Times*, wrote a subsequent law review article in which he cautiously concurred in Kalven's assessment of the case.[8] Today it is widely assumed that Meiklejohn's theory is predominant in our First Amendment thinking, and the *New York Times* case is accordingly viewed as the North star for free speech questions. Any First Amendment analysis seems incomplete unless it begins with a citation or quotation from either or both of these sources.

* Associate Professor of Law, University of Michigan.

It is not my purpose here to offer a revisionist view of the *New York Times* decision, to argue that the Court there did not mean to adopt the Meiklejohn thesis. At this late stage, what the opinion has become in our minds is probably far more important than whatever it was originally intended to be. Rather, I am prepared to take Kalven's interpretation as given and wish to discuss what seems to me the more vital question: namely, the extent to which we have been willing to commit ourselves to the world view offered in the writings of Alexander Meiklejohn and the opinion in *New York Times*. I shall argue here that our First Amendment jurisprudence in fact evidences a profound ambivalence about the fundamental premises of the Meiklejohn thesis, an ambivalence that limits its centrality in our thinking. It is not that the Meiklejohn theory is somehow logically untenable, but that the empirical observations about human nature which underlie it are a matter of some considerable confusion for us. We are, in short, of two minds on the "central meaning of the First Amendment," and this unresolved posture is reflected in various areas of the First Amendment, but principally that of broadcast regulation. But before describing this tension and its First Amendment consequences, we must first probe more deeply into Meiklejohn's analysis to locate the source of the ambivalence.

Meiklejohn's book *Free Speech and Its Relation to Self-Government* was written against the backdrop of two decades of suppression of radical speech which had followed the formulation of the clear and present danger test. His overarching purpose was to make a case for the absolute protection of "political speech." To do this he attempted to link together the political theory which he believed underlies the Constitution and a theory of freedom of speech and press. Finding the essence of our political system to be the concept of self-government, Meiklejohn reasoned that we all must, as citizen-governors, have access to all speech that people have to offer. The "government" cannot tell us that some things are too dangerous for us to hear. To allow it to do so would not only be demeaning but would also cut against our choice to assume the risk of unwise political decisions. It is not possible, or desirable, to insure against that risk by shifting decision-making power to "wiser" people. The most that we can tolerate, and remain consistent with our original principles, is a Robert's Rules of Order adapted to political discussion. I take the liberty of burdening the reader with the following lengthy excerpt from Meiklejohn because it both articulates this thesis in his own words and because, as an exhortation, it also reveals his implicit confidence in the capability of citizens to implement a plan of self-government, the matter with which I am ultimately concerned:

> We Americans, in choosing our form of government, have made, at this point, a momentous decision. We have decided to be self-governed. We have measured the dangers and the values of the suppression of the freedom of public inquiry and debate. And, on the basis of that measurement, having regard for the public safety, we have decided that the destruction of freedom is always unwise, that freedom is always expedient. The conviction recorded by that decision is not a sentimental vagary about the "natural rights" of individuals. It is a reasoned and sober judgment as to the best available method of guarding the public safety. We, the People, as we plan for the general welfare, do not choose to be "protected" from the "search for truth." On the contrary, we have adopted it as our "way of life," our method of doing the work of governing for which, as citizens, we are responsible. Shall we, then, as practitioners of freedom, listen to ideas which, being opposed to our own, might destroy confidence in our form of government? Shall we give a hearing to those who hate and despise freedom, to those who, if they had the power, would destroy our institutions? Certainly, yes! Our action must be guided, not by their principles, but by ours. We listen, not because they desire to speak, but because we need to hear. If there are arguments against our theory of government, our policies in war or in peace, we the citizens, the rulers, must hear and

> consider them for ourselves. That is the way of public safety. It is the program of self-government.[9]

We find in this excerpt an unqualified endorsement of the domestic ideal. It is, to be sure, an ideal that has undeniable roots in our culture and heritage. Bernard Bailyn has demonstrated how one of the transforming ideas of the American revolutionary movement involved a shift in thinking about the concept of "sovereignty" as a power necessarily residing in an independent agency of "government" to a power held by the "people."[10] What is of immediate interest, however, is not the historical origins of the thesis nor its specific political content, but rather its underlying conception of the human personality.

One finds beneath Meiklejohn's rhetoric a particular view of the ordinary citizen: He is a person who is essentially rational, able to discern his true interests and willing and capable of acting on the basis of those insights. The citizen is mature, open-minded, cautious, independent, responsible and self-reliant. Nowhere is this better illustrated than in Meiklejohn's choice of the town meeting as the central point of reference for his analysis of free speech theory.[11] The image selected suggests conscientious citizens quitting their homes to meet, hear argument, discuss and then resolve all relevant arguments on matters affecting their community. These are people, to use one of Rawl's terms, who are in the state of "reflective equilibrium." And it is of a piece with the general libertarian position that as long as the government leaves the people alone, the society will flourish and liberty will reign.

This, it seems to me, is precisely the point at which one begins to see doubts arise. In fact, we are not wholly comfortable with the proposition that the "people" are capable of self-government, at least a self-government that preserves liberty and the "good life" we strive for. Cannot the "people" be brought to do things which in a calmer moment they would regard as against their better interests? Even the most traditional libertarians have occasionally exhibited some inclination to affirm the truth of that rhetorical question. Milton himself was not prepared to leave room for the dangerous doctrine of Catholicism.[12] Bailyn also speaks about the concern of the framers over the thin line between democracy and mob rule, of mass ignorance giving way to dictatorship.[13] And even some of the original articulations of the marketplace metaphor turn from the optimistic belief that "truth" will always emerge to the more agnostic view that the marketplace must remain open even though noxious doctrine may thereby succeed; a plea for freedom gilded with elitism.[14]

But, as the experiences of this century have pressed upon us, this shadow over the belief in the capacities of citizens to maintain their freedoms has darkened dramatically. To see this one need only think for a moment about the dominant concerns of the social sciences in the past several decades. They stand in stark contrast to the nineteenth century libertarian and eighteenth century enlightenment writings. No longer is the challenge to simply remove the fetters on man's essential good nature, but to understand the complex processes that can bring about the horrors of Nazism and to a lesser degree the refusal to accept the demands of liberty and the phenomena of alienation and apathy. Intellectual thought in this century treats such matters as the complexity of the cognitive processes and its extensive irrational components, the rise of the masses and the concomitant break between knowledge and power, and the seemingly innate human impulse for security and release from fear which can open a society to violence and self-destruction. Such intellectual trends have seemingly given birth to a new form of elitism, which casts considerable doubts on the premises of popular sovereignty. I do not mean to overstate the case; the elitism I speak of does not rest solely on a concern over a new rise in fascism or its late twentieth century equivalent. There is more currently a focus on the integrity of the political process, of certain techniques of political salesmanship, for example. The point is simply that we have been offered new grounds for distrusting the open marketplace.

The magnitude of this shift in perception, from an abstract to a concrete concern, can be glimpsed in some of our most thoughtful literature on the First Amendment. One finds, for example, in Alexander Bickel's, *The Morality of Consent* the statement with respect to the self-righting thesis that "we have lived through too much to believe it. . . . Disastrously, unacceptably noxious doctrine can prevail," he insisted, "and can be made to prevail by the most innocent sort of advocacy."[15] What distinguished Bickel's from earlier First Amendment writings is a deep skepticism about the capacity of the "masses" to exercise sound judgment on public questions. One sees in Kalven too a recognition of this dilemma for freedom of speech. Speaking of the group libel decision in *Beauharnais v. Illinois*[16] in his book *The Negro and the First Amendment*,[17] Kalven acknowledged the powerful and realistic concerns of many about the potential exploitation of mass paranoia through defamation of societal groups. He noted David Riesman's observation that, while certain speech has always carried with it a threat to liberty, what makes it so problematic now is "the existence of a mobile public opinion as the controlling force in politics and the systematic manipulation of that opinion by the use of calculated falsehood and vilification."[18]

While these books illustrate the extent to which our First Amendment thinking has been affected by our contemporary experience and intellectual currents, they also show a common tendency in legal writing, namely to withdraw from the logical consequences of the concern over manipulation. There appears to be a uniform inclination to seek comfort in the prudential argument that, while manipulation is surely possible, in the end we have no one to trust who can accurately separate good speech from destructive speech. "[W]e err—on the right side perhaps," Bickel concludes his discussion, "but we err." It may be a problem, but the government can do nothing about it.[19]

Insofar as this purports to be a description of reality, I think it is mistaken. It would be surprising to find that this profound ambivalence was reflected only in our scholarly literature and not in our actual decision-making. This distrust of the ordinary citizen's ability to decide wisely on matters of importance to them, and to us all, appears to be too pervasive to remain always in the wings. And, in fact, traces of its effects can be seen occasionally, though in widely disparate areas. The *Beauharnais* case, of course, is a specific instance in which "dangerous" speech was allowed to be excluded from the marketplace. Usually, however, the effects of the ambivalence are more subtle and exist on the periphery of speech questions. There is an aspect to the obscenity decisions which, I think, reflects a choice of protecting people against themselves; and this seems to be especially so in the area of movies, where one often hears vague arguments about the special "impact" on audiences offered in justification of special restrictions.[20] Perhaps the most explicit illustration, however, is in the largely unobserved areas of labor and securities law, where the government has undertaken an extensive effort to censor speech to protect the integrity of the internal political process. It is interesting to see in the case of securities regulation, for example, how willing the courts have been to permit government scrutiny of partisan commentary, in order to enjoin misrepresentations. For a long time the SEC completely forbade the making of predictions in proxy solicitations, and there are some delightfully explicit statements in judicial opinions about how this is justified because investors are gullible people, easily taken advantage of by "experts."[21]

But within the First Amendment realm, the most vital area affected by this ambivalence has been the electronic media. It is here, within the context of an elaborate government regulatory machinery, that our skepticism of the self-government notion has most successfully intruded into our system of expression. As one ought perhaps to expect, the indicia of that intrusion require careful attention to discern, but they are there and the effects have not been small.

From whatever angle the broadcast regulatory enterprise is viewed, it has unquestionably constituted a major challenge to traditional assumptions about the proper relationship between the government and the press. The search for a constitutional justification for this potentially explosive development is fascinating. For much of its life, of course, the regulatory structure was the beneficiary of that social policy known as "benign neglect." It was the heated political and social controversies of the 1960's and early 70's that first served as an alembic to bring into pure form questions relating to the legitimacy of regulation. The resultant pressure for public access finally brought into dramatic relief more fundamental questions about the very premises of the entire regulatory structure. The Supreme Court's answer to those questions in *Red Lion Broadcasting Co. v. FCC*[22] posed an intriguing development in First Amendment theory. Rather than announcing a new theory to justify the legislative choice to regulate, it merely worked within the confines of traditional thought. The argument was simple: The First Amendment is premised on the belief that truth, or the wisest decisions, will emerge from the full interplay of ideas; but, when mounting concentration restricts the major outlets of information, thereby threatening that premise, the government can legitimately intervene to assure a freer flow of ideas and information. Here again is the professed faith in the ultimate rationality of the people. Self-government is the goal, and the fullest expression the surest path to it. *Red Lion*, and nearly all the debates over the need and legitimacy of access, was apparently derivative of Meiklejohn.[23]

But the absence of an elitist flavor to the *Red Lion* analysis does not demonstrate its irrelevance to the reality of broadcast regulation. One of the especially intriguing features of the Communications Act is how the duality of thinking about the concept of self-government tends to coalesce to legitimize regulation. Fear of manipulation can be satisfied, or at least mollified, by the existence of regulation. Since the two currents of thought converge to support the same result, one strain may hide comfortably in the crevices of the structure sanctioned by the other. Thus, one must be skeptical of the professed adherence to the Meiklejohn perspective in the broadcast context.

There is, moreover, plenty of reason for skepticism, for no other technology of communication has raised more concerns over the problem of manipulation than the electronic media, and particularly television. The characteristics of that medium intensify the problem. Since television appeals to more of our senses than does print, its impact is commonly suspected of being greater, in the same way that movies are sometimes thought to limit the opportunities for reflection. But, in contrast to movies, television has become, in some respects at least, the predominant organ of political discourse and source of information for the general populace. This raises the ambivalence to its peak, for on the one hand political speech according to the Meiklejohn perspective is the most vital to a functioning democracy, and therefore most in need of protection, while on the other hand, the elitist perspective sees in such a context the spectre of manipulation and therefore the greatest need for caution and restraint.

The problem of television's impact on its vast audience has, accordingly, been a subject of considerable attention in the literature about the technology. Generally the discussion is somewhat abstract, or tentative, especially because of the difficulty of measuring "impact," let alone defining it, is so problematic. Discussions range from a recognition of the potential problem and a recommendation that we be attentive to it[24] to the suggestion that the special opportunities for manipulation offered by television provide an independent justification for regulation. One of many possible examples one could give of attention to this perceived "impact" of broadcasting is Professor Schmidt's recent book *Freedom of the Press vs. Public Access*. In trying to uncover the broad acceptance of broadcast regulation, Schmidt posits the explanation that:

> Television has become the symbol of the media's mammoth power in the post-industrial age. It is the focus of late twentieth-century anxieties about the adequacy of an eighteenth-century First Amendment to govern the relationship between government and the media, not only because of its technical novelty, but also because its social force is vastly greater than that of any other communications medium in history.[25]

Schmidt goes on to point out the evidence that television is the major and most believed source of information for the public, that its audience is composed of the least educated sectors of the society and that the television audience tends to rely on television as its exclusive source of information. Schmidt concludes that in view of this reality "it is not surprising that access rights leave the realm of conjecture when it comes to radio and television."[26]

This concern over the possibilities of manipulation through the television technology has not escaped judicial attention either. The most explicit statement came in the cigarette commercial case of *Banzhaf v. FCC*.[27] In a decision upholding the Commission's power to require licensees to air anti-smoking announcements under the fairness doctrine, Chief Judge Bazelon placed explicit reliance on the impact thesis as a justification for regulation:

> Moreover, the broadcasting medium may be different in kind from publishing in a way which has particular relevance to the case at hand. Written messages are not communicated unless they are read, and reading requires an affirmative act. Broadcast messages, in contrast, are "in the air." In an age of omnipresent radio, there scarcely breathes a citizen who does not know some part of a leading cigarette jingle by heart. Similarly, an ordinary habitual television watcher can *avoid* these commercials only by frequently leaving the room, changing the channel, or doing some other such affirmative act. It is difficult to calculate the subliminal impact of this pervasive propaganda, which may be heard even if not listened to, but it may reasonably be thought greater than the impact of the written word.[28]

Though Bazelon's thesis has not resurfaced as a judicially articulated basis to support regulation, its expression stands as a firm acknowledgment of the power of the concern over the social dangers of the television medium.

In all these discussions about "impact" of television there seems to be something more than the simple thesis of *Red Lion* that as long as there are opportunities for counter messages the system will work according to the traditional optimistic view of the marketplace of ideas, that truth or good sense will emerge victorious. The concern appears to drive much deeper, into the premise that the ordinary man is capable of self-direction even with all the advantages of multifarious ideas. The possibilities for emotionalism gaining dominance over intellectualism, of caution giving way to irresponsibility, seem frightening. And, so with the cigarette commercials, total exclusion, and not just "fairness," was ultimately thought to be necessary.[29]

But it is important to see that what underlies the handling of the cigarette commercial issue is really only symptomatic of a much more extensive undercurrent that affects all broadcast issues, including cases involving political speech. The best, and most important, illustration of this extension of *Banzhaf* into the political sphere is the Supreme Court's decision in *Columbia Broadcasting System, Inc. v. Democratic National Committee*,[30] decided in 1973. In that case the Democratic National Committee and the Business Executives' Move for Vietnam Peace argued that the First Amendment afforded "responsible" members of the public the right to purchase available commercial air time in order to present political advertisements. A majority of the Court rejected that claim. The opinion of the Court seemed to rely on the problems of administration and the need for journalistic discretion as the primary reasons for its result. It was this latter theory of the case that caused the decision to be hailed by the press and by those favoring freedom for broadcasters as representing a substantial shift in the Court's thinking from that found in *Red Lion*. The move was from an emphasis on the "public's" right to control the airwaves to a recognition of the right and power of broadcast journalists to control what was broadcast. But, the opinion is deceptive on that score; for the emphasis on journalistic discretion did not arise from a pure belief in the wisdom of journalists but rather from a perceived need to maintain control of the content of broadcasting in the hands of those who live under the aegis of government scrutiny.

One paragraph in particular in the Court's opinion provides an insight into the Court's thinking. Near the end of the opinion Chief Justice Burger advanced the argument that "in a very real sense listeners and viewers constitute a 'captive audience.'"[31] He then quoted with approval the statement of Judge Bazelon in *Banzhaf*, referred to previously, and closed with the cryptic statement that "[i]t is no answer to say that because we tolerate pervasive commerical advertisements we can also live with its political counterparts."[32] The idea offered is ambiguous. The "captive audience" concept suggests the problem of unfair intrusion. But there is more here, and it is reflected in the Chief Justice's inclusion of the *Banzhaf* quotation. Bazelon's fears of "subliminal impact" and "pervasive propaganda" connote more of the problem of thought control, of manipulation, than mere invasion of privacy. This concern in the *CBS* opinion becomes even clearer when one notes the frequently encountered statement in the opinion that it is important for the "public" to maintain control over those who use the airwaves.[33] The difficulty with the claim of BEM and DNC was that it opened the broadcast doors to people who were not made "responsible" through the subtle processes of government selection and oversight. And the possibilities of exploitation of mass public opinion on such vital matters as the war effort, through techniques of distortion and emotional appeals, was a more pressing danger than any commercial speech; political demagoguery can undermine the entire system, not just cause cancer.

All of this is to suggest that elitist view colored the thinking of the Court in *CBS*, as it has in other areas of broadcast regulation. The phenomenon cannot be explained away as simply the reactionary stance of conservative justices to anti-war speech. Whatever one thinks of the outcome of the *CBS* case, the fear of manipulation as a motivating factor in our thinking is not a distinctive characteristic of any particular ideological group. It also supports the position, advocated by many liberals, that something ought to be done to remove or lessen the amount of violence on television.

The purpose of this essay has been to identify an undercurrent of thought that cuts against our most vital assumptions about the First Amendment. Ambivalence about such a central matter is difficult to establish with the certainty of logic; to some extent one must be satisfied with asking whether others share the writer's intuition on the matter. The reasons why doubts about the Meiklejohn thesis tend to remain somewhat obscure are readily seen. Judges, officials and scholars naturally shy away from expostulating what seem vague, unprovable ideas. In the case of the "impact" thesis with respect to broadcasting, for example, one frequently suspects upon encountering it in a discussion that the author does not know quite what to do with it. It seems amorphous, not subject to empirical verification, yet still powerfully attractive as an intuitive proposition. But, compounding the problem is the fact that the elitist view is in a way unthinkable. It cuts against deep-seated beliefs. It seems wholly inconsistent with things we would prefer to believe about the public, and about ourselves as well. We prefer a view of ourselves as self-reliant, responsible, fully capable of self-determination, and we loathe the thought that we may be subject to manipulation against our better interests. For judges, of course, this difficulty is magnified. Their role seems to demand that they emphasize the positive, that they service the illusion rather than candidly acknowledge that they and other elites share powerful doubts about the ability of the masses to decide what is best for themselves. This is, moreover, probably for the better. People may attain more of their potential if the positive is emphasized; they may aspire to greater heights if their better side is appealed to. In any case, all of this combines to cloud the ambivalence.

Nevertheless, one can, as I have tried to do, piece together various data which suggest that the Meiklejohn view does not have such an exclusive hold on our legal doctrine as many appear to believe, or would have us believe. It is important to understand the sources of weakness in that position and to see that our thinking about even the most fundamental issues is considerably complex. To perceive the separate, indeed quite inconsistent, strains of thought that together make up our beliefs about such a critical problem as the viability of the concept of self-government is to better understand our First Amendment jurisprudence and, more particularly, the legal process in vital areas like that of broadcast regulation.

Notes

1. 376 U.S. 255 (1964).
2. *Id*. at 276.
3. *Id*. at 273.
4. H. Kalven, *The New York Times Case: A Note On "The Central Meaning of the First Amendment,"* 1964 SUP. CT. REV. 191 (1964) (hereafter cited as Kalven I).
5. *Id*. at 194.
6. A. Meiklejohn, *Free Speech and Its Relation to Self-Government*, reprinted in POLITICAL FREEDOM (1948).
7. Kalven I, note 4 *supra*, at 221 n. 125.
8. *See*, Brennan, *The Supreme Court and the Meiklejohn Interpretation of the First Amendment*, 79 HARV L. REV. 1 (1965).
9. A. MEIKLEJOHN, POLITICAL FREEDOM 57 (1948).
10. B. BAILYN, THE IDEOLOGICAL ORIGINS OF THE AMERICAN REVOLUTION 172-74 (1967).
11. MEIKLEJOHN, POLITICAL FREEDOM 24-28 (1948).
12. *See* F. SIEBERT, *et al*, FOUR THEORIES OF THE PRESS 45 (1974).
13. B. BAILYN, THE IDEOLOGICAL ORIGINS OF THE AMERICAN REVOLUTION 282 (1967).
14. *See* Gitlow v. New York, 268 U.S. 652, 673 (Holmes, J., dissenting). *See also* A. BICKEL, THE MORALITY OF CONSENT 72 (1975) (hereafter cited as BICKEL).
15. BICKEL, note 14 *supra*, at 71, 72.
16. 343 U.S. 250 (1952).
17. H. KALVEN, THE NEGRO AND THE FIRST AMENDMENT 8-15 (1965).
18. *Id.*, at 9, quoting from Riesman, *Democracy and Defamation: Control of Group Libel*, 42 COLUM. L. REV. 727, 730 (1942).
19. BICKEL, note 14 *supra*, at 78.
20. *See, e.g.*, A. BICKEL, THE LEAST DANGEROUS BRANCH 140 (1962).
21. *See, e.g.*, SEC v. May, 134 F. Supp. 247 (S.D.N.Y. 1955), *aff'd* 229 F. 2d 123 (2d Cir. 1956); Union Pacific Railroad Co. v. Chicago and Northwestern Railway Co., 226 F. Supp. 400 (N.D. Ill. 1964). The SEC's disallowance of predictions has been reversed. SEC Release No. 33-5362, 34-9984, § 23,508 (Feb. 2, 1973).
22. 395 U.S. 367 (1969).
23. The Court's opinion reads like a classic text:

> It is the purpose of the First Amendment to preserve an uninhibited marketplace of ideas in which truth will ultimately prevail, rather than to countenance monopolization of that market, whether it be by the Government itself or a private licensee. . . . "[S]peech concerning public affairs is more than self-expression; it is the essence of self-government." *Garrison v. Louisiana*, 379 U.S. 64,

74-75 (1964). *See* Brennan, The Supreme Court and the Meiklejohn Interpretation of the First Amendment, 79 Harv. L. Rev. 1 (1965). It is the right of the public to receive suitable access to social, political, esthetic, moral, and other ideas and experiences which is crucial here. That right may not constitutionally be abridged either by the Congress or by the FCC.

Red Lion, 395 U.S. at 390.

24. *See, e.g.,* L. TRIBE, CHANNELLING TECHNOLOGY THROUGH LAW 29 (1973):

Almost as difficult as conceiving of cumulative trends is imagining the effects of scale. Barely 100,000 television receivers were in use in the United States in 1948. In the next year there were a million. A decade later there were 50 million. The social and psychological consequences of such phenomenal growth are hard even to contemplate, let alone predict. Indeed, in the case of television these effects are still a matter of debate, and apparently adequate research tools for measuring or evaluating them do not yet exist.

25. B. SCHMIDT, FREEDOM OF THE PRESS V. PUBLIC ACCESS 120 (1976).
26. *Id.* at 120-21.
27. 405 F. 2d 1082 (D.C. Cir. 1968), *cert. denied* 396 U.S. 842 (1969).
28. *Id.* at 1100-01, n. 77.
29. 15 U.S.C.A. § 1335.
30. 412 U.S. 94 (1973).
31. *Id.* at 127.
32. *Id.* at 128.
33. *Id.* at 124, 125, 130.

First Amendment and Broadcasting
By Henry Geller*

I. The Different Treatment of Broadcasting

Broadcasting is treated differently under the First Amendment than the print media. The best and most obvious illustration of this is, of course, to compare *Miami Herald Publishing Co., Inc.* v. *Tornillo*[1], with *Red Lion Broadcasting Co.* v. *FCC*[2] In *Tornillo*, the Supreme Court struck down a Florida statute that gave political candidates who had been editorially attacked in the press the right to reply. The opinion states:

> [T]he Florida Statute fails to clear the barriers of the First Amendment because of its intrusion into the function of editors. A newspaper is more than a passive receptacle or conduit for news, comment, and advertising. The choice of material to go into a newspaper, and the decisions made as to limitations on the size of the paper, and content, and treatment of public issues and public officials—whether fair or unfair—constitutes the exercise of editorial control and judgment. It has yet to be demonstrated how governmental regulation of this crucial process can be exercised consistent with First Amendment guarantees of a free press as they have evolved to this time.[3]

The opinion does not cite or mention *Red Lion*, decided five years previously, which involved the right of reply in the broadcast field. In the *Red Lion* case the Court unanimously sustained an FCC regulation that had given a political candidate, attacked on the air, the right to reply over the same broadcast facilities. The Supreme Court held:

> There is nothing in the First Amendment which prevents the Government from requiring a licensee to share his frequency with others and to conduct himself as a proxy or fiduciary with obligations to present those views and voices which are representative of his community and which would otherwise, by necessity, be barred from the air waves.[4]

In both cases, the argument was made that there would be a chilling effect on robust debate. In both cases, there was no evidence on the point. Yet in *Tornillo*, the Court found such an effect, stating:

> Faced with penalties that would accrue to any newspaper that published news or commentary arguably within the reach of the right-of-access statute, editors might well conclude that the safe course is to avoid controversy. Therefore, under the operation of the Florida statute, political and electoral coverage would be blunted or reduced. Government-enforced right of access inescapably "dampens the vigor and limits the variety of public debate," *New York Times* v. *Sullivan* . . .[5]

In *Red Lion*, the Court sloughs aside the possibility of a chilling effect as "at best speculative," further stating:

> . . . if licensees should suddenly prove timorous, the Commission is not powerless to insist that they give adequate and fair attention to public issues.[6]

*Assistant Secretary of Commerce for Communications and Information. This paper was prepared when Mr. Geller was a Communications Fellow, Aspen Institute Program on Communications and Society; Former General Counsel of the FCC. (Ed. Note)

The contrast between *Tornillo* and *Red Lion* is thus startling and clear. The Court treats broadcasting as "unique."[7] The critical issue is why broadcasting is "unique" and so closely regulated despite its First Amendment protection.

II. THE BASIS FOR BROADCASTING'S UNIQUENESS

There are a number of latter day explanations for this "unique" status. It is urged that broadcasting has unique impact upon the American people: radio is everywhere, in the car, in the home, the transistor held to the youth's ear; and television has even greater impact in light of the amount watched on the average (close to seven hours a day).[7] But while several former Government officials would subscribe to this power or impact theory,[8] and it may now unconsciously influence the attitude of some jurists towards broadcasting, it simply can not stand as a valid basis for singling out broadcasting for close governmental regulation. First, it cannot seriously be argued that WQXR-FM, the Times' radio station in New York City, has greater impact and power than the *Times*—yet the former comes within a fairness obligation and the latter does not. Even more important, if television has too much power (and certainly the existence of only three national TV networks raises a serious problem), the answer is not to pervert the Constitution but to use the antitrust or similar trade regulation laws, and, above all, to expand the number of news media sources by policies favoring cable, direct satellite broadcasting, etc.

Another recent rationale for according broadcasting lesser First Amendment status is the so-called "captive audience" concept—that broadcast messages are "in the air", omnipresent", and cannot be avoided as a practical matter.[9] This rationale has support in the language of both the Court[10] and the Commission.[11] But it also does not withstand analysis. First, the listener or viewer has the choice to tune to another station or to click off the set. And second, even assuming *arguendo* some basis to the concept, it does not follow that the Government can intervene to license or regulate speech because of its special efficacy.[12]

As a final example, there is the argument that broadcasting is essentially an entertainment medium, and thus entitled to lesser First Amendment protection. But this argument is nowhere stated by the Courts. On the contrary, the Supreme Court rejected the notion of such a distinction in *Winters* v. *New York*.[13] Further, it is belied by two facts: (i) broadcasting is a medium of the press[14]; and (ii) more and more, TV entertainment programs can and do make presentations on issues like abortion, premarital sex, and the Vietnam War.

I believe that the basis for the Court's different treatment of broadcasting does not lie in any of these *post hoc* rationalizations but rather is that stated by the Court in *NBC* v. *U.S.* and *Red Lion*:

(a) Because of the pattern of frequency interference in the 1920's, the Government soundly decided to license users of radio.

(b) Licensing, in itself, distinguishes broadcasting from print, but it is simplistic to base the present structure of regulation solely on the fact of licensing. The Government could have auctioned the frequency, or given leases with "rent" payments, or used a common carrier or similar approach where access would be assured to many.[15] Congress decided, however, to give short-term licensees solely on the condition that the recipient volunteers to serve, and shows at time of renewal that it has served, the public interest.

Broadcasting's unique treatment thus stems from two factors—(1) that radio is inherently not open to all, and requires Government licensing to prevent chaotic interference; and (2) the decision to license upon a public trustee basis. Two comments are crucial here.

First, there is still the need to license. It is argued that radio frequencies are no longer scarce—that there are thousands more radio broadcast licensees than daily newspapers.[16] But the matter is not a question of the scarcity of broadcast facilities as compared to daily newspapers. Whatever the economics of the daily newspaper field, it is technologically open to all. Radio is inherently not so open. The government must license or there will be a pattern of frequency interference. It chooses one licensee for a frequency and forecloses all others—a crucial difference from the print media. And choose it must, because there are many more applicants than frequencies available. As the Court pointed out in the *Red Lion* case[17], in the large markets with the great majority of the U.S. population, there is not one AM, FM, or VHF broadcast frequency available, and most of the allocated UHF assignments are being used; indeed, others covet the broadcast band for nonbroadcast use. When Government then chooses, for example, one entity to operate on VHF Channel 2 in New York City, it must do so on some basis—lot, auction, "rent", or public trustee.[18]

This brings me to the second comment—that if licensing is still necessary, the Government's basis for licensing—the public trustee concept—is not necessary or ordained. It can be argued that in light of government licensing, some form of issue access is constitutionally required.[19] But even so, there are many ways to provide such access.[20] As a matter of both sound policy and constitutional principle, the Government should select the approach that accomplishes this purpose with the least interference or unnecessary burden on other important First Amendment rights.[21] Congress, however, never approached the issue in these terms. It did not want censorship, but decided upon the public trustee notion, not really knowing what would develop. In effect, it said to the agency: "Here is a new, dynamic field; without censoring, license and regulate it in the public interest, whatever that means."[22]

Congress thus placed the Commission in a dilemma. As the Court in *CBS* v. *DNC* notes, the Commission is the "overseer" and "ultimate arbiter and guardian of the public interest";[23] programming is the essence of service to the public; yet the Commission is not to censor. This regulatory scheme, Chief Justice Burger states, calls for "a delicate balancing of competing interests", and the "maintenance of this balance for more than 40 years has called on both the regulators and the licensees to walk a 'tightrope' to preserve the First Amendment values written into the . . . Communications Act."[24] As I shall show within, there have been frequent stumbles from this regulatory tightrope.

But if the Congress failed to consider the approach that would least interfere with the First Amendment values, the courts should have passed upon the matter. But here the answer lies in the statement made in another context, "Legal theory is one thing; [but] the practicalities are different."[25] When the Courts considered the issue, the practicalities foreclosed reversal. Thus, when the issue reached the Court for the first time in the 1943 *NBC* v. *U.S.* case, the system of government regulation in the public interest had become well entrenched. The Court had yet not become so concerned with First Amendment values, and it sloughed off the serious problem. The Court noted the need for licensing and thus for governmental regulation, and then stated:

> The right of free speech does not include, however, the right to use the facilities of radio without a license. The licensing system established by Congress in the Communications Act of 1934 was a proper exercise of its power over commerce. The standard it provided for the licensing of stations was the "public interest, convenience, or necessity." Denial of a station license on that ground, if valid under the Act, is not a denial of free speech.[26]

There was thus no analysis of why this public interest approach to licensing is constitutional.

When the matter next came before the Court in 1969 in the *Red Lion* case, there had now been over 40 years of operation under the public trustee scheme. The issue before the Court was the constitutionality of the fairness doctrine, but this in turn raised the question of the legality of the whole public trustee scheme. For the fairness doctrine is an essential element of that scheme: ". . . adherence to the Fairness Doctrine is the *sine qua non* of every licensee."[27] Suppose, for example, that there are only three VHF channels in a community. While many would like to use the channels, only three parties are given the license to use them, with all others enjoined by the government from their use. These parties do not purchase the privilege, but rather are given the short-term license to use the frequencies solely on the ground that they will operate in the public interest. Suppose further that one or indeed all these parties present only viewpoints with which they agree on matters of great concern.[28] The consequence would clearly be a pattern of operation inconsistent with the statutory scheme of a public trustee—of a fiduciary given the use of scarce radio frequencies as a proxy for the entire community.

Indeed, as I shall show within, *striking down the fairness doctrine, without invalidating the whole public trustee scheme, would not accomplish much, and in particular would not place the broadcast journalist on the same footing as the print counterpart.* The Court, after so much time, was naturally reluctant to wipe out this long and well established system. It did not do so, rather affirming in broad terms both the fairness doctrine and the Commission's authority to regulate the licensee's overall programming performance.

In view of the above analysis, the difference between *Tornillo* and *Red Lion* can be found very largely in Justice Holmes' famous aphorism: "The life of the law has not been logic. It has been experience." In print, the experience over centuries makes governmental intrusion to license or insure fairness anathema; in broadcasting—a wholly new medium—the experience allowed for such a governmental experiment and militated against invalidation after decades of operation.

III. Placing the Fairness Doctrine in the Overall Setting of Public Trustee Regulation

One of the pegs of the above analysis is that the fairness doctrine is just one facet of the public trustee scheme, and that its elimination would not be effective, so long as the public interest scheme is restrained. I develop that point here, first by giving some notion of how the scheme works:

(1) *Requirement of local programming.* Both the Congressional and the Commission scheme of TV allocations is based on local outlets.[29] Thus, it is possible to have the 15 TV stations assigned to Los Angeles also serve San Diego by simply allowing them to increase height and power. But such service would not be *local*, presenting San Diego officials or covering issues of importance in San Diego only (e.g., bond issues; local elections). The Commission has therefore decided upon a nationwide allocations scheme of thousands of channels so that communities like San Diego will have local outlets. This is a large expenditure of valuable and scarce spectrum space. If a television station does not serve in a significant way as a local outlet—if it is, in effect, a network spigot or mere purveyor of non-local film programming, there has been a waste of valuable spectrum space and an undermining of the basic allocations scheme. Accordingly, the Commission requires the licensee to devote a reasonable amount of its broadcast day to local programming, and at least in theory will not grant an initial license or renewal without a showing of such devotion.[30] But this is turn raises the difficult issue, what is a reasonable amount of local programming sufficient to obtain renewal?

(2) *Informational programming.* There is another basic allocations purpose—the provision of informational programming. The Commission has stressed that it has allotted so much spectrum space to broadcasting, as against other claimants for spectrum, because of the contribution which it can make to an informed electorate. It therefore requires broadcasters to devote a reasonable amount of time to the discussion of issues of public concern.[31] The

Commission has accordingly held that if the broadcaster does not present a significant amount of controversial issue programming, it "is undermining the basic allocations scheme."[32] There is again the difficult issue of just what is a reasonable amount of informational programming warranting renewal.

(3) *The ascertainment problems/programming list process.* In addition to the obligation to provide reasonable *amounts* of time to local and informational programming, the Commission requires the licensee "equitably and in good faith" to serve the needs and interests of the local audience.[33] It therefore calls upon the licensee to ascertain those needs or problems by contacting local leaders or groups[34] and to present programs designed to cover the ascertainment problems.[35] And at renewal, the Commission examines the problems/program list to determine whether the licensee has reasonably ascertained and met the needs and interests of its area.

(4) *The comparative process.* The foregoing has focused on the noncomparative renewal process. The Congress, however, has provided that at the end of the three year license term, newcomers can file competing applications for the channel.[36] This possibility of challenge provides a competitive spur to the existing licensee to provide a substantial (strong, solid) service. If the incumbent provides such service, it receives a "plus of major significance" that will normally assure its renewal.[37] If it provides just mediocre service or service barely warranting renewal in a non-comparative situation, it does not receive this "plus", and, in theory, this should be "determinative, in and of itself, against the renewal applicant."[38] Thus, under the statutory scheme, the critical issue is the incumbent's record, and programming is the essence of that record.

(5) *Rules of the game.* The preceding has been a brief discussion of the licensing process (initial, renewal; comparative and non-comparative). Under the broad public interest standard, the Commission can also prescribe rules that markedly affect how broadcast stations operate, and indeed, whether a station may be licensed to a particular entity. Two examples of such regulation are the Prime Time Access Rule (PTAR)[39] and the multiple ownership rules.[40] The former deals with the dominance of the three national TV networks. It limits the networks to three hours of programming out of four in prime time for affiliates in the top 50 markets, to open the market to first run syndicated programs.[41] The multiple ownership rules limit the number of VHF stations that one entity can control (five) and proscribes certain duopoly situations.[42] It is important to bear in mind that these restrictions, while economic in nature, do not depend upon any finding of violation of the antitrust laws. Rather, the Commission has much more flexibility to act under the public interest standard, in order to diversify the sources of information coming to the American people,[43] and can accordingly adopt more stringent policies than those required under the antitrust laws.

This thumbnail sketch illustrates that there is permitted considerable Government involvement with broadcast operations: licensing and renewal in the public interest; comparative hearings; public interest regulation such as prime-time access, multiple ownership, etc. Because of the existence of this pervasive public interest regulatory scheme, elimination of the fairness doctrine would not accomplish the goal sought by its critics—placing broadcast journalism in the same position regarding the Government as print journalism. There has been legitimate concern that Government might use improper means to "chill" critical journalistic efforts.[44] But an Administration with such an improper purpose would be most unlikely to proceed through haphazard, skewed fairness rulings, which in any event would be subject to searching judicial review.[45] The Government (the FCC) can affect the economic health of the licensee or network in so many important vital respects—for example, by delaying the renewal, changing the multiple ownership rules applicable to networks or large VHF stations, or changing the network programming process through prime-time access and syndication rules. Thus, so long as the public interest licensing/regulatory scheme is maintained (as contrasted with the notion of the Government as only a traffic officer), elimination of the fairness doctrine will not insulate broadcast journalism from the possibility of improper Government activity, but it will have the result of protecting the public interest in flagrant situations such as *Lamar Broadcasting Co. (WLBT-TV)*. Fairness and the public trustee notion are integrally linked.

IV. THE RESULTING FIRST AMENDMENT STRAINS

The consequences of the public trustee scheme have been, I believe, severe First Amendment strains. Again, I shall give only some examples of what has become a substantial and spreading problem. The reason for the increasing strains has been aptly noted by Clay T. Whitehead, former director of the Office of Telecommunications Policy: For many years, the Communications Act was a dormant instrument; the Act called for public participation, but until the militant 1960's and the rise of the consumer movement, there was little interest on the part of public groups. With the 1965 breakthrough in the famous *Church of Christ* case,[47] there has been a rising tide of litigation in which the public participant insists that the Act means what it says—that the licensee must act as a public trustee, and therefore must serve the needs and interests of its area, must present a reasonable amount of local and informational programming, must cover controversial issues fairly, and so on. The Commission and the broadcaster no longer have a "free ride": Very difficult issues in this most sensitive programming field now have to be faced.

(1) *Fairness*. For years the Commission rested on the general principle set out in the 1949 *Editorializing Report, supra*. But inherent in the general principle that licensees must afford a reasonable opportunity for the presentation of contrasting viewpoints on issues which they cover, are a host of difficult problems, brought to the fore by a new breed of complainants pressing hard for access for their viewpoints.

(a) *Defining balance or reasonable opportunity*. The doctrine requires that *reasonable* opportunity be afforded the contrasting viewpoints on an issue. There has therefore always been lurking in the doctrine's administration a very difficult question—namely, at what ratio (i.e., 2 to 1, 3 to 1, etc.) would the FCC say that the opportunity for presenting opposing viewpoints has not been *reasonable*? Further, how does frequency of presentations or choice of time (e.g., prime or non-prime time) affect this evaluation? Not only have these problems arisen recently,[48] but this basic issue of reasonable balance had led to other difficulties.

(b) *The "stop-watch" problem*. In order to ascertain whether there has been reasonable balance, the FCC literally has used a stop-watch to time the presentations that have been made on the various sides on an issue.[49] Even more difficult can be the problem of judging whether a program segment is for, against, or neutral in regard to a particular issue. In the gray areas that are bound to arise in this respect, it is not appropriate for a governmental agency to make such sensitive programming judgments.

(c) *The "stop-time" problem*. An associated problem arises from the fact that during and after the period in which the FCC makes a decision on a fairness complaint, a broadcaster frequently continues his coverage of an issue for a number of reasons (e.g., new developments). The FCC then finds that the circumstances upon which it made its decision have changed significantly. For example, in one case, during the period between the time of the original FCC decision on the complaint and the Commission's action on reconsideration, the licensee broadcast several presentations that crucially affected the FCC's judgment on whether reasonable opportunity had been presented.[50]

(d) *The "super-editor" problem.* Even with the above burden on the complaint, the number of fairness complaints has increased greatly in the last few years, and the FCC has accordingly been called upon to make a greater number of rulings. An analysis of those rulings in the first six months of 1973 shows the wide variety of judgments that the FCC has been asked to make; e.g., whether vegetarianism (in contrast to a meat diet) or the men's position on women's liberation are "opposing" viewpoints that should be afforded time; whether passing references in a commentary require opposing statements; whether reasonable balance has been achieved in several varying factual situations.[51] This host of rulings raises the issue of whether the FCC has become a "super editor" in the broadcast journalism process. One particularly noteworthy matter in the study is the *KREM-TV* Spokane case.[52] I believe that this case—routinely issued by the Commission—is of such significance that I have attached my analysis as Appendix A. It shows a chilling effect on robust, wide-open debate as a result of the Commission's case-by-case implementation of the fairness doctrine. Yet the Commission would probably cite this routine case as another instance of the doctrine's success, because in the end the licensee's judgment was sustained![53]

(e) *The FCC's policies on rigged or slanted news.* The Commission's present policy is to investigate every "extrinsic evidence" case of abuse by some newsman within the extensive news organization maintained by broadcasters.[54] But the Commission is intervening here in the most sensitive journalistic area. No really hard-hitting journalistic enterprise can flourish in an atmosphere where there is, in effect, a deep intrusion by the government into the journalistic processes—either by direct FCC investigation, or by the FCC's review of the licensee's investigation.

The FCC investigation of the WBBM-TV Pot Party newscasts illustrates these difficulties. In this case,[65] WBBM-TV telecast a pot party at the Northwestern University campus to show the pervasiveness of this kind of drug violation. The party depicted was authentic in that it did involve pot smoking by students at campus rooming house; further, the public obviously knew that "this was a televised pot party—an inherently different event from a private, nontelevised pot-smoking gathering."[56] But the FCC found that the public was incorrectly ". . . given the impression that WBBM-TV had been invited to film a student pot gathering that was in any event being held, whereas, in fact, its agent [a young newsman] had induced the holding of the party."[57] Since this newsman had encouraged the commission of a crime, the FCC called for stricter policy guidelines to the licensee's staff in this respect. This exhaustive hearing, during which WBBM-TV's renewal was in jeopardy, did not serve any overriding policy need, but it clearly could have a chilling effect on other broadcasters who might have been interested in breaking new ground in TV investigative journalism. The Commission has forgotten the Court's admonition in the *CBS* case that "calculated risks of abuse are taken in order to preserve higher values."[58]

(f) *The first duty under the fairness doctrine.* The first duty under the fairness doctrine is to devote a reasonable amount of time to the discussion of public issues. There would appear to be considerable confusion as to the standard applicable to this first duty. The standard could appropriately be termed as "reasonable amount of time", with reasonableness determined either generally[59] or on an *ad hoc* basis. But in denying a recent petition on this issue, the Commission stated that ". . . petitioners would have to show . . . that specific issues of public importance were not afforded a reasonable amount of broadcast time . . ."[60] This "specific issue" standard for implementing the first part of the fairness doctrine is entirely inappropriate in view of the First Amendment considerations. The FCC should not be concerned with whether a broadcaster covered specific issues to a degree shown to be reasonable to the agency, but rather only whether the licensee generally has devoted a reasonable amount to public issues.

In this connection, the Commission's recent action in *In re Complaint of Representative Patsy Mink (WHAR)*,[64] would appear to have a very narrow scope. The Commission noted that while the choice of issues is for the licensee, there could be a "rare exception" where the issue is "so critical or of such great importance that it would be unreasonable for the licensee to ignore [it] completely. . . ."[62] The strip mining controversy in *WHAR* was held to be such an issue in the Clarksburg, West Virginia community. Clearly, if this principle is extended beyond the above narrow formulation, the FCC would be called upon to set the issue agenda for roughly 9000 broadcasters—an impossible task violative of the First Amendment.

(2) *Renewal, -Non-Comparative.* As we have seen, the non-comparative renewal raises several difficult problems: what is a reasonable amount of time to be devoted to local or informational programming? Further, in processing the renewal application,[63] the Commission looks at "the programming broadcast by a licensee to meet ascertained problems during the past license period (problems-program list evaluation)."[64] Such an examination is not only subjective but involves the Commission deeply in evaluating daily broadcast programming decisions. In an address to the International Radio and Television Society on September 14, 1973, Chairman Burch stated (at 3):

> If I were to pose the question, what are the FCC's renewal policies and what are the controlling guidelines, everyone in the room would be on equal footing. You couldn't tell me. I couldn't tell you—and no one else at the Commission could do any better (least of all the long-suffering renewals staff).

This raises serious First Amendment issues, under *NAACP* v. *Button* and *Greater Boston Television Corp.* v. *FCC*.

The Commission now does have a processing standard for its renewal staff: it is to bring to the Commission any application that falls below 10% non-entertainment in TV, 8% in AM, and 6% in FM.[65] But this generous standard passes virtually every TV and AM station as a rule, causing a problem only for the classical music station. The latter is hassled by the FCC staff to add a talk program at 5:30 or 6:00 a.m., so that it can grant the renewal. Renewal today is thus a stultifying process.[66]

(3) *Renewal-Comparative.* This area is equally flawed from the standpoint of the First Amendment. This is shown by examination of the Commission's most recent decision in this field. *Cowles Florida Broadcasting, Inc.*,[67] the licensee of WESH-TV, was challenged by a newcomer (Central), and won the comparative hearing, despite a serious deficiency involving an illegal main studio move. Cowles' victory is based very largely on its past broadcast record. The Commission's handling of that record is most instructive in this First Amendment context.

In its original opinion, the Commission rejected the Administrative Law Judge's standard for judging past records—"thoroughly acceptable"—as "too vague to be meaningful."[68] The Commission found that the applicable standard is "superior" past service and that Cowles' operation of WESH-TV met that standard. But in the same opinion the Commission also states that "Central has long known that if it wished to displace Cowles it would have to prove, *inter alia*, that Cowles' past performance was below average."[69] Further, the Commission concedes that "a measure of subjectiveness is unavoidably involved, given the absence of standards defining superior service, and that its conclusion is based on our own administrative "feel" acquired through years of overseeing television operations."[70]

Nor does the confusion end there. On reconsideration, the Commission, *sua sponte*, scrapped "superior", and asserted that the applicable standard is "substantial", meaning, "solid, favorable" as contrasted with service just minimally qualifying for renewal in the absence of competing applications."[71] The Commission does not engage in any new analysis or explain why Cowles' service is "substantial." Whatever the label is, WESH-TV meets it because the Commission subjectively "feels" it does.

The Commission thus concedes that its present *ad hoc* manner of proceeding—without any general guidelines—is "subjective."[72] In its November, 1976 *Comparative Renewal Report to Congress*, at par. 105, it termed the process "inherently subjective and arbitrary . . ." In prior testimony to the Congress, the Commission's spokesman (Chairman Burch) stated that the absence of any guidance ". . . is an invitation to the exercise of unbridled administrative discretion . . . that does not serve the public."[73] Finally, the Senate Committee on Governmental Affairs, 95th Cong. 1st Sess., *Study on Federal Regulation*, found the Commission's policy provided "little guidance" and demonstrated "a clear example of how inadequate standards for decision can produce protracted proceedings that are a jumble of issues and parties." The report found that:

> the Commission has as yet been unable to provide adequate guidance on the relative importance of past service of the licensee compared to offered service of a competing applicant, or even which aspects of past service—news coverage, community service, reinvesting profits into the station, or others—will be most persuasive.[73]

The area has thus become one of "unbridled" or "subjective" discretion, contrary to sound First Amendment principles governing the regulation of free speech, and particularly a press medium. As the Court point out in *Greater Boston Television Corp. v. FCC*:

> . . . a question would arise whether administrative discretion to deny renewal expectancies, which must exist under any standard, must not be reasonably confined by ground rules and standards—a contention that may have increased significance if First Amendment problems are presented on renewal application by a newspaper affiliate, including the possibility that TV proceedings may come to involve over-view of newspaper operations.[74]

The Commission's retention of such complete, subjective discretion presents no countervailing statutory or First Amendment benefit, but only the probability of an enlarged government invasion of the very rights the First Amendment and 47 U.S.C. § 326 were designed to preserve. For under the statutory scheme the critical issue is the incumbent's record and programming is the essence of that record. The question is whether in this sensitive area involving an important press medium the First Amendment is served by examination of an incumbent's programming without any objective standards to which the licensee has had the opportunity to conform.

(4) *Prime Time Access Rule.* The foregoing has been a discussion of the renewal process and fairness. Application of rules can also raise very difficult First Amendment problems. To give but one example, the Commission adopted the Prime Time access rule in 1970, which required network affiliates in the top 50 markets, in effect, not to present network or off-network programming during the 7-8 p.m. time slot. Waiver requests were filed, and the Commission found itself in a First Amendment quagmire, granting some and denying others without any rationale.[75] In a subsequent revision, the Commission exempted from the rule's coverage, *inter alia*, both "off network" and network programs if designed for children in the ages 2-12 or if documentaries or public affairs programs. But this again raised serious First Amendment problems.

Upon appeal, the court recognized that the Commission was clearly employing the exemptions as "bait to the stations to use . . . program categories believed to be in the 'public interest;'"[76] and that the Commission had "never before considered what types of programs may be played at particular times." The court nevertheless affirmed, saying:

> The only way that broadcasters can operate in the "public interest" is by broadcasting programs that meet somebody's view of what is in the "public interest." That can scarcely be determined by the broadcaster himself, for he is in an obvious conflict of interest.
>
> Since the public cannot through a million stifled yawns convey that their television fare, as a whole, is not in their interest, Congress had made the FCC the guardian of that public interest.
>
> The Commission surely cannot do its job . . . without interesting itself in general program format and the kinds of programs broadcast by licensees.[77]

This is, I believe, an extraordinary analysis of the problem. But there was another hurdle for the court: In order to present a program at 7:00 or 7:30 p.m., the network must establish that it is indeed a children's program. But that means that there can be heated disputes on what constitutes a children's program (CBS, for example, argued that Walt Disney, the FCC's one example, is *not* a children's program).

Citing *Lafayette Radio Electronics Corp.* v. *FCC*, the FCC answered that if in doubt, it would give declaratory rulings. This pre-censorship or pre-clearance scheme horrified the court, which forbade it, saying that the Commission is to examine complaints in this area at renewal only on the basis of overall programming. But what if a syndicator protests a particular network show as not being a child's program and asks for a cease-and-desist order citing the rule and Section 312 (b) of the Act? These considerations show how deep into the programming mire the FCC can get with a rule like PTAR.

(5) *Program Format.* This is an area the Commission has entered under prodding from the Court of Appeals for the District of Columbia Court. The Commission wishes to leave the choice of entertainment format to the licensee's judgment based on market forces.[79] The Court of Appeals for the District of Columbia Circuit, however, has insisted that the Commission treat this issue in an evidentiary hearing on a transfer or assignment when the station format is being switched from a unique one (e.g., classical music format) to "popular" music.[80] The hearing is to delve into the "extent of support for the formats themselves,"[81] and if financial loss is cited as a reason, whether there are such losses attributable to an economically unfeasible format. Again, very difficult First Amendment issues arise. What is a unique format (e.g., is a classical music station different from a "fine arts" one—see *WEFM, supra*)? What if the unique format is supported by 9% of the area population but the new format is, say, a second black service for a 45% minority? What is the effect of the Court's holding on experimentation? Communications lawyers now advise their clients never to adopt a unique format, because they will be "locked in"; and broadcasters have testified to this reluctance.[82]

(6) *"Lifted Eyebrow."* The FCC, often under pressure from Congressional sources, acts improperly through a "lifted eyebrow" or similar technique. Two examples are "topless radio" and the family viewing concept.

(7) *Topless radio.* Several radio stations changed their telephone call-in shows to deal largely with explicit discussion of sexual relations. The shows became quite popular, but raised considerable controversy at the FCC and Congress. The Commmission initiated a Notice of Inquiry (FCC 73-331, March 27, 1973), and the next day, Chairman Burch, in a speech before the NAB, attacked the shows as "prurient trash" and stated:

> And the price [of ignoring this 'problem'] may be high. Because this comes at a time when broadcasters are seeking greater stability in the renewal process, longer license

terms, selective de-regulation, and less detailed intrusion into journalistic discretion . . .

All these matters are now pending before the Congress or the Commission. All are dependent on the notion of the responsible public trustee . . .

The Commission has now acted [by releasing the notice of inquiry] and will take further action in this difficult field as necessary. It is my hope and the purpose of this statement to make further government action moot.[83]

This "lifted eyebrow" process was successful. Thus, as Judge Bazelon recites:

. . . Storer Broadcasting ended all sexual discussions on its widely syndicated talk show originating in Los Angeles on March 29, one day after Burch's speech. The Executive Vice-President of Storer stated this action was due to the Chairman's speech and the notice of inquiry and added [citation omitted]: '[R]ather than add to the problems of an industry which already has enough major difficulties in the area of governmental relations, we prefer to be responsive." WHN of the Metromedia took similar action and its general manager stated [citation omitted]: 'We didn't feel it was a big enough part of our format to be worth the hassle, or worth looking over our shoulder and wondering what Big Brother thought of our topic yesterday.' Several other stations including Station WDEE of Detroit followed suit and by June of 1973, a NAB survey found almost a total absence of sex discussion on the radio. One anonymous broadcaster stated [citation omitted]: 'You have to understand, . . . [we] are a member of a group that operates a number of stations and are going to cable TV, and our growth depends on FCC approval. We live or die still by the FCC gun.'[84]

The Commission imposed a forfeiture on the licensee with the most egregious program, and this was sustained in the cited case. But in my view, the petitioners missed the boat. The Commission, through the Chairman, had wiped out *all* these shows, many of which were not "obscene" or "indecent." The appeal should have focused on this broadside action, not the single worst broadcast. As to the Court's holding that Chairman Burch's speech is not a "final order" of the Commission but rather "merely represents the unofficial expression of the views of one member of the Commission," this clearly blinks reality. The Commission was duty-bound to repudiate the coercive thrust of its leading spokesman. There was no such repudiation but rather a clear pattern (Notice of Inquiry by the Commission; Chairman's speech; forfeiture action by the Commission against the licensee broadcasting the most flagrant program).

(b) *Family Viewing.* In April of 1975, the National Association of Broadcasters (NAB) adopted an amendment to the Television Code, providing generally that the first hour of network prime time and the preceding hour will not consist of programming unsuitable for viewing by the entire family. But the FCC was most active in the process that led to this industry "self-regulatory" action. The House Appropriations Committee in 1974 directed the Commission to submit a report "outlining specific positive actions taken or planned by the Commission to protect children from excessive programming of violence and obscenity."[85] FCC Chairman Wiley met with network officials several times in the latter part of 1974, making proposals to them, including that programs inappropriate for viewing by children not be broadcast prior to 9 p.m. The networks agreed fully to the family viewing concept, and the Chairman played a significant role in its adoption by the NAB and by the other industry elements (the independents; public broadcasting).

The Chairman was acting in his official capacity as the head of the agency. He was using his time, office space, and staff to discharge his official duties. So the question is: What responsibilities was he discharging? It is not enough to glibly cite the Commission's promotional role or the First Amendment. The Chairman's official duties are circumscribed by the Act. He—and the agency—can "perform any and all acts, . . . not inconsistent with this Act, as may be necessary in the execution of its [or his] functions."[86] But the act in question *was* inconsistent with the Act: Section 326 expressly forbids Governmental intrusion into this area. And the Chairman and the Commission concede that the agency lacks power to adopt the family viewing concept.[87] How then can the Chairman justify initiating discussion of the concept; urging its adoption as an NAB rule; trying to hasten and facilitate the process of adoption; and above all, taking steps to reduce opposition and promote industry-wide acceptance by the independents and public broadcasting?[88]

V. Conclusion

The foregoing is by no means an exhaustive list of the First Amendment problems stemming from the public trustee scheme, but it suffices to show how serious and pervasive the strains are. I would make a few final observations on this score.

First, these First Amendment problems have led the Commission to adopt broad—indeed, rather vague—policies that are then treated in a horatory fashion. Thus, in the *Children's Television Report*,[89] the Commission held that licensees ". . . must provide programs for children, and that a reasonable part of this programming should be educational in nature . . ." (par. 19), with ". . . some effort made for both pre-school and school aged children . . ." (par. 25) and with "reasonable scheduling" of children's programming throughout the week (par. 27).[90] The Commission supported this "cautious" approach by quoting the following Court language:

> [I]n applying the public interest standard to programming, the Commission walks a tightrope between saying too much and saying too little. In most cases it has resolved this dilemma by imposing only general affirmative duties—e.g., to strike a balance between various interests of the community, or to provide a reasonable amount of time for the presentation of programs devoted to the discussion of public issues. The licensee has broad discretion in giving specific content to these duties . . . Given its long-established authority to consider program content, this approach probably minimizes the dangers of censorship or pervasive supervision.[91]

This holding is echoed in the later *NAIPTD* case[92] where the Court specifically approves "broad and flexible restriction on speech in a forum where only a limited number of persons may speak at one time", stating:

> In the field of broadcasting, program categories must remain somewhat vague to avoid the indication that the guideline is rigid enough to be censored . . . When we deal as the Commission must, with the worlds of visual arts and of the intellect, too precise a series of definitions might end in a stylized format close to censorship.[93]

But this approach, making a virtue out of vagueness, flies in the face of other precedents in this sensitive First Amendment area.[94] The area simply becomes one of "unbridled administrative discretion."[95]

Further, experience shows that, in part because of these First Amendment considerations, the Commission does not implement policy statements like those in the *Children's TV Report*. In its 1946 Policy Statement (the Blue Book),[96] the Commission stressed as "essential" the "reasonable provision for local self-expression" and that "in particular, public interest requires that [local live] programs should not be crowded out of best listening hours."[97] It also stated that the carriage of programs devoted to the discussion of public issues ". . . in reasonable sufficiency, and during good listening hours, is a factor to be considered in any finding of public interest."[98] The Commission revised its application forms to obtain data on the foregoing essential aspects of public interest operation, and stated that it would implement these policies at renewal.[99]

However, the FCC has never effectively implemented the above local live or informational requirements. It has been over a quarter of a century since the Blue Book; it has been exactly thirty years since the issuance of the Editorializing Report,[100] where the Commission again stressed that broadcast licensees must devote a reasonable amount of time to the discussion of controversial issues of importance. Yet not once has the Commission ever designated a renewal application for hearing on the ground that the applicant had not rendered reasonable local live or informational service, either in amount or scheduling during good listening hours. This would be a remarkable record for the thousands of licensees and thousands of renewals over the years. The fact is that the Commission has simply not implemented these basic policies.[101]

I believe that this failure may be related, in part, to the above First Amendment concerns. Because terms such as "reasonable amount of time" do not really inform the licensee of its responsibilities in these basic areas (local, informational, and children's programming), it may well follow that there is a tendency to protect the incumbent in the face of a challenge to its operation on this score. Broadcasters are operating in the dark because of *Commission* failure, and the agency is thus a partner to the station's dilemma at renewal. If the Commission moves against the broadcaster in these "subjective" circumstances, is there not both unfairness and serious problems under the First Amendment?[102]

Appendix A

Station KREM-TV in Spokane, Washington, one of whose top officials was associated with a proposed Expo '74, editorialized strongly in favor of the project and its supporting bond issue. There was considerable disparity in the amount of time actually afforded the anti-bond viewpoints, and the station rejected one of the spokesmen for that viewpoint. But the station had a reasonable explanation for its rejection (i.e., the spokesman did not appear to represent groups for which he claimed to speak), and showed that it solicited opposing viewpoints.[a] Further, the station actively sought to obtain the views of leading spokesmen for the opposition and did present them. On the basis of these facts, the FCC staff ruling found that the licensee had afforded reasonable opportunity.

However, the FCC process for resolution of the significant issues was a long, arduous one—licensee response to complaint on October 12, 1971; further investigation on June 5 through 9, 1972; licensee response on February 6, 1973; and finally, the decision on May 17, 1973, 21 months after the broadcasts in question. The licensee's letter of February 6, 1973 concludes:

> Finally, apart from the merits of the controversy engendered by the Hecht complaint, we desire to comment briefly upon the procedures followed here. With due respect for the Commission's important responsibility in administering the fairness doctrine, we think there is a grave question whether it serves the public interest to require a station to account in such minute detail for everything it has said and done on a particular issue. We cannot believe that such a requirement contributes to an atmosphere of licensee independence or robust presentation of issues; we know that it is tremendously burdensome. We hope the Commission can find a way to give reasonable consideration to individual fairness complaints without the kind of exhaustive investigation that has apparently been thought necessary here.[b]

In order to quantify the extent of burden, the author inquired of the licensee as to the amounts of time and money expended in the handling of this fairness complaint. The licensee reported legal expenses of about $20,000, with other expenses (e.g., travel) adding considerably to the total;[c] this is not an insubstantial amount, in light of the fact that the total profits reported by all three TV stations in Spokane for 1972 was about $494,000.[d] However, from this licensee's standpoint, the important factors were the amount of time spent by top-level station personnel and the emotional strain on them.

Thus during the period from September 14, 1971 to May 18, 1973, the president and vice-president of the station devoted a total of about 80 hours; the station manager, 207 hours; and six members of his staff, an additional 194 hours. The station pointed out:

> In round numbers, then, 480 man hours of executive and supervisory time was spent on this matter. This, of course, does not include supporting secretarial or clerical time attendant to the work carried out. This represents a very serious dislocation of regular operational functions and far more important in that sense than in the simple salary dollar value.[E]

Finally, there is the factor of deferral of license renewal. The KREM-TV renewal would normally have been granted on February 1, 1972; because of the fairness complaint, however, its application for renewal (and that of its companion AM station) was placed on deferred status until May 21, 1973. The FCC has recognized that placing the renewal in jeopardy because of licensee activity in the news field can have a serious inhibiting effect and should be done only when a most substantial and fundamental issue is presented.[f]

Consider here the possible impact of such deferral upon a station manager or news director. Because of editorials such as that on Expo 74, the renewals of the station's license can be put in question and for a substantial period. What effect—perhaps even unconscious —does this have on the manager or news director the next time he is considering an editorial campaign on some contested local issue? What effect does it have on other stations? These questions raise a most important consideration—namely, that what may be crucially significant here is not the *number* of fairness rulings adverse to the broadcaster, but the *effect* of a ruling such as KREM's.

Thus the fact that KREM-TV was absolved of all charges does not obviate a significant question: Is the FCC's manner of proceeding, while in good faith in light of substantial issues, nevertheless discouraging the presentation of programming on controversial issues? Although it is not possible to give a definitive answer, the question is one that must be taken into account in formulating policy in this sensitive area.

All the above considerations in the KREM-TV case raise a basic issue: Is the goal of promoting robust, wide-open debate better served by focusing on whether the licensee has been fair in handling a particular issue or on whether he has generally remained faithful to the concept of a public trustee over his license period?

A. The station's editorial, with an offer of time to respond, was mailed to 194 community leaders and 200 members of the public; the station contacted 22 area organizations.

B. KREM-TV letter of February 6, 1973, pp. 31-32.

C. Verbal statement of the licensee and his law firm to the author.

D. TV Broadcast Financial Data, 1972, FCC 05693, Table 17; FCC financial data is publicly available only on an aggregate market basis, in order to protect the confidentiality of individual station profits and losses.

E. Letter of September 7, 1973 to Mr. J. Roger Wollenberg.

F. See *CBS* ("Hunger in America"), 20 FCC 2d 143, 150 (1969).

Notes

1. 418 U.S. 241 (1974).
2. 325 U.S. 367 (1969).
3. 418 U.S. at 258 (footnote omitted).
4. 395 U.S. at 389.
5. 418 U.S. at 257.
6. 395 U.S. at 393.
7. National Broadcasting Co. v. United States, 319 U.S. 190, 226 (1943); Red Lion, at 390. See also Virginia State Bd. of Pharmacy v. Virginia Citizens Consumer Council, Inc. 425 U.S. 748, 773 (1976); Bigelow v. Virginia. 421 U.S. 809, 825, n. 10 (1975); NAACP v. FPC, 425 U.S. 662, 670, n. 7 (1976). And the Court of Appeals for the Second Circuit, in finding constitutional a regulation that prescribes the particular types of programs that can be broadcast at particular times, stated:

> . . . *we recognized that First Amendment protection is applicable to the broadcast industry {citation omitted} but that the peculiar characteristics* of the broadcast media require the application of constitutional standards to their regulation which differ from those applicable to other types of communication. National Association of Independent Television Producers and Distributors v. FCC, 516 F. 2d 526, 531 (2d. Cir. 1975 (emphasis added).

7. 1976 BROADCASTING YEARBOOK, A-2.
8. See, e.g., statements of President Nixon, The Washington Post, September 6, 1977, at 1, and of Vice-President Spiro Agnew, The New York Times, November 14, 1969, at 24.
9. Banzhaf v. FCC, 405 F. 2d 1082, 1100-01 (D.C. Cir. 1968), cert. denied, 395 U.S. 842 (1969).
10. See, e.g., *CBS INC.* v. Democratic National Committee, 412 U.S. 94, 127 (1973); cf. Lehman v. City of Shaker Heights, 418 U.S. 293 (1974); Kovacs v. Cooper, 336 U.S. 77 (1949); Public Utilities Commission v. Pollak, 343 U.S. 451, 469 (1952).
11. See Eastern Educational Radio, 24 F.C.C. 2d 408, 411 (1970); Sonderling Corp., 27 Pike & Fischer R.R. 2d 285, 288, *recon. denied,* 41 F.C.C. 2d 477 (1977); REPORT ON THE BROADCAST OF VIOLENT, INDECENT, AND OBSCENE MATERIAL, F.C.C. 75-202 (1975).
12. The differing nature of the medium can be taken into account in applying concepts like obscenity. See Joseph Burstyn, Inc. v. Wilson, 343 U.S. 495, 503 (1952); Ginsberg v. New York, 390 U.S. 629 (1968) (obscenity and children); Illinois Citizens Commission for Broadcasting v. FCC, 515 F. 2d 391 (D.C. Cir. 1974), (obscenity, children and broadcasting).
13. 333 U.S. 507, 510 (1948). It is true that as to another "entertainment" medium, films, the Court has sustained laws calling for prior censorship aimed at the obscene—a process that would not be allowed as to books or magazines. See, e.g., Times Film Corp. v. City of Chicago, 365 U.S. 413 (1961). But it has specified strict procedures to be followed in this area. Freedman v. Maryland, 380 U.S. 51 (1965).
14. The all news radio station in the larger market is now a familar format. As to television, it has been estimated that 65% of the population looks to it as the principle source of its news. ROPER ORGANIZATION, TRENDS IN PUBLIC ATTITUDES TOWARD TELEVISION AND OTHER MASS MEDIA, 1959-74, at 3-4 (1975).
15. *Red Lion, supra,* at 390-91; Option Papers, House Subcommittee on Communications, Comm. 95-13, 95th Cong., 1st Sess (1977), at 90-91.
16. See Brandywine-Main Line Radio, Inc. v. FCC, 473 F. 2d 16, 75-76 (D.C. Cir. 1973) (dissenting opinion), *cert. denied,* 412 U.S. 922 (1973); *Statement of Walter Cronkite* in Hearings before Senate Subcommittee of Constitutional Rights, Judiciary Committee, 92d Cong., 1st Sess., p. 83.
17. 395 U.S. at 396-400.
18. It is not persuasive to cite cable development as eliminating scarcity in television. Cable is making little inroads in the major markets where the great bulk of the population resides. It may be that with new developments like the Warner Cable project in Columbus, Ohio (see *Broadcasting Magazine,* February 14, 1977, at 33), cable will eventually achieve a breakthrough. But that is by no means assured. The "wired nation" is not here or imminent, and policy for the last quarter of a century cannot be based on such speculative development. See Price, *Requiem for the Wired Nation; Cable Rulemaking at the FCC,* 61 VA. L. REV 541 (1975).
19. See *Red Lion,* supra, at 389. The argument can be stated by analogy; Suppose the Government were to license the use of the main park in Jackson, Mississippi to one party, the White Citizens Council, for three years, and allow no one else to use that park for parades, rallies, etc. And suppose black groups sought the right to present their parades or rallies. Clearly they would succeed in striking down the above governmental action as unconstitutional. But the Government has done the equivalent as to Jackson Channel 3.
20. *Red Lion, supra,* at 390-91. See *Options Papers, op.* cited at n. 15, at 90-91.

21. See Keyishian v. Board of Regents, 385 U.S. 589, 609 (1967); Shelton v. Tucker, 364 U.S. 478, 488 (1960). In the latter case the Court, after noting that considerable leeway is afforded the legislative judgment in the economic regulatory area, stated as to the sensitive First Amendment field:

> though the governmental purpose be legitimate and substantial, that purpose cannot be pursued by means that broadly stifle fundamental liberties when the end can be more narrowly achieved [footnote ommitted]. The breadth of legislative abridgment must be conceived in light of less drastic means for achieving the same basic purpose. . . . *Id.*

22. See H. FRIENDLY, THE FEDERAL ADMINISTRATIVE AGENCIES 12 (1962). (The public interest standard was used first in the Transportation Act of 1920, and has since been used in several acts, e.g., FPC, CAB.)

23. 412 U.S. at 117.

24. *Id.* at 117.

25. Ashbacker Radio Corp. v. FCC, 326 U.S. 327, 332 (1945).

26. 319 U.S. at 226-27.

27. Office of Communication of United Church of Christ v. FCC, 359 F. 2d 994, 1009 (D.C. Cir. 1966).

28. This is not a fanciful situation. In the *Church of Chirst* case, the licensee stated that it would not cover the issue of integration for fear of inducing community violence—yet it had no trouble presenting editorials against school integration (on the grounds that its editorial stand involved "state rights," not school integration). See Lamar Life Broadcasting Co., 38 F.C.C. 1143, 1146-47 (1965).

29. See *Notice of Inquiry in Docket No. 19154*, 27 F.C.C. 2d 580, 581 (1971); Section 307 (b), 47 U.S.C. 307 (b); S. Rept. No. 526; 87th Cong., 2d Sess. (1962).

30. See, e.g., Simmons v. FCC, 169 F. 2d 670 (D.C. Cir. 1948), *cert. denied*, 335 U.S. 846 (1948).

31. See, *Red Lion, supra*, at 294; Section 315 (a), 47 U.S.C. 315 (a); Storer Broadcasting Co., 11 F.C.C. 2d 678 (1968); *Report on Editorializing by Broadcast Licensees*, 13 F.C.C. 1246, 1248 (1949).

32. *Notice of Inquiry in Docket No. 19154*, 27 F.C.C. 2d 580, 581 (1971).

33. *See Commission Policy on Programming*, 20 PIKE AND FISCHER R.R. 1901, 1913-15 (1960).

34. *See Ascertainment of Community Problems by Broadcast Applicants*, 41 Fed. Reg. 1372 (1976).

35. *See FCC Report to the Congress re Comparative Hearing Process*, November, 1976, pars. 81-98, for a succinct discussion of this process.

36. See FCC v. Sanders Bros. Radio Station, 390 U.S. 470, 475 (1940); Citizens Communications Center v. FCC, 447 F. 2d. 1201 (D.C. Cir. 1971).

37. Citizens Communications Center v. FCC, *supra*, at 1213, n. 35. But see Geller, *The Comparative Hearing Process in Television*, 61 VA. L. REV. 271, 489-503 (1975).

38. *Policy Statement on Regular Comparative Renewal Hearings*, 22 F.C.C. 2d 424, 428 n. 4 (1970), *reversed on other grounds*, Citizens Comminications Center v. FCC, *supra*.

39. See Sec. 73.658 (j) (k) 47 C.F.R. 73.658 (j) (k) (1970).

40. See Section 3.636, 47 C.F.R. 73.636

41. See *Report and Order*, 23 F.C.C. 2d 395 (1970); *affirmed*, Mt. Mansfield Television, Inc. v. FCC, 442 F. 2d 470 (2d Cir. 1971).

42. See *Report and Order*, 18 Fed. Reg. 7796 (1953), *affirmed*, U.S. v. Storer Broadcasting Co., 351 U.S. 192 (1956).

43. See *Second Report and Order*, 50 FCC 2d. 1046 (1975), *reversed on failure to require divestiture*, NCCB v. FCC. Thus, for a time the Commission considered adoption of a rule which would limit holdings in the top 50 markets to only two. VHF Stations. See *Report and Order*, FCC 68-138, 12 PIKE AND FISCHER R.R. 2d 1501 (1968).

44. See Brandywine-Main Line Radio, Inc. v. *FCC, supra*, 473 F. 2d at 78 (Bazelon, C.J. dissenting); Bazelon, *FCC Regulation of the Telecommunications Press*, 1975 DUKE L.J. 213, 214-16; F. Friendly, *Policizing TV*, COLUMBIA JOURNALISM REV., March-April 1973, at 9; H. ASHMORE, FEAR IN THE AIR (1973).

45. See, e.g., National Broadcasting Co., Inc. (The Pensions Case) v. FCC, 516 F. 2d 1101 (D.C. Cir., 1971), vacated, *cert. denied*, 424 U.S. 910 (1976); Straus Communicatons, Inc. v. *FCC*, 530 F. 2d 1001, (D.C. Cir. 1976).

46. 38 F.C.C. 1143, 1146-47 (1965).

47. Office of Communication of the Church of Christ v. *FCC, supra*.

48. See Concurring Statement of Chairman Burch in Complaint of the Wilderness Society against NBC (ESSO), 31 F.C.C. 2d 729, 734-39 (1971); Public Media Center, 59 FCC 2d 494 (1976). Indeed, there is some confusion as to the standard to be applied in fairness cases. The Commission, citing Green v. FCC, 447 F. 2d 323, 329 (D.C. Cir. 1971), has stated that ". . . the essential test of fairness must be whether the public has been 'left uninformed' as to contrasting viewpoints on an issue." Public Media Center, *supra*, at par. 44 Under this

test, it would be unnecessary to look to how much the initial side had been presented in amount, frequency or audience times; all that would be needed is to determine whether the public has been left uninformed about the contrasting viewpoint. But the statutory standard is not stated in terms of "uninformed" but rather "reasonable opportunity." See Section 315 (a), 47 U.S.C. 315 (a); Brandywine-Main Line Radio, Inc. v. *FCC, supra,* 473 F. 2d at 46: "The ultimate test in this area is reasonableness. The critical issue is whether the sum total of the licensee's efforts, taking into account his plans when the issue is a continuing one, can be said to constitute a reasonable opportunity to inform the public on the contrasting viewpoint—one that is fair in the circumstances.'"

Despite its "uninformed" formulation, the Commission does look to reasonableness in the particular circumstances (i.e., amount, frequency, audiences). *Fairness Report*, 48 F.C.C. 2d 1, 17 (par. 44) (1974); Public Media Center, *supra*. What emerges is the Commission's strong desire to avoid any ratio (three-to-one or five-to-one) or formula (*ibid.*). But while this desire for flexibility is understandable, it presents constitutional problems when licensees and the public are left in doubt in this sensitive First Amendment area, and the Commission can rule "flexibly" after the fact: "Yes, this is fair" or "No, it is not." See NAACP v. Button, 371 U.S. 415, 438 (1963), where the Court stated that "precision of regulation must be a touchstone" in the area of freedom of expression; Greater Boston Television Corp. v. FCC, 143 U.S. App. D.C. 383, 444 F. 2d 841, 854 (1970), *cert. denied*, 402 U.S. 1007 (1970), 403 U.S. 923 (1971).

Further, a kind of formula does emerge if one analyzes the decisions the Commission is forced to reach. Thus, in its most recent decision, *Public Media Center, supra*, the Commission has, in effect, established that if the two sides have had roughly the same amount of time, the frequency and audience factors are not to be considered. *See, e.g.*, decision as to *KJOY* (par. 49), *KPAY* (par. 51), and *KVON* (par. 57), where the Commission found "reasonable opportunity" relying solely on roughly the same amount of time, despite great disparities as to frequency (but see Clarence F. Massart, 10 F.C.C. 2d 968 (1967); George E. Cooley, 10 F.C.C. 2d 969, 970 (1967) where the Commission found unfairness in two political editorializing cases because of an imbalance in frequency even though overall time was roughly the same); and see *KSRO* (par. 55), where there was a four-to-one disparity, so the Commission looked to "frequency and audience"). A formula of sorts thus emerges: Disparity in total time (at least if four-to-one and probably less) will result in consideration of frequency and audience. My point is that the area is confused and contradictory, when it should be clear and consistent. Cf. Friends of Earth v. *FCC*, 449 F. 2d 1164, 1169-70 (D.C. Cir. 1971); Garrett v. FCC. 513 F. 2d 1056, 1060-61 (D.C. Cir. 1971); CBS, Inc. v. FCC, 454 F. 2d 1018, 1026 (D.C. Cir. 1971); Melody Music, Inc. v. FCC, 345 F. 2d 730, 732-33 (D.C. Cir. 1965).

49. Complaint of Wilderness Society against NBC (ESSO), 31 F.C.C. 2d at 735-39. In that case the staff set forth the following "stop-watch" analysis of the material broadcast on the issue (pp. 738-39):

Date of Broadcast	Pro	Anti
June 7, 1970	4:40	5:35
September 10, 1970	:20	1:00
January 13, 1971	:06	:15
February 14, 1971	——	:10
February 16, 1971	:49	1:05
February 24, 1971	:15	1:30
February 28, 1971	1:32	——
June 4, 1971	1:58	——
July 11, 1971	:27	2:15
August 6, 1971	:45	1:10
August 26, 1971	——	:15
September 15, 1971	——	8:00
Total	10:52	21:15

see also Sunbeam TV Corp., 27 F.C.C. 2d 350, 351 (1971).

50. Complaint of Wilderness Society Against NBC (ESSO), *supra*, 31 FCC 2d at 733.

51. See H. Geller, The Fairness Doctrine in Broadcasting: Problems and Suggested Courses of Action, The Rand Corporation, R-1412-FF, December 1973, App. D, 114-132.

52. Complaint of Sherwyn H. Heckt, 40 F.C.C. 2d 1150 (1973).

53. In addition to the FCC's problems in administering the fairness doctrine, there is also the consideration of its possible abuse by the Executive. Thus, Fred Friendly has shown how both Republican and Democratic Administrations sought to use the fairness doctrine to chill anti-Administration viewpoints. See F. Friendly, "Politicalizing TV", Columbia Journalism Rev. March-April 1973, p. 9; The New York Times Magazine

Section, March 30, 1975, p. 8; THE GOOD GUYS, THE BAD GUYS, AND THE FIRST AMENDMENT, 201-02 (1976).

54. *Fairness Report*, 48 F.C.C. 2d at 21; Letter to ABC, 16 F.C.C. 2d 650, 657 (1969); CBS ("Hunger in America"), 20 F.C.C. 2d 143, 151 (1969).

55. CBS (WBBM-TV), 18 F.C.C. 2d 124 (1960).

56. Id. at 133.

57. Id. at 134.

58. CBS v. DNC. *supra*, 412 U.S. at 125.

59. FCC Order 76-419; amending Section O. 281 (a) (8((i), 47 C.F.R. O. 281 (a) (B) (i); Notice of Inquiry in FCC Docket No. 18154, 22 F.C.C. at p. 64.

60. American Broadcasting Co. (KGO-TV), 56 F.C.C. 2d 275, 283 (1975); see Public Communications, Inc., 50 F.C.C. 2d 395, 399-400 (1974).

61. FCC 76-529.

62. Fairness Report, 48 F.C.C. at 10.

63. *Report to the Congress Re Comparative Renewal Process*, November 1976, at par. 97.

64. Since 1967 there have been an increasing number of petitions to deny filed by public interest groups—333 petitions. But only nine have been granted, and the renewals designated for hearing. In 1972, the FCC granted 99.32% of all renewals filed, in 1973, 99.19%, and in 1974, 99.69%. Worse, the standards applied are subjective. Address to Chairman Torbert MacDonald, before the 1975 NAB Convention, Chicago, Illinois, pp. 4-5.

65. See 47 C.F.R. 0.281(a) (8) (i).

66. To give one example, KIBE-AM, a San Francisco classical music station, bowing to the Commission dictates, substituted a 6:00 a.m. talk show for a baroque music program, in order to gain renewal without going through an expensive hearing which it could ill afford. (Letter of April 6, 1976, from Edward Davis, station manager to author.) It felt that by doing so, it was causing the least damage to its schedule, and yet giving lip service to the FCC standards. But the audience reaction was clear: hostility and bewilderment that a program enjoyed by many was now gone because of Government fiat.

Does this really serve the public's interest? Is this not bureaucracy having its way? Indeed, the charade could have further consequences. The licensee is to present programs dealing with its community's problems "based upon its good faith judgment as to when broadcast reasonably could be expected to be effective." FCC Ascertainment Primer, Question 31, 41 Fed. Reg. at 1383. What if there were a petition to deny that this talk show is not being reasonably scheduled to be "effective" at 6:00 a.m.? (And of course it is not.) What would the FCC do then to "protect" the public interest?

67. 60 F.C.C. 2d 372 (1976); *reconsid. denied*, 62 F.C.C. 2d 953 (1977); *additional views on denying reconsid.*, 40 PIKE AND FISCHER R.R. 2d 1627 (1977); appeal docketed sub nom., Central Florida Enterprise Inc. v. FCC, No. 76-1742 (D.C. Cir. August 16, 1977).

68. 60 F.C.C. 2d 417, § 137.

69. 60 F.C.C. 2d 421, 422.

70. 60 F.C.C. 2d at 422.

71. 62 F.C.C. 2d 953, 855-56 § 9.

72. *Cowles*, 60 F.C.C. 2d at 433.

73. Hearings on Broadcast License Renewal Before the Subcommittee on Communications and Power of the House Committee on Interstate and Foreign Commerce, 93rd Congress, 1st Session, ser. 93-35, at 1119 (1973) (testimony of FCC Chairman Burch). Vol. IV at 160-61.

74. 444 F. 2d at 854. For an example of possible abuse in this area, see the Watergate disclosures concerning the threat by the Nixon Administration to make it "awfully rough" for the *Washington Post* television stations when they seek renewal and could be challenged comparatively. NCCB V. PCC, *supra*, 555 F. 2d at 954 (1977); Geller, *The Comparative Renewal Process in Television: Problems and Suggested Solutions*, 61 VA. L. REV. 498, n. 143 (1975).

75. See, e.g., Mutual Insurance Co. of Omaha, 33 F.C.C. 2d 583 (1972) (waiver granted for "Wild Kingdom"); Campbell Soup Co., 35 F.C.C. 2d 758, 761 (1972) (waiver denied for "Lassie"); Time-Life, 35 F.C.C. 2d 773, 775 (1972) (waiver granted for "Six Wives of Henry VIII").

76. NAITPD v. FCC, 516 F. 2d 526, 536 (2d Cir. 1975).

77. *Id.*

78. 345 F. 2d 278 (9th Cir. 1965).

79. See *Memorandum Opinion and Order*, 37 PIKE AND FISCHER, R.R. 2d 1679 (1976); *Notice of Inquiry in Docket No. 20682*, 57 F.C.C. 580 (1975).

80. See, e.g., Citizens Committee to Save WEFM v. *FCC*, 506 F. 2d 246 (D.C. Cir. 1974); Citizens Committee v. FCC (WCKA), 436 F. 2d 263 (D.C. Cir. 1970); Citizens Committee to Preserve Progressive Rock, 478 F. 2d 926 (D.C. Cir. 1973).

81. Citizens Committee to Save WEFM v. *FCC, supra*, 526 F. 2d at 962.

82. E.g., Statement of Mr. James Gabbert, on Aug. 3, 1977, on Broadcast Overview, House Subcommittee on Communications (transcript not yet printed).

83. Quoted in the dissenting opinion of Chief Judge Bazelon in Illinois Citizens Committee for Broadcasting v. FCC, 515 F. 2d 391, 408 (D.C. Cir. 1975).

84. *Id*. at 409.

85. H. Rept. No. 1139, 93rd Cong., 2d Sess., at 15 (1974); see also S. Rept. No. 1056, 93rd Cong., 2d Sess., at 17 (1974).

86. Section 4 (i) of the Communications Act, 47 U.S.C. 154 (i).

87. Thus, in *KCOP Television, Inc.*, FCC 76-576, par. 15, the Commission rejected claims of ". . . excessive violence in KCOP's programming available for child viewing . . ." with the short statement: "Section 326 of the Communications Act of 1934, as amended prohibits censorship by this agency. Thus, we believe that it is inappropriate for the Commission to enter into this sensitive area of licensee programming."

88. Because of the governmental taint, the Court invalidated the concept in Writers Guild of America, Inc. v. FCC, 423 F. Supp. 1064 (C.D. Cal. 1976), *appeal pending*. For another example of the "lifted eyebrow" technique, see the history of the "drug lyrics" controversy, Memorandum Opinion and Order, 31 F.C.C. 2d 377, 385, 401 (1971), *aff'd. sub nom.*, Yale Broadcasting Co., v. FCC 478 F. 2d 594, en banc rehearing denied, 478 F. 2d 602 (D.C. Cir. 1973); (see dissenting opinion of C.J. Bazelon), *cert. denied*, 414 U.S. 914 (1973).

89. 50 F.C.C. 2d 1 (1975).

90. *Id*. at 6-8.

91. Banzhaf v. FCC, 405 F. 2d 1082, 1095 (D.C. Cir. 1968), *cert. denied sub nom.* Tobacco Institute v. FCC, 396 U.S. 842 (1969).

92. 516 F. 2d at 537.

93. *Id*. at 537.

94. See Hynes v. Mayor of Oradell, 96 S.Ct. 1755, 1760 (1976); NAACP v. Button, 371 U.S. 415, 433 (1963)—(in the First Amendment area "government may regulate . . . only with narrow specificity"); Gelling v. Texas, 343 U.S. 960 (1952); Greater Boston Television Corp. v. FCC, *supra*, 444 F. 2d at 854.

95. See Hearings, cited at n. 62, at 119 (Statement of Chairman Burch).

96. *Report on Public Service Responsibility of Broadcast Licensees*, 1946.

97. *Id*. at p. 56.

98. *Id*.

99. *Id*. at pp. 57-59.

100. *Report on Editorializing by Broadcast Licensees*, 13 F.C.C. 1246, 1248 (1949). See also *Fairness Report*, *supra*, 48 F.C.C. 2d at 9-10.

101. See, e.g., Herman C. Hall, 11 F.C.C. 2d 344 (1968) (granted even though the applicant proposed *zero* programming in news/public affairs) 14 F.C.C. 2d 1, 12-13; FCC Public Notice-B-13087, February 20, 196; 18 F.C.C. 2d 268, 269 (1969); 21 F.C.C. 2d 35 (1969).

102. See Greater Boston Television Corp. v. FCC, 143 U.S. App. D.C. 383, 444 F. 2d 841, 854 (1970), *cert. denied*, 402 U.S. 1007 (1970), 403 U.S. 923 (1971).

For the American Press: The Freedom to Be Responsible
BY DONALD McDONALD*

Government, under the First Amendment, not only is obliged to refrain from making any laws *abridging* freedom of the press; it is also obliged to *protect* that freedom, prevent it from being abridged by any person, group, or institution, including, in some instances, the press itself. This twofold obligation has been attested to in a number of court decisions based on the nature and needs of a self-governing political society.

Although some still question whether the people have a right to know, the more fundamental and, I think, self-evident truth about a democratic society is that the people have a need to know, and from this need flows their right to know.

The philosopher Richard McKeon has said that democracy is a community based on communication.[1]

Mr. Justice Douglas, in his *Branzburg v. Hayes* dissent, said: "The press has a preferred position in our constitutional scheme, not to enable it to make money, not to set newsmen apart as a favored class, but to bring fulfillment to the public's right to know. . . . Knowledge is essential to informed decisions."[2]

And James Madison, in a letter to W. T. Barry in 1822, maintained: "A popular government, without popular information, or the means of acquiring it, is but a prologue to a farce or a tragedy, perhaps both. Knowledge will forever govern ignorance: and a people who mean to be their own governors must arm themselves with the power which knowledge gives."[3]

Madison and the other founding fathers adopted the First Amendment precisely because they recognized this fundamental political need of the people to know, they knew that the press was a principal vehicle for knowledge, and they had learned from experience that, left to themselves, government officials inevitably seek to limit, if not destroy, the freedom of the press.

But what if, over the intervening two centuries, the threat to the flow of public information is no longer monopolized by government? What if the mass media themselves restrict that flow and dangerously narrow the scope of "popular information"? Does the First Amendment permit—or even command—government to take appropriate protective action? I think it does and that the language of the courts in our time supports this position.

In delivering the Supreme Court's 1945 decision in *Associated Press v. United States,* Mr. Justice Black emphasized: "It would be strange indeed if the grave concern for freedom of the press which prompted adoption of the First Amendment should be read as a command that the government was without power to protect that freedom."

The First Amendment, contended Mr. Justice Black,

> rests on the assumption that the widest possible dissemination of information from diverse and antagonistic sources is essential to the welfare of the public, that a free press

* Editor, THE CENTER MAGAZINE.

is a condition of the free society. Surely a command that the government itself shall not impede the free flow of ideas does not afford non-governmental combinations a refuge if they impose restraints upon that constitutionally guaranteed freedom. Freedom to publish means freedom for all and not for some. Freedom to publish is guaranteed by the Constitution, but freedom to combine to keep others from publishing is not. Freedom of the press from governmental interference under the First Amendment does not sanction repression of that freedom by private interests.[4]

Now it is true that the Court was addressing a particular instance of "private interests" repressing the freedom of the press. In this case, the by-laws of the Associated Press which gave member newspapers veto power over the admission of competing newspapers to membership and, hence, access to the Associated Press wire service, were found in violation of the First Amendment. It is equally true that not every demonstration of the media's constriction of the free flow of public information warrants government intervention. But it requires no strained interpretation of the Court's language to see that what the Court established in *Associated Press* was the general principle that government has both the power and the obligation to protect the freedom of the press whenever that freedom is jeopardized, from whatever source.

Almost a quarter of a century after *Associated Press,* the Supreme Court again affirmed—this time in the 1969 *Red Lion* decision—the primacy of the people's right to know, the subordination of the broadcasters' freedom to that right, and the government's duty to enforce that subordinate relationship. *Red Lion* upheld the Federal Communication Commission's constitutional right to compel broadcasters to give adequate coverage to controversial issues of public importance and to see that such coverage is fair and accurately reflects opposing views.

Speaking for the Court, Mr. Justice White said: "It is the right of the viewers and listeners, not the right of the broadcasters, which is paramount. . . . It is the right of the public to receive suitable access to social, political, aesthetic, moral, and other ideas and experiences which is crucial here."

Justice White pointed out that

> A license permits broadcasting, but the licensee has no constitutional right to be the one who holds the license or to monopolize a radio frequency to the exclusion of his fellow citizens. Thee is nothing in the First Amendment which prevents the Government from requiring a licensee to share his frequency with others and to conduct himself as a proxy or fiduciary with obligations to present those views and voices which are representative of his community and which would otherwise, by necessity, be barred from the airwaves.

In language reminiscent of Justice Black's in *Associated Press,* Justice White continued, "It is the purpose of the First Amendment to preserve an uninhibited marketplace of ideas in which truth will ultimately prevail, rather than to countenance monopolization of that market, whether it be by the government itself or a private licensee."[5]

But what, then, are we to make of a subsequent Supreme Court decision, that of *Miami Herald Publishing Co., Inc. v. Tornillo,* in 1975? In that case, the Court ruled unanimously that a Florida statute compelling newspaper publishers to print the reply of public officials attacked in their papers was unconstitutional. Chief Justice Burger argued that the Florida law was a "compulsory access law," and, after describing a newspaper's decision-making process regarding choice and treatment of news and editorial matter to be printed, he said: "It has yet to be demonstrated how governmental regulation of this crucial process can be exercised consistent with First Amendment guarantees of a free press as they have evolved to this time."[6]

In a concurring opinion, Mr. Justice White added: "[T]he balance struck by the First Amendment with respect to the press is that society must take the risk that occasionally debate on vital matters will not be comprehensive and that all viewpoints may not be expressed."[7]

In effect, when broadcast journalists are unfair, government must intervene; when newspaper journalists are unfair, government may not intervene.

I do not wish either to try to reconcile *Red Lion* and *Tornillo,* or to rationalize what may be an irreconcilability between them. I do assert that *Tornillo* does not undermine my claim that government, precisely because of the First Amendment, has an obligation to protect the press from "repression of [its] freedom by private interests."

Nor does Chief Justice Burger's statement in *Tornillo,* that "press responsibility is not mandated by the Constitution and, like many other virtues, it cannot be legislated," undermine my claim of the government's affirmative obligations under the First Amendment.

I do not argue that press responsibility—particularly editorial responsibility—can be either mandated by the Constitution or legislated. What *is* mandated by the Constitution is the government's obligation to insure the free flow of public information. And what can be legislated are the conditions which will best promote this free flow, which will at least make possible "the widest possible dissemination of information from diverse and antagonistic sources" and "preserve an uninhibited marketplace of ideas in which truth will ultimately prevail."

When those conditions have deteriorated and, in some cases, no longer exist, and when the press itself is the cause of the deterioration or absence of those conditions which are "essential to the welfare of the public," then the government must act to restore those conditions. In so acting, it is not seeking to "legislate" press responsibility, nor is it substituting its judgment for the judgment of editors and publishers with regard to content, i.e., with regard to what shall be printed or broadcast. Indeed, with the exception of proven defamatory falsehoods, in which case publication of retraction can be compelled under defamatory statutes, the government has no business telling either publishers or broadcasters what they must print or broadcast.

But can government promote the free flow of popular information and the "widest possible dissemination of information from diverse and antagonistic sources" without dictating what and how public information shall be handled by print and broadcast journalists? I think it can. But before demonstrating that possibility, a different question must be answered. Do present conditions in the mass media in fact require remedial intervention? I think they do, and in an earlier article[8] I described those conditions in some detail. I shall not review that article exhaustively here, but instead will select some of its evidence and add new evidence I have discovered since the article appeared.

Ownership of the mass media is becoming increasingly concentrated with each passing year. In 1910, there were 2,400 daily newspapers in the United States owned by 2,351 individual publishers (13 publisher groups owned 62 of these papers)—all serving a population of one hundred million. By 1977, the American population had more than doubled—it is now about 220,000,000—but the number of daily newspapers had dropped to 1,762. Even more significant, the number of individual publishers had dropped to 882, because 1,047 of these daily newspapers are now owned by 167 publisher groups. These groups own sixty per cent of the daily newspapers in the United States and account for seventy-one per cent of the total circulation of the dailies and seventy-eight per cent of the circulation of Sunday and weekend newspapers.

In a recent series of articles in the *Washington Post,* the reporters—William H. Jones and Laird Anderson—declared that "within two decades, virtually all daily newspapers in

America will be owned by perhaps fewer than two dozen major communications conglomerates."[9]

In 1920, just before the beginning of radio, 552 American cities had competing daily newspapers. In 1945, prior to the advent of television, there were 117 cities with competing newspapers. Today, fifty-five cities have competing daily newspapers, but twenty-one of these have joint publishing arrangements, sanctioned by the Newspaper Preservation Act, which insures no real competition for advertising and no Sunday competition of any kind.

Nor does the existence of almost nine thousand commercial and educational radio and television stations appreciably affect this ownership-concentration situation. The most cogent analysis of that situation has been that of Morton Mintz and Jerry Cohen in their book, *America, Inc.*[10]

> In the twenty-five top markets, [they write,] there are a total of ninety-seven VHF [television] stations. In addition to the fifteen owned and operated by C.B.S., N.B.C., and A.B.C., newspapers as of early 1960 were operating thirty-four. Of the thirty four, twenty-six are affiliates of one of the networks. . . .
>
> Consider communities outside of metropolitan areas and which have populations of between five thousand and fifty thousand. In each of sixty-eight such communities where there is one daily newspaper and one AM station, the paper has an interest in the station. In twenty-eight similar communities where there are two stations, the single newspaper has an interest in one of them.
>
> Now consider communities in metropolitan areas with populations of 175,000 to two million or more. In eight such communities, a newspaper owns fifty to one hundred per cent of the only radio station. In six similar communities, where there are two stations, the paper owns a majority interest in one of them. . . .
>
> All fifteen of the network-owned VHF television stations are in the nation's twenty-five largest markets, including New York, Chicago, and Los Angeles. The eleven largest cities do not have even one VHF station that is not in the hands of a network, a newspaper, a newspaper chain, an owner of a group of stations, or an industrial or financial conglomerate.

Mintz and Cohen also cite a Justice Department study which "showed that in each of fifty major urban markets a single owner controlled two or more broadcast media and/or at least one TV station plus one daily newspaper. In several such markets a newspaper chain or dominant newspaper owned network-affiliated TV, AM, and FM stations."[11]

Federal communications records as of 1970 showed that 231 of the nation's daily newspapers are owned by broadcasting licensees in the same city.

More recent data, available from both industry and government sources, indicate that media ownership concentration, including newspaper-broadcasting cross-ownership, continues to be one of the striking characteristics of the communications media in this country. For example, a 1974 map of the United States, prepared by American Research Bureau (Arbitron Television) shows the "areas of dominant influence" (a U.S. market measurement) in which a daily newspaper and a television station are commonly owned. At least half of the geographical area and much more than half of the population fall into this category, since cross-ownership naturally tends to concentrate where the people and the markets are. About forty-five per cent of the American people live in Standard Metropolitan Statistical Areas in which there is newspaper-television station cross-ownership.

The fact of ownership concentration, the highly profitable nature of both broadcasting and newspaper properties, and the enormous capital that would be required to start one of these media virtually insures that only the very wealthy and/or those who have access to the needed capital can afford to become a part of the media industry.

While information on the extent to which non-media interests own media properties is difficult to assemble in any comprehensive fashion, one piece of evidence does add an important dimension to the picture of media ownership. It concerns the holdings, as of July 5, 1972, in the broadcast industry by the twenty-five largest bank trust departments, and an analysis of the number of shares and the percentage of various broadcast companies' stock held by these banks.[12]

Among other things, this report shows that Morgan Guaranty Trust owns substantial holdings in twenty-four broadcasting companies, including 3,381,646 shares of Westinghouse, and more than five million shares of the Travelers Corporation. Chase Manhattan Bank owns 3,309,683 shares of Radio Corporation of America; more than two million shares of Westinghouse; almost four million shares of Columbia Broadcasting System; more than six million shares of General Electric; and substantial holdings in another sixteen broadcasting companies.

When one looks at the individual broadcasting companies and the extent to which they are owned by major banks, one finds, for example, that in 1972, 34.8 per cent of the America Broadcasting Company, Inc.'s total shares were held by eight of the twenty-five largest banks in the United States. Thirty-six per cent of the shares of Dun & Bradstreet (owners of five television stations) was owned by eight of these banks; thirty-eight per cent of C.B.S. stock was held by eleven banks; thirty-three per cent of Capital Cities Broadcasting Corporation, owner of seventeen broadcasting stations, was held by eleven banks; and twenty-three per cent of Metromedia, Inc., which owned sixteen broadcasting stations in 1972, was held by four of these banks.

Information is not available on the extent to which these same twenty-five banks hold stock in insurance companies and investment trusts which, in turn, own shares in these same broadcasting companies.

In the media ownership pattern that has now developed in this country, it is not surprising that certain kinds of public information and certain kinds of public affairs reporters fare badly. Again, my earlier article[13] contains representative examples of what has been happening to the "free flow" of "popular information" in the American mass media. I will not recount them here, but the picture is a sorry one. It includes reporters and editors fired or "re-assigned" after they had filed articles containing information displeasing to media owners and advertisers. It includes the case of the Chicago *Tribune,* which failed to carry a single story of an important eleven-day trial of Sears, Roebuck and Company before an administrative law judge of the Federal Trade Commission. Sears had been charged with systematically engaging in bait-and-switch selling tactics. The *Tribune,* which, each year, receives five million dollars in advertising from Sears, filed a four-paragraph rewrite of a *Wall Street Journal* story on the trial, a week after the trial ended.

In 1970, the National Commission on the Causes and Prevention of Violence said in its final report:

> The news media can play a significant role in lessening the potential for violence by functioning as a faithful conduit for intergroup communication, providing a true marketplace of ideas, providing full access to the day's intelligence, and reducing the incentives to confrontation that sometimes erupts in violence. . . .
>
> It should become habitual editorial policy to display fairly and clearly the opinions, analyses, and solutions offered by a wide variety of people, expert and non-expert covering the spectrum, regardless of the proprietor's personal position.
>
> Too many news organizations fear social ideas and social action. As a result, they stimulate, dissatisfy, and arouse anxiety, only to fall silent or limit themselves to irrelevant clichés when thoughtful solutions are required. Alternative solutions to our

most urgent social problems, based on the work of our most imaginative social thinkers, and written with the clarity that only a good journalist can produce, ought to be standard practice. . . .

We strongly recommend that the news media examine carefully the problems posed when equivalent access to the media is denied.[14]

Because of the commercial nature of broadcasting and the pressure on management to show stockholders an ever-increasing return on their investment, the competition among networks as well as among stations in the same market is not over which company can serve the public interest best. It is over which company can capture the largest audience and, consequently, the greatest advertising revenue. The results in both entertainment and news and public affairs programming are predictable. And the evidence is there for all to see and hear every time we turn on our television or radio receiver.

Is government intervention the answer to this media situation? I think it is, and permit me to draw from Professor Emerson's *The System of Freedom of Expression*[15] for my rationale.

Professor Emerson points out that it is no longer enough to protect the freedom of the press from government interference in order to guarantee freedom of expression. Today, "the overpowering monopoly over the means of communication acquired by the mass media" constitutes "the most significant threat" to our system of freedom of expression.

At the same time,

modern government, by virtue of its size, resources, control of information, and links to the mass media, plays a more dominant and narrowing role in the system. . . . [Too,] costs of all methods of communication steadily rise beyond the means of the individual or the ordinary group. The result is that the system is choked with communications based upon the conventional wisdom and becomes incapable of performing its basic function.

Search for the truth is handicapped because much of the argument is never heard or heard only weakly. Political decisions are distorted because the views of some citizens never reach other citizens, and feedback to the government is feeble.

The possibility of orderly social change is greatly diminished because those persons with the most urgent grievances come to believe the system is unworkable and merely shields the existing order.[16]

"Under these circumstances," Emerson continues,

it becomes essential, if the system is to survive, that a search be made for ways to use the law and legal institutions in an affirmative program to restore the system to effective working order.

In general, the government must affirmatively make available the opportunity for expression as well as protect it from encroachment. This means that positive measures must be taken to assure the ability to speak despite economic or other barriers. It also means that greater attention must be given to the right of the citizen to hear varying points of view and the right to have access to information upon which such points of view can be intelligently based. Thus, equally with the right and ability to speak, such an approach would stress the right to hear and the right to know.[17]

Emerson is quite aware of what he calls the "grave administrative and procedural problems" posed by any effort to employ governmental authority to facilitate operation of the system of freedom of expression.

The attempt to use governmental power to achieve some limited objective, while at the same time keeping the power under control, is always a risky enterprise. Nowhere is this truer than in the area of freedom of expression. Nevertheless, there is no alternative. The weaknesses of the existing system are so profound that failure to act is the more dangerous course. Moreover, the government is already deeply involved at many points

—some of great importance—as in its regulation of radio and television. The same kind of movement may be found in other areas of individual rights today, such as the development of the affirmative aspects of the equal protection clause.[18]

"The only prudent course, then," according to Emerson,

is to formulate principles and devise techniques that use social power to facilitate freedom of expression while holding the instrument of that power in check. The initial responsibility of the government is to maintain the basic conditions that a system of freedom of expression requires in order, not just to exist, but to flourish.

The crucial need is that the society act with vigor and imagination to give affirmative support to the system of freedom of expression. This is especially important in the very broadest areas of affirmative action—the maintenance of fundamental economic, political, and social conditions necessary for a system of freedom of expression to survive at all.[19]

As stated earlier in this article, it is the media conditions, not the actual journalistic process, with which government remedial action can appropriately and constitutionally deal. Editorial, publishing, and broadcasting decisions relating to what information shall be made public and how it shall be made public should not be the concern of government. The Fairness Doctrine rule of the Federal Communications Commission was established for sound historical and technological reasons. But if the reforms recommended below are made, i.e., if certain conditions are changed, that part of the Fairness Doctrine which enables government officials to tell broadcasters which public issues must be reported and what constitutes fairness in their reporting might well be dropped.

Here are my recommendations for government action:

(1) Elimination of newspaper-broadcasting station cross-ownership in the same city. The United States Court of Appeals for the District of Columbia was, of course, first to rule that "divestiture is required except in those cases where the evidence clearly discloses that cross-ownership is in the public interest." The court said that the Federal Communication Commission's "limiting divestiture to small markets of 'absolute monopoly' squanders the opportunity where divestiture might do the most good." The F.C.C.'s order, said the court, is "inconsistent with its long-standing policy that 'nothing can be more important than insuring that there is a free flow of information from as many divergent sources as possible.'"[20] Recently, the Supreme Court has held differently.[21]

(2) Limiting of the number of newspapers that one person or one corporation may own.

(3) Development of the Public Broadcasting Service into a "fourth network," a genuinely professional public affairs and entertainment radio and television network with funds derived wholly or in great part from a government-imposed and collected levy on the revenues of commercial radio and television stations and networks who are deriving great financial profit from this public resource, the airwaves. This network would be insulated from all government interference through the creation of a representative board of overseers to whom the network's management would be accountable. The overseers themselves would be accountable to the public at large, and would be required publicly to evaluate the performance of P.B.S. at regular intervals.

(4) Requiring commercial radio and television stations, for at least a defined (but possibly renewable) interim period, say, three years, to make free prime time regularly available to individuals and groups in the community for whatever messages they wish to deliver. The amount of public access time should be adequate to the needs of the community but not so great as to result in a severe loss of revenue to the station owners.

(5) Through tax subsidies, low-interest loans, technical help, and other devices, facilitating the entry of new voices in both the print and electronic media. The object here is not

only to diversify the ideas, views, and information reaching the public, but also to achieve what Emerson recommends in his book, the creation of "an open market with a new form of economic base," since the goal of a truly free and open system of freedom of expression "cannot be reached by mere enforcement of the antitrust laws. It will undoubtedly be necessary to go to the economic root of the problem. . . ."

(6) Re-examination, legislatively and/or judicially, of the Newspaper Preservation Act to determine whether Congress' waiver of certain parts of our antitrust law is constitutional. One of the effects of the Newspaper Preservation Act is to make it difficult, if not impossible, for a third newspaper to enter a city and compete for both advertising and readers where two existing papers have entered the now-sanctioned joint publishing arrangement.

(7) Strict enforcement of F.C.C. rules limiting the percentage of broadcasting company stock which banks may own. It is an open secret that the F.C.C. has routinely permitted violations of these rules.

(8) Legislative hearing to determine whether American journalists need and/or want due-process guarantees of protection in the performance of their duties: the investigating, writing, editing, and printing or broadcasting of public affairs reports. As matters stand, reporters and editors have little or no recourse when information they have gathered is dropped, re-shaped, or cut so deeply as to amount to mortal mutilation of the original truths in their stories, all on the orders of and under practices established by the owners and managers of the employing newspaper, broadcasting station, or network.

If the people have a right and a need to know the facts about the public affairs of their political society, then a communication system in which any person or institution can interfere with the information-gathering process and defeat the public interest must, it seems to me, be looked at for possible remedies.

Television reporter Daniel Schorr's experience with his employer, the Columbia Broadcasting System, is instructive here. Schorr came into possession of a secret House committee report on United States intelligence activities. When C.B.S. refused to make public this information, Schorr went to *The Village Voice* with it, whereupon C.B.S. suspended him from active duty. In a speech to the Individual Rights and Responsibilities section of the American Bar Association in August, 1976, Mr. Schorr said:

> If government should not control news, then no one should. The First Amendment says only that Congress shall make no law abridging the freedom of the press and speech. Perhaps it is time for an unofficial First Amendment that says no enterprise shall make rules abridging individual freedoms of speech and press.
>
> I am not suggesting that reporters have any right to decide what their employers will publish or broadcast. What I am talking about is the extent to which a journalist—part of a large news enterprise, subject to its disciplines when engaged in its process—still retains personal freedom of expression outside it. . . . A newspaper reporter who takes elsewhere a story that his editor has decided—perhaps for valid reasons—not to print may be severely disciplined, or even fired. That has happened.
>
> When did freedom of the press evolve into a franchise to be exercised through large enterprises?. . . I would suggest that the First Amendment is not only the news establishment's First Amendment, but it is every journalist's and every American's individual right and, what's more, individual responsibility.[22]

Admittedly this due-process recommendation for reporters and editors is a delicate matter. It reaches into the heart of the journalistic decision-making process. But I believe it is possible for both the journalistic profession and the government to collaborate in setting up due-process procedures by which editors and reporters can request and get public hearings, in which their peers will sit in judgment, when they feel their communications work in the public interest is being systematically vitiated by their superiors. Ideally the media should set this process up on their own, with the government brought in only if the media cannot or will not do the job. The government can be brought in appropriately with regard to broadcast journalists because of the licensure procedure and the government's obligation to insure the licensees' fulfilling of their public trust in the exploitation and operation of this public resource—the air waves.

None of this would invite or permit government officials to substitute their judgment for that of the owners and/or news officials of a newspaper or broadcasting station. It would simply establish another media condition conducive to a freer flow of public information. It would mandate greater public accountability by media owners to the people concerning their stewardship of the public trust reposed in them.

The National News Council is already beginning to accomplish some of this, but the Council can only request, not compel, a public statement of accountability from media owners and managers. Nor is the Council set up to serve as a forum for due-process hearings for individual reporters and editors who have grievances.

Were these eight recommendations put into effect, a number of things would happen. Commercial broacasters would, for the first time, be free from governmental regulation of program content; they would be subject only to the present laws and statutes relating to slander, obscenity, and libel.

The Public Broadcasting Service, adequately funded, would be able to recruit the best professional talent in public affairs journalism and make available to this talent the opportunity to use the broadcast medium imaginatively, freely, and conscientiously in the public interest.

The P.B.S. would be a yardstick by which the public could measure the news and public affairs performance of the commercial broadcasters. The public would have access to the kinds of public information which commercial broadcasters now either scant or ignore because it is offensive to powerful advertisers (e.g., the oil companies) and/or because the audience for documentary journalism is not large enough to offset the revenues that could otherwise be gained from the broadcasting, say, of a sports event, a soap opera, a police action drama, or a girlie situation comedy in that same time period.

There would still be among both newspaper and broadcasting station owners a profound conflict of interests. The media owners' function, A. J. Liebling once said, is "to inform the public," but their "role is to make money."[23] This conflict remains; but its serious public consequences would be greatly diminished if these remedies were applied.

It was the same Liebling who observed that "freedom of the press is guaranteed only to those who own one."[24] My first two recommendations would help to deconcentrate media ownership. My fifth recommendation would help to expand the ownership of the press. And over-all, the recommendations seek to enliven, diversify, and guarantee the free flow of public information in this self-governing society. That, it seems to me, is why the press was included in the protection afforded by the First Amendment.

Notes

1. McKeon, *Communication—Making Men of One Mind in Truth* in PROBLEMS OF COMMUNICATION IN A PLURALISTIC SOCIETY 1-21 (1956).

2. 408 U.S. 665, 721 (Douglas, J., dissenting).

3. THE COMPLETE MADISON 337 (1953).

4. Associated Press v. United States, 326 U.S. 1, 20 (1945) (footnote omitted).

5. Red Lion Broadcasting Co. v. FCC, 395 U.S. 367, 389–90 (1969).

6. Miami Herald Publishing Co., Inc. v. Tornillo, 418 U.S. 241, 258 (1974).

7. *Id.* at 260 (White, J., concurring).

8. McDonald, *The Media's Conflict of Interests,* THE CENTER MAGAZINE 15-35 (Nov./Dec. 1976).

9. The Washington Post (July 24, 1977).

10. M MINTZ & J. COHEN, AMERICA, INC. (1970).

11. *Id.* at 140.

12. *Disclosure of Corporate Ownership,* released in 1974 by the Senate Subcommittees on Intergovernmental Relations, and Budgetng, Management, and Expenditures.

13. See note 8 *supra.*

14. *The New York Times* (January 13, 1970).

15. T. EMERSON, THE SYSTEM OF FREEDOM OF EXPRESSION (1961).

16. *Id.* at 628.

17. *Id.* at 629.

18. *Id.* at 630.

19. *Id.*

20. National Citizens Committee for Broadcasting v. FCC, 2 MEDIA L. RPTR. 1405 (1977).

21. The Supreme Court has now ruled that, although "diversification of ownership" does further "statutory and constitutional policies," it is "unable to find anything in the Communications Act, the First Amendment or the Commission's past or present practices that would require the Commission to 'presume' that its diversification policy should be given controlling weight in all circumstances." FCC v. National Citizens Committee for Broadcasting, 98 S. Ct. 2096 (1978).

22. *Editor & Publisher* 19 (August 21, 1976).

23. A. LIEBLING, THE PRESS (1964).

24. *Id.* at 30.

Privacy of Information
By John H. F. Shattuck*

If you are looking for a revolution in the field of information privacy, I am afraid you are going to be disappointed. This is probably the first example in history in which there has been a counter-revolution before the revolution has begun. I will canvass this counter-revolution, but I only promise to finish with a few hopeful notes and see if there is something from the ashes that we can put together from this information privacy field.

I want to make two points; let me review them at the beginning. First, I will explore the question of why privacy of information is so important—why should we be fighting for it—why is it a central constitutional value even if it is not explicitly mentioned in the Constitution? I need only say that we are now five years from 1984, although in many respects it is already upon us, and all you have to do is look around you and engage in banking and crediting and job-seeking and various other functions that everyone has to do in the society and you will understand why privacy of information is so important.

In my second point, I will look at the major constitutional roadblock to the development of a strong information privacy right in the Fourth Amendment area. I will focus on the Fourth Amendment, confident that Alan Westin will touch upon the rights of privacy in the First, Fifth and Fourteenth Amendment areas as well.

What, then, is information privacy? I start from the premise that information is the principal commodity of power in our society. It was once fashionable to say that power comes from the barrel of a gun, but I think it is more realistic to say that power in a modern technological society comes out of a computer or a databank. It is no accident that many of the governmental power abuses that have been revealed in recent years—many of which go far back in our contemporary history—revolve around information practices. What, after all, was Watergate but an attempt to find out as much as possible in secret about the opposition—from wiretapping to enemies lists to political surveillance. So Alan Westin was right when over 10 years ago he hit upon the rather novel idea that privacy is the right to control information about one's self. Looked at in this way, privacy is stripped of its rather Victorian image and can be viewed as a question of solitude or the right to be let alone.

Privacy is a political and technological issue which cuts across all races and classes. The technology of record-keeping in our society today is so vast that no one escapes. As a result of the federal Privacy Act of 1974,[1] for example, we have learned that the federal government has more than eight thousand separate record systems filling an equivalent of ninety-two billion pages—all of them containing personal information (not statistical information or economic data, but personal information) about the citizens of the country. A simple listing of these systems fills three thousand one hundred pages of small type. Perhaps because of this, we no longer hear at the ACLU what we used to hear about the privacy issue: "If you haven't done anything wrong you have nothing to worry about."

* Executive Director, American Civil Liberties Union, Washington Office.

When people begin to see the scope of the record-keeping effort by the federal government alone, they realize that privacy is a central issue for them. This is even reflected in the public opinion polls, which are beginning to focus upon this issue.

In March of 1977, for example, the Harris poll showed for the first time that a majority of people polled—54% in a national sampling—believed that personal information is being kept in government files somewhere for unknown purposes which may damage them. Five years ago, in 1974, only 40% of the people believed that. While I don't think we should submit civil liberties to the public opinion pollers, I believe it is significant that privacy is beginning to percolate through the society as an issue that concerns everyone.

On the other hand, it should be emphasized that the evidence is overwhelming that information-control most affects those who are at the lower levels of the society. The non-conformists, the poor, minority groups—people who are not in positions of power—are those who are the most likely to be affected by information-gathering practices.

Consider, for example, an arrest record. Years ago, arrest records were kept primarily for the purpose of making sure that there were no secret arrests. These records were kept at the bottom of the police station house and they became dusty and disappeared in a short period of time and had no particular effect upon those who were arrested. But today, arrest records are a major commodity of information. They are circulated throughout the society for many purposes—for employment screening, for determining eligibility for all kinds of social benefits, as well as for law enforcement purposes. Consider, therefore, the impact of an arrest record on an urban black male, whom the President's Commission on Crime Control has demonstrated has a 90% statistical probability of being arrested sometime during the course of his life, as opposed to 60% for white urban males and only 47% for all males.

So if you are black and you live in the city, you are going to have an arrest record and you are going to be hurt by it when you look for a job. 55% of all states, 56% of all counties and 77% of all cities ask about arrest records in their civil service application forms. A study recently conducted in New York, demonstrates that 75% of employment agencies would not accept for referral an applicant who had an arrest record, even if there was no conviction.

Consider one other example of the impact of modern information practices on the people at the bottom of the social heap. Under the 1975 amendments to the federal Social Security Act, a welfare mother who wishes to receive child support payments must become an agent of the state in helping to track down a missing father and must turn over whatever information she has about the father to the Social Security authorities, who then can search all federal records for whatever information they can find about him. If they locate the father, then he has to provide support, all of which hardly help the financial situation of either of the parties.

From this overview of the importance of information privacy, let us look at the rather sorry state of the law in this area, at least the Fourth Amendment law. The traditional legal protections of information privacy are very few. As in most areas of rapid social change, the law has not kept pace with reality.

The most difficult roadblock is the fact that in our legal system the rights of property are very deeply imbedded and have a great deal to say about constitutional rights, particularly in the Fourth Amendment area. This, in turn, impacts heavily on information privacy. To understand why, we have to look at the roots of the Fourth Amendment.

If you look at the case of *Entick v. Carrington,*[2] which was decided 10 years before the outbreak of the American revolution and is the case on which Fourth Amendment principles were built, you find that a broad search, conducted by officers of the Crown for political literature in England, was invalidated on the grounds of an intrusion into the houses of the people who were being searched, rather than the nature of the information that was being seized. In the words of the Court, as Lord Camden put it, "Papers are the owner's goods and chattels. They are his dearest property and are so far from enduring a seizure that they will hardly bear an inspection and although the eye cannot, by the laws of England, be guilty of a trespass, yet where private papers are removed and carried away, the secret nature of those goods will be an aggravation of the trespass."

This decision, in other words, is cast in terms of an invasion, an intrusion, a trespassory action which ends up in the seizure of papers, and the result, of course, is the Fourth Amendment as we know it, which protects a person's house, papers and effects.

Now to be sure, the view of privacy as a property right has protected many aspects of the rights of privacy in the two centuries since *Entick v. Carrington,* but it has not been very helpful in protecting the right of information privacy.

Today, we don't keep most of our personal records within the four walls of our houses. The bulk of private records and personal information is maintained at distant points by faceless entities over whom we have very little control. Indeed, the concept of records, or papers as physical objects is really not of any particular concern to us in the development of information privacy. Instead, we are concerned only about the information contained in a record, regardless of its physical form. Whether it is pencilled notes or images on a microfilm or electronic notations on a computer tape or intangible microwaves in the air, it is the information we are concerned about, not the form in which it is contained.

This information describes us, defines us, chronicles our lives, but is it really our property? That is the question. Certainly it is not in the traditional sense since it is customary for those institutions which maintain the records to claim that the information belongs to them and that any rights in the information should be exercised by them.

Now it is true that the courts do not today always interpret the Fourth Amendment in property terms. There is another strain of Fourth Amendment law. Over the last 12 years, the courts have been attempting to define "reasonable expectation of privacy" as a formula for determining the constitutional boundaries of a person's right to be free from intrusion. This line of reasoning began with the *Katz*[3] decision in 1967 which held, for the first time, that wiretapping not involving a physical trespass was in fact an invasion of some constitutionally protected area. But the reasonable expectation of privacy formula has been extremely slippery for us. It has been hard to apply in the area of information privacy. There is a catch in the *Katz* case — how do we know in what circumstances we may justifiably rely on an assumption of privacy?

Justice Harlan in that case thought that there should be two criteria — an actual expectation of privacy and an expectation that society is prepared to accept as reasonable. The problem with this formula is that when a person reveals information about himself to others, the courts will often find that his privacy rights are waived or that he implicitly consented to the turning over of this information. This is exactly what has happened in the area of informants or undercover agent activities. When they have been challenged as Fourth Amendment violations based on intrusion, it is assumed that the person with whom the informant was dealing was in fact implicitly consenting to the turning over of any information that he may have given to the informant.

The same thing is true with respect to information in records. Bank records illustrate the problem. People generally trust that when they write a check or deposit money in their accounts that such transactions are confidential. That trust supposedly lies at the heart of the banking institution, but the myth of the banker as the discrete, closed-mouth keeper of financial confidence is just that — a myth.

It is generally the practice for governments to obtain bank records without subpoena, without any process, but simply on the cooperation and willingness of banks to turn over these records.

What do the courts say about that? There are two conflicting lines of interpretation. The first one—and I am afraid the dominant one, because it is the Supreme Court speaking —has focused on constitutional challenges to the federal Bank Secrecy Act of 1970. The Bank Secrecy Act requires banks to make and preserve copies of almost every check and other banking records that they process and to report to the Treasury Department transactions over $10,000.00. This means that the government records anything that might be reflected in those transactions—the bank records and all of the receipts of the transaction. According to the legislative history of this statute, the premise of these requirements is that bank records "have a high degree of usefulness in crime, in criminal, tax and regulatory investigations and proceedings." This is undoubtedly true, but I question whether that should automatically lead to the turning over of all banking records to the government. Both the number of records to be kept and the length of time they are to be preserved under the Bank Secrecy Act far exceeds the normal business practices of most banks.

In 1972, an unholy alliance of the ACLU and the California Bankers' Association went to court and challenged this statute on Fourth Amendment grounds. A three-judge federal district court agreed with the plaintiffs in part and struck down the reporting provisions of the statute as a violation of the Fourth Amendment rights of the bank customers and held for the first time, that bank customers have a reasonable expectation of privacy when they turn over information about themselves through their bank records to the banks.

Two years later, the Supreme Court had contrary thoughts about this and reversed.[4] In a six to three decision, the Court held that the challenge to the reporting requirement was premature because the information obtained from the records had not actually been used against the plaintiffs in the case. But this door, which we thought was open, was soon closed. In a decision in 1976, *United States v. Miller*,[5] which is the high point to date of the counter-revolution in information privacy, the Supreme Court again ruled on the rights of bank customers under the Bank Secrecy Act. This time the question was whether a customer could challenge, on Fourth Amendment grounds, a subpoena from the IRS to a bank for records to be used in a criminal proceeding.

In a seven to two decision the Court held in *Miller* that when a customer goes to a bank, he knowingly and voluntarily discloses certain information about himself and takes the risk that the bank will disclose it to the government or to other people. According to the Court, the bank customer has no legitimate expectation of privacy for two independent reasons. First, the bank records belong to the bank, and second, the customer voluntarily discloses the information about himself.

A contrary view of this problem was reached in 1974 by the California Supreme Court in a decision which gives us, I think, a more acceptable sense of where the information privacy issue should be going. The case, *Burrows v. Superior Court*,[6] involved the constitutionality of the seizure of a criminal suspect's bank records without a subpoena or any other search warrant, but simply upon "request"—the prevalent practice when bank information is sought by goverment investigators. The California court invalidated this practice as a violation of the suspect's privacy on independent California constitutional grounds, so those from California can rest assured that at least they can enjoy some degree of information privacy.

Although the California decision is overshadowed by *Miller*, it demonstrates a judicial understanding of this issue which is necessary if the right of information privacy is to grow. Let me briefly quote from the opinion to indicate that the California court perceived that the property interest resides in the bank customer, rather than the bank. The court said:

> For all practical purposes, the disclosure by individuals or business firms of their financial affairs to a bank is not entirely volitional since it is impossible to participate in

the economic life of contemporary society without maintaining a bank account. In the course of such dealings, a depositor reveals many aspects of his personal affairs, opinions, habits, and associations. Indeed, the totality of bank records provides a virtual current biography. . . . Development of photocopying machines, electronic computers and other sophisticated instruments have accelerated the ability of government to intrude into areas which a person normally chooses to exclude from prying eyes and inquisitive minds. Consequently judicial interpretations of the reach of the constitutional protection of individual privacy must keep pace with the perils created by these new devices.[7]

In short, there is a ray of hope in that opinion, as far as the development of a right of information privacy is concerned.

Let me conclude by outlining what I believe the elements of that right should be.

Although the governmental access issue is only a part of the overall subject of information privacy, it is the most important part because it goes to the heart of the new technologies of information control that I was thinking about earlier. In searching for a solution to the problems created by *Miller* and traditional Fourth Amendment law, three obvious principles come to mind.

First, the record subject's right of privacy should be established by law and no government access to private records should be permitted except by the uncoerced consent of the subject or by formal legal process, enforceable by a court. In this way, the interests of the record subject, rather than the record keeper, would become central. Such a principle would recognize the record subject's own interest in the information, a property interest if you will, and his reasonable expectation of privacy in the records. No longer would a telephone call from the local police or the flashing of a badge or an FBI letterhead to the record maintainer be sufficient to open the records to the investigator.

A second principle which I would like to see in legislative form, if it's not going to be recognized by the courts, is that the use of legal process would require notification to the record subject — to the person whose real interests are at stake — and a delay in the delivery of records to the government sufficient to permit a challenge — either a court challenge or a decision not to challenge, but at least an opportunity to decide whether there are interests to be protected.

A third principle is that the obligation of prior notice to the record subject should be overcome only by a demonstration of evidence sufficient to obtain a search warrant. This should include a showing that the records would be destroyed if the record subject were informed or that the person would flee if notified before the search.

Let me close by attempting to put these obvious but important principles into perspective and again mention why I think it's important that we begin the modest revolution that this field may be able to have if the California Supreme Court approach is adopted.

There is a mystique about the use of record searches in the law enforcement community — and after all, that is really what we are talking about here. Somehow the "paper trail" is regarded as more important — more incriminating — than the physical evidence that was generally thought to be the proper area of Fourth Amendment protection. In fact, there is such a mystique about records and the desire of the police to obtain them that the old-fashioned rules have been thought not to apply.

But in constitutional terms, the same old-fashioned issues arise in this field — the illegality of the kind of general search at issue 200 years ago in the *Entick* case, and the judgment of a neutral magistrate that a limited search is justified but not a general fishing expedition. While there has been much talk about the need for broad search powers to combat organized crime and white-collar crime, the traditional protections of the Fourth Amendment should not be an impediment to effective law enforcement — they certainly are not in other areas and there is no reason to believe that they should be in this new area of information control.

The impact of these Fourth Amendment protections should be greatest not in the area of law enforcement (where probable cause can be shown that a crime has been committed and that there is evidence in the records that are going to be obtained), but rather in the gathering of political intelligence and in all of the abuses of the record process that we know about through the Watergate period and on into today. It is important to realize that in articulating information privacy interests, we are not engaged in an attempt to cut back effective law enforcement. To the contrary, we are seeking to eliminate other improper purposes which can so easily be involved in the searching of personal records.

Notes

1. 5 U.S.C. §552a (Supp., Feb. 1975).
2. 19 Howell's State Trials 1029 (1765).
3. *Katz v. United States,* 389 U.S. 347 (1967).
4. *California Bankers Assn. v. Shultz,* 416 U.S. 21 (1974).
5. *United States v. Miller,* 425 U.S. 435 (1976).
6. *Burrows v. Superior Court,* 13 Cal. 3d 238, 529 P.2d 590, 118 Cal. Rptr. 166 (1974).
7. *Id.,* 13 Cal. 3d at 247–48, 529 P.2d at 596, 118 Cal. Rptr. at 172.

The Personal and Political Dimensions of Privacy
By Alan F. Westin*

Let us go back to the beginning and examine the politics of privacy, taking a deeper look at what privacy means in this society. In so doing, I want to reconsider what the functions of privacy are or should be, given the kind of society we are. Hopefully, this may tell us about our options — political options — in advancing the right to privacy.

First, there is what is called informational privacy. That is what I was referring to in 1966[1] when I said that, in one sense at least, the claim to privacy is the claim of an individual or group to determine what information about himself or herself, or the organization should be revealed to others and under what conditions. How much? At what time? With what bargains and constraints on the revelation and the use? That, then, deals with the flow of information outward from people and organizations, including the government.

Next, there is the other facet of a comprehensive right of privacy dealing with autonomy, or what personal actions an individual can engage in as individual decisions free from the intrusion of governmental control — though, obviously, there will always be social mores and social pressures and other kinds of forces acting upon the individual making that decision. If you marry privacy of information and personal autonomy, you have a pretty good understanding of what the claim to privacy is intended to cover.

In one sense, privacy — just as all rights in the American Constitution — can be viewed as an instrumental rather than an ultimate or final right. That is, we claim free speech or freedom of religion in order to serve larger values, such as the pursuit of truth, whether it is truth in the social order, or truth in a courtroom contest over whether somebody is guilty of a crime or not. In that sense, privacy is a particularly instrumental claim in a free society in two senses.

First of all, the claim to privacy relates to a constantly shifting balance within each of our individual psychic orders. At some time, you want to be completely alone, out of the sight and surveillance of every other person. You need solitude. It is only in the act of solitude that you can reflect on something or capture some idea. But nobody could live that kind of life all the time. So every person at other times needs to be in the company of an intimate. They need somebody with whom they can share very private parts of themselves. Their husband or wife or drinking companion or parent or other trusted person (a confidential advisor, a lawyer or priest, etc.) is someone to whom they can disclose aspects of themselves without fear of its being used against them in harmful ways, or put into some kind of record system that they will have to confront later.

There are other times when we want to be in the company of larger numbers of people — at a ball game or sitting in a bar or on a plane or train — and to reveal things about ourselves. We disclose things about our personal situations or thoughts, essentially because we are talking to strangers who do not continue in our life and will also not exercise control

*Professor of Political Science, Columbia University.

over us. These people with whom we share our thoughts are passersby in our lives. Communication with them permits us to let off steam, and to be part of the social crowd in various ways.

Finally, there are times when we act under various conventions of reserve. Here, we reveal certain things under the clear understanding that there are rules of the game as to what is revealed and how it will be used. Those settings are still other aspects of privacy.

If you think about the psychodynamics of the individual, then, you realize that nobody could live a life of pure privacy. Nor could anyone live a life of total immersion in the social whirlpool. We are constantly shifting our desires for privacy, depending on the hour of the day or the week, and our changing personal and interpersonal developments.

Likewise, at the level of the social order, privacy is closely related to the shifting balance between the public and the private sectors, as well as to what is considered legitimate social activity. It is related to legitimacy because the person who occupies a legitimate status in the society is not, as a broad general matter, fearful about the publication of facts about their basic condition or status, since publication of those facts will not produce judgments that deny the individual rights, benefits, or opportunities. But if you are a homosexual, you may fear that information about that condition will bar employment, block obtaining a license, or prevent you from renting an apartment.

Or, if you are a woman on welfare who has sex with a man, you may be worried whether a welfare worker is going to report you as having had a man in the house, since that might affect your entitlement to continued aid for dependent children. The claim to privacy in such situations is an effort by people whose life styles or conditions are not considered legitimate to withhold information to authorities about those matters. The claim to privacy is a shield for groups while they fight to win from the larger society an acceptance and legitimacy that would then allow that activity to be publicly known.

Political systems obviously set the general balances of privacy within which their individual and group claims are asserted. Totalitarian societies dismiss privacy as a bourgeois claim — a rejection of the communal order. Any withholding of assent, or claim of private action or belief, is something subversive of state morality. The idea of ideas unexpressed, or loyalties partially held, of activities that are not to be within the ken of the guardians of the state, defies the notion of a total, good society and has been assailed from Plato's time to the modern totalitarian state.

On the other hand, democratic societies start out with a commitment to protect individuals and groups against unlimited disclosure and surveillance powers by the state or other social authorities. The democratic society assigns a vital role to privacy in the development of individual and associational contributions to the total society, including criticism of and dissent from prevailing government programs and social mores. Privacy is essential for the organizing of alternatives to state action, or of alternatives to prevailing notions of wisdom in the good society.

Accordingly, a democratic society sets a liberal or libertarian balance among three values — the claim to individual and group privacy; the need for public disclosure or freedom of information, to reveal who is doing what and why in the society's power centers; and the need for social order.

Given the realities of living in a complex, highly technological, all too terror-ridden state, there are always legitimate needs of surveillance to protect individuals and property in society. Therefore, properly limited information-collection and surveillance by constituted authority is a legitimate general principle in a democratic state. Just as the individual needs to balance changing states of privacy in managing a sound individual life, so at the political level, society needs to balance privacy, disclosure, and surveillance in order to manage a democratic system.

With this background, let's turn to the legal dimensions of privacy. The word privacy, of course, does not appear in the American Constitution or in the Bill of Rights. Throughout most of our constitutional history, while great clauses like the Commerce Clause were being litigated, privacy was mentioned in the Supreme Court decisions or in major constitutional discussions only as a desired purpose of such relatively narrow constitutional clauses as the fourth amendment's guarantee of reasonable searches and seizures and the fifth amendment's protection against compulsory self-incrimination. It is only within the past decade that we have begun to establish an independent constitutional law of privacy in both the informational-privacy and in personal-autonomy aspects.

The United States Supreme Court, in my view, has done very badly in the last decade in responding to the need of developing a new conception of informational-privacy.[1] It has failed to perceive the new dimensions of the organizational and technological society of which we are now a part, and it has been insensitive to the role of formal records and data-processing systems in reshaping our open society into a credential and gate-keeper oriented organizational arrangement.[2]

On the whole, the Court has done much better in the personal autonomy area. However, recent decisions in the abortion[3] and obscenity[4] areas, along with the unwillingness of the Court to deal with some of the issues in areas like homosexuality[5] or sodomy[6] statutes suggest that the Court still is unwilling to reach some of the clear doctrinal adjudications that are needed in the personal autonomy realm as well.

Basically, the Court, for reasons that puzzle me, has simply not seemed to grasp the nature of our times in terms of the issues of informational privacy. Despite all the lessons to be learned from Watergate and all the writing that scholars have done to explain why privacy is so important in a high-technology society, there has been little understanding inside the United States Supreme Court as to the real nature of these issues and how to use judicial authority to protect them—Justices Douglas and Brennan excepted.

Since those of us who feel this way have been as persuasive as we could be and have not yet persuaded the Supreme Court, perhaps the verdict has to be that one ought probably to write this Supreme Court off, for the time being, in terms of developing the kind of forward doctrinal movement on informational privacy that I think we need here. That does not suggest that we go into the monastery and achieve more solitude, but that we should recognize that when one arena of governmental innovation is closed to you, you simply turn your attention to the other arenas of innovation.

Thus for the next decade, short of a turnabout in the United States Supreme Court's thinking, it is in two other arenas that our political action in behalf of a sound balance on privacy issues ought to be focused. One is in the area of organizational policy, such as organizational management decisions; the second is in the legislative area. Since Mr. Shattuck's paper has already addressed some of the things that we might want to do in the legislative area,[7] let me start with organizational action, with managers and their decisions, where I believe we have considerable opportunity.

I am talking essentially about educating the people who are managing the new information functions of our society—corporation executives; heads of executive agencies and governments at the federal, state, and local levels; and managers of various non-profit organizations such as universities, religious organizations, unions, etc. Let me note that I believe it is in the self-interest of those managers, in advancing their organizational goals, responding to the wishes of these employees, clients, and beneficiaries, and promoting public approval of their behavior, that they develop new privacy policies, not because I believe such managers have become unique keepers of the constitutional flame in the country.

Why do I assume it is in their interests to be innovators here? Largely because American society in the last decade has created the kind of new concepts about rights of individuals that makes it exceedingly risky for such organizational managers to keep to their old ways.

For example, the informational privacy issue, in one dimension, is a question of social allocations in society. What are the standards that will be used to make judgments about who gets access to the rights, benefits, and opportunities of our society? Who will have opportunities to get credit or welfare, or good jobs and promotions, and all the other things that are now controlled by various organizational information collectors and record maintainers?

Twenty years ago, the answers were fairly clear. It didn't help much if you were black rather than white. It didn't help if you were female and not male. It didn't help if you had ever been arrested for various kinds of offenses, especially political offenses. It certainly was no help to you if you dressed differently or cut your hair differently or if your sexual activity was not within the accepted norms. A set of sharp disqualifications had been built into the machinery of judgment about people.

In part, the claims to privacy and the claims to equality are closely connected here. But there is a difference. In some areas, we fight for equality because we know that people are inescapably visible in some aspect of their lives. If they are black and their skin color is anything other than pink, then they are not going to escape being perceived as being black. Women are noticeably different than men for the most part and therefore, if you are a woman, you are seen as a woman.

In these instances, it is the equality claim that we push when we say that you may not ask whether a person is black or a woman in order to make credential judgments. Since these conditions are visible, American law says it will police how organizations record and use facts about race, sex, etc. to insure that judgments do not discriminate.

Other aspects of personal identity are not immediately visible—your political affiliations, your personality and ideological characteristics, your sexual preferences. They have to be the subject of investigation or compulsory disclosure, either by checking normally confidential records, asking neighbors, and other kinds of inquiries. It is here that the privacy claim is the primary one. Employers, insurers, and credit-grantors, for example, can be convinced that they ought not to collect information to enforce judgments that are not acceptable in privacy terms.

Consider one example of what I am referring to. It has been traditional for many life insurance companies, whenever a larger than usual life insurance policy is involved, to investigate the sexual activity of the individual as part of its "life-style" check. They have done this largely because actuarial studies—which, of course, point backward—suggest that homosexuals have earlier mortality rates and higher suicide rates than heterosexuals. Since taking prudent risks and making profits are what insurance companies are all about, they investigate sexual activity in order to see whether somebody is a homosexual and, therefore, a bad risk.

In the area of race, we decided as a society to socialize risk. We do not allow insurance companies to make judgments on the basis of what may be statistically provable, e.g., earlier mortality rates and higher crime rates in areas that are disproportionately black in central cities. We simply say you cannot use that as a factor in making individual decisions in insurance.

We have a similar right to socialize privacy risks in insurance. We should say to insurance companies, by public protest or by legislation if needed, that if everybody has to pay a few dollars more on a $100,000, or $1 million policy, in order that nobody's sex life gets investigated to separate the homosexuals from the heterosexuals, that is the privacy interest of the society. No longer will a business motive be allowed to justify that kind of investigation and decision-making based on a non-visible characteristic of an individual.

Thus, I start with the conviction that there are many areas in which an informed press, and an informed consumer and civil liberties movement, and an interested public can persuade managers of many of the gate-keeper organizations in our society to come up with new policies and new ways of handling information that leave people's autonomy alone, and will not require the United States Supreme Court to issue any new constitutional decisions at all.

However, such organizational actions may require the credible threat of legislation, and perhaps the enactment of some minimum-standards legislation. Exemplary new privacy policies by organizations like Bank of America, IBM, and others have often been to anticipate public or employee concerns and to forestall sweeping legislation. Managers of these leading-edge organizations would much rather innovate by themselves than have another federal or state regulatory agency or detailed and costly legislation.

What kind of legislation do we need to keep private and public organizational leaders moving ahead to assure privacy rights? First, we need an instrument for inquiry, publicity, and recommendation at the federal level. The Privacy Act of 1974[8] was a great step forward in defining fair information practices and providing various rights of individual challenges and access but it did not create either a permanent monitoring agency or an enforcement agency. The Privacy Protection Study Commission that the Act created is now out of business. While I do not favor creating a comprehensive licensing board of the Swedish or West German variety, I think we need a continuing force for investigation, publication, exposure, recommendation of legislation, and other kinds of momentum-creating activities. The absence of that is a serious flaw in the present federal Privacy Act structure.

As we know, nine states have passed similar fair information practices laws at the state level, covering state government agencies. That approach is useful and very important, and needs to be extended to all the states. Alongside it, however, must be efforts to enact minimum-standards legislation in specific areas such as medical records and health data, criminal justice information systems, personnel records, banking and customer records, insurance, and a few others. Here we ought to write pinpointed statutes, using a fine-tuned approach to problems in the private sector that will not be well treated by omnibus-type laws. Since I treat privacy as a subtle and shifting value, I believe it is difficult and even self-defeating to try to write general codes that are not anchored in the bargains we engage in when we give information to our doctor, employer, insurer, or bank. In each case, there are different expectations about privacy, different levels of revelation, different assumptions by us (and society) about how the information should be used, and different types of fiduciary relations. Legislation at its best should try to recognize the essential nature of those bargains about disclosure and confidentiality, and police the boundaries within which they are given.

To sum up, we have become an organizationally dominated, records-based, and technologically driven society, in which people's individuality and status is very difficult to protect with a few words in a constitution or even by judicial interpretation of a right to privacy. It calls for specific, detailed, area-sensitive kinds of interventions, responsive, of course, to broad public notions of fair procedure and standards. Legislation and regulation tend to be more fitting instruments than judicial decisions, despite our tendency to seek a judicial thunderbolt that will resolve it all and put everything in place. In fact, despite the bad assumptions of the rulings, the Justices may not be entirely wrong when they say, for example, as they did in the *Miller* case,[9] that Congress can lay out the privacy rights that need protection in the banking area, and other legislation (federal or state) can deal with the criminal justice, personnel, medical, and other areas. It may be fitting, for the kind of majoritarian society that we are, that the Court says to us, "we are not going to make this a matter of constitutional absolutes." If through the legislative process society wants to create a legally enforceable expectation of confidentiality in bank accounts or medical records, or to give right of access to information in criminal justice systems, we should pass a law.

If I felt that the American public was growing hostile to the new claims to privacy, I would feel more worried than I do. But, as all the recent public opinion polls document, the public cares strongly about privacy, is still worried about intrusions by government and business, and wants more protections. Privacy is thus a rather good growth stock in our American constitutional system. What else is there that can unite the John Birch Society and the Wall Street Journal on the one hand and the *Nation* and the ACLU on the other—or put the American Bankers Association and the ACLU on the same side of test case litigation and legislative efforts? Concern over privacy unites all those who treasure difference and autonomy in our society, and is a cause that can be successfully advanced through the legislative and lobbying processes. It is in that area that I think we will be doing most of our work in the future.

Notes

1. Westin, *Science, Privacy, and Freedom: Issues and Proposals for the 1970's,* 66 COLUM. L. REV. 1003, 1205, 1210–12 (1966).

2. *See* United States v. Miller, 425 U.S. 435 (1976); California Bankers Ass'n v. Shultz, 416 U.S. 21 (1974).

3. *See* Bellotti v. Baird, 428 U.S. 132 (1976); Planned Parenthood of Cent. Mo. v. Danforth, 428 U.S. 52 (1976); Doe v. Bolton, 410 U.S. 179 (1973); Roe v. Wade, 410 U.S. 113 (1973).

4. *See* Young v. American Mini Theatres, 427 U.S. 50 (1976); Miller v. California, 413 U.S. 15 (1973). *See also* Huffman v. Pursue, 420 U.S. 592 (1975).

5. *See, e.g.,* Gaylord v. Tacoma School Dist. No. 10, 88 Wash. 2d 286, 559 P.2d 1340, *cert. denied,* 98 S. Ct. 234 (1977); Acanfora v. Board of Educ., 359 F. Supp. 843 (D. Md. 1973), *aff'd,* 491 F.2d 498 (4th Cir.), *cert. denied,* 419 U.S. 836 (1974); McConnell v. Anderson, 316 F. Supp. 809 (D. Minn. 1970), *rev'd,* 451 F.2d 193 (8th Cir. 1971), *cert. denied,* 405 U.S. 1046 (1972). *But see* Gay Lib v. University of Mo., 416 F. Supp. 1350 (W.D. Mo. 1976), *rev'd,* 558 F.2d 848, *petition for cert. filed sub nom.* Ratchford v. Gay Lib, 98 S. Ct. 1276 (Sept. 20, 1977) (No. 77–447) (the Justices have requested respondent Gay Lib, to file a reply to appellant's petition for certiorari, which suggests that the case may not be disposed of summarily).

6. *See, e.g.,* Lovisi v. Slayton, 539 F.2d 349 (4th Cir.), *cert. denied sub nom.* Lovisi v. Zahradnick, 429 U.S. 977 (1976); Doe v. Commonwealth's Attorney, 403 F. Supp. 1199 (E.D. Va. 1975), *aff'd mem.* 425 U.S. 901 (1976); Buchanan v. Batchelor, 308 F. Supp. 729 (N.D. Tex. 1970), *vacated on other grounds sub nom.* Wade v. Buchanan, 401 U.S. 989 (1971); Arizona v. Bateman, 113 Ariz. 107, 547 P.2d 6 (1976), *cert. denied,* 429 U.S. 864 (1977), Washington v. Rhinehart, 70 Wash. 2d 649, 424 P.2d 906, *cert. denied,* 389 U.S. 832 (1967).

7. *See* Shattuck, *Privacy of Information, supra.*

8. Privacy Act of 1974, Pub. L. No. 93–579, 88 Stat. 1896.

9. United States v. Miller, 425 U.S. 435 (1976).

The Exclusionary Rule—A Relic of the Past?

By James L. Oakes*

There exists an important need to reflect upon the increasingly maligned exclusionary rule. The rule operates to exclude from evidence the fruits of law officers' unconstitutional or illegal conduct. As legal doctrines go, the exclusionary rule is a relative newcomer. It has been around for just 63 years.[1] It has been the subject of controversy since it was six.[2] In a series of relatively recent Supreme Court decisions its scope has been limited. Its conceptual basis has been attacked,[3] later modified,[4] and now replaced.[5] In Ronald Dworkin's terminology,[6] its character has been changed from a "secondary" rule of constitutional law consisting of a personal right and a concomitant governmental obligation, to a "primary" rule of evidence, if not merely a "principle," governing the judiciary's supervisory power to "deter" some police officers sometimes. One might question whether it is any longer worth discussing at constitutional law symposia.

I think it is. I choose to examine the exclusionary rule because it is embattled and because its defenders are few. I would defend today against its abolition or abandonment. One may think of Don Quixote and his windmills, but for me it is somewhat like rooting for the team that's behind 16–0 with less than a minute to play; there are those who will remember Harvard's tying Yale in that impossible situation. More importantly, the recent analyses of the exclusionary rule raise, but leave unanswered, fundamental questions pertaining to the nature of government and particularly to our form of government, or at least to the role of government in law. For the purposes of this occasion, I paint with a broad brush a picture of the rule as it was and the rule as it is, and then examine some of those questions I call fundamental.

Thomas Schrock and Robert Welsh have perceptively written[7] that the exclusionary rule commenced as a constitutional requirement. Explicated by Mr. Justice Day for a unanimous court in 1914 in *Weeks v. United States*,[8] a Court that included Justices White, McKenna, Holmes, Hughes, Lamar and Pitney, the exclusionary rule represented a personal right of a criminal defendant. Simply put, a criminal defendant was entitled to prevent his government in the form of the judicial branch from utilizing evidence to help convict him where that evidence had been obtained by an unconstitutional search or seizure. Said Justice Day, "There was involved in the order refusing the application [for suppression of the illegally seized evidence] a denial of the *constitutional rights of the accused*. . . . In holding [the evidence] and permitting [its] use upon the trial, we think prejudicial error was committed."[9]

Correlative with this personal right of the accused, according to the unanimous Court in *Weeks*, was a duty—not just of the searching or prosecuting executive branch but a duty of all government, including the criminal-trial-conducting judicial branch:

> The effect of the Fourth Amendment is to put the courts of the United States and Federal officials, in the exercise of their power and authority, under limitation and restraints as to the exercise of such power and authority, and to forever secure the people, their

*Judge, United States Court of Appeals, Second Circuit. Many of these thoughts were taken from a May 1977 commencement address to Tulane Law School. Since that address was not published I feel at liberty to draw upon it.

persons, houses, papers and effects against all unreasonable searches and seizures under the guise of law. This protection reaches all alike, whether accused of crime or not, and the duty of giving to it force and effect is *obligatory upon all entrusted under our Federal system with the enforcement of the laws.*[10]

Thus, the governmental duty aspect of the *Weeks* vision rests on two interrelated and dependent concepts. First, all branches of the Government are treated as one unit. For purposes of the exclusionary rule, there is no concept of separate branches of government. Second, unitary government has a duty in relation to its citizens. That duty does not permit separation of the means, the search or the seizure, from the ends, the subsequent use of the evidence seized by the search at the trial. The governmental duty makes not only the Fourth but the Fifth and Sixth Amendments meaningful in the sense that the judiciary avoids validating or sanctioning unconstitutional conduct by closing its eyes. This personal-rights, governmental-duty theory underlies the exclusionary rule as set forth in *Weeks*. There is not a mention in *Weeks* of deterrence of police misconduct, the weak reed that the rule is now said to rest upon.

The *Weeks* conceptual basis is further explicated by Mr. Justice Holmes for the Court in *Silverthorne Lumber Co. v. United States*,[11] again excluding illegally seized evidence and its fruits. Not a mention does Holmes make of deterrence. So, too, in the rhetorically moving Brandeis and Holmes dissents in *Olmstead*.[12] The Government is a whole; its agents, the courts, cannot ignore the illegal acts of its other agents, the police, without investing those acts with the authority and sanction of Government. In the eyes of Justice Brandeis, illegally seized evidence that is not suppressed ratifies the past illegal act and in the eyes of Justice Holmes, it implicates the Government in the practice of illegal seizure. This same view is, of course, the one subsequently developed for the California Supreme Court by Chief Justice Traynor in *People v. Cahan*,[13] perhaps the most well written of the state court decisions.

Any ensuing deterrence effect is merely a side result, which may or may not occur. It is not the underlying basis of the exclusionary rule, as the rule was conceived and promulgated. Intellectually candid debate over the exclusionary rule must therefore take into account Justices Day, Holmes, and Brandeis and their concept of personal constitutional right and corresponding governmental duty; they cannot be brushed to one side.[14]

But now we are told by the Supreme Court that this original concept is wrong. The exclusionary rule is not "a personal constitutional right of the party aggrieved."[15] It is not a constitutional right at all.[16] Rather, "it is a judicially created remedy designed to safeguard Fourth Amendment rights generally through its deterrent effect."[17] And as one would expect, the correlative of this judicial remedy characterization is the fragmentation of the unitary government concept. Thus, the courts are viewed as separate from the executive branch, their function as "neutral truth seekers" being merely to assure a fair trial.[18] Under this view, the police who illegally violate a person's privacy are treated for evidentiary purposes as if they were acting discretely, on their own; meanwhile, the courts are concerned only that the defendant's trial be "fair," so that in certain instances—perhaps all—the courts may admit illegally obtained evidence.

What are those instances? If deterrence is the basis for the rule then obviously the evidence comes in if deterrence may not be accomplished. This is the import of Mr. Justice Blackmun's opinion in *United States v. Janis*,[19] holding that evidence illegally obtained by state officials (and hence perhaps excludable in state proceedings) may nevertheless be used in a federal proceeding. At the very least the illegally obtained evidence may be admitted when the marginal increment in deterrence is outweighed by the social cost of suppressing relevant evidence,[20] as in grand jury proceedings,[21] and possibly in federal habeas corpus from a state court conviction.[22] The Chief Justice would have us "balance" the "reliability" of the evidence sought to be suppressed, "the irrelevancy of the constitutional claim to the criminal defendant's factual guilt or innocence, and the . . . deterrent effect . . . on police misconduct."[23] On this basis he would justify, at least in a habeas corpus context, admission of incriminating statements made in violation of the Sixth Amendment, and presumably admission of evidence obtained in violation of the Fourth Amendment. Indeed, it is "absurd," "bizarre," "remarkable," "intolerable," the Chief Justice says, for the majority of the Court to hold otherwise.[24]

Thus we have two entirely different models of the exclusionary rule: the early model, that the rule reflects an obligation of a unitary government enforceable in the courts as a personal constitutional right of the accused; and the present model, that the rule's deterrent impact is to be balanced by the courts, utilitarian-style, in the sanitized context of a trial against the social cost of suppressing relevant evidence.

Let us scrutinize the arguments of those who would deconstitutionalize the exclusionary rule. Professor, now Dean, Dallin Oaks (no relation to the author) as the leading nonjudicial proponent of today's model, notes a measure of inconsistency between the governmental-obligation notion and the doctrine of *Frisbie v. Collins*[25] and *Ker v. Illinois*.[26] These two cases, one decided in 1952, the other in 1886, permit a person to be tried even though brought before the court by illegal means such as by kidnapping, arrest without probable cause or arrest upon an illegal or insufficient warrant.[27] *Ker* and *Frisbie* are inconsistent with the Brandeis-Holmes *Olmstead* dissents, the argument runs; thus governmental obligation or at least governmental integrity cannot be a precedential basis for the exclusionary rule. Moreover, as Chief Justice Burger himself pointed out in 1964, "we may have come the full circle from the place where Brandeis stood . . . a vast number of people are losing respect for law and the administration of justice because they think that the Suppression Doctrine is *defeating* justice."[28]

Are *Ker* and *Frisbie* really sound? Is the exclusionary rule, or, as the Chief Justice prefers, the Suppression Doctrine, in fact "defeating justice"? Do the public demands for law and order in the streets necessitate the abandonment of the rule? What of the "truth"? And, irrespective of these arguments, where do we go from here?

First as to *Ker* and *Frisbie*. We note that the Court went out of its way in 1975 to reaffirm them.[29] Perhaps this was due to a series of widely-commented-upon cases in the Second Circuit,[30] involving governmental kidnaping of drug dealers in South America and in one case alleged participation in torture, in which cases *Ker* and *Frisbie* were under severe attack, as they had been from the commentators. *Ker* and *Frisbie* were shown themselves to be inconsistent with the due process notions of, among other cases, *Rochin v. California*;[31] in the process, Brandeis' *Olmstead* dissent was evoked,[32] despite the "full circle" alluded to by the Chief Justice in 1964.

Moreover, in 1975 America was, as it still is, wrestling with the Watergate revelations—revelations not just of government playing dirty tricks, but of government engaging in illegal surveillance,[33] exercising, to say the least, questionable political pressures and carrying out other unlawful, unconstitutional, and outrageous conduct. This post-Watergate ambiance, therefore, could have further psychologically impaired the continuing vitality of *Ker* and *Frisbie*. But *Ker* and *Frisbie* were reaffirmed, unnecessarily and unwisely in my opinion.

Yet, even though as reaffirmed these cases may support a precedential argument against the exclusionary rule, they are hardly pillars of judicial strength. In a day when all civilized nations are opposing not only the politics but the tactics of terrorism, including kidnaping and torture, can our courts condone government's engaging in these tactics even for the purpose of bringing serious crime defendants to trial? Does the end always justify the means?

I suggest that *Ker* and *Frisbie*, rather than being bedrocks of the law, at most set forth, to borrow Dworkin's terminology, only "principles" reflecting a view of "due process," and in a context that can be modified, as in the South American drug-dealer cases, to cast grave doubt on their continued wisdom.

Is the exclusionary rule really *"defeating* justice"? A poll would clearly say, "It is outrageous (if not 'bizarre') that illegally obtained evidence cannot be admitted to convict the guilty." This is a substantive objection to the exclusionary rule, irrespective of whether the Fourth, Fifth or Sixth Amendments create individual rights, stemming from a gut feeling of indignation at a guilty person going "free" for a particularly ugly crime. There is, after all, that crime out there—there is another Kitty Genovese being murdered. But one answer to this substantive argument is fairly simple and need not implicate in our limited time the complex question of what causes crime. How many people actually do go *free* because of the exclusionary rule? I suspect very few. After all, not only must law officers engage in unconstitutional or illegal conduct, but in addition the suspect must plead not guilty and have a lawyer competent enough to raise the exclusionary rule issue. Next, the factfinder must conclude that the police conduct was illegal and not consented to. And finally, a court must find both that the suspect has standing to raise the question and that the rule is applicable to the facts at hand. Even in those few cases when the exclusionary rule is applied, and it usually is not, the rule seldom need affect the judgment. If there is other— untainted—evidence, convictions may still be obtained.

I do not think that it can be experientially proven that more than a very few out of 1,000 cases in our criminal courts are affected by the exclusionary rule to the point of acquittal. True, the cases that get to the rarefied atmosphere of the courts of appeals and the even rarer atmosphere of the Supreme Court often involve conviction or acquittal, because for the most part we get only close cases where there has been a conviction on the basis principally or wholly of illegally obtained evidence—the cases where it is worth making the exculsionary rule argument. In our court last year, I would be surprised if ten cases resulted in new trials because of the exclusionary rule; maybe two or three resulted in acquittal.[34] Usually the best the appellant can do is to obtain a new trial. And most of these cases can be explained in terms of sloppy police work—the failure to concentrate police effort on scientific gathering of evidence. Decent ordinary police work will generally do the job.

At least the burden of proof is on the opponents of the exclusionary rule to show that because of the "constable's blunders" any considerable per cent of guilty people go free. I suggest that the substantive effects of the exclusionary rule are minimal at most and in a well-run police force they should be virtually nonexistent.

Another reason that I find the contention that the exclusionary rule "defeats" justice unpersuasive is that the rights of criminals today often become the rights of citizens tomorrow; the rules of evidence and due process which today are interpreted to protect society and not to safeguard defendants' rights can be used tomorrow by an arbitrary government against any citizen. Therefore, far from defeating justice, the exclusionary rule advances it, insofar as it ultimately protects all citizens from governmental impingement on their personal freedoms.

If *Ker* and *Frisbie* provide weak precedential support for exclusionary rule antagonists, and if the rule does not "defeat" justice to any appreciable degree, what about Chief Justice Burger's concern with appearances? He has reminded us[35] that the "public will be outraged" at courts it already thinks are soft-hearted, perhaps soft-headed. One answer is simply that judges do not, or should not have to, run for office. The substance of the Constitution, not public feeling, is what the business of judging is all about. The popularity of a constitutional rule is not the measure of its rightness. To be sure, the Supreme Court is said to follow the election returns and the returns of 1968 and 1972 might be thought to have promoted a return to "law and order," in reaction to the supposed "permissiveness" of the Warren Court. But would anyone seriously suggest that election returns are a reliable guide for constitutional interpretation? The day that this country abandons substance for style in its judicial branch, as it has from time to time in its legislative or executive branches, and permits popular passions to direct the outcome of constitutional decisionmaking, is the day that the death knell of our democracy will sound.

Well, what, then, of "truth"? This piece has suggested that substantively abolition of the exclusionary rule would do little for law and order and that "style" of the judiciary is to be virtually disregarded in a genuine democracy. Is, then, the underlying rationale of *Weeks* and Justices Day, Holmes and Brandeis ultimately to prevail? What of the opposing titans — the Chief Justice's "truth" — yes, Cardozo's and Wigmore's view that in the end the purpose of the law of evidence is the search for "truth." The great Dean Wigmore opposed the artificiality of a number of the rules of evidence — those against the admission of hearsay, illegally obtained evidence, remote evidence that interferes with the search for truth — and he has influenced, and influenced persuasively, I daresay, everyone in the legal profession and not least your speaker. We have abandoned many silly artificialities. But are we to throw out the baby of human rights with the bathwater of technicalities?

Blind devotion to Wigmore's views carries its own illogic. I yield to no one in the search for truth, but as Diogenes asked, what is truth? If truth is what the State says it is, is the State always correct? If a state is untrammeled by rules of evidence, its agents can plant evidence; plant the idea of and effectuate the execution of crime; burst down doors of a house in the night and seize anything in or out of sight; obtain admissions from a defendant in the absence of his lawyer; extract confessions by hook, crook or force. Despite the fact that all this evidence would be admissible in the name of "truth," what is to differentiate that state from a police state?

An accommodation between the often competing values of truth and human rights may be necessary. I would suggest that the exclusionary rule usually strikes an appropriate balance; it restrains the truth-creating tendency of a state's law enforcement apparatus and at the same time permits the police to gather evidence which is generally adequate to convict the guilty. The rule strikes this balance and thereby nurtures personal freedoms without unduly hindering the criminal justice process. The exclusionary rule is not unlike many rules of evidence which limit the search for truth in the recognition of stronger social policies.[36]

Mr. Weeks, Mrs. Mapp, Mr. Wade and Mr. Simmons, yes, Messrs. Entick and Carrington, may not have been very savory characters — and I suspect James Otis and Sam Adams were not either — at least in the Crown's eyes. But the search for "truth" is not the sole end of law in a society that recognizes human rights.

Denigration of the exclusionary rule in the name of "truth" raises a false hope because actually attaining "truth" may prove to be elusive. Let someone tell me after the fact from an appellate judge's chair when an accused is *truly* "guilty" or "innocent"; I want to know only whether he has been convicted or acquitted properly under our rules of law and if those rules have sound reason and history behind them and apply to our present and future society and to the case. If the Fourth Amendment is bothersome because it obstructs the search for truth, what of the Sixth, or the Fifth? Shall we repeal them by judicial fiat? The argument from "truth" against the exclusionary rule states too much.

Where do we go from here? I am not sure. At the end of its 1976 term the Supreme Court decided a curious case which it was careful to point out did not involve the exclusionary rule. In *United States v. Chadwick*,[37] the Chief Justice for the Court, with only Justices Blackmun and Rehnquist dissenting, held that the Fourth Amendment Warrant Clause was not limited just to private dwellings and a few other "high privacy" areas and that it did not, absent "exigency," permit the search of a double-locked footlocker seized contemporaneously with the defendant's arrest even though there was probable cause to suspect that the footlocker contained contraband.[38] The decision as such is not that remarkable; indeed, one might have thought it compelled by the precedents.[39] What is curious is a footnote which states that, because the question was limited to whether a search warrant is required, "this case presents no issue of the application of the exclusionary rule."[40] Yet the district court had suppressed the marijuana found in the footlocker, a decision which had been affirmed by the First Circuit. The illegally obtained evidence was thus excluded. The "application" of the exclusionary rule may not have been involved but the "operation" of the exclusionary rule was. The exclusionary rule, then, even in the Fourth Amendment context, is not yet a relic of the past. It is not in the Sixth Amendment context.[41] It is not in the Fifth.[42]

But its application has been limited, some would say dangerously so. I have attempted to show that this has occurred in the context of rising crime rates and public "demand" as expressed at the polls for "law and order" and to show how the underlying conceptual basis of the rule has been changed to meet its new limited application.

What will occur if Congress extends *Bivens* liability to the officers who conduct the illegal activity? Suppose Congress makes the government liable instead of the police or federal employees individually, as Attorney General Bell has suggested, in the context of certain suits against the CIA and FBI.[43] Suppose that the defense of "good faith" is no longer available to the the government, that a minimal amount of damages must be awarded, that a truly satisfactory (and "deterrent") piece of legislation could be devised to permit civil responsibility toward the injured citizen.[44] Would that warrant abandonment of the exclusionary rule?

Any answer to this may depend, I suggest, on one's approach to the *Olmstead* vs. *Ker-Frisbie*, governmental integrity question. It may depend on whether one prefers to rest individual protections in statutes as opposed to constitutions. It may depend on one's view of the sturdiness or fragility of our internal institutions in terms of resisting malevolent governmental intrusions. In the meanwhile, at least, I believe that the exclusionary rule still serves a beneficent purpose and perhaps does not serve it with all of the evil consequences its critics suggest.[45]

Notes

1. *Weeks v. United States*, 232 U.S. 383 (1914).
2. Wigmore, *Using Evidence Obtained by Illegal Search and Seizure*, 8 A.B.A.J. 479 (1922).
3. *E.g.*, *People v. Defore*, 242 N.Y. 13, 150 N.E. 585 (1926); Oaks, *Studying the Exclusionary Rule in Search and Seizure*, 37 U. CHI. L. REV. 665 (1970).
4. *See Linkletter v. Walker*, 381 U.S. 618, 636–37 (1965).
5. *See, e.g.*, *Stone v. Powell*, 428 U.S. 465 (1976); *United States v. Calandra*, 414 U.S. 338 (1974).
6. R. DWORKIN, TAKING RIGHTS SERIOUSLY (1977), ch. 1 *passim*.
7. Schrock & Welsh, *Up from Calandra: The Exclusionary Rule as a Constitutional Requirement*, 59 MINN. L. REV. 251 (1974).
8. 232 U.S. 383.
9. *Id.* at 398 (emphasis added).
10. *Id.* at 391–92 (emphasis added).

11. 251 U.S. 385, 392 (1920).

12. *Olmstead v. United States*, 277 U.S. 438 (1928).

13. 44 Cal. 2d 434, 445, 282 P. 2d 905, 912 (1955).

14. For valuable analyses of the exclusionary rule, see Amsterdam, *Perspectives on the Fourth Amendment*, 58 MINN. L. REV. 349, 432 (1974); Dellinger, *Of Rights and Remedies: The Constitution as a Sword*, 85 HARV. L. REV. 1532, 1553 (1972); Schrock & Welsh, *supra* note 7. Professor Amsterdam is quoted in, *e.g.*, *Stone v. Powell*, 428 U.S. at 487 n.25, for his earlier statement in *Search, Seizure and Section 2255: A Comment*, 112 U. PA. L. REV. 378, 388–89 (1964), that the rule may inflict "gratuitous harm on the public interest. . . ." But as Amsterdam develops in his *Perspectives*, 58 MINN. L. REV. 349, the exclusionary sanction "is a necessary evil because the supposed alternatives to it are pie in the sky," *id.* at 429, and "[i]t is the linchpin of a functioning system of criminal law administration that produces incentives to violate the fourth amendment." *Id.* at 432.

15. *United States v. Calandra*, 414 U.S. 338, 348 (1974); *see Stone v. Powell*, 428 U.S. 464, 486 (1976).

16. *United States v. Calandra*, 414 U.S. 338, 348.

17. *Id.*

18. Wigmore, *supra* note 2; *see* Schrock & Welsh, *supra* note 7, at 255 & n.16.

19. 428 U.S. 433 (1976).

20. *Id.* at 453–54; *United States v. Calandra*, 414 U.S. 338, 351.

21. *United States v. Calandra*, 414 U.S. 338, 351.

22. *See United States v. Janis*, 428 U.S. at 493.

23. *Brewer v. Williams*, 430 U.S. 387, 415, 427 (Burger, C.J., dissenting).

24. *Id* at 415, 416, 417, 428.

25. 342 U.S. 519 (1952).

26. 119 U.S. 436 (1886).

27. Oaks, *supra* note 3, at 669. *Frisbie* was also cited with approval in Justice Powell's opinion in *Stone v. Powell*, 428 U.S. 465 (1976).

28. Burger, *Who Will Watch the Watchman?*, 14 AM. U. L. REV. 1, 22 (1964).

29. *Gerstein v. Pugh*, 420 U.S. 103, 119 (1975).

30. *United States v. Lira*, 515 F.2d 68 (2d Cir. 1975); *United States ex rel. Lujan v. Gengler*, 510 F.2d 62 (2d Cir. 1975); *United States v. Toscanino*, 500 F.2d 267, 271 (2d Cir. 1974); *see, e.g.*, Note, *The Greening of a Poisonous Tree: The Exclusionary Rule and Federal Jurisdiction over Foreign Suspects Abducted by Government Agents*, 50 N.Y.U.L. REV. 681 (1975).

31. 342 U.S. 165 (1952); *see United States v. Russell*, 411 U.S. 423, 431–32 (1973) (dictum); *Mapp v. Ohio*, 367 U.S. 643 (1961).

32. 500 F.2d at 274; *see* 515 F.2d at 72 (Oakes, J., concurring). The concurring opinion in *Lira* also refers to *Harris v. United States*, 331 U.S. 145, 172–73 (1947) (Frankfurter, J., dissenting), and *United States v. Kirschenblatt*, 16 F.2d 202, 203 (2d Cir. 1926) (L. Hand, J.). The Frankfurter and Hand opinions are doctrinally similar to and accord with the Brandeis and Holmes dissents in *Olmstead*.

33. *See United States v. United States District Court*, 407 U.S. 297 (1972); *United States v. Giordano*, 416 U.S. 505 (1974).

34. *United States v. Karathanos*, 531 F.2d 26 (2d Cir.), *cert. denied*, 428 U.S. 910 (1976); *see generally* Note, *Formalism, Legal Realism, and Constitutionally Protected Privacy Under the Fourth and Fifth Amendments*, 90 HARV. L. REV. 945, 983 & n.235 (1977), for the proposition that "neither deterrence nor direct societal cost are empirically demonstrable results of exclusion." *Id.*

35. *Brewer v. Williams*, 430 U.S. 387, 415 (Burger, C.J., dissenting).

36. *E.g.*, Fed. R. Evid. 407 which precludes introduction of subsequent remedial measures to prove negligence in order to encourage safety. Fed. R. Evid. 403, Advisory Committee note.

37. 433 U.S. 1 (1977).

38. *Id.* at 7–15.

39. *See Mapp v. Ohio*, 367 U.S. 643, 649 (1961).

40. 433 U.S. 1, 7 n.3 (1977).

41. *Brewer v. Williams*, 430 U.S. 387 (1977).

42. *See Michigan v. Tucker*, 417 U.S. 433, 447 (1974).

43. N.Y. Times, Sept. 3, 1977, at 30, col. 1.

44. Professor Amsterdam has argued persuasively that suggested alternatives to the exclusionary rule such as damage suits, criminal prosecutions or administrative hearings, are "pie in the sky." Amsterdam, *Perspectives on the Fourth Amendment*, 58 MINN. L. REV. 349, 429 (1974). Cf. ALI Model Code of Pre-Arraignment Procedure § 150.3 Commentary (Proposed Draft, April 15, 1975) (retaining exclusionary rule for "substantial violations" of code or for exclusions constitutionally required) [hereinafter ALI Model Code]. The burden, it seems to me, is upon those who would abolish or even limit the exclusionary rule to establish that they have an effective, workable

alternative which maintains both the constitutional sanctity of the individual Amendments invoked and preserves governmental integrity in respect of the means used and of the ends sought by our criminal justice system.

45. This essay is directed against the outright abandonment of the exclusionary rule and perforce does not deal with middle-ground limitations upon it. One proposed limitation is to lift federally imposed standards on state courts by overruling *Mapp v. Ohio*, 367 U.S. 643 (1961); *see* Miles, *The Ailing Fourth Amendment: A Suggested Cure*, 63 A.B.A.J. 364 (1977). Application of the rule in federal habeas corpus from state court convictions has of course already been limited by *Stone v. Powell*, 428 U.S. 465 (1976). A third middle-ground approach would confine the impact of the rule to cases of gross police misconduct. *Cf. Rizzo v. Goode*, 423 U.S. 362, 371, 379 (1976) (no injunction against police misconduct absent a plan or policy on the part of department officials authorizing misconduct); *Younger v. Harris*, 401 U.S. 37, 53, (1971) (no injunction against state criminal proceedings absent "bad faith" and "harassment"). While the time and space allotment for this piece does not permit dealing with the many objections that can be made to each of these or any other middle-ground proposals, some obvious points can be made. In response to the overruling of *Mapp*, I would suggest that there is a greater likelihood of police misconduct in the states where, in many cases, the police receive low salaries and poor training. If the gross abuse limitation were adopted as to *constitutional* violations, the Fourth and perhaps the Fifth and Sixth Amendments would in effect be constitutionally redundant in light of the due process clause. The "shock-the-conscience" test of *Rochin v. California*, 342 U.S. 165, 172 (1952), however well conceived as a last resort for the protection of rights when no more explicit refuge exists, is still subject to the objections voiced so well by Mr. Justice Black dissenting in *Adamson v. California*, 332 U.S. 46, 68–123 (1947): that, if all the safeguards of the Bill of Rights are to be read merely in terms of due process limitations, constitutional protection is ad hoc, episodic, nebulous and accordion-like. This objection incidentally applies in an entirely different way to the federalism argument above which seeks the overruling of *Mapp*.

I do not speak to the ALI proposal, note 44 *supra*, since as I read it, it *preserves* the exclusionary rule in the case of constitutional violations and in a highly sophisticated way proposes its use in the case of "substantial" code violations. *See* ALI Model Code, *supra* note 44, at 404 & n.39. Of course, if the constitutional test were to be the substantiality test proposed by the ALI, we would be dealing with a different proposition.

Federal Sentencing Reform:
The Emerging Constitutional Issues
By Gerald F. Uelmen*

During the past decade, the need for basic reform of the federal sentencing process has been convincingly demonstrated. The unbridled discretion placed in the hands of sentencing judges has resulted in unacceptable disparities in the punishment meted out to similar offenders for similar crimes.[1] The Federal Criminal Code presented to in Congress[2] proposes a dramatic change in sentencing to meet this need, by narrowing the range of choices available to the sentencing judge, and creating explicit factual guidelines to control those choices, subject to appellate review. This approach is strikingly similar to the Uniform Determinate Sentencing Act adopted in California.[3] The California Act confronts a judge who is sentencing a defendant to prison with three choices: a middle term, a lesser term when circumstances of mitigation are shown, and a greater term when circumstances of aggravation are shown.[4] A similar process is envisioned by the federal proposal, although the choices will be expressed in "ranges." The judge will be expected to sentence within a "range" established for the applicable category of offense and the applicable category of defendant. If that range is exceeded, the judge must articulate the reasons, and the defendant can challenge that decision on appeal. If the judge falls short of the range, reasons must again be offered, and the prosecutor can appeal. The "ranges" are to be established by a specially created "Sentencing Commission," based upon aggravating and mitigating circumstances.[5] An example of what the Sentencing Commission is expected to formulate was offered by Senator Edward M. Kennedy, a principal co-sponsor of the proposal. He suggested four ranges might be formulated for the crime of burglary:[6]

> 1. When committed when the home is occupied and when the defendant brandishes a weapon in the presence of the occupants; 2.8 years to 3.5 years;
> 2. When committed while the occupants were at home but when the defendant, although armed with a weapon, did not brandish it; 1.5 years to 2 years;
> 3. When committed in an occupied dwelling by a defendant armed with a weapon; 6 months to 1.2 years;
> 4. When committed in an unoccupied dwelling by an unarmed defendant, 3 months to one year.[7]

While these reforms may correct the most serious disparities in sentences, they inject procedural changes into the sentencing process which raise substantial issues of constitutional magnitude. If the sentencing judge is required to make new factual findings to justify the sentence a whole panoply of procedural rights within the rubric of "due process" may apply, including the right to standards which are not "vague," adequate notice, confronta-

* Professor of Law, Loyola Law School of Los Angeles; J.D., 1965; LL.M., 1966, Georgetown University Law Center. The author wishes to acknowledge the editorial assistance of Allan Ides, Loyola Law School '79, in the preparation of this article.

tion and cross examination of witnesses, proof beyond a reasonable doubt, a jury trial, explicit findings for appellate review, and the right to exclude unlawfully obtained evidence. The magnitude of the impact such changes could have upon the criminal justice system is rather stark; while only 15 percent of federal defendants now avail themselves of all of the procedural rights of a trial,[8] all convicted defendants are ultimately subjected to the sentencing process, including the 85 percent who plead guilty. If the full panoply of due process rights is injected into every sentencing, we face the possibility of a vast multiplication of the commitment of judicial resources to what is now a rather routine and expeditious process.

As the law has evolved thus far, two basic models of the sentencing process have emerged. The traditional model, which we can label the "discretion" model, allows a sentencing judge untrammelled access to information relevant to the sentence. *Williams v. New York*,[9] in which the U.S. Supreme Court upheld imposition of a death penalty on the basis of information contained in a presentence report, offers the rationale for the "discretion" model: "Modern concepts individualizing punishment have made it all the more necessary that a sentencing judge not be denied an opportunity to obtain pertinent information by a requirement of rigid adherence to restrictive rules of evidence properly applicable to the trial."[10] The Court did *not* hold that the sentencing process is immune from due process scrutiny, however, noting that the defendant was represented by counsel, and was not deprived of an opportunity to present evidence.[11] Only the rights to reasonable notice of the charges and an opportunity to examine adverse witnesses were explicitly rejected.

The second model, which we will call the "enhancement" model, finds its paradigm in *Specht v. Patterson*.[12] There the Court confronted a proceeding whereby a defendant convicted of indecent liberties, carrying a maximum sentence of ten years, could be found to be a "threat of bodily harm to the public" or a "habitual offender" and given an indeterminate sentence of one day to life.[13] The finding was made on the basis of a psychiatric report submitted to the Court. Noting that the finding defendant was a public threat or habitual offender was a new finding of fact that was not an ingredient of the offense charged, the Court concluded the situation was "radically different" from *Williams v. New York*. This difference entitled the defendant to the "full panoply of the relevant protections which due process guarantees in state criminal proceedings,"[14] including "that he be present with counsel, have an opportunity to be heard, be confronted with witnesses against him, have the right to cross-examine, and to offer evidence of his own. And there must be findings adequate to make meaningful any appeal that is allowed."[15] The absence of a right to proof beyond a reasonable doubt and a jury trial from this catalogue may simply be explained by noting that the cases holding these rights to be incorporated within "due process" had not yet been decided.[16]

The essential difference between the "discretion" model and the "enhancement" model is the existence of an explicit factual predicate for punishment which was not an essential element of the underlying crime. But these two models are not mutually exclusive; it would be more accurate to characterize them as representing opposite ends of a spectrum. "Due Process" is no longer the "all or none" proposition suggested in *Specht v. Patterson*. As stated by the Court more recently in *Morrissey v. Brewer*:[17]

> Once it is determined that due process applies, the question remains what process is due. It has been said so often by this Court and others as not to require citation of authority that due process is flexible and calls for such procedural protections as the particular situation demands.

The purpose of this paper will be to review the major procedural protections encompassed within "due process," and consider their applicability to the sentencing procedures envisoned in the federal proposal. We will find that these procedures do not always fit comfortably into *either* the "discretion" or the "enhancement" models. But in seeking the answer to "what process is due," the ambiguous terrain we tread is not untrod. At least two other legislative devices raise a similar galaxy of issues.

First, we have the death penalty statutes enacted in response to the holding in *Furman v. Georgia*[18] that a discretionary death penalty violates the eighth amendment proscription of "cruel and unusual punishment." These statutes require the finding of specified "aggravating circumstances" to justify the imposition of a penalty of death. This separate factual finding may take these provisions outside the realm of *Williams v. New York*. Yet the "enhancement" model of *Specht v. Patterson* might be distinguished, since the "aggravating circumstances" frequently bear a close relationship to the underlying crime. Significantly, each of the death penalty statutes subsequently upheld by the Supreme Court[19] provided an explicit list of aggravating circumstances,[20] an opportunity to confront and cross-examine adverse witnesses,[21] the right to present evidence on one's own behalf,[22] proof beyond a reasonable doubt to a jury,[23] and explicit factual findings which were subject to appellate review.[24] In the one state where the judge was vested with discretion to disregard the jury's recommendation and impose a death penalty, the Court, in *Gardner v. Florida*,[25] held that a presentence investigation report relied upon by the sentencing judge in such circumstances must be disclosed in its entirety to defense counsel, thus limiting its prior holding in *Williams v. New York* to non-capital cases.

A second parallel is the "Dangerous Special Offender" sentencing provisions presented in the Organized Crime Control Act of 1970[26] and the Comprehensive Drug Abuse Prevention and Control Act of 1970.[27] Both provide a defendant convicted of a felony may receive a sentence in excess of the normal maximum, up to a maximum of twenty-five years, upon a finding he is a "dangerous special offender." Special Offenders are defined to include those with two prior convictions, those who committed the offense "as part of a pattern of conduct" which constituted a substantial source of income, and those who participated in a supervisory capacity in a conspiracy of three or more.[28] The statute specifically provides that a notice of the prosecutor's intent to rely upon the Dangerous Special Offender provisions be filed prior to trial, and that the defendant has a right to counsel, compulsory process, cross-examination, specific factual findings and appellate review of the determination a defendant is a Dangerous Special Offender.[29] The statute does, however, permit reliance upon hearsay in presentence reports, limited non-disclosure of such reports, and provides that the burden of proof is merely a preponderance of the evidence, to be determined by a judge sitting without a jury.[30] This middle position was justified by the draftsmen as follows:

> The requirements of Specht v. Patterson . . . are inapplicable, since no separate charge triggered by an independent offense is at issue. Only circumstances of aggravation of the offense for which the conviction was obtained are before the court.[31]

This carefully constructed compromise has been abandoned in the proposed Federal Criminal Code, however. Rather than triggering a special evidentiary hearing, the same circumstances will be included in the sentencing "guidelines" as a basis for "a substantial sentence of imprisonment."[32]

As we review the procedural rights in the due process panoply, it will be enlightening to compare the judicial treatment of these two legislative parallels.

I. DEFINING AGGRAVATING CIRCUMSTANCES: THE PROBLEM OF VAGUENESS

The task of defining the "ranges" of punishment under the proposed Federal Criminal Code will be delegated to a specially created "Sentencing Commission."[33] The task of drafting reasonably detailed and explicit standards is a formidable one, perhaps best done by an administrative body. The Commission will have two years to complete this task, since it will be created immediately upon enactment of the bill, while other provisions will take effect twenty-four months after enactment.[34]

The constitutional issues raised by the formulation of these standards are serious ones. The right to explicit definitions which are not vague is an essential of due process of law. Two rationales support this doctrine of "vagueness": the lack of fair notice to potential defendants,[35] and the danger of discriminatory application where the law is vague.[36] While both rationales apply with greater force to the definition of the crime itself than the definition of the punishment, one cannot simply dismiss the vagueness doctrine as inapplicable to sentencing enhancement provisions. This much is now abundantly clear from the Supreme Court opinions considering the constitutionality of statutes defining the "aggravating circumstances" under which the death penalty may be imposed. The precision with which those circumstances were defined was of central concern to the Court. In *Gregg v. Georgia*,[37] for example, the Court carefully examined each of ten categories of aggravating circumstances in the Georgia statute in terms of vagueness or overbreadth. The Court noted with approval that the Georgia Supreme Court, in *Arnold v. State*,[38] had already declared one statutory ground for capital punishment was unconstitutionally vague, and had narrowly construed other grounds.

The conclusion that the vagueness doctrine applies to sentence enhancement provisions does not, of course, mean that it applies with the same force as the doctrine is applied to definition of crime. The doctrine has always been applied with varying strictness, depending upon the context. The strictest application has always been reserved for cases where first amendment liberties were at stake.[39] Similarly, a higher standard of strictness is recognized where the statute defines the availability of capital punishment.[40] At the other end of the spectrum are cases suggesting "greater leeway" with respect to "regulatory statutes governing business activities."[41] This variable standard is consistent with the Supreme Court's interpretation of the standards of procedural due process.

The first step in applying the constitutional test of "vagueness" to definitions of aggravating circumstances is to ascertain the *extent* of aggravation permitted. The extent of aggravation should not, however, be measured in purely quantitative terms: the real issue is one of proportion. For example, the aggravation of a one year sentence to a two year sentence under Senator Kennedy's burglary example permits a 100% increase in the punishment being meted out; at the other end of the spectrum, adding one year to a six year sentence is an increase of less than 17%. The subtlety of this distinction was not lost on the draftsmen of the Dangerous Special Offender provisions contained in current federal law. The increased sentence permitted upon a finding that the defendant is a dangerous special offender is limited to a term "not disproportionate in severity to the maximum term otherwise authorized by law."[42] Apparently, this limitation was intended as an end-run around *Specht v. Patterson*, in the belief *Specht* only applies where a separate charge triggered by an independent offense is at issue. The proportionality limitation was designed to insure that the increased sentence did not represent a penalty for a different crime. At least one court was persuaded by this argument,[43] although it contradicts rather specific language in *Specht*:

> The Sex Offenders Act does not make the commission of a specified crime the basis for sentencing. It makes one conviction the basis for commencing another proceeding under another act to determine whether a person constitutes a threat of bodily harm to the public, or is an habitual offender and mentally ill. This is a new finding of fact that was not an ingredient of the offense charged.[44]

A persuasive argument can be made that, even if *Specht* is limited to a "separate offense," whether the aggravating circumstance states a separate offense should be determined by a comparison of that circumstance and the nature of the offense, rather than looking to the extent of aggravation permitted. Using this standard, it is clear that many of the "aggravating circumstances" specified in the Dangerous Special Offender provisions *do* state a "separate offense," at least to the same extent the Colorado Sex Offender Act did. A sentence can be aggravated if the defendant has engaged in a "pattern of conduct," if he has two or more prior convictions, or if he participated in a conspiracy with three or more other persons.[45] Similarly, the new federal proposal will utilize "separate offenses" to aggravate if Senator Kennedy's burglary example is utilized as the model. The harshest penalty is reserved for a defendant who "brandishes a weapon in the presence of the occupants." This conduct can add from .8 to 1.5 years to the sentence.[46] The same conduct, however, is defined in the Code as the separate crime of "Menacing,"[47] a Class A Misdemeanor punishable by up to one year imprisonment.[48]

The test of proportionality remains a more significant part of the equation, however. Whether the aggravating circumstance is characterized as a "separate offense" or not can quickly engage us in a label game. The real focus of our inquiry should be what's at stake for the defendant. If the example offered by Senator Kennedy is a sample of the guidelines to be promulgated by the Federal Sentencing Commission, the stakes may be rather high: proof of aggravating circumstances could mean the difference between a sentence of 3 months or 3.5 years.

The second step in our "vagueness" analysis should be to ascertain the extent of "free play" in the definition of aggravating circumstances, to insure that prosecutors and judges are held to ascertainable standards in utilizing them. When we confront an aggravating circumstance which is so broad and amorphous it could be plausibly utilized against *any* defendant, we face the very danger that the vagueness doctrine is designed to prevent: the prosecutor can pick and choose the defendants against whom the provision will be utilized virtually at whim.

This danger appears to be greatest when attempting to define aggravating circumstances relating to the defendant's personal background. The Sentencing Commission is directed, for example, to establish categories of defendants based upon their "mental and emotional condition," "community ties," and "degree of dependence upon criminal activity for a livelihood."[49]

II. Giving Notice to the Defendants of Aggravating Circumstances To be Invoked

The proposed Federal Criminal Code provides for a determination by the sentencing judge of what sentencing range is "applicable," but affords no notice to the defendant of what factual basis for a particular range is being considered.[50] Thus, a defendant facing sentencing will have no advance notice that circumstances in aggravation will be asserted, much less be informed what particular circumstances will be relied upon.

The absence of notice in these provisions stands in sharp contrast to the state death penalty procedures upheld by the Supreme Court, which require the "aggravating circumstances" be alleged before trial,[51] and the Dangerous Special Offender statutes, requiring a notice be filed by the prosecuting attorney a reasonable time before trial "setting out with particularity the reasons why such attorney believes the defendant to be a dangerous special offender."[52] The requirement of particularity has been strictly construed by the Courts applying this statute.[53]

Three rationales can be offered in support of a requirement of advance notice of "aggravating circumstances." First, a defendant cannot voluntarily, knowingly and intelligently enter a plea to the underlying charge unless he is fully aware of the consequences.[54] While it might be argued that the imposition of the maximum or "aggravated" sentence is a possible consequence for every defendant, this argument overlooks the realities of the decision to enter a plea. A defendant may be aware of the "aggravating circumstances" specified by

Sentencing Commission guidelines, and enter a plea of guilty fully confident that these circumstances do not apply and that the middle sentence or range is applicable, only to learn at the time of sentencing that the judge is considering an aggravated sentence.

Secondly, the notice provides a basis for judicial review of the decision to invoke the aggravation procedure.[55] If the prosecutor is required to specify the grounds for aggravation to be invoked and the facts which will be relied upon to prove those grounds, a lengthy hearing might be avoided by allowing the judge to determine, in advance, that even if the facts are proven, the aggravated term would not be justified.

Finally, the notice serves a vital apprisal function, to enable a defendant to prepare a defense for the hearing on the applicability of aggravating circumstances.[56] It is unrealistic to expect a defendant to respond to every possible aggravating circumstance that might be asserted, especially where a veritable catalogue of possibilities is presented.

The first rationale really raises an issue as to the validity of a plea, rather than the validity of the sentence. If a defendant who entered a plea of guilty were to receive an aggravated sentence without notice, the appropriate remedy would be to vacate the conviction and permit withdrawal of the plea, rather than mere invalidation of the sentence.[57] The second rationale is concededly non-constitutional. While the avoidance of unnecessary hearings is a laudable legislative goal, it is not compelled by the Constitution.[58] The insufficiency of a factual basis can be reviewed on appeal following a full hearing. It is the last rationale, the apprisal function, that gives rise to the most serious constitutional objections to the lack of requirements for advance notice in the federal proposal.

Clearly, counsel is given an adversarial role to play. Rule 32 of the Federal Rules of Criminal Procedure requires the court to afford counsel an opportunity to comment on the presentence report and to speak on behalf of the defendant. The prosecutor must be given an equivalent opportunity to speak.[59] To expect counsel to perform this role in the absence of any advance specification of aggravating circumstances is not only unrealistic, it is basically unfair.

It might be argued that counsel's role will not be very different from that under the conventional "discretion" model, where counsel frequently discovers only at the time of sentencing that the judge is considering imposing the maximum senence based on some unanticipated antipathy to the circumstances of the crime. But the whole object of the federal reform proposal is to formalize and rationalize this exercise of judicial discretion. The opportunity to challenge the sentence on appeal has little meaning if one has no meaningful opportunity to challenge factual findings at the time they are made. And a meaningful challenge at the sentencing hearing demands advance notice and an opportunity to prepare.

It might also be suggested that the disclosure of the presentence report in advance of sentencing will itself function as a notice of aggravating circumstances to be relied upon. Such a suggestion could only be made by someone who has never read a presentence report. It is akin to suggesting the investigative report of a police officer can serve in lieu of an indictment. In any event, the federal proposal allows aggravating circumstances to be found from sources other than the contents of the probation report.[60]

III. USE AND DISCLOSURE OF PRESENTENCE REPORTS: THE RIGHT TO CONFRONTATION

Pursuant to §2002 of the proposed Federal Criminal Code,[61] a presentence investigation will be conducted by a probation officer, and a report submitted to the Court before sentencing. The Court will not be limited to the report in considering what sentence is appropriate, however. An "open door" policy is adopted for sentencing hearings by virtue of §3714 of the proposal:

> Any relevant information concerning the history, characteristics, and conduct of a person found guilty of an offense may be received and considered by a court of the United States for the purpose of ascertaining an appropriate sentence to be imposed, regardless of the admissibility of the information under the Federal Rules of Evidence . . . [62]

These provisions raise two issues in terms of the constitutional right to confrontation of witnesses. First, to what extent must a presentence report which will be utilized as a basis for an aggravated sentence be disclosed to the defendant? Secondly, assuming the report is disclosed, can it be relied upon without affording the defendant an opportunity to cross-examine the sources of information utilized in the report?

To some extent, the issue of a right to disclosure of the report may seem academic, since the Federal Rules of Criminal Procedure were recently amended to require disclosure of the report. An exception is recognized, however: if disclosure would result in some harm the court may summarize the factual information contained in the report which will be relied upon.[63] A persuasive argument can, and has, been made that even in the context of the traditional "discretion" model of sentencing, the constitution requires full disclosure of the presentence report to the defendant.[64] These arguments apply with even greater force to the "enhancement" model, as can be illustrated by the parallels to both capital punishment and Dangerous Special Offender sentencing.

In *Gardner v. Florida*,[65] the U.S. Supreme Court held that a defendant was denied due process when a death sentence was imposed on the basis of a presentence report to which he was not given access. While the decision is clearly bottomed on the "significant constitutional difference" between the death penalty and lesser punishment for crime, the Court gave substantial emphasis to the nature of the factual determination which was a prerequisite to imposition of the death penalty. In rejecting the argument that trial judges could be trusted to responsibly exercise their discretion in reviewing secret information, Justice Stevens remarked:

> [T]he argument rests on the erroneous premise that the participation of counsel is superfluous to the process of evaluating the relevance and significance of aggravating and mitigating facts. Our belief that debate between adversaries is often essential to the truth-seeking function of trials requires us also to recognize the importance of giving counsel an opportunity to comment on facts which may influence the sentencing decision in capital cases.[66]

Again, in holding that counsel's failure to request access to the report was not a waiver, the Court noted the report's importance to appellate review of the factual determination made by the trial judge:

> since the judge found, in disagreement with the jury, that the evidence did not establish any mitigating circumstance, and since the presentence report was the only item considered by the judge but not the jury, the full review of the factual basis for the judge's rejection of the advisory verdict is plainly required. For if the jury, rather than the judge, correctly assessed the petitioner's veracity, the death sentence rests on an erroneous factual predicate.[67]

The application of these arguments to the sentencing procedure envisioned by the federal proposal is obvious. The imposition of a particular sentence will be based upon a finding of factual circumstances which should be open to adversarial debate and subject to appellate review. Both processes require that counsel have full access to the presentence report.

Another parallel can be found in the Dangerous Special Offender sentencing provisions. Although enacted five years prior to the amendment of Rule 32 of the Federal Rules of

Criminal Procedure requiring disclosure of presentence reports, these statutes provided:

> The Court shall permit the United States and counsel for the defendant . . . to inspect the presentence report sufficiently prior to the hearing as to afford a reasonable opportunity for verification. In extraordinary cases, the court may withhold material not relevant to a proper sentence, diagnostic opinion which may seriously disrupt a program of rehabilitation, any source of information obtained on a promise of confidentiality, and material previously disclosed in open court. A court withholding all or part of a presentence report shall inform the parties of its action and place in the record the reasons therefore.[68]

The exceptions for irrelevant or previously disclosed material raise no issue of denial of a right to confrontation. The exceptions for diagnostic opinion and confidential sources now appear, in almost identical language, in Rule 32 (c) (3).[69] The Rule goes beyond the statute, however, in requiring the judge to summarize the undisclosed information and give the defendant an opportunity to comment on it. Both of these rationales for non-disclosure were considered and rejected by the *Gardner* court. The possible disruption of a program of "rehabilitation" was not a very persuasive rationale to justify non-disclosure to a defendant who was about to be executed.[70] It is equally implausible in the context of aggravation of a prison sentence. Once a decision has been made to imprison a defendant, disruption of "rehabilitation" is hardly justification to withhold the information being relied upon to determine how many years the defendant will be confined. As to confidential sources, the Court noted that an assurance of secrecy *increases* the risk of unreliability, and the interest in reliability plainly outweighs the state's interest in preserving confidences.[71]

Even in the context of a capital case, however, the Court did not explicitly reject the alternative of summarizing instead of full disclosure. To the contrary, it distinguished the holding in *Williams v. New York* as inapplicable, because the material facts in the undisclosed presentence report *had* been described in detail by the trial judge in open court.[72] "Summarization" may seriously hamper the ability of counsel to challenge the information, however. As the Court stated in a closely related context:

> Adversary proceedings are a major aspect of our system of criminal justice. Their superiority as a means for attaining justice in a given case is nowhere more evident than in those cases, such as the ones at bar, where an issue must be decided on the basis of a large volume of factual materials, and after consideration of the many and subtle inter-relationships which may exist among the facts reflected by these records. As the need for adversary inquiry is increased by the complexity of the issues presented for adjudication, and by the consequent inadequacy of *ex parte* procedures as a means for their accurate resolution, the displacement of well-informed advocacy necessarily becomes less justifiable.[73]

The second issue, the extent to which the presentence report can be relied upon without affording the defendant an opportunity to cross-examine the sources relied upon was not reached in *Gardner v. Florida*, but this is the battleground on which both *Williams v. New York* and *Specht v. Patterson* were fought. While the right to cross-examine was rejected for the "discretion" model in *Williams*, it was mandated as part of the "full panoply" of due process rights which the Court recognized in the context of the "enhancement" model of *Specht*. While it can certainly be argued that the sentence aggravation procedure envisioned by the federal proposal bears a closer resemblance to the "enhancement" model of *Specht* than to the "discretion" model of *Williams*, such an argument will not be dispositive, since the Court has explicitly abandoned the "full panoply" approach to due process since *Specht* was decided. The focus of our inquiry should rather be upon the significance of cross-examination to truth finding in the context of the factual questions being resolved.[74] The greatest enlightenment in resolving this inquiry can be found in the Supreme Court's approach to parole and probation revocation proceedings in *Morrissey v. Brewer*[75] and *Gagnon v. Scarpelli*.[76] In both of these contexts, the Court concluded due process includes the right to confront and cross-examine adverse witnesses. Parole and probation revocation, unlike sentencing under the "discretion" model, involves a specific factual allegation which must be proved. Thus, just as at a trial, the right of cross-examination must be afforded to assure the "accuracy of the truth-determining process."[77] The parallel between parole or probation revocation hearings and the factual determinations to be made to justify an "aggravated" sentence is readily apparent. The potential loss of liberty may be even greater in the context of sentence aggravation.

Even with respect to parole or probation revocation hearings, however, the Court recognized a significant limitation upon the right of cross-examination which has not been recognized as a limitation on the right of confrontation at trial: the right can be disallowed if "the hearing officer specifically finds good cause for not allowing confrontation."[78] Little guidance is available as to what might constitute "good cause" for denial of the right. On the one hand, the Court suggests the process "should be flexible enough to consider evidence including letters, affidavits, and other material that would not be admissable in an adversary criminal trial."[79] Since the reason such evidence is excluded at a trial is because it is hearsay and the party has no opportunity to cross-examine its author, this suggests mere unavailability may be "good cause." On the other hand, the Court suggests a stricter test in delineating the circumstances when a defendant can cross-examine those who supplied adverse information at a preliminary hearing before he is returned to prison: "if the hearing officer determines that the informant would be subjected to risk of harm if his identity were disclosed, he need not be subjected to confrontation and cross-examination."[80] While no clear standard of "good cause" emerges, it is clear that the burden is upon the state to show specific reasons why the right must be limited. Such a showing cannot be based upon arguments which apply to parole or probation procedures in general.

The confrontation and cross-examination of witnesses permitted in sentencing hearings under the federal proposal should be at least as great as that required in parole and probation revocation proceedings. The routine reliance upon presentence reports apparently envisioned by Federal Criminal Code §3714 is clearly at odds with the standards announced in *Morrissey* and *Gagnon*. In the absence of a compelling showing of particular reasons to dispense with the right, a defendant contesting a showing of aggravating circumstances should have the right to cross-examine all adverse witnesses.

IV. PLAYING THE LABEL GAME: THE PROBLEM OF BURDEN OF PROOF

To understand the burden of proof issues posed by the proposed Federal Criminal Code, the fragility of the labels "element of the crime," and "aggravating" or "mitigating" circumstances must be comprehended. It is now axiomatic that due process in criminal proceedings requires that every element of the crime must be proven beyond a reasonable doubt.[81] At least under the "discretion" model, however, this burden does not apply to factual issues at a sentencing hearing. Thus, if a state defined two separate crimes of "burglary," carrying a penalty of 1 year, and "armed burglary," carrying a penalty of 2 years, the jury would have to find beyond a reasonable doubt that the defendant was armed before he would be liable for the 2 year sentence. Can this result be avoided by simply defining the crime of burglary, punishable by up to 2 years, and decreeing that being armed is an "aggravating circumstance" which justifies the 2 year sentence?

Such legislative sleight of hand has apparently won the approval of the United States Supreme Court. In *Mullaney v. Wilbur*,[82] the Court held that due process requires the prosecution to prove beyond a reasonable doubt the absence of heat of passion on sudden provocation before a defendant could be convicted of murder, reasoning that absence of provocation was an essential element of the malice required for murder. Two years later, in *Patterson v. New York*,[83] the Court upheld a New York law which required the defendant to prove the "extreme emotional disturbance" which would result in a verdict of manslaughter rather than murder, distinguishing *Mullaney* on the ground that the New York statute made "extreme emotional disturbance" an affirmative defense, whereas the Maine statute construed in *Mullaney* resulted in a "presumption" of the absence of provocation which the defendant had to overcome. Protesting this "label game," Justice Powell, author of the *Mullaney* opinion, dissented in *Patterson:*

> With all respect, this type of constitutional adjudication is indefensibly formalistic. A limited but significant check on possible abuses in the criminal law now becomes an exercise in arid formalities. What *Winship* and *Mullaney* had sought to teach about the limits a free society places on its procedures to safeguard the liberty of its citizens becomes a rather simplistic lesson in statutory draftsmanship. Nothing in the Court's opinion prevents a legislature from applying this new learning to many of the classical elements of the crimes it punishes.[84]

The degree of burden of proof to be imposed should not depend upon the label attached to a fact. Rather, the standard of proof required by due process should depend upon the consequences of an erroneous factual determination.[85] Erroneous factual findings in the context of Senator Kennedy's burglary example may have dire consequences for a defendant, increasing the amount of time he must spend in prison as much as fourteen times. While the Court in *In Re Winship*[86] premised the requirement of proof beyond a reasonable doubt upon *both* the possible loss of liberty and the accompanying stigma of conviction, these results can also be seen to flow from aggravation of a sentence. Since the factual premise upon which aggravation is based is made a part of the record, the defendant may be "stigmatized" to the same extent a juvenile is by delinquency proceedings, or a sexual psychopath is by mentally disordered sex offender proceedings. In fact, the factual basis for sentence aggravation may be based on a finding the defendant is "engaging in a pattern of racketeering activity."[87] Certainly being labeled a "racketeer" carries as great a social stigmatization as being labeled a "juvenile delinquent." To argue that the loss of liberty or stigmatization is of less consequence because the defendant has already been convicted of an underlying crime overlooks the difference between the factual issues involved in the underlying crime, and the factual issues involved in the finding of aggravation. In a closely related context, the California Supreme Court concluded that "the fact that the issues at the criminal trial were judged by the reasonable doubt standard has no bearing on how the distinct issues at the mentally disordered sex offender proceeding must be proved."[88] This suggests a distinction might be made between aggravating circumstances based on facts relating to the crime, and aggravating circumstances relating to the defendant. Since a finding of facts related to the crime might involve no greater stigmatization than the conviction itself, a small increment in the sentence might be justified without the necessity of proof beyond a reasonable doubt.

Whether or not proof beyond a reasonable doubt is required by due process, an argument can certainly be made that proof beyond a reasonable doubt (and a jury trial) are required, in some circumstances, by the constitutional right to equal protection of the laws. Returning to the burglary example of Senator Kennedy, we have already seen that the same facts might be alternatively used *either* as a separate charge *or* as an aggravating circumstance, with approximately the same net gain in maximum sentence.[89] The protection of the double jeopardy clause would apparently preclude use of the same fact for *both* an additional charge and aggravation.[90] If the facts are used for a separate charge, they would have to be pleaded and proved to a jury beyond a reasonable doubt. If the aggravation route were used, these rights would be denied.

This choice of procedures is analogous to that presented to the Supreme Court in *Humphrey v. Cady*.[91] In *Humphrey*, the petitioner had been committed under the Wisconsin Sex Crimes Act, which did not provide for a jury trial, even though the procedure for commitment under the general Mental Health Act did grant a right to jury trial. Noting that the two Acts were not mutually exclusive, the Court remanded for a full evidentiary hearing, noting: "The equal protection claim would seem to be especially persuasive if it develops on remand that petitioner was deprived of a jury determination or of other procedural protections, merely by the arbitrary decision of the State to seek his commitment under one statute rather than the other."[92] Similar reasoning was adopted by the California Supreme Court in holding that a unanimous jury verdict was required for commitment of mentally disordered sex offenders, inasmuch as commitment of mentally disordered persons under the Lanterman-Petris-Short Act requires jury unanimity.[93]

V. THE RIGHT TO JURY TRIAL

The proposed Federal Criminal Code does not provide for a jury determination of the facts utilized for aggravation of a sentence. This may present the same sort of "label game" involved in the burden of proof, since the same fact may be alternatively labeled an "aggravating circumstance" or an element of the crime. To argue that due process requires a jury determination in these circumstances, however, would require us to ignore the strong parallel to other contexts in which the Supreme Court has upheld the denial of a right to a jury trial, even though other procedural rights, including burden of proof beyond a reasonable doubt, *were* required.

In *McKeiver v. Pennsylvania*,[94] the Court declined to require jury trials in juvenile court proceedings. Many of the practical considerations which buttressed this ruling are equally applicable to sentencing proceedings. Although stated as "different" reasons, the Court repeatedly restated essentially the same reason for concluding a jury trial was not a constitutional requirement: the formality this would inject into the proceedings.

> If the jury system were to be injected into the juvenile court system as a matter of right, it would bring with it into that system the traditional delay, the formality, and the clamor of the adversary system and, possibly the public trial.[95]

Much the same argument could be made with respect to sentencing proceedings, even under the "enhancement" model. Substantial delays would be added to an already overburdened system, at little gain in terms of the reliability of the fact finding function.

More recently, the Court has intimated that due process does not require a jury determination of aggravating facts utilized to impose a death penalty. In upholding the Florida death penalty statute in *Proffitt v. Florida*,[96] the Court noted that the sentence is ultimately determined by the trial judge rather than the jury, concluding that this may lead to even greater consistency in the imposition of capital punishment than if the issue were entrusted to less experienced juries. The Court was also impressed by the appellate review system, under which the evidence of aggravating and mitigating circumstances is reviewed and reweighed to determine independently whether the sentence is warranted. If imposition of the ultimate penalty of death is permissable without a jury determination of aggravating facts, one is hard put to argue such a procedure is required for the imposition of lesser penalities, unless the protections alluded to by the Court in *Proffitt* are unavailable under the proposed Federal Criminal Code. As will be seen, such an argument *can* be made, since the scope of appellate review of sentences under the proposed Code is significantly narrower than the Florida procedure considered in *Proffitt*.

VI. APPELLATE REVIEW: THE NEED FOR FINDINGS

While there is no recognized constitutional right to appellate review of a judgment of conviction, much less of a sentence, where appellate remedies *are* made available by statute, due process requires that there must be findings adequate to make meaningful any appeal that is allowed.[97] The absence of any right to appellate review has rendered findings unnecessary under the traditional "discretion" model of sentencing,[98] with rare exceptions.[99] With the broader scope of appellate review envisioned by the proposed Federal Criminal Code, however, will findings be a constitutional requirement?

The proposal requires that the Court state in open court the general reasons for its imposition of the particular sentence, and if the sentence is outside the "range" established by the Sentencing Commission, the reason for imposition of a sentence outside the range.[100] The key factual determination in this scheme will, of course, be the determination of what "range" is applicable. Whether a sentence is within a particular "range" is an issue that can be resolved by simple mathematics; the issue that will be hotly contested in the sentencing court is the factual basis for finding a particular range applicable. Yet, as the Code is presently drafted, this determination will not be reviewable. The defendant is permitted to file a notice of appeal only if the sentence exceeds the guidelines "that are found by the sentencing court to be applicable to the case."[101] And in considering the appeal, the court of appeals is not authorized to review the factual basis for determination a particular range is applicable, but is limited to determining whether the sentence is "clearly unreasonable" in terms of the reasons stated by the trial judge and the factors to be considered in imposing a sentence.[102]

The federal proposal also allows an appeal by the government if the sentence is lower than the guidelines found by the sentencing judge.[103] In either case, if the court of appeals finds the sentence "clearly unreasonable," it can only impose a new sentence itself.[104] A greater sentence can only be imposed on an appeal by government, however.[105]

In asking whether these provisions meet the due process requirement of findings adequate to make appellate review meaningful, the limited scope of appellate review becomes very significant. The judge is apparently not required to make *factual* findings to support the conclusion a particular sentencing range is applicable. Only the "general reasons" for imposition of a particular sentence need be stated. From the standpoint of constitutionality, this would present no problem, since the determination of the applicability of a particular sentencing guideline is apparently unreviewable. From the stand point of sound public policy, however, this limitation upon the scope of appellate review will serve to perpetuate many of the worst abuses of present sentencing disparity. At present, a sentencing judge can impose any sentence within the statutory limit, and the sentence ordinarily will not be disturbed on appeal if the record is silent.[106] The judge who announces the basis for the sentence, however, does so at the risk that this basis will be declared unacceptable by a reviewing court, and the sentence set aside.[107] While an attempt is made to eliminate this anomaly by requiring a statement of "general reasons" for every sentence, the failure to require reviewable factual findings invites the same sort of disingenuousness that characterizes the present system. An apt illustration can be drawn from the lone example of possible sentencing ranges offered by Senator Kennedy. A defendant convicted of the offense of burglary might receive a sentence ranging from 3 months to 3.5 years, depending upon factual findings whether he was "armed" or "brandished a weapon," and whether the dwelling was occupied or not. Yet a judge who concludes the defendant brandished a weapon in an occupied dwelling and imposes a 3.5 year sentence need only state the "general reason" for the sentence. Some of the "general reasons" that might be offered are suggested in §2003(a):

> (A) to afford adequate deterrence to criminal conduct;
> (B) to protect the public from further crimes of the defendant;
> (C) to reflect the seriousness of the offense, to promote respect for law, and to provide just punishment for the offense; and
> (D) to provide the defendant with needed educational or vocational training; medical care, or other correctional treatment in the most effective manner.[108]

Since the sentence was within the guidelines found to be applicable by the sentencing judge, no reason for imposition of a sentence outside the range needs to be stated, and the sentence will not even be appealable. Thus, the "general finding" is no better than the silence of the sentencing judge at present; it may even be worse. At least relief is available at present where a sentencing judge states an impermissible basis for the sentence.[109] Under the proposed revision, as long as sentence is "within guidelines," an appeal is not even permitted. Thus, the availability of appellate review may be restricted, rather than expanded.

If an objective of the proposed Federal Criminal Code is to promote greater uniformity and fairness in sentencing, this process must start with a fact-finding process which is rational, visible and subject to appellate review. To do otherwise will not only perpetuate sentencing disparity, but further camouflage it under a system of appellate review that is, at best, an illusion.

VII. APPLICABILITY OF THE EXCLUSIONARY RULES TO SENTENCING

While the right to exclude illegally obtained evidence is embodied in due process, it is a right subject to a list of limitations and exceptions which seems to grow with each passing term of the Supreme Court. The Court has permitted a number of "collateral uses" of illegally obtained evidence on the theory that suppression for these uses would not further the rule's purpose of deterring official lawlessness.[110] While the Supreme Court has yet to rule on the question, among the collateral uses permitted by many lower courts is the consideration of an appropriate sentence.[111] From this perspective, the provision of §3714 of the proposed Federal Criminal Code rendering all evidence admissible for the purpose of ascertaining an appropriate sentence is hardly surprising.

It is worth a moment's reflection, however, to ask whether the same result should follow in the context of the factual findings required for aggravation under the federal proposal. If a defendant were on trial for armed burglary, the gun allegedly used in the burglary would certainly be suppressed at trial if it were illegally seized. Should the result be different where the defendant has been convicted of burglary, and the illegally seized gun is offered as evidence to aggravate the sentence by showing the defendant was armed?

The rationale relied upon by those courts allowing illegally obtained evidence to be admitted at that time of sentence is that applying the exclusionary rule at sentencing would not add in any significant way to the deterrent effect of the rule: "It is quite unlikely that law enforcement officials conduct illegal electronic auditing to build up an inventory of information for sentencing purposes, although the evidence would be inadmissible on the issue of guilt."[112] This assumption may have some validity in the context of evidence not directly related to the underlying crime. Significantly, each of the cases admitting unlawfully seized evidence at the time of sentencing dealt with evidence of unrelated criminal activity offered to show the character of the defendant.[113] Where the unlawfully seized evidence related directly to the circumstances of the underlying crime, such as a confession disclosing details of the crime, courts have been more reluctant to consider the evidence for purposes of sentencing.[114]

This distinction assumes even greater significance where the illegally obtained evidence is used to aggravate a sentence. A police officer is highly motivated to obtain evidence which will elevate the degree of the crime. For example, a homicide detective who has evidence the defendant committed a murder will certainly seek evidence of premeditation with diligence, to justify a conviction of first degree murder. To argue this motivation will somehow be diminished because premeditation is no longer an element of the crime but has been classified as an aggravating fact is, of course, totally specious. The catalogue of facts which serve to aggravate a sentence will be well known to every federal officer, and gathering evidence of those facts will be a vital part of every federal investigation. Thus, the deterrent purpose of the exclusionary rule will be well served by applying it to evidence offered to prove aggravating circumstances of the crime at the time of sentencing.

Where the aggravating facts relate to the character of the defendant, however, a different result can be justified. Such evidence may have been sought in an independent investigation for a different purpose, and the purpose of the exclusionary rule would be little served by suppressing the evidence for an unanticipated use.

CONCLUSION

In its present form, the proposed Federal Criminal Code will go a long way towards eliminating unjustifiable disparities in federal sentencing. But this goal may be achieved at considerable cost in terms of the constitutional guarantee of due process of law. A monumental task of drafting awaits the Federal Sentencing Commission to avoid the pitfalls of vagueness in drafting sentencing guidelines. A defendant may face substantial aggravation of a prison sentence with no notice of the aggravating circumstances being relied upon and no opportunity to confront and cross-examine the sources of those "facts." Facts which would require proof beyond a reasonable doubt and a jury trial if labeled elements of the crime need be established by only a preponderance of evidence to the Court through the simple expedient of relabeling them "aggravating circumstances." The appellate review provided is largely illusory, since the most significant factual determination is not reviewable. And evidence which would be excluded at the trial on constitutional grounds may be admitted at the sentencing under the guise of "aggravation."

Many of the same constitutional issues are raised by the California Uniform Determinate Sentencing Act. The definitions of "aggravating circumstances" compiled by the California Judicial Council are hardly models of precision.[115] A requirement of notice to the defendant of aggravating circumstances was eliminated from the Act in an eleventh hour amendment,[116] and a finding of aggravating circumstances may be based upon information in presentence reports, with no opportunity to confront or cross-examine witnesses.[117] The denial of a requirement of proof beyond a reasonable doubt and a jury trial raises even more serious equal protection problems than the federal proposal, because the prosecutor is given an option of pleading and proving facts as "enhancement," which requires proof beyond a reasonable doubt to a jury, or relying upon the same facts to show aggravation.[118] At least the appellate review provided allows an inquiry into the sufficiency of evidence to establish the aggravating circumstances however.[119] These shortcomings in the California law led this author to predict that its aggravation provisions will shortly become a useless and impractical "dead letter" law, leaving the judge with a choice of only the middle term or the lesser term.[120] The same fate may befall the federal proposal unless steps are taken to correct the most obvious constitutional deficiencies. The laws defining the availability of capital punishment may provide a useful model in their precision of definition of aggravating circumstances, requirement of notice, opportunity to confront and cross-examine, and for appellate review of factual findings. All of these features should be incorporated in the federal proposal. The necessity of proof beyond a reasonable doubt to a jury can be avoided by carefully limiting aggravating circumstances to facts that are not equally susceptible to proof as an independent crime.

Notes

1. E.g., M. FRANKEL, CRIMINAL SENTENCES; LAW WITHOUT ORDER (1973); K.D. Harris and R.P. Lura, *Geography of Justice: Sentencing Variation in U.S. Judicial District*, 57 JUDICATURE 392 (1974); W.J. Zumwalt, *Anarchy of Sentencing in Federal Courts*, 57 JUDICATURE 96 (1973).

2. S. 1437, 95 Cong., 1st Sess. (1977) [hereinafter referred to as S. 1437].

3. Uniform Determinate Sentencing Act of 1976, 1976 Cal. Stats., ch. 1139.

4. CAL. PEN. CODE §1170 (b). *See* M. Oppenheim, *Computing a Determinate Sentence . . . New Math Hits the Courts*, 51 CAL. S.B.J. 604 (1976).

5. S. 1437, tit. I. §§2003, 3725.

6. Burglary is defined as follows in the new Code:

> A person is guilty of an offense if at night, with intent to engage in conduct constituting a crime . . ., and without privilege, he enters or remains surreptitiously within a dwelling that is the property of another.

S. 1437, tit. I, §1711 (a). The offense is a Class C felony, punishable by a term of imprisonment of not more than twelve years. *Id.* at §§1711 (b), 2301 (b).

7. E.M. Kennedy, *Criminal Sentencing: A Game of Chance*, 60 JUDICATURE 208, 213–14 (1976), *reprinted in* Congressional Record, January 11, 1977 at S407.

8. Administrative Office of the United States Courts, "Federal Offenders in the United States Courts, 1970," August 1972, at 2.

9. 337 U.S. 241 (1948).

10. *Id.* at 247.

11. *Id.* at 244.

12. 386 U.S. 605 (1967).

13. Colorado Sex Offenders Act, COLO. REV. STAT. ANN. §§ 39-19-1 to 39-19-10 (1963).

14. 386 U.S. at 609, quoting Gerchman v. Maroney, 355 F. 2d 302 (3rd Cir. 1962).

15. 386 U.S. at 610.

16. The right to jury trial was incorporated one year later, Duncan v. Louisiana, 391 U.S. 145 (1968), while incorporation of the right to proof beyond a reasonable doubt came three years later, *In re* Winship, 397 U.S. 358 (1970).

17. 408 U.S. 471, 481 (1972).

18. 408 U.S. 238 (1972).

19. Jurek v. Texas, 428, U.S. 262 (1976); Proffitt v. Florida, 428 U.S. 242 (1976); Gregg v. Georgia, 428 U.S. 153 (1976).

20. GA. CODE ANN. § 27-2534.1(b) (1975); TEXAS PENAL CODE § 19.03 (1974); FLA. STAT. ANN. § 921.141 (5) (1976).

21. GA. CODE ANN. § 27-2503 (1975); TEXAS CODE OF CRIM. PROC. Art. 37-071 (a) (1974); FLA. STAT. ANN. § 921.141 (1) (1976).

22. *Id.*

23. GA. CODE ANN. § 27-2534.1(c) (1975); TEXAS CODE OF CRIM. PROC. Art. 37.071 (a), (c) (1974); FLA. STAT. ANN. § 921.141 (1) (1976). The jury, under Florida law, serves only in an advisory capacity in the sentencing process. However, if the jury recommends a life sentence, the judge may not impose the death

penalty unless, ". . . the facts suggesting a sentence of death should be so clear and convincing that virtually no reasonable person could differ." Tedder v. State, 332 So. 2d 908, 910 (1975).

24. GA. CODE ANN. § 27-2534.1(c) and 27-2537 (1975); TEXAS CODE OF CRIM. PROC. Art. 37-071 (f) (1975); FLA. STAT. ANN. § 921.141 (3), (4).

25. 430 U.S. 349 (1977).

26. 18 U.S.C. § 3575 (1977).

27. 21 U.S.C. § 849 (1977).

28. 18 U.S.C. § 3575 (e); 21 U.S.C. § 849 (e).

29. 18 U.S.C. §§§ 3575 (a)-(b), 3576; 21 U.S.C. §§§ 849 (a)-(b), (h).

30. 18 U.S.C. § 3575 (b); 21 U.S.C. § 849 (b).

31. S. Rep. No. 91-617, 91st Cong., 1st Sess., at 163 (1969).

32. S. 1437, tit. II, part E, § 994 (e).

33. *Id.* § 991. The Commission will consist of nine members designated by the Judicial Conference of the United States.

34. S. 1437, tit. III, § 263.

35. Lanzetta v. New Jersey, 306 U.S. 451 (1939).

36. Grayned v. City of Rockford, 408 U.S. 104 (1972); Giacco v. Pennsylvania, 382 U.S. 399 (1966); *see* Note, *The Void-For-Vagueness Doctrine in the Supreme Court*, 109 U.PA. L. REV. 67 (1960).

37. 428 U.S. 153, 164-68 (1976).

38. 236 Ga. 534, 224 S.E. 2d 386 (1976), holding the following definition of an aggravating circumstance was void for vagueness: "The offense . . . was committed by a person . . . who has a substantial history of serious assaultive criminal convictions."

39. Smith v. California, 361 U.S. 147 (1959).

40. Arnold v. State, 236 Ga. 534, 224 S.E.2d 386, 392 (1976).

41. Papachristou v. City of Jacksonville, 405 U.S. 156, 162 (1972).

42. 18 U.S.C. § 3575 (b); 21 U.S.C. § 849 (b).

43. United States v. Stewart, 531 F.2d 326 (6th Cir. 1976).

44. 386 U.S. at 608.

45. 18 U.S.C. § 3575(e); 21 U.S.C. § 849(e).

46. *See* text at note 7, *supra*.

47. S. 1437 tit. I, §1614 defines "menacing" as follows: "A person is guilty of an offense if he engages in physical conduct by which he intentionally places another person in fear of imminent bodily injury."

48. S. 1437, tit. I, §2301 (b).

49. S. 1437, tit. II, part E, §994 (d) (4), (8), (11).

50. S. 1437, tit. I, §2003.

51. GA. CODE ANN. §27-2503 (1975) provides: ". . . only such evidence in aggravation as the State has made known to defendant prior to the trial shall be admissible." Texas Penal Code §19.03 (1974) makes the aggravating circumstances an element of the crime which must be pleaded in the initial charge. *But cf.* FLA. STAT. ANN. §921.141(1) (1976), which allows the court to consider evidence, ". . . as to any matter that the court deems relevant to sentencing."

52. 18 U.S.C. §3575 (a); 21 U.S.C. §849 (a). *See* Statement of Henry S. Ruth, *The Organized Crime Control Act: Hearing on S. 30 Before the Subcomm. on Criminal Laws and Procedures of the Senate Comm. on the Judiciary*, 91st. Cong., 1st Sess. at 345 (March 19, 1969).

53. In United States v. Kelley, 384 F. Supp. 1394 (W.D. Mo. 1974), *aff'd* 519 F.2d 251 (8th Cir. 1975), the court held that notice filed by the prosecutor of his intention to invoke §3575 was defective in that the notice contained nothing more than an ". . . unsupported conclusory allegation" that defendant was dangerous within the meaning of 18 U.S.C. §3575. The court suggested that a statement of the factual basis upon which the allegation rested was a necessary concomitant of proper notice. 384 F. Supp. at 1399. A similar result was reached in United States v. Duardi, 384 F. Supp. 856, 861, 871, 874, (W.D. Mo. 1974), *aff'd*, 529 F. 2d 123 (8th Cir. 1975). *See also* Klein, *Extended Terms for Dangerous Offenders Under the Proposed Federal Criminal Code (S.1): The Emerging Legislative History*, 8 LOY. UNIV. L.J. 319, at 323-327 (1976).

54. Fed. R. Crim. P. 11(c) (1); United States v. Edwards, 379 F. Supp. 617, 621 (D. Fla. 1974); United States v. Kelly, 384 F. Supp, 1394, 1400 (WD. Mo. 1974), *aff'd*, 519 F.2d 251 (8th Cir. 1975).

55. *See* United States v. Duardi, 384 F. Supp. 856 (W.D. Mo. 1974), *aff'd* 529 F. 2d 123 (8th Cir. 1975); Klein, *supra* note 53, at 330.

56. Klein, *supra* note 53, at 329.

57. United States v. Blair, 470 F.2d 331, 339-40 (5th Cir. 1972).

58. *See* Klein, *supra* note 53, at 330-31.

59. Fed. R. Crim. P. 32 (a) (1), (b) (3) (A).

60. S. 1437, tit. I, §3714.

61. *Id.* §2002.

62. *Id.* §3741.

63. Fed. R. Crim. P. 32(c) (3) (A) and (B).

64. Note, *Procedural Due Process at Judicial Sentencing for Felony*, 81 HARV L. REV. 821 (1967).

65. 430 U.S. 349 (1977).

66. *Id.* at 360.

67. *Id.* at 362.

68. 18 U.S.C. §3575 (b); 21 U.S.C. §849 (b).

69. Fed. R. Crim. P. 32 (c) (3) (A) and (B). *Cf.* ABA STANDARDS, SENTENCING ALTERNATIVES AND PROCEDURES §4.4 (Approved Draft, 1968).

70. 430 U.S. at 360.

71. *Id.* at 358-59.

72. *Id.* at 356-57.

73. Alderman v. United States, 394 U.S. 165, 183-84 (1969).

74. Chambers v. Mississppi, 410 U.S. 284, 295 (1972); Dutton v Evans, 400 US. 74, 89 (1970).

75. 408 U.S. 471 (1972).

76. 411 U.S. 778 (1973).

77. Chambers v. Mississippi, *supra*, note 74.

78. Morrissey v. Brewer, 408 U.S. 471, 489 (1972).

79. *Id.*

80. *Id.* at 487.

81. *In re* Winship, 397 U.S. 358 (1970).

82. 421 U.S. 684 (1975).

83. 432 U.S. 197 (1977).

84. *Id.* at 224 (Powell, J., dissenting).

85. *In re* Winship, 397 U.S. 358 (1970).

86. *Id.* at 363.

87. S. 1437, tit. II. §994 (e).

88. People v. Burnick, 14 Cal. 3d 329, 330, 121 Cal. Rptr. 488, 504 (1975).

89. *See* text at note 46 *supra*.

90. Jeffers v. United States, 432 U.S. 137 (1977).

91. 405 U.S. 504 (1972).

92. *Id.* at 512.

93. People v. Feagley, 14 Cal. 3d 338, 121 Cal. Rptr. 509 (1975).

94. 403 U.S. 528 (1971).

95. *Id.* at 550.

96. 428 U.S. 242 (1976).

97. Specht v. Patterson, 386 U.S. 605, 610 (1967).

98. United States v. Thompson, 541 F.2d 794 (9th Cir. 1976); United States v. Carden, 428 F.2d 1116 (8th Cir. 1970).

99. *See e.g.,* United States v. Capriola, 537 F.2d 319 (9th Cir. 1976).

100. S. 1437, tit. I, §2003 (b).

101. *Id.* §3725 (a).

102. *Id.* §3725 (d).

103. *Id.* §3725 (b).

104. *Id.* §3725 (e) (1) (A). At present, a reviewing court which finds a sentence unlawful cannot itself impose a new sentence, but must remand the case for resentencing. United States v. Wilson, 450 F.2d 495, 498 (4th Cir. 1971). A remand for resentencing can direct that the new sentence be imposed by a different judge than imposed the original sentence. United States v. Robin, 553 F.2d 8 (2nd Cir. 1977) (en banc).

105. S. 1437, tit. I, §3725 (e) (1) (B). The ABA STANDARDS, APPELLATE REVIEW OF SENTENCES (Approved Draft, 1968) §3.46 oppose the increase of sentences on appeal by the government on grounds of "serious constitutional difficulties" under the double jeopardy provision of the fifth amendment, citing Ocampo v. United States, 234 U.S. 91 (1914); Trono v. United States, 199 U.S. 521 (1905); Kepner v. United States, 195 U.S. 100 (1904).

106. A shocking example of the premium this places on judicial silence appears in United States v. Hartford, 489 F. 2d 652 (5th Cir. 1974). There three defendants, all young first offenders, appeared before the same judge for sentencing on the same day. In case #1 *(Hartford),* the defendant had been convicted of simple possession, punishable by a one-year maximum sentence. The judge declared one year was not sufficient, and

instead sentenced the defendant under the Federal Youth Corrections Act, which carries an indeterminate sentence of up to four years. In case #2 *(Bowdoin)*, the defendant was given the 5 year maximum sentence for distribution of LSD, the court declaring he imposed the maximum sentence in all narcotics cases, and "if I could give him any more I would give it to him." In case #3 *(Newton)*, the judge simply imposed the maximum 5 year prison sentence for distribution of hashish without comment. The Appellate Court reversed the sentences in cases #1 and #2, finding an abuse of discretion, but affirmed the sentence in case #3. The obvious lesson for trial judges is that the less they say, the more likely the sentence will be upheld.

107. *See* United States v. Grayson, 550 F.2d 103 (3d Cir. 1976).

108. S. 1437, tit. I, §2003 (a).

109. United Sates v. Grayson, 550 F.2d 103 (3d Cir. 1976).

110. *E.g.,* United States v. Janis, 428 U.S. 433, (1976); Oregon v. Hass, 420 U.S. 714 (1975); United States v. Calandra, 414 U.S. 338 (1974); Harris v. New York, 401 U.S. 222 (1971).

111. United States v. Patrick, 542 F.2d 381 (7th Cir. 1976); United States v. Vandemark, 522 F.2d 1019 (9th Cir. 1975); United States v. Schipani, 435 F.2d 26 (2d Cir. 1970).

112. United States y. Schipani, 435 F.2d 26, 28 (2d Cir. 1970).

113. *See* cases cited in note 111, *supra*.

114. United States *ex rel.* Rivers v. Myers, 384 F.2d 737 (3d Cir. 1976); United States *ex rel* Brown v. Rundle, 417 F.2d 282 (3d Cir. 1969); United States *ex rel.* Cleveland v. Casscles, 354 F. Supp. 114 (S.D.N.Y. 1973).

115. *See* CALIFORNIA RULE OF COURT, rule 421 (a) (3), (a) (8), (a) (11) (Amendments Eff. July 1, 1977).

116. CAL. PENAL CODE §1170 (b) (West Supp. 1978), as amended by A.B. 476, June 29, 1977.

117. *Id.* Presentence reports are fully disclosed to a defendant as a public record under California law. CAL. PENAL CODE §1203 (a) (West Supp. 1978).

118. Compare CALIFORNIA RULES OF COURT, rule 421 (a) (1), (a) (2), (a) (10) and (b) (3) *with* CAL. PENAL CODE §§12022, 12022.5, 12022.6, 12022.7 and 667.5 (West Supp. 1978).

119. CAL. PENAL CODE §§1237, 1259-1260 (West 1970).

120. Uelmen, *Proof of Aggravation Under the California Uniform Determinate Sentencing Act: The Constitutional Issues,* 10 LOY. L.A.L. REV. 725 (1977).

Eliminating Disparities and Disproportionality in Sentencing

By Constance Baker Motley*

When one looks at our criminal justice system today, one sees an institution long beset by multi-faceted problems which seem to defy lasting solutions. Among the more intractable of these problems are two in the area of criminal sentencing which have been recently highlighted by legal scholars, judges, prison administrators and legislators.

One of these is the problem of disparities in criminal sentences given, for what appears to be the same crime, to defendants who appear to have similar backgrounds and character traits. There are disparities in the sentences meted out by the same judge. Disparities exist in criminal sentences as between different judges of the same court. There are regional disparities in sentencing for the same crime. Disparities have been found in sentences given to white and black defendants apparently similarly situated. And there is the curious disparity in sentencing between white collar criminals and non-violent blue collar criminals. Another problem which has been dramatically thrusted to the fore by the Supreme Court's decision in *Coker v. Georgia*[1] is the problem of disproportionate and excessive punishment. In that case the Court concluded that a sentence of death for the crime of rape of an adult woman is grossly disproportionate and excessive punishment barred by the cruel and unusual punishment clause of the Eighth and Fourteenth Amendments to the Federal Constitution. Of course, Mr. Justice Brennan and Mr. Justice Marshall reiterated their well-known view that the death penalty itself is violative of the Eighth Amendment in that it is both excessive punishment and morally unacceptable.

I. THE NEW YORK EXPERIENCE

Somewhat recently I had occasion to rule in the case of *Carmona v. Ward*[2] that the mandatory indeterminate life sentences imposed upon two women for possession and sale of small quantities of cocaine as decreed by New York's 1973 Drug Law are so grossly disproportionate to the nature of their offenses as to constitute excessive punishment in violation of the cruel and unusual punishment clause of the Eighth (and Fourteenth) Amendment. Here sentences were found to be significantly more severe than those which have been imposed for the same offenses in any other jurisdiction in the United States, and are more severe than those imposed for many serious and violent crimes in the state of New York itself. The statutory scheme pursuant to which they were imposed does not differentiate, in imposition of this maximum punishment, among offenders of varying degrees of culpability, nor does it allow for consideration of any mitigating circumstances in the case unless the accused persons can provide the prosecutors with sufficient new and material intelligence information that they become eligible for a probation recommendation. Even in view of the admitted severity of the drug abuse problem in New York, it seems clear that New York's legitimate interests in both deterrence and isolation of drug offenders could be as well served by such sentences of

*Judge, United States District Court, Southern District of New York.

shorter duration as are provided for in other jurisdictions, including the federal system where many New York City and State drug offenders are regularly tried, convicted, and sentenced.

Traditionally, criminal penalties have been viewed as serving at least four goals: retribution, preventive detention, deterrence, and rehabilitation. However, as indicated, in the last few years, two broad areas of the sentencing process have been the focus of concern. With respect to the first area, there has recently arisen a new consciousness that there are grave disparities in sentences given to those alleged to be similarly situated persons. Second, the "law and order" mood abroad in our nation today has led to "tougher" and "surer" sentences for certain crimes as a means of deterring criminal conduct. As a result of the emergence of these two areas of concern, many states are experimenting with new approaches to sentencing. For example, in California, the legislature recently eliminated the system of indefinite sentences in an effort to provide a surer, more equitable punishment system and to eliminate the anxiety of the convict who has no idea of when he will be finally released by the parole board.[3] Moreover, at the federal level, Senator Edward Kennedy proposed a dramatic break with sentencing tradition which contemplated the establishment of a sentencing commission which would set guidelines for sentences meted out by federal judges.[4] The purported objective of this legislative proposal was the elimination of disparities in sentencing in the federal system.

It should come as no surprise to a student of constitutional law who is focusing on the area of criminal justice that the "get tough" sentencing proposals could lead to some discrete Eighth Amendment problems. What may be a bit surprising, however, is that proposals which seek to eliminate disparities in sentencing may also run into constitutional hurdles.

One example of a "get tough" sentencing scheme which has presented some perplexing constitutional law issues is the 1973 New York State Drug Law.[5] This piece of legislation was reputedly the culmination of a long series of efforts to deal effectively with the ever increasing traffic in drugs and the social havoc which it has wrought, particularly in our urban centers. In the past, the State of New York had sought to deal with this new societal scourge by the establishment of drug treatment centers, education programs, and stricter law enforcement, all of which were viewed in 1973 as failures. The new approach embodied in the 1973 law was to make the penalties for drug trafficking so severe that persons would be effectively deterred from selling narcotics in New York State.

To give some idea of how severe these penalties were, a simple example should suffice: A college student is found with one ounce of a white, powdery substance on his or her person. An analysis indicates that 1/10 of the one ounce substance is cocaine, the rest is a dilutant. He or she has never before been convicted or even arrested for any crime. If convicted of this simple possession charge, a Class A felony under New York's 1973 law, the defendant must be sentenced to a mandatory minimum of six years and a mandatory maximum of life imprisonment. The convicted defendant will not be eligible for parole until the six year minimum sentence has been served. If parole is granted at that time and the defendant released, the defendant would remain on lifetime parole. The mandatory lifetime parole provision was recently eliminated to provide for release from parole as in all other felony cases. The heart of the matter—a mandatory life sentence—remains. This sentencing scheme eliminates all discretion for the court to take into account any special circumstances surrounding the particular case or the defendant before it. The defendant's criminal record is irrelevant, as well as family ties, school and employment background. The sentence is simply the quintessence of toughness.

Needless to say, the law came under immediate attack in the state courts. The constitutional springboard was the Eighth Amendment's cruel and unusual punishment prohibition. Despite heavy reliance on this Bill of Rights prohibition, the New York Court of Appeals ruled the penalties constitutional.[6] Since then the 1973 New York drug law has been attacked in numerous respects, notably (1) the mandatory indeterminate life sentences for Class A drug offenders; (2) the preclusion of plea bargaining for a narrow class of A felony offenders; (3) the mandatory lifetime parole provision without possiblity of discharge; (4) the predication of probation, in part, upon a recommendation from the prosecutor due to the defendant's cooperation; and (5) the denial of bail pending appeal from any Class A felony conviction. It has been charged that, both on their face and also as enforced, these various provisions deny rights to due process and equal protection of law as well as the right to be free from cruel and unusual punishment.

Referring again to the simple possession example case outlined above, the most serious challenge to the 1973 New York Drug law is the claim that the mandatory indeterminate life sentence is so disproportionate to the offense—simple possession of an ounce of a substance containing 1/10 part cocaine—as to violate the cruel and unusual punishment bar embodied in the Eighth Amendment to the Federal Constitution.

It is, at this point in our constitutional jurisprudence, a truism to note that the power to define crimes and to establish punishments rests with the legislature in the first instance. However, the exercise of that power is subject to judicial scrutiny to ensure that it does not transgress any constitutional prohibitions. The final judgment as to whether the punishment decreed by any criminal statute exceeds constitutional limits is a function reserved to the judiciary.

The cruel and unusual punishments clause of the Eighth Amendment, however, infrequently invoked by the Supreme Court, has served as an important and controversial check upon the legislature's power to define and punish crimes. In appropriate cases, the Supreme Court has not hesitated to rely upon that clause in declaring the imposition of a particular punishment constitutionally impermissible.

The Supreme Court's recent decision in *Coker v. Georgia* reaffirmed its previous holding in *Gregg v. Georgia*[7] that a punishment is excessive and unconstitutional if it (1) makes no measurable contribution to acceptable goals of punishment and hence is nothing more than the purposeless and needless imposition of pain and suffering; or (2) is grossly out of proportion to the severity of the crime. A punishment might fail the test on either ground.

Although it is entirely possible, and indeed probable, that in our example the convicted defendant would be released from prison substantially before the expiration of the maximum life term, the defendant would have no *right* to be released at an earlier time. His or her release would be within the parole board's discretion. Accordingly, for Eighth Amendment purposes, a court must view the severity of the punishment by looking to the maximum term possible.

A punishment may be constitutionally impermissible under the Eight Amendment not only because of its nature or mode but because of its severity or harshness. A punishment, otherwise appropriate, may be so disproportionate to the offense for which a defendant has been convicted and the circumstances of the case that it may violate the Constitution. The Supreme Court in *Robinson v. California*[8] warned that "imprisonment for ninety days is not, in the abstract, a punishment which is either cruel or unusual. But the question cannot be considered in the abstract. Even one day in prison would be cruel and unusual punishment for the 'crime' of having a common cold." While the United States Supreme Court has never held a sentence of imprisonment invalid under the Eighth Amendment solely because of its length, some state and federal courts have not been so reluctant.[9] And there is obviously nothing in the Eighth Amendment standards enunciated by the Supreme Court which prevents their application to periods of imprisonment alone.

Application of either the concept of disproportionality or the more nebulous Eighth Amendment test of whether a challenged punishment comports with the dignity of man— the basic concept underlying the Eighth Amendment—obviously presents difficulties of interpretation upon which reasonable persons can and do differ. However, recent cases in the Supreme Court have provided some guidance.

Manifestly, the application of such general and value-laden principles calls for the utmost in judicial self-restraint consistent with the conscientious discharge of the Court's constitutional responsibilities. While the Eighth Amendment is an evolving concept, "draw[ing] its meaning from the evolving standards of decency that mark the progress of a maturing society,"[10] the Supreme Court has made clear that the process of divining such contemporary standards does not give federal judges license to apply to challenged punishments their own subjective perceptions of proper penology. Insofar as possible, the constitutional propriety of a challenged punishment is to be judged by objective indicia rather than by subjective judicial reaction.

Thus, the essential question remains whether New York can *constitutionally* punish the possession of an ounce of cocaine by life imprisonment.

Although by no means dispositive of a punishment's constitutionality, the enactments of legislative bodies, both in New York and elsewhere, serve as some index of community standards and values. They give some indication of a punishment's general moral acceptability.

In New York, all Class A non-capital felony offenders must receive an indeterminate sentence with a maximum duration of life imprisonment. Thus, Class A drug offenders, irrespective of the degree of their involvement in the drug trade, receive the same maximum sentence as those felons convicted of first degree murder, first degree arson, and kidnapping in the first degree. Additionally, Class A drug offenders are punished *more* severely than felons convicted of such crimes as second degree arson, first degree rape, first degree manslaughter, first degree burglary, and second degree kidnapping, all of which are classified as B felonies carrying a maximum term of imprisonment of 25 years. Not only is the treatment of A felony drug offenders unique in its severity among non-capital crimes in New York, it is also virtually unique among all the States of the Union. The New York Court of Appeals duly noted when the 1973 challenged law was before it in *People v. Broadie*[11] that drug trafficking is punished more severely in New York as a result of the 1973 law than in other jurisdictions.

It appears that only two states—California and Louisiana—require a court to impose a life sentence for certain drug offenses. However, as of July 1, 1977, California eliminated the mandatory indeterminate life sentence and substituted definite sentences of up to five years for a first offender, depending on the nature of the offense. Even under the Louisiana scheme, the maximum penalty for simple possession is five years imprisonment. Thus, it is clear that even in those two states with relatively severe penalties for drug offenses, the defendant in our example would have received a substantially less onerous sentence than in New York.

Under federal law, possession with intent to sell cocaine (or, for that matter, heroin and many other narcotic drugs) is punishable in the case of a first offense by probation or imprisonment up to 15 years, a fine of up to $25,000, or both, along with a mandatory special parole term of at least three years following any term of imprisonment.

This brief survey is sufficient to make it clear that the penalty mandated by the New York law is "unusual" in its severity, both when compared with punishments for other offenses within New York, and also when matched against punishments for similar offenses in other jurisdictions. This disparity is powerful evidence that the challenged punishment of life imprisonment does not comport with prevalent moral notions of what constitute just, temperate, and appropriate punishments for these offenses. This evidence should weigh heavily in the scales against the constitutionality of such a sentence.

Finally, under the New York law a person never before involved with the law, who is convicted of agreeing to give *any* amount (up to one-eighth of an ounce) of a narcotic drug to a friend receives the same life sentence as does the major purveyor of heroin. This total failure to tailor the maximum indeterminate sentence in any meaningful way to the culpability of the offender, the gravity of the offense, and the peculiar circumstances of each case must also render the life sentences imposed under New York law constitutionally suspect.

The New York drug law is an example of an attempt to solve a major criminal justice problem with a penalty which is both severe and mandatory—yet raises at least one grave constitutional issue. As we have seen, in determining whether a punishment violates the Eighth Amendment, a court must necessarily compare the punishment imposed on the defendant with the punishments imposed on similarly situated persons in other courts. When the disparity is too great, the more severe punishments become constitutionally suspect.

II. The Emerging Federal Trend

The same sentencing disparities which can give rise to Eighth Amendment problems have given impetus to the current movement to standardize sentences in the federal courts. It has long been recognized that the discretion of the district judge is a two-edged sword: on the one hand it allows the judge to tailor the sentence to the individual, but on the other hand, the statistics seem to indicate that very few judges give the same sentence as some other judge in what appears to be a similar case. The result appears to be a wide variation in the sentences imposed on those defendants who have committed essentially identical crimes and whose backgrounds and characters would not justify any significant difference in punishment.

Senate Bill 1437, as presented to Congress, was sponsored by Senators Kennedy and McClellan. The bill would recodify the federal criminal code, Title 18. Chapters 20 to 23 of the proposed new Title 18 would radically change federal sentencing procedures in an attempt to insure that similar defendants convicted of similar crimes would receive similar sentences. The irony of this laudatory attempt is that in attempting to bring a new measure of fairness into the federal sentencing scheme, the new bill raised a variety of new constitutional questions.

Professor Gerald F. Uelmen has very ably presented the multiple facets of the constitutional problems in his article, *Federal Sentencing Reform: The Emerging Constitutional Issues*.[12] As Professor Uelmen has pointed out, the proposed Senate Bill 181 would establish the Federal Sentencing Commission. The Commission would have two years to formulate sentencing guidelines before the recodification became effective. S. 181 contemplates that any given crime may have more than one sentencing range depending on the "applicable category of offense committed by the applicable category of defendant." For example, the Commission may set a high sentencing range for a bank robbery in which shots were fired by the robbers, or which was, say, the second bank robbery committed by the defendant.

In sentencing, the judge's task would be two-fold. First, the judge must determine which of the Commission's sentencing ranges is the appropriate range for this particular crime. Then, sentence must be imposed based on the factors listed in S. 1437. These include the very general notions of the need for deterrence, the need to promote respect for the law, the need to provide the defendant with educational or vocational training, and other considerations. If the judge imposes a sentence outside the Commission's range, the defendant can appeal if the sentence is higher, and the Government can appeal if the sentence is lower than the range. However, it does not appear that the defendant can appeal the judge's choice of sentencing range.

Professor Uelmen's analysis of the constitutional problems inherent in this sentencing scheme points out the peculiar irony in this Congressional attempt to rationalize the sentencing of federal defendants. Under the present sentencing regime, there are few constitutional constraints on the sentencing judge. He or she may use all kinds of information gleaned from post-conviction investigations by the probation office—including hearsay accounts. There is no appellate review of sentences, and if the judge's sentence is within the range specified in the statute, that sentence can be overturned on appeal only in the most extraordinary instances—usually articulated in lack of due process terms.

But now, with an attempt by Congress to bring a measure of fairness to sentencing, as Professor Uelmen suggests, this praiseworthy attempt may be laced with that very same constitutional problem. One problem will be the degree of proof required to establish those factors which would either (1) put the defendant in a higher sentencing range established by the Commission or (2) convince the judge that the defendant should receive a sentence which is higher than the range suggested by the Commission. Must these aggravating factors be proved beyond a reasonable doubt? For example, if the Commission rules that a simple bank robbery should draw a sentence of from 0 to 3 years, and that armed robbery should be punished by a sentence of from 3 to 5 years, has the Commission really defined the new offense of armed robbery, and, if so, should not this aggravating factor really be considered an "element" of the crime which, like all elements of the crime, must be proven beyond a reasonable doubt?

There are other, closely connected constitutional issues. Is it clear that the same burden of proof applies both to the defendant's factors in mitigation of sentence as to the prosecution's factors in aggravation of the sentence? Should the aggravating factors be generally stated in order to preserve the traditional discretion of the sentencing judge, or would such vague formulations raise constitutional objections of notice to the defendant? And must the defendant be given notice of any aggravating factors which the prosecution intends to prove? Does the establishment of a new "sentencing adversarial process" necessarily carry with it the panoply of due process rights which have traditionally guarded the rights of criminal defendants?

There are, of course, a host of other potential constitutional problems. But the irony in the sentencing proposal is now apparent. Where before, the unbridled discretion of the sentencing judge was subject to little constitutional restraint, now the new and liberal sentencing scheme—designed at least in part to make the whole process more fair—appears to be rife with potential problems. Perhaps this apparent contradiction is explained by the fact that the prosecutor is invited to prove not only that the defendant committed the crime, but that the defendant deserves a harsher punishment. The sentence is now part and parcel of the adversary process, and, being such, entitles the defendant to his or her constitutional protections.

It is also true that under the present scheme, a large degree of unfairness does intrude into the sentencing process. But there is the conviction on the part of some that since the sentencing is in the hands of an impartial judge, the unfairness will be minimal and will not reach constitutional dimensions. However, when the sentencing process is put, in part, in the hands of the prosecutor, the sense of fairness which is institutionalized in the present system is partly dissipated and extrinsic safeguards, namely, due process guarantees, may be deemed necessary.

In 1973, I suggested in an article[13] a different solution to the problem of disparate sentences for those convicted of the same crime. The proposal contemplated that the appropriate legislative body would determine a sentence for each crime, including its various degrees. The suggested scheme contemplated that the legislatively determined penalty would mandatorily be imposed after the first offense. The proposed scheme further contemplated that the sentencing judge would not take into account the many variables in the particular defendant's background and character, the thought being that these variables are the real culprit as judges bring to bear their own subjective notions of an individual's societal worth.

My proposed sentencing scheme would also embody a system of escalating mandatory sentences based solely on the number of prior convictions for the particular defendant. These sentences would be relatively short, and, as indicated, imposed only in conjunction with a system which grants every first offender a suspended sentence and an appropriate period of probation, with an exception in the case of first offenders for certain particularly heinous offenses such as premeditated murder. After the first offense, a short mandatory prison term of up to one year, which has been legislatively defined for each crime, would be imposed. Under my proposal, if there are exceptional or unusual mitigating circumstances, a suspended sentence may be recommended by the sentencing judge whose written recommendation and reasons for same must receive the approval of a reviewing panel. For the third offense, a much longer mandatory sentence of up to three years for each crime would be legislatively provided. Future offenses would receive proportionately greater mandatory sentences of up to five years. Thereafter, a recidivist would receive a maximum of five years for each conviction after the fifth conviction.

This system contemplates that parole boards would continue to exist only for the release of prisoners for a compelling humanitarian reason. Also, the judge would continue to have the power, as presently exists in the federal system, to treat juvenile offenders and young adult offenders as they presently are treated in the federal system. They would be continually eligible for suspended sentences, for example. Finally, victimless crimes would not be dealt with by the traditional criminal justice system. The chief objective of the proposal is to eliminate from the prison system all but the most intractable criminals. Another objective is to require a recognition of the fact that costly rehabilitation programs—if same could be effectively implemented in prisons—have never been and perhaps never will be provided by our society—certainly not in the foreseeable future.

CONCLUSION

Sentencing practices and procedures are under scrutiny all over the country. And it is apparent that existing sentencing goals and philosophies are being seriously questioned in many places. The judiciary, itself, has moved to set its own house in order by the appointment of sentencing committees whose task is to suggest remedies for disparities in sentencing. A long indifferent Congress has been alerted to the problems of sentence disparities. Prison unrest is said to have its origins in no small degree to a knowledge of such disparities. State legislative bodies are making radical changes in their sentencing goals and philosophies. The result is that we seem to be undergoing an unchartered revolution in sentencing philosophies and goals and sentencing practices and procedures.

There appear to be two main currents of thought at the base of this revolution. First, there is the conviction on the part of some that punishment should be certain and sentences imposed more often for certain crimes—regardless of the background and character of the defendant. This conviction is embodied in the 1973 New York Drug law. But at the same time that surer punishment is being sought irrespective of background and character of a defendant, there is the pervasive and perhaps even countervailing conviction that defendants should be punished individually but similarly if they have committed similar crimes and have similar backgrounds and character traits. This latter school of thought is evidenced by bills such as S. 1437 which seek to eradicate a history of unconscionable sentencing disparities. The most difficult problems with respect to this latter conviction are that it is no simple task to determine when we are dealing with similarly situated defendants with respect to a particular crime and what weight to give to certain background and character traits. This latter consideration obviously gives rise to wide disparities in sentencing. There is also the problem of trying to give proper weight to the seriousness of a white collar crime versus a nonviolent blue collar crime in order to close the gap between the punishments meted out in the two categories of cases.

The need seems clearly to be a kind of national consensus on sentencing philosophies and goals to give this revolution a rational base and the structuring of sentencing procedures and practices in such a way as to eliminate both disproportionality and disparities.

Finally, what is common in both the "get tough" and "fairness" sentencing philosophies is that complex constitutional problems arise when changes are made in an attempt to satisfy either or both of these two goals. The timeliness and appropriateness of these concerns are thus apparent. It cannot be denied that future constitutional law cases in the criminal justice area will include some new and perplexing constitutional law claims relating to disproportionality and disparities in criminal sentences which deserve the attention of able minds.

Notes

1. 433 U.S. 584 (1977).
2. 436 F. Supp. 1153 (1977), *rev'd* 576 F.2d 405 (2nd Cir. 1978).
3. California Uniform Determinate Sentence Act of 1976, CAL. PENAL CODE §1168 (West Supp. 1977).
4. S.B. 1437, Chs. 20-23.
5. N.Y. PENAL CODE §§220.00-.60 (McKinney Supp. 1978).
6. People v. Broadie, 37 N.Y. 2d 100, 371 N.Y.S. 2d 471, 332 N.E. 2d 338 (1975), *cert. denied*, 423 U.S. 950 (1975).
7. 428 U.S. 153 (1976).
8. 370 U.S. 660, 667 (1962).
9. *See, e.g.,* Downey v. Perini, 518 F.2d 1288, 1290 (6th Cir.), *vacated and remanded,* 423 U.S. 993 (1975); Hart v. Coiner, 483 F.2d 136, 140 (4th Cir. 1973), *cert. denied*, 415 U.S. 983 (1974); In re Lynch, 8 Cal. 3d 410, 503 P.2d 921, 105 Cal. Rptr. 217 (1972); Ralph v. Warden, 438 F.2d 736 (4th Cir. 1970), *cert. denied*, 408 U.S. 942 (1972); United States v. McKinney, 427 F.2d 449 (6th Cir. 1970), *cert. denied*, 402 U.S. 982 (1971); Workman v. Commonwealth, 429 S.W.2d 374 (Ky. 1968).
10. Trop v. Dulles, 356 U.S. 86, 101 (1958).
11. 37 N.Y.2d 100, 332 N.E.2d 338, 371 N.Y.S.2d 471, *cert. denied*, 423 U.S. 950 (1975).
12. *Infra.*
13. Motley, *"Law and Order" and the Criminal Justice System*, 64 J. OF CRIMINAL L. & CRIMINOLOGY 259 (1973).

Changing Conceptions of Administrative Due Process
By Bernard Schwartz*

What Madison once said of power—that it is of an encroaching nature[1]—is also true of administrative due process. The right to be heard prior to administrative action has increasingly been extended by the courts into areas which had previously been beyond the procedural pale. The result has been "a due process explosion in which the Court has carried the hearing requirement from one new area of governmental activity to another, an explosion which gives rise to many questions of major importance to our society."[2]

The starting point of the current "due process explosion" was the seminal decision in *Goldberg v. Kelly*.[3] That decision was not, however, written upon a tabula rasa. Before its implications can be understood, it is necessary for a word to be said about the pre-*Goldberg* law on administrative due process.

Pre-Goldberg v. Kelly Due Process

Our administrative law has been based upon Justice Frankfurter's oft-quoted assertion that "the history of liberty has largely been the history of the observance of procedural safeguards."[4] The American system has emphasized administrative procedure more than any other. The starting point in such emphasis has, of course, been the constitutional command of due process. "Audi alteram pertem—hear the other side!—a demand made insistently through the centuries, is now a command, spoken with the voice of the Due Process Clause."[5]

As Justice Douglas reminds us, "Notice and opportunity to be heard are fundamental to due process of law."[6] But our law has gone far beyond the "hear the other side" minimum. Building upon the due process foundation, American administrative law has constructed an imposing edifice of formal procedure. The consequence has been a virtual judicialization of the agencies—a consequence that became apparent soon after the creation of the first modern agency, the Interstate Commerce Commision. "You have organized the National Commission," wrote a commissioner to Thomas M. Cooley, first ICC chairman, when the latter retired, "laid its foundations broad and strong and made it what its creators never contemplated, a tribunal of justice, in a field and for a class of questions where all was chaos before."[7] From establishment of the ICC to the present, the administrative process has been set in the judicial mold.

Until *Goldberg v. Kelly*, however, this was true only in the ICC-type regulatory agencies. Before *Goldberg* the prevailing rule was that due process rights existed only in regulatory cases, for the law was based on what the Supreme Court now calls "the wooden distinction between 'rights' and 'privileges.'"[8] As a leading case put it, "Due process of law is not applicable unless one is being deprived of something to which he has a right."[9] If the

*Webb Professor of Law, New York University.

individual was being given something by government to which he had no preexisting *right*, he was being given a mere *privilege*. Grant of a privilege created no vested right; the privilege "may be withdrawn at will and is not entitled to protection under the due process clause."[10]

The privilege concept was widely used, in such diverse fields as licensing, immigration, government employment, and government contracts.[11] But its broadest potential was in the burgeoning field of social welfare—the field that has been the expanding area of present-day administrative law. During the past generation government has been assuming benefactory functions in a geometric progression. Under the privilege concept, all this public largess involved mere privileges. This meant insulation of an ever-larger area of administrative power from the safeguards of procedural due process. As recently as 1966, a federal court could dismiss a suit by a welfare recipient on the simple ground that there was no "right" to welfare.[12] At the beginning of 1967, only that one action by welfare claimants had been finally decided in the federal courts.

Goldberg v. Kelly

All this has been changed by *Goldberg v. Kelly*.[13] At issue there were New York City regulations governing the termination of welfare benefits. The regulations provided for notice "of proposed discontinuance or suspension . . . together with the reasons for the intended action," and allowed the recipient to "submit in writing a statement or other evidence to demonstrate why his grant should not be discontinued." The agency could then decide that benefits should cease. The terminated recipient was at that point entitled to what the regulations termed a "fair hearing," which was a full trial-type proceeding with all the essentials of formal adjudicatory procedure.

The Supreme Court held that the procedures so provided were constitutionally inadequate. In the Court's view, due process requires "a full 'evidentiary hearing'" *before* termination of welfare benefits. Most important for our purposes was the Court's specific rejection of the privilege concept. "The constitutional challenge cannot be answered by an argument that public assistance benefits are a 'privilege' and not a 'right.'" It is no longer accurate to think of welfare benefits as only privileges. "Such benefits are a matter of statutory entitlement for persons qualified to receive them." In this sense, they are "more like 'property' than a 'gratuity.'"[14] Welfare cases, like regulatory cases, must now be considered to involve state action that adjudicates important rights. "The same governmental interests which counsel the provision of welfare, counsel as well its uninterrupted provision to those eligible to receive it; pre-termination evidentiary hearings are indispensable to that end."[15]

Entitlements and Judicialization

The pre-*Goldberg* privileges, removed from the reach of procedural due process, have been transformed by *Goldberg* into *entitlements*, fully qualified for due process protection. It is true that *Board of Regents v. Roth*[16] shows that, even since *Goldberg*, "the range of interests protected by procedural due process is not infinite."[17] Though the right-privilege distinction has been rejected, the word "property" in the Due Process Clause must still be given some meaning. "To have a property interest in a benefit, a person clearly must have more than an abstract need or desire for it. He must have more than a unilateral expectation of it. He must, instead, have a legitimate claim of entitlement to it."[18]

But the usual recipient of governmental largess does have a statutory entitlement in the *Goldberg-Roth* sense—i.e., if he comes within the terms of the statutory scheme, he is entitled to the benefits provided under it. The post-*Goldberg* cases, particularly those in the lower courts, rapidly applied its hearing requirement to virtually the entire benefactory apparatus of the Welfare State. "The trend in one area after another has been to say, 'If there, why not here?'"[19] The right to be heard as a matter of due process was extended en masse to all the benefactory areas of administrative power, from the welfare benefits involved in *Goldberg* itself to disability,[20] medicare,[21] unemployment,[22] and veterans' benefits,[23] as well as education[24] and housing.[25]

Does abandonment of the privilege concept, however, necessarily mean that the whole range of benefactory administration must be held to the full panoply of adversary requirements traditionally imposed on regulatory administration?

Complaints of undue judicialization of administration procedure have long been heard. As Judge Friendly has noted, "cases before the old-line regulatory agencies have been characterized by enormous records (read by no one), great expense, and giant delays."[26] Perhaps the problem was not as pressing so long as it was confined to the regulatory agencies. "Burdensome though it is, the cost of [formal] procedure is often but a small part of the amount involved in any regulatory case of consequence and can be borne without difficulty by a multi-million dollar corporation of the kind commonly regulated by the big federal agencies. That class of *administrés* can be left to take care of itself."[27]

Since *Goldberg* formal procedural requirements are no longer limited to cases involving "that class of *administrés*." This led Judge Friendly to assert that "over-judicialization in the regulatory agencies in the United States is as nothing compared to what would result if all the safeguards of the Administrative Procedure Act were to be applied to the denial, withdrawal, or curtailment of welfare, medical and unemployment payments, and other benefits. . . . The United States would be buried under an avalanche of paper, like Professor Fulgence Tapir in Anatole Frances' Penguin Island—if indeed enough reporters to type the records could be found."[28]

Due Process Ad Absurdum?

Judge Friendly asserts that "there must be some floor below which no hearing of any sort is required"[29] and gives as an example a case cited by the present writer: "One wonders whether even the most outspoken of the Justices would require one on the complaint of an AFDC recipient, recounted by Professor Bernard Schwartz, that 'I didn't receive one house-dress, underwears. . . . They gave me two underwears for $14.10 . . . it should have been $17.60 instead of $14.10.'"[30]

But the case cited was one in which a trial-type hearing *was* held before the agency decision on the adequacy of the underwear grant.[31] Under the governing statutes, a full "fair hearing" might be demanded as of right whenever the welfare agency refused to grant the full amount applied for in any special-grant application, however small the amount at issue was.

This case constitutes the veritable reductio ad absurdum of the recent "due process explosion." Perhaps the *Goldberg* plaintiff whose benefits are being terminated should be afforded the same procedural protection as a business adversely affected by a regulatory decision. But must the same be true of the decision denying $3.50 of the amount requested in a special grant for underwear—where the amount involved does not even begin to cover the cost of transcribing the record?

The post-*Goldberg* cases have tended to rebuff welfare agencies when they have sought to reduce the right to be heard to what they claimed was a manageable scope. An attempt by welfare agencies to deal with the hearing glut caused by the broadside hearing requirement in welfare cases was rejected in *Carleson v. Yee-Litt*.[32] Relying on the principle that hearings are required only where there are no disputed issues of fact,[33] the California welfare agency issued regulations permitting the reduction or termination of welfare benefits prior to a hearing whenever the Chief Referee determined that the recipient's appeal raised only issues of policy and no issue of fact or judgment. The three-judge district court held that the

California regulations violated the minimum due process standard laid down in *Goldberg*. The fact-policy distinction was found to be unclear and unmanageable, and that necessarily led to erroneous hearing denials. The Supreme Court affirmed without opinion.

A dissent in the district court noted that the errors alleged by plaintiffs in administration of the California fact-policy distinction applied to only a minute percentage of the cases. Of 4,090 hearing requests filed in October, 1972, plaintiffs alleged only 49 cases where welfare recipients were erroneously denied aid pending a hearing. Of these only five involved alleged errors in administering the fact-policy distinction.[34]

In adopting the district court view that the only way the law could ensure against erroneous hearing denials was to require hearings before reduction or termination in all cases, was not the Supreme Court losing sight of Judge Learned Hand's famous dictum that "due process of law does not mean infallible process of law"?[35]

In a more recent case regulations under the Social Security Act provided that benefits were not to be reduced, suspended, or terminated without notice and hearing rights. The regulations contained exceptions in cases where there had been a clerical or mechanical error in effectuation of a determination or decision or the facts indicating suspension, reduction, or termination action were supplied by the recipients and the conclusions to be drawn from such facts were not subject to conflicting interpretations. In cases involving these exceptions benefits might be reduced, suspended, or terminated without notice and hearing. The court ruled the exceptions invalid. Even in cases involving clerical or mechanical errors in agency determinations awarding benefits *Goldberg* applies. "In arguing that a full oral evidentiary hearing is unnecessary in the context of his exceptions, defendant evades the more fundamental issue presented by this case, i.e., whether advance written notice and thus some opportunity for a hearing, whatever its form, can be denied when it is demonstrated that SSI benefits may be denied to eligible recipients. The cases teach that such a denial is unfair and violative of due process."[36]

What such a decision means in practice is illustrated by a New York case. A welfare recipient had informed the county welfare agency that his monthly earnings were $563.33. The agency then determined that the adjusted gross income of the recipient was in excess of the eligibility standards. The court held that, even in such a case, the recipient had the *Goldberg* right to a pretermination hearing (with payments in the interim): "This right cannot be denied by virtue of any argument that the recipient himself supplied the information on which the Department bases its determination to discontinue the assistance."[37]

Consider the situation of this welfare recipient. He has informed the welfare agency that he has obtained a job which makes him ineligible for further welfare payments. Under the court's decision he must now be given notice of intent to terminate which must inform him of his right to a prior hearing (with a right to continued payment of benefits in the interim). Is there any doubt that he will opt for a hearing, which means he must continue receiving payments until the hearing and decision, even though he himself has furnished information of employment which makes him completely ineligible?

Retreat from Goldberg?

Two approaches may be followed to avoid the ludicrous results involved in extending the full hearing requirement to the whole range of benefactory administrative action. The first is to retreat from *Goldberg* itself and refuse to follow its implication of wholesale application of the pretermination hearing demand to all public largess decisions. As already noted, the post-*Goldberg* cases extended its hearing requirement to cases involving comparable benefits, such as disability, medicare, unemployment, and veterans' benefits.[38] More recent Surpeme Court decisions indicate, however, that such extension was unwarranted.

The decisions referred to are those in *Arnett v. Kennedy*[39] and *Mathews v. Eldridge*,[40] where the Court held that due process did not require hearings before a government employee was discharged or disability payments were terminated. Though the holding in *Arnett* on the validity of discharge without a prior hearing was clear, internal fragmentation (the Justices divided three-three-three) prevented agreement in any majority opinion. Though six Justices (the three concurring and three dissenting Justices) did hold that the government employee had an entitlement in his job protected by due process, the same number also held that no pretermination hearing was required (the three-man plurality, who held that no hearing at all was required, and the three concurring Justices, who held that due process requirements were satisfied by a postdischarge hearing).

If *Arnett* stood alone, its precedential value would be blurred because of the fragmented nature of the decision. But it has now been joined by *Eldridge*, where the opinion of the Court was joined by six Justices, with only two dissents. The issue in *Eldridge* was whether due process required that prior to the termination of social security disability payments the recipient be afforded an opportunity for an evidentiary hearing. The statute and regulations provided that after an initial determination by the Social Security Administration terminating payments, the recipient could seek reconsideration and then an evidentiary hearing before an SSA administrative law judge. Payments were to be terminated after the initial determination, but if the recipient were to prevail after the reconsideration, hearing, or a later agency appeal, he would be entitled to retroactive payments. The lower courts ruled that the interest of the disability recipient in uninterrupted benefits was indistinguishable from that of the welfare recipient in *Goldberg* and held that due process required a pretermination hearing. The Supreme Court reversed, holding that due process was satisfied by the posttermination procedures provided in the agency.

The lower courts had concluded that the post-*Goldberg* decisions had demonstrated that the *Goldberg* requirement was not limited to situations involving the deprivation of vital necessities. The Supreme Court stressed that *Goldberg* involved the "brutal need" of persons on the very margin of subsistence where termination "may deprive an eligible recipient of the very means by which to live while he waits."[41] Eligibility for disability benefits, in contrast, was said not to be based upon financial need. Yet, as the *Eldridge* opinion recognizes, even with respect to the degree of deprivation, the difference between welfare and disability termination can be overstated. The disability recipient is normally virtually as dependent upon his payments as the welfare recipient.

Mathews v. Eldridge shows that the law may be moving toward the point where *Goldberg v. Kelly* stands virtually alone in vindicating the due process right to a pretermination hearing, at least where monetary benefits are at stake. *Goss v. Lopez*[42] (where the Court held that due process required a hearing before even short school suspensions) shows that cases not involving money payments may still stand on a different footing. There is a line between the two types of case, in the relative ability to repair the effects of an improper decision. One may question, however, whether the results in *Eldridge* and *Goss* are consistent. The *Eldridge* opinion emphasizes that "the degree of potential deprivation that may be created by a particular decision"[43] is a key factor to be considered in determining whether there is any due process right to a pretermination hearing. If that is the case, who suffers the greater deprivation, the pupil subject to a short suspension or the disabled worker whose payments are ended?

There is a comparable inconsistency between the results in *Goldberg* and *Arnett*. It may be wrong for the welfare recipient to have inferior procedural rights as compared to the civil servant, even though the latter performs services for the payments received. But for him to have superior rights is justice turned bottom-side-up.

In addition, it is unreal to say, as the plurality and concurring *Arnett* opinions do, that the discharged civil servant is not really hurt because, if vindicated on appeal after full hearing, he will be reinstated with back pay. To be sure, the deprivation is less than that involved in *Goldberg* where termination in face of the "brutal need" of the welfare recipient "may deprive an eligible recipient of the very means by which to live while he waits."[44] But the Due Process Clause protects against *deprivation*, not only *destitution*.

Despite these inconsistencies, *Goldberg v. Kelly* will probably continue to be followed, but will be confined to the welfare termination case. In cases involving other types of public largess, the procedural theme will be set by *Arnett* and *Eldridge*. This does not mean no due process protection, but only that a pretermination hearing is not necessary. It should not be forgotten that six Justices in *Arnett* held that procedural due process does protect the government employee's entitlement to his job. The concurring opinions (the swing votes in the decision) stated that the due process demand was met by the postremoval hearing provided in the case. The right to a posttermination hearing was reaffirmed in *Mathews v. Eldridge*, where the Court stressed the claimant's right to an evidentiary hearing on administrative review of the decision terminating his disability benefits.

Even so, the practical effect of *Eldridge* will be to reduce substantially the number of hearings which nonwelfare benefactory agencies will be required to hold. Far fewer people will insist upon their hearing rights if they can demand the hearing only after the agency decision had gone into effect. The result may be to make the due process requirement workable by drastically cutting down the number of hearings held by nonregulatory agencies. One is nevertheless left with a modest doubt on whether postdecision hearings alone are really enough to give those affected the fundamentals of fair play[45] which due process demands. Is the *Arnett-Eldridge* retreat from *Goldberg* the only way to avoid the opposite extreme of imposing the details of judicialized adversary procedure upon the entire benefactory decision process?

Flexible Due Process

A second approach to the problems involved in overbroad extension of judicialized procedural requirements involves the dilution of *Goldberg v. Kelly* in another important respect. The *Goldberg* Court indicated that, where due process required a hearing, a full evidentiary hearing was demanded. The opinion of Justice Brennan did state that a full judicial-type hearing was not necessary.[46] This disclaimer must not, however, be given too much weight. "After the usual litany that the required hearing 'need not take the form of a judicial or quasi-judicial trial', Mr. Justice Brennan proceeded to demand almost all the elements of one."[47] In *Mathews v. Eldridge*, the Court itself conceded that, in *Goldberg*, "the Court held that a hearing closely approximating a judicial trial is necessary".[48]

The *Goldberg* requirement of a judicial-type evidentiary hearing may pose a serious dilemma for a system of administrative law which has extended procedural requirements from the traditional regulatory field to the expanding area of social welfare. However fair in theory, fully judicialized procedure may frustrate effective administration in fields such as welfare and social security. This is true not only because of the nature of the cases involved, but also because of their number. When we move from the Interstate Commerce Commission-type agencies to those administering benefactory statutes such as the Social Security Act, we move into mass administrative justice, where cases are measured not in the thousands but in the millions. "To impose in each case even truncated trial-type procedures might well overwhelm administrative facilities. . . . Moreover further formalizing the . . . process and escalating its formality and adversary nature may not only make it too costly . . . but also destroy its effectiveness."[49]

In areas of mass administrative justice, such as social security with its over 100,000,000 decided claims a year,[50] formal adjudicatory procedure may have to give way where it can serve only to frustrate effective administration. As the Supreme Court has put it, with regard to the social security system, "The system's administrative structure and procedures, with essential determinations numbering into the millions, are of a size and extent difficult to comprehend. . . . 'Such a system must be fair—and it must work.'"[51]

If our administrative law system is to be workable as well as fair, it will have to realize that due process is a flexible concept. The Procrustean notion[52] that when due process demands a hearing it must demand a full-scale judicial-type trial in every case has already started to give way. The Supreme Court itself has recently declared that "The judicial model of an evidentiary hearing is neither a required, nor even the most effective, method of decisionmaking in all circumstances."[53] The law must recognize that due process need not necessarily mean traditional adversary process, "procedural process in the administrative setting does not always require application of the judicial model."[54] Administrative procedure must develop as a compromise between what a British judge once called the methods of natural justice and those of courts of justice.[55]

For this to be accomplished the law will have to go beyond the *Arnett* and *Eldridge* retreat from *Goldberg* which permits agency action without a pretermination hearing. It must also recognize that the still-required posttermination hearing need not necessarily conform to all the requirements of the traditional adjudicatory hearing in every case.

As Judge Friendly has urged, it is only "some kind of hearing"[56] that is required by due process. The type of hearing required may vary with the seriousness of the particular case. "This is not to suggest that benefits can be precisely quantified in dollar terms or that some excess of the costs would call for reconsideration of the required procedures. As Mr. Justice Brennan has rightly said, administrative fairness usually does entail 'some additional administrative burdens and expense'. But if the excess of costs over estimated benefits were, say, four-fold, with the concomitant likelihood that, in the Chief Justice's words, 'new layers of procedural protection may become an intolerable drain on the very funds earmarked for food, clothing, and other living essentials', one would at least wish to examine whether it would not be possible to devise some less cumbersome but nevertheless fair procedures."[57]

Under Judge Friendly's approach, due process requirements should depend upon incremental analysis—i.e., gains versus losses for each additional procedure required. Full judicialization may be demanded in cases with the most serious consequences, such as welfare termination or school expulsion. In other cases, the process may demand less. Since there are alternatives less burdensome than fully judicialized hearings, the law should choose the less burdensome alternatives, where the incremental gain in the more burdensome procedure would be outweighed by the marginal costs, e.g., in time and expense.[58] In other words, as the Supreme Court affirmed in 1975, determination "of the precise dictates of due process requires consideration of both the governmental function involved and the private interests affected by official action. . . . [T]he formality and procedural requisites for [a due process] hearing can vary, depending upon the importance of the interests involved and the nature of the subsequent proceedings."[59]

The Supreme Court has recently indicated its agreement with this incremental approach. *Ingraham v. Wright*[60] dealt with the question of whether imposition of disciplinary corporal punishment in public schools was consonant with the requirements of due process. The Court found that corporal punishment implicated a constitutionally protected liberty interest. It did not, however, conclude from this that, as in *Goss v. Lopez*[61] notice and hearing were required by due process prior to imposition of the disciplinary penalty. In this case, said the Court, traditional common law remedies were fully adequate to afford due process.

It went on to say, however, that "even if the need for advance procedural safeguards were clear, the question would remain whether the incremental benefit could justify the cost."[62] Prior hearing as a universal constitutional requirement in corporal punishment cases would unduly burden school discipline. "'At some point the benefit of an additional safeguard to the individual affected . . . and to society in terms of increased assurance that the action is just, may be outweighed by the cost. . . . We think that point has been reached in this case."[63]

In *Ingraham* the burden imposed by requiring administrative safeguards of notice and hearing were so much greater than any benefit to be derived that predisciplinary hearings should not be required. Previously *Goss v. Lopez* itself had recognized that, even where due process is held to require a hearing, the hearing requirement itself may still be flexible. *Goss*, as already noted, held that due process prohibited the summary suspension of public school pupils. Even where only short suspensions of up to ten days were involved, school authorities were not free from notice and hearing requirements. *Goss*, however, stopped "short of construing the Due Process Clause to require, country-wide, that hearings in connection with short suspensions must afford the student the opportunity to secure counsel, to confront and cross-examine witnesses . . . or to call his own witnesses."[64]

More formal procedures may be required for longer suspensions or expulsions. Full judicialization may be demanded in cases with the most serious consequences, such as welfare termination or school expulsion. The hearings demanded for them should approach trial-type proceedings, with all the requirements demanded by *Goldberg*.

In other cases, due process requirements should depend upon the already-mentioned incremental analysis. Since there are alternatives less burdensome than fully judicialized hearings, the law should choose the less burdensome alternatives, where the incremental gain in the more burdensome procedure would be outweighed by the marginal costs, e.g., in time and expense.

"[T]he probable value, if any, of additional . . . procedural safeguards" must be balanced against "the [state] interest, including the function involved and the fiscal and administrative burdens that the additional . . procedural requirement would entail."[65] The drastic consequences involved in the cutting off of welfare led *Goldberg* to demand all but full judicialization for welfare termination hearings. In *Goss* where school suspensions were subject to due process procedural requirements, the Court stated only that students facing suspension "must be given *some* kind of notice and afforded *some* kind of hearing."[66] Since the impact on the student of a short suspension was slight compared with the undesirable consequences of subjecting routine school discipline to the formalities of trial-type procedures, an informal hearing was all that was required. In the "informal give-and-take between student and disciplinarian," it was up to the latter whether to summon the accuser, permit cross-examination, allow the student to present witnesses, or permit counsel.[67] Though both welfare terminations and short student suspensions adversely affect individual entitlements and are consequently subject to due process requirements, the detailed procedures demanded are not the same in both cases.

Judge Hufstedler has, however, reminded us that there may be dangers in the flexible approach to due process. In a ninth circuit case, the court held that tenants in federally financed housing projects had a due process right to be heard before permission for rent increases was granted their landlords by the Federal Housing Administration. However, the Court went on to recognize that trial-type procedure would be inappropriate here, because of the "sheer number of tenants involved," the technical issues presented, and the lengthy delay that would ensue. All that was required was notice of a proposed rent increase, an opportunity to make written objections, and the receipt of a concise statement of the FHA's reasons for its action.[68]

Judge Hufstedler, dissenting, objected that the decision was one that eviscerated the due process protections that it purported to grant. "The great procedural protections of due process are reduced by the majority to little more than a right to send and receive mail. Procedural due process is flexible, but it is not flaccid."[69] Due process, said Hufstedler, requires as a minimum, a meaningful evidentiary hearing, with the right to appear, to call and examine witnesses, and to present documentary evidence.

The courts must be vigilant in ensuring that flexible due process does not result in a general dilution of due process. The danger is that, by a legal counterpart of Gresham's Law, second-class procedures will be permitted to take over the administrative field. At the same time, a flexible due process concept will enable the law to avoid trial-type adversary procedure as the exclusive medium, regardless of cost or efficacy, for resolving all cases to which the due process right to be heard now applies. Where the theoretical gain in the appearance of justice through a full-scale trial is outweighed by the inappropriateness of judicial process (as where the individual interests at stake are less than the costs of conducting the proceeding) agencies should be permitted to "hear" through something less than the full panoply of traditional adversary process.

Conclusion

Writing in a case involving FCC regulation, Judge Bazelon asserts that "The life of the law in this area is . . . surely not logic. I would be less concerned if I were sure it was experience; however, surveying the field after twenty-five years of work, I have serious doubts that the experience of nonregulation or the history of regulation really were the cause of all this startling, even radical departure from our traditions."[70]

Too much of our administrative law is grounded neither on logic nor experience. Particularly in a period of explosive change there is danger that the personal predilections of the judge, justified by post hoc rationalizations, have become the decisive factor.

In 1970, the Supreme Court laid down the broadside *Goldberg v. Kelly*[71] pretermination evidentiary hearing requirement in entitlement (*née* "privilege") cases. Since the requirement was stated in due process terms, it was one which presumably could not be diluted or dispensed with by statute. Only four years later, however, in *Arnett v. Kennedy*,[72] a statute doing just that was given effect, though the Court could not agree on any rationale which commanded the concurrence of more than three Justices. A year later, in *Goss v. Lopez*,[73] the pendulum swung back to *Goldberg* (or even beyond), when the Court ruled that short school suspensions must be preceded by due process hearings. Then in 1976, *Mathews v. Eldridge*[74] went back to the *Arnett* result, holding that due process did not require pretermination hearings before disability benefits were terminated.

Is the difference in result to be explained less in terms of legal logic—or even experience—than of the swinging back and forth of one or two Justices on the procedural due process issue? It reminds one of T.R. Powell's comment on the Court of the mid-thirties. "Years ago, that learned lawyer John Selden in talking of 'Council' observed: 'They talk (but blasphemously enough) that the Holy Ghost is President of their General Councils when the truth is, the odd Man is still the Holy Ghost.'"[75]

Such a comment, applied to the subject of this paper, may be unduly cynical. The post-*Goldberg* cases do fit into a logical pattern, inconsistent though it may be with the implications of *Goldberg* itself. The *Goldberg* pretermination hearing requirement is now applied only in cases involving welfare and nonmonetary benefits. That is why the requirement was imposed in school suspension cases by *Goss v. Lopez,* but not in the public employment and disability cases at issue in *Arnett v. Kennedy* and *Mathews v. Eldridge.*

Some might say that *Ingraham v. Wright*[76] (which held that corporal punishment might be imposed in schools without prior notice and hearing) is inconsistent with the *Goss-Eldridge* dividing line. According to the Court, however, there is no such inconsistency. In *Goss*, the school suspension interrupted the student's entitlement to education; the corporal punishment at issue in *Ingraham* had no such result. "Unlike *Goss v. Lopez* . . ., this case does not involve the state-created property interest in public education. The purpose of corporal punishment is to correct a child's behavior without interrupting his education."[77]

Welfare cases aside (at least as long as *Goldberg v. Kelly* continues to be followed), the dividing line so far as the due process right to a pretermination hearing is concerned appears to be that between the *Goss* and *Eldridge* cases—i.e., that between monetary entitlements (where reimbursement after later hearing and decision reversing the original termination decision can, in theory at least, make the individual whole for his temporary loss of benefits) and entitlements other than money payments, such as that to public education. One may not agree with the line in terms of fairness to those on either side (e.g., the question already posed of who is hurt more and hence has the greater need for precedural protection—the pupil subject to a short suspension or the disabled worker whose disability payments are ended). But it is a workable line and one which will substantially reduce the number of hearings which must be held, as compared with the number which would be required if *Goldberg* had not been modified by the *Arnett* and *Eldridge* cases.

In addition, administrative due process itself is coming to be construed as a flexible concept, so that not every case to which due process applies must necessarily demand a full evidentiary hearing. Not long ago such a flexible intepretation would have been deemed inconsistent with due process demands. As Judge Friendly puts it, "When a hearing is required, what kind of hearing must it be? Specifically, how closely must it conform to the judicial model? For a long time we had labored under the illusion that the two latter questions could be answered rather easily. We needed only to determine whether the issue was one of adjudicative or of legislative fact. If the former, a full trial-type hearing was demanded . . . the Supreme Court. . . . yielded too readily to the notions that the adversary system is the only appropriate model and that there is only one acceptable solution to any problem."[78]

Now all this has changed. Even when agency action "implicates a constitutionally protected interest,"[79] i.e., an interest protected by due process, a hearing may not be required (as *Ingraham v. Wright*[80] shows) where the incremental benefit does not justify the cost. And, even where a hearing is required, a judicialized evidentiary hearing is not necessarily required in every case. *Goss v. Lopez*[81] shows that, even when a hearing must be held, the due process demands are flexible. When the burden of a full evidentiary hearing far outweighs the benefit of judicialization it is only "some kind of hearing" that must be held. It is this flexible notion of due process that makes the burden imposed on school administration by the *Goss* decision tolerable.

Nobody outside Bedlam can suppose that the reason why due process requires administrative hearings is to give the greatest amount of work to the greatest number of lawyers. Yet that is the inevitable result of an unflexible application of *Goldberg v. Kelly* to the entire administrative process. The more flexible concept that is starting to be applied avoids such a situation and makes due process workable. As Judge Friendly stated in a foreword to a book co-authored by the present writer, "If due process is interpreted as a mechanical yardstick, unalterable regardless of time, place, and circumstances, it may make government unworkable. . . . The Constitution does not require full judicialization in every conceivable case."[82]

Post-Script[83]

The most important more recent case on the due process right to be heard was *Board of Curators of University of Missouri v. Horowitz.*[84] Respondent brought an action challenging her dismissal as a student from the medical school of a state university, alleging that petitioners had not accorded her procedural due process prior to her dismissal. The dismissal had been based upon faculty dissatisfaction with respondent's clinical performance. The Council of Evaluation, which assessed academic performance, had recommended that she be dropped. As an "appeal" of that decision, respondent was permitted to take examinations under seven physicians. Only two of them recommended her graduation. The Council then reaffirmed its decision. The recommendation was approved by the faculty coordinating committee and dean and sustained, on appeal, by the provost.

The Court rejected respondent's due process claim. According to it, a different result was not compelled by *Goss v. Lopez,*[85] which had ruled that the due process right to be heard applied where students were suspended from public schools for disciplinary reasons. There are differences between disciplinary decisions and decisions taken for academic reasons which may call for hearings in connection with the former but not the latter. Academic evaluations, in contrast to disciplinary determinations, bear little resemblance to the fact-finding proceedings to which the hearing requirement has traditionally been attached. A decision which rests on academic judgments is more subjective and evaluative than the typical fact questions presented in the average disciplinary decision. The determination to dismiss for academic reasons is comparable to the decision as to the proper grade for a student in a course; like the latter, it requires an expert evaluation of cumulative information and is not readily adapted to adjudicatory procedural tools. Under these circumstances, the Court declined to ignore the historic judgment of educators and formalize the academic dismissal process by requiring a hearing. A school must remain an academic institution, not a courtroom or an administrative hearing room.

In more traditional terms, the *Horowitz* decision is justified by an accepted exception to the due process right to be heard: what has been termed the "pure administrative process"— i.e., cases where decisions are made on the basis of observation by technical experts or tests. When the decision evaluates the skill or competence of an individual, a trial-type proceeding is inappropriate. What is needed is a test of the individual's competence. In an academic setting, evaluation of performance by the appropriate educational authorities is all that is required.

It is, of course, elementary that there is a due process right to be heard only when "life, liberty, or property" are adversely affected by *governmental* action. As a general proposition, due process furnishes no protection against summary *private* action: the State, not the private individual, is the addressee of the Due Process Clause. *Jackson v. Metropolitan Edison Co.*[86] all but aborted a prior trend toward what may be termed "corporate due process." The Court there held that due process restraints might not be extended to privately-owned utilities. Hence, termination of electric service without notice and hearing did not violate due process. The fact that the utility was subject to pervasive state regulation did not by itself convert its action into that of the state for due process purposes.

Memphis Light, Gas & Water Division v. Craft[87] holds that a different result must be reached where the utility in question is publicly owned. At issue was the termination of utility service supplied by a municipal utility (owned and operated by a division of the city of Memphis). In such a case, where the utility may not terminate service "at will" but only "for cause," respondent customers asserted a "legitimate claim of entitlement" within the protection of the Due Process Clause. Due process required that the municipal utility provide its customers with some administrative procedure prior to termination of service.

In these more recent cases, the Supreme Court has continued to apply the flexible balancing approach to due process noted in this paper. The *Horowitz* opinion recognized that, while the value of some form of hearing in a disciplinary context outweighed any resulting harm to the academic environment, the same conclusion did not follow in the academic context. The incremental gains involved in enlarging the judicial presence in the academic community would be clearly outweighed by the marginal costs: "a hearing may be 'useless or even harmful in finding out the truth as to scholarship.'"[88]

The Court, in its *Memphis* holding that procedural due process protected the municipal utility customer, did not impose formal trial-type procedural requirements upon the decision to terminate service. It stressed again that only "some kind of hearing" is demanded in such a case. Under the balancing approach, some administrative procedure for entertaining customer complaints prior to termination was required. All that was necessary here was notice and an opportunity to present objections prior to termination. The latter requirement could be met by opportunity for a meeting with a responsible employee empowered to resolve the dispute. As so construed, the "some kind of hearing" requirement should not prove burdensome.

Notes

1. THE FEDERALIST, No. 48.
2. Friendly, *Some Kind of Hearing,* 123 U. PA. L. REV. 1267, 1268 (1975) [hereinafter *Friendly*].
3. 397 U.S. 254 (1970).
4. McNabb v. United States, 318 U.S. 332, 347 (1943).
5. Caritativo v. California, 357 U.S. 549, 558 (1958) (Frankfurter, J., dissenting).
6. Joint Anti-Fascist Refugee Comm. v. McGrath, 341 U.S. 123, 178 (1951) (Douglas, J., concurring).
7. SCHWARTZ, THE LAW IN AMERICA: A HISTORY 141 (1974).
8. Board of Regents v. Roth, 408 U.S. 564, 571 (1972).
9. Bailey v. Richardson, 182 F.2d 46, 58 (D.C. Cir. 1950), *aff'd by equally divided Court,* 341 U.S. 918 (1951).
10. Gilchrist v. Bierring, 14 N.W.2d 724, 730 (Iowa 1944).
11. The cases are discussed in B. SCHWARTZ, ADMINISTRATIVE LAW 215-19 (1976) [hereinafter SCHWARTZ].
12. Smith v. Board of Commissioners, 259 F. Supp. 423 (D.D.C. 1966), *aff'd,* 380 F.2d 632 (D.C. Cir. 1967).
13. 397 U.S. 254 (1970).
14. 397 U.S. at 262.
15. *Id.* at 265.
16. 408 U.S. 564 (1972).
17. *Id.* at 570.
18. *Id.* at 576-7.
19. Friendly, *supra* note 2, at 1300.
20. Richardson v. Wright, 405 U.S. 208 (1972).
21. Martinez v. Richardson, 472 F.2d 1121 (10th Cir. 1973).
22. California Human Resources Dep't v. Java, 402 U.S. 121 (1971).
23. Plato v. Roudebush, 397 F. Supp. 1295 (D. Md. 1975).
24. Goss v. Lopez, 419 U.S. 565 (1975).
25. Escalera v. Housing Authority, 425 F. 2d 853 (2d Cir. 1970).
26. Foreword to SCHWARTZ AND WADE, LEGAL CONTROL OF GOVERNMENT: ADMINISTRATIVE LAW IN BRITAIN AND THE UNITED STATES xvi-xvii (1972).

27. *Id*. at 113.
28. *Id*. at xviii.
29. Friendly, *supra* note 2, at 1275.
30. *Id*.
31. *See* SCHWARTZ AND WADE, *supra* note 26, at 243.
32. 412 U.S. 924 (1973).
33. *See* SCHWARTZ, *supra* note 11, at 243.
34. Yee-Litt v. Richardson, 353 F. Supp. 996, 1001 (N.D. Cal. 1973).
35. Schechtman v. Foster, 172 F.2d 339, 341 (2d Cir. 1949).
36. Cardinale v. Mathews, 399 F. Supp. 1163, 1175 (D.D.C. 1975).
37. Damiano v. Shuart, 343 N.Y.S. 2d 723, 725 (Sup. Ct. 1973).
38. *Supra* notes 20-23.
39. 416 U.S. 134 (1974).
40. 424 U.S. 319 (1976).
41. Goldberg v. Kelly, 397 U.S. at 264.
42. 419 U.S. 565 (1975).
43. 424 U.S. at 341.
44. Goldberg v. Kelly, 397 U.S. at 264.
45. FCC v. Pottsville Broadcasting Co., 309 U.S. 134, 143 (1940).
46. 397 U.S. at 266.
47. Friendly, *supra* note 2, at 1299.
48. 424 U.S. at 333.
49. Goss v. Lopez, 419 U.S. at 583.
50. During the 1976 fiscal year, the Social Security Administration processed over 129,000,000 claims.
51. Richardson v. Perales, 402 U.S. 389, 399 (1971).
52. Compare Friendly, in SCHWARTZ AND WADE, *supra* note 26, at xviii.
53. Mathews v. Eldridge, 424 U.S. at 348.
54. Dixon v. Love, *431* U.S. *105, 115* (1977).
55. Local Government Board v. Arlidge, [1915] A.C. 120, 138.
56. *See* Friendly, *supra* note 2, *passim*.
57. *Id*. at 1303-04.
58. See Goldberg v. Kelly, 397 U.S. at 263.
59. See Goldberg v. Kelly, 397 U.S. at 263.
59. Fusari v. Steinberg, 419 U.S. 379 (1975).
60. 430 U.S. 651 (1977).
61. 419 U.S. 565 (1975).
62. 430 U.S. at 680.
63. *Id*. at *682* (quoting Mathews v. Eldridge, 424 U.S. at 348).
64. 419 U.S. at 583.
65. Ingraham v. Wright, *430* U.S. at *675* (quoting Mathews v. Eldridge, 424 U.S. at 345).
66. 419 U.S. at 579.
67. *Id*. at 584.
68. Geneva Towers Tenants Organization v. Federated Mortgage Inv., 504 F.2d 483 (9th Cir. 1974).
69. *Id*. at 498.
70. Citizens Committee v. FCC, 506 F.2d 246, 282 (D.C. Cir. 1974) (Bazelon, J., concurring).
71. 397 U.S. 254 (1970).
72. 416 U.S. 134 (1974).
73. 419 U.S. 565 (1975).
74. 424 U.S. 319 (1976).
75. Quoted in B. SCHWARTZ, THE SUPREME COURT 20 (1957).
76. 430 U.S. 65 (1977).
77. *430* U.S. at 674 n. 43.
78. Friendly, *supra* note 2, at 1268, 1316.
79. Ingraham v. Wright, *430* U.S. at *672*.
80. 97 S. Ct. 1401 (1977).
81. 419 U.S. 565 (1975).
82. SCHWARTZ AND WADE, *supra* note 26, at xix, quoting *id*. at 130-1.
83. At the editor's request, this post-script has been added, in an attempt to cover the important cases decided since 1977, when this paper was written. (*Editor's note:* These additions were completed prior to the Court's decision in Mackey v. Montrym, 47 U.S.L.W. 4798 (June 25, 1979).)

84. 435 U.S. 78 (1978).
85. *Supra* note 42.
86. 419 U.S. 345 (1974).
87. 436 U.S. 1 (1978).
88. 435 U.S. at 90.

Limitations Upon The Power of Impeachment: Due Process Implications

BY CHARLES WIGGINS*

I.

During the spring and summer of 1974, the American people were witness to the exercise by the Congress of a power so awesome as to cause this Representative to shudder. A presidency was destroyed and a President confined to exile. Stripped to its essentials, a peaceful coup d'etat occurred before our eyes.

Commentators, delighted with the end, assured us that the means were proper. "The system works," we were assured. And indeed it did if we understand the "system" to mean a constitutional process for terminating the tenure of an incumbent President when it becomes politically imperative to do so.

Literal readers of the Constitution may be taken aback by such a characterization of the impeachment power. The designation of specific grounds for impeachment in the Constitution is surely an illusory limitation upon the power itself, so long as impeachment will lie, for example, for conduct which the Congress may declare to be an "abuse of power."[1]

I do not hold that there are no practical limits upon impeachment. Quite to the contrary, the very forces which can raise a simple political squabble to the level of an impeachment crisis—public opinion—can also prevent the misuse of the power. In essence, then, I have come to the conclusion that the scope of the impeachment power, and such limitations as may exist with respect to its exercise, are political decisions committed to a political body for resolution.

The Nixon experience, which some have called the "finest hour of the House of Representatives" and "proof that no man is above the law," only reinforces my conclusion. We have had three serious impeachment efforts against significant figures in our history— Justice Chase, President Andrew Johnson, and President Nixon—and each involved a major struggle between contending political forces in which the impeachment process was deployed as the ultimate political weapon.

The recent events involving President Nixon cannot be fully explained by scholars who focus upon the historical meaning of "high crimes and misdemeanors," nor by those who dwell upon the legal niceties involved in the few American impeachment precedents. Just as in the case of Justice Chase and President Johnson, the great forces leading to the "Constitutional Crisis" of 1974 were essentially political. Make no mistake of this point. The law was only martialled as a justification for a political objective—the removal of President Nixon, an objective which powerful forces both in and out of Congress equated with the public interest.

Few who wielded the levers of power in this country are, or were, neutral concerning Richard Nixon. His political career inspired feelings which ranged from passionate loyalty to

* Former U.S. Representative (Republican, California); partner, Musick, Peeler & Garrett (Los Angeles, California).

an abiding conviction of his irredeemable immorality. And nowhere were these feelings more intensely held than in the partisan halls of Congress, where the power to impeach reposed.

The Watergate break-in was the flagrant act which unleashed, slowly at first, the years of accumulated political animus toward Richard Nixon and which ultimately lead to his downfall. Once the dam was breached, every aspect of his Administration was reviewed hypercritically and served up as further justification for his impeachment. For example, when the House Judiciary Committee solemnly undertook to examine whether Mr. Nixon had committed impeachable misconduct, its initial agenda included:

(1) allegations concerning domestic surveillance activities conducted by or at the direction of the White House, including 1969 wiretaps, the Houston plan, the activities of Messrs. Caulfied and Ulasewicz, the activities of the so-called "Plumbers Unit," and the activities surrounding the Ellsberg trial;

(2) allegations concerning the intelligence activities conducted by or at the direction of the White House for purposes of the presidential election of 1972, including White House "dirty tricks," intelligence activities by the Committee to Re-Elect the President, the Diem cables, the alleged plan to burglarize and firebomb the Brookings Institution, and Operation Sandwedge;

(3) allegations concerning the Watergate break-in and related activities, including alleged efforts by persons in the White House to "coverup" such activities, the so-called Liddy plan, the destruction of files, documents and other evidence, the payment of money to Watergate defendants, the relationship between the CIA and the Watergate investigation, alleged offers of clemency, the role of John Dean, the firing of Mr. Cox, and the content of presidential tapes;

(4) allegations concerning alleged improprieties in connection with the personal finances of the President, including tax deductions taken with respect to a gift of vice-presidential papers, expenditures attributed to the San Clemente and Key Biscayne property, the sale of his New York apartment, deductions with respect to property owned by him in Whittier and Florida, and the possible income which should be imputed to him by reason of his personal use of governmental facilities and services;

(5) allegations concerning efforts by the White House to use agencies of the executive branch for political purposes and alleged White House involvement with illegal campaign contributions including the alleged misuse of the IRS, the so-called "enemies list," the allegations concerning ITT and alleged contributions by the dairy industry; and

(6) the allegations concerning other misconduct that do not fall within any of the foregoing categories such as the secret bombings of Cambodia, and the impoundment of funds (or, one might add, any other charge which comes to mind).

It must be clear beyond serious question that such an extensive catalog of potential offenses did not suddenly spring from a "second-rate" burglary.[2]

It is true, of course, that the steady accumulation of power in the presidency beginning long before Nixon would ultimately have been called into question with or without a Watergate. But President Nixon was not simply the unfortunate occupant of the White House when the inevitable day of reckoning occurred. Challenges to the exercise of presidential power long condoned[3] were directed at *Nixon's* exercise of that power rather than the *institutional* problem it represented. Indeed, precious little of substance has been done post-Watergate to strip the Imperial Presidency of its trappings.

Once the Watergate dam had broken, a steady drumbeat of shrill criticism against the Nixon Administration mounted in intensity for some eighteen months prior to the impeachment hearings. Far from being immune from the impact of that criticism, individual congressmen were among the cheerleaders. I recall a colleague on the Judiciary Committee telling me with emotion, "Nixon committed his first impeachable offense when he raised his right hand to take the oath of office in 1969. He lied then and we should have impeached him a long time ago."

The point of all of this is that by 1974 there existed in the country, and especially in Washington, D.C., a supercharged political atmosphere which had become clearly and emphatically anti-Nixon. It was in and because of this atmosphere that Congress undertook to flex its long-dormant impeachment muscle. The crowd cheered and gave thumbs down to Nixon. Politicians more concerned with pleasing the crowd than the rights of the gladiator in the arena delivered the fatal blow.

Nixon resigned and the accumulating pressure on the country was relieved. In the end, the truth or falsity of the specific allegations were largely immaterial. Whether justified or not, the presidency of Richard Nixon had been effectively destroyed. The country desperately needed a new President and quickly. I have no doubt that the country would have survived a trial in the Senate but I am equally certain that the country would have suffered further during that process.

After resisting articles of impeachment against Mr. Nixon on the basis of evidence before the Judiciary Committee, I ultimately urged his resignation and failing that act on his part would have voted for the first article of impeachment relating to an obstruction of justice. The tape of June 23, 1972, revealed, after the Judiciary hearings had been concluded, precious little evidence of a crime[4] justifying the impeachment of a President; but it was *some* evidence and a principled basis upon which the overriding need of the country for a new President could be recognized.

It is idle to expect any future President to be subjected to the impeachment process in an antiseptic, politics-free atmosphere. At least with respect to major figures, impeachment and politics go hand in hand. Just as in the case of Chase, Johnson, and now Nixon, impeachment is an extension of politics, just as war is a continuation of politics by other means.

So much for the Nixon experience. My present concern is with the procedure of impeachment. Adherence to common sense rules can and hopefully will temper the political excesses of the game. The questions I wish to explore are these:

(1) What rights should be accorded the respondent in the course of investigating the alleged grounds for his impeachment?;

(2) What should be the rights of a respondent in a Senate trial of those grounds?; and

(3) Is there any recourse to judicial review to correct alleged errors in the congressional impeachment process?

II.

Impeachment is a hybrid process. It has many of the hallmarks of a judicial proceeding. But it is clearly something more. It also resembles the legislative-investigative function, and yet that image is imperfect as well. In the final analysis, impeachment appears to be an amalgam of traditional legislative and judicial functions designed, as Hamilton correctly observed, "as a method of NATIONAL INQUEST into the conduct of public men."[5]

An accurate characterization of the process of impeachment may not be particularly important in itself. It assumes significance only in deciding which model—the legislative or judicial—is to govern the rights of a respondent caught up in its workings. Total acceptance of the judicial model is to pursue the impossible dream. That model would, of course, maximize the procedural rights of an official subject to impeachment. If the impeachment scenario were played out in the fashion of most judicial proceedings, however, individual rights would be exalted and political imperatives disregarded. So long as the process is under the supervision of politicians, there is little likelihood that political imperatives will fall before the niceties of the law.

On the other hand, the legislative model is also an unsatisfactory standard for fixing the procedural rights of an impeachment respondent. To be sure, a witness before a Senate or House investigative body is not stripped bare of procedural rights, but he is not armed with a full panoply of judicially enforceable due process protections either. For example, the conduct of an impeachment "trial" along the lines of a Senate or House investigation would be intolerable. It is not at all uncommon for legislative hearings to be structured so as to justify a preconceived result with witnesses selected accordingly. Whatever may be the right of an impeachment respondent to challenge such a procedure, it is clear that this legislative model is not to be preferred.

Whichever standard is deemed as more appropriate for adoption by analogy in an impeachment proceeding, it is not to be consistently applied throughout that process. Clearly, the process which is due a potential respondent during a pre-impeachment investigation is significantly less than would be due at a Senate trial. Because the rights which should be accorded an impeachment respondent differ during the course of the proceedings, the process should be examined chronologically.

A. Pre-Impeachment Investigation

Although simple respect for a co-equal branch would suggest that charges of sufficient magnitude to justify the removal of a Federal official from office would warrant a careful investigation before adoption of an impeachment resolution by the House, such has not been the uniform historical practice.

The first impeachment was that of Senator Blount in 1779. The House acted upon ex parte evidence submitted in confidence by the President. The Senator did not participate in any way. The second impeachment, that of Judge John Pickering in 1803, followed a similar pattern.

Only a year later, however, when the House considered the case of Justice Samuel Chase, a committee undertook an investigation of the charges. It acted upon ex parte evidence in recommending impeachment and Justice Chase was accorded no "courtroom rights" in that investigation.

The Judge Peck impeachment in 1830 appears to be the first occasion when the House permitted participation by the respondent in its investigation. The role of the respondent was restricted to a limited cross-examination of charging witnesses, however, which triggered a heated floor debate in the House on the fairness of the committee's procedures. This debate culminated in a belated offer to the Judge to submit explanatory materials. His acceptance of the offer did not save him from impeachment.

The next impeachment was that of Judge West H. Humphreys in 1862. The Judge was a secessionist and the House, through its Judiciary Committee, had little trouble recommending impeachment without the necessity of Judge Humphreys' participation.

The Andrew Johnson investigation in the House both with respect to the unsuccessful impeachment attempt in 1867 and the later successful effort in 1868 was similarly an ex parte affair. It does not appear that the President was represented nor participated in any way.

Secretary of War Belknap in 1876 fared somewhat better than earlier respondents. He was represented by counsel during the House investigation and the key adverse witness was subject to cross-examination. Belknap was offered an opportunity to appear and testify under oath, but he refused. He apparently was denied the opportunity to introduce other witnesses of his own, however.

In all impeachments occuring in this century, Judge Swayne in 1904, Judge Archibald in 1912, Judge Londerback in 1933, and Judge Ritter in 1936, the respondents were accorded extensive rights of participation by the House investigation committee. The opportunity to be present, in person and by counsel, to cross-examine witnesses and to offer testimony, was offered and exercised fully.[6]

In the case of President Nixon, of course, the Judiciary Committee, properly I believe, followed the modern precedents.

The recent precedents of the House affording expanded procedural rights to a respondent stand for no more than an *ad hoc* exercise of discretion by that body. A respondent is entitled to no more than what a majority of the House is willing to give him, and this is as it should be. At the House level, the constitutional function is that of framing the charges only. No irredeemable legal prejudice to a respondent occurs upon the making of an allegation against him. (Alas, the political damage is unavoidable and uncontrollable.) Absent such prejudice, the need for formalistic procedural rights is unnecessary. Albeit unnecessary, it is clearly desirable to extend to an impeachment respondent considerable freedom to participate in the investigatory phase. The argument that the committee should proceed as a grand jury and limit participation accordingly is not a good one. Limited witness participation exists before a grand jury, in part, because of the necessity of secrecy and because the grand jury's probable cause standard does not require the precision of proof which an adversary proceeding would provide. But in an impeachment investigation the grand jury reasons for secrecy do not exist and could not be maintained in any event when the facts revealed by the investigation must be debated in public before the full House. In addition, the standard of proof required by the House to impeach should be greater than mere probable cause.[7]

Once a respondent is invited to participate at all, questions inevitably arise as to the extent of those rights he shall enjoy before the committee.

There should be no serious debate that a witness must retain his Fifth Amendment right against self-incrimination. Although precedents do not abound, surely the right would be subject to judicial protection, by habeas corpus, for example, if Congress were to confine a witness for failure to answer an incriminating question. But the plot thickens if the respondent himself raises the Fifth Amendment claim. Presumably a court would protect the right in any criminal or habeas context, but who is to defend the constitutional right if the House chooses to impeach for failure to answer the incriminating question, or, more likely, for raising a Fifth Amendment claim with respect to certain subpoenaed documents?[8]

It is to be recalled that the third article of impeachment against Mr. Nixon was based upon his failure to respond to congressional subpoenas. To some, the presidential reluctance was merely a continuation of the cover-up, but accepting the position of the President as a good faith one, he was raising objections to the subpoenas both on constitutional and procedural grounds. The Committee did not agree with the President's claim, and voted to impeach him because of his persistence, without providing a forum before the full House or in court to test his good faith claims.[9]

Had President Nixon objected to the compelled production of subpoenaed documents on Fifth Amendment grounds, I suspect that the Committee would have respected this constitutional claim, although it gave short shrift to his constitutional arguments on other grounds.

Whatever the action of the House, one would hope that the Senate would respect a Fifth Amendment defense.[10] However, this is surely an illustration where legalisms would give way to political realities. It is exceedingly unlikely that an impeachment respondent would be permitted to continue in office after asserting a Fifth Amendment claim at any point in the impeachment process. On the record, of course, he would not be impeached for asserting the defense; but one could confidently predict that he would be impeached nevertheless.

Although I am less certain, it is to be presumed that the attorney-client privilege and similar evidentiary privileges would also be respected by the House investigative committee. The history of judicial recognition of such privileges before grand juries is too long to be overlooked and the policy reasons for recognizing such privileges clearly apply with equal force to a House investigation of impeachment. The question was avoided in the Nixon investigation by the President waiving the attorney-client privilege and may have been overcome in any event because the various attorneys called to testify were viewed by the Committee as co-conspirators to the crimes under investigation.

Before the House of Representatives, then, a respondent may be impotent to enforce sensible rules for his benefit as a matter of right. But he is not without a remedy. His appeal is to the public for fairness. And I have no doubt that the House will respond favorably to that appeal in future cases—especially where a grant of fair treatment will not interfere with the political ends sought by the investigation itself.

B. The Senate Trial

Several constitutional provisions provide a point of beginning for the consideration of the rights of an impeached federal officer in a Senate trial.

Article I, Section 3 states: "The Senate shall have the sole Power to try all Impeachments. When sitting for that Purpose, they shall be on Oath or Affirmation."[11] And section 5 of Article I provides: "Each House may determine the Rules of its Proceedings. . . ."[12]

The standing rules of the Senate do not provide a detailed procedure for the trial of impeachments. Rather, it has been the practice to adopt rules for the conduct of a specific trial when confronted with that responsibility. The rules of procedure in former cases, however, stand as precedents which clearly outlined the judicial flavor of the proceedings.

In summary form, the established procedure has been as follows:

After adopting Articles of Impeachment,[13] the House selects managers[14] and designates a chairman;[15]

The House formally advises the Senate of its action by message;[16]

The Senate receives the message,[17] in due course adopts an order that it is prepared to receive the Articles[18] and communicates its action to the House;[19]

The House managers appear before the Senate,[20] present the written Articles,[21] the chairman impeaches the respondent at the bar of the Senate by oral accusation,[22] and requests the Senate to order a trial;[23]

The Senate thereupon organizes for trial[24] and notifies the House[25] and the respondent of the date fixed;[26]

The accused may appear in person or by attorney,[27] or not at all,[28] in which case the trial proceeds as if upon a not guilty plea;[29]

The accused may demur to the impeachment on the ground that he is not a civil officer[30] or that the offense alleged is not impeachable under the Constitution;[31]

Briefs on the legal issues may be filed;[32] and

The trial commences in a manner which is described as follows:

> The presiding officer of the Senate directs the Sergeant at Arms to make a proclamation to the effect that "All persons are commanded to keep silent, on pain of imprisonment, while the House of Representatives is exhibiting to the Senate of United States articles of impeachment against . . . " After such proclamation, the articles are exhibited by the managers of the House, and the presiding officer of the Senate then informs the managers that the Senate will take proper order in the subject of impeachment and give the House notice thereon. The Senate then proceeds to consider the articles of impeach-

ment and continues to be so engaged until final judgment is rendered. All members of the Senate sitting are required by the Constitution to be sworn before consideration of impeachment charges (III: 2055). The presiding officer has power to issue all orders, mandates and writs needed to compel the attendance of witnesses or to enforce obedience of its orders. The presiding officer rules on all questions of evidence and incidental questions which may arise. He may, however, at his option, submit questions to a vote of the members of the Senate, in which case the vote shall be without a division unless the Yeas and Nays be demanded by 1/5 of the members present. Witnesses are sworn and examined by the managers of the House and may be cross-examined by the respondent or his counsel.[33]

Although the history recorded in these precedents need not be followed in future cases, there is every reason to believe that they would be, and in fact that more care would be given to insure the appearance, if not the fact, of fairness to the accused. The watchful eye of television would surely be on the Senators in the future, and that body, properly concerned with its own image, would doubtlessly proceed with great caution. But some elements of due process, essential in a trial, would be lacking nevertheless.

Notwithstanding the special oath taken by the Senators, genuine objectivity and the absence of bias would not be present. In the political atmosphere of impeachment, many Senators could be expected to have expressed prior opinions respecting guilt or innocence. The Senate could not be sequestered, of course, and it would be inevitably exposed to (if not playing a direct role in) an unparalleled media spectacle. Moreover, attendance at all stages of the trial by the senatorial jurors would be spotty and the level of attention by individual jurors subject to wide and uncontrollable variations.

Any one of these deviations from the judicial norm might be a denial of due process in a trial setting; but given the political nature of the proceedings held before a political body, such variations are only a part of the unique process which is due an impeachment respondent.

I believe there are certain minimum rights which in all events must be respected, if the process is to be characterized as a "trial" at all.

The respondent must be informed of the charges against him, be afforded the opportunity to be present and to be represented by counsel if he wishes. He must be afforded an opportunity to make his defense, on the law or on the facts; to offer testimony in his own behalf; to utilize the processes of the Senate to compel the attendance of witnesses; and be able to confront and cross-examine adverse witnesses. His self-incrimination rights must be respected and the House must carry the overall burden of making its case. All of the fine points of evidence, I believe, need not be applied, even if the Confrontation Clause[34] be implicated.

Perhaps the foregoing is not an exhaustive listing, but any Senate trial which affords such rights as a minimum to an accused would have the essentials of fairness which are necessary to avoid converting a political trial into a political spectacle.

I have not the slightest doubt that any impeachment respondent in the future would enjoy these minimum rights. It is idle to speculate that the Senate might run amok and disregard both history and common sense in the future. More real is the possibility that, in the view of the respondent, the Senate may err in its application of the law or the facts within the context of a fair impeachment proceeding. What then?

So much has been written on the subject of judicial review of the judgment of impeachment that I doubt my ability to add to the learning on the subject.[35] From all that has been written, however, it is obvious that the Supreme Court need not take such a case, assuming that an action raising fundamental constitutional questions were filed in some appropriate lesser forum,[36] and there is every reason to doubt that it would do so given the opportunity.

It is one thing for the court to acknowledge its fundamental responsibility "to say what the law is"[37] where the consequences of its declaration do not jeopardize the continuity of government itself, and it's quite another matter to tell a President that he must vacate the White House.[38] Surely such would be the consequences of any purported judicial nullification of the judgment of impeachment of a sitting President. If there ever were a case where finality of decision is required, and the instant transfer of power imperative, it is with respect to a judgment of impeachment following a Senate trial of a President. If there is room to maneuver with intellectual honesty, no court would subject the country to such turmoil. And there is ample room to maneuver, whether it be in the "sole Power to try all Impeachments"[39] language in the Constitution or the flexible standards of justiciability found in *Baker v. Carr.*[40]

Of course, the test might come in less earth-shaking circumstances, such as the impeachment of a minor civil officer or judge; but whatever the context, the issue is pure dynamite which need not be handled by the court at all. It is fanciful to assume that a majority of the House and two-thirds of the Senate would commit such a monumental error (such as the purported impeachment of a governor, for instance) as would tempt the Court to abandon a sensible policy of hands off.

Some have contended that, absent judicial supervision, the power to impeach becomes an instrument for legislative usurpation of powers not granted by the Constitution.[41] And indeed it could be, just as the self-proclaimed judicial power to declare an act of Congress unconstitutional is subject to abuse. But there is an ultimate check in a society governed by democratic principles. The people can reverse a blatantly wrong decision by the Senate. And it is the threat of this power to retaliate politically that is likely to prevent gross abuses in the first instance.

III.

To those of us who have been trained to think in terms of rights and judicial remedies, impeachment is apt to be an alien process. Once that process is understood to be political, however, and not simply a novel legal problem to which traditional legal remedies apply, perception is clear. Political "wrongs," I believe, are best remedied within the political system. Reliance upon the political system may be of small comfort to individuals who have been aggrieved and who have no immediate judicial remedy; but in seeking the national interest in conflicts between institutional contenders, the country will be better served by placing the ultimate power of decision in the people, rather than yielding absolute supremacy to any one contending institution, even if individuals may suffer as a result.

Notes

1. Although the legitimacy of such a ground for impeachment has never been tested in the Senate, there was widespread support for Artice II— the so-called "Abuse of Power" Article—by eminent scholars in the Nixon case.

2. Others were even more exhaustive in their specification of Nixon's "crimes." See W. Dobrovir, J. Gebhardt, S. Buffone, & A. Oakes, The Offenses of Richard M. Nixon: A Guide for the People of the United States (2 nd. ed. 1974).

3. If the misdeeds of others chronicled in the book, V. Lasky, It Didn't Start With Watergate (1977), are only half-right, the political excess of Mr. Nixon by comparison to his predecessors would be unexceptional.

4. It was not my view then, nor now, that impeachment will lie only for criminal misconduct. In the Nixon case, however, I believe it was essential to establish criminality on the part of the President in order to gain public acceptance of the harsh remedy of removal of one so recently and overwhelmingly re-elected. Had the President been found blameless on the criminal allegations, but condemned for his "political" abuses, I saw the specter of a nation divided over the issue of whether the President had been driven from office by his political adversaries. In my view, the risk was not worth running, nor essential to the political objectives of his adversaries, given the convenience of the more credible criminal grounds for impeachment.

5. 2 A. HAMILTON, THE FEDERALIST No. 65, at 209 (New York 1778) (original text, Library of Congress). Of course Hamilton wrote of the political nature of impeachment because, in his view, the violations justifying the remedy related to the "public trust" and were injuries to "society itself." *Id.* at 208. But I am less philosophical in my description of impeachment as a political process. At least in the major impeachments seriously undertaken, the basic underlying forces were contending political factions seeking to assert power and control over the operations of government. And, unless some unpopular future Executive is so helpful as to commit a public crime, I suspect it will always be thus.

6. I have made mention of only those instances in which the House voted Articles of Impeachment and the case reached the Senate for trial. In all, there have been seventy officials subject to an impeachment investigation by the House. Many involved no more than a cursory examination of charges too serious to overlook. Others appear to have resulted in a serious investigation of the charges with the respondents being accorded some degree of participation. Most impeachment inquiries involved federal judges but several, undertaken with varying degrees of enthusiasm, involved major political figures. In 1843, a House committee summarily disposed of charges amounting to treason against President Tyler. In 1868, charges against a Supreme Court Justice were dismissed in such an expeditious and discreet fashion that his name does not appear in available records. Vice President Colfax was subject to an investigation in 1873 for his alleged involvement in scandalous conduct occurring while a Member of Congress and before becoming Vice-President. Attorney General Daugherty in 1922 and Secretary of the Treasury Mellon in 1932 were also the object of impeachment investigations. And, of course, the Justice Douglas matter in 1970 is within recent memory. In addition, there have been literally hundreds of impeachment resolutions introduced by individual Congressmen which have been ignored entirely, the most recent of which to my knowledge is a resolution to impeach Federal Trade Commissioner Paul Rand Dixon for allegedly describing Ralph Nader as a "dirty Arab."

7. This point was much debated during the Nixon impeachment investigation. Some argued for a probable cause standard, analogizing to the grand jury rule and invoking the English precedents; others argued that since the House would be charged with the prosecution of the case in the Senate, it would be unethical to take a case to trial without sufficient proof to sustain a conviction. The committee ultimately settled upon the "clear and convincing" standard.

8. Boyd v. United States, 116 U.S. 616 (1886).

9. On this issue, see Van Alstyne, *The Third Impeachment Article: Congressional Bootstrapping*, 60 A.B.A.J. 1199 (1974); and Bickel, *Should Rodino Go to Court?*, The New Republic, June 8, 1974, at 11.

10. The Supreme Court has condemned "the practice of imputing a sinister meaning to the exercise of a person's constitutional right under the Fifth Amendment." Slochower v. Bd. of Educ., 350 U.S. 551, 557 (1956).

11. U.S. Const., art. I, sec. 3, cl. 6.

12. *Id.* at sec. 5, cl. 2.

13. 6 C. CANNON, CANNON'S PRECEDENTS OF THE HOUSE OF REPRESENTATIVES OF THE UNITED STATES, secs. 500, 514 (1935) (hereinafter cited as CANNON'S PRECEDENTS).

14. *Id.*; 3 A. HIND, HIND'S PRECEDENTS OF THE HOUSE OF REPRESENTATIVES OF THE UNITED STATES, secs. 2300, 2345, 2417, 2448 (1907) (hereinafer cited as HIND'S PRECEDENTS).

15. 3 HIND'S PRECEDENTS, *supra* note 14, at sec. 2448.

16. *Id.* at secs. 2413, 2419, 2446.

17. *Id.* at secs. 2078, 2419.

18. *Id.* at secs. 2435, 2419.

19. *Id.* at secs. 2325, 2419.

20. *Id.* at sec. 2420; 6 CANNON'S PRECEDENTS, *supra* note 13, at sec. 501.

21. 3 HIND'S PRECEDENTS, *supra* note 14, at sec. 2420; 6 CANNON'S PRECEDENTS, *supra* note 13 at sec. 501.

22. 3 HIND'S PRECEDENTS, *supra* note 14, at secs. 2413, 2446, 2473; 6 CANNON'S PRECEDENTS, *supra* note 13, at sec. 501.

23. 6 CANNON'S PRECEDENTS, *supra* note 13, at 501.

24. *Id.* at sec. 502.

25. *Id.* at sec. 503.

26. *Id.* at sec. 504, 3 HIND'S PRECEDENTS, *supra* note 14, at sec. 2127.

27. 3 HIND'S PRECEDENTS *supra* note 14, at secs. 2127, 2424.

28. *Id.* at 2307, 2333, 2393.

29. *Id.* at 2127, 2424; W. BROWN, CONSTITUTION, JEFFERSON'S MANUAL, AND RULES OF THE HOUSE OF REPRESENTATIVES OF THE UNITED STATES, NINETY-FIFTH CONGRESS, H.R. Doc. No. 663, 94th Cong., 2d Sess., sec. 611 (1977).

30. 3 HIND'S PRECEDENTS, *supra* note 14, at sec. 2310.

31. *Id.* at sec. 2481.

32. 6 CANNON'S PRECEDENTS, *supra* note 13, at sec. 480.

33. LEGAL MATERIALS ON IMPEACHMENT, SPECIAL SUBCOMMITTEE ON H. RES. 920 OF THE COMMITTEE ON THE JUDICIARY, 91st Cong., 2d Sess. 3 (1970).

34. U.S. CONST., amend VI.

35. The celebrated book by Professor R. BERGER, IMPEACHMENT: THE CONSTITUTIONAL PROBLEMS (1973), and Professor Goldberg's critical review, *An Essay On Raoul Berger's Thesis For Judicial Intervention In the Process of the Removal of the President of the United States*, 1975 WISC. L. REV. 414, make all of the arguments adequately.

36. Ritter v. United States, 84 Ct. C1. 293 (1936), *cert. denied* 300 U.S. 668 (1937).

37. Marbury v. Madison, 5 U.S. (1 Cranch) 137, 177 (1803).

38. Powell v. McCormack, 395 U.S. 486 (1969), has been repeatedly cited as a precedent upon which the Supreme Court might wish to rely in choosing to review a judgment of impeachment. But the stakes were relatively low in *Powell*. He had been re-elected by his constituency following his improper exclusion from the House. Upon re-election, he was seated. Congress proceeded with its business without a ripple. There is a chasm of practical difference between challenging the action of one branch of the legislature with respect to one of its Members and the reinstatement of a deposed President at the expense of a sitting one. The enormity of following the *Powell* precedent in a presidential impeachment case would not be lost on the Justices.

39. U.S. CONST., art. I, sec. 3, c1. 6.

40. Baker v. Carr, 369 U.S. 186 (1962).

41. This contention appears to be the point of beginning for Professor Berger's analysis. R. BERGER, *supra* note 35, at 53.

A Judicial Short-Circuiting of The Equal Protection Promise

By Nathaniel R. Jones*

Permit me to begin these observations with a comment, which may or may not be amusing: Something funny happened when we were on our way to the promise of the Equal Protection Clause. It was an election in 1968. That election was something of an omen of things to come and the *Milliken*[1] decision of 1974, I think, bore that out. The turning point, in my view, of the promise of *Brown* v. *Board of Education*[2] and the Equal Protection Clause occurred in that decision. The Detroit case, which is *Milliken I*, marked the turning point at which the Supreme Court switched signals and directions. It had in *Swann*[3] stated that transportation was an acceptable tool of desegregation and reiterated that school zone lines could not be used as barriers to full vindication of constitutional rights. Earlier the Court held in *Davis*[4]—the Mobile, Alabama case—that such things as super-highways could not be used as barriers to avoid an effective remedy. And there was *Wright* v *Emporia*.[5] Prior to that decision there were the *Green*[6] and *Monroe*[7] cases, wherein various subtle artifacts of obstruction were knocked out by the Supreme Court, as they were asserted for purposes of delay in granting full relief.

What we found in *Milliken I* was the Supreme Court doing what Judge Learned Hand in 1951 had urged not be done, *i.e.* a rationing of justice. He suggested at that time that we needed a new commandment: "thou shalt not ration justice."[8]

Clearly in the Detroit case we saw the beginnings of the Supreme Court doing precisely that. The extension of the principles that were enunciated in *Milliken I*—namely that the nature of the violation determined the scope of the remedy—were enunciated in earlier cases but not in such a restricted fashion. Since then have come the cases of *Washington* v *Davis*[9] and *Village of Arlington Heights*[10] with yet further refinements of that equitable principle as a predicate for enjoyment of the spirit of the Fourteenth Amendment's Equal Protection Clause. When it extended this principle into these other fields of civil rights, the Supreme Court was indeed constructing a higher barrier. It thus increased the difficulty for Blacks and other minorities who seek to obtain relief against a violation of their constitutional rights.

I find it sad that the Supreme Court, 83 years after *Plessy*,[11] and over 122 years after *Dred Scott*,[12] and some 114 years plus after the Emancipation Proclamation requires that Blacks prove that the lingering manifestations of segregation and of deprivation stem from certain kinds of state actions that were intentionally conceived before entitlement to judicial relief.[13] Such a standard and such a requirement are, in actuality, perpetuating the very substantive violation that was supposedly being redressed.

The substantive promise of *Brown* and the various legislative enactments that have since been bottomed on the Equal Protection Clause remain empty and elusive until and unless an effective remedy is at the same time placed within reach.

In other words, what I am saying is that the constant tampering by the Supreme Court with the vitality of *Brown* moves beyond one's reach the relief which must come before

---

*General Counsel, NAACP. This article was adapted from a speech delivered in September, 1977 (editor's note).

209

Brown has any meaning. This amounts to a cruel hoax. The direction in which the Supreme Court has taken us ensures further delay and frustrates the effort to end these historic wrongs.

All this does is to short-circuit, even more, the onward movement toward the creation of a single society. Without effective relief from the courts, the pain of racially-based injury remains unabated. Thus, the remedy standard, fashioned by the Supreme Court—and I emphasize this—constitutes a clear limit on the equal protection guarantee. What the Court has done has been to elevate to a higher plane of concern the objections of the ruling majority and of the dominant group. It does this at the sacrifice of and at the cost of the constitutional rights of the victims of historic discrimination.

In the area of school desegregation, the Supreme Court has utilized the traditional remedy formulation, namely, the *nature* of the violation determines the scope of the remedy. It had done this, as we had hoped, in a way that would weaken and ultimately eliminate the artificial distinction between *de facto* and *de jure* discrimination. But what it now has done in several cases has been to reaffirm and to strengthen that distinction, myth though it be. It has taken a constricted view of the word "nature."

Brown v. *Board of Education* targeted state mandated or deliberately maintained dual school systems as constitutionally offensive. In efforts to define that segregation which was deliberately maintained and constitutionally offensive, the Court focused on the school board's purpose or intent to segregate. As the movement toward desegregation came North and West, there were those who contended that the proscriptions of and promise of *Brown* really had no application in these regions, but rather, were proscriptions and mandates that were directed at the 17 Southern states and the District of Columbia. When the battle lines were actually drawn in the North and West, it became clear that the conditions complained of by minorities were not the result of accident, were not the result of happenstance. They resulted, rather, from intentional and purposeful conduct and represented the vestiges of the badges of slavery. Therefore, there was an affirmative duty on the part of the school districts and the state to eliminate them. Current segregation causation appears obvious to Blacks.

In these Northern cases, as was established in *Keyes*,[14] it was possible to catalog the general techniques and devices that have been used by agencies of the state in concert with private discriminators to bring about segregated conditions.

In that nearly every Northern school system has practiced *de jure* segregation—and this can be shown under the *Keyes* standard at least inferentially—the courts had broad mandates to grant relief by means including the restructuring of a school system, even though some components of the segregated system might not have been the subject of direct proof. Thus, courts under *Keyes* are freely permitted to engage in inferences and presumptions which would characterize areas as *de jure* segregated even though beyond the scope of the direct proof.

In efforts to restore vitality to the *de jure/de facto* distinction, the Supreme Court has more recently held, in another context, that only that which can be specifically proved to have been purposely or intentionally segregated is subject to a court ordered remedy under equal protection claims. That is the teaching of *Washington v. Davis* and *Arlington Heights*. The "purpose" requirement is prevailing over the "impact" reality.

With remedy being the all important focus of a school desegregation suit for instance, it has become essential for litigators to expend a vast amount of time, effort and money to spread the *Keyes* formulation over as many facets of a school system as possible. Thus with the threatened extension of this *de facto de jure* fiction into employment and into housing, it is now more difficult for relief to be made available to victims of discrimination, except under specific statutes.

What is difficult for a layperson who is Black or Brown to understand is this constant reminder from the Supreme Court that one is entitled to relief for historic discrimination or the vestiges thereof on equal protection grounds *only* if there is a showing of specific intent. At this time in history one would assume that courts would allow presumptions to shift the burden of proof to school boards, employers and others.

The Court's specific intent requirement is reminiscent of a story that I once heard. A person walked the same course every day along a certain street and periodically he would be sprinkled with a very hot substance that would singe his skin. He would attempt to rub it off with his handkerchief while all the time absorbing the pain. Thereafter he would go about his business. One day as he walked along this street, he was suddenly doused by a bucket of that burning substance. It turned out to be water and lye. He was in front of a fire station. He dashed into a nearby firehouse, where he saw a group of firemen sitting around waiting for an alarm. He asked for some help, "Would you please help me," he asked, "I'm burning up. Would you spray me? I'm burning!" The fireman replied, "Well now, let's see, we work for the taxpayers of this city. Our water is provided by the taxpayers—all publicly provided. We do understand you are in distress. And we can see by looking at you and by the tone of your voice that you are in agony. There is no question about your excruciating pain. The effects of whatever happened outside are obvious. But before we can expend any of the public resources—such as our labor, our skill, our water, and use this equipment—we have got to conduct a little inquiry to determine whether the person or persons responsible for your condition did it accidentally or intentionally." The natural reply was: "I could not care less, I need relief." Nevertheless, the process and the inquiry continued while the man suffered.

That is the position and the mood of racial minorities in this country who are constantly being told of the specific discriminatory intent standard which operates as a predicate to relief. Blacks are told this despite the fact that under our rules of evidence, the courts can take judicial notice of the obvious. When a history is so obvious, proof of intent should not be required for equal protection relief.

We are talking about the victims of historic discrimination, persons who come from a group whose descendants and forebearers were brought to this country in slavery, who were subjected to all kinds of indignities; persons over whom the Civil War was fought; whose emancipation had to be pronounced by a President followed thereafter by the Thirteenth, Fourteenth and Fifteenth Amendments to the Constitution; a class of people who conducted their lives in the pollution of *Plessy v. Ferguson*, yielding all the while to the harsh realities of second-class citizenship. That is the slate upon which life for Blacks has been drawn.

So to be told in 1977 by the Supreme Court that the only way they can get relief from school segregation is to prove that it was intentionally brought about,[15] that the only way they can get relief for employment discrimination is to prove that it was intentionally conceived,[16] and told even before they can get relief under Title VII[17] for discriminatory seniority systems one must prove that the seniority system was put into effect for the express purpose of discriminating against their group,[18] is, I think, to perpetuate virtually discriminatory conditions. It represents a backing away from the commitment and the obligations of the Equal Protection Clause.

Now if I may focus for a moment on the turning point which I previously indicated was *Milliken I*. The question largely comes down to why and what this case was really all about. Like most lawyers and scholars, we try to work out problems in a logical and reasoned way. We have problems doing that with *Milliken I* because the Supreme Court's majority decision in the case was the sad but inevitable culmination of a national anti-Black strategy. Consequently, examination of that decision cannot be limited to a simple legal analysis of the majority's severely flawed construction of the evidential record, but should be also viewed in the light of the *political* climate created by a former administration—the head of which now stands ignominiously repudiated by the nation. The political climate that was then created was so polluted with hypocrisy, racism, and cynicism that the healthy constitutional precedents—*Brown* and its progeny—simply wilted.

The architects of that strategy, with the Detroit *Dred Scott* type decision under their belts, have, frankly, obtained what they wanted, namely, a slowdown of civil rights advances. Should there be any doubt of that, all one has to do is to examine what has happened in the wake of *Milliken I*.

As we do that, let us first consider some warnings. In his widely quoted lecture at the Harvard Law School[19] on the occasion of the 20th anniversary of the *Brown* decision, in May, 1974, Judge J. Skelly Wright predicted that if the Supreme Court were to hold—which it later did[20]—that the crossing of school district lines in segregation cases was impermissible, then, the national trend toward residential, political and economic apartheid will not only have been greatly accelerated, but will have been rendered legitimate and virtually irreversible by force of law. Moreover, Justice William O. Douglas, in his *Milliken I* dissent, prophetized: "When we rule against the metropolitan area remedy, we take a step that will likely put the problems of the Blacks and our society back to the period of time that antedated the separate but equal regime of *Plessy v. Ferguson*."[21]

We all know that such recent decisions as *Washington v. Davis* and *Arlington Heights v. Metropolital Housing Corporation* have wrought certain things because in these cases the courts rejected the "effects" test and the "impacts" test as a basis for relief on equal protection grounds and have reinforced the *de facto/de jure* myth. This development is forcing plaintiffs to prove some intentional and purposeful conduct before their entitlement to relief under the Constitution.

For a dramatic illustration of the way in which the remedy limitations and equal protection claims result in substantive denial of rights, let us look at the *Milliken I* case.[22]

Faced with the realities of Detroit life and the strange interpretation put on these realities by the Supreme Court, the District Court and the Court of Appeals, post *Milliken I*, have been grappling with the difficult problem of seeking to vindicate the rights previously held to have been violated. The plan adopted by one District Court in 1975[23]—pursuant to the Supreme Court mandate—impacted on a system numbering 247,000 students, 70% of whom were Black. Under the plan, 28,000 students were reassigned, 22,000 of these 28,000 required bus transportation. The plan contained, as the Court of Appeals said, "glaring defects that could never pass constitutional muster and would not be countenanced by this court in a different factual situation."[24]

In other words, the Supreme Court's restrictions on inter-district relief in *Milliken I* are compelling the lower courts to trifle with the constitutional rights of the minority children. Full relief is denied due to the deference the Court insists be shown to school district lines, which the guilty parties themselves laid out. The U.S. Court of Appeals for the Sixth Circuit, which had affirmed the principle of metropolitan relief,[25] before it was reversed by the Supreme Court,[26] has now been forced to wrestle with the consequences of the Supreme Court's reversal of its holding in *Milliken I*.

The plaintiffs argued in the appellate court that under the plan approved by the District Court on that remand, there was left over 100 all-Black schools in three sub-regions of the Detroit system—the very areas most savagely hit by the segregation policies of the state and the Detroit school authorities.

The following reply was given in the August 4, 1976 opinion by the Sixth Circuit in a remand order to the District Court which directed further modifications. The court was troubled by the fact that the very core of Detroit, which represented the part of the system that was most severely impacted by the segregation policies of the State of Michigan and the Detroit School Board, was untouched by this plan. The court said:

> We cannot hold that where unconstitutional segregation has been found, a plan can be permitted to stand which fails to deal with the three regions where the majority of the most identifiably Black schools are located.
>
> We recognize that it would be appropriate for us at this point to supply guidelines to the district judge as to what he should do under this remand. Omission of such guidelines is not based on any failure to consider the problems in depth, it is based upon the conviction which this court had at the time of its *en banc* opinion in the case—and for the reasons carefully spelled out therein—that genuine constitutional desegregation cannot be accomplished within the school district boundaries of the Detroit School District.[27]

Not long ago attorney Louis Lucas of Tennessee was still conducting hearings before the district judge on ways of vindicating the constitutional rights of some 100,000 Black children in Detroit whose rights were found by the District Court to have been violated[28] back in 1971. That opinion had been upheld by the Court of Appeals on three different occasions.[29] Three years after *Milliken I,* Mr. Lucas, Thomas Atkins, and others were still in the District Court trying to fashion a way to vindicate those constitutional rights, primarily because of the way the Supreme Court developed relief standards which limit the real reach of the Equal Protection Clause.

In order for the aggrieved insular minority to realize the promise of the Equal Protection Clause and *Brown*, there now must be applied enormous resources and staying power, to say the least.

Having said all of this, the natural question arises—What happened? What caused this derailment of this forward movement toward the promised land. Justice Thurgood Marshall, in his dissenting opinion in *Milliken I*, laid out the cause: "Today's holding, I fear, is more a reflection of a perceived public mood that we have gone far enough in enforcing the Constitution's guarantee of equal justice than it is the product of neutral principles of law."[30]

Such a public mood, as Justice Marshall warned, is perilous because it fails to recognize the reality of the racial situation in America today. The issues presented in the *Bakke*[31] case bring this nation face to face with the question of whether the Equal Protection Clause of the Fourteenth Amendment will be applied as to advance the opportunities of those victims of historic racism and discrimination, or whether it will be construed in such a way as to choke those opportunities.

Black and other minorities feel strongly that the rules of the game are being altered in ways that impact most adversely upon them at the most inopportune times. Nowhere is this more evident than with respect to the affirmative efforts to eliminate the vestiges of discrimination.

Regarding the *Bakke* issues, there are a number of questions which beg answering. The Supreme Court's disposition of the *Bakke* issue can weigh very heavily on the destiny of minorities and may determine once and for all—or at least for a long time—whether the Equal Protection Clause is going to be used as a sword to strike down the vestiges of discrimination or as an instrument of decapitation.

Notes

1. Milliken v. Bradley, 418 U.S. 717 (1974).
2. 347 U.S. 483 (1954).

3. Swann v. Charlotte-Mecklenburg Bd. of Educ., 402 U.S. 1, *reh. denied*, 403 U.S. 912 (1971).

4. Davis v. Board of School Comm'rs of Mobile County, 402 U.S. 33 (1971).

5. Wright v. Council of Emporia, 407 U.S. 451 (1972).

6. Green v. County School Bd., 391 U.S. 430 (1968).

7. Monroe v. Board of Comm'rs, 391 U.S. 450 (1968).

8. The reference is from a speech Judge Hand made at the seventy-fifth anniversary dinner of the Legal Aid Society. It can be found in the proceedings of a Special Session of the Court of Appeals commemorating fifty years of federal judicial service by Judge Hand. 264 F.2d 35 (2d Cir. 1959) (April 10, 1959 - 3: 30 P.M. Room 506, United States Courthouse. Foley Square, New York, N.Y.) Note: pagination in the reporter refers to the published proceedings of a special session of the United States Court of Appeals for the Second Circuit, and *not* to the official cite pagination.

9. 426 U.S. 229 (1976).

10. Village of Arlington Heights v. Metropolitan Housing Dev. Corp., 429 U.S. 252 (1977).

11. Plessy v. Ferguson, 163 U.S. 537 (1896).

12. Dred Scott v. Sandford, 60 U.S. (19 How.) 393 (1857).

13. See notes 15-18 *infra* & accompanying text.

14. Keyes v. School Dist. No. 1, Denver, Colo., 413 U.S. 189, *reh. denied*, 414 U.S. 883 (1973).

15. Milliken v. Bradley, 433 U.S. 267 (1977) (Milliken II).

16. Washington v. Davis, 426 U.S. 229 (1976).

17. 42 U.S.C. §§ 2000 *et seq.* (1970 ed. and Supp. V) (Title VII of the Civil Rights Act of 1964).

18. International Bhd. of Teamsters v. United States, 431 U.S. 324 (1977).

19. Lecture by Judge J. Skelly Wright at Harvard, on the 20th anniversary of the *Brown* decision (May 1974).

20. *See* notes 3-7, *supra*.

21. 163 U.S. 537 (1896).

22. Milliken v. Bradley, 418 U.S. 717 (1974), *on remand*, 402 F. Supp. 1096 (E.D. Mich. 1975).

23. Bradley v. Milliken, 411 F. Supp. 943 (E.D. Mich. 1975), *aff'd*, 433 U.S. 267 (1977) (Milliken II).

24. Bradley v. Milliken, 540 F.2d 229, 237 (6th Cir. 1976), *aff'd*, 433 U.S. 267 (1977) (Milliken II).

25. Bradley v. Milliken, 433 F.2d 897 (6th Cir. 1970).

26. *See* note 24, *supra*.

27. 540 F.2d at 224 (6th Cir. 1976).

28. Bradley v. Milliken, 338 F. Supp. 582 (E.D. Mich. 1971).

29. Bradley v. Milliken 484 F.2d 215 (6th Cir. 1973); 519 F.2d 679 (6th Cir. 1975); 540 F.2d 229 (6th Cir. 1976).

30. 418 U.S. 717, 814 (Marshall, J., dissenting).

31. Regents of the University of California v. Bakke, 98 S.Ct. 2733 (1978). (Decided after the preparation of this article.) EDITOR'S NOTE: *As this book was going to print, the United States Supreme Court handed down four decisions that bear upon the matters discussed in Mr. Jones' article. For the benefit of the reader, Mr. Jones has agreed to appendix a few remarks on those decisions in order to reveal the general direction of his thought. More extended discussion of these decisions he reserves for another occasion. His observations follow:*

While much of the focus of post-*Bakke* analysis has been on "quotas," such a concentration of attention is misplaced—recall, Mr. Bakke *was* ordered admitted to the University of California at Davis Medical School. Credible civil rights commentators, by contrast, have insisted that the Court's express approval of race-sensitive remedies is of far greater importance—something that the California Supreme Court had held ran afoul of the Fourteenth Amendment.

The Justices who voted to overturn the Davis plan did so not on Fourteenth Amendment grounds, but on Title VI grounds—there having been no showing on the record of past exclusion of minorities.

Reading Mr. Justice Powell's plurality opinion along with the other *Bakke* opinions, it seems clear that racial quotas are not per se constitutionally or statutorily barred. Furthermore, it is evident from reading the various opinions that one of the circumstances under which explicit race-sensitive quotas are permissible is when a finding of discrimination is made by a body with the expertise and/or authority to render such a finding. Congress, certainly, is such a body.

The decision in *United States Workers of America v. Weber,* 47 U.S.L.W. 4851 (June 27, 1979), turned on a *statutory* construction of Title VII. The 5-2 Supreme Court decision upheld, over statutory challenge, a voluntary plan of affirmative selection of black trainees for craft jobs on a one-to-one ratio with whites. The Court took this action even though the trial record did *not* contain proof of intentional past discrimination. (Such proof, it should be noted, did and continues to exist.)

Speaking for the Court, Mr. Justice Brennan held that such a plan was not prohibited by Title VII of the 1964 Civil Rights Act. This is altogether consistent with the issue addressed by Congress in enacting the law, that is, Congress was concerned "with the plight of the Negro in our economy."

Throughout this article I have taken issue with the judicial trend of burdening discrimination victims with the duty to prove the obvious—past discrimination—when courts can easily enough deal with the matter by invoking presumptions or through judicial notice. In this regard, it was encouraging to note what Mr. Justice Brennan declared in footnote 1 of *Weber,* which in relevant part provides: "Judicial findings of exclusion from crafts on racial grounds are so numerous as to make such exclusion a proper subject for judicial notice."

The Court's acceptance of the "judicial notice" evidentiary rule represents one of *Weber's* significant aspects. Yet there remains the need to extend this rule to the housing and educational areas, where likewise there have been numerous enough findings to render the matter "a proper subject for judicial notice."

On April 24, 1979, the Court heard tandem arguments in the cases of *Columbus Bd. of Education v. Penick* and *Dayton Bd. of Education v. Brinkman.* Decisions were handed down on July 2, 1979, upholding the rulings of the United States Court of Appeals for the Sixth Circuit. At issue was whether the record in each case contained sufficient findings of constitutional violations to justify the system-wide remedies sanctioned by the Circuit Court.

Mr. Justice Byron White wrote for the majority in each case (7-2 in *Columbus,* 47 U.S.L.W. 4924 (July 2, 1979), and 5-4 in *Dayton,* 47 U.S.L.W. 4944 (July 2, 1979), affirming the system-wide desegregation remedies.

Many feared that after Mr. Justice William Rehnquist dramatically imposed an eleventh hour stay in the *Columbus* case last year—this after a denial of a similar request presented to Mr. Justice Potter Stewart—and after the granting of certiorari in the case, that given these occurrences the Court was contemplating a further retreat from desegregation remedies.

Though the *Bakke, Weber, Columbus* and *Dayton* decisions are not a constitutional breakthrough in the *Brown* sense, they are significant for their reaffirming aspects. They have lifted some of the doctrinal fog over whether the vestiges of separate racial treatment may be effectively uprooted through race-sensitive legal remedies. These four decisions represent something of a retreat from the judicial trend that discounted the disproportionate impact or results test in equal protection cases and the emerging legislative trend to abandon legislation directed toward remedying past discrimination.

For a long time after *Milliken I* the signals from the Court tended to be unclear. This fed the popular notion that equal protection guarantees could be circumvented, or at least restricted by imposing limits on remedy tools. Buzz words like "reverse discrimination" and "forced busing" became weapons in the arsenals of anti-affirmative action and anti-desegregation forces. Public confusion, and to some extent judicial bewilderment, stemmed from the *Milliken I* and *Dayton I* holdings. In short, the lie was that the Fourteenth Amendment had already been fully realized and that there existed no further need for race-sensitive remedies.

It is now clear from the latest quartet of Supreme Court decisions bearing on race that race-conscious remedies remain necessary and viable, whether constitutionally or statutorily rooted or whether the product of intentional action. To *that* extent, the pursuit of racial justice is back on the track—for the time being.

Gender in the Supreme Court: The 1976 Term
By Ruth Bader Ginsburg*

I. INTRODUCTION

On November 22, 1971 a unanimous Burger Court decision, *Reed v. Reed,*[1] attracted front page attention.[2] Speaking for the Court, the Chief Justice announced that an Idaho statute giving men preference over women in administering estates denied would-be administrator Sally Reed the equal protection of the laws. The *Reed* decision marked the first solid break from the Supreme Court's consistent rejection of women's complaints of unconstitutional gender discrimination.[3]

Sex-based discrimination was an area in which the Warren Court, like all of its predecessors, had paid utmost deference to legislative judgments. By contrast, the Burger Court, in the years 1971–1975, compiled a record remarkable for a Court characterized as "restrained" or "non-interventionist."[4] In *Frontiero v. Richardson* (1973),[5] the High Court held married women in the uniformed services entitled to the same fringe benefits as married men. Under the laws declared unconstitutional, married men automatically received a housing allowance and health care for their wives, while married women received these benefits only if they supplied all their own support and more than half of their husband's. In *Taylor v. Louisiana* (1975),[6] the Burger Court overturned the Warren Court's 1961 *Hoyt v. Florida*[7] decision and declared unconstitutional a Louisiana jury selection system that limited service by women to volunteers. In *Weinberger v. Wiesenfeld* (1975),[8] the Court struck down one of a series of Social Security Act sex lines. It held a widowed father entitled to the same benefits to care for his child that a widowed mother receives. In *Stanton v. Stanton* (1975),[9] the Court ruled inconsistent with the equal protection principle a Utah law that required parents to support a son until he is twenty-one, but a daughter only until she is eighteen. And in landmark January 1973 rulings, *Roe v. Wade*[10] and *Doe v. Bolton,*[11] the Court struck down anti-abortion laws found to intrude arbitrarily into the decision of a woman and her doctor to terminate a pregnancy.

These 1971–1975 "activist" decisions indicated that women had become "one of the Burger Court's new constituencies, as blacks were of the Warren Court."[12] But there were counter-indications during those years. In *Kahn v. Shevin* (1974),[13] the Court upheld exclusion of widowers from a Florida statute that grants widows a real property tax exemption. And, most significantly, in *Geduldig v. Aiello* (1974),[14] the Court upheld against an equal protection challenge a California statute that excluded women disabled by pregnancy from a workers' income protection disability insurance plan.

1976 Term returns, overall, disappointed expectations of women's rights advocates. The Court did render decisions continuing in the new direction charted from *Reed* through *Stanton.* In *Craig v. Boren* (1976),[15] and *Califano v. Goldfarb* (1977),[16] explicit sex-role stereotyping in legislation was condemned more forcibly than in earlier decisions. An important synthesis was essayed in *Califano v. Webster* (1977),[17] in which the Court addressed the distinction between impermissible adverse discrimination and permissible rectification for past injustices.

*Professor of law, Columbia University.

However, in an area of critical importance to women, the Court overwhelmingly rejected the arguments of female litigants and the groups supporting them. In *General Electric Co. v. Gilbert* (1976),[18] the Justices confronted a private employer's plan providing nonoccupational sickness and accident benefits to all employees, save only those with disabilities arising from pregnancy. Construing Title VII of the Civil Rights Act of 1964,[19] the Court expanded its reasoning in *Aiello* and declared the exclusion entailed no gender-based discrimination at all. Finally, in a set of stunning decisions announced at the Term's end (*Beal v. Doe, Maher v. Roe,* and *Poelker v. Doe,* 1977),[20] the Court declared that neither the Constitution nor current federal law requires states to spend Medicaid funds for nontherapeutic abortions and that public hospitals are not required by the Constitution to provide or even permit nontherapeutic abortions.

II. Invalidation of Classifications Based on Casual Assumptions About "The Way Women (or Men) Are": *Craig v. Boren* and *Califano v. Goldfarb*

The laws at issue in *Reed, Frontiero, Taylor, Wiesenfeld* and *Stanton* shared a salient characteristic. Each reflected a lump judgment about "the way women (or men) are." The challenged legislation rested on the gross assumption that females are concerned primarily with "the home and the rearing of the family," males with "the marketplace and the world of ideas."[21] The challengers did not assert that these propositions were inaccurate description for the generality of cases. But they questioned the reasonableness of treating the growing numbers of men and women who do not fit the stereotype as if they did, and of using gender pigeonholing in lieu of neutral, functional description. The Court's response displayed increasing awareness that the traditional legislative approach had all the earmarks of self-fulfilling prophecy. Thus, in *Stanton,* the Court reasoned:[22]

> A child, male or female, is still a child. . . . Women's activities are increasing and expanding. . . . The presence of women in business, in the professions, in government and, indeed, in all walks of life where education is a desirable, if not always a necessary antecedent, is apparent and a proper subject of judicial notice. If a specified age of minority is required for the boy in order to assure him parental support while he attains his education and training, so, too, it is for the girl. To distinguish between the two on educational grounds is to be self-serving: if the female is not to be supported so long as the male, she hardly can be expected to attend school as long he does, and bringing her education to an end earlier coincides with the role-typing society has long imposed.

In *Craig v. Boren*[23] and *Califano v. Goldfarb,*[24] the Court developed 1971– 1975 precedent rejecting legislative resort to a gender criterion as a proxy for some other individual or social characteristic. For the first time, explicit statement of a heightened standard of review for sex-based classifications attracted majority support.

Craig v. Boren was a challenge to an Oklahoma law that permitted girls to buy 3.2 beer (and work in an establishment where "near beer" was sold) at age eighteen, but required boys to wait until age twenty-one. Building on *Stanton,* the High Court held that Oklahoma's "boy protective" legislation could not withstand equal protection measurement.

Prior to *Craig,* the Court purported to apply the restrained, "rational basis" standard of review to sex lines in the law. In *Frontiero v. Richardson,*[25] four of the Justices, in a plurality opinion, ranked sex as a "suspect" criterion, entitled to the same stringent review the Court gives to classifications based on race, national origin or religion.[26] After *Frontiero,* however, no fifth vote emerged to elevate sex to the "suspect" categories.[27] But in *Craig,* Justice Brennan, writing for the Court, tendered a new formulation: classification by gender, to comport with the equal protection principle, must "substantially" further "important" governmental objectives.[28]

Under restrained or lower-tier equal protection review, legislation survives Supreme Court inspection if "rationally related" to a "legitimate" governmental objective. Classification by race, national origin or religion, on the other hand, is subjected to rigorous, upper-tier review: the legislative objective must be "compelling" and the classification must be "necessary" to its accomplishment.[29] Sex-based categorization, the *Craig v. Boren* majority declared, is governed by an intermediate or middle-tier standard—"something in between" upper-tier compelling interest and lower-tier rational relationship.[30]

In *Craig v. Boren,* the Court stood 7–2, but the case argued in tandem with it, *Califano v. Goldfarb,*[31] proved a cliffhanger. *Goldfarb* concerned social security provisions qualifying a deceased wage earner's widow for survivor's benefits automatically, but qualifying a widower for benefits only upon proof that his wage-earning wife supplied at least three-fourths of the couple's support (all her own support plus at least one-half of his). The case bore a marked kinship to two earlier High Court adjudications. In *Frontiero v. Richardson,*[32] the Court had invalidated a virtually identical sex line in the context of fringe benefits for married members of the uniformed services. In *Weinberger v. Wiesenfeld,*[33] the Court had declared unconstitutional exclusion of widowed fathers from the Social Security Act's provision of child-in-care benefits for widowed mothers. Although *Frontiero* yielded an 8–1 vote,[34] and *Wiesenfeld* a unanimous judgment,[35] *Goldfarb* was a 5–4 decision.[36]

Perhaps accounting for the sharp division on the Court, *Goldfarb* was the first successful gender discrimination claim that carried a substantial price tag. The Government estimated an annual cost in excess of $500 million to provide spouses of female wage earners the benefits accorded spouses of male wage earners. By contrast, in *Frontiero* the Government conceded that, in the military context, striking the one-way dependency test would have scant impact on the fisc. (Relatively few women served in the armed forces, fewer still were married, even fewer were married to civilians.) And in *Wiesenfeld,* the annual cost of extending child-in-care benefits to widowed fathers had been estimated at $20 million, less than 4% of the cost implicated in *Goldfarb.*[37]

For five members of the Court, the vastly augmented amount at stake did not deter adherence to the *Fronteiro* and *Wiesenfeld* precedents. Adverting to the heightened review standard declared in *Craig v. Boren,*[38] the Court again condemend knee-jerk classification by gender. The plurality opinion, patterned closely on *Wiesenfeld,*[39] described the one-way dependency test as denigrating the efforts of the wage-earning woman by providing her spouse less protection than that provided the spouse of a wage-earning man. Rationalizing the scheme as an effort to redress economic discrimination against women would be pure afterthought. For the legislative history left no doubt that Congress had in fact acted solely on the then generally accepted premise that men are breadwinners first and foremost, while women are primarily wives and mothers. In other words, Congress indulged the familiar assumption that women depend on men but not vice versa. Congress did not invoke a "need" (income) test as a criterion for benefits, nor did it contemplate ameliorating job market discrimination against women. Rather, the lawmakers simply equated the terms "widow" and "dependent."

In a concurring opinion, Justice Stevens associated himself with the opening point made by the dissenting Justices—that social security benefits are neither contractual nor a form of compensation for services. Social security, though requiring payments by employers and employees, is not an insurance scheme, it is a tax.[40] Thus benefits to covered workers are not so sharply distinguishable from benefits paid out of general revenues—welfare benefits, for example. This starting point led Justice Stevens to focus on the discrimination against the surviving male spouse, not the discounted return on contributions made by the married female wage earner. Why this discrimination against a class of men, Justice Stevens asked. Not because Congress entertained the slightest desire to compensate females for the disadvantageous treatment to which they are exposed in economic endeavor. On the contrary, the disparate treatment Congress ordered for widows and widowers simply reflected longstanding "habit"; the discrimination encountered by widower Goldfarb was "merely the accidental byproduct of [the legislators'] traditional way of thinking about females." (Women are "the weaker sex," "more likely to be child-rearers or dependents.")[41]

A bare majority of the Court thus understood that equations of the kind embraced in the Social Security Act, still pervasive in federal and state lawbooks, channel and constrain individuals. Laws of this genre, ranking men independent, women dependent, inhibit both men and women from choosing the paths they will pursue in life based on their individual talents and preferences. The classification at issue in *Goldfarb,* the prototypical sex-line in the law,[42] was indeed "self-serving," and "coincide[d] with the role-typing society has long imposed."[43] But four members of the Court, in dissent, rehearsed again the historic argument: the sex-based classification accurately reflects the station in life of most women, it operates benignly in their favor, and it is administratively convenient.[44]

Follow-up judgments, announced a few weeks after *Goldfarb,*[45] dealt summarily with the identical gender line in the context of derivative old-age (wives and husbands) social security benefits. Once more, the one-way dependency test was invalidated. The same day, in a per curiam ruling in *Califano v. Webster,*[46] the Court's majority—the five Justices responsible for the *Goldfarb* judgment—dealt with the nervous question of affirmative action in the context of sex.[47]

III. A CORRIDOR FOR AFFIRMATIVE ACTION: *Califano v. Webster*

Califano v. Webster[48] distinguishes from knee-jerk categorization by sex a law deliberately enacted to compensate women for past employment discrimination. *Webster* upheld a classification, effective from 1956 to 1972, establishing a more favorable social security benefit calculation for retired female workers than for retired male workers.

Old-age insurance benefits are based on the wage earner's "average monthly wage." Before 1972, women could exclude from the computation of their average monthly wage three more low earning years than men could exclude. The provision sanctioned disparate treatment solely on the basis of sex. But this scheme, unlike the one before the Court in *Goldfarb,* had been enacted in direct response to the adversely discriminatory conditions women encountered in the labor market—depressed wages for "women's work," early retirement routinely forced on women but not upon men. Congress sought to reduce the carryover impact on the working woman's retirement years of past wage and job placement bias against her.

In 1972, Congress phased out the differential. It did so not by removing the three low earning years exclusion for women, but by extending this exclusion to men. Congress took this action after the Equal Pay Act (1963)[49] and Title VII of the Civil Rights Act of 1964[50] were made applicable to most sectors of the economy. Those laws prohibited the discriminatory employer practices that supplied the *raison d'etre* for the 1956 sex-specific classification.

The *Webster* majority opinion stresses that, in contrast to *Goldfarb,* the provision at issue involved no "romantically paternalistic" view of women as men's dependents or appendages. Two points are prominent in the *Webster* majority ruling: (1) When, as in *Webster,* legislation directly addresses historic disadvantageous treatment and serves to remedy or ameliorate it, disparate treatment of the sexes, at least as an interim measure, is constitutional. (2) When, as in *Goldfarb* and *Craig v. Boren,* disparate treatment is rooted in traditional role-typing and is not deliberately and specifically aimed at redressing past injustice, disparate treatment based on sex is unconstitutional. If the Court adheres to the *Webster* synthesis, it will uphold a gender classification justified as compensatory only if in fact adopted by the legislature for remedial reasons rather than out of prejudices about "the way women (or men) are," and even then, only if the classification neatly matches the remedial end.

The *Webster* majority opinion thus attempts to preserve and bolster a general rule of equal treatment while leaving a corridor open for genuinely compensatory classification. The line between impermissible adverse discrimination and permissible rectification sketched in *Webster* may bear significantly on "affirmative action" questions now reaching the High Court.[51]

IV. THE COURT DISARMED: *Vorchheimer v. School District of Philadelphia*

Craig v. Boren and *Califano v. Goldfarb* suggest a Court—at least a slim majority— gaining appreciation of what sex discrimination is and how deeply it pervades the nation's history and laws. But a month after *Goldfarb,* in *Vorchheimer v. School District of Philadelphia,*[52] the Court wavered. Philadelphia reserves for scholastically-superior boys its Central High School, the City's oldest, most celebrated public secondary school. Girls' High, a sister institution, is reserved for academically-gifted female students. Split down the middle 4–4, the Justices could reach no decision on Susan Vorchheimer's claim for admission to Central High, and the judgment below (2–1 for the School District) remains the last word in the controversy.

The *Vorchheimer* record presented scant evidence of tangible differences in the two schools. The record perhaps led some members of the Court to conclude Philadelphia's sex-segregated Central and Girls' schools afforded equivalent educations. On this basis, the School District argued separation of boys from girls was non-stigmatic—though separate, the schools were "equal." No precedent had paved the way for a challenge to separate but equal education of boys and girls. *Brown v. Board of Education,*[53] the landmark decision holding separate education of the races inherently unequal, had been preceded by a long line of cases in which decision turned on the markedly inferior opportunities afforded blacks, on inequalities solidly demonstrated at trial.[54]

Nonetheless, given a society in which women have been regarded as members of "the second sex,"[55] and secure precedent in the race discrimination area, a strong case could have been made that reservation of an educational institution to males is "likely to be a witting or unwitting device for preserving tacit assumptions of male superiority—assumptions for which women eventually must pay."[56] And if the Court had accepted that sex-based classification, like classification based on race, religion or national origin, should attract rigorous, upper-tier equal protection scrutiny rather than intermediate or middle-tier review, a decision for Susan Vorchheimer should have been assured. But as the *Vorchheimer* trial judge put it, the "something in between" standard gives lower courts insufficient guidance, it leaves them with "an uncomfortable feeling, somewhat similar to a man playing a shell game who is not absolutely sure there is a pea."[57]

V. OTHER 1976 TERM DECISIONS

An array of other issues touching on gender occupied the Justices. In *Trimble v. Gordon,*[58] the Court overturned an Illinois intestacy law that qualified a child born out of wedlock for succession to the mother's property, but not to the father's. On the other hand, in *Fiallo v. Bell,*[59] the Court upheld a federal statute recognizing for immigration purposes parent-child relationships between mother and offspring born out of wedlock, but not between father and out-of-wedlock offspring. In so ruling, the Court relied on the plenary authority of Congress to regulate immigration.

In *Coker v. Georgia,*[60] the Court ruled it cruel and unusual punishment to impose the death penalty for rape of an adult woman. Several women's rights groups, in amicus curiae argument, contended that the death penalty for rape originated in a view of the crime as theft of a man's property, and that excessive punishment had the nullifying effect of making triers reluctant to convict.

Two Title VII rulings in the 1976 Term bear significantly on women's prospects in the job market: *Dothard v. Rawlinson*[61] and *International Brotherhood of Teamsters v. United States*.[62] In *Dothard v. Rawlinson*,[63] the Court held invalid Alabama's statutory minimum height and weight requirements for prison guards. These requirements automatically disqualified a disproportionately large percentage of women. At the same time, the Court upheld a regulation barring women from "contact" positions in Alabama's violent, overcrowded, understaffed male maximum security penitentiaries. Based on the abnormal circumstances prevailing in these prisons, the Court concluded male gender constituted a "bona fide occupational qualification" for the contact guard post. But the "bfoq" ruling was tightly framed. Emphasizing that very few jobs fit under that rubric, the Court stated: "We are persuaded—by the restrictive language of [the exception], the relevant legislative history, and the consistent interpretation of the Equal Employment Opportunity Commission—that the bfoq exception was in fact meant to be an extremely narrow exception on the general prohibition of discrimination on the basis of sex."

International Brotherhood of Teamsters v. United States[64] held Title VII does not prohibit maintenance of a seniority system that perpetuates the effects of discrimination occurring before the effective date of the Act. While the charge was race discrimination, the Court's reasoning is fully applicable to sex discrimination claims.

VI. A Pregnant Problem: *General Electric Co. v. Gilbert*

The Court's first encounters with the pregnant problem, and the first major setback for feminist advocates in the 1970's, occurred in the 1973 Term. In *Geduldig v. Aiello*,[65] the Court upheld, as consistent with the "equal protection" principle, a California statute that excluded women disabled by pregnancy from a state-operated workers' income protection disability insurance plan. (Institutionalized drug addicts, alcoholics, and sexual psychopaths completed the list of exclusions.) The pregnancy exclusion was reviewed under the minimum rationality, lower-tier test generally applicable to economic and social legislation. Use of an intermediate standard was not considered, for the Court reasoned California had not excluded anyone from benefit eligibility "because of gender." Rather, the program simply "divide[d] recipients into two groups—pregnant women and *nonpregnant persons*."[66]

Yet earlier in the 1973 Term, in *Cleveland Board of Education v. LaFleur*,[67] the High Court had held that school teachers may not be dismissed or placed on involuntary leave arbitrarily at a fixed stage in pregnancy. And in the 1975 Term, in *Turner v. Department of Employment Security*,[68] the Court announced that pregnant women ready, willing, and able to work may not be denied unemployment compensation when jobs are closed to them.

The *LaFleur* and *Turner* decisions issued under a due process-conclusive presumption rubric. The Court said that the rules in question irrebuttably presumed the unfitness of the pregnant woman and impermissibly burdened her exercise of the fundamental right to bear a child. Conclusive presumption analysis, though popular for a spell in the High Court, has not fared well under critical analysis. As one student writer pointed out, conclusive or irrebuttable presumptions are not "evidentiary rules involved in the process of fact-finding," they "are nothing more than statutory classifications."[69] And at the end of the 1974 Term, in *Weinberger v. Salfi*,[70] the Court indicated that it would not spread the doctrine to new areas.

Underlying the Court's divergent responses in *LaFleur* and *Turner* on the one hand, *Aiello* on the other, may be a factor not fully acknowledged in the written opinions. Perhaps the *able* pregnant woman seeking only to do a day's work for a day's pay is a sympathetic figure before the Court, while the woman disabled by pregnancy is suspect. (Is she really sick or recovering from childbirth, or is she malingering so that she may stay "where she belongs"—at home with baby?)[71]

Despite *Aiello,* disadvantageous treatment of pregnancy in employment contexts, including exclusions from employee insurance plans, remained a live issue under Title VII. Title VII prohibits sex discrimination, just as it prohibits race discrimination, in all terms and conditions of employment.[72] In contrast to the Constitution's equal protection requirement, which has not been read to address sex discrimination with the same vigor as race discrimination. Title VII places race and sex on the same line. Title VII Sex Discrimination Guidelines issued by the Equal Employment Opportunity Commission provided:[73] "Disabilities caused or contributed to by pregnancy, miscarriage, abortion, childbirth, and recovery therefrom are, for all job-related purposes, temporary disabilities and should be treated as such under any health or temporary disability insurance or sick leave plan available in connection with employment." Courts of Appeals in most of the Circuits had accepted the EEOC's interpretation.[74] They reasoned that Title VII required rigorous review of employment practices which place women at a disadvantage in the labor market, not the restrained brand of equal protection review applied in *Aiello.*

But on December 7, 1976, in *General Electric Co. v. Gilbert,*[75] the Court extended the *Aiello* approach to Title VII's domain. At issue was GE's plan providing non-occupational disability benefits to all employees (without regard to the "voluntariness" or sex-specific nature of the disabling condition), save only those with disabilities arising from pregnancy. Exclusion of women disabled due to pregnancy, the Court held, did not violate the statute, for leaving out pregnant persons was not sex-based discrimination at all. The pregnancy classification was assessed as "neutral," signalling neither a gender-based purpose nor a discriminatory effect.[76]

The Court's unwillingness to acknowledge the existence of gender discrimination in the pregnancy disability exclusion could lead to intolerable results if similar myopia attended other group-specific exclusions. For example, would the Court uphold as "neutral" an employer's plan singling out sickle-cell anemia for exclusion from health or disability insurance coverage?

Yet the likelihood that childbirth will occur nowadays normally twice in a working woman's life, and the cost generated by insurance coverage for pregnancy-related absences, no doubt influenced the Court's ruling—its determination to remit the issue for explicit decision in the political arena rather than to resolve it by constitutional adjudication (in *Aiello*) or statutory interpretation (in *Gilbert*). If Congress is genuinely committed to eradication of sex-based discrimination, it will respond by providing firm legislative direction assuring job security, health insurance coverage, and income maintenance for child-bearing women.[77] For women will remain more restricted in their options than men so long as the pregnancy problem is brushed under the rug by the nation's lawmakers.

VI. STUNNING CURTAILMENT OF DOCTRINE BOLDLY ANNOUNCED: *Beal v. Doe, Maher v. Roe,* AND *Poelker v. Doe*

In landmark January 1973 rulings, *Roe v. Wade*[78] and *Doe v. Bolton,*[79] the Supreme Court struck down anti-abortion laws as unwarranted state intrusions into the decision of a woman and her doctor to terminate a pregnancy. Until June 20, 1977, it appeared that in no other area of the law had the Burger Court acted more intrepidly.

The 1973 reproductive freedom decisions have been typed aberrational—highly activist decisions[80] from a bench normally deferential to legislative judgments. Significantly, the opinions in *Roe v. Wade* and *Doe v. Bolton* barely mention "women's rights." They are not tied to any equal protection or equal rights theory. Rather, the Court anchored stringent review of abortion prohibitions to concepts of bodily integrity, personal privacy or autonomy, derived from the due process guarantee.

Some speculated that the 7−2 judgments in the 1973 cases were motivated, at least in part, by population concerns and the spectre of unwanted children born into impoverished families. But in a trilogy of decisions announced June 20, 1977,[81] the Court stood 6−3 against extending the 1973 rulings to require state support for an indigent woman's non-therapeutic abortion.[82] The majority declared that although the state could not interfere arbitrarily with the decision of a woman able to pay for an abortion, government could encourage childbirth by refusing Medicaid reimbursement for nontherapeutic abortion and by banning such abortions in public hospitals.

The Court asserted the 1977 decisions "signal[led] no retreat from *Roe {v. Wade}* or the cases applying it."[83] But in practical terms, the recent rulings augur that in many localities poor and unsophisticated women will find access to abortion at best difficult, too often impossible. Nor can the political process be relied upon to respond to the plight of the indigent woman. As Justice Blackmun said in dissent: "Why should any politician incur the demonstrated wrath and noise of the abortion opponents when mere silence and nonactivity accomplish the results the opponents want?"[84]

VII. CONCLUSION

Summing up the 1976 Term, one Supreme Court watcher observed: "This was the year the women lost."[85] But with respect to explicit sex lines in the law, an important advance was made. *Craig v. Boren*[86] and *Caifano v. Goldfarb*[87] articulated a tighter equal protection review standard for gender-based classifications. And *Califano v. Webster*[88] delineated a narrow channel for affirmative action in the context of sex.

On the loss side, *General Electric Co. v. Gilbert,*[89] the pregnancy benefits Title VII ruling, has broad potential impact. But legislative overruling of the decision has been proposed in both the House and Senate, and has attracted strong support.[90]

Most unsettling of the losses are the decisions on access by the poor to elective abortions. Although leaving "the poor alone ineligible for abortion defies justice, common sense, rational policy and the Federal budget,"[91] movement in the political forum is blocked. Ultimately, however, the courage lacking in legislative chambers may become less significant. For, in time, development of safer, more effective, easily utilized or administered contraceptives and abortifacients may place securely in the hands of women the means of controlling individual reproduction and perhaps the national fertility as well.[92] Women at every economic level firmly in control of the decision whether and, if so, when to bear children should have a profound impact on the shape of future society.

Notes

1. 404 U.S. 71 (1971).
2. See New York Post, November 22, 1971, p. 1 (AP dispatch).
3. *See generally,* BABCOCK, FREEDMAN, NORTON & ROSS, SEX DISCRIMINATION AND THE LAW, ch. 1 (1975); DAVIDSON, GINSBURG & KAY, SEX-BASED DISCRIMINATION, ch. 1 (1974); Johnston, Jr. & Knapp, *Sex Discrimination by Law: A Study in Judicial Perspective,* 46 N.Y.U.L. REV. 675 (1971).
4. *See generally* Ginsburg, *Gender and the Constitution,* 44 U. CIN. L. REV. 1 (1975); Ginsburg, *Gender in the Supreme Court: The 1973 and 1974 Terms,* 1975 SUP. CT. REV. 1; Ginsburg, *Sex Equality and the Constitution,* 52 TULANE LAW REV. 451 (1978).
5. 411 U.S. 677 (1973).
6. 419 U.S. 522 (1975).

7. 368 U.S. 57 (1961).

8. 420 U.S. 636 (1975).

9. 421 U.S. 7 (1975).

10. 410 U.S. 113 (1973).

11. 410 U.S. 179 (1973).

12. Oelsner, *Supreme Court's Year is Marked by Changes in Patterns of Voting,* New York Times, July 4, 1977, p. 1.

13. 416 U.S. 351 (1974).

14. 417 U.S. 484 (1974).

15. 429 U.S. 190 (1976).

16. 430 U.S. 199 (1977).

17. 430 U.S. 313 (1977).

18. 429 U.S. 125 (1976).

19. 42 U.S.C. § 2000e. Congress prospectively overruled the *General Electric Co. v. Gilbert* decision in October 1978 by defining sex-based classification to include classification based on pregnancy. P.L. 95–555, 92 Stat. 2076.

20. 432 U.S. 438, 526, 519 (1977).

21. Stanton v. Stanton, 421 U.S. 7, 14 (1975).

22. *Id.* at 14–15.

23. 429 U.S. 190 (1976).

24. 430 U.S. 199 (1977).

25. 411 U.S. 677 (1973).

26. The plurality opinion, written by Justice Brennan, was joined by Justices Douglas, Marshall and White. Rejecting Government arguments as to the "benignity" and administrative convenience of the sex classification, Justice Brennan said:

> There can be no doubt that our Nation 'has had a long and unfortunate history of sex discrimination. Traditionally, such discrimination was rationalized by an attitude of "romantic paternalism" which, in practical effect, put women not on a pedestal, but in a cage.

411 U.S. at 684. Justice Stewart's terse concurring opinion states only that the particular statutes before the Court "work[ed] an invidious discrimination." *Id.* at 691. Justice Powell, joined by Chief Justice Burger and Justice Blackmun, concurred on the basis of *Reed,* but thought it "premature and unnecessary" to decide whether sex constitutes a "suspect" category pending consideration by the states of the proposed Equal Rights Amendment. *Id.* at 692. Justice Rehnquist was the sole dissenter.

27. Justice Stevens, who was not on the Court when *Frontiero* was decided, may be edging toward that position. *See, e.g.,* Mathews v. Lucas, 427 U.S. 495, 520–21 (1976) (dissenting opinion): "Habit, rather than analysis, make it seem acceptable and natural to distinguish between male and female. . . ; for too much of our history there was the same inertia in distinguishing between black and white."

28. 429 U.S. at 197. Separate concurring opinions were filed by Justices Powell, Stevens, Stewart and Blackmun. Chief Justice Burger and Justice Rehnquist filed separate dissenting opinions. In a footnote to the *Craig v. Boren* majority opinion, the Court disapproved Goesaert v. Cleary, 335 U.S. 464 (1948). 429 U.S. at 210, n.23. *Goesaert,* upholding a Michigan statute prohibiting women from working as bartenders, had sanctioned the authority of the legislatures to draw "a sharp line between the sexes." 335 U.S. at 465.

29. *See generally* Gunther, *In Search of Evolving Doctrine on a Changing Court: A Model for a Newer Equal Protection,* 86 HARV. L. REV. 1 (1972); *Developments in the Law—Equal Protection,* 82 HARV. L. REV. 1065 (1969).

30. *Cf.* Stanton v. Stanton, 421 U.S. 7, 17 (1975). Justice Powell, in his *Craig v. Boren* concurring opinion, was reluctant to acknowledge a middle tier, but noted: "[C]andor compels the recognition that the relatively deferential 'rational basis' standard of review normally applied takes on a sharper focus when we address a gender-based classification." 429 U.S. at 210–11 n.*.

31. 430 U.S. 199 (1977).

32. 411 U.S. 677 (1973).

33. 420 U.S. 636 (1975).

34. *See* note 26 *supra.*

35. Justice Brennan's opinion for the Court in *Wiesenfeld* rejects the Government's justification of the classification as "benign" (420 U.S. at 648) and, in addition to emphasizing the statute's denigration of gainfully-employed females (420 U.S. at 645), objects to the provision's anti-male facet. 420 U.S. at 652. Justice Powell's concurring opinion, joined by Chief Justice Burger, stresses the discrimination against the female wage earner. Justice Rehnquist's separate concurring opinion rests on the irrationality of the scheme from the viewpoint of the surviving child. Up to 1978 *Wiesenfeld* remained the only case in which Justice Rehnquist had

joined his brethren in striking out a classification under the equal protection principle. This uncharacteristic vote was not counted in Shapiro, *Mr. Justice Rehnquist: A Preliminary View,* 90 HARV. L. REV. 293, 308 (1976).

36. Justice Brennan wrote the plurality opinion in which Justices White, Marshall and Powell joined. Justice Stevens concurred separately.

37. *Compare* Brief for the Appellant at 22, Weinberger v. Wiesenfeld, 420 U.S. 636 (1975) (No. 73–1892), *with* Brief for the Appellant at 8, 39, 1A–6A, Califano v. Goldfarb, 430 U.S. 199 (1977) (No. 75–699).

38. *See* text at notes 28–30 *supra.*

39. *See* note 35 *supra.*

40. But note the misleading title employed by Congress, the "Federal Insurance Contributions Act."

41. 430 U.S. at 223; Califano v. Webster, 430 U.S. 313, 317 (1977). Justice Stevens also questioned the soundness of the Court's decision in Kahn v. Shevin, 416 U.S. 351 (1974), text at note 13, *supra.* He pointed out "that case involved a discrimination between surviving spouses which originated in 1885; a discrimination of that vintage cannot reasonably be supposed to have been motivated by a decision to repudiate the 19th century presumption that females are inferior to males. . . . [T]he Court upheld the Florida statute on the basis of a hypothetical justification for the discrimination that had nothing to do with the legislature's actual motivation." 430 U.S. at 224.

42. *See* GINSBURG & FASTEAU, THE LEGAL STATUS OF WOMEN UNDER FEDERAL LAW 10–11, 202–205 (Columbia Law School Equal Rights Advocacy Project 1974); Johnston, Jr. & Knapp, *Sex Discrimination by Law: A Study in Judicial Perspective,* 46 N.Y.U.L. REV. 675 (1971).

43. Stanton v. Stanton, 421 U.S. 7, 15 (1975).

44. Authored by Justice Rehnquist, the *Goldfarb* dissenting opinion relies heavily on Mathews v. Lucas, 427 U.S. 495 (1976), in which the Court sustained a Social Security Act provision disadvantaging certain children born out of wedlock. But in *Lucas,* the Court distinguished illegitimacy from race and sex as classifying factors: "[P]erhaps in part because illegitimacy does not carry an obvious badge, as race or sex do, this discrimination against illegitimates has never approached the severity or pervasiveness of the historic legal and political discrimination against women and Negroes." 427 U.S. at 506. Moreover, the *Lucas* opinion, citing *Wiesenfeld,* referred to the invalidity of sex classifications based on the "overbroad" assumption that males are the wage earners that count in the family unit. 427 U.S. at 513. If these statements of Justice Blackmun, author of the Court's opinion in *Lucas,* are difficult to reconcile with his dissenting vote in *Goldfarb,* it is even more difficult to reconcile the position of Chief Justice Burger in *Goldfarb* with the concurring opinion to which he subscribed in *Wiesenfeld.* See 420 U.S. at 654 (discrimination against the female wage earner identified as the principal flaw requiring invalidation of the social security classification).

45. Silbowitz v. Secretary of Health, Educ. and Welfare, 397 F. Supp. 862 (S.D. Fla. (1975)), *affirmed sub nom.* Califano v. Silbowitz, 430 U.S. 924 (1977); Jablon v. Secretary of Health, Educ. & Welfare, 399 F. Supp. 118 (D. Md. 1975), *affirmed sub nom.* Califano v. Jablon, 430 U.S. 924 (1977).

46. 430 U.S. 313 (1977).

47. Chief Justice Burger wrote a concurring opinion in *Webster* for the four *Goldfarb* dissenters.

48. 430 U.S. 313 (1977).

49. 29 U.S.C. §206(d).

50. 42 U.S.C. §2000e.

51. In University of California Regents v. Bakke, 98 S.Ct. 2733, 2766, 2783–2784 (1978), Justice Brennan, dissenting in part, cited *Webster* as a pathmarker. In contrast, Justice Powell, author of the prevailing opinion, considered gender-based classification precedent inapposite. *Id.* at 2755.

The match between persons who in fact experienced past discrimination and the benefited class might be regarded as closer in *Webster* than in *Bakke.* On the other hand, it is arguable that "compensation" for past injustice, the issue in *Webster,* merits greater suspicion than measures directed at eliminating current prejudice and opening equal opportunity for the future. *See* Note 89 HARV. L. REV. 95 (1975).

52. 400 F. Supp. 326 (E.D. Pa. 1975), *rev'd,* 532 F.2d 800 (3d Cir. 1976), *aff'd by an equally divided Court,* 430 U.S. 703 (1977).

53. 347 U.S. 438 (1954).

54. The most immediate *Brown* predecessors in a prolonged litigation campaign were Sweatt v. Painter, 339 U.S. 629 (1950), and McLaurin v. Oklahoma, 339 U.S. 637 (1950).

55. *See generally* S. DE BEAUVOIR, SECOND SEX (1949); E. JANEWAY, MAN'S WORLD, WOMAN'S PLACE (1971); W. CHAFE, THE AMERICAN WOMAN (1972).

56. C. JENCKS & D. REISMAN, THE ACADEMIC REVOLUTION 297–98 (1968).

57. *Vorchheimer,* 400 F. Supp. at 340–41.

58. 430 U.S. 762 (1977). *But see* Lalli v. Lalli, 47 U.S.L.W. 4061 (December 11, 1978) (upholding New

York statute that allows illegitimate child to inherit from intestate father only if, prior to father's death, there has been a judicial declaration of paternity).

59. 430 U.S. 787 (1977).

60. 433 U.S. 584 (1977).

61. 433 U.S. 321 (1977).

62. 431 U.S. 324 (1977). *See also* United Air Lines, Inc. v. Evans, 431 U.S. 553 (1977) (stewardess who, without timely challenge, was terminated under "no-marriage" rule later declared unlawful under Title VII and who was subsequently reinstated but without retroactive seniority cannot at time of reinstatement challenge otherwise neutral seniority system).

63. 433 U.S. 321 (1977).

64. 431 U.S. 324 (1977).

65. 417 U.S. 484 (1974). Justice Brennan dissented in an opinion joined by Justices Douglas and Marshall.

66. 417 U.S. at 496–97 n.20.

67. 414 U.S. 632 (1974).

68. 423 U.S. 44 (1975).

69. Note, 87 HARV. L. REV. 1534, 1556 (1974). *See generally* Bezanson, *Some Thoughts on the Emerging Irrebuttable Presumption Doctrine,* 7 IND. L. REV. 644 (1974); Note, 72 MICH. L. REV. 800 (1974); Note, 27 STAN L. REV. 499 (1974). *But see* Tribe, *Structural Due Process,* 10 HARV. CIV. RTS. —CIV. LIB. L. REV. 269 (1975).

70. 422 U.S 749 (1975).

71. *See* Johnston, Jr., *Sex Discrimination and the Supreme Court—1971–1974,* 49 N.Y.U.L. REV. 617, 646–47, 678–80 (1974); Bartlett, *Pregnancy Under the Constitution: The Uniqueness Trap,* 62 CALIF. L. REV. 1532, 1535, 1563–66 (1974); Note, 75 COLUM. L. REV. 441 (1975).

72. *But see* International Brotherhood of Teamsters v. United States, 431 U.S. 324 (1977), described *supra,* text at note 64, interpreting 42 U.S.C. 2000e-2(h) to permit employers to apply different conditions based on otherwise neutral, legitimate seniority systems that may perpetuate pre-Title VII discrimination. A narrowly construed "bona fide occupational qualification" exception to Title VII's nondiscrimination requirement (42 U.S.C. §2000e-2(e)) applies to religion, sex and national origin, but not to race. *See* Dothard v. Rawlinson, 433 U.S. 321 (1977), described *supra,* text accompanying note 63.

73. 29 C.F.R. 1604.10(b).

74. *See* Communication Workers v. American Tel. & Tel. Co., 513 F.2d 1024 (2d Cir. 1975); Wetzel v. Liberty Mutual Ins. Co., 511 F.2d 199 (3d Cir. 1975), *vacated on jurisdictional grounds,* 424 U.S. 737 (1976); Gilbert v. General Electric Co., 519 F.2d 661 (4th Cir. 1975), *rev'd,* 429 U.S. 125 (1976); Tyler v. Vickery, 517 F.2d 1089, 1097–99 (5th Cir. 1975); Satty v. Nashville Gas Co., 522 F.2d 850 (6th Cir. 1975), *aff'd in part,* 434 U.S. 136 (1977); Hutchinson v. Lake Oswego School District, 519 F.2d 961 (9th Cir. 1975).

75. 429 U.S. 125. Justices Brennan, Marshall and Stevens dissented.

76. But see Brooklyn Union Gas Co. v. New York State Human Rights Appeal Board, 41 N.Y. 2d 84, 390 N.Y.S. 2d 884 (1976) (interpreting sex discrimination prohibition in state human rights law to encompass discrimination based on pregnancy). In the 1977 Term, the Court held that stripping women disabled due to pregnancy of accrued job-bidding seniority violates Title VII. Nashville Gas Co. v. Satty, 434 U.S. 136 (1977).

77. Congress overturned *Gilbert* in October 1978 by explicitly defining sex-based classification for Title VII purposes to include classification based on pregnancy. P.L. 95–555, 92 Stat. 2076.

Ironically, job security and income protection for childbirth did not figure in "women-only" protective labor legislation once in vogue in the United States. In this respect, the United States differs from almost every other Western industrial country. *See generally* A. COOK, THE WORKING MOTHER: A SURVEY OF PROBLEMS AND PROGRAMS IN NINE COUNTRIES (N.Y. State School of Industrial and Labor Relations, rev. ed. 1978); *cf.* Heffermehl, *The Status of Women in Norway,* 20 AM. J. COMP. L. 630, 640–41 (1972) (recounting that in the first part of this century, farsighted feminists in Norway steadfastly and successfully opposed "women-only" protective legislation except with respect to benefits for the childbearing woman).

78. 410 U.S. 113.

79. 410 U.S. 179.

80. *See* Ely, *The Wages of Crying Wolf: A Comment on Roe v. Wade,* 82 YALE L.J. 920 (1973).

81. Beal v. Doe, 432 U.S. 438 (1977); Maher v. Roe, 432 U.S. 526 (1977); Poelker v. Doe, 432 U.S. 519 (1977). Justices Brennan, Marshall, and Blackmun dissented.

82. *But cf.* Carey v. Population Services International, 431 U.S. 678 (1977) (striking down New York provisions making it a crime for any person to distribute contraceptives to minors over sixteen, for anyone but a licensed pharmacist to distribute contraceptives to persons over sixteen, and for anyone, including pharmacists, to advertise or display contraceptives).

83. Maher v. Roe, 432 U.S. 464, 475 (1977). Writing for the majority, Justice Powell sharply distinguished government-imposed obstacles to abortion, *e.g.,* the criminal sanctions in Roe v. Wade, 410 U.S. 113 (1973), and the spousal consent requirement in Planned Parenthood v. Danforth, 428 U.S. 52 (1976), from a state policy to promote childbirth. The former attract rigorous review, he declared, the latter merits judicial deference. The majority acknowledged that a state may fund all abortions if it so chooses, and left open the question whether refusal to fund "medically necessary" abortions would be constitutional.

84. Beal v. Doe, 432 U.S. 438, 463 (1977). Blockage in the political processes has long supplied a prime reason for close judicial scrutiny of legislation. *See* United States v. Carolene Products, 304 U.S. 144, 152–53 n.4 (1938).

85. Oelsner, *Recent Supreme Court Rulings Have Set Back Women's Rights,* New York Times, July 8, 1977, p. 8A (attributing the comment to a 1977 Term clerk for a Supreme Court Justice).

86. 429 U.S. 190 (1976).

87. 430 U.S. 199 (1977).

88. 430 U.S. 313 (1977).

89. 429 U.S. 125 (1976).

90. The legislation overruling *General Electric Co. v. Gilbert* passed in October 1978. P.L. 95–555, 92 Stat. 2076.

91. Wicker, *Kitchen-Table Justice,* New York Times, June 28, 1977, p. 31.

92. *See generally* DAVIDSON, GINSBURG & KAY, SEX- BASED DISCRIMINATION, Text Note on Control of the Body 390, 417–18 (1974).

Wealth Discrimination in The Supreme Court:
Equal Protection for The Poor From GRIFFIN to MAHER

BY BARBARA BRUDNO*

Questions concerning the constitutional status of inequalities based on poverty, or of discrimination against the poor, can cut to the quick of the American psyche. Merely raising such questions requires acknowledging a duality—what the President's Commission on Income Maintenance Programs labeled a "paradox"[1]—that all too many Americans prefer and can afford to ignore.[2] That duality is the seemingly paradoxical conflict between, on the one hand, the traditional ideal of "equality for all," more modestly expressed in contemporary terms as "equality of opportunity," and, on the other hand, the stratified nature of our society and the enormous amount of poverty endemic to it.

The magnitude of this poverty and stratification is indicated most readily by U.S. Census data documenting both the millions of people living below the officially-defined "poverty level"[3] and the vast and persistent disparities in the share of national aggregate income received by the lower and upper fifths of the population. In 1975, for example, almost 26 million individuals were officially "poor"; and families in the bottom twenty percent received only 5.4% of national aggregate income compared with the 41.1% and 15.5% shares retained by families in the top one-fifth and the highest 5%, respectively.[4] Moreover, these inequalities in relative shares of income are neither fluctuating nor randomly distributed. Rather such inequalities have remained relatively constant over the past three decades,[5] and, they are suffered disproportionately by racial minorities, women, the aged and children.[6]

The constitutional significance of these economic disparities and their consequences stems from the Fourteenth Amendment's guarantee of equal protection of the laws.[7] However, questions concerning the equal protection status of discrimination on the basis of poverty continue to be especially troubling to the legal community. Their intelligible articulation, let alone intelligent resolution, requires that one first deal with two intrinsically interrelated sets of perennially difficult questions.

The first set of such questions is primarily definitional or analytical in nature. The three most critical of these questions are: (1) How should the relevant form of discrimination be artculated for purposes of Equal Protection analysis?; (2) How should "poverty" be defined and a class or classes of the "poor" be delineated for Equal Protection purposes?; and, (3) How much and what sort of "equality" is implied by guaranteeing "*equal* protection" to the poor?

The second set of such questions is primarily institutional and doctrinal in nature. They concern the appropriate role of the judiciary, especially that of the United States Supreme Court, in resolving claims of unconstitutional discrimination against the poor. More particularly, these questions ask how actively the Court should review the discrimination

*B.A., 1963, M.A., 1964, J.D., 1967, University of California, Berkeley. Professor of Law, University of California, Los Angeles.

229

challenged by such claims and how much, if any, special protection the Court should afford the poor against majoritarian abuse.

This second set of questions also raises two of the most crucial as well as familiar Equal Protection-poverty issues. Those two issues are, first, when, if ever, the poor as a class, or poverty as a classifying criterion, should be accorded suspect[8] or semi-suspect[9] status; and, second, whether, and to what extent, the response to the first issue should depend on the nature of the interest or right at stake. Insofar as the Court responds negatively to these issues, as it has with its 1977 *Maher* decision,[10] the Court in effect decides that its role in reviewing claims of unconstitutional discrimination against the poor is no different than its role in resolving analogous discrimination claims made by business entities. Such judicial deference is just as troubling when the Equal Protection-poverty claim at issue involves the poor's inability to exercise constitutional rights which are essential to a person's status as an autonomous individual and equal citizen,[11] as it would be when the claim involves the poor's lack of effective access to the courts[12] or the ballot.[13]

An adequate, let alone comprehensive, treatment of these two sets of questions, or of the two key Equal Protection-poverty issues raised by the second set, is beyond the parameters of this or any one undertaking. I will therefore limit my discussion to two of the most important Equal Protection-poverty decisions: *Griffin* v. *Illinois*[14] and *Maher* v. *Roe.*[15]

Griffin is the first Supreme Court decision addressing the constitutionality of discrimination against the poor. In that seminal decision the Court held that the poor as well as the affluent have a Fourteenth Amendment right to "equal justice."[16] In so holding, the Court recognized three basic "equality" principles constitutive of that right. These principles, which provide the essential framework for analyzing Equal Protection claims of unconstitutional discrimination against the poor, are the primary focus of my discussion in Part I.

The right of the poor to equal justice, first proclaimed in *Griffin,* has come under increasing attack by the Burger Court.[17] The most recent manifestation of this attack is the decision in *Maher* and its companion case, *Poelker* v. *Doe.*[18] Applying the deferential "any rational basis" non-standard of review, *Maher* held that states constitutionally may refuse to provide Medicaid funds to otherwise eligible poor pregnant women who seek to exercise their constitutional right to an elective abortion.[19] This holding, and, even more so, the Equal Protection approach advanced in Justice Powell's majority opinion in *Maher,* represent a dangerous departure from both *Griffin's* three "equality" principles and related constitutional doctrines protective of the dependent poor developed within the *Griffin*-equal justice tradition. The nature of this departure is the primary focus of my discussion in Part II.

I. *Griffin's* "Equality" Principles

Griffin's basic overreaching principle of equality was a response to what Justice Black, author of the Court's plurality opinion, characterized as "an age-old problem" of justice. This principle holds that both the "poor and rich, weak and powerful alike" are entitled to "equal justice."[20] Although the precise contours of this right to "equal justice" were not spelled out in *Griffin* itself, the Court made one of its key aspects clear:

> [The] constitutional guaranties of due process and equal protection both call for procedures in criminal trials which allow no invidious discriminations between persons and different groups of persons. . . . In criminal trials a State can no more discriminate on account of poverty than on account of religion, race, or color.[21]

This first key aspect of the Fourteenth Amendment's guarantee of equal justice gives rise to the first of *Griffin's* three "equality" principles. This first equality principle declares that, in some contexts, or with respect to some interests, poverty is (almost) as constitutionally "suspect" a classifying criterion as race. That is, for purposes of Equal Protection review, some claims of unconstitutional discrimination against the poor are subject to (almost) the same strict scrutiny as are claims of unconstitutional discrimination against racial minorities.[22]

Griffin's second equality principle follows from the context in which its above-quoted first principle was applied. The context in *Griffin* was *not* criminal *trials*, but criminal appeals. Griffin's complaint was not that he had been denied his constitutional right to present at a defense trial solely because he was poor. Rather, his complaint was that he had been denied an otherwise generally available opportunity for full appellate review solely because he was financially unable to purchase the transcript necessary to raise trial errors on appeal. This opportunity of which Griffin was deprived, however, is one which the states constitutionally can deny altogether.[23] That is, a state has, in the first instance, no constitutional obligation to provide *any* system of appellate review. Therefore, as the *Griffin* dissenters argued and the majority conceded, Griffin was not deprived of any interest which he otherwise could claim entitlement to as a matter of constitutional right.[24] Nonetheless, concluded the majority, determination of Griffin's equal justice claim does not turn on any such distinction between "rights" and state-afforded "privileges."[25]

Stated generally, then, *Griffin's* second equality principle declares that the equal protection standard appropriate to review the constitutionality of a state allocation of benefit X which deprives some persons of equal or effective[26] access to X solely because they are poor does not depend conclusively on whether a state has, in the first instance, any affirmative constitutional obligation to set up some system providing X or otherwise to refrain from denying X outright. In other words, *Griffin's* second equality principle holds its first equality principle applicable to a state's allocation-of-X independently of the constitutional status of X. *Griffin* thus stands as a landmark decision rejecting the "right-privilege" distinction which, as will be noted below, now has been resurrected in all but name only by the Burger Court.[27]

Griffin's third equality principle follows from the nature of the challenged discrimination to which its first two equality principles were applied. The discrimination at issue in *Griffin* resulted from the state's requirement that appellants purchase their own transcripts. Although this requirement, as written and administered, applied uniformly to all appellants, it effectively deprived poor appellants, *i.e.*, appellants unable to purchase a transcript, of appellate review of alleged trial errors. This payment requirement thereby in effect classified all defendants who were otherwise statutorily entitled to full appellate review into two sub-classes according to whether or not an appellant could afford the price of a transcript.

Thus, *Griffin's* third equality principle rejects as constitutionally irrelevant any distinction between, on the one hand, state-imposed conditions which "discriminate against [or exclude] 'indigents' *by name*,"[28] and, on the other hand, facially neutral and uniformly applied access fees which, if not waived for the poor, constitute "an effective bar" to the poor's access to X.[29] In effect, then, *Griffin's* third equality principle declares constitutionally irrelevant any differences between discriminations against the poor which are merely "de facto" and those which are "de jure." Thus, a state system allocating X which has the *effect* of depriving those unable to pay some access fee or cost from effective or adequate, let alone equal,[30] access to X, solely because of their poverty, may violate Equal Protection even if that allocation system is neutral both on its face and as applied.

The significance of this third equality principle is evidenced most clearly in the debate it precipitated between Justices Frankfurter (concurring) and Harlan (dissenting). One key doctrinal and institutional Equal Protection issue on which that debate focused is whether *the state* can be said to *discriminate* against the poor, or against those unable to pay, when the only "state action" apparent on the face of the challenged legislation is the requirement of a user fee. Thus, Justice Harlan argued that *Griffin* was not "a case where *the State's own action* has prevented a defendant from appealing. . . . All that Illinois has done is to *fail to alleviate* the consequences of differences in economic circumstances that *exist wholly apart from any state action.*"[31]

In the view of Harlan—and now, given *Maher,*[32] of the Burger Court as well—a state cannot be considered responsible, at least legally, for anyone's poverty. Therefore, a case like *Griffin*, in Harlan's view, involves no more than a mere "omission" by the state to grant "affirmative" relief to the poor; or, conversely, it does not involve any "act" by which the state can be said to "discriminate" against anyone. What this legal pedantry comes down to is another variation of the anachronistic Tort Law "act-omission" doctrine.[33] Frankfurter's inimitable retort to Harlan's attempted elevation of this distinction to one of constitutional dimensions is uniquely eloquent:

> Law addresses itself to actualities. It does not face actuality to suggest that Illinois affords every convicted person, financially competent or not, the opportunity to take an appeal, and that it is not Illinois that is responsible for disparity in material circumstances. Of course a State need not equalize economic conditions. . . . But when a State deems it wise and just that convictions be susceptible to review by an appellate court, it cannot by force of its exactions draw a line which precludes convicted indigent persons . . . from securing such a review merely by disabling them from bringing to the notice of an appellate tribunal errors of the trial court which would upset the conviction were practical opportunity for review not foreclosed [by requiring all criminal appellants, whatever their (in)ability to pay, to purchase their own stenographic transcript].
>
> To sanction such a ruthless consequence, inevitably resulting from a money hurdle erected by a State, would justify a latter-day Anatole France to add one more item to his ironic comments on the "majestic equality" of the law. "The law, in its majestic equality, forbids the rich as well as the poor to sleep under bridges, to beg in the streets, and to steal bread."[34]

This "*state*-discrimination" issue raised by *Griffin's* equality principles, especially the third principle, may be confused all too easily with an even more basic Equal Protection (and/or Due Process)[35] question. That question is the "affirmative duty" question which is inherent in all Equal Protection claims challenging so-called "de facto" discriminations against the poor. That this "*state*-discrimination" issue may be so easily confused with the more basic "affirmative duty" question is because the former may appear to lend itself to restatement in the following terms: Must a state (or the federal government), as a matter of guaranteeing Equal Protection to the poor, provide X free-of-charge (or at proportionately reduced rates) to the poor when it allows all others to enjoy X on payment of some user fee?

This confusion between the "*state*-discrimination" issue debated in *Griffin* and the "affirmative duty" question first raised generally by Harlan in his *Griffin* dissent,[36] can occur only if one first misconstrues the three *Griffin* equality principles as constituting a series of independent, rather than a set of mutually interdependent principles, and, then, proceeds to ignore *Griffin's* second equality principle while applying the first and third separately and out of context. This will be more evident from a comparison of the nature of the discrimination at issue in *Griffin*, and two subsequent equal justice cases, *Douglas* v. *California,*[37] and *Gideon* v. *Wainwright.*[38]

The Equal Protection issue in *Griffin* arose because the state chose to have an appellate system for reasons unrelated to any concern about the distribution of income. Once a state sets up such system and prescribes the conditions of access, the Equal Protection issue then is whether the state may include among those conditions a payment requirement which effectively excludes an entire class of otherwise entitled appellants solely on the basis of their poverty. If such an access condition, *e.g.*, a filing fee, or the cost of a necessary transcript, is held unconstitutional under *Griffin's* three equality principles because the Court concludes, as it did in *Griffin*, that depriving a convicted defendant of an opportunity to appeal solely on the basis of the defendant's poverty is not justified by a sufficiently strong state interest related to the purpose of the state's having an appellate system,[39] then the state may remedy this unconstitutional inequality in one of three basic ways.

The first remedy available to the state under *Griffin* is to dismantle its criminal appeals system altogether, or discontinue, for all defendants, any form of appellate review necessitating a transcript. Second, the state may provide transcripts free of charge to all appellants, *i.e.*, finance the production and distribution of transcripts out of general revenues rather than via user fees. Or, third, the state can waive the payment requirement for those appellants who, like Griffin, otherwise would be barred from full appellate review.

A state has these three remedy options under *Griffin* because it has no duty to provide a system of appellate review in the first instance. That the state may choose to continue its system of appellate review and eliminate the unconstitutional exclusionary access condition by adopting the third rather than the more expensive second option does not mean, however, that a state is thereby under a duty affirmatively to discriminate in favor of poor defendants—as opposed to a duty to remove a discriminatory condition violative of Equal Protection—anymore than a state's choice of the second remedy alternative would imply a similar affirmative duty to ensure free access to appellate review for all defendants. In short, that waiver of payment for those too poor to pay an access fee or cost requirement is one acceptable remedy under *Griffin* does not mean that there was unconstitutional discrimination in *Griffin* only because the state failed to satisfy some affirmative duty to poor appellants.

The specific affirmative duty question asking whether a state must, as a matter of guaranteeing Equal Protection to the poor, provide X free, or at reduced rates, to those unable to pay the access fee for X, makes constitutional sense only in a case like *Gideon* where the X in question is a constitutional right.[40] As Harlan pointed out in his *Douglas* dissent,[41] *Gideon* could have been decided on Equal Protection rather than Sixth Amendment— Fourteenth Amendment Due Process grounds.[42] However, the constitutional violation alleged in *Gideon*, unlike that in *Douglas* or *Griffin*, did not rest only or primarily on an asserted right to be free from discrimination based on poverty. Rather, the constitutional claim in *Gideon* rested on an asserted right to actual enjoyment of the Sixth Amendement's counsel guarantee, which meant, in effect, a right to appointed counsel for those defendants unable to retain a private attorney.

Since the discrimination against the poor held unconstitutional in *Gideon*, unlike that struck down in *Griffin*, involved the deprivation of a constitutional right, the state in *Gideon* did not have available the same remedy options it would have under *Griffin*. That is, a state could not cure the discrimination against the poor held unconstitutional in *Gideon* either by dispensing with criminal trials altogether or by disallowing representation by counsel for all criminal defendants. Rather, the only remedy available to the state was to provide lawyers free of charge either to all criminal defendants or at least to those too poor to retain private counsel. *Gideon*, therefore, unlike *Griffin*, involved an unconstitutional discrimination against the poor, or an unconstitutional deprivation on the basis of poverty, *because* the state has a constitutional obligation under the Sixth Amendment affirmatively to guarantee representation by counsel for all criminal defendants.[43]

The discrimination at issue in *Gideon* differs from that in *Griffin* in one other crucial respect: the degree of direct state responsibility for, or involvement in, the deprivation based on poverty. That is, unlike *Griffin*, the deprivation in *Gideon* did not result from the state pricing or regulating the availability of lawyers. Since *Douglas* raises essentially this same "*state*-discrimination" issue while sharing *Griffin's* absence of a constitutional right, it is more useful at this point to focus on the nature of the discrimination at issue in *Douglas* vis-à-vis that in both *Gideon* and *Griffin*.

The discrimination at issue in *Douglas* is similar to that in *Gideon* and dissimilar to that in *Griffin* in two important ways. First, the discrimination against poor appellants struck down in *Douglas*, unlike that invalidated in *Griffin*, did not result from an access fee or cost requirement *imposed* by the state. Rather, the discrimination at issue in *Douglas*, like that in *Gideon*, resulted from the prohibitive cost of retained counsel for poor defendants. Second, the discrimination in *Douglas*, unlike that in *Griffin*, and analogously to that in *Gideon*, involved, not access to, but the "adequacy"[44] of, appellate review. However, unlike the unconstitutional deprivation in *Gideon*, the discrimination held unconstitutional in *Douglas*, like that in *Griffin*, constitutionally could have been remedied by dispensing altogether with criminal appeals.

The remedy options available to the state in *Douglas* nonetheless differ in one significant respect from those available under *Griffin*. Unlike the alternative of eliminating altogether transcripts or transcript-necessary review, a state could not remedy the discrimination held unconstitutional in *Douglas* by disallowing representation by counsel for all defendants on appeal—assuming, of course, a Due Process right to the participation of retained counsel on appeal.[45] Thus, *Douglas* involved much more of an omission, or a failure to take affirmative steps to alleviate the adverse consequences of poverty, than did *Griffin*. Hence, Harlan's objection in *Griffin* that the *state* there "discriminated" only in the sense that it failed to comply with an affirmative duty to alleviate an inequality resulting from the defendant's poverty applies much more readily and meaningfully in the context of *Douglas*.

Nonetheless, *Griffin's* third equality principle, even as applied in a case like *Douglas*, poses constitutional issues, especially remedial ones, significantly different from those raised by the specific affirmative duty question which meaningfully can be asked only with respect to the type of discrimination at issue in a case like *Gideon*. The latter type of discrimination, unlike that at issue in either *Griffin* or *Douglas*, is analogous to the discrimination involved in *Maher* in that it presents no issue with respect to the application of *Griffin's* second equality principle. This type of discrimination thus presents the most compelling case for applying *Griffin's* first equality principle in favor of the poor.

II. *Maher's* Departure from *Griffin's* "Equality" Principles

It is difficult to think of an easier case of discrimination suffered by[46] the poor than *Maher*, other than a hypothetical one involving a statute which *on its face* and "by name"[47] deprived only those pregnant women who are "poor," or—closer to *Maher's* facts—only those pregnant women who are financially and otherwise eligible for pregnancy-or abortion-related medical benefits under Medicaid,[48] of access to constitutionally protected nontherapeutic abortions.

Maher seems such an easy case for several reasons. First, like *Griffin*, the disadvantaged class in *Maher* is composed entirely of poor individuals *all* of whom are equally disadvantaged, or deprived, by the challenged statutory allocation system. Moreover, all members of this class, unlike some members of the class of criminal appellants to which *Griffin* applies, are "poor" under even the most restrictive approaches to defining poverty.[49] In fact, the individual pregnant women denied the Medicaid funds necessary to exercise their constitutional right to obtain an abortion who comprise the disadvantaged class in *Maher*, unlike their *Griffin* counterparts, are *all* among the poorest of the poor. That is because the former, unlike the latter, are all financially eligible, *i.e.*, sufficiently needy under state standards lower than the federal government's official "poverty-line"[50] to qualify for Medicaid assistance.[51] Thus, *Maher* involves no class-delineation problems whatsoever.[52] Nonetheless, Powell's majority opinion never makes clear exactly how the disadvantaged class in *Maher* is delineated for purposes of its Equal Protection analysis.[53]

Second, the class "singled out"[54] by that portion of the state Medicaid legislation challenged in *Maher*, which denies medical benefits altogether to those otherwise eligible pregnant women seeking "nontherapeutic" abortions,[55] would appear on its face to satisfy the Burger Court's two conditions for meaningful review of Equal Protection-poverty claims announced just four years earlier in *San Antonio Independent School District v. Rodriguez.*[56] Those conditions are first, that the disadvantaged class be ascertainable on the basis of an income-line or functional indigency approach to defining poverty,[57] and second, that the challenged discrimination be attributable to "complete inability to pay" resulting in an "absolute deprivation."[58]

The *Maher* majority, however, either disagrees with the foregoing to the point of finding it unworthy even of mention, or holds, implicitly if not expressly, that satisfaction of *Rodriguez's* discrimination criteria as well as its class-delineation requirements cannot in itself suffice to trigger an Equal Protection standard of review stricter than that of the "any rational basis" test. That is, *Maher* may hold that discrimination on the basis of poverty does not warrant active review, even if the discrimination at issue otherwise appears to satisfy *Rodriguez's* two-prong test for applying the strictest possible scrutiny. Under that test an allegedly unconstitutional discrimination is strictly scrutinized if it involves either a suspect class[59] or "a fundamental right explicitly or implicitly protected by the Constitution."[60]

If the above correctly characterizes *Maher's* holding, the Supreme Court now has said that it refuses to recognize any similarity between claims of discrimination by the poor and otherwise indistinguishable claims of discrimination by semi-suspect let alone suspect classes,[61] however ascertainable, discrete and insular the particular class of poor alleging the unconstitutional discrimination might be, *and*, however imporant to the poor *or* constitutionally "fundamental" the interest or right at stake might be.[62] This interpretation of *Maher* finds further support in Justice Powell's numerous footnotes narrowing to insignificance not only *Griffin*, [63] but all other inconsistent post-*Griffin* Equal Protection-poverty decisions which had any vitality left after Justice Powell's comparable but relatively less ambitious re-interpretation of *Griffin* and related precedents in his *Rodriguez* opinion.[64]

If, on the other hand, *Maher* implicitly holds that there is no basis whatsoever for finding any "absolute deprivation" within the meaning of *Rodriguez*, then *Maher*, in effect, has redefined and further restricted this Equal Protection concept announced for the first time four years earlier by Justice Powell. More significantly, *Maher* has limited this concept's triggering of a standard of review stricter than that of "any rational basis" to include only those deprivations which are "*state*-created," as well as "absolute" and causally attributable to the poor person's "inability to pay." Such a judicial pronouncement is essentially meaningless, *unless* it is just another variation on *Maher's* purportedly independent holding based on its new requirement of an "infringement."

Maher's new infringement doctrine declares that discriminations involving fundamental rights, even as narrowly defined in *Rodriguez*, will be reviewed under some strict scrutiny standard only if the right at stake is "infringed." *Maher* defines "infringement" to include only those forms of "*state*-discrimination" which would satisfy the arguments of Harlan in both his *Griffin*[65] and *Douglas* dissents.[66] Insofar as *Maher* relegates to review under the "any rational basis" non-standard *any* Equal Protection-poverty challenge to a non-infringing but otherwise discriminatory denial of state benefits, *Maher* constitutes a clear repudiation of *Griffin's* third equality principle.[67]

That *Maher's* new infringement doctrine contravenes *Griffin's* third equality principle is especially evident from comparing Powell's discussion of a *"state*-created obstacle"[68] with Harlan's *Griffin* dissent, discussed in Part I above.[69] The *Maher* majority apparently believes that there is a constitutionally significant difference between, on the one hand, a state's failure to waive an access fee it uniformly imposes on everyone, including those unable to pay it, and, on the other hand, a state's failure to uniformly extend an in-kind[70] benefit to all otherwise eligible recipients. This is so even though the basis for the latter exclusion is the desire to exercise a constitutional right, which desire is frustrated solely because of the otherwise eligible recipients' financial inability to acquire the same benefit from a private source. That is, the *Maher* majority apparently believes that the state failure to waive constitutes "direct state interference" with the exercise of a constitutional right, while the state exclusion, or failure to extend uniformly, constitutes only "state encouragement of an alternative activity [in *Maher*, forced childbirth for those women unable to afford a private legal abortion] consonant with legislative policy."[71]

The conflict between *Maher's* infringement requirement and *Griffin's* third equality principle is evident also from a comparison of *Maher* and *Douglas*. As noted above,[72] *Douglas* extended this principle to a discriminatory deprivation of appellate counsel which resulted, not from a *state*-imposed bar or "money hurdle," but from the prohibitive cost of retained counsel for the relatively poor. If this constitutes discrimination within the meaning of *Griffin's* third principle, it is difficult to understand why the deprivation of access to elective abortions in *Maher* does not.[73] Moreover, the remedy options which would be available to the state under a contrary ruling in *Maher* parallel those under *Douglas*. Here the state could either opt out of the Medicaid system altogether or extend pregnancy-related Medicaid benefits to the discriminated-against class. The former remedy is analogous to a state's decision to dismantle the criminal appeals system under *Douglas*, while the latter entails none of the affirmative steps necessary to provide appointed counsel for those appellants unable to afford retained counsel. Nor does the latter entail any increased expenditure or reallocation of general state revenues. In fact, unlike the impact of *Griffin*, *Douglas*, and *Gideon*, the state would actually save money had *Maher* struck down the discriminatory allocation of Medicaid benefits among poor pregnant women.[74]

In addition to its inconsistency with *Griffin's* third equality principle and apparent limitation on *Rodriguez's* absolute deprivation concept, some of the more troubling aspects of *Maher's* infringement requirement include the following. First, six members of the Burger Court apparently believe that denial of Medicaid funds *by state law* to otherwise eligible poor pregnant women who seek to exercise their constitutional right to choose an abortion "places no obstacle—absolute or otherwise—in the pregnant woman's path to an abortion."[75] Moreover, they find *no* such "obstacle" even when that same state law provides funds to otherwise similarly situated women who either opt for childbirth or necessarily (as defined by state law) undergo an abortion.[76]

Powell's "no obstacle" statement quoted above reflects, on the part of the *Maher* majority, either incredible naiveté and socio-economic myopia, or disingenuousness and an unprincipled willingness to distort or disbelieve uncontested factual matters.[77] Unfortunately—and particularly for the poor—this is not the first time a Burger Court majority opinion has reflected either of these.[78]

Second, *Maher's* "state-created obstacle" test for the requisite degree of "infringement" seem to be equated with one if not both of the following two "affirmative duty" issues: (1) whether "[t]he Constitution imposes [any] obligation on the States to pay the pregnancy-related medical expenses of indigent women, or indeed to pay any of the medical expenses of indigents";[79] and (2) "if [a state] had elected not to fund either abortions or childbirth . . .

[whether] the Constitution *requires* such [abortion-expenses] assistance for all indigent pregnant women."[80] These explicit suggestions in Powell's *Maher* majority opinion, that the "*state*-created obstacle" and either one or both of the above two "affirmative duty" issues are all one and the same for Equal Protection purposes, reflect precisely the same confusion as that generated by Harlan's use of "affirmative duty" language in his *Griffin* dissent when discussing the "*state*-discrimination" issue over which he joined debate with Frankfurter, as noted above.[81]

Third, *Maher's* suggested equation of and confusion between the two above "affirmative duty" issues and the "*state*-created obstacle" test for an "infringement" contravenes *Griffin's* second as well as its third "equality" principle. *Maher*, therefore, not only resurrects but stands on its head the "right-privilege" distinction which *Griffin*, via its second equality principle, rejected.[82] *Maher* holds constitutional a state Medicaid law which in effect says to the otherwise eligible poor pregnant woman who desires but does not "need" an abortion: "If you want the Medicaid benefits to which you are otherwise entitled then you must forfeit your constitutional right to choose an 'elective' abortion." This is a classic case of an "unconstitutional condition."[83] Therefore, to uphold the constitutionality of any law imposing such a condition is to repudiate *Griffin's* rejection of the "right-privilege" distinction.[84]

Finally, *Maher's* Equal Protection approach departs from *Griffin's* first equality principle as well as its second and third. Focusing on the combined impact of the two reasons Powell gives for applying the "any rational basis" test makes this clear. The second of those two reasons is discussed above[85]—namely, the absence of that "infringement" *Maher* now requires for any degree of actual scrutiny of discriminatory deprivations of constitutionally fundamental rights. The first reason for *Maher's* applying this non-standard is, in Justice Powell's words:

> This case involves no discrimination against a suspect class. An indigent woman desiring an abortion does not come within the limited category of disadvantaged classes so recognized by our cases. Nor does the fact that the impact of the regulation falls upon those who cannot pay lead to a different conclusion. In a sense, every denial of welfare to an indigent creates a wealth classification as compared to non-indigents who are able to pay for the desired goods or services. But this Court has never held that financial need alone identifies a suspect class for purposes of equal protection analysis.[86]

This passage mistakenly assumes that the disadvantaged class in *Maher* is composed of indigent women seeking an abortion and that poverty is the sole classifying criterion. However, even if the above-quoted statement correctly characterized the discrimination at issue, the question whether "financial need *alone*" identified a suspect class would be as beside the point here as it was in *Griffin*.[87] Rather, the question should have been whether, in a case at least as strong as *Griffin*, [88] the controlling Equal Protection standard is *Griffin's* first equality principle or the deference-to-the-legislature stance of traditional economic discrimination cases. *Maher's* response to this question is a mechanical invocation of *Rodriguez's* two-tier Equal Protection approach and a footnote confining *Griffin* and its "underlying principles" to criminal procedure cases.[89] Such a reinterpretation of *Griffin*, which is even more restrictive than that announced by Powell four years earlier in his *Rodriguez* opinion,[90] lacks support in both precedent and reasoned argument, and neither is offered in *Maher*.

The *dicta* in *Maher* suggesting that its Equal Protection approach would have been the same had the disadvantaged class been ascertainable solely on the basis of poverty thus represents unfortunate confusion at best, and, at worst, an indication of the Burger Court's probable future resolution of Equal Protection claims of unconstitutional discrimination against the poor which raise directly the viability of *Griffin's* first equality principle.

Contrary to the assumption implicit in the above-quoted passage, however, *Maher* involves discrimination *among*, not against, the poor. That is, the disadvantaged class in *Maher* is not all poor pregnant women seeking abortions, but is rather a sub-class of poor pregnant women seeking abortions—namely, those women who would be eligible for pregnancy-related Medicaid benefits but for their attempt to exercise their constitutional right to choose abortion over childbirth.[91] The Equal Protection-poverty issue in *Maher*, therefore, is analogous, not to that in *Griffin*, *Douglas* or *Rodriguez*,[92] but rather to that in *Danridge* v. *Williams*[93] and *Shapiro* v. *Thompson*.[94]

Dandridge, upon which *Maher* relied,[95] and *Shapiro*, which *Maher* distinguished,[96] both involved discrimination among AFDC recipients. The two decisions reached opposite results primarily because *Dandridge* was thought to involve only a discriminatory allocation of admittedly inadequate welfare funds, while *Shapiro* involved a discriminatory denial of welfare funds on the basis of the exercise of a constitutional right.[97] However, as I have argued elsewhere,[98] the discrimination sustained in *Dandridge* rested on an unconstitutional condition analogous to that struck down in *Shapiro*. In the former, the reciprocal right of mothers and children to choose to live with members of their own immediate family was at stake; in the latter, it was the right to travel interstate. In both cases, as in *Sherbert* v. *Verner*,[99] the state effectively put otherwise eligible welfare claimants to the choice of either receiving the benefits to which they were otherwise entitled or exercising their constitutional rights. As noted above,[100] this is the same type of forced choice imposed by the state in *Maher*.

The *Maher* majority treats the unconstitutional conditions doctrine and prior contrary precedent in the same unjustifiably restrictive, re-interpretative manner as it treats *Griffin*. And, again, *Maher's* new infringement doctrine[101] supplies the main doctrinal explanation for the departure. Thus, according to the *Maher* majority, in cases like *Shapiro* and *Sherbert*, the state "acted" by "penalizing" the exercise of a constitutional right—the so-called penalty being the denial of welfare benefits to which the claimant was otherwise entitled.[102] In *Maher*, on the other hand, the state does not refuse Medicaid funds *because* the otherwise eligible pregnant woman has exercised her constitutional right to an elective abortion; therefore, concludes the *Maher* majority, there is no action by the state in response to, *i.e.*, no penalty for or infringement of, the exercise of a constitutional right.

Neither prior caselaw nor the reasons underlying the Warren Court's development of the unconstitutional conditions doctrine justify this penalty-infringement distinction enunciated in *Maher*.[103] Moreover, the discriminatory deprivation of the constitutional right at stake in *Maher* is even more serious and less justified than that in *Shapiro* or *Sherbert*.

First, an overriding state interest in the unconstitutional conditions-welfare cases, as well as in Equal Protection-poverty cases like *Griffin* and *Douglas*, is saving money and/or allocating limited resources in what the state decides is the least costly manner.[104] In *Maher*, however, unlike all other Equal Protection-poverty cases, the discrimination costs rather than saves the state money.[105] The only apparent state interest involved in *Maher*, then, is to prod dependent poor pregnant women into giving birth rather than exercising their constitutional right to an elective abortion.[106] It is difficult to imagine a more pernicious example of the sort of discriminatory treatment against which the unconstitutional conditions doctrine was developed to protect those dependent on government largess.[107]

Second, the negative effect on the otherwise eligible welfare recipient's ability to exercise her constitutional right in *Maher* is much more severe than that in *Shapiro* or *Sherbert*. The benefit disqualification at issue in the latter cases was held unconstitutional because it "chilled" the exercise of the otherwise eligible recipient's constitutional rights. In *Maher*, the benefit disqualification is sustained despite the fact that it renders it impossible for most if not all otherwise eligible recipients even to be able to exercise their constitutional rights. Thus, in *Maher*, in contrast to *Shapiro* and *Sherbert*, the poor pregnant woman in reality has no *choice* between exercising her constitutional right and receiving the benefits to which she is otherwise entitled.

Finally, the Medicaid-abortion disqualification sustained in *Maher* perpetuates poverty in a way and to a degree that is unparalleled in either unconstitutional conditions cases such as *Shapiro* or Equal Protection-poverty cases such as *Griffin*. Not only does the impoverished pregnant woman otherwise eligible for Medicaid become more dependent on welfare and less able to escape poverty by being effectively forced to bear another child, but both the size of her family and of the state's welfare rolls also is increased thereby.[108] Nonetheless, protests the *Maher* majority:

> We certainly are not unsympathetic to the plight of an indigent woman who desires an abortion, but . . . when an issue involves policy choices as sensitive as those implicated by the public funding of nontherapeutic abortions, the appropriate forum for their resolution in a democracy is the legislature.[109]

Maher's retreat from prior unconstitutional conditions precedent thus signals the same unwillingness on the part of the Burger Court majority to ensure the poor's participation in our society as rights-bearing citizens as does *Maher's* analogous departure from *Griffin's* equality principles. Together, these two interrelated stands of the majority's Equal Protection approach in *Maher* pose a serious threat to a constitutional system of equal justice for poor and rich, weak and powerful alike, heralded by the *Griffin* decision.

Notes

1. *See* the Commission's November 1969 report, entitled POVERTY AMID PLENTY: THE AMERICAN PARADOX, *especially* at 23.

2. *See generally* M. HARRINGTON, THE OTHER AMERICA 9-24 (1969); MacDonald, *Our Invisible Poor*, in POVERTY IN AMERICA 7-24 (L. Ferman, J. Kornbluh & A. Haber, eds. 1968); *see also* REPORT OF THE NATIONAL ADVISORY COMMISSION ON CIVIL DISORDERS 281-82, 389-401, 407-08 (New York Times ed. 1968). For both a historical and an empirical analysis of Americans' views about the poor generally, and welfare recipients in particular, *see* J. FEAGIN, SUBORDINATING THE POOR: WELFARE AND AMERICAN BELIEFS 15-16, 24-44, 50-55, 91-126 (1975). For discussion of the ambivalent nature of Americans' attitudes toward the poor, *see* Diamond, *The Children of Leviathan: Psychoanalytic Speculations Concerning Welfare Law and Punitive Sanctions*, 54 CALIF. L. REV. 357, 360-66 (1966); Jacobs, *America's Schizophrenic View of the Poor*, in POVERTY: VIEWS FROM THE LEFT 39-57 (1970).

3. This "poverty level" represents an income cut-off line which separates those who are officially "poor" from everyone else. Poverty level statistics are based on a "poverty index" developed by the Social Security Adminstration in 1964. This index is based primarily on the Agriculture Department's "economy" food plan (multiplied by 3) and provides a range of income levels adjusted according to various demographic data, *e.g.,* family size, sex of family head. *See generally* S.M. MILLER & P. ROBY, THE FUTURE OF INEQUALITY 25-29 (1970); U.S. DEPT. OF HEALTH, EDUCATION, AND WELFARE, THE MEASURE OF POVERTY 5-18 (Apr. 1976).

In 1975, the average poverty level for a nonfarm, male-headed family of four was $5,502.00, annually. For a female-headed family the corresponding figure was $5,473.00. The average poverty level for a single male under 65 years old was $2,902.00, annually, and for a single woman under 65, $2,685.00. The corresponding figures for single men and women over 65 are lower. U.S. BUREAU OF THE CENSUS, STATISTICAL ABSTRACT OF THE UNTED STATES: 1976, at 415 (97th ed. 1976) [hereinafter cited as STATISTICAL ABSTRACT].

4. STATISTICAL ABSTRACT, *supra* note 3, at 406, 415. The corresponding figures for unrelated individuals reveal an even greater inequality: 4.0% compared with 47.9% and 18.7%. *Id.* at 406.

5. See S.M. MILLER & P. ROBY, *supra* note 3, at 37-39; STATISTICAL ABSTRACT, *supra* note 3, at 406; Lapman, *What Does It Do For the Poor? - A New Test for National Policy*, in THE PUB. INTEREST, Winter 1974, at 71-72; Schiller, *Equality, Opportunity, and the "Good Job,"* in THE PUB. INTEREST, Spring 1976, at 111-12.

6. *See* STATISTICAL ABSTRACT, *supra* note 3, at 407-08, 414; *see generally* B. BLECHMAN, E. GRAMLICH & R. HARTMAN, SETTING NATIONAL PRIORITIES: THE 1975 BUDGET 166-82 (1974); S.M. MILLER & P. ROBY, *supra* note 3, at 29-34, 37, 40-41; *cf.* Beal v. Doe, 97 S. Ct. 2394, 2397 & nn. 3-4 (1977) (Marshall, J., dissenting).

7. U.S. CONST. amend. XIV.

8. Suspect classifications are those which are presumptively "invidious." They thus receive the strictest judicial scrutiny. *See* Karst, *Foreword: Equal Citizenship Under the Fourteenth Amendment*, 91 HARV. L. REV. 1, 22-26 (1977); *Developments in the Law-Equal Protection*, 82 HARV. L. REV. 1065, 1087-1104 (1969) [hereinafter cited as *Developments*]; Note, *The Supreme Court, 1970 Term*, 85 HARV. L. REV. 38, 125-26 n. 19 (1971).

Racial criteria which discriminate *against* a disadvantaged minority are the primary example of suspect classifications. *See, e.g.,* Loving v. Virginia, 388 U.S. 1, 11 (1967); McLaughlin v. Florida, 379 U.S. 184, 192 (1964); Korematsu v. United States, 323 U.S. 214, 216 (1944) (*dictum*). On the other hand, racial criteria utilized to overcome the adverse effects of past discrimination against racial minorities—so-called "benign" racial classifications—do not share the same presumptive discriminatory motivation or purpose. Therefore, they do not warrant the same strict scrutiny. *See, e.g.,* Bakke v. Regents of the University of California, 18 Cal. 3d 39, 67-69, 78-80, 553 P. 2d 1152, 1174-76, 1182-83, 132 Cal. Rptr. 680, 702-04, 710-11 (1976) (Tobriner, J., dissenting), *cert. granted*, 429 U.S. 1090 (1977); United Jewish Organizations v. Carey, 430 U.S. 144, 165-68 (1977) (White, J., plurality); *Id.* at 179-80 (Stewart, J., concurring); *noted in The Supreme Court, 1976 Term*, 91 HARV. L. REV. 284-94 (1977). *See generally*, Brest, *Foreword: In Defense of the Antidiscrimination Principle*, 90 HARV. L. REV. 1, 16-22 (1976); *Developments, supra*, 82 HARV. L. REV. at 1104-20.

Alienage is the only other classifying criteria which the Surpeme Court has accorded suspect status. *See, e.g.,* Nyquist v. Maucet, 97 S. Ct. 2120, 2124-27 (1977). However, discrimination on the basis of alienage has been upheld in circumstances where analogous discrimination on the basis of race would be struck down. *See e.g.,* Mathews v. Diaz, 426 U.S. 67, 78-80, 84-85 (1976) (durational residency requirement for federal Medicare benefits for aliens); Sugarman v. Dougall, 413 U.S. 634, 647-49 (1973) (state exclusion of aliens from the right to vote and hold office).

9. I use the term "semi-suspect" to refer to those classifying criteria which trigger an Equal Protection standard of review which is less strict than the "compelling" interest test applicable to suspect classifications, note 8, *supra*, and constitutionally fundamental rights, note 60, *infra*; but which is significantly more active and less deferential than the "any rational basis" test applicable to an ever-expanding category of social and economic regulations, note 93, *infra*. For a recent example of the sort of business regulation for which this latter non-review standard was developed, *see* City of New Orleans v. Dukes, 427 U.S. 297, 303-06 (1976), *noted in The Supreme Court, 1975 Term*, 90 HARV. L. REV. at 132-33.

During the 1976 and 1977 Terms, the Supreme Court explicitly accorded semi-suspect status to classifications on the basis of both sex and illegitimacy. *See* Trimble v. Gordon, 430 U.S. 762, 767, 769 (1977) (state intestacy provision discriminating against illegitimates invalidated); Califano v. Goldfarb, 430 U.S. 199, 204-07, 212-13 (1977) (Social Security Act provision discriminating against widowers invalidated); Craig v. Boren, 429 U.S. 190, 197 (1976) (state prohibition on the sale of beer to males between the ages of 18 and 21 invalidated); Mathews v. Lucas, 427 U.S. 495, 505-09 (1976) (Social Security Act provision discriminating against illegitimates upheld); *see generally*, Note, *The Supreme Court, 1976 Term*, 91 HARV. L. REV. at 177-88 (1977).

10. Maher v. Roe, 97 S. Ct. 2376 (1977), discussed in text accompanying notes 46-109, *infra; see also* notes 18-19; *infra* & accompanying text.

11. The right of a pregnant woman to control both her own reproductive processes and her future by choosing whether to abort or undergo childbirth is a striking example of such a right. *See* Roe v. Wade, 410 U.S. 113, 153 (1973); *but see* Maher v. Roe, *supra* note 10, 97 S. Ct. at 2382-86; Poelker v. Doe, 97 S. Ct. 2391, 2392 (1977), note 18, *infra. See* Karst, *supra* note 8, 91 HARV. L. REV. at 4, 57-59:

> The substantive core of . . . the equal protection clause is a principle of equal citizenship, which presumptively guarantees to each individual the right to be treated by the organized society as a respected, responsible, and participating member. . . .

> The equal citizenship principle comes to bear on [cases such as *Roe v. Wade*] . . . in recognizing that there is great weight in a woman's claim of the right to control her own social roles. . . . The focus

of equal citizenship here is . . . a right to take responsibility for choosing one's own future. [The] use of the word "autonomy" to describe the right in question is apt; to be a person is . . . to be an active participant in society rather than an object. . . .

Last Terms decisions in *Maher v. Roe* and *Poelker v. Doe*, in any case, utterly fail to satisfy the principle of equal citizenship. . . . [T]he Court [there] subordinated interests which are central to . . . women's status as respected, participating members of the community. . . . The sensitivity of the Justices in the *Maher* and *Poelker* majority ended at the boundary of their own social class. . . .

See also Tribe, *Foreword: Toward A Model of Roles in the Due Process of Life and Law*, 87 HARV. L. REV. 1, 42-50 (1973).

12. *See* Griffin v. Illinois, 351 U.S. 12, 16-19 (1956): *see also* Bounds v. Smith, 430 U.S. 817, 821-25 (1977); Mayer v. Chicago, U.S. 189, 193, 196-97 (1971); Boddie v. Connecticut, 401 U.S. 371, 374-76, 380-82 (1971); Douglas v. California, 372 U.S. 353, 355, 357-58 (1963); *but see*, United States v. MacCollom, 426 U.S. 317, 324-26 (1976); Ross v. Moffitt, 417 U.S. 600, 611-12, 614-16 (1974); United States v. Kras, 409 U.S. 434, 443-46, 449-50 (1973). *See generally* B. BRUDNO, POVERTY, INEQUALITY, AND THE LAW, ch. 2, § 1 (1976) [hereinafter cited as BRUDNO], *especially* at 136-48; Karst, *supra* note 8, 91 HARV. L. REV. at 29-31.

13. *See* Harper v. Virginia Bd. of Elec., 383 U.S. 663, 666-68, 670 (1966); *see also* Bullock v. Carter, 405 U.S. 134, 142-44 (1972); Kramer v. Union Free School District, 395 U.S. 621, 626-29 (1969); *but see* Gordon v. Lance, 403 U.S. 1, 4-5, 7 (1971); James v. Valtierra, 402 U.S. 137, 141-43 (1971). *See generally* BRUDNO, *supra* note 12, ch. 2, § 2, *especially* at 232-35 & 256-58; Karst, *supra* note 11, 91 HARV. L. REV. at 27-29.

14. 351 U.S. 12 (1956).

15. 97 S.Ct. 2376 (1977).

16. 351 U.S. at 16, 19.

17. *See e.g.,* United States v. MacCollom, 426 U.S. 317 (1976); Simon v. Eastern Kentucky Welfare Rights Organization, 426 U.S. (1976); Weinberger v. Salfi, 422 U.S. 749 (1975); Ross v. Moffitt, 417 U.S. 600 (1974); Ortwein v. Schwab, 410 U.S. 656 (1973); United States v. Kras, 409 U.S. 434 (1973); Lindsey v. Normet, 405 U.S. 56 (1972); James v. Valtierra, 402 U.S. 137 (1971); Wyman v. James, 400 U.S. 309 (1971); *see also* Mathews v. Eldridge, 424 U.S. 319 (1976). *Cf.* Village of Arlington Heights v. Metropolitan Hous. Dev. Corp., 429 U.S. 252 (1977); Milliken v. Bradley, 418 U.S. 717 (1974); Jefferson v. Hackney, 406 U.S. 535 (1972).

See generally Brudno, *Fairness and Bureaucracy: The Demise of Procedural Due Process for Welfare Claimants*, 25 HASTINGS L. J. 813 (1974); Clune, *The Supreme Court's Treatment of Wealth Discriminations Under the Fourteenth Amendment*, 1975 SUP. CT. REV. 289.

18. 97 S. Ct. 2391 (1977). *Poelker* held that municipalities constitutionally can withhold publicly financed hospital benefits to poor pregnant women who choose to terminate their pregnancy rather than undergo childbirth. This discrimination among poor pregnant women otherwise equally eligible for pregnancy-related public hospital benefits presents the same Equal Protection issues as those sustained in *Maher*. See 97 S. Ct. at 2392; text accompanying notes 87-94, *infra*.

19. Only the first trimester is involved in *Maher*. *See* 97 S.Ct. at 2378 n.1. Therefore, under Roe v. Wade, 410 U.S. 113, 163-64 (1973), neither the state's interest in the mother's health nor that in the potential life of the fetus is sufficiently compelling to justify any interference with the right of those in the disadvantaged class in *Maher* to decide, in consultation with their doctor, whether or not to terminate their pregnancy. *See* 97 S.Ct. at 2390-91 (Brennan, J., dissenting); *see generally* Tribe, *supra* note 11, at 10-41.

20. 351 U.S. at 16, 19.

21. 351 U.S. at 17.

22. See note 8, *supra*.

23. *See* 351 U.S. at 18; *see also* Ross v. Moffitt, 417 U.S. 600, 611 (1974); McKane v. Durston, 153 U.S. 684, 687-88 (1894); *Developments, supra* note 8, 82 HARV. L. REV. at 1178.

24. *See* 351 U.S. at 18 (Black, J.); *id*, at 21 (Frankfurter, J., concurring); *id.*. at 27 (Burton, J., dissenting); *id*. at 36-37 & n. 9 (Harlan, J., dissenting).

25. *See generally* B. BRUDNO, *supra* note 12, at 558-64 and authorities cited therein; *see also* note 83; Goldberg v. Kelly, 397 U.S. 254, 262 (1970); Brudno, *supra* note 17, 25 HASTINGS L. J. at 820-23 & nn. 22 & 28 & authorities cited therein.

26. On the difference between equal and effective access to the judicial sysem and the extent to which *Griffin's* equal justice principle guarantees "equality," *see* B. BRUDNO, *supra* note 12, at 55, 58-68, 176, 181-82, 215; *cf. id.* at 436-37. *See also* note 30, *infra*.

27. *See* text accompanying notes 82-84, *infra*.

28. *See* 351 U.S. at 35 (Harlan, J., dissenting).

29. *See* 351 U.S. at 24 (Frankfurter, J., concurring).

30. The question of how much and what sort of equality is entailed by *Griffin's* equal justice principle represents a specific instance of the third definitional question inherent in all Equal Protection-poverty claims noted in the Introduction. *See* paragraph following text accompanying note 7, *supra*. Justice Black's seemingly interchangeable use of the phrases "equal justice" and "adequate appellate review" in his plurality *Griffin* opinion, along with the *Griffin* majority's express refusal to require states to provide poor defendants verbatim transcripts in *all* cases, suggest that *Griffin's* three equality principles speak to relative rather than absolute equality. *See also* Mayer v. City of Chicago, 404 U.S. 189, 194-96 (1971); Draper v. Washington, 372 U.S. 487, 495-96 (1963). *Compare* the *Mayer-Draper* notion of "adequate and effective" appellate review with Professor Frank Michelman's concept of "minimum protection," in *Foreword: On Protecting the Poor through the Fourteenth Amendment*, 83 HARV. L. REV. 7, 13-16, 33-39 (1969). *See generally* B. BRUDNO, *supra* note 12, at 55, 58-68, 176, 181-82; *see also* note 26, *supra*.

31. 351 U.S. at 34 (emphasis added); *see also* Douglas v. California, 371 U.S. 353, 361-62 (Harlan, J., dissenting); *compare Maher's "state*-created obstacle" requirement, 97 S.Ct. at 2382 (emphasis added); *see* text accompanying notes 68-71 & 79-81, *infra*.

32. *See* 97 S.Ct. at 2382-83; note 31, *supra*; text accompanying notes 75-78 & 108-09, *infra*.

33. *See generally* 2 F. HARPER & F. JAMES, THE LAW OF TORTS 1044-53 (1956); W. PROSSER, LAW OF TORTS 338-50 (4th ed. 1971).

34. 351 U.S. at 23, *quoting* J. COURNOS, A MODERN PLUTARCH 27.

35. I add this qualification for two reasons. First, Justice Black's plurality opinion in *Griffin* rests upon a hybrid Equal Protection-Due Process approach. *See* 351 U.S. at 17-18; text accompanying note 21, *supra; see also*, Douglas v. California, 371 U.S. 353, 357-58; *cf.* Ross v. Moffitt, 417 U.S. 600, 608-09 (1974); *see generally* BRUDNO, *supra* note 12, at 51, 181; Willcox & Bloustein, *The Griffin Case—Poverty and the Fourteenth Amendment*, 43 CORNELL L. Q. 1, 10-13 (1957).

Second, assume that there was no Medicaid or analogous medical care system involved in *Maher*. *See* 97 S.Ct at 2386 n. 13. *If* that had been the case, then the challenged discriminatory deprivation of the right to choose between abortion and childbirth would have been a challenge to the government's (Congress') failure to guarantee that poor as well as more affluent women in fact have such a choice. *Cf.* paragraph following text accompanying note 107, *infra*. Such a challenge could have been made on the basis of Equal Protection (focusing on the discriminatory nature of the deprivation), Due Process (focusing on the nature of the right at stake), or both. *Cf.* Douglas v. California, 372 U.S. 353, 363 (1963) (Harlan, J., dissenting); text accompanying notes 41-43, *infra*. I do not address this latter constitutional issue here.

36. *See* 351 U.S. at 34-35; text accompanying notes 31-33, *supra*.

37. 372 U.S. 353 (1963). *Douglas* held *Griffin* applicable to denial of appointed counsel for indigent appellants, at least for the first appeal granted as of right. *Douglas*, like *Griffin*, rested on a hybrid Equal Protection-Due Process approach. *See* note 35, *supra; see also* Anders v. California, 386 U.S. 738, 741-42 (1967); *but see*, Ross v. Moffitt, 417 U.S. 600, 608-09 (1974).

38. 372 U.S. 335 (1963). *Gideon* held that the Sixth Amendment's guarantee of counsel, including the right of indigent federal defendants to appointed counsel, was part of the due process guaranteed to state defendants by the Fourteenth Amendment. Thus, under *Gideon*, state defendants too poor to hire private counsel have the same right to appointed counsel under the Due Process Clause of the Fourteenth Amendent as their federal counterparts do under the Sixth Amendment. *Cf.* Douglas v. California, 372 U.S. 353, 363 (1963) (Harlan, J., dissenting); text accompanying notes 41-42, *infra*.

39. *See* 351 U.S. at 17-18 (Black, J.); *id.* at 21-22 (Frankfurter, J., concurring).

40. In *Gideon*, the X in question was the Sixth Amendment right to counsel which, for purposes of state criminal proceedings, is "incorporated" by the Due Process Clause of the Fourteenth Amendment. *See* note 38, *supra*. Similarly, the X in question in *Maher* was the right of choice between abortion and childbirth which is included within the more general right to personal privacy guaranteed by the Due Process Clause (as part of "liberty"). *See* notes 11 & 19, *supra* & authorities cited therein. However, unlike *Gideon*, *Maher* did not involve discriminatory deprivation of a constitutional right *solely* on the basis of poverty. *See* text accompanying note 91, *infra; see also* note 35, *supra*; notes 43 & 46, *infra*.

41. 372 U.S. at 363.

42. *See* note 38, *supra*.

43. *Compare* the nature of the challenged discriminatory deprivation in *Maher*, which arose because the state chose to finance childbirth and "necessary" abortions for Medicaid-qualified poor pregnant women but refused to pay the analogous expenses of otherwise eligible pregnant women who sought elective abortions. *See* text accompanying note 91, *infra*; note 51, *infra*, & accompanying text; *see also* note 40, *supra*.

44. See BRUDNO, *supra* note 12, at 176; *cf.* Ross v. Moffitt, 417 U.S. 600, 607 (1974); Case Comment, *Indigent Prisoner Defendants' Rights in Civil Litigation: Payne v. Superior Court*, 90 HARV. L. REV. 1029, 1036-38 (1977).

45. *Cf.* Gagnon v. Scarpelli, 411 U.S. 778, 783 n.6 (1973); *see generally* BRUDNO, *supra* note 12, at 194-95 fn. *j.*

46. *Maher*, unlike *Griffin*, involves discrimination *among*, rather than *against*, the poor. *See* text accompanying notes 86-94, *infra; see also* notes 35 & 40, *supra*. Although this difference between *Maher* and *Griffin* is not significant for purposes of the discussion at this stage, I use the neutral phrase "suffered by" here to avoid confusion on this issue.

47. *See* Griffin v. Illinois, *supra*, 351 U.S. at 35 (Harlan, J., dissenting).

48. Medicaid, 42 U.S.C. §§ 1396-1396j (1976), provides medical care to specified categories of financially needy persons. All recipients of Aid to Families with Dependent Children (AFDC), 42 U.S.C. §§ 601-10 (1976), and Supplemental Security Income for the Aged, Blind, and Disabled (SSI), 42 U.S.C. §§ 1381-83c (1976), are eligible for Medicaid. Poor persons who fall within the category of the "medically indigent"—*i.e.*, those persons whose income and/or assets render them financially ineligible for AFDC or SSI, but who would be eligible if their medical expenses were included in calculating need for purposes of AFDC or SSI—may be covered by Medicaid at the option of each individual participating state. Poor persons who do not meet the non-need eligibility criteria for AFDC or SSI are not eligible for Medicaid regardless of how destitute they may be. *See generally* B. BRUDNO, POVERTY, INEQUALITY, AND THE LAW 489, 499-501, 518-21 fn. *u*, 579-784 (1976). *See also* Beal v. Doe, 97 S.Ct. 2366, 2368-69 & n. 1 (1977).

49. *See* the second of the three basic definitional questions inherent in Equal Protection-poverty claims noted in the Introduction, paragraph following text accompanying note 7, *supra*. As I argue in an article currently in progress, the definitional approach adopted by the majority in San Antonio Indep. School Dist. v. Rodriguez, 411 U.S. 1, 18-28, 61 n.6 (1973), to delineate a disadvantaged class of poor for purposes of meaningful Equal Protection review is the most restrictive possible approach. *See generally* BRUDNO, *supra* note 48, at 435-37; *see also* text accompanying notes 56-58, *infra*.

50. *See* note 3, *supra; see generally* BRUDNO, *supra* note 48, at 5-6 & fn. *a*.

51. The Medicaid eligibility of most poor pregnant women rests on their eligibility for AFDC. *See* note 48, *supra*. The financial need eligibility criteria for AFDC are set by the states and typically fall well below the federal government's official poverty level. For example, in 1975, the poverty level for a female-headed family of four was $5,473.00 annually, or approximately $456.00 per month; for a family of three, $4,175.00 annually, or approximately $348.00 per month. *See* U.S. BUREAU OF THE CENSUS, STATISTICAL ABSTRACT OF THE UNITED STATES: 1976, at p. 415, Table No. 672 (97th ed. 1976). By comparison, the average monthly AFDC payment per family in December, 1975, without regard to family size, was $229.75, with the average AFDC family consisting of 3.2 members. *See* 40 *Current Operating Statistics*, SOC. SEC. BULL. 6 (Dec. 1977). The poverty level for the average female-headed family, which is lower than the corresponding figure for the average male-headed family of the same size, is used here because most AFDC families are headed by women. *See generally*, B. BLECHMAN, E. GRAMLICH & R. HARTMAN. SETTING NATIONAL PRIORITIES: THE 1975 BUDGET 174-77, 179-81, 195 (1974); THE PRESIDENT'S COMMISSION ON INCOME MAINTENANCE PROGRAMS, POVERTY AMID PLENTY: THE AMERICAN PARADOX 116-20 (1969).

52. *Compare, e.g.,* San Antonio Indep. School Dist. v. Rodriguez, 411 U.S. at 19-20, 25-28; Gordon v. Lance, 403 U.S. 1, 5 (1971); *see* BRUDNO, *supra* note 48, at 261-62, 434-35.

53. *See* 97 S.Ct. at 2380-81; text accompanying notes 86-94, *infra*.

54. *Maher*, unlike *Griffin*, involves *de jure* discrimination.

55. *I.e.,* abortions which are not established as "medically necessary" under state law. *See* 97 S.Ct. at 2378-79 & nn. 2-3.

56. 411 U.S. 1, 20, 22-23 (1973). See also note 49, *supra*; Beal v. Doe, 2394, 2397 (1977) (Marshall, J., dissenting); *but see* note 46, *supra*.

57. *See* 411 U.S. at 19, 22.

58. *See id.* at 20; *but see id.* at 117-19 (Marshall, J., dissenting). For a persuasive critique of these latter two criteria announced in *Rodriguez, see* Clune, *The Supreme Court's Treatment of Wealth Discriminations Under the Fourteenth Amendment*, 1975 SUP. CT. REV. 289, 336-43.

59. *See* 411 U.S. at 17, 28. *See also* note 8, *supra*.

60. *See* 411 U.S. at 17, 29, 33-35. For the view that *Rodriguez's* constricted test of fundamental rights renders an Equal Protection analysis on the basis of fundamental interests redundant, *see* Karst, *Foreword: Equal Citizenship Under the Fourteenth Amendment*, 91 HARV. L. REV. 1, 33 n. 183 (1977).

This "either-or" test for strict scrutiny of Equal Protection claims is typically invoked by the Burger Court to rationalize use of the "any rational basis" non-standard. *See, e.g.,* Maher v. Roe, 97 S.Ct. 2376, 2380-81,

2385 (1977); Massachusetts Bd. of Retirement v. Murgia, 427 U.S. 307, 312-14 (1976); *see also* text accompanying notes 85-86, *infra*. Justice Marshall repeatedly has objected to this so-called "two-tier" Equal Protection approach. *See, e.g.*, Beal v. Doe, *supra*, 97 S.Ct. at 2396; Massachusetts Bd. of Retirement v. Murgia, *supra*, 427 U.S. at 318-21.

61. *See* notes 8 & 9, *supra* & accompanying text.

62. *See* text accompanying note 10, *supra*. The right at stake in *Maher* clearly fits within *Rodriguez's* circumscribed category of fundamental rights. *See* 411 U.S. at 34 n. 76.

63. *See* 97 S.Ct. at 2381 n. 6; *see also* note 73, *infra*.

64. *See* 97 S.Ct. at 2380 n. 5 (*Boddie*); *id.* at 2381 n. 6 (*Douglas*); *cf.* 97 S.Ct. at 2383 n. 8 (Shapiro v. Thompson, 394 U.S. 618 (1969), *infra* at text accompanying notes 94-103).

For Justice Powell's restrictive re-interpretation of *Griffin*, *Douglas*, and related Equal Protection-poverty precedents in *Rodriguez, see* 411 U.S. at 20-22. *Compare* Marshall's analysis of these same precedents in his *Rodriguez* dissent, 411 U.S. at 117-24.

65. *See* 351 U.S. at 34-35; text accompanying notes 31-33, *supra*.

66. *See* 372 U.S. at 361-62; text following note 45, *supra*.

67. *See* text accompanying notes 28-30, *supra*.

68. *See* 97 S.Ct. at 2382-83.

69. *See* text accompanying notes 31-33, *supra*.

70. *Cf.* Justice Cardozo's oft-criticized distinction between those forms of "inaction" which result "positively or actively in working an injury" and those which result only "negatively merely in withholding a benefit," in H.R. Moch v. Rensselaer Water Co., 247 N.Y. 160, 162, 159 N.E. 896, 898 (1928).

71. *See* 97 S.Ct. at 2382; *but see id.* at 2387-88 (Brennan, J., dissenting); Beal v. Doe, *supra*, 97 S.Ct. at 2394, 2398-99 (Blackmun, J., dissenting).

72. *See* text following note 43, *supra*.

73. The only explanation suggested in *Maher* for such a distinction between *Griffin* and *Maher* is the majority's unsupported assertion in a footnote that *Griffin* and "the principles underlying *Griffin* and *Douglas*" apply only in criminal procedure cases, 97 S.Ct. at 2381 n.6; *see also* note 63, *supra*, & accompanying text; note 89, *infra*, & accompanying text.

74. *See* 97 S.Ct. at 2385; *id.* at 2391 (Brennan, J., dissenting); Beal v. Doe, *supra*, 97 S.Ct. at 2399 (Blackmun, J., dissenting); *see also* text accompanying notes 104-06, *infra*.

75. *See* 97 S.Ct. at 2382.

76. *See* 97 S.Ct. at 2381-83, *criticized in The Supreme Court, 1976 Term*, 91 HARV. L. REV. 137, 141-44 (1977).

77. *See* Beal v. Doe, *supra*, 97 S.Ct. at 2395-97 & nn. 1-2 (Marshall, J., dissenting); *see also id.* at 2399 (Blackmun, J., dissenting).

78. *See e.g.*, United States v. Kras, 409 U.S. 434, 449 (1973); Wyman v. James, 400 U.S. 309, 318-24 & nn. 8 & 11; *see generally* Brudno, *Fairness and Bureaucracy: The Demise of Procedural Due Process for Welfare Claimants*, 25 HASTINGS L.J. 813, 852-54, 858-59, 862-66 (1974); *see also* BRUDNO, *supra* note 48, at 757-58; note 96, *infra*.

79. 97 S.Ct. at 2380; *but see* note 40, *supra*.

80. 97 S.Ct. at 2386 n. 13; *but see* note 35, *supra*; note 43, *supra*, & accompanying text.

81. *See* text accompanying notes 31-36, *supra*.

82. *See* note 25, *supra*, text accompanying notes 25-27, *supra*.

83. That aspect of the right-privilege distinction which is most inimical to the maintenance of liberty and the rule of law in the welfare state is its corollary which views the power to withhold altogether benefits deemed "privileges" (*e.g.*, in *Maher*, Medicaid benefits; in *Griffin*, access to appellate review) as including the lesser power to impose *any* condition upon eligibility for those benefits. The leading decision expressly repudiating this corollary is Sherbert v. Verner, 374 U.S. 398 (1963). *Sherbert* struck down an Unemployment Insurance disqualification provision as applied to a Seventh-Day Adventist because the provision effectively required her to choose between receiving the benefits to which she was otherwise entitled and following the precepts of her religion. Therefore, ruled *Sherbert*, absent a "compelling" state interest, such a condition is unconstitutional under the First Amendment's Free Exercise Clause. *See generally* BRUDNO, *supra* note 48, at 565-68 & authorities cited therein; *see also* text accompanying notes 99-103, *infra*.

84. *See* text accompanying notes 23-27, *supra*.

85. *See* text accompanying notes 65-84, *supra*.

86. 97 S.Ct. at 2381.

87. *See* text accompanying notes 20-22, *supra*.

88. *See* text preceding note 46, *supra*; note 46, *supra*; text accompanying notes 48-58, *supra*; text accompanying note 91, *infra; see also* note 11, *supra*, & accompanying text.

89. *See* 97 S.Ct. at 2380-81 & n. 6; *see also* text accompanying note 63, *supra*; note 73, *supra*, & accompanying text.

90. *See* 411 U.S. at 20-21; note 64, *supra*.

91. The discrimination in *Maher*, therefore, is directly analogous to that upheld in Wyman v. James, 400 U.S. 309 (1971). *James* represents the most significant, as well as the most blatant, pre-*Maher* example of the Burger Court's resurrection of the right-privilege distinction. That these two most egregious examples of retreat from the unconstitutional conditions doctrine both involve welfare mothers asserting rights of self-determination available to other citizens cannot be a mere coincidence. *See generally* Brudno, *supra* note 78, at 841-54, 857-60, 862-66. *See also* note 96, *infra*.

92. *Rodriguez* is comparable to *Griffin* and *Douglas* in that all three cases involved discrimination against the poor, or discrimination solely on the basis of poverty. However, unlike *Griffin* and *Douglas*, *Rodriguez* involved discrimination against poor groups (*i.e.*, residents of property-poor school districts), not poor individuals. Contrary to the majority's reasoning then, *Rodriguez* is even less relevant to *Maher* than *Griffin* or *Douglas*.

93. 397 U.S. 471 (1970). *Dandridge* upheld a maximum per-AFDC-family grant rule which discriminated among otherwise equally eligible AFDC recipients solely on the basis of family size. Conceding that the Equal Protection claim at issue involved "the most basic economic needs of impoverished human beings," 397 U.S. at 485, the *Dandridge* majority nonetheless concluded that state welfare regulations are no different than business regulations for purposes of Equal Protection review, since both fall into the category of "state economic or social regulation." Therefore, the "any rational basis" test was invoked and any inquiry into actual justification for the over- and under-inclusiveness of the challenged regulation was eschewed. *See* 397 at 486-87; *cf.* Maher v. Roe, 97 S.Ct. 2376, 2385 (1977). *See also* note 60, *supra*, & accompanying text; text accompanying note 10, *supra*. *See generally* B. BRUDNO, POVERTY, INEQUALITY, AND THE LAW 723-26 & nn. *d-e* (1976), & authorities cited therein.

94. 394 U.S. 618 (1969. *Shapiro* struck down one-year waiting requirements for AFDC eligibility. The majority, emphasizing that both "the very means to subsist" and the constitutional right to travel interstate were at stake, 394 U.S. at 627, 629-30, concluded that the asserted state interests were either constitutionally impermissible (*e.g.*, deterring in-state migration of welfare claimants), or insufficiently strong (*e.g.*, conserving fiscal and administrative resources). 394 U.S. at 631-38. And, of particular import for subsequent Equal Protection-poverty cases, the *Shapiro* majority noted that "the saving of welfare costs cannot justify an otherwise invidious classification." 394 U.S. at 633; *see also* Mayer v. Chicago, 404 U.S. 189, 197 (1971); Boddie v. Connecticut, 401 U.S. 371, 381-82 (1971); *but see* Jefferson v. Hackney, 406 U.S. 535, 549 (1972).

95. *See* 97 S.Ct. at 2381, 2385.

96. *See* 97 S.Ct. at 2383 n.8. Ironically, the mandatory "home visit" upheld against a Fourth Amendment, unconstitutional condition challenge in Wyman v. James, 400 U.S. 309 (1971), note 91, *supra*, would have been struck down had the *James* majority adopted *Maher's* "penalty" interpretation of *Shapiro*. *See* note 102, *infra*, & accompanying text.

97. *See* Dandridge v. Williams, 397 U.S. 471, 484 n. 16 (1970); *see also* San Antonio Indep. School Dist. v. Rodriguez, 411 U.S. 1, 32 n. 71 (1973); *see generally,* BRUDNO, *supra* note 93, at 726-28 & nn. *f-g*, & authoritis cited therein.

98. *See* BRUDNO, *supra* note 93, at 729-33 & nn. *h-k*. The constitutional right of choice with respect to living with members of one's family, for which I argued there, recently has been recognized by four members of Court. *See* Justice Powell's plurality opinion in Moore v. City of East Cleveland, 97 S.Ct. 1932, 1935-39 (1977), *noted in The Supreme Court, 1976 Term*, 91 HARV. L. REV. 128-37 (1977).

99. 374 U.S. 398 (1963); *see* note 83, *supra*.

100. *See* text accompanying note 83, *supra; see also* text accompanying notes 75-78, *supra*.

101. *See* text immediately preceding & accompanying notes 65-67, *supra*.

102. *See* 97 S.Ct. at 2383 n. 8.

103. *See generally,* BRUDNO, *supra* note 93, at 565-79 & authorities cited therein; Jones, *The Rule of Law and the Welfare State*, 58 COLUM. L. REV. 143 (1958); Linde, *Constitutional Rights in the Public Sector: Justice Douglas on Liberty in the Welfare State*, 40 WASH. L. REV. 10 (1965); O'Neil, *Unconstitutional Conditions: Welfare Benefits With Strings Attached*, 54 CALIF. L. REV. 443 (1966); Reich, *Individual Rights and Social Welfare: The Emerging Legal Issues*, 74 YALE L.J. 1245 (1965); W. Van Alstyne, *The Demise of the Right-Privilege Distinction in Constitutional Law*, 81 HARV. L. REV. 1439 (1968); *see also* F. HAYEK, THE ROAD TO SERFDOM (1950).

104. *See generally* Bennett, *Liberty, Equality, and Welfare Reform*, 68 NW. U.L. REV. 74, 98-103 (1973); *see also* BRUDNO, *supra* note 93, at 68, 97-98, 167, 215-16, 723-27; Michelman, *Foreword: On Protecting the Poor Through the Fourteenth Amendment*, 83 HARV. L. REV. 7, 27-33 (1969); note 94, *supra*, & authorities cited therein.

105. *See* 97 S.Ct. at 2385; *see also* 97 S.Ct. at 2391 (Brennan, J., dissenting); Beal v. Doe, 97 S.Ct. 2394, 2399 (1977) (Blackmun, J., dissenting); note 106, *infra*.

106. *See* 97 S.Ct. at 2382-83, 2385:

> *Roe* . . . implies no limitation on the authority of a State to make a value judgment favoring childbirth over abortion, and to implement that judgment by the allocation of public funds. . . . The State may have made childbirth a more attractive alternative, thereby influencing the woman's decision. . . . The State unquestionably has a "strong and legitimate interest in encouraging normal childbirth". . . . The medical costs associated with childbirth . . . are significantly greater than those normally associated with elective abortions during the first trimester. The subsidizing of costs incident to childbirth is a rational means of encouraging childbirth.

107. *See* Beal v. Doe, 97 S.Ct. 2394, 2395-98 (1977) (Marshall, J., dissenting); *id.* at 2399 (Blackmun, J., dissenting); Note, *The Supreme Court, 1976 Term*, 91 HARV. L. REV. 137, 142-46 (1977); *see also* Karst, *Foreword: Equal Citizenship Under The Fourteenth Amendment*, 91 HARV. L. REV. 1, 57-59 (1977); note 11, *supra*.

108. *See* Beal v. Doe, *supra*, 97 S.Ct. at 2397 (Marshall, J., dissenting).

109. 97 S.Ct. at 2385-86.

"Mr. Chief Justice; May It Please the Court:"
By Louis H. Pollak*

> Last spring I was one of a group of lawyers who prepared an *amicus* brief filed by four private universities—Columbia, Harvard, Stanford and Pennsylvania—in support of petitioner in *The Regents of the University of California v. Allan Bakke.* Working on that brief merely whetted my appetite. In the ensuing months I have found myself indulging fantasies of participation in the oral argument (representing, I hasten to add, only myself as would-be *amicus*—not the Regents, and not the four private universities on whose *amicus* brief I was privileged to work). Finally, in September, one month before the real argument is to take place, I have put my fantasies on paper. The paragraphs which follow are those I would like to say to the Court in a presentation so lucid and persuasive that none of the Justices would find it necessary to interrupt the even tenor of my rhetoric with questions.

15 September 1977.   LHP

Mr. Chief Justice; may it please the Court:

This case brings back to this Court the momentous issues raised, but put off to a later day, in *DeFunis v. Odegaard.*[1] There, as Your Honors will recall, the Supreme Court of Washington,[2] overturning a judgment of the Washington Superior Court, rejected the contention that the University of Washington's special admissions program was, as to an unsuccessful white applicant, a denial of the equal protection of the laws. In *DeFunis,* the plaintiff had, pursuant to the judgment of the Superior Court, been enrolled in law school throughout the appellate phases of the litigation, with the result that, after certiorari was granted and argument had in this Court, it became apparent that the plaintiff would shortly receive his degree in law whatever the outcome of his law suit. Wherefore, on determining that the controversy was moot, this Court dismissed its writ of certiorari.

In the present case, this Court has granted certiorari to review a decision of the California Supreme Court[3] in conflict with that of the Washington Supreme Court. The present case arose when respondent Allan Bakke, denied admission in 1973 and again in 1974 to the Davis Medical School of the University of California, went to court to compel petitioner, the Regents of the University of California, to admit him to medical school. It is undisputed that respondent's so-called "benchmark score"—an aggregate quantification by the Davis admissions committee not only of an applicant's academic record but also of the committee's appraisal of the applicant's personality, strengths, career plans, etc.—was higher than the "benchmark score" of those minority applicants (black, Chicano and other Spanish-surname, Asian-American, Native American) who were admitted in 1973 and 1974 pursuant to the Davis program of reserving sixteen of the one hundred seats in the first-year class for qualified minority applicants.

*United States District Judge for the Eastern District of Pennsylvania. This essay was prepared in 1977 when the author was Dean and Albert M. Greenfield University Professor of Human Relations and Law, University of Pennsylvania Law School.

The record before this Court does not disclose whether, in either of the years in question, any white applicant with a "benchmark score" lower than Bakke's was admitted to one of the eighty-four seats for which white applicants were eligible.[4] Nor does the record before this Court admit of an authoritative answer to the question whether, in either year, respondent would have gained admission had the special admissions program not been in effect. It is, for example, entirely possible that Bakke, who is in his thirties, would in any event have lost out to other applicants (whether white or not) whose quantified credentials, academic and other, summed to lower numbers but who enjoyed the comparative advantage of youth—a qualification much admired, perhaps overly admired, by American medical schools. But there does not appear to be any ready means of pursuing this conjecture: for the California Supreme Court has elected to place on the University's officials the burden of proving that in the absence of the special admissions program, Bakke still would not have been admitted, and those officials have acknowledged that they cannot make this showing.[5] It is of course arguable that the propriety of this allocation of burden of proof—which goes to respondent's standing to raise a federal question—is itself a federal question on which this Court has the last word. But it seems hard to make the case that allocating the burden of proof in this way was inherently unreasonable. And so I would urge this Court to regard this case as one in which respondent has standing to complain about an admissions process—a process under which whites, including respondent, were not eligible for sixteen per cent of the seats in each entering class of medical students, in a state in which twenty-five percent of the population, but no more than four percent of the physicians, are minority persons—which has operated to his probable detriment. In short, I would ask this Court to address the merits of respondent's claim, sustained by the California Supreme Court, that implementation of the Davis special admissions program was, as to respondent, a denial of the equal protection of the laws.

Before proceeding to the merits, I think certain preliminary observations are in order. Although this case is a law suit arising from one applicant's complaint against a particular medical school, it is perceived as presenting constitutional issues of general significance for the nationwide academic community. The issues are primarily of concern to state colleges and universities, since the defendant at trial (the petitioner here) is the governing body of a state institution which must conform its policies and processes to the fourteenth amendment. But the way this case is decided can be expected to affect most private educational institutions as well, since a broad network of federal and state statutes and implementing regulations impose on such institutions—properly, in my view—constraints comparable with constitutional norms. In short, this private law suit—not, at its inception, even denominated a class action—has in its progress through the California courts become transformed into public litigation of the most widespread and momentous application and implication.

This seems to me to bear importantly not only on this Court's resolution of the merits of the case but also on the form of the decision. At the risk of appearing to instruct Your Honors in the obvious, I would urge you—whichever way you rule—to eschew constitutional pronouncements broader than those required for the disposition of this case. Thus, although the Davis program is broadly representative of programs in force at hundreds of colleges and universities, there are so many variations of criteria and administrative practice that an opinion sustaining the Davis program ought not to be so broadly phrased as to appear to extend this Court's *non obstat* uncritically to any and every race-aware admissions program advertised as remedial: if there are programs whose purposes are obscure, whose criteria are porous, or whose operations are slip-shod, reversal of the judgment below should not insulate them from judicial scrutiny. Conversely, if this Court votes to affirm—as I trust you will not—it would, I respectfully submit, be incumbent upon Your Honors to confine this Court's disapproval of the Davis program to exactly that feature which fails to pass constitutional muster. If, for example, this Court, disagreeing with what I shall later argue, is persuaded that the inclusion of Asian-Americans among the benefited minority categories is constitutionally unwarranted, notwithstanding California's long and dishonorable record of *de jure* discrimination against Asian-Americans, precise limitation of the Court's holding in this respect would be of great consequence, inasmuch as many race-aware admissions programs at other institutions do not include Asian-Americans within their "minority" categories. Similarly, if this Court concludes (erroneously, as I see the matter) that some constitutional infirmity inheres in what respondent denominates a "quota"—namely, the reservation of a fixed number of seats in an entering class for qualified minority applicants— careful tailoring of the Court's opinion in that respect would be very significant, since a great many race-aware admissions programs follow the slightly different pattern of establishing a so-called "goal" (whether stated as a particular number of seats or as a percentage of the entering class) the approximate achievement of which may involve race-aware choices among minority and non-minority applicants with respect to every seat in the entering class.

For my part, I am bound to say that I find the "quota" v. "goal" distinction of limited semantic value, and of even less value as an instrument of constitutional analysis. Under either rubric, the legitimacy of the method must depend, so it seems to me, on assurance that (1) all those admitted are qualified—a proposition not challenged in the instant case, and (2) the percentage of the class tentatively allocated to minority matriculants bears a reasonable relationship to the objective of enlarging the cadre of minority professionals—a reasonableness hardly open to challenge in the context of the Davis program, reserving only a sixth of the seats for minority matriculants in a state in which minority persons are a fourth of the population and minority physicians are so very few.

My plea that decision either way be confined to the constitutional necessities of the case entails a corollary. It has frequently been asserted—in briefs *amici* in this case, and in public commentary on the case—that the record made below does not offer an adequate basis for confident adjudication of the complex constitutional issues presented. It may well be that a case which appeared relatively straightforward at trial has grown in legal complexity at appellate levels, so that the record now seems a shaky platform for issues which have become weightier and weightier with the filing of each new *amicus* brief and the publication of each new law review critique. Nonetheless, I am satisfied that the record, taken together with the essentially undisputed data and experience this Court can properly cull from the briefs of the parties and the briefs *amici,* will be found to support a final judgment here—a judgment of reversal. But if the Court is of a different view—if the Court feels that critical factual questions remain open—then remand for appropriate amplification of the record would seem the proper course. Surely the constitutional issues tendered are of too great a magnitude to be resolved, either way, on the basis of the Court's perception that one or the other party may have failed to present evidence which, if proffered, might have changed the disposition of the case. The case was a private grievance at its inception. But it is now a public controversy involving major constitutional issues in whose proper resolution all Americans have a vital stake. Deciding these issues today must take second place to deciding them right.

Because the time for oral argument is so brief, I shall praetermit discussion of a number of matters which have already been extensively canvassed in the opinions below and in the briefs filed in this Court. In particular, I will not undertake to explore in detail the several important remedial objectives served by giving affirmative weight to minority status in admissions decisions at the University of California and at other colleges and universities— both state and private, both large and small—throughout the country. I would only stress that in my view the primary objective is not to achieve a more heterogeneous and hence an intellectually more challenging classroom environment; nor is it to neutralize those cultural biases which may tend to skew academic competition in favor of white students. Both of these are important objectives and, indeed, it is certainly arguable that pursuit of the second of these should be regarded as a constitutionally obligatory aspect of the admissions process in a state institution. But I submit that the societal objective of far greater significance is the achievement of a major increase in the number of minority Americans trained at graduate and professional levels. I take it, furthermore, that the judgment that this is an objective of compelling importance is not seriously disputed — either as a general matter or as it bears on the particular issues confronting this Court in this case. Thus, I read the opinion of Mr. Justice Mosk for the court below to acknowledge that in California, as elsewhere, there is a great dearth of minority physicians, and that this is a matter of proper concern for the responsible officers of administration and instruction of a state university. I would add that the gross under-representation of minority persons among California's physician population is not only a major social problem, but one for which the state of California may properly be charged with at least some measure of official accountability, given the degree to which minority educational achievement has been hobbled by, *inter alia,* the *de jure* racial segregation practiced in various California public school systems.[6] I am not suggesting that anything in this record, or *dehors* the record, would show the University of California to have been one of the state agencies blameworthy in this regard. But I do suggest that for the Davis Medical School faculty to address this major problem as it did was a particularly appropriate fulfillment of the educational responsibility of a state university. Actions taken by the Davis medical faculty (and other medical faculties of the University of California) to increase the number of minority physicians should in the near term help to alleviate grave short-falls in the delivery of health services to millions of minority persons in California and elsewhere, and should in the long term significantly enlarge the cadre of minority persons occupying positions of leadership in the health sciences in California and across the nation. And what holds true for medicine would also appear to hold true for law — and, in significant measure, for other advanced academic disciplines whose special admissions policies have been placed at risk by the decision below.

It is tempting to devote some attention to one portion of Mr. Justice Mosk's analysis which seems central to his legal reasoning but which, I submit, is wholly unsupported by the record in this case. I refer to his assumption that substantial enlargement of the numbers of minority matriculants in medicine (and, presumably, in law and other graduate disciplines) can be achieved through admissions processes which do not give affirmative weight to the racial identity of minority applicants.[7] This critical assumption is quite erroneous, and must not be allowed to obscure the argument and decision in this Court. Happily, a number of the briefs filed in this Court have abundantly demonstrated that this assumption is entirely undermined not merely by what little testimony there is of record, but by all the experience and information available to educators versed in these matters. These briefs make it clear that to find in the Constitution an insistence on race-blindness in graduate admissions would turn the nation's clock back to the time, only a decade ago, when degree candidacy in medicine, law, and the other advanced academic disciplines which largely define the values and quality of American life was almost off limits to blacks and other minority Americans. For the Constitution's equal protection clause to compel such malign consequences — consequences so subversive of the very purposes which brought the fourteenth amendment into being — would be a strange and tragic irony. But I submit that no such irony is commanded by the Constitution.

For the past forty years the decisions of this Court have been uniform in declaring that race-defined or ethnic group-defined governmental policies are subject to the most demanding judicial scrutiny, and properly so. But these decisions are not authority for the proposition that race or ethnicity can never be the touchstone of government policy. Especially in remedial contexts, akin to the setting in which this case arose, this Court's decisions sound a very different note. As Mr. Justice Brennan observed last Term, concurring in *United Jewish Organizations of Williamsburgh v. Carey,* "we have authorized and even required race-conscious remedies in a variety of corrective settings."[8] Moreover, as Mr. Justice Brennan added by way of footnote, the principle involved is not confined to instances of court-fashioned remedies:

> Of course, it could be suggested that the remedial rules upheld in these earlier cases acquired added legitimacy because they generally arose in the form of judicial decrees rather than affirmative legislative or executive action. Arguably, a court-imposed remedy to correct a ripe finding of discrimination should be accorded particular respect. Yet, the role of the judiciary is not decisive.[9]

Indeed, the official action sustained in *Williamsburgh*—race-conscious legislative redistricting designed to give blacks and Puerto Ricans a more nearly proportional share of effective voting strength in the election of state legislators from the borough of Brooklyn—was not judicially fashioned or mandated and was not predicated on a judicial finding of prior illegality. Whether viewed as upholding state legislative compliance with federal legislative and executive mandates pursuant to the Voting Rights Act of 1965, or as validating an independent state legislative initiative building on the principles announced in *Gaffney v. Cummings,*[10] the decision in *Williamsburgh* is a clear affirmation of legislative and/or executive race-conscious remedial action.

It may be urged that the *Williamsburgh* doctrines are without application here for the reason that respondent Bakke has suffered a cognizable legal injury and that the *Williamsburgh* plaintiffs—whose own entitlement to vote was in no way curtailed—did not. Arguably so. But without pausing to examine the nature of the wrong asserted by the *Williamsburgh* plaintiffs—did they lack standing?, or were they unable to demonstrate "harm" in some sense known to the law?—I submit that the purported distinction is in any event unavailing to explain away two other decisions of this Court sustaining what were in fact, if not *in haec verba* so denominated, legislatively mandated race-conscious (or, perhaps, ethnic group-conscious) allocations of entitlement detrimental to those challenging the legislation. I have in mind *Morton v. Mancari,*[11] and *Katzenbach v. Morgan.*[12] In *Morton v. Mancari,* as Your Honors will recall, this Court upheld a federal statute (and conforming administrative practice) which accorded tribal Native Americans a preference with respect to certain hiring and promotional opportunities in the Bureau of Indian Affairs. And in *Katzenbach v. Morgan* this Court upheld a federal statute which extended the suffrage to tens of thousands of New Yorkers of Puerto Rican origin theretofore disenfranchised by virtue of New York's constitutional and legislative insistence on literacy in English as a qualification for voting.

That the plaintiff class in *Morton v. Mancari*—handicapped, by virtue of white or other non-tribal status, in securing federal employment—suffered a detriment akin to that complained of by Bakke is, I think, clear. In *Katzenbach v. Morgan* the plaintiffs were, it is true, not precluded from voting as a consequence of Congress' extension of the franchise to others theretofore ineligible to vote. But, manifestly, the plaintiffs perceived that their influence on the New York voting process would, *pro tanto,* be diluted by the operation of the federal statute—otherwise, it is not apparent what standing they would have had to complain.

I recognize that this Court based its decision in *Morton v. Mancari* on the "unique" history and status of Native Americans, especially those still tribally grouped. But this Court did not suggest that this special history and status freed Congress from constitutional restraints in defining the relationships between tribal Native Americans and other Americans. In the present case, I would point out that the University of California has shaped its remedial policies with care to address the needs not only of Native Americans but of other Americans whose history and status are, in somewhat differing ways, unique:

The United States Reports of relatively recent vintage amply illustrate the degradations officially imposed by the United States and by California on Asian-Americans, and the comparable degradations imposed by many states on Chicanos and other Spanish-surname Americans.

As for blacks, the tragic uniqueness of the slave experience and its still ramifying *sequelae* hardly need argument before this Court. But what bears decisively on the issues presented by this case is the history of the Freedmen's Bureau[13] canvassed in detail in the *amicus* brief of the NAACP Legal Defense Fund. That history shows that the very Congress which submitted the fourteenth amendment for ratification also authorized, over Presidential veto, a large remedial apparatus for the education and economic advancement not of Americans generally, but, specifically, of the freedmen. What could more clearly show that the fourteenth amendment, far from precluding remedial programs particularly designed to assist those groups battered by American history, was expected to be implemented in just such ways? Unaided by comparable legislative history, this Court has—correctly in my view—recently sustained rationally grounded governmental policies preferring women to men in the allocation of certain entitlements.[14] Wherefore, the carefully tailored remedial program challenged in the instant case would seem, *a fortiori,* to pass constitutional muster.

"Justice is pictured blind and her daughter, the Law, ought at least to be color-blind."[15] So wrote Albion W. Tourgée just over eighty years ago, in his brief filed in this Court on behalf of Homer Plessy. In lonely acquiescence, the elder Justice Harlan, dissenting in *Plessy v. Ferguson,* said, "in view of the Constitution, in the eye of the law, there is in this country no superior, dominant, ruling class of citizens. There is no caste here. Our Constitution is color-blind, and neither knows nor tolerates classes among citizens."[16]

The question in the present case is whether the special programs so belatedly undertaken by American universities contradict the great ideal which the Justice so eloquently declared.

I submit that they do not. The Justice was challenging Jim Crow laws designedly enacted by white majorities (the "superior, dominant, ruling class of citizens"[17]) to degrade every freedman—not merely keeping him in "his place" but, as Professor C. Vann Woodward has so trenchantly observed, "constantly pushing the Negro further down."[18]

But the policies challenged here, like the policies pursued by Congress in establishing the Freedmen's Bureau, have not created a caste—they have been fashioned and implemented to break down the pernicious castes which are our legacy. Nor are these the policies of self-defense of a "superior, dominant, ruling class of citizens." Now, as in 1866, whites are numerically, economically and culturally the controlling group, and the policies which Bakke and other whites challenge are pursued at the sufferance and under the authority of white political majorities. The Regents of the University of California, on behalf of the people of California, have acted affirmatively—beyond what the Constitution minimally requires—to hasten the day of full equality. If the white majority of California's population, finding these remedies imprudent in concept or in practice, wishes to overrule the Regents, it presumably has the political and constitutional authority to do so.[19] Indeed, it may well be that the white majority of the national population, through its representatives in Congress, also has the political and constitutional authority to supersede the University of California's initiative—this is, at least, one possible implication of this Court's decision in *Katzenbach v. Morgan.*[20]

In citing *Katzenbach v. Morgan* for this conjectured proposition, I am not arguing that Congress could properly adjudge the Davis program "unconstitutional" if this Court sustains it: I am, I must confess, leery of the implication in *Katzenbach v. Morgan* that Congress has a power to readjudicate constitutional issues resolved by this Court. Rather, I am suggesting that Congress, under section 5 of the fourteenth amendment, has an enforcement power superior to the states—one which would authorize Congress both to undo state remedial programs which Congress deems unwise, and to establish national remedial programs which may not have commended themselves to state legislatures or other agencies vested with state authority.

But my central point is simply this: that since the policies here challenged can be altered or terminated through conventional political processes—processes in which Bakke and all other whites can fully and effectively participate—the case for judicial intervention is unpersuasive. I do not mean to be understood as saying that whites are unprotected by the equal protection clause. Of course they are protected—as all Americans are—from stigma or irrationality given the force of law. And, as a group, whites would also be protected from group oppressions they are politically powerless to resist. Thus, I would expressly deny the extraordinary dictum contained in Justice Brown's opinion for the Court in *Plessy,* that Jim Crow laws adopted by a black majority would not be perceived by a white minority as an unconstitutional degradation.[21] What I do say is that when America's white majorities impose burdens on themselves in order modestly and rationally to redress (not compensate for, but redress) the decades and centuries of handicaps of America's minorities, to the resultant advantage of the entire nation, those whites who disagree with such policies are not the "discrete and insular minorities" whose political helplessness gives them a special claim on this Court's protective authority.[22] To be sure, if America's white majorities singled out a particular ethnic subset of whites for disadvantaged treatment—building perhaps on the grotesque xenophobia of Quebec's current francophone government which has just pushed through the provincial parliament legislation intended to strangle the schools, language, and culture of Quebec's anglophone minority—such a program would clearly be unconstitutional.[23] But that is not this case. I am prepared to argue the wisdom of the Davis and other special admissions programs at greater length in the proper forum; but I believe—and this is central to my submission—that a court, even this Court, is not the proper forum for that debate. I would simply say that I subscribe, as I think we all subscribe, to the ideal of a nation in which there is no caste, governed by a Constitution which is color-blind. We have not yet attained that ideal. We strive for it. And meanwhile I share the view, articulated by the Court of Appeals for the First Circuit, that "our society cannot be completely color-blind in the short term if we are to have a color-blind society in the long term."[24]

For these reasons, I respectfully submit that the judgment of the California Supreme Court should be reversed.

Notes

1. 416 U.S. 312 (1974).
2. DeFunis v. Odegaard, 82 Wash. 2d 11, 507 P.2d 1169 (1973).
3. Bakke v. Regents of the Univ. of Cal., 18 Cal. 3d 34, 553 P.2d 1152, 132 Cal. Rptr. 680 (1976).
4. *But see* Fitt, *In Fact, There is No New Wrong,* N.Y. Times, Sept. 12, 1977, at 32.
5. 18 Cal. 3d at 63–64, 553 P.2d at 1172, 132 Cal. Rptr. at 700.
6. Brief for NAACP Legal Defense and Education Fund, as *Amicus Curiae,* app. B, Regents of the Univ. of Cal. v. Bakke, *cert. granted,* 429 U.S. 1090 (No. 76–811, 1976 Term).
7. 18 Cal. 3d at 53–56, 533 P.2d at 1165–67, 132 Cal. Rptr. at 693–95.
8. 430 U.S. 144, 171 (1977) (Brennan, J., concurring in part).

9. *Id.* at 172 n.2.

10. 412 U.S. 735 (1973).

11. 417 U.S. 535 (1974).

12. 384 U.S. 641 (1966).

13. Freedmen's Bureau Act, 39th Cong., 1st Sess., ch. 200 (1866).

14. Califano v. Webster, 430 U.S. 313 (1977); Kahn v. Shevin, 416 U.S. 351 (1974). *Cf.* Craig v. Boren, 429 U.S. 190 (1976).

15. Brief for Plaintiff in error at 19, Plessy v. Ferguson 163 U.S. 537 (1896).

16. 163 U.S. 537, 559 (1896).

17. *Id.*

18. C. WOODWARD, THE STRANGE CAREER OF JIM CROW 93 (1957).

19. *Compare* Reitman v. Mulkey, 387 U.S. 369 (1967) *and* Hunter v. Ericson, 393 U.S. 385 (1969), *with* James v. Valtierra, 402 U.S. 137 (1971).

20. 384 U.S. 641 (1966).

21. 163 U.S. at 551.

22. *See* United States v. Carolene Prods. Co. 304 U.S. 144, 152 n.4 (1938); Ely, *The Constitutionality of Reverse Racial Discrimination,* 41 U. CHI. L. REV. 723 (1974); *cf.* Sandalow, *Racial Preferences in Higher Education: Political Responsibility and the Judicial Role,* 42 U. CHI. L. REV. 653 (1975).

23. *Cf.* Meyer v. Nebraska, 262 U.S. 390 (1923).

24. Associated Gen. Contractors of Mass., Inc. v. Altshuler, 490 F.2d 9, 16 (1st Cir. 1973), *cert. denied,* 416 U.S. 957 (1974).

Author's Note: Because this imagined oral argument was prepared before the actual oral argument took place, it only addresses the *constitutional* question presented by the petition for certiorari, and not the *statutory* question (the relevance, if any, of Title VI of the Civil Rights Act of 1964) which the Court, subsequent to the argument, asked the parties to address in supplemental briefs. Succinctly put, my view on the statutory question is as follows: (1) If, on the basis of appropriate committee hearings and reports, Congress were to conclude that pursuit of racially aware admissions programs would impede achievement of the goals of the equal protection clause, Congress, pursuant to its authority under section 5 of the fourteenth amendment, (a) would probably have authority to direct state universities to desist from the implementation of such programs (see text, *supra,* at note 20), and (b) might have comparable authority with respect to private universities receiving substantial federal and/or state subventions. (2) Conversely, if on the basis of appropriate committee hearings and reports, Congress were to conclude that pursuit of such programs would promote achievement of the goals of the equal protection clause, Congress, might well have authority to require the adoption and implementation of such programs by all universities, state and private, which receive substantial federal subventions, as a condition reasonably annexed to the receipt of federal funds. (3) The legislative history of Title VI, and the legislative and administrative record since its enactment, do not establish that Title VI (which is addressed to federally funded institutions, state and private) was intended either to preclude or to require the adoption and implementation of racially aware university admissions programs.

LHP

Racially Discriminatory Admission
To Public Institutions of
Higher Education

By Lino A. Graglia*

Should public institutions of higher education, as a matter of social policy, and may they, as a matter of constitutional law, grant preferences in admission of students on the basis of race or ethnic group? The basic difficulty, of course, is that to grant preference to members of some racial or ethnic groups is to disadvantage members of other racial or ethnic groups. From the point of view of the latter, therefore, the question becomes: May a person be denied admission to a public institution of higher education on the grounds that his government now perfers some races to others and that his is not one of the preferred races? To state the question in this form is, for most people, to make it virtually self-answering. The violation of fundamental principle seemingly involved and the sense of gross injustice necessarily engendered seem so great that adoption or continuance of such a policy should not be contemplated except upon a clear showing of overwhelming benefits obtainable in no other way. No such showing has been or can be made by the proponents of racial preferences in higher education.

An argument based upon principle is often not the most persuasive, especially before an audience of academics and intellectuals who know that no principle is absolute, that a serious problem is a problem, not because a fundamental principle is involved, but because principles come into conflict, and that arguments on principle often are resorted to when purely "practical" considerations seem insufficient to support the position being advanced.

Nonetheless, I believe that the proponents of racial preferences seriously underestimate the power and value of the principle that they would have us abandon or seriously weaken. The principle that no person should be disadvantaged by government because of race—a corollary of the basic democratic ideal of individual human worth, dignity, and responsibility—is one of enormous appeal and persuasiveness and, in a multi-racial and multi-ethnic society, of enormous usefulness. It is perhaps as valuable and as close to an absolute as any principle we have.

Because the principle is now under attack, it may be useful to recall what it has so far accomplished. It was the basis and justification for the Brown[1] decision, prohibiting school racial segregation, and for later decisions, prohibiting racial segregation in all areas of public life.[2] Its apparent unanswerability allowed Thurgood Marshall, counsel for the NAACP and now a Supreme Court justice, to argue in Brown that "the only thing that this Court is dealing with . . . [is] whether or not race can be used. . . . [W]hat we want from this Court is the striking down of race."[3] By the mid-1960's, the principle had gained sufficient acceptance to overcome the entrenched and powerful interests served by racial segregation and to make the abolition of state-imposed racial segregation a reality in all areas of public life. Finally, the principle gave us the great Civil Rights Acts of 1964 and 1968 and the Voting Rights Act of 1965, the passage of each of which was made irresistable by the claim

*Rex G. Baker and Edna Heflin Baker Professor in Constitutional Law, University of Texas School of Law.

that it would simply end state-imposed racial discrimination. The basic and strongest argument of opponents of the great civil rights advance represented by the 1964 Act was not that racial discrimination could be justified, but that the Act would somehow lead to demands for the use of racial discrimination to increase school racial integration. Senator Humphrey, the Senate floor manager of the bill that became the Act, responded that "bogeymen and hobgoblins have been raised to frighten well-meaning Americans."[4] As the *DeFunis*[5] and *Bakke*[6] cases illustrate, the fears of the opponents of the 1964 Act were well founded and are "bogeymen and hobgoblins" no longer.

Flushed with victories in the cause of racial equality, proponents of racial preferences would now abandon or undermine the very principle that made those victories possible. They forget, I think, that majorities can ultimately protect themselves because of their numerical superiority and that it is minorities who should be most apprehensive of proposals that would weaken accepted and effective principles of justice and equality. As the philosopher Carl Cohen has written:

> The principle that a person's race is simply not relevant in the application of the laws is a treasured one. If we are prepared to sacrifice that principle now and then, in an attempt to achieve some very pressing and very honorable objective, we will have given up its force as constitutional principle.
>
> Preferential admission systems present instances of this sometimes agonizing tension between important ends and impermissible means. . . . In facing dilemmas of this kind long experience has taught the supremacy of the procedural principle. With societies, as with individuals, the use of means in themselves corrupt tends to corrupt the user, and to infect the result.[7]

But, proponents of racial preferences may ask, can we not make a distinction between discrimination by government against members of nonwhite racial minorities and discrimination by government against members of the white racial majority? Perhaps we can, although the so-called white majority turns out on inspection to be only an aggregation of ethnic minorities. The capacity of the human mind, particularly when trained in law, to make distinctions is very great. The relevant question, however, is not whether such a distinction is logically possible, but whether it will be persuasive to many of those who will have to be persuaded if the principle is not to be effectively destroyed and if intensification of racial hostility is not to be the result. Alexander Bickel and Philip Kurland, in an amicus brief filed in the Supreme Court in the *DeFunis* case, said:

> For at least a generation the lesson of the great decisions of this Court and the lesson of contemporary history have been the same: discrimination on the basis of race is illegal, immoral, unconstitutional, inherently wrong and destructive of democratic society. Now this is to be unlearned and we are told that this is not a matter of fundamental principle but only a matter of whose ox is gored.[8]

Perhaps that is only rhetoric, but it is powerful rhetoric, frequently quoted as if dispositive of the issue and unshakably believed by most opponents of racial preferences. Whether or not we agree with it, its power is a fact that proponents of racial preferences must overcome, and I do not think it can or should be overcome.

Can we now successfully argue that the true fundamental principle is not that *all* racial discrimination by government is illegal, immoral, unconstitutional, inherently wrong, and destructive of democratic society, but that only *some* such discrimination is? Certainly no such distinction was ever suggested before. But, a proponent of racial preferences can answer, there was no need or occasion to make that distinction before; judges and lawyers can no more foresee the future than can others. Surely we are not now trapped by a principle stated more broadly than was then necessary. No, we are not trapped by principles when they do not serve our immediate purposes, but that is the very reason we should seek to preserve, as best as we can, those principles that have proven their worth. Perhaps it can be demonstrated that discrimination by government against persons classified as belonging to nonwhite minority races is inherently wrong and immoral but that discrimination by government against persons classified as belonging to the white majority race is sometimes permissible. But, even putting aside all the difficulties involved in making those classifications,[9] I lack confidence in my ability to demonstrate either branch of the proposition, and certainly to demonstrate the complete proposition, to the satisfaction of one whose interests incline him to disagree. I would continue to place my hope for justice and equality on the ring of self-evident truth and the apparent moral stature of the principle that *all* racial discrimination by government is evil. The proposition that government may not discriminate against nonwhites but may discriminate against whites does not have that ring or that stature, and seems a very unlikely candidate for a fundamental principle of justice and morality. I, for one, am not at all sure that we are so far removed from discrimination against nonwhite minorities that we can safely begin to consider the circumstances in which racial or ethnic discrimination is permissible. Those who believe that a principle permitting discrimination against whites but prohibiting it against nonwhites can be made acceptable to many of those it would disadvantage must have had experiences and have perceptions so different from mine as to make communication between us on this subject difficult.

What benefits can possibly be claimed to follow from the use of racial preferences in higher education sufficient to justify the violation of fundamental principle involved? Amazingly, the justifications offered by supporters of racial preferences are singularly unimpressive. The basic argument, or at least the most frequent assertion, in the articles, books, and legal briefs of proponents of racial preferences is simply that the preferred minority groups are "underrepresented" or, more typically, "grossly underrepresented" in our public institutions of higher education and in the professions to which those institutions lead. The more thoughtful proponents go on to explain, usually very briefly, why greater "representation" of these groups would be beneficial, but even these proponents weave the "underrepresentation" assertion into all parts of their argument as if it alone provided a basis for granting racial preferences. For example, the brief filed in the Supreme Court for the University of California in the *Bakke* case, prepared by exceptionally able counsel, consists of eighty-seven pages and has twenty headings and sub-headings. Surely one would expect to find a major heading and a substantial discussion for each of the alleged benefits of racial preferences in admission to medical school. It appears, however, that not more than two pages and part of one sub-heading specifically address the question. The first of the ends to be achieved by racially preferential admission is, according to the brief, simply "reducing the historic deficit of traditionally disfavored minorities in medical schools and in the medical profession."[10] But this, of course, is in itself no argument at all; it amounts to no more than the tautology that the number of persons from certain racial and ethnic groups is to be increased in order that that number be increased. The argument does not tell us *why* the number should be increased—even at the cost of official racial discrimination. It gives no reason why government should concern itself with determining the race of students and of members of the professions, or with seeking to adjust racial proportions. We certainly have no principle that requires that all or any particular racial or ethnic groups in the nation be "represented," proportionately or otherwise, in all institutions and occupations, or that authorizes government to discriminate racially if necessary to produce particular racial or ethnic proportions.

When the use of racial preferences in admitting students to institutions of higher education was first begun about ten years ago, the principal justification given was that the usual admission criteria (grade point average and performance on standard admission tests) were, for some inexplicable reason, inaccurate in predicting the academic performance of nonwhites and that nonwhites would actually perform better in colleges and graduate schools than their grade point averages and test scores would indicate. If this were true, the use of different admission criteria for nonwhites clearly would be justified and necessary; there can be no justification for using a measuring device that does not measure.[11] Unfortunately for proponents of racial preferences, their basic assumption proved not to be true, as nearly all will now concede.[12] The usual admission criteria do not underpredict the academic performance of nonwhites in colleges and graduate schools, and, for some nonwhite groups, they may even overpredict. Establishment of this fact, however, did not lessen the drive for the use of racial preferences in higher education. A peculiar aspect of this subject is that showing the arguments of proponents of racial preferences to be baseless causes none or very few of those proponents to favor the use of racial preferences any less; it only causes them to move on to other arguments.

The basic arguments offered today for the use of racial preferences in higher education are, first, that they will provide educational "diversity"—which, for one reason or another, is always found to be particularly important in the type of school that happens to be under discussion—and, second, that they will lead to the increased availability of professional services to members of the preferred groups. Additional arguments often made for racial preferences are that they will help provide "role models" for and lead to increased educational aspirations by members of the preferred groups; that they will help overcome unfavorable racial and ethnic stereotypes; and that they will compensate for past injustices. None of these arguments has merit, as even a very brief discussion of each should suffice to show.

In support of the "diversity" argument, proponents of racial preferences usually argue that such preferences are analogous to the geographical preferences sometimes used by institutions of higher education in order to obtain students from a variety of areas. In my opinion, this "geographical discrimination," too, is difficult to justify even though, unlike racial discrimination as practiced today, it generally has been used only in choosing between students who were otherwise equally or almost equally qualified. As practiced by major educational institutions in the Northeast, it usually meant that some students from New York City were denied admission so that some students from, say, South Dakota could be admitted. If this geographical diversity provided any educational benefit, I failed to discern it during my attendance at a school that sought such diversity. I suspect that the presumably more able students who were excluded would have contributed more than did those who were admitted for geographical diversity, and I am pleased that geographical discrimination —always practiced more by private schools than by public schools—seems to be on the wane. In any event, we have no fundamental principle prohibiting interstate geographical discrimination; we do have, or had, such a principle prohibiting racial discrimination.

The theory of racial and ethnic diversity is, apparently, not that such diversity is valuable for its own sake, but that one's racial or ethnic group is a reliable indicator of other things that are valuable, such as differences in points of view, attitudes, or other traits. I doubt, however, that race or ethnicity is such an indicator. I think that differences in economic status, for example, are much more important indicators of different experiences and perceptions. But, of course, there are economically advantaged and economically disadvantaged persons in every racial and ethnic group; indeed, there are many more whites than nonwhites living below federally established poverty lines. In answer to this, the Catch 22-like argument is sometimes made that even if there are no significant differences between whites and nonwhites, this is itself an important fact that may be learned by mixing members of the two groups. Thus, racial preferences in admission to higher education are justified if important differences are associated with race or if they are not. I suspect, however, that most college and graduate school students have already learned that people are much the same regardless of race; those who have not learned this are likely to "learn" only that members of the preferred racial and ethnic groups are not as qualified for higher education as are members of other groups—hardly a prescription for enhanced interracial understanding and respect. On the other hand, if race is significantly associated with differences important to higher education, it would be most unwise for government to emphasize those differences and their importance by using race or ethnic group as a basis for action. Our historic national policy has been, as Nathan Glazer has recently pointed out, neither to suppress nor to encourage such racial or ethnic differences as may exist, with the result that we have been able to have a degree of interesting cultural diversity and to maintain necessary social cohesion.[13]

All other things being equal, one might prefer racial or ethnic diversity to racial or ethnic homogeneity—about this reasonable persons can differ—but other things are not equal when diversity can be obtained only by denying persons advantages because of their race. In any event, we would have no *DeFunis* or *Bakke* cases to discuss today if racial preferences were granted by institutions of higher education only on an all-other-things-being-equal basis, or even only within the normal range of administrative discretion in selecting students for admission. In each of those cases, admission to a state-operated graduate school was granted to nonwhites who would not have come close even to being considered for admission if they had been white; standards were not merely bent or shaved, but were virtually abandoned in order to obtain the desired number of nonwhites. Mr. Bakke, for example, was denied admission to the University of California at Davis Medical School—in fact he was not even placed on the "alternate list"—although he had a 3.5 college grade point average and scored in the 90th percentile on the Medical College Admission Test (MCAT). Preferred nonwhites, however, were admitted with college grade point averages as low as 2.1, and the majority of nonwhites admitted scored below the 50th percentile on the MCAT.[14]

The emptiness of the "diversity" argument for racial preferences in higher education is demonstrated by the fact that, in practice, diversity of possibly significant traits is not in fact sought or necessarily obtained. An individual who is a member of a preferred racial or ethnic group may gain admission though he is otherwise indistinguishable from the average white, while a better qualified individual not of a preferred ethnic group, say one of Italian, Greek, or Polish descent, is denied admission regardless of the unusualness of his experiences or traits—and regardless, it should be added, of the fact that his ethnic group may be even more "underrepresented" in the school's student body than are the preferred racial or ethnic groups.

Nor can racial preferences in higher education be justified on the ground that they will lead to the greater availability of professional services to members of the preferred groups. It is doubtful that racial preferences do serve this objective significantly, and, in any event, it is clear that it can be better served in other ways. Nonwhite graduates of our professional schools probably will have at least as many professional opportunities today as white graduates of similar qualifications, and the availability of professional services is primarily determined not by race but by economics. There is no reason to think that nonwhites will or should be less concerned than whites with economic incentives. In any event, opportunities for contributions to society are not confined to or peculiarly concentrated in poor areas, and there is, therefore, no reason to encourage nonwhite professionals to confine or concentrate their practice in such areas.

It is sometimes said that some members of nonwhite groups would prefer to be served by professionals of the same group. Whether or not such a preference exists to any significant extent, it is clearly one that we can accept in the interest of honoring individual choice, even the choice to racially discriminate, but not one that we should encourage or take extra-ordinary steps to satisfy. As was said in connection with the "diversity" argument, the law should take the position that the individual's race is irrelevant, in the hope that the educative effect of law will help make this so even where it is not so already. Further, any preference that some members of minority racial or ethnic groups may have for being served by professionals from the same group will undoubtedly be much diminished when they come to realize, as they eventually must, that those professionals have not always been required to meet the educational standards applied to whites. I take it that no one is advocating racial preferences in higher education on the grounds that the preferred will do poorly in school, thus have limited professional opportunities, and thus be economically required to serve those who can afford no better. If we are concerned, as we should be and are, with increasing the availability of professional services to the poor, that concern can be met simply, directly, and appropriately by subsidizing such services by payments to the poor or to those who serve them.

The argument that a large number of professionals from nonwhite groups is needed to provide "role models" for and to increase the educational aspirations of young people of those groups is also insufficient to justify racial preferences in higher education. First, it appears that members of the nonwhite groups to which preferences are typically granted do not, in fact, have lower aspirations than do whites; they frequently have higher aspirations.[15] Second, it is already clear to most, and should soon be clear to all, that members of all nonwhite minority groups are more than welcome and can and do succeed in all profes-sions.[16] Most important, we cannot convincingly demonstrate to anyone that nonwhites can successfully compete with whites by acting on the basis that they can not and by applying lower standards to them than to whites. We hardly need or want as "models" persons who were not expected to and did not meet the standards applicable to whites. In short, the "role model" argument seems to depend upon the assumption that young people of the preferred racial and ethnic groups can and will be fooled. For example, young blacks are to notice that there are now more blacks in law school, but they are not to realize that these blacks are there only because of their race. When this realization does come, it can hardly be a source of pride; if increased aspiration results, it will likely be only the aspiration to receive preferential treatment, to be exempted from the standards applicable to whites, and to be required to meet only the standards considered suitable for blacks.

Far from reducing unfavorable stereotypes of racial and ethnic minority groups, it seems obvious that racial preferences in higher education must reinforce and corroborate such stereotypes. If the preferentially admitted are in fact the equal of whites, why is it necessary that they be preferred? Proponents of racial preferences answer, of course, that blacks have suffered slavery, segregation, and other racial discrimination, and that the other preferred groups also have been unfairly disadvanted. But this explanation cannot be persuasive to those disadvantaged by racial preferences, because not all of the racially or ethnically preferred will have been exceptionally disadvantaged—some in fact will have been exceptionally advantaged—and some of those not preferred will have been disadvantaged. Nonwhites with a middle or upper economic class background and highly educated parents (both being university professors, for example) are regularly accorded preferential admission while better qualified whites with a lower economic class background and parents with very little educa-tion are denied admission. The "exceptional disadvantages" explanation is, therefore, simply invalid, and its invalidity can only become more obvious with the passage of time. Pro-ponents of racial preferences tell us that such preferences are meant to be only temporary, merely "transient," but they also tell us that they will clearly be necessary for a very long time—more than one or two generations—to counteract the effects of past mistreatment.

But slavery ended over 100 years ago; state-imposed segregation was practiced primarily in the South, and ended even there about fifteen years ago; the constitutional prohibition of racial discrimination is now a quarter of a century old, and statutory prohibitions (*e.g.*, the 1964 Civil Rights Act) are more than a decade old. The argument is further weakened by the ever more obvious fact that persons of Chinese and Japanese descent, easily distinguishable racially and among the most disadvantaged and discriminated against in our history, also are among those least in need of preferential treatment in higher education.

At some point, additional explanations for racial and ethnic preferences will be required; indeed, additional explanations are being sought and offered even now, as the increased interest in questions of innate racial differences shows. Perhaps the greatest value of an official policy of governmental neutrality in regard to race is that it makes questions of possible differences in innate racial characteristics irrelevant and makes concern with any such differences, in discussions of law, almost inherently improper and offensive. An explicit policy of racial discrimination, however, makes such concerns and inquiries relevant and inevitable.

Finally, racial preferences in higher education cannot be justified as compensation for past unfair disadvantages. First, as already noted, not all and not only members of the preferred groups have suffered such disadvantages. Second, preferential admission to institutions of higher learning is an inappropriate means of compensation in any event. It places the burden of compensation not on society as a whole, but on the more qualified persons who are denied admission even though they are not responsible for the supposed disadvantage being compensated for and even though they may be disadvantaged themselves. Further, it places members of the preferred racial and ethnic groups into competition with clearly more qualified whites, which can serve only to reinforce unfavorable stereotypes and lead to frustration and resentment.

As Carl Cohen predicted, a program of racially preferential admissions tends to corrupt all it touches.[17] The program generally is implemented as surreptitiously as possible; publicity to the general public and to state legislators and other officials is avoided. The program is typically misrepresented as being one, not for certain racial or ethnic groups as such, but for the "culturally deprived," and it is usually justified as necessary to correct a "cultural bias" in the standard admission criteria that is known not to exist. A racially preferential admissions policy almost inevitably leads to demands for and the practice of racially preferential grading. Students admitted at such cost in principle can hardly be permitted to fail in large numbers. Professors who balk at personally practicing racial discrimination in grading can adopt a policy of simply failing no one or almost no one, thereby eroding educational standards generally. If the ordinary standards are not applicable to nonwhite students, they are easily found inapplicable to nonwhite applicants for faculty and administrative positions as well; "role models" and "diversity" are soon found to be important in these positions too. In the legal profession, however, an obstacle external to law schools sometimes exists—the difficult bar examination required in many states. When it was discovered that students admitted to and graduated from law schools on the basis of race failed these examinations in disproportionate numbers, as was to be expected, the cry arose that these tests, too, were "culturally biased" or were graded by examiners biased against nonwhites (even though the race of the test-taker is never stated on the test paper) and a campaign is now underway to have such examinations abolished. The final step, of course, is the institution and strict enforcement of "affirmative action" programs in employment, and we will then have as many nonwhite "doctors," "lawyers," "engineers," and so on, as may be desired.

One of the most serious harms resulting from the use of racial preference is that it casts doubt and aspersion upon the achievement of every member of the preferred racial and ethnic groups. My reaction to the news that the City University of New York recently has decided that Italian-Americans are members of a specially disadvantaged "minority" group entitled to preferential treatment was one of gratitude that I had been admitted to and graduated from City College (part of the City University system) before this policy went into effect. It is no answer that very few of the preferred individuals reject preferential treatment because of its unavoidable stigmatizing effect. It is easy to believe that it is better to be a suspect student or a suspect lawyer or doctor, say, than not to be admitted or not be a lawyer or doctor at all, especially since further preferential treatment may be expected. Many members of preferred groups who do not require preferential treatment do vigorously object to it. For example, the eminent economist, Thomas Sowell has written:

> What all the arguments and campaigns for quotas are really saying, loud and clear, is that *black people just don't have it*, and that they will have to be given something in order to have something. The devastating impact of this message on black people— particularly black young people—will outweigh any few extra jobs that may result from this strategy. Those black people who are already competent, and who could be instrumental in producing more competence among the rising generation, will be completely undermined, as black becomes synonymous—in the minds of black and white alike— with incompetence, and black achievement becomes synonymous with charity or pay-offs.[18]

Kenneth P. Clark, another black and an eminent educational psychologist, has argued:

> Racism emerges in both blatant and in more difficult to answer, subtle, manifestations. In the academic community, it began to be clear in the 1960's that apparently sophisticated and compassionate theories used to explain slow Negro student performance might themselves be tainted with racist condescension. Some of the theories of "cultural deprivation," "the disadvantaged," and the like, until recently popular in educational circles and in high governmental spheres, and still prevalent in fact, were backed for the most part by inconclusive and fragmentary research and much speculation. The eagerness with which such theories were greeted was itself a subtly racist symptom. The theories obscured this orientation, but when challenged, some of their advocates posed more overt racist formulations.[19]

Further, to admit a student to an institution of higher education on the basis of his race for the purpose of increasing his race's "representation" in the school is to make him an officially recognized representative of his race and, thereby, to place burdens upon him and other members of his race that neither he nor they should be required to bear. As a preferentially admitted black law school graduate wrote:

> There were seventeen black students in my law school class, and we were all scared; perhaps more than the white students. Traditionally, first-year law students are supposed to be afraid, or at least awed; but our fear was compounded by the uncommunicated realization that perhaps we were not authentic law students and the uneasy suspicion that our classmates knew that we were not, and, like certain members of the faculty, had developed paternalistic attitudes toward us. The silence, the heavy sense of expectation, fell on all of the blacks in a classroom whenever one of us was called upon for an answer. We waited, with the class, for the chosen man to justify the right of all of us to be there.[20]

The losses from and dangers of racially preferential admissions seem so great and the reasons offered in support so clearly invalid or insubstantial that it is difficult to see the issue as other than one-sided. But why then do so many well-meaning and intelligent people favor racially preferential admissions? I am forced to speculate that some factor or factors must be operating that proponents of racial preferences have failed to express. Perhaps it is a factor noted by Max Lerner[21] that may be called "historical momentum." For over two decades we have had a magnificent, exhilarating, and enormously successful crusade to end all forms of state-imposed racial discrimination. There is, I think, an understandable reluctance to see such a crusade come to an end merely because it has attained its announced objective. Success beyond all expectation can more easily lead to a search for new conquests than to total satisfaction. The battle for black equality under law was an apparently unambiguous struggle between good and evil; one could define and establish one's decency and humanity and give significance to one's life by joining it. When and where will such an opportunity present itself again?

Another possible explanation for the position of proponents of racial preferences in higher education is that in their heart of hearts, or perhaps even subconsciously, they believe or fear, as Thomas Sowell and Kenneth Clark have noted, that blacks are not and cannot become able to compete with whites on equal terms. Finding this belief unacceptable, devoutly wishing it not to be so, they finally determine to support their wish with the force of law. If large numbers of black doctors and lawyers, for example, cannot be had on the basis of performance and ability, let them be had by legal fiat.

Conclusion

To say that the use of racial and ethnic preferences in higher education is indefensible and likely to prove socially destructive is not to say, however, that the Supreme Court should hold it unconstitutional. These are, or should be, two very different questions. This raises the central question of constitutional law: What, if anything, justifies the Supreme Court in holding a law or other official action unconstitutional? I do not doubt that the framers and ratifiers of the fourteenth amendment did not imagine that it would prohibit good faith efforts to improve the condition of blacks or other minority racial groups. But this argument proves too much. It is equally clear that the fourteenth amendment was not intended to prohibit school segregation either. What justified the *Brown* decision, I would argue, is the wide acceptance and enormous persuasiveness of the principles that no person should be disadvantaged by government because of his race. But this principle, of course, equally prohibits the use of racial preferences intended to benefit blacks and other racial minorities, and, as I have argued, to qualify the principle is effectively to destroy it. The Court would, therefore, be most justified in acting to preserve the principle in full force, at least where no better reason to permit its violation appears than the reasons offered by proponents of racial preferences in higher education.

The Supreme Court would also be justified in striking down racial preferences as unconstitutional because the present widespread use of such preferences is largely attributable to the Court itself; the Court would, in effect, be partially correcting its own mistake. The use of racial preferences in higher education is simply a part or outgrowth of what is euphemistically referred to as "affirmative action," that is, the use of racial discrimination to increase racial integration in the name of prohibiting or combatting racial discrimination. This idea was introduced into constitutional law by the Surpeme Court in the *Green*[22] case in 1968, and it came to full flower in the *Swann*[23] case in 1971. In these cases the Court held, in effect, that racial discrimination was constitutionally required when necessary to increase school racial integration. That this requirement is indefensible is perhaps best illustrated by the fact that the Court has never admitted that there was such a requirement and has never attempted to defend it on its own merits. The Court instead has consistently maintained that the requirement was, not integration for its own sake, but only "desegregation," the undoing of only that racial separation shown to be the effect of past racial discrimination.[24] Nonetheless, it is these decisions that have led to and have been used to justify the use of racial preferences in public higher education. If the fourteenth amendment could *require* racial discrimination to increase racial integration (albeit in the name of "desegregation") in grade schools, as in *Green* and *Swann*—to the extent of requiring that children be bused out of their neighborhoods and away from their neighborhood schools because of their race— surely it would at least *permit* such discrimination in admission to higher education. The pernicious idea of racial preferences in higher education almost surely would not have arisen or gained a foothold except for the Supreme Court's apparent approval and encouragement (indeed, in grade schools, requirement) of racial discrimination to increase integration. It is, therefore, peculiarly appropriate that the Supreme Court should lay the idea to rest.

Notes

1. Brown v. Board of Educ., 347 U.S. 483 (1954).

2. *See, e.g.,* Gayle v. Browder, 352 U.S. 903 (1956) (buses); Holmes v. Atlanta, 350 U.S. 879 (1955) (municipal gold courses); Mayor of Baltimore v. Dawson, 350 U.S. 877 (1955) (public beaches and bath houses).

3. 49A LANDMARK BRIEFS AND ARGUMENTS OF THE SUPREME COURT OF THE UNITED STATES: CONSTITUTIONAL LAW 1154 (P. Kurland & G. Casper eds. 1975) (Brown v. Board of Educ., 347 U.S. 483 (1954)).

4. 110 CONG. REC. 6552 (1964) (remarks of Sen. Humphrey).

5. DeFunis v. Odegaard, 416 U.S. 312 (1974).

6. Bakke v. Regents of the Univ. of Cal., 18 Cal. 3d 34, 553 P.2d 1152, 132 Cal. Rptr. 680 (1976), *cert granted,* 429 U.S. 1090 (1977) (No. 76-811, 1976 Term).

7. Cohen, *Race and the Constitution,* THE NATION, Feb. 8, 1975, at 16-17.

8. Brief of the Anti-Defamation League of B'nai B'rith *Amicus Curiae* at 16, DeFunis v. Odegaard, 416 U.S. 312 (1974).

9. See Bittker, *The Case of the Checker-board Ordinance: An Experiment in Race Relations,* 71 YALE L.J. 1387 (1962); Kaplan, *Segregation Litigation and the Schools—Part II: The General Northern Problem,* 58 Nw. U.L. REV. 15 (1963).

10. Brief for Petitioner at 32, Regents of the Univ. of Cal. v. Bakke, *cert. granted,* 429 U.S. 1090 (No. 76-811, 1976 Term). The other asserted benefits are "countering the effects of educational deprivation and societal discrimination, and obtaining the educational and societal benefits that flow from racial and ethnic diversity in a medical school student body." *Id.* at 32. Other benefits mentioned are "increasing aspirations among minorities" to become doctors, and destroying "pernicious stereotypes" that it is not proper for "minorities" to become doctors. *Id.* at 32-33.

11. *See* Posner, *The DeFunis Case and the Constitutionality of Preferential Treatment of Racial Minorities,* 1974 SUP. CT. REV. 1, 7 (if inaccuracy of standard predictors were the justification, the case would not be "one of preferential treatment at all").

12. *See, e.g.,* Brief *Amicus Curiae* for the Association of American Law Schools in Support of Petitioner at 13, Regents of the Univ. of Cal. v. Bakke, *cert. granted,* 429 U.S. 1090 (1976) (No. 76-811, 1976 Term): "We know . . . that the [Law School Admission Test] is not racially biased. Five separate studies have indicated that the test does not underpredict the law school performance of blacks and Mexican-Americans."

13. N. GLAZER, AFFIRMATIVE DISCRIMINATION: ETHNIC INEQUALITY AND PUBLIC POLICY (1975).

14. Bakke v. Regents of the Univ. of Cal., 18 Cal. 3d 34, 42-44, 553 P.2d 1152, 1158-59, 132 Cal. Rptr. 680, 686-87, (1976).

15. *See, e.g.,* Armor, *The Evidence on Busing,* 28 PUB. INTEREST 90, 101-02 (1972).

16. In the legal profession, for example, both a justice of the United States Supreme Court (Thurgood Marshall) and the Solicitor General of the United States (Wade McCree) are black. No person of Italian descent, for example, has ever occupied either position.

17. *See generally* Graglia, *Special Admission of the "Culturally Deprived" to Law School,* 119 U. PA. L. REV. 351 (1970).

18. T. SOWELL, BLACK EDUCATION—MYTHS AND TRAGEDIES 292 (1972) (emphasis in original).

19. Clark, *The Social Scientists, The Brown Decision,* and *Contemporary Confusion,* in ARGUMENT xxxi, xli (L. Friedman ed. 1969).

20. McPherson, *The Black Law Student: A Problem of Fidelities*, ATLANTIC, April 1970, at 99.

21. *See* LERNER, *Four Ways of Looking At the Court—And a Fifth, infra.*

22. Green v. County School Bd., 391 U.S. 430 (1968).

23. Swann v. Charlotte-Mecklenburg Bd. of Educ., 402 U.S. 1 (1971).

24. *See* L. GRAGLIA, DISASTER BY DECREE: THE SUPREME COURT DECISIONS ON RACE AND THE SCHOOLS (1976).

Affirmative Action: A Plea For A Rectification Principle
By Charles B. Renfrew

More than twenty years ago, in *Brown v. Board of Education*,[1] the Supreme Court provided the impetus for ending racial discrimination in public schools. Since that time, university officials have embarked upon novel courses of action designed to implement that goal. Ironically, the Supreme Court must now decide whether the Constitution necessarily inhibits efforts specifically designed to increase minority participation in higher education. The mootness decision in *DeFunis v. Odegaard*[2] forestalled a resolution of the preferential admissions controversy, but the opinion reflected the Court's belief that the issue was likely to be presented again quickly. "If the admissions procedures of the law school remain unchanged, there is no reason to suppose that a subsequent case attacking those procedures will not come with relative speed to this Court, now that the Supreme Court of Washington has spoken."[3] The Court referred directly only to the admissions policies at the University of Washington which Marco DeFunis challenged. Yet, given the prevalence of preferential minority admissions programs in state universities nationwide, the statement carried much broader predictive significance. The Supreme Court's recent decision to review the determination of the California Supreme Court in *Bakke v. Regents of the University of California*[4] means that a decision on the merits is likely.

The magnitude of the issue, coupled with the certainty of its imminent reassertion after the *DeFunis* decision, prompted widespread discussion in the legal community. In law review articles and in *amicus curiae* briefs submitted in connection with the cases, many of our most eminent scholars have addressed the central social, political and constitutional questions which this issue poses. Are racial classifications,[5] whatever their motivation and whoever their beneficiaries, necessarily so pernicious as to be constitutionally untenable? The question evades easy resolution. One can advance cogent arguments, buttressed by an impressive array of case analysis and significant socio-political or economic theory, both for and against the reverse discrimination inherent in preferential minority admissions. There is simply no sharp line which separates the permissible from the impermissible in this context, and thus I cannot offer any firm or certain conclusions. I would, however, like to share some of the concerns which dominate my thinking on the subject and offer a possible approach which focuses more sharply upon the circumstances in which preferential treatment is afforded.

I begin with the assumption that the primary purpose of preferential minority admissions programs in graduate schools is to increase significantly the number of minority persons in the various professions, rather than to afford greater access to education to the culturally and economically deprived or to enrich the educational experience of all students at a particular institution.[6] In short, although greater cultural and economic heterogeneity within student bodies may be a valuable by-product of increased minority admissions, the

* © 1977 by Charles B. Renfrew, United States District Judge for the Northern District of California. I wish to express my gratitude to my law clerk, Jane E. Genster, for her invaluable assistance in the preparation of this article.

immediate goal is racial and ethnic diversity in the professions. Thus, the classification is based upon race and/or national origin and, I think, necessarily so. Weighting admissions programs in favor of minorities is the only available method practically adapted to achieve this goal within the next several generations.[7] Finally, I accept the fact that preferential minority admissions do deprive members of the Caucasian majority of educational opportunities which they would have enjoyed, but for their race.

Under these circumstances, are preferential minority admissions ever constitutionally permissible? If so, are they equally justifiable regardless of the nature of the institution responsible for their creation? Finally, does the constitutionality of special admissions programs depend upon the ethnic or racial minority which they are designed to benefit?

The first question—the legality of reverse discrimination—has been the subject of voluminous commentary. Proponents of preferential admissions programs have generally advanced five interests to justify the policy: (1) fulfillment of legal obligations imposed by federal and state affirmative action programs, (2) correction of the discriminatory effects of traditional admissions criteria, (3) representation of a cross-section of society in institutions of higher learning,[8] (4) promotion of increased minority representation in the professions, and (5) correction of the effects of past discrimination.[9] Of these five potential interests, only the nexus of the fourth and fifth appears to me to be a strong enough basis for judicial validation of a flat racial or ethnic preference.

Reference to affirmative action obligations imposed by state or federal law cannot inform the constitutional question. Quite clearly, if a sufficient number of qualified minority professionals are not available to fill positions in the required percentages, the demands of affirmative action programs will have to be restructured to conform with the number of available professionals. Affirmative action goals must follow constitutional interpretation rather than dictate it.

Likewise, speculation about the possible discriminatory effect of traditional admissions criteria, particularly standardized tests, is not a convincing rationale for the programs. Professor Posner is surely correct in stating that if the examinations were proven inaccurate as predictors of educational success with respect to disadvantaged minorities, the issue would not be one of preferential treatment at all.[10]

Finally, the concept that a racial classification becomes permissible if it accords with a university's or court's sense of a healthy and interesting racial, ethnic, and cultural blend is unprincipled. The diversity of experience may enrich education, but it is not clear that the constitutionality of racial classifications can vary with the proclaimed goals of any institution. The chief goal of a manufacturing plant is productivity. Yet it is fatuous to suggest that an employer who hired only men because he strongly believed that the presence of women impedes productivity would pass muster under Title VII of the Civil Rights Act,[11] or that a public employer who hired exclusively members of one race to forestall the distractions generated by perceived racial tensions would receive constitutional approval. Moreover, defining certain goals as constitutionally protected and others as legally suspect would serve only to insure that the permissible goals would be advanced by any challenged institution. The difficulty of proving the motivation which actually inspired any given program would be insurmountable.

It is rather the fact of minimal minority representation in the professions coupled with a history of past discrimination which sets reverse discrimination apart from other racial classifications. If preferential admissions policies are constitutionally permissible, the justification must necessarily be that a minority's current underrepresentation in a particular field can be said, with some certainty, to be the result of a pervasive and longterm pattern of de jure discrimination by the Caucasian majority.

Those who argue that preferential admissions are constitutionally impermissible frequently emphasize the importance of developing and adhering to neutral principles applicable to all racial and ethnic classifications, regardless of the group identity of the beneficiary and victim. Professor Posner's contention that "the distribution of benefits and costs by government on racial or ethnic grounds is impermissible"[12] is the clearest example of this approach.

The value of racially neutral principles, in securing both the appearance and actuality of justice, can hardly be denied. Their value can, however, be overstated. Were we, in the Rawlsian fashion, to step behind the veil of ignorance and formulate governing principles for a newly organized society,[13] I have no reason to doubt that we would choose a racially neutral principle such as Professor Posner suggests. And were a society to evolve according to such a principle, justifying deviation from it at any future point would be exceedingly difficult.

Racially neutral principles seem to promise justice when adopted by a society without a past. Yet they guarantee no more than the appearance of justice when elected by an existing society without regard to its past. If the current distribution of societal advantages has been shaped to a significant extent by past inequities toward a particular racial or ethnic minority, the imposition of Posner's principle will prolong the effects of the historical discrimination and thus further hinder the disadvantaged group. Under these circumstances, it would appear that the only just legal principle is one designed to compensate for unrectified historical wrongs.[14] It is one I call the rectification principle.[15]

Assuming momentarily that a case for reparations can be made by various minority groups, the first question is whether either the equal protection clause of the fourteenth amendment, or the case law interpreting it, poses an absolute barrier to the use of such a principle in the context of preferential admissions. The language of section 1 of the fourteenth amendment is straightforward: "No State Shall . . . deny to any person within its jurisdiction the equal protection of the laws." Despite the fact that the amendment was principally directed at remedying the legal inequalities that accompanied slavery, the congressional debate on bills which preceded the fourteenth amendment and on the fourteenth amendment itself suggests the legislators' awareness of the scope of the clause, and its possible application to persons other than freedmen and, indeed, other minorities.[16] Yet, given the context of the times, it is not surprising that the legislative history offers little assistance in addressing the issue of preferential minority admissions. It is difficult to believe that mid-nineteenth century congressmen gave any serious consideration to the possibility that minorities might some day be the beneficiaries of favorable discrimination at the expense of the white majority. Thus, the legislative history contains no blueprint for meeting a situation in which the prohibitive language of the amendment conflicts with its ameliorative purpose.

Alexander Bickel's painstaking study of the legislative history led him to conclude that the amendment's framers, aware that they were formulating a constitution, intentionally chose "language capable of growth," "whose future effect was left to future determination."[17] He suggested, although in a different context, that "the record of history, properly understood [leaves] the way open to, in fact invite[s], a decision based on the moral and material state of the nation [at the present time], not 1866."[18] Thus, the legislators of the past seem to direct us to the evolved wisdom of the present to resolve modern fourteenth amendment controversies.

A study of equal protection precedent regarding race suggests that the fourteenth amendment can accommodate a rectification principle, although that message is not unqualified. The fourteenth admendment guarantee of equal protection is a personal right,[19] "universal in [its] application, to all persons . . . without regard to any differences of race, of color, or of nationality. . . ."[20] Classifications based upon race have become the paradigm of suspect classifications, and when subjected to strict scrutiny have been found constitutionally impermissible. The Supreme Court so found in *McLaughlin v. Florida*:[21]

> [W]e deal here with a classification based upon the race of the participants, which must be viewed in light of the historical fact that the central purpose of the Fourteenth Amendment was to eliminate racial discrimination emanating from official sources in the States. This strong policy renders racial classifications "constitutionally suspect," . . . and subject to the "most rigid scrutiny," . . . and "in most circumstances irrelevant" to any constitutionally acceptable legislative purpose.[22]

Whether strict scrutiny is the appropriate standard of review for discrimination which favors rather than hinders minorities has been the subject of extensive debate. Strict scrutiny *is* a standard of review—a formula designed by the judiciary to ensure the fulfillment of the equal protection clause guarantee—rather than a constitutional mandate itself. It is rooted in the judiciary's special solicitude for discrete, historically disadvantaged minority groups to whom the political process can be expected to be, and has in fact been, unresponsive.[23] This fact suggests that the propriety of strict scrutiny depends upon a showing of majority action which victimizes a minority, and has prompted some to contend that the catalyst for extraordinary judicial review is lacking when majority action hinders the majority, as in the preferential admissions context.[24]

The argument is a strong one, recommended by the traditional notion of separation of powers and, to some extent, by the Supreme Court's recent decision in *United Jewish Organizations of Williamsburgh, Inc. v. Carey*.[25] Given the profound intellectual ambivalence which the issue creates, and the societal values which compete for recognition in this context, the resolution of the controversy will undoubtedly entail some consideration of a societal ideal and a balancing of the respective veils of color-consciousness and color-blindness toward its attainment. Such a decision is more appropriately relegated in the first instance to the legislature than to the courts:

> When such choices must be made, the effort ought to be to draw from the legislature, as the most broadly representative, politically responsible institution of government, a focused judgment about the appropriate balance to be struck between competing values. Once the legislature has made such a judgment, courts ought to be extremely hesitant to uspset it, for if the values to which law gives expression are to change over time, the legislature's warrant for making the necessary decisions is a good deal stronger than that of the courts.[26]

However persuasive this argument might be, it is largely irrelevant to the issue of preferential admissions as it has been presented to the courts.[27] The admissions practices in question are not the product of legislative deliberation and enactment, but rather the formulations of more insulated groups of university officials.[28] University officials may design admission policies under authority properly delegated to them by state legislatures, and thus, in law and in theory, many such policies may be labelled legislative judgments. Yet, if greater judicial deference is owed a legislative decision to discriminate against the majority than a similar decision to discriminate against a minority, that deference must stem from the fact, rather than the fiction, of the broad-based fact-finding, debate, and publicity which would presumably precede such a legislative decision.

One might decide that a majority which chooses through the representative political process to discriminate against itself is constitutionally entititled to do so.[29] Yet I find no convincing support for the proposition that a state-imposed racial classification, even if it does represent the considered judgment of the majority whom it injures, is entitled to a presumption of constitutionality. Others can debate whether such a classification must be "necessary to promote a *compelling* governmental interest"[30] or "must serve important governmental objectives and must be substantially related to achievement of those objectives."[31] For purposes of this discussion, I will assume that the standard of review is strict scrutiny.

Not since *Hirabayashi v. United States*[32] and *Korematsu v. United States*[33] has the Supreme Court permitted the use of racial classification, except to remedy prior illegal discrimination. This prior discrimination exception exposes the contradiction in the law as applied to the preferential admissions controversy, and may lay the foundation for the development of a broader rectification principle. Despite the fact that equal protection is an individual rather than a group right, the federal courts have in the past temporarily subjugated personal interests to group interests to rectify racial injustice. However suspect racial classifications may be, the courts have frequently sanctioned and in fact have required the use of race-conscious remedies to redress past discrimination.[34] The courts have moved cautiously in this area, acutely aware of the thorny problems of reverse discrimination which racial preferences and quotas entail. They have universally required a showing of a discriminatory status quo, *i.e.*, a demonstration of present disparate minority representation in a field which is reasonably believed to stem from past illegal discrimination. But the precedent for relief based upon such a showing is open-ended.

Those who would restrict the precedent set by race-conscious remedies frequently characterize their use as a carefully circumscribed response to specific, past, proven discrimination. From this characterization flows the contention that preferential admissions are justifiable only for a university proven guilty of past discrimination, and only in favor of the minorities against whom that particular school has discriminated. Given the operation of the judicial system, the courts' prescription of race-conscious remedies tends to be triggered by a finding of illegal discrimination on the part of a defendant and tailored to correspond to the extent and degree of the illegality. Yet, this does not describe the outer ambit of judicial validation of remedial racial preferences. Courts have, for example, upheld employment quotas imposed by state and federal contracting requirements, not upon a demonstration of past discriminatory practices by particular, challenged defendants, but instead upon a general showing by the government that an industry is racially imbalanced and that the imbalance stemmed from past, broad-based discrimination.[35] Therefore, general approval for preferential admissions programs following proof that academia has widely discriminated against identifiable minority groups is not such a novel step.

Similarly, the present accepted remedial response is often described as narrowly formulated to benefit only proven victims of discrimination rather than their children and their children's children. This description is followed by the argument that preferential admissions deviate from past remedial practices in benefiting groups rather than individuals. Courts have indeed expressed concern that the boundaries of relief be restrictively drawn and, where the facts of the case permit, prescribed preferential treatment only for those proven injured.[36] But surely relief which consists of a hiring quota for a given period of time carries a broader, more general preference, extending beyond those individuals who actually suffered discrimination at the hands of a defendant to a gross, group preference[37]—much like that afforded by preferential minority admissions programs.

One could continue to point out the limitations of each potential basis for distinguishing race-conscious remedies presently used by the courts from racially perferential admissions policies. Exhausting the list would, I believe, ultimately demonstrate only that the cases offer no dispositive ground for rejecting as a matter of constitutional doctrine the use of a rectification principle in university admissions. The dangers of and motivation for the two forms of race-consciousness are identical. The evils of racially based remedies are, in substance, the same as those of preferential admissions: At some point, for some segment of affected individuals, race becomes the definitive factor. The catalyst for the imposed remedies and the rectification principle is likewise the same: A minority's minimal representation in a particular field is reasonably believed to result from racial discrimination. And, in the final analysis, the justification is the same: In the absence of an extraordinary societal response, a status quo derived from race discrimination is most likely to be reinforced and prolonged.

The hesitation to read past precedent to permit preferential minority admissions programs stems, in large part, from the seemingly boundless nature of the license to classify upon racial and ethnic grounds to which affirmation might extend. Many have expressed the fear that, once given judicial approval, such preferences could be extended for an indeterminate period of time to innumerable racial and ethnic groups. Such concerns are not entirely baseless. In addition to special programs for blacks, Spanish-surnamed, American Orientals, and American Indians, the Office of Federal Contract Compliance Program has set up outreach and positive recruitment programs for individuals of Eastern, Middle, and Southern European ancestry, such as Jews, Catholics, Italians, Greeks and Slavs.[38] While these programs deal with employment matters, there is every reason to believe that any group, once it has received special benefits because of its particular ethnic identity, will obtain, or seek to obtain, special preference in other areas such as education if some type of statistical parity program is adopted as the touchstone. The potential scope and duration of preferential admissions programs does set them apart from most of the remedies adopted by the courts to date. If validated by the Supreme Court, the programs would undoubtedly be maintained by many schools which presently operate under them and perhaps instituted by some which presently have no such program. Moreover, their cessation is more likely to depend upon the diminution of public support for their continuance, than upon the expiration of a court order.

However, judicial affirmance of a rectification principle in the context of preferential admissions would entail some clear theoretical limits. The principle of reparations gives no carte blanche to preferential admissions, but is grounded upon the basic premise of remedial case law: "[W]hile quotas merely to attain racial balance are forbidden, quotas to correct past discriminatory practices are not."[39] The rectification principle does not authorize a grand scheme of social engineering which proceeds blindly toward the goal of statistical parity in the professions. Nor does it ignore the fact that various racial, ethnic, and cultural groups may value some occupations more highly than others, and freely orient themselves professionally consistent with those priorities. Nor does it assume that minimal representation necessarily stems from pervasive discrimination, without considering the practical, expected difficulties posed by recent immigration, cultural disorientation, and language barriers.

Proponents of preferential admissions programs ordinarily refer to "minorities," without distinguishing among the various groups. *Yet minortity status, standing alone, is insufficient to justify preferences under the legal theory which I have advanced. In order to invoke a rectification principle, minority status must be paired with a history of pervasive discrimination by the majority. Finally, minority status and past discrimination are not sufficient conditions. In order to justify racially conscious remedies, it must be satisfactorily proven that the effect of the discrimination is an underrepresentation in a particular field; that is, there must be a demonstrable current social problem caused by historical injustice.*

The rationale of the rectification principle poses a problem rarely addressed by legal thinkers. Our national history not only evinces discrimination of varying nature and degree against a series of minority groups, but also suggests that the lingering effects of such injustice differ with respect to the various groups. Although the quantum relationship between past discriminatory practice and present group status cannot be estimated with any certainty, an extensive link is clear in some cases. More than a century ago, Alexis de Tocqueville recorded the existence of "three races" in the United States—the European, the Indian, and the Negro.[40] Today, we could probably gain general societal agreement that the discriminatory behavior of the white majority is quite directly responsible for the disadvantaged position of the American Indian and the American Black. The historical basis for this societal perception requires little elaboration.

De Tocqueville commented only briefly upon the plight of the American Indian: "The Indians will perish in the same isolated condition in which they have lived. . . ."[41] Although isolation has not been the goal of modern governmental policy toward the Indians, the treatment afforded the American Indian by the white majority has resulted in their continuing seclusion from the mainstream of American life. The conduct of the white majority was early characterized by extremes: The plunder and fragmentation of Indian society by early European settlers was followed by the federal government's announced broad solicitude for the tribes' future, a paternalism not without its opportunism. The majority's behavior has since been characterized by ambivalence: Governmental policy has wavered between the goal of cultural integrity and autonomy for the Indian and the goal of cultural assimilation. Whatever the wisdom or benefits of these approaches, they have not notably advanced the end of social equality for the American Indian.

The history of Black Americans is one with which we are all painfully familiar—a people whose very presence on the continent resulted from physical brutality and coercion, who first experienced life in this country as slaves, whose emancipation fostered the thirteenth and fourteenth amendments, and whose continuing battle for social equality has been the mainstay of equal protection litigation ever since. De Tocqueville commented that "slavery recedes, but the prejudice to which it has given birth is immovable."[42] While his vision has not proved fully accurate, it long remained more correct than any of us can comfortably admit. We do not and cannot know precisely how the distribution of societal advantages between blacks and whites might differ if blacks had been able to and had chosen to immigrate to the United States as free persons, or had de jure racial prejudice proved amenable to rapid extinction. But we know that the composition of our professions would be very different and, for that reason, the moral responsibility of the white majority vis-a-vis the blacks seems clear.

The history of extensive and long-lived de jure discrimination distinguishes those minorities from all others in the United States. Once we move beyond those minorities whose inferior status was governmentally approved, it becomes increasingly difficult—if not impossible—to estimate our historic debt. Can we determine with any precision the degree of past discrimination necessary to justify national remedial action? The difficulty of this inquiry is illustrated by reference to the Spanish-surnamed Americans. How do we evaluate the claim of this group to preferential treatment, in light of the more regionalized, less pervasive, but clearly discernible prejudice which they have suffered?

The fact of such prejudice is undisputed. Yet has it been the pervasive de jure and nationwide discrimination suffered by blacks and native Americans? The greater number of these Americans either came to this country voluntarily or are the descendants of those who did. What effect does this have when contrasted with the experience of blacks and native Americans? How do we rationally justify a difference in the treatment given an immigrant from Cuba from that given an immigrant from India? The definition of Spanish surname or Hispanic given by the EEOC is also broader than the class of persons who may have suffered any prejudice. Hispanic is defined as "all persons of Mexican, Puerto Rican, Cuban, Central or South American, or other Spanish culture or origin, regardless of race."[43] Should a

Portuguese immigrant receive less favorable consideration than one from Spain simply because of the difference in national origin? This is not to say that there may not be, indeed should be, programs giving recognition to persons from culturally or economically deprived backgrounds, but participation in such programs should not be restricted by race or national origin.

The task of calculating the impact of discrimination against any group other than American Indians and blacks is likewise elusive. Focusing upon the professional achievements of Asian Americans may help to illustrate the problems of this sort of assessment. It is indisputable that during the late nineteenth century the Chinese suffered widespread discrimination in the western United States. It is often pointed out that Chinese Americans are minimally represented in the legal profession in this country. Yet is it clear that the relatively small number of Chinese attorneys results from majority prejudice? Chinese culture has traditionally respected very little the legal profession and has stressed achievement in the sciences. Given the much greater number of Chinese Americans in the fields of medicine and engineering in this country, it may be that the group's representation in the two professions is a result of cultural background and choice, rather than a product of past discrimination. If this is the case, the conditions of the rectification principle cannot be met. Past discrimination without lingering pronounced social effects does not stimulate a remedial response.

Fairly analyzed, a rectification principle imposes a rather heavy burden upon the group which claims entitlement to its benefits. Because no other group can cite a history of de jure discrimination of similar magnitude, nor claim comparably egregious results, a national rectification principle must perhaps, fairly and logically, be limited to American Indians and blacks. Such a restriction admittedly cleaves a distinction which ignores some unsavory American history. But law making consists largely of line drawing, and the threshold for judicial affirmance of racial preferences is a very high one. Objectively viewed, a rectification principle is not a panacea for the social problems created or exacerbated by limited minority representation in the professions. The Supreme Court may in its wisdom decide that the questions posed by *Bakke* are more appropriately answered by resort to a different legal theory. Congress may perhaps decide that the social ills caused by economic and educational disparity among various ethnic and racial groups require a broader, more inclusive response. However, if the standard of review is strict scrutiny and the justification is past majority injustice with marked continued effects, the license for preferential minority admissions may be less expansive than those who support the university policies have previously recognized.

Notes

1. 347 U.S. 483 (1954).
2. 416 U.S. 312 (1974).
3. *Id.* at 319 (per curiam) (footnotes omitted).
4. 18 Cal. 3d 34, 553 P.2d 1152, 132 Cal. Rptr. 680 (1976), *cert. granted*, 429 U.S. 1090 (No. 76-811, 1976 Term).
5. While racially mixed ancestry may make difficult the racial determination of any individual, current EEOC definitions add to these difficulties. For example, "white," with the effect of exclusion from an affirmative action program, is defined as "[a]ll persons having origins in any of the original peoples of Europe, North Africa, the Middle East, or the Indian subcontinent." 41 Fed, Reg. 17,601, 17,602 (1976); 1 EMPL. PRAC. GUIDE (CCH) § 1710.

6. The structure and operations of the special admissions programs which have come to the courts' attention support this assumption. At the law school of the University of Washington at the time relevant to DeFunis' complaint, the special consideration afforded a portion of the applicants was triggered solely by an applicant's avowal that he or she was a member of one of four minority groups which the University believed warranted special attention—Black Americans, Chicano Americans, American Indians, and Phillippine Americans. DeFunis v. Odegaard, 82 Wash. 2d 11, 507 P.2d 1169, 1174, (1973). The question of cultural and economic disadvantage was irrelevant in the decision making process. 507 P.2d at 1198 (Hale, C.J., dissenting).

During the time period relevant to Bakke's complaint, the special admissions program at the medical school at the University of California at Davis purported to be open to individuals from economically or educationally disadvantaged backgrounds. Bakke v. Regents of the Univ. of Cal., 18 Cal. 3d 34, 40n.5, 553 P.2d 1152, 1156-57 n.5, 132 Cal. Rptr. 680, 684-85 n.5 (1976). In one respect, the program is less inclusive of minorities than the program utilized by the University of Washington; it excludes from special consideration a minority group member who cannot demonstrate disadvantage to the committee's satisfaction. At the same time, it is more inclusive of minorities in that it recognizes a broader range of minority groups. However, in operation, the special admissions program is certainly as exclusive of majority group members as that used by the University of Washington. Since the program began in 1969, no nonminority individual has ever been admitted under its auspices. Rather the trial court found, and the University did not challenge upon appeal to the state supreme court, that nonminority applicants were barred from participation in the special admissions program. *Id.* at 44, 553 P.2d at 1159, 132 Cal. Rptr. at 687.

In short, despite a disadvantaged background and the diversity which he or she might bring to the institution, the Appalachian Caucasian need not apply.

7. The July 25, 1977, San Francisco Chronicle reported that a study prepared by Franklin Evans, a researcher with the Education Testing Service in Princeton, New Jersey, concluded that if schools had followed a racially-blind admissions policy, only one in five black students admitted last fall would have been accepted.

Dissenting in *DeFunis*, Mr. Justice Douglas suggested that admissions of minority students could be adequately increased through a racially neutral selection process which afforded special consideration to culturally and/or economically disadvantaged students. DeFunis v. Odegaard, 416 U.S. 312, 320 *passim* (Douglas, J., dissenting). This seems unlikely. It has been estimated that in order to maintain a minority representation of 15-20%, an institution which shifted to a racially neutral admissions program for the disadvantaged would have to admit 40-50% of its students under this category. Sandalow, *Racial Preferences in Higher Education: Poltical Responsibility and the Judicial Role*, 42 U. Chi. L. Rev. 653, 690 n.113(1975). It is highly unlikely that the institutions could support the increased financial aid demands which such admissions would entail, and it is impossible to believe that the professions could benefit from the exclusion of those students best qualified under traditional criteria from such a large percentage of its places.

8. The goal of representation of a cross-section of a society in all institutions of higher learning too easily falls into the statistical parity described with unusual insight by Nathan Glazer in Affirmative Discrimination: Ethnic Inequality and Public Policy (1975). He pointed out that such a goal, despite its avowed good intentions, may cost more than it benefits. Not only does it promote ethnic and racial groupings, causing division and disharmony among races, but it replaces our concern for individual claims to consideration on the basis of justice and equity with a concern for rights for publicly determined and delimited racial and ethnic groups.

9. The conglomerate of interests served are summarized in O'Neil, *Racial Preference and Higher Education: The Larger Context*, 60 Va. L. Rev. 925, 942 (1974).

10. Posner, *The DeFunis Case and the Constitutionality of Preferential Treatment of Racial Minorities*, 1974 Sup. Ct. Rev. 1, 7.

11. 42 U.S.C. § 2000e *et seq.* (Supp. II, 1972).

12. Posner, *supra* note 10, at 22.

13. J. Rawls, A Theory of Justice (1971).

14. It is interesting to note that the conservative social philosopher Robert Nozick views the rectification of historical wrongs as a legitimate basis for the redistribution of holdings. *See* Nozick, *Distributive Justice*, 3 Phil. & Pub. Affairs 45, 48-49, 125-26 (1973). Nozick's theory of entitlement generally eschews Rawlsion redistribution to maximize the position of the least advantaged. Nozick notes, however, that the entitlement theory cannot be used "to condemn any particular scheme of transfer payments, unless it is clear that no considerations of rectification of injustice could apply to justify it." *Id.* at 126.

15. Support for this principle may be found in Morton v. Mancari, 417 U.S. 535 (1974), in which the Supreme Court held that the Indian preference provided by the Indian Reorganization Act of 1934 was not in violation of Title VII of the Civil Rights Act as extended to federal employees.

16. *See generally* Bickel, *The Original Understanding and the Segregation Decision*, 69 Harv. L. Rev. 1 (1955).

17. *Id.* at 63, 64.

18. *Id.* at 65.

19. Shelley v. Kraemer, 334 U.S. 1, 22 (1948).

20. Yick Wo v. Hopkins, 118 U.S. 356, 369 (1886).

21. 379 U.S. 184 (1964).

22. *Id.* at 191-92 (citations omitted).

23. *See e.g.,* United States v. Carolene Prod. Co., 304 U.S. 144, 152-53 n.4 (1938).

24. *See* Ely, *The Constitutionality of Reverse Racial Discrimination*, 41 U. Chi. L. Rev. 723 (1974).

25. 430 U.S. 144 (1977), especially the concurring opinion of Justice Brennan at 176.

26. Sandalow, *supra* note 7, at 700-01.

27. This point is similarly made by Sandalow, *id.* at 698.

28. It is questionable whether the nature of a university enables it to engage in vital public debates and evaluation concerning the implementation of preferential admissions programs. Experience in the late sixties points out that the university appears to be peculiarly vulnerable to pressure from aggressive special interest groups which seem to threaten its existence. *See* Hauser, *Political Actionism in the University*, 2 Daedalus 265 (1975).

29. It should be recognized that this formulation presents a series of questions which are more easily posed than answered. For instance, would legislation passed by a state be entitled to the same deference as legislation enacted by Congress pursuant to section 5 of the fourteenth amendment? If so, would not a state whose collective minority population exceeds that of its Caucasian population be barred from instituting preferential minority admissions? It has been estimated that it will be so in California by the middle 1980's. Is the majority upon which the theory focuses determined by the racial and ethnic backgrounds of the voters or of the legislators?

30. Dunn v. Blumstein, 405 U.S. 330, 342 (1972), *quoting* Shapiro v. Thompson, 394 U.S. 618, 634 (1969) (emphasis in original).

31. Craig v. Boren, 429 U.S. 190, 197 (1976).

32. 320 U.S. 81 (1943).

33. 323 U.S. 214 (1944).

34. *E.g.,* United Jewish Organizations of Williamsburgh, Inc. v. Carey, 430 U.S. 144 (1977) (remedial voting redistricting); Swann v. Charlotte-Mecklenberg Bd. of Educ., 402 U.S. 1 (1971) (school desegregation); United States v. Montgomery Bd. of Educ., 395 U.S. 225 (1969) (school desegregation); NAACP v. Allen, 493 F.2d 614 (5th Cir. 1974) (employment discrimination); Vulcan Soc'y of New York City Fire Dep't, Inc. v. Civil Serv. Comm'n, 490 F.2d 387 (2d Cir. 1973) (employment discrimination); Carter v. Gallagher, 452 F.2d 315 (8th Cir. 1971), *cert. denied,* 406 U.S. 950 (1972) (employment discrimination).

35. *E.g.,* Associated Gen. Contractors of Mass., Inc. v. Altschuler, 490 F.2d 9, 16-19 (1st Cir. 1973), *cert. denied,* 416 U.S. 957 (1974).

36. *See, e.g.,* Chance v. Board of Examiners, 534 F.2d 993, 998 (2d Cir. 1976); Kirkland v. New York State Dep't of Correctional Servs., 520 F.2d 420, 430 (2d Cir. 1975), *cert. denied,* 429 U.S. 823 (1976).

37. *See, e.g.,* Vulcan Soc'y of New York City Fire Dep't, Inc. v. Civil Serv. Comm'n, 490 F.2d 387, 398-99 (2d Cir. 1973).

38. 41 C.F.R. § 60-50.1 (b) (1976).

39. United States v. Wood, Wire & Metal Lathers Local 46, 471 F.2d 408, 413, and cases cited therein (2d Cir.), *cert. denied,* 412 U.S. 939 (1973).

40. A de Tocqueville, Democracy in America 370 (Vintage ed. 1945).

41. *Id.*

42. *Id.* at 373.

43. 41 Fed. Reg. 17,601, 17,602 (1976); 1 Empl. Prac. Guide (CCH) § 1710.

Minority Preferences
In
*Law School Admissions**
By Terrance Sandalow†

Introduction

In addressing the subject of "reverse discrimination," I want to caution at the outset against permitting the use of the word "discrimination" to prejudice consideration of the subject. "Discrimination" has, in recent years, become a bad word. It tends to be used as a shorthand for "unjustifiably unequal treatment." In its original and still proper meaning, however, the word is quite neutral. Discrimination merely means differentiation. It comes from a Latin word that means "to distinguish." Accordingly, when we discriminate—i.e., when we differentiate or distinguish—among people, the propriety of our action depends upon the reasons that we have acted as we have. If we wish to know whether an act of discrimination is proper, we must inquire whether the distinction we have made is consistent with our moral principles.

That is, of course, the question that the United States Supreme Court will be addressing in the *Bakke* case.[1] The question presented by that case is whether a professional school, in particular a medical school, is entitled to adopt an admission policy that discriminates in favor of the members of certain minority groups in order to increase the enrollment of those groups within the school's student body. The California Supreme Court has held that the program of the Davis Medical School was unconstitutional under the federal Constitution. Although it avoided a decision that race could never be taken into account in the admission process, it held that in this situation an adequate justification had not been made out by the university for doing so.

I do not want to address in any great detail what I think most people would call the legal issues that are presented by the *Bakke* case. They are difficult and complex, involving questions about the role of courts in our society, among other things,[2] and I simply cannot deal with all those issues adequately on this occasion. Instead, I want to discuss the social context within which the constitutionality of so-called "special admission" programs must be determined. I shall consider first the purposes that are served by the programs and, second, the reasons why the programs must exist if those purposes are to be achieved.

Now, though I have said that I am not going to address the legal issues, it must nevertheless be understood that I really am addressing the legal issues when I consider the purposes behind the programs, their importance, and the reasons why the programs are necessary if these purposes are to be achieved. For these "social" questions are almost certain

*This article is a revised and enlarged version of a paper delivered at the Southwestern University Law Review's First West Coast Conference on Constitutional Law on September 18, 1977. It is drawn in major part from the Association of American Law School's Brief *amicus curiae* in *The Regents of the University of California v. Bakke* which I co-authored with Professor David E. Feller and Dean Ernest Gellhorn.

†Dean and Professor of Law, The University of Michigan.

to prove determinative as the Supreme Court considers the legal issues. The Court has never held that race cannot ever be taken into account by governmental bodies making decisions of one sort or another. At most, it has said that when a racial criterion is used, the validity of that use must be judged under the strictest constitutional standard—a standard of strict scrutiny. To meet the test of strict scrutiny, the Court has told us, classification must be "necessary to serve a compelling governmental purpose."[3] My purpose in discussing the social context of "special admission" programs is to demonstrate that the programs meet that test.

I. The Objectives of "Special Admission" Programs

Preliminarily, we must recognize that the purposes served by "special admission" programs cannot be considered in isolation from the historical and social conditions that have created the need for the programs. The decisions of the Supreme Court—from *Dred Scott v. Sanford*[4] to *Strauder v. West Virginia*,[5] to *Brown v. Board of Education*[6] and beyond—amply record the efforts to exclude racial minorities from full participation in American life. Until very recently, racial minorities were almost entirely foreclosed from a role in the nation's public life, not only by excluding them from elective and appointive office in national, state, and local government but, in many sections of the country, by denying them the fundamental rights and obligations of citizenship, including the franchise and the opportunity to serve on grand and petit juries. Their children were required to attend segregated and generally inferior schools. They often received lower levels of governmental services than whites and some services were at times simply withheld from them. In the private sector, minorities fared no better. By custom, and occasionally by law, they were relegated to the least desirable employment, to jobs that paid substantially less than those open to whites and that offered neither an opportunity for advancement nor a chance to participate in the many important decisions made in the private sector. The housing available to them displayed a similar pattern. Life in the ghetto and the barrio not only deprived minorities of contact with the dominant society, it subjected them to crowding, inadequate public services, and often to housing that failed to meet the minimal standards of our society. The unpleasant but inescapable truth is that, the Constitution notwithstanding, there existed in the United States a virtual caste system.

The legacy of that history is the reality we now confront. Despite the important beginnings that have been made since enactment of the Civil Rights Act of 1964, racial minorities are not—and are not close to being—full participants in American life. By every social indicator they continue to constitute an underclass in our society. Their income, life expectancies, and educational attainments are lower than those of whites. They are disproportionately the victims and the perpetrators of crime. Finally, and of more immediate concern for the *Bakke* case, racial minorities constitute approximately 17% of the total population but, as of the 1970 census, barely more than 1.9% of the membership of the bar.[7]

The nation is now committed to eliminating this legacy of racism. We have undertaken to remove the vestiges of caste from our society, not only by improving the conditions of life among historically disadvantaged minorities, but also by creating a racially integrated society. The question presented in *Bakke* is whether, now that we have made that commitment, the Constitution should be construed to forbid measures that are essential to its performance.

Any effort to achieve racial equality must, if it is to succeed, begin with an awareness that, in the United States today, race is a socially significant characteristic. Race, in other words, is not merely a superficial aspect of "deeper" social problems such as poverty or inadequate education. It is integral to those problems. Many Americans, but especially those who are members of the groups that are the immediate beneficiaries of special admission programs, live in communities and belong to organizations that are defined in racial and ethnic terms. The direction of their loyalties and their sympathies are significantly determined by their racial and ethnic identifications. Whether, or to what extent, that is desirable is currently the subject of much debate. Such identification may, as some contend, lead only to divisiveness. Or, as others maintain, it may foster a sense of belonging and a pride in cultural origins. But whether it is good or bad, it is a reality with which law and the institutions of American life must contend.

In these circumstances, the question whether racial minorities are substantially represented in law school classes and at the bar assumes crucial importance. Gross underrepresentation of these groups has consequences quite different from those that would result from, say, gross underrepresentation of persons with one blue and one green eye. Individuals who share that characteristic have not historically been segregated by our society, nor otherwise subjected to generations of invidious discrimination. Governmental decisions do not affect them differently than they affect other persons and, conversely, their views on issues of public policy are likely to be distributed in the same way as in the general population. In each of these respects individuals who share only a socially irrelevant characteristic differ from the members of racial minorities. And, it is precisely because of these differences that gross underrepresentation of the latter in law schools and at the bar is a pressing social problem.

A. *The Need For More Minority Lawyers*

The most important reason for special admissions programs in the law schools is, quite simply, that there is a critical need for more minority lawyers. The 1970 census, as noted above, reported that racial minorities, which constitute approximately 17% of the population, represented barely more than 1.9% of the bar. However dramatic, this gross statistic does not begin to convey the desperate shortage of minority lawyers. A 1968 survey revealed that before special admissions programs began to have an effect there were, in the entire South, only 506 black lawyers. In Mississippi, where the black population was nearly 1,000,000, there were nine practicing black lawyers. In Alabama, with an even larger population of blacks, there were but 20 and in Georgia only 34.[8]

In drawing attention to this data, I do not mean to suggest that any of the compelling reasons for increasing minority representation at the bar that are detailed below require representation proportional to the percentage of the minority in this population. Opponents of special admissions programs have at times sought to characterize the programs as an attempt to achieve such representation among lawyers, an attempt that would, they then contend, necessarily imply maximum quotas for each racial and ethnic group in the profession. Stated bluntly, this objection is simply a "red herring." Neither now nor in the foreseeable future can there be any question of proportional representation in the bar. The serious question is whether publicly-supported schools can take steps to assure that the representation of minorities at the bar will be more than negligible. Reasons of compelling social importance require an affirmative answer to that question.

(1) The Public Role of the Legal Profession

Nearly 150 years ago, de Tocqueville described the crucial role of the legal profession in the United States. Lawyers, he wrote,

> are naturally called upon to occupy most of the public stations. They fill the legislative

assemblies and they conduct the administration; they consequently exercise a powerful influence upon the formation of the law, and upon its execution.[9]

Time has added prescience to the keenness of these observations. Even more than in De Tocqueville's time lawyers now "form the highest political class" in the nations. No other professional group, no other single class of citizens, exercises or comes close to exercising as pervasive an influence upon the operations of government.

Of the nearly 400,000 lawyers in the United States today, approximately 50,000 are employed by federal, state, and local governments. They serve as legislators and as staff to legislatures; as policy makers, administrators, and litigators within the executive departments; and as judges and staff to the judicial system. Nor is the public role of lawyers confined to the public offices they hold. Acting on behalf of private interests, they exert a powerful influence on public policy, serving not only as intermediaries between citizens and their governments, but also as the architects of law reform aimed at making government responsive to the needs and interests of the citizenry. No less important, if often less fully appreciated, lawyers interpret the actions of government to their clients and their communities, and thereby serve a crucial role in achieving public understanding and acceptance of those actions.

The public influence of lawyers extends far beyond their formal roles in government or in representing clients in their dealings with government. Despite the importance of government in the modern world, the direction of our society and the quality of our national life depend not only, and perhaps not even most importantly, upon the decisions of government, but also upon the myriad decisions made in the private sector. Here too the influence of lawyers is pervasive. Lawyers frequently serve as members of the governing boards, as well as advisors to, private foundations, educational and charitable institutions and corporations. The play an important role in the labor movement. They are often in positions of leadership in the extraordinary variety of community and other organizations that play so vital a role in American life. In all these varied roles, lawyers are influential molders of public policy.

Because of the public importance of the legal profession, there is an imperative need that it include qualified representatives of the diverse groups that constitute our society. Since pre-Revolutionary times, Americans have been committed to the democratic ideal that government derives legitimacy from the consent of the governed, an ideal that we have historically understood to require the active and continuous participation of the governed in their government, either directly or by representation. For this reason, the frequency with which lawyers are elected to public office alone suggests the importance of increasing minority membership in the bar. But as my preceding comments demonstrate, representation does not depend solely upon elected representatives.

In a society as complex as ours, representation throughout the vast network of public and private institutions which shape our national life is required to achieve the active and continuous participation in the governance of society upon which consent is founded. Decisions significantly affecting the lives of minority group members are made daily by zoning boards of appeal, transportation departments, regulatory agencies—everywhere that decisions are made affecting the lives of Americans. At times, perhaps often, these decisions will have a different impact upon minority communities than upon the white community. A minority presence in the decision-making process increases the likelihood that those differences will be recognized and taken into account. Similarly, a minority presence in Wall Street law firms, corporate law departments, labor union legal staffs, law faculties, and the boards of foundations and community organizations—indeed, in all the institutions in which the influence of lawyers is felt—is likely to alter the behavior of those institutions in a host of subtle and perhaps not so subtle ways, making them more responsive to the varying needs of minority communities. No less significantly, the presence of minorities in these institutions provides evidence to the members of minority groups that these important centers of American life are open to their members, evidence that may be expected to have an important influence upon their acceptance of the institutional framework of American society.

A single illustration may help to demonstrate the urgency of increasing minority representation at the bar. One of the harshest indicators of the economic and social conditions of America's racial minorities is the fact that their members are disproportionately both the victims and the perpetrators of reported crimes. Nationwide, 28% of all persons arrested are members of a racial minority. Unless the number of minority lawyers is raised beyond that which existed prior to the commencement of special admission programs and which will continue in the absence of such programs, the consequence must be a system of criminal justice in which many of the defendants are black or Chicano but in which nearly all judges, prosecutors, and even defense counsel are white. Given the history of racial injustice in the United States, it is not to be expected that such a system can maintain the respect and confidence of the minority communities that is so essential to its mission. I do not, of course, suggest that the fairness and credibility of the criminal justice system depend upon minorities or non-minorities being prosecuted, defended, or judged only by members of their own groups. But it is true nonetheless that the visible presence of minorities as prosecutors, defense counsel, and judges is essential to the appearance of justice, as well as to its reality.

The importance of a visible, and therefore a substantial, minority presence is obviously not limited to the criminal justice system. It exists wherever decisions are made that affect minorities, and that means that it exists wherever decisions are made affecting Americans. To be sure, it is neither possible nor necessary to have minorities represented wherever decisions affecting minorities are made. But substantially increased numbers of minority lawyers will inevitably have the effect of rendering the decision-making process of our society more cognizant of the distinctive interests of minorities.

(2) Serving the Legal Needs of Minority Communities

Increasing the number of minority lawyers is necessary also to serve adequately the legal needs of the members of minority communities. In stating the existence of this need, we should be mindful of the ideal eloquently expressed by Justice Douglas in his *DeFunis* dissent, that "[t]he purpose of [a state university] cannot be to produce Black lawyers of Blacks, Polish lawyers for Poles, Jewish lawyers for Jews, Irish lawyers for the Irish. It should be to produce good lawyers for Americans."[10] This is a compelling social and political ideal. Constitutional law ought not, however, in the single-minded pursuit of that ideal, ignore the existence of other values or the reality of the society in which we live. Although it would be absurd to suppose that only a Jewish lawyer can adequately represent a Jew or that only a black lawyer can adequately represent a black, it is true nonetheless that many Jews and many blacks (like many persons of other backgrounds) would prefer to be represented by lawyers with an ethnic and racial identity similar to their own. Nor should the existence of these preferences occasion surprise. Beyond the natural affinity that many persons feel with persons of a common cultural background, the history and in some measure the present reality of our society afford the members of some racial and ethnic minorities ample reason to perceive the dominant society as alien and to regard it with suspicion and even hostility. When the need for legal assistance arises, often at a time of anxiety or crisis, they may feel the need to turn to a lawyer whom they trust to understand and to empathize with their situation. Law schools need not endorse these feelings to recognize their existence and the importance of providing some outlet for them.

In a society in which racial and ethnic identities play an important role in everyday life, moreover, a lawyer's racial or ethnic background may have an important bearing on his ability to serve his client. Many of the tasks that lawyers perform for their clients require an understanding of the social context in which the client's problem arises. A brilliant and effective tax specialist is, for that reason, unlikely to be an effective representative in a labor negotiation. The reason is not simply that he is unfamiliar with the law of labor relations, it is also and perhaps primarily that he lacks an understanding of the practical problems of labor relations, of the customs that have developed in dealing with those problems, and of the style and manners of collective bargaining. To the extent that racial and ethnic groups form distinctive subcultures within our society, the representation of some of their members in connection with some of their legal needs may involve similar difficulties for the "outsider." The ability to "speak the language" of the client, to understand his perception of his problem, and to deal with others in the community on his behalf are qualities essential to being a "good lawyer." These qualifications are more likely to be found among lawyers who share the client's racial or ethnic identity, at least to the extent that the client's life is bound up in a community defined in these terms.

B. Racial Diversity and the Objectives of Legal Education

At least since the time of Plato it has been understood that those who govern require an understanding of the governed. The need is common to all forms of government, but in a democracy it is critical. In the United States, as I have previously noted, lawyers play a crucial role in the governance of the nation. Successful performance of that role requires an understanding of the diverse elements that comprise our pluralistic society. The need for such an understanding is hardly less important to successful performance of the lawyer's role in the representation of private interests.

For these reasons, a major objective of legal education is to assist students in acquiring an understanding of the social environment within which legal decisions are made. It is inevitable that this understanding, so far as it can be gained in an academic setting, will be acquired largely from books. To a substantial degree, however, it is also acquired by interaction among students, through exposure to differing points of view in class discussion and in less formal settings. The importance of these interactions to the education of lawyers was recognized by the Surpeme Court more than a quarter century ago in *Sweatt v. Painter*.[11] "[A]lthough the law is a highly learned profession," Mr. Chief Justice Vinson wrote for the Court,

> we are well aware that it is an intensely practical one. The law school, the proving ground for legal learning and practice, cannot be effective in isolation from the individuals and institutions with which the law interacts. Few students and no one who has practiced law would choose to study in an academic vacuum, removed from the interplay of ideas and the exchange of views with which the law is concerned.[12]

The Court's concern in *Sweatt* was, of course, the need of black law students to interact with their white counterparts. But there is no less need for whites to interact with blacks.

The importance that the law faculties attach to achieving diversity within their student bodies will be obvious to those who are familiar with the admission practices of the law schools. Of course, with respect to many of the characteristics that are socially significant in our pluralistic society, substantial heterogeneity is achieved without deviating from admission criteria concerned only with predicting the level of an applicant's academic performance. Thus, even though on the average white applicants from low income families have lower LSAT scores and GPAs than those from more affluent families, substantial numbers do qualify for admission, without special consideration, at schools which have varying admissions standards.[13] To the extent that diversity is not achieved in this way, the schools commonly rely upon non-academic factors to achieve it, always subject to the requirement that an applicant's predicted level of performance exceeds a school's minimum standards. Thus, some schools give preference to students from geographical areas that otherwise would not be represented in their student bodies. Many, perhaps most, are likely to prefer a student who has an uncommon background—e.g., substantial experience in business or law enforcement or, perhaps advanced training in economics or psychology—to others who have scored higher on predictors of academic success. The admission decision in all such cases rests upon the judgment of schools that the existence of this diversity will contribute to the education of other students in the class.

In view of the importance of race in American life and the importance that it is certain to have for the indefinite future, it would be startling if faculties had not concluded that the absence of racial minorities in law schools, or their presence only in very small numbers, would significantly detract from the educational experience of the student body. As a consequence of our history, race accounts for some of the most important differences in our society. Precisely because race is so significant, prospective lawyers need knowledge of the backgrounds, views, attitudes, aspirations, and manners of the members of racial minorities. It is true, of course, that the members of a minority group often differ with respect to these characteristics, and that with respect to some or all of them some members of minority groups are indistinguishable from many whites. Encountering these diversities and similarities is, however, an important part of the educational process. Well intentioned whites, no less than bigots, need to learn that there is not a common "black experience" and to appreciate the oversimplification of such statements as "blacks want (believe, need, etc.). . . ." Moreover, the distribution of attitudes among blacks, or among the members of other racial minorities, undoubtedly is not the same as it is among whites. And that too is worth knowing. If the distribution of perceptions and views about politics or crime or family is different among the several minority groups than among whites, that in and of itself may exert a shaping influence upon law and public policy, an influence to which law students must become sensitive if they are adequately to serve their future clients and perform successfully their future roles as community leaders.

The educational objectives of a minority presence in law school, finally, encompass more than increased understanding of minority groups. There is also a need to increase effective communication across racial lines. The difficulties that stand in the way of achieving such communication are not always obvious. Thus, as I have written elsewhere,

> I cannot imagine that any law teacher whose subject matter requires discussion of racially sensitive issues can have failed to observe the inability of some White students to examine critically arguments by a Black, or the difficulty experienced by others in expressing their disagreements with Blacks on such issues. Yet, these skills are not only a professional necessity, they are indispensable to the long-term well-being of our society.[14]

C. Increasing The Social Mobility of Racial Minorities

The special admission programs that have been undertaken by the law schools must be seen as part of a larger effort by the nation to improve the conditions of life of some of its most disadvantaged citizens. In part, that effort involves an attempt to accelerate the growth of a "middle class" within those racial and ethnic minority groups that historically have been denied the opportunity to participate fully in the richness of American life. The justification for minority preferences within that overall strategy is not difficult to discern: because of the continuing importance of racial and ethnic identifications and loyalties, there is reason to anticipate that the strengthening of the black, Chicano, or Puerto Rican middle class through such preferences will have a catalytic effect. Increased numbers of black and Hispanic lawyers and other professionals should encourage the aspirations of black and Hispanic children. The organizational talent and financial resources of a minority middle class, experience suggests, will to some extent be put at the service of less advantaged members of minority groups. The hope, in short, is to set in motion a chain reaction leading to the breakdown of a complex of conditions that today condemn large numbers to lives of poverty and desperation.

But if this chain reaction is to occur it must begin. Professional education is the last step in a long educational process. The ability of an applicant to compete successfully for law school admission is the product not only of 16 years of previous schooling but also of the applicant's cultural background, a background intimately related to the educational attainments of the applicant's parents and of other adults who have influenced his or her development. Even if there were now to be immediate and effective compliance with the command of *Brown v. Board of Education*, and equal educational opportunity in primary and secondary schools were suddenly to become a reality, considerable time would have to elapse before the effect of these changes could significantly affect the number and quality of minority applicants to law school. The command of *Brown* is not completely obeyed, however, even after nearly a quarter century. And equal educational opportunity does not exist.

To deny professional schools the power to employ race-conscious admissions standards is, thus, to withhold from minorities, for a generation and perhaps longer, an important avenue of social mobility. The costs of withholding realistic opportunities for professional education from the current generation of minority students will not be borne only by them. It will be borne also by other members of minority groups who will be denied the service that would have otherwise been provided to their communities. It will be borne by the next generation of minority children who, like those of previous generations, will lack a visible demonstration of the potential rewards of aspiration and effort. And, not least, it will be borne by white Americans who, once again, will have failed to meet their commitment to achieve racial equality.

II. THE NEED FOR SPECIAL ADMISSION PROGRAMS

If, as I hope, you are persuaded that the purposes I have discussed are of compelling social importance, it remains only to consider whether special admission programs are necessary to the achievement of those purposes. Accordingly, I turn to that question. With regret, I must report that the answer is not in doubt.

The unpleasant but unalterable reality is that affirmance of the California Supreme Court's decision would mean, for the law schools, a return to the virtually all-white student bodies that existed prior to the Civil Rights Act of 1964 and subsequent congressional enactments which, after so many years of default, finally committed the nation to the goal of racial equality. More specifically, as a result of the current admission practices of the nation's law schools, 1700 black and 500 Chicano students were admitted to the Fall, 1976 entering class. They represented 4.9% and 1.3%, respectively, of the total of 43,000 who were admitted. If the schools had not taken race into account in making their admission decisions, but had otherwise adhered to the admission criteria they employ, the number of black students would have been reduced to no more than 700 and the number of Chicanos to no more than 300.[15] It is virtually certain, however, that the reduction would have been much greater and it is not at all unlikely that even this reduced number would have again been reduced by half or more. Thus, the nation's two largest racial minorities, representing nearly 14% of the population, would have had at most a 2.3% representation in the nation's law schools and, more likely, no more than about 1%.

These conclusions are drawn from the *Evans Report*[16] which studied characteristics of applicants for admission to the 1976 law school class. The length and complexity of that study preclude any effort to set out its findings and supporting data in detail, but it may be useful to set forth briefly the data underlying the conclusions stated in the preceding paragraph and summarize several additional findings that further demonstrate the devastating impact that race-blind admission standards would have upon minority enrollment in law schools.

The ineradicable fact is that, as a group minorities in the pool of law school applicants achieve dramatically lower LSAT scores and GPAs than whites. Illustratively, 20% of the white and unidentified applicants, but only 1% of blacks and 4% of Chicanos receive both an LSAT score of 600 or above and a GPA of 3.25 or higher. Similarly, if the combined LSAT/GPA levels are set at 500 and 2.75 respectively, 60% of the white and unidentified candidates would be included but only 11% of the blacks and 23% of the Chicanos.[17] Such disparities exist at all LSAT and GPA levels. Their effect, under a race-blind system, must inevitably be to curtail sharply the number of blacks and Chicanos admitted to law school.

In 1976, there were more than 80,000 applicants for approximately 39,000 seats in the first-year class. Law schools commonly employ an index number combining LSAT and GPA scores as one means of predicting the probable law school performances of applicants. If all applicants for the 1976 class were to be assigned an index number, computed under two widely-used prediction formulas, the number of blacks in the top 40,000 would have been 370, on one formula, and 410 on the other. The equivalent figures for Chicanos are 225 and 250.[18]

Of course, law schools do not select students solely by "the numbers." Although an important factor in determining who will be admitted to law school, they are not the only one. To determine the number of blacks and Chicanos who would have been admitted to law school under a race-blind standard, it is necessary to estimate how they would have fared if non-quantitative predictors of success (letters of recommendation, experience, etc.) and other nonracial criteria affecting admissions (e.g., the school's interest in student diversity) were taken into account. Obviously, this cannot be done directly. It seems reasonable to assume, however, that if race were not a factor in the admission process, the applications of minorities would be affected by such factors in precisely the same way as those of whites.

On that assumption, the *Evans Report* calculated the acceptance rates for whites for each LSAT-GPA combination.[19] These acceptance rates were then applied to black and Chicano students who had the same combination of LSAT scores and GPAs.[20] On this basis, 700 blacks and 300 Chicanos would have been admitted, a number equal to 40% of the blacks and 60% of the Chicanos actually admitted.

These figures, 700 black and 300 Chicanos, state the outside limit that would have been admitted under a race-blind standard. It is virtually certain, however, that they substantially overstate the number that would actually have enrolled as first-year students. By employing aggregate national acceptance rates, the study in effect treats all law schools as a single school. As the report notes, the implicit assumption of such a procedure is "that minority candidates would apply to and be willing to attend" any school.[21] Common sense rebels against any such assumption. Geographical considerations alone are bound to limit a potential applicant's choice of schools. Moreover, the schools to which these 700 blacks and 300 Chicano students would have been admitted are predominantly the least selective law schools in the country. Since those schools lack the financial aid resources of the more selective institutions, a large portion of the high percentage of minority students who require financial assistance would, for that reason alone, be unable to attend the only schools to which they could gain admission.[22]

No one knows with any certainty how far these factors would reduce the number of blacks and Chicanos attending law school below the maximum eligibility figures of 700 and 300, perhaps by 25%, perhaps by 50%, perhaps by more. Since substantially more than half of both black and Chicano applicants were from low-income families,[23] however, and in view of the limitations imposed by geography, a reduction of 50% seems not at all implausible. On that basis, the number of black and Chicano students enrolled in the first-year class in 1976 would have been approximately 1% of the entering class, roughly the same as in 1964. The progress of a decade would have been wiped out.

The drastic impact of an affirmance in *Bakke* is also demonstrated by the *Evans Report's* findings that under a race-blind admission standard 12 of the nation's most selective law schools, which during 1975 had total minority enrollment of approximately 1,250, nearly 15% of the national total, would have enrolled no "more than a handful of minority students."[24] Yet, these are the schools from which, over the years, many of the leaders of the bar and the nation have been drawn. They are, moreover, the wealthiest institutions and, therefore, those with the greatest resources for the financial aids so sorely needed by many minority students.

The importance of *Bakke* to the future of minority student enrollment in the law schools of this country cannot be overstated. If the schools are prohibited from using race as a factor in admissions, minority enrollment will plummet and the hopes of a generation schooled in the traditions of equal opportunity enunciated by *Brown* will be dashed. This becomes even clearer when one examines the alternatives that have been suggested and realizes that in fact they offer no realistic prospect of substantial minority enrollments.

Arguments have been made from time to time, most notably by the California Supreme Court and by Justice Douglas dissenting in *DeFunis*, that substantial minority enrollments in professional schools can be maintained without using racial admission criteria. If there are means by which that can be done, they are not known to the law schools. We do know, however, that none of those that have been suggested would work. None would permit the enrollment of minority students in numbers even close to those that now exist and some would, in addition, have a destructive effect upon the quality of legal education and of the profession, requiring law schools to admit students—white and black—who are less qualified to study and practice law than students now being admitted.

The California Supreme Court suggested that universities "might increase minority enrollment by instituting aggressive programs to identify, recruit, and provide remedial schooling for disadvantaged students of all races. . . ."[25] Law schools have, however, already directed precisely such efforts toward minority students. An expansion of these efforts to other groups would not increase the number of minority applicants, but it would enlarge the number of whites is competition with them. Recruitment efforts directed toward minorities have been sufficiently successful that for the past several years the ratio of law school applicants to baccalaureate degrees granted has been the same for blacks and Chicanos as for whites.[26] There can be no doubt that this growth in the number of minority applicants is directly related to the existence of the special admissions program. For without these programs, it would have been pointless for most of the minority applicants, including most of those admitted, to have applied to law school at all.

A whole family of other suggestions for maintaining minority enrollments, while avoiding the use of race as an admission factor, depend upon reducing the influence of the quantitative predictors in the admission process. These range from Justice Douglas' extreme suggestion that the LSAT be abandoned to more moderate proposals that would have the schools place greater reliance on personal interviews, recommendations, and the like as a way of predicting academic performance and potential contribution to the society. Some of these suggestions rest upon the assumption that the LSAT is "culturally biased," i.e., that it underpredicts the probable academic performance of minority applicants. Five separate studies conducted over the past half dozen years have found that assumption is wrong.[27] In the light of these findings, to call for abolition of the LSAT amounts to a demand that the messenger who brings the bad news be shot or, more accurately, that some other messenger who will bring better tidings be substituted.

For both majority and minority students, the combination of LSAT and GPA, with all their limitations, is the best available predictor of academic achievement, especially at the levels of difference which separate majority and minority applicants in nearly all law schools. If they are, for that reason, to be given weight in the admission process, minority students' nonquantitative predictors of academic performance (such as letters of recommendation) would, on the average, have to be a good deal more favorable than those of whites if the former are to compete successfully for admission. But there is not the slightest reason to suppose that they are; indeed, there is no reason to suppose that such subjective factors are distributed on other than a random basis among applicants of different races. There is, accordingly, no reason to suppose that greater emphasis upon "soft data" would lead to admission of any but a very small number of minority applicants.[28]

The same is true with respect to the suggestion that schools should, in the interest of "flexibility" place greater emphasis on factors other than predicted academic performance. Whatever may be the wisdom or unwisdom of such a proposal, there is not a shred of evidence that reliance on any of the nonacademic factors suggested would, unless used as a covert method of applying a racial preference, greatly enlarge the number of minority admissions. Some greater number of minority applicants might be admitted than if purely academic predictors of success were to be employed, but it is by no means obvious that that would be so. It is entirely possible that an admissions process employing standards as flexible as those suggested by the California Supreme Court would disadvantage minority students, favoring instead those applicants who had letters of recommendation from influential persons, or who were most similar to law school professors and admissions office professionals. And the cost of greatly diminishing the role of the best predictors of academic competence would be so intolerable as inevitably to cause abandonment of the endeavor.

We can put aside quickly the suggestion of the California court that professional schools specifically rely more on "matters relating to the needs of the profession and society, such as an applicant's professional goals" as a method of increasing the number of minority lawyers. If "the needs of the profession and society" are defined to include a need for more minority lawyers, the alternative is no alternative at all but a restatement of precisely the admission program that the California court declared unconstitutional. Similarly, if "professional goals" are defined to include an intention specifically to serve minority communities, their use as an admission criterion may be subject to the same attack as the use of the race of applicants in the admissions process. In any event, reliance on the stated goals of applicants for admission is pursuit of a chimera: applicants will inevitably say that which they believe will secure admittance and there is often—we think usually—little relationship between even the sincerely expressed goals of an applicant not yet in school and the professional career eventually pursued.

There is, moreover, a far greater difficulty. If the schools are to admit students upon the basis of their stated professional goals, they must inevitably evaluate and rate these goals comparatively. Is it better, for example, to train a lawyer who says he wants to attack corporations or one who seeks to defend them? Is a practice in the field of securities regulation more or less valuable to society than the representation of labor unions? Choices among applicants on any such basis would thrust the schools into an unwanted and unauthorized role of social arbiter. They can properly assess the community's overall need for lawyers; they should not be placed in the position of evaluating those objectives.

Another, superficially more plausible, means that has been suggested for maintaining minority enrollment is to convert special admission programs into programs for the economically disadvantaged. The underlying theory seems to be that a substantial number of minority group members will gain admission to law schools under such a program because minorities are disproportinately included among the economically disadvantaged. Here again, the theory depends upon ignoring the facts. Although racial minorities are disproportionately included among the economically disadvantaged, approximately two-thirds of all disadvantaged families are white.[29] Even if we were to assume that disadvantaged minorities would apply for admission to law school in proportion to their numbers, the size of special admissions programs would have to be trebled to maintain the present representation of minorities in law schools. A school that now specially admits 10% minorities would be required to extent its program to 30% of the class.[30] But there is no reason to believe that there would be anything like that proportion of minority applicants presenting credentials equal to those of white applicants with whom they would be in competition.

The best data now available as to the probable composition of any such disadvantaged special admissions program suggest that, among the present pool of applicants, over 90% of those who would be admitted under such a program would be neither black nor Chicano.[31] And even this necessarily understates the problem. However schools advertise their special admission programs, it is understood that the programs are essentially limited to members of minority groups. But once it is learned that an applicant of any race possessing academic credentials substantially lower than those ordinarily required for admission can gain admission if the applicant shows economic disadvantage, it can be predicted with certainty that two things will happen: (i) there will be a substantial number of unverified and unverifiable claims of childhood economic disadvantage and (ii) there will be a large number of potential applicants who now do not apply who will seek to take advantage of the program.

Moreover, one effect of a racially neutral disadvantaged program, as distinct from a minority program, would be to eliminate those blacks and other minorities who now are able to gain admission but who could not reasonably claim a disadvantage other than race. Among minorities, as among whites, applicants who come from low-income families have, in general, substantially lower LSAT scores and GPAs than those who do not.[32] Many of these latter applicants constitute the most promising of those admitted under the present special admission programs. Yet it is just these applicants who will be denied admission under a racially neutral program for the disadvantaged.

There is, regrettably, one final alternative still to be considered. The suggestion that professional schools abandon special minority admissions programs in favor of programs for the disadvantaged or that they seek to maintain minority enrollments by reducing reliance on quantitative predictors of academic performance may rest upon the premise that either of these alternatives would permit race to be taken into account *sub rosa*. I do not imply that the court below meant to invite such an interpretation of those suggestions, but there are others who have suggested that in the effort to achieve racial equality "we cannot afford complete openness and frankness on the part of the legislature, executive or judiciary."[33] It need hardly be said in response that a constitutional principle designed to be flouted should not be imposed on schools dedicated to teaching the role of law in our society.

Notes

1. Bakke v. Regents of the Univ. of Cal., 18 Cal. 3d 34, 553 P.2d 1152, 132 Cal. Rptr. 680 (1960), *cert. granted*, 429 U.S. 1090, *aff'd in part and rev'd in part*, 98 S. Ct. 2733 (1978).

2. *See* Sandalow, *Racial Preferences in Higher Education: Political Responsibility and the Judicial Role*, 42 U. CHI. L. REV. 653 (1975).

3. *See* L. TRIBE, AMERICAN CONSTITUTIONAL LAW § 16-6 (1978).

4. 60 U.S. (19 How.) 393 (1857).

5. 100 U.S. 303 (1880).

6. 347 U.S. 483 (1954).

7. BUREAU OF THE CENSUS, DETAILED CHARACTERISTICS OF THE POPULATION, Table 223 (1970).

8. *See* Gellhorn, *The Law Schools and the Negro*, 1968 DUKE L. J. 1069, 1073-74.

9. 1 A. DE TOCQUEVILLE, DEMOCRACY IN AMERICA 329-30 (Schocken ed. 1961).

10. DuFunis v. Odegaard, 416 U.S. 312, 342 (1974).

11. 339 U.S. 629 (1950).

12. *Id.* at 634.

13. *See* F. EVANS, APPLICATIONS AND ADMISSIONS TO ABA ACCREDITED LAW SCHOOLS: AN ANALYSIS OF NATIONAL DATA FOR THE CLASS ENTERING IN THE FALL 1976, at 63 (Law School Admission Council 1977) [hereinafter cited as EVANS REPORT].

14. Sandalow, *Racial Preferences in Higher Education: Political Responsibility and the Judicial Role*, 42 U. CHI. L. REV. 653, 684 (1975).

15. EVANS REPORT, *supra* note 13, at 44.

16. *Id.* at 35.

17. *Id.* at 49-50.

18. Illustratively, of those whites who had an LSAT score between 600-649 and a GPA between 3.00-3.24, 83% received at least one offer of admission from a school to which they had applied. Of those who had an LSAT between 550-599 and a GPA between 2.75-2.99, 60% received such an offer. These illustrations, and the full range of calculations set out in the EVANS REPORT, demonstrate that, as might be expected, the lower an applicant's quantitative predictors, the lower his or her chance of admission.

19. For example, since 60% of whites who had LSAT scores between 550-599 and GPAs between 2.75-2.99 were accepted by at least one school, it was assumed that the same percentage of blacks with such credentials would have received at least one offer of admission. Since there were 37 blacks in this group, the assumption is that 22 would have received an offer. In fact, 30 of the 37 blacks in this group received at least one offer.

20. *Id.* at 44.

21. *Id.* at 45.

22. *Id.* at 57.

23. *Id.* at 29 & 59.

24. *Id.*

25. Moreover, low income whites perform sufficiently well on the LSAT and GPA to qualify for admission, in substantial numbers, at schools with varying standards. *Id.* at 63.

26. Compare ALTESEK & GOMBERG, BACHELOR'S DEGREES AWARDED TO MINORITY STUDENTS 1973–1974, at 4 (1977) (baccalaureate degrees) with EVANS REPORT, *supra* note 13, at 29 (law school applicants).

27. *See* Schrader, Pitcher & Winterbottom, *The Interpretation of Law School Admission Test Scores for Culturally Deprived and Non-white Candidates*, LSAC 66-3, in 1 LAW SCHOOL ADMISSION RESEARCH 375 (1976); Flickinger, *Law School Admissions and the Culurally Deprived*, printed with Schrader & Pitcher, *The Interpretation of Law School Admission Test Scores for Culturally Deprived Candidates: An Extension of the 1966 Study Based on Five Additional Law Schools*, LSAC 72-5, in 2 LAW SCHOOL ADMISSION RESEARCH 277 (1976); Schrader & Pitcher, *Predicting Law School Grades for Black American Law Students*, LSAC 73-6, in 2 LAW SCHOOL ADMISSION RESEARCH 451 (1976); Schrader & Pitcher, *Prediction of Law School Grades for Mexican American and Black American Students*, LSAC 74-8, in 2 LAW SCHOOL ADMISSION RESEARCH 715 (1976).

Research has also been done as to whether there is any possible source of bias in the "speededness" of the test, i.e., the question whether minority candidates may not finish the test in as large a proportion as whites. The first study indicated that, although speededneess had a slight effect on scores, there was no differential in that effect. Evans & Reilly, *A Study of Speededness as a Source of Test Bias*, LSAC 71-2, in 2 LAW SCHOOL ADMISSION RESEARCH 111 (1976) and in 9 J. EDUC. MEASUREMENT 123 (1972). A second, extended study confirmed the absence of any differential effect. Evans & Reilly, *The LSAT Speededness Study Revisited: Final Report*, LSAC 72-3, in 2 LAW SCHOOL ADMISSION RESEARCH 191 (1976).

28. Ironically, it is this very reliance on unverifiable "soft data" which the equal employment regulations seek to limit. *See Employee Selection Guidelines*, 41 Fed. Reg. 51733 (Nov. 23, 1976) (issued jointly by the Departments of Justice and Labor and the Civil Service Commission); *EEOC Guidelines on Employee Selection Procedures*, 29 C.F.R. 1607.1 (1976). *See also* Rowe v. General Motors Corp., 457 F.2d 348, 358 (5th Cir. 1972) (promotions).

29. Bureau of the Census, CURRENT POPULATION REPORTS, Series P-60, No. 103, *Money Income and Poverty Status of Families and Persons in the United States: 1975 and 1974 Revisions* (Advance Report 1976).

30. Even if the schools were willing to expand the programs to this extent, their inability to provide financial assistance to so sharply increased a number of disadvantaged students would necessarily lead to a very substantial reduction in the number of minority students, if the programs were to operate in a racially neutral manner.

31. EVANS REPORT, *supra* note 13, at 62.

32. *Id.* at 61.

33. Kaplan, *Equal Justice in an Unequal World: Equality for the Negro—The Problem of Special Treatment*, 61 Nw. U.L. REV. 361, 410 (1966).

Congress' Power to Confer Standing
in the Federal Courts
By Scott H. Bice*

> *No principle is more fundamental to the judiciary's proper role in our system of government than the constitutional limitation of federal court jurisdiction to actual cases or controversies. . . . The concept of standing is part of this limitation.*[1]

So said Justice Powell writing for the Court in *Simon v. Eastern Kentucky Welfare Rights Organization.*[2] Justice Powell also repeated the now well-known doctrine that the concept of standing also has nonconstitutional ingredients — ingredients sometimes referred to as "prudential" limitations on federal judicial power.[3] This distinction between the constitutional and nonconstitutional or "prudential" aspects of standing seems important. First, presumably the Court cannot make exceptions to the constitutional aspects of standing, while it can relax the prudential limitations[4] in appropriate circumstances. Second, and probably more important, the distinction may affect Congress' power to alter the standing doctrine. Those dissatisfied with the Supreme Court's recent interpretations of the standing requirement may seek to expand the Court's interpretations through remedial legislation.[5] But some judicial[6] and scholarly opinion[7] suggests that Article III prevents Congress from giving federal courts jurisdiction if the Court has previously decided that persons in the plaintiffs' position lack standing in the constitutional sense.[8] This paper discusses the validity of this opinion.

I

The constitutional requirements of standing to challenge governmental action are that a plaintiff challenging the action must, first, allege that he is suffering an "injury in fact"[9] which, second, is causally linked to the allegedly illegal governmental action.[10] As the Court had phrased it, "the relevant inquiry is whether . . . the plaintiff has shown an injury to himself that is likely to be redressed by a favorable decision."[11] The constitutional requirements serve two important functions, according to the Court. First, they supposedly insure that the plaintiff has a sufficient "personal stake" in the outcome of litigation to provide "the concrete adverseness which sharpens the presentation of issues upon which the court so largely depends for illumination of difficult . . . questions."[12] Second, they prevent the Court from rendering "gratuitous" decisions.[12]

Two notable Supreme Court decisions clearly illustrate these two requirements. In *Schlesinger v. Reservists Committee to Stop the War,*[14] the plaintiffs sued as citizens and taxpayers, challenging the constitutionality of Congressmen serving as officers in the armed forces reserves. The plaintiffs alleged that such service violated the incompatibility clause of the Constitution which provides that "no Person holding any Office under the United States, shall be a Member of either House during his Continuance in Office."[15] According to plaintiffs, the Congressmen's membership in the armed forces reserves deprived the plaintiffs — and all other citizens — "of the faithful discharge" of the Congressmen's duties, a discharge "to which all citizens and taxpayers are entitled."[16] The Supreme Court, in an

* © 1977 Scott H. Bice. Professor, University of Southern California Law Center.

opinion by Chief Justice Burger, held that the plaintiffs lacked standing to challenge the Congressmen's commissions. Addressing the plaintiffs' standing as "citizens,"[17] the Court ruled that the plaintiffs had not alleged an "injury in fact" but had instead alleged only an "abstract" injury, one indistinguishable from the injury suffered by all citizens who have a "generalized interest"[19] in constitutional governance. Harm to such a generalized citizen interest, the Court made clear, is not sufficient for standing, even though that might mean that no individual would have standing to test the constitutionality of the Congressmen's commissions.[20]

Simon v. Eastern Kentucky Welfare Rights Organization[21] involved a challenge to the legality of a revenue ruling issued by the Internal Revenue Service. The revenue ruling concerned a hospital's eligibility for treatment as a nonprofit organization. Under the Internal Revenue Code, hospitals are eligible for such treatment only if they are "organized and operated exclusively for . . . charitable purposes. . . ."[22] The Code does not further define this requirement, and the IRS has determined the status of each hospital on a case-by-case basis. Prior to 1969, the IRS had required a hospital "to be operated to the extent of its financial ability for those not able to pay for the services rendered. . . ."[23] In 1969, the Service issued the challenged ruling indicating that a hospital was entitled to nonprofit status even if it gave those unable to pay only *emergency* aid.[24] Apparently recognizing that the new ruling was inconsistent with its previous standard, the IRS modified the standard to remove the requirements relating to caring for patients without charge. . . ."[25]

According to the plaintiffs, the new ruling was inconsistent with the Code's requirement that tax exempt hospitals be operated "exclusively for charitable purposes." The plaintiffs alleged that they were indigent and that the new revenue ruling hindered them in obtaining hospital treatment, because it eliminated the important incentive of tax exempt status for the hospitals to provide treatment to them. The plaintiffs each described an instance in which he or a member of his family had been disadvantaged because of indigence in seeking needed hospital services.

The Supreme Court, in an opinion by Justice Powell, held that the plaintiffs lacked standing to challenge the legality of the revenue ruling. Apparently recognizing that the plaintiffs alleged an "injury in fact" by claiming increased difficulty in gaining access to hospital services,[26] the Court held that plaintiffs failed to allege a causal connection between the new revenue ruling and their difficulty in obtaining hospital service. According to the Court, whether the denials of service specified in the complaint could fairly be traced to the revenue ruling or traced instead to decisions unrelated to tax considerations was "purely speculative."[27] Therefore, whether a decision on the legality of the ruling would mitigate the plaintiffs' injury was, according to the Court, also too speculative to warrant federal judicial determination of the legality of the new revenue ruling.

II

These decisions can of course be evaluated in terms of their consistency with previous standing decisions[28] and in terms of the desirability of the judicially defined limits that they establish on federal jurisdiction.[29] Our present concern is not with the consistency or wisdom of the Court's standing decisions, however, but rather with the scope of Congress' power to confer standing on plaintiffs like those in *Reservists* and *EKWRO*, thereby altering the scope of federal jurisdiction which those decisions appear to establish as a matter of constitutional law.

Let us first consider two types of statutes that Congress might enact to change the result in *EKWRO*. Congress might amend the "solely for charitable purpoess" provision of the

Internal Revenue Code to make clear that one purpose of the requirement is to *encourage* hospitals to provide free care to indigents. Plaintiffs in the position of the complainants in *EKWRO* could then allege that the new revenue ruling fails to provide the encouragement required by the Code (arguing that the IRS would, at a minimum, have to require that hospitals *admit some* indigents) and that the IRS's failure to encourage the hospitals invades the beneficial interest that Congress has conferred on indigents. In *EKWRO* the Court assumed that the new IRS policy gave less encouragement to hospitals, but it thought that the plaintiffs had not alleged injury because they failed to allege that the reduced incentive caused the hospitals to *deny* the plaintiffs medical care. If Congress makes clear that indigents are entitled to have the IRS encourage hospitals to provide care, then the plaintiffs would have a congressionally created interest which the *EKWRO* Court apparently thought Congress had not created. This interest would be infringed regardless of whether or not the reduced incentive actually caused the hospitals to deny the plaintiffs aid, since the interest in having the IRS send certain "economic signals"[30] is infringed by the IRS's failure to send such signals.[31] If such a statute were passed, the issue would be whether Congress has the constitutional power to create such beneficial interests and, if so, whether it can require federal courts to give them judicial protection.

Second, Congress might attempt a broader overruling of *EKWRO* by providing that "any person may challenge the legality of IRS action which grants tax exempt status to a taxpayer." Persons who are denied tax exempt status may be expected to litigate the legality of the IRS action, but those granted such status will of course not bring the court challenges. Congress might conclude, however, that the possibility of illegal conduct in the granting of an exception is sufficient to allow any person who believes that the tax exemption is unlawful to challenge the IRS action in court. Congress would in effect thus create what we shall call a "citizen interest" in the lawful conduct of governmental affairs.[32] If such a statute were enacted, the issues would again be whether Congress has the power to confer such interests and whether it can make them enforceable in the federal courts.

While there are substantial alternative methods of changing the result in *EKWRO*, the creation of a citizen interest seems to be the most plausible method for Congress to use to change the result in *Reservists*. Congress could, for example, enact a statute providing that "any person may challenge, under the incompatibility clause, the constitutionality of members of Congress holding other positions in the federal government." Because the statutes creating such judicially enforceable citizen interests seem clearly to provide the broadest expansion of standing in the federal courts, we shall focus our discussion on Congress' power to enact such statutes. For if Congress can create citizen standing, it would seem to follow that it could create standing in citizens who have been given interests in addition to or instead of citizen interests in the legality of the government's conduct.

Some of the Court's more recent opinions suggest that Article III prevents Congress from creating judicially enforceable citizen interests.[33] In *Reservists,* for example, the district court had upheld citizen standing, recognizing that even though the alleged injury from the Congressmen's status in the armed forces was hypothetical,[34] the incompatibility clause gave citizens the right to be free from the *potential* harms that conflicts of interest can cause. The Supreme Court indicated that "if the Congress enacted a statute creating such a legal right, the requisite injury for standing would be found in an invasion of that right."[35] But, the Court continued, to satisfy the Article III prerequisite "the complaining party would still be required to allege a specific invasion of the right suffered by him. Standing could not be found — as it is not here — in a citizen who alleged no more than the right of all other citizens to have government conducted without what he perceived, without himself having suffered concrete harm, to be proscribed conflicts of interest."[36] The Court's meaning is unclear, but it appears to be saying that although Congress can create citizen interest to be free from the *potential* harm necessarily created by conflicts of interest, only those citizens who suffer "concrete harm" from the conflict may go to court to challenge its legality. Thus the Court appears to be saying that Congress can, on the one hand, create citizen interest in freedom from conflicts of interest but that, on the other hand, only those citizens who are somehow specifically "injured" by the conflicts can vindicate the general citizen interests.[37]

If this is what the Court means, its position seems internally inconsistent. If Congress can create an interest in all citizens to be free from the potential of harm caused by constitutionally prohibited conflicts of interest in the federal government, then any citizen who alleges the existence of the unconstitutional conflict must have alleged injury in fact. The Court's statement that only those injured in some additional sense by the conflict may sue is comprehensible only if the Court means that Congress *cannot* create a *judicially enforceable* interest in citizens in general to be free from constitutionally proscribed conflicts of interest.

In *EKWRO*, the Court used similar—and similarly confusing—language to describe Congress' power to confer standing. Quoting approvingly from another notable standing case, the Court noted that "[a]lthough the law of standing has been greatly changed in [recent] years, we have steadfastly adhered to the requirement that, *at least in the absence of a statute expressly conferring standing*, federal plaintiffs must allege some threatened or actual injury resulting from the putatively illegal action before a federal court may assume jurisdiction."[38] Having thus raised the possibility of standing conferred by statute where it would not otherwise exist, the Court cautioned in a footnote that the reference to a statute expressly conferring standing "was in recognition of Congress' power to create new interests, the invasion of which will confer standing. . . . [but that] [w]hen Congress has so acted, the requirements of Art. III remain: '[t]he *plaintiff still must allege a distinct and palpable injury to himself*, even if it is an injury shared by a large class of other possible litigants.'"[39]

Again, it is difficult to understand what the "distinct and palpable injury" requirement could mean if Congress has the power to create citizen interests in the lawful conduct of governmental affairs. If Congress has power to create judicially enforceable citizen interests in lawful governance, the claim that the government is not acting lawfully logically should constitute an allegation of an "injury in fact." If it does not, it must be because Congress cannot create the judicially enforceable citizen interest it has purported to create.

These cases[40] suggest, therefore, that the Article III case or controversy provision which requires plaintiffs to allege "injury in fact" prevents Congress from creating judicially enforceable citizen interests. We turn, then, to a discussion of the validity of that view of Article III.

III

The case and controversy limitation on federal jurisdiction and the associated non-constitutional prudential limitations can, taken together, be referred to as the "justiciability" doctrines. These doctrines are commonly thought to serve two related but nonetheless distinct policies. First, the justiciability doctrines play a separation of powers role, enabling the Court to define the necessary independence of the federal judiciary[41] and to prevent the federal judiciary from transgressing on the prerogatives of the other branches.[42] The "finality" requirement is a good example of a doctrine that protects judicial independence. This doctrine prevents federal courts from adjudicating an issue if the Court's resolution is subject to executive or legislative revision.[43] The Court has said that the political question doctrine is a justiciability doctrine that prevents judicial intrusion on the affairs of other branches.[44]

Second, the justiciability doctrines provide the Court with a means of insuring that the federal judicial power will be exercised in an efficient manner.[45] They seek to insure that the parties will present a well-argued case, to increase the probability that the legal issues will be capable of a resolution which can be limited to a concrete factual situation, and to insure that the parties have finally reached an impasse. The "ripeness"[46] and "adverseness"[47] requirements are examples of justiciability doctrines that in substantial measure serve to structure the presentation of issues in a fashion conducive to efficient judicial resolution.

Congressional power over the justiciability doctrines which set the judicial independence necessary for a viable separation of powers is, almost by definition, quite limited. The point of these aspects of the justiciability doctrines is to provide judicial autonomy from the other branches: that policy would of course be undermined to the point of extinction if the other branches could overrule the Court's determination of the necessary elements for judicial independence.[48] Thus Congress generally cannot, for example, command the Court to render a decision subject to executive or legislative revision in violation of the finality limitation.[49]

Congress probably has greater power over the justiciability doctrines which prevent the judiciary from impinging on the other branches. This is because Congress may be able to "waive" some of the protections against judicial intrusion which the Court has established.[50] But Congress' power to waive these protections is no doubt limited by the Constitution's separation of powers — a division of decision-making authority aimed at preventing concentration of governmental power in too small a group of individuals. Amorphous as the concept of separation of powers is, the constitutional division of "legislative," "executive," and "judicial" functions must mean that there are some issues that the courts cannot resolve, even though Congress has consented to the Court's action, and even though they satisfy judicial efficiency concerns and do not threaten judicial independence. The line is a difficult one to draw in the abstract, but it might be articulated in terms of the "essential functions" established by the Constitution for each branch.[51]

The Supreme Court could not, for example, accede to a congressional directive that the Court rather than the Senate determine whether the president's nominees were suitable for judicial appointment. On the other hand, even though the Court has said that it will not inquire into the regularity of the congressional enactment process, if Congress provided that fraud in the enactment process should vitiate legislation and gave the federal courts jurisdiction to determine in a proper suit whether acts of fraud had occurred, the courts could probably assume jurisdiction in spite of the earlier pronouncements that such issues constituted "political questions."[52]

The difference between these two situations is this: the Constitution establishes a *political* check on the President's appointment power — a check to be exercised in each case of appointment. The Senate cannot avoid the responsibility of providing that political check. The *Senate's collective judgment* on the qualification of each nominee is what the Constitution requires. Thus even if Congress gave the Court specific guidelines to judge the acceptability of the nominees[53] and provided an adverse advocate to argue against the nomination, the Court should refuse to act.[54] But discovering and remedying fraud in the legislative process is, on the other hand, not an exclusive province of any branch, except to the extent that due process requires judicial participation in the application of some remedies. Congress can provide for its own investigation and remedy procedures, but it does not necessarily abrogate "the legislative power" by providing that if fraud is proved to a court, the court should not enforce the legislation.

Although we have, for the purposes of discussion, distinguished separation of powers issues which concern judicial independence from those which concern the abrogation of an "essential function" of another branch, various congressional actions could of course concern both aspects of separation of powers. This most notably occurs when Congress creates a vague but judicially enforceable right. Suppose, for example, that Congress provided that each citizen has a judicially enforceable interest in a reasonably healthful environment, but that Congress did not further define "reasonably healthful." Such a statute might well raise questions about whether the Congress was abrogating its "legislative" function by refusing to set intelligible standards.[55] But it could also raise judicial independence issues by forcing courts to resolve complex issues of public policy that involve significant·trade-offs between efficiency and equity in the absence of either statutory or common law standards. In the absence of such standards the Court's resolution of these complex issues might be given little respect as principled adjudication, thereby undermining the judiciary's claim to respect in areas of constitutional adjudication where similar trade-offs must sometimes be made.

Those aspects of the justiciability doctrines which primarily concern the efficient performance of the judicial function are subject to the greatest congressional control. In substantial part, this is because those aspects of the justiciability doctrines are most often referred to as "prudential limitations" and thus their alteration does not raise constitutional questions. But the difference is not traceable solely to the attachment of the "constitutional" or "prudential" label to the particular doctrines. Questions concerning the efficient use of judicial services involve policy choices about the allocation of the federal government's resources. Such policy choices have traditionally been recognized as particularly appropriate for legislative resolution. Thus, for example, the Court has recognized congressional power to require federal courts to hear cases at an earlier stage than the courts, in absence of the congressional directive, would have done so.[56] To be sure, there are Article III limits on Congress' power, but they are probably approached only when the Congress so impairs the efficient functioning of the judiciary as to in effect threaten the independence of the judicial branch.

In assessing Congress' power to create judicially enforceable citizen interests, the relevant inquiry is thus to what extent the injury in fact requirement — which appears to stand in the way of the creation of citizen interests — should be viewed as related to judicial independence, to protection against judicial infringement on the political branches or to the efficient functioning of the federal judiciary. In other words, if the injury in fact requirement insures judicial independence, the Court is correct in intimating that Congress cannot confer standing in its absence. But, if the injury in fact requirement is only a means of preventing intrusion on the other branches of the federal government or of determining which cases are "worth" judicial resolution, congressional power to confer standing in the absence of injury in fact would be greater, though still perhaps limited in some fashion by Article III.

A relationship between the injury in fact requirement and judicial independence is difficult to perceive. But an argument for such a relationship might be formulated along the following lines. Requiring injury in fact provides the courts with a method of preventing feigned or collusive suits — suits which threaten judicial independence. Feigned or collusive suits occur when one of the parties controls both sides of the litigation thereby depriving the court of an adversary presentation.[57] The injury in fact requirement reduces the possibility of such suits because someone who is injured is much less likely to be a "sham" party. Feigned or collusive suits undermine judicial independence because they can present facts and frame issues so as to "preordain" the judicial result, and thus can manipulate the judiciary to achieve outcomes just as executive or legislative revision manipulates the judiciary by accepting the Court's judgment only when that judgment coincides with the views of the executive or legislative revisor.

But even if one accepts the argument that feigned or collusive suits threaten judicial independence, one can seriously question whether the injury in fact test can be of much assistance in preventing collusive suits. First, the Court has defined injury in fact so that objective proof of injury is difficult. It has said, for example, that injury to aesthetic interests can be sufficient, [58] but such aesthetic interests seem clearly subjective to the plaintiff and thus the allegation of injury in fact provides little assurance that the party is not actually friendly to the government's action. If, as the Court has said, a person can allege injury in fact by claiming that the construction of a resort will spoil his interests in an aesthetically pleasing environment,[59] the injury in fact requirement cannot be viewed as a meaningful objective test of actual adversary concern. A proponent of economic development could, for example, allege such an injury.

Second, even if the Court had not recognized such subjective harms as injury in fact, the requirement would still seem to be an undesirable method of preventing collusive or feigned suits. While there may be some correlation between palpable economic injury and the absence of feigned or collusive suits, the injury in fact requirement is neither a sufficient nor a necessary test for non-collusiveness. It is not sufficient because those suffering economic harm can be bribed to maintain collusive suits. Indeed those intent on maintaining collusive suits would probably be well acquainted with the bribe as a technique of selecting a hospitable "adversary." Injury in fact is not a necessary test because many who could not show objective economic harm could nevertheless care passionately about the legality of the government's action and could maintain a truly superb adversary presentation.[60] But it bears repeating that palpable economic injury is not the only invasion which constitutes injury in fact, and so long as this is true — which of course it should be in a society in which various non-monetary interests are recognized as "real" — there is no substantial relationship between the injury in fact requirement in actions against the government and the protection of judicial independence. Thus considerations of judicial independence do not prevent Congress from creating citizen interests — either in viewing the unspoiled wilderness or in "observing" a federal government that acts constitutionally.

It is easier to see a relationship between injury in fact and prevention of judicial intrusion on the other branches. As the *Reservists* case shows, the requirement prevents persons from litigating "generalized grievances" about the conduct of government, and it thus insulates the legislative and executive branches from judicial inquiry when all that a potential plaintiff can allege is that he is outraged by the government's conduct. This means citizens whose only claim is outrage at the government's action will have to resort to the other branches for relief, most notably to the units of those branches charged with investigation and punishing governmental misconduct. In a government with separation of powers, it does seem sensible to leave the executive and legislative branches to police their own houses so long as the purported misconduct "injures" no one.

But the Court's wisdom in refusing generally to recognize citizen outrage as a sufficient trigger for judicial inquiry does not settle the issue of Congress' power to waive its protection and require the courts to recognize citizen interests. If the legislative and executive branches consent to judicial inquiry, and if the outraged citizen presents a claim otherwise susceptible of judicial resolution, the citizen suit does not, by itself, constitute an abrogation of one of the essential functions of those branches. To be sure, Congress might violate the separation of powers by allowing some citizen challenges to Congress' exercise of its essential functions. For example, a court should refuse to accept jurisdiction over a congressionally authorized citizen suit charging that the Senate's confirmation of a Supreme Court justice resulted from an inappropriate weighing of the nominee's judicial philosophy.[61] But the separation of powers violation would result from the nature of the "legal" issue submitted to the Court, not from the nature of the plaintiff's interest in it. Thus the courts should refuse to decide such challenges even if they were brought by persons with cases pending in the Supreme Court or by disappointed nominees.[62] Since it is the nature of the issue tendered, not the identity of the party presenting it, that gives rise to separation of powers problems, the injury in fact requirement should not be viewed as a bar to the creation of citizen interests on separation of powers grounds.

The injury in fact requirement is clearly related to the competent and efficient functioning of the federal judiciary. The Court, as noted above, has said as much directly. Requiring "injury in fact" insures that plaintiffs will have a "personal stake" and hence will make an adversary presentation.[63] Injury in fact also serves to screen out cases which, even though presented in an adversary context, are not "worth" the judiciary's time in light of other questions pressing for judicial resolution.[64] Assuring an adversary presentation and screening out cases that are not worth the time it takes to decide them are both desirable attributes of a judicial system.

But as the discussion of the use of injury in fact to identify collusive suits indicated, there is reason to doubt whether the injury in fact requirement is necessary to insure adverse presentations.[65] Litigants, especially institutional litigants, often will be superbly adverse plaintiffs even though injured only in the sense that they are outraged at the government's behavior. But let us assume, for purposes of argument, that the injury in fact test makes sense as a rough judicial test for adverseness. Indeed, one can sympathize with the judicial reluctance to develop standards for granting standing to some uninjured citizens and denying it to others. But when Congress creates judicially enforceable citizen interests, it in effect creates a different test for adverseness, namely the willingness to spend the time and undergo the expense of bringing suit.[66] Unless the court determines that the citizen who actually brings suit is a collusive plaintiff, Congress' determination that filing suit is sufficient proof of a "personal stake in the outcome" should be accepted by the courts. In other words, unless the injury in fact test were necessary to insure an adverse presentation, which it surely is not, injury in fact should be viewed as a test for adverseness developed in part to give appropriate weight to separation of powers considerations,[67] and in part to serve judicial administration or judicial economy interests.[68] Neither of these considerations is offended by the Congress' recognition of another *prima facie* test for "personal stake" and hence for adverseness. Of course both plaintiffs "injured in fact" and those vindicating citizen interests should be dismissed if it is shown that they are collusive parties.

Using the injury in fact requirement as a method of screening out cases not "worth" judicial resolution seems, at least at first impression, to be a persuasive justification of the test. Requiring the plaintiff to allege some injury to himself seems a plausible manner of eliminating less important cases. However, even this efficiency rationale has been substantially undermined by the Court's recognition of trifling harms as sufficient to constitute injury in fact[69] and by the commentators' arguments that institutional litigants may often present issues quite worthy of judicial resolution, even though they allege no injury. But even assuming that the efficiency rationale provides adequate support to a judicially imposed injury in fact requirement, Congress has enormous power to determine which otherwise reviewable issues are worthy of judicial resolution. Congress can, for example, set minimum amounts in controversy[70] and decide that whole classes of cases — for example diversity actions — are not worthy of federal judicial resolution.[71] Although there is substantial scholarship and some case law which suggest limits on Congress' power to decide what is worthy of federal judicial resolution,[72] there can be little doubt that Congress' power to determine the subjects worthy of federal judicial resolution is very significant indeed.

If Congress decides that citizens should be able to challenge Congressmen's behavior under the incompatibility clause or attack the granting of an exemption to a taxpayer, it has of course thereby determined that the resolution of such disputes is worthy of judicial attention. Congress could probably create special federal agencies to monitor the legality of these governmental actions and to seek federal judicial relief for illegal government activities. But if Congress chooses instead to leave the matter to private litigation, Article III gives the judiciary no basis to deny Congress this choice. So long as the elements of the justiciability doctrines which insure the appropriate judicial independence and legislative responsibility are satisfied, Article III does not require an injury in fact beyond the alleged invasion of a congressionally created citizen interest in constitutional or lawful governance.[73]

If the foregoing analysis is correct, the injury in fact requirement should not, by itself, be viewed as prohibiting Congress from conferring standing through the creation of citizen interests. Limitations on Congress' power to create citizen interests must be traced to one or more of the following types of constitutional provisions: first, those which insure the separation of powers; second, those which recognize the interest-creating and interest-regulating autonomy of state governments; and third, those which protect individual interests from government intrusion. A full discussion of these limitations is beyond the scope of this paper; two examples will illustrate the constraints not already discussed. While Congress can create many citizen interests in the lawful conduct of the federal government and also create citizen interest in the constitutional conduct of state governments, notions of intergovernmental immunity implicit in the Tenth Amendment would probably preclude Congress from creating a citizen interest in the conduct of state government in accordance with state law.[74] Similarly, Congress could not create a citizen interest in having the government enforce a statute requiring privately owned newspapers to print only truthful material, for the Congress would be creating a citizen interest in the enforcement of a statute which itselfs violates the prohibitions of the First Amendment, as the Court has defined them.[75]

Congress has not, of course, generally created citizen interests, nor is it likely to do so. For even though several states have created what amounts to citizen standing,[76] there is a strong respect at the federal level for the combination of policies that underly the injury in fact requirement. This respect means that citizen interests will probably be created only in those instances in which there is reason to suppose that the Court's current interpretation of the injury in fact requirement will effectively preclude — or at least make quite difficult — judicial review of otherwise reviewable governmental action. Indeed, one reading of *Flast v. Cohen*[77] — to me the most plausible reading — is that the Court itself recognized citizen standing to challenge the legality of expenditures under the establishment clause, perhaps because other traditional "injured in fact" plaintiffs were unlikely to appear to challenge those expenditures. The *Flast* Court in effect recognized a citizen interest to have government respect the constraints of the establishment clause. In *Reservists*, the Burger Court refused to recognize a similar citizen interest in government respect for the incompatibility clause. But Congress can create the citizen interest which the Court failed to recognize.

While Congress will often be able to create citizen interests, it will also often not have to do so to confer standing on those denied it by the courts. As the discussion of *EKWRO* showed,[78] Congress can create more specific beneficial interests for narrower classes than "all citizens" or "all persons." One would expect that the more modest course would often be preferred.

Let us conclude by considering two notable congressional attempts to create standing where it arguably would not otherwise have existed. One has gone to the Supreme Court and been approved. The other has divided the lower courts.

In *Trafficante v. Metropolitan Life Insurance Company*,[79] two residents of an apartment house that was subject to the nondiscrimination-in-housng provisions of the Civil Rights Act sued charging that the the apartment owner discriminated on the basis of race. The two tenants, one white and one black, claimed that they lost the social benefits of living in an integrated community, lost the business and professional advantages of living in an integrated commuity and suffered both social and economic disadvantage from being viewed as residents of a white ghetto.[80] Section 810(d) of the Civil Rights Acts provides that suit may be commenced by "the person aggrieved"[81] by the allegedly illegal action, and the Act further defines a "person aggrieved" as "any person who claims to have been injured by a discriminatory housing practice."[82] Even though the two plaintiffs themselves had not been denied housing, the Court thought that they had alleged sufficient injury to establish standing. Noting that members of the racial minorities discriminated against were not the only persons who suffered from the effects of racial discrimination,[83] the Court concluded that Congress intended to allow tenants of "the same housing unit that is charged with discrimination"[84] to sue to prevent the discrimination.

The plaintiffs' allegations were more concrete than generalized grievances about the conduct of government,[85] and perhaps they would have been sufficient to constitute injury in fact if the apartment house had been a state actor and the suit had been brought directly under the Fourteenth Amendment without the benefit of any congressional action. But Justice White, writing for himself and Justices Blackmun and Powell, expressed doubts about the sufficiency of the allegations in the absence of congressional action.[86] "I would have 'great difficulty,'" Justice White wrote, "in concluding that the plaintiffs presented a case or controversy absent the Civil Rights Act."[87] Thus, he was apparently saying that absent congressional action creating interests in those living in the apartment to dwell in a building which complied with the Civil Rights Act, the plaintiffs' allegations would have constituted abstract generalized complaints which are insufficient to establish federal jurisdiction. Justice White's recognition of standing in *Trafficante* does not settle his view concerning Congress' power to confer citizen standing, for the plaintiffs alleged invasions of their interests more particular than the general citizen interest in government being conducted according to law. We do not know, for example, how he would react to a statute defining "person aggrieved" as "any resident of the city in which the apartment house is located." His view is nevertheless not inconsistent with congressional power to confer such citizen standing.

Congress has now enacted what may well be an attempt to create citizen standing. In the Clean Air Act, Congress provided that "any person" may sue to challenge noncompliance with certain provisions of the Act.[88] Although one circuit court has indicated substantial doubt as to whether Congress can authorize non-injured plaintiffs to sue,[89] the District of Columbia Circuit has ruled squarely that Congress may authorize such suits.[90] Assuming that Congress meant to authorize these citizen suits, the D.C. Circuit Court seems quite correct.

Notes

1. Simon v. Eastern Ky. Welfare Rights Org., 426 U.S. 26, 37 [hereinafter EKWRO]. The standing doctrine "[u]nlike other associated doctrines . . . 'focuses on the party seeking to get his complaint before a federal court and not on the issues he wishes to have adjudicated.'" *Id.* at 37–38. *See also* Flast v. Cohen, 392 U.S. 83, 98 (1968).

2. 426 U.S. 26 (1976).

3. *Id.* at 38. *See also* Warth v. Seldin, 422 U.S. 490, 499–503 (1975); Barrows v. Jackson, 346 U.S. 249, 255–56 (1953).

4. The standing doctrine, which prevents persons from asserting the rights of third parties, is commonly thought to be a prudential limitation. *See, e.g.*, Eisenstadt v. Baird, 405 U.S. 438, 444 (1972) ("We think . . . that our self-imposed rule against the assertion of third-party rights must be relaxed in this case. . . ."); Barrows v. Jackson, 346 U.S. at 255–56.

5. For a recent statement of dissatisfaction, see Supreme Court Denial of Citizen Access to Federal Courts to Challenge Unconstitutional or other Unlawful Actions: The Record of the Burger Court (Statement of the Board of Governors of the Society of American Law Teachers).

6. *E.g.*, EKWRO, 426 U.S. at 64 (Brennan, J., concurring in the judgment) ("Of course the most disturbing aspect of today's opinion is the Court's insistence on resting its decision regarding standing squarely on the irreducible Art. III minimum . . . thereby effectively placing its holding beyond congressional power to rectify.")

7. *E.g.*, Leedes, *Mr. Justice Powell's Standing*, 11 U. RICHMOND L. REV. 289 (1977).

8. Any attempt to discuss the standing doctrine is confronted with a serious conceptual problem, a problem not unlike that faced by one attempting to discuss the clothes of a naked king. For as numerous commentators have recognized, it is difficult to discern any significant difference between the concept of "standing to sue" and the concept of a "claim upon which relief can be granted." *See, e.g.*, Albert, *Standing to Challenge Administrative Action: An Inadequate Surrogate for Claim for Relief*, 83 YALE L.J. 425 (1974); Tushnet, *The New Law of Standing: A Plea for Abandonment*, 62 CORNELL L. REV. 663 (1977). Standing is supposedly a doctrine that relates to jurisdiction to decide, while the concept of a "claim upon which relief can be granted" is related to the merits of a case over which the court has jurisdiction. But so long as the party seeking judicial relief alleges some invasion of his own interests, there is simply no logical difference between telling him that he cannot sue because he lacks "standing" and telling him that he cannot prevail because the particular invasion of his interests is not entitled to judicial protection under the existing constitutional, statutory, and common laws. This means that any discussion of Congress' power to confer standing cannot logically be divorced from a discussion of Congress' power to create judicially enforceable "claims upon which relief can be granted."

9. Association of Data Processing Serv. Org. v. Camp, 397 U.S. 150, 153 (1970); *cf.* Sierra Club v. Morton, 405 U.S. 727, 734 (1972).

10. EKWRO, 426 U.S. at 45 (to meet the "minimum requirement of Art. III . . . [plaintiff must] establish that, in fact, the asserted injury was the consequence of the defendants' actions, or that prospective relief will remove the harm."); Warth v. Seldin 422 U.S. 490, 505 (1975); Linda R.S. v. Richard D., 410 U.S. 614, 618–19 (1973). *But see* United States v. SCRAP, 412 U.S. 699 (1973).

11. EKWRO, 426 U.S. at 38.

12. Baker v. Carr, 369 U.S. 186, 204 (1962).

13. EKWRO, 426 U.S. at 38.

14. 418 U.S. 208 (1974).

15. U.S. Const., art. I, § 6.

16. 418 U.S. at 213.

17. The Court also addressed and dismissed the plaintiffs' standing as taxpayers, finding that the plaintiffs had failed to satisfy the requirements for taxpayer standing enunciated in Flast v. Cohen, 392 U.S. 83 (1968). Plaintiffs had failed to allege the violation of a "specific constitutional limitation" on the "congressional taxing and spending power." 418 U.S. at 229.

18. 418 U.S. at 221.

19. 418 U.S. at 228. The Court noted that the "proposition that all constitutional provisions are enforceable by any citizen simply because citizens are the ultimate beneficiaries of those provisions has no boundaries." *Id.*

20. *Id.* ("The assumption that if respondents have no standing to sue, no one would have standing, is not a reason to find standing.").

21. 426 U.S. 26 (1976).

22. I.R.C. § 501 (c)(3), 26 U.S.C. § 501 (c)(3).

23. Rev. Rul. 56–185, 1956–1 C.B. 202.

24. Rev. Rul. 69–545, 1969–2 C.B. 117.

25. *Id.*

26. 426 U.S. at 40: "The obvious interest of all respondents, to which they claim actual injury, is that of access to hospital services."

27. 426 U.S. at 42.

28. It is difficult, for example, to reconcile the Court's treatment of the standing issue in United States v. SCRAP, 412 U.S. 699, with its decision in EKWRO, *supra* note 1. The Court's purported attempt to do so amounts to nothing more than a statement that the two cases are "different." *See* 426 U.S. at 45. n. 25.

29. The scholarly evaluation of the standing doctrine is voluminous. For criticism of the more recent cases, consult K. DAVIS, ADMINISTRATIVE LAW IN THE SEVENTIES 485–528 (1976); Beach, *Unchain the Courts—An Essay on the Role of the Federal Courts in the Vindication of Social Rights*, 1976 ARIZ. ST. L.J. 437; Tushnet, *supra* note 8; Note, 90 HARV. L. REV. 205 (1976).

30. The phrase is Justice Brennan's. EKWRO, 426 U.S. at 55 (Brennan, J., concurring in the result and dissenting).

31. Justice Brennan makes a forceful argument for such a construction of the plaintiff's allegations of harm in EKWRO itself. *Id.*

32. We use the term "citizen interest" to designate the interests of a person in officials of his government, observing the relevant constitutional, statutory, and common laws. Noncitizens may also have such interests, and by using the term "citizen," we do not mean to imply that aliens have no such interests in the conduct of government. Whether Congress' power is more limited in conferring interests on aliens than on citizens is a topic that we do not address here.

33. Earlier cases had suggested a broad congressional power. *E.g.*, Sierra Club v. Morton, 405 U.S. at 732 n. 3; Trafficante v. Metropolitan Life Ins. Co., 409 U.S. 205, 212 (1972) (White, J., concurring); Linda R.S. v. Richard D., 410 U.S. at 616 n. 3.

34. Reservists Comm. to Stop the War v. Laird, 323 F. Supp. 833, 840 (D.D.C. 1971).

35. Schlesinger v. Reservists Comm. to Stop the War, 418 U.S. 208, 224 n. 14 (1974).

36. *Id.*

37. The distinction is not unknown in the law of standing. In Sierra Club v. Morton, 405 U.S. 727 (1972), the Court summarized earlier decisions that had talked of a person's standing to vindicate the public interest or his standing as a private attorney general as follows: "Taken together, [these cases] thus established a dual proposition: the fact of economic injury is what gives a person standing to seek judicial review under the statute, but once review is properly invoked, that person may argue that public interest in support of his claim that the agency has failed to comply with its statutory mandate. It was in the latter sense that the 'standing' of the [plaintiff in one of the cases] . . . existed only as a 'representative of the public interest.' It is in a similar sense that we have used the phrase 'private attorney general' to describe the function performed by persons upon whom Congress has conferred the right to seek judicial review of agency action." 405 U.S. at 737–38.

38. EKWRO, 426 U.S. at 41 (quoting Linda R.S. v. Richard D., 410 U.S. at 617) (emphasis added).

39. EKWRO, 426 U.S. at 41 n. 22 (emphasis added).

40. *See also* United States v. Richardson, 418 U.S. 166, 178 n. 11 (1974).

41. *See* A. BICKEL, THE LEAST DANGEROUS BRANCH 114–15 (1962); P. BATOR, P. MISHKIN, D. SHAPIRO, H. WECHSLER, HART AND WECHSLER'S THE FEDERAL COURTS AND THE FEDERAL SYSTEM 64–70, 85–93 (1973.)

42. Flast v. Cohen, 392 U.S. 83, 95 (1968).

43. *E.g.*, Hayburn's Case, 2 U.S. (2 Dall.) 409 (1792).*Cf.* Glidden Co. v. Zdanok, 370 U.S. 530 (1962); United States v. Klein, 80 U.S. (13 Wall.) 128 (1872).

44. Flast v. Cohen, 392 U.S. at 95.

45. *Id. See generally* P. BATOR *et al.*, *supra* note 41, at 66–70.

46. *E.g.*, Abbott Laboratories v. Gardner, 387 U.S. 136 (1967); United Public Workers v. Mitchell, 330 U.S. 75 (1947). *See generally* Scharpf, *Judicial Review and the Poltical Question: A Functional Analysis*, 75 YALE L.J. 518, 529–33 (1966).

47. *E.g.*, Baker v. Carr, 369 U.S. 186, 204 (1962) ("concrete adverseness" required to "sharpen . . . the presentation of issues. . . .").

48. The statement in the text of course assumes that judicial review is established. The mere fact that one institution can define the jurisdiction of a second institution does not mean that the first institution will deprive the second institution of the independence necessary to satisfy separation of powers requirements.

49. *See* cases cited in note 43 *supra*.

50. *See, e.g.*, Brown *Qius Custodiet Ipsos Custodes — The School Prayer Cases*, 1963 SUP. CT. REV. 1, 15; Monaghan, *Constitutional Adjudication: The Who and the When*, 82 YALE L.J. 1363 (1973).

51. *See* L. JAFFE, JUDICIAL CONTROL OF ADMINISTRATIVE ACTION 31 (abridged student ed. 1965); *cf.* Ratner, *Congressional Power Over the Appellate Jurisdiction of the Supreme Court*, 109 U. PA. L. REV. 157 (1960).

52. Field v. Clark, 143 U.S. 649 (1892). *See also* Coleman v. Miller, 307 U.S. 433 (1939); Lester v. Garnett, 258 U.S. 130 (1922).

53. The absence of standards to judge the qualifications of the nominees could be thought to raise judicial independence problems. *See* the discussion accompanying notes 61–62 *infra*.

54. This is not to say that all issues "relating to" Senate Confirmation of Supreme Court Justices should be immune from judicial inquiry. For example, if Congress created citizen interests in the observance of the incompatibility clause, a citizen suit challenging the seating of a Supreme Court Justice could be authorized.

55. A discussion of the valid contours of the delegation doctrine is beyond the scope of this paper.

56. *Compare* Aetna Life Ins. Co. v. Haworth, 300 U.S. 227 (1937) (federal declaratory judgment act upheld) *with* Willing v. Chicago Auditorium Ass'n, 227 U.S. 274 (1928) (federal courts will not issue declaratory judgments).

57. *E.g.*, Moore v. Charlotte-Mecklenburg Bd. of Educ., 402 U.S. 47 (1971); United States v. Johnson, 319 U.S. 302 (1943); Lord v. Veazie, 49 U.S. (8 How.) 251 (1850). The doctrine of collusive suits does not

necessarily prevent courts from taking jurisdiction of actions in which the parties have reached agreement by the time the suit is filed. The judicial acceptance of guilty pleas and jurisdiction over consent judgments, and the naturalization of aliens have been entertained. *See* C. WRIGHT, HANDBOOK OF THE LAW OF FEDERAL COURTS (2d ed. 1970). It is the fact that one party is financing and directing the conduct of the suit, often if not always surreptitiously, that seems to be important, if not always essential.

58. *E.g.*, United States v. SCRAP, 411 U.S. 687, 686 (1973).

59. Sierra Club v. Morton, 405 U.S. 727, 738 (1972).

60. *See* Scott, *Standing in the Supreme Court — A Functional Analysis*, 86 HARV. L. REV. 645 (1973).

61. *See* notes 52–54 and accompanying text *supra*.

62. The Court has allowed persons subject to the jurisdiction of federal courts to challenge the qualifications of the judges, even though the parties alleged no specific harm from the judge's lack of proper qualifications. *E.g.*, Palmore v. United States, 411 U.S. 689 (1973); Glidden Co. v. Zdanok, 370 U.S. 530 (1962).

63. *See* notes 57–60 and accompanying text *supra*.

64. *See* notes 56–57 and accompanying text *supra*.

65. *See* notes 59–60 and accompanying text *supra*.

66. *See* Scott, *supra* note 60.

67. The requirement prevents federal courts from entertaining grievances about conduct which are more appropriately considered by the other branches. *See* notes 48–54 and accompanying text *supra*.

68. The requirement saves the courts from developing tests to select among litigants who suffer no harm.

69. *See* K. DAVIS, ADMINISTRATIVE LAW IN THE SEVENTIES 181 (1977 Supp.).

70. *See* 28 U.S.C. § 1331.

71. It was not until 1875 that Congress decided to extend federal question jurisdiction to the federal courts.

72. For a collection of the cases and articles, see P. BATOR *et al.*, *supra* note 41, at 309–75.

73. This conclusion is consistent with most of the scholarly criticism of the present formulation of the standing doctrine. For example, Mr. Berger concludes from an historical analysis of English and early American practice that there is no constitutional requirement of standing. Berger, *Standing to Sue in Public Actions: Is it a Constitutional Requirement?*, 78 YALE L.J. 816 (1969). Professor Jaffe has also urged that an injury in fact is not constitutionally required. Jaffe, *The Citizen as Litigant in Public Actions: The Non-Hohfeldian or Ideological Plaintiff*, 116 U. PA. L. REV. 1033 (1968). Even Professor Davis, who disagrees with Professor Jaffe's conclusion in the absence of congressional action, acknowledges the power of Congress to create standing in the absence of injury in fact. K. DAVIS, *supra* note 69, at 526. *See also* Monaghan, *supra* note 50; Scott, *supra* note 60.

74. *See* National League of Cities v. Usery, 426 U.S. 833 (1976).

75. *See, e.g.*, Gertz v. Robert Welch, Inc., 418 U.S. 323 (1974).

76. This is generally accomplished through the allowance of taxpayers' suits even though the taxpayer will not benefit economically from a cessation of the challenged governmental action.

77. 392 U.S. 83 (1968).

78. *See* notes 29–32 and accompanying text *supra*.

79. 409 U.S. 205 (1972).

80. *Id.* at 208.

81. Civil Rights Act of 1968, § 810(a).

82. *Id.*

83. 409 U.S. at 210.

84. *Id.* at 212.

85. *See* notes 34–40 and accompanying text *surpa*.

86. 409 U.S. at 212 (concurring opinion).

87. *Id.*

88. 42 U.S.C. § 1857h–2(a).

89. National Resources Defense Counsel v. E.P.A., 481 F.2d 116 10th (Cir. 1973).

90. Metropolitan Washington Coalition for Clean Air v. District of Columbia, 511 F.2d 809 (D.C. Cir. 1975).

Our Constitutional Liberties: Myths or Realities?

BY WILLIAM M. KUNSTLER*

The founding fathers—and I wish there had been some founding mothers of this country—would find the interpretation of the Bill of Rights unrecognizable were they, by some miracle, to be restored to life. They would see the petition for redress of grievances destroyed by the ongoing Kent State case in which the land on which four students were killed and many wounded on May 4, 1970, is becoming the location of a gymnasium despite the fact that the Interior Department is now in the process of determining whether it should be preserved as a historical site. All the great arguments of John Quincy Adams and James Buchanan, when gag rules were blocking the petitions against slavery in the 1830's in the halls of Congress, are now comparatively meaningless in light of a proliferation of such orders by the courts.

The search and seizure protections of the fourth amendment—surely one of the bedrocks of the Revolution, the Declaration of Independence, and the Constitution—have been virtually destroyed. The privilege against self-incrimination has been eradicated by immunity laws which do not give full immunity yet take away the privilege. The right to counsel of the sixth amendment has been destroyed by the Supreme Court in state prosecutions so that defendants in such cases find no constitutional basis to have an out-of-state attorney represent them. The excessive bail of the eighth amendment has been more honored in the breach than in the observance and excessive bail is the rule throughout the United States. Cruel and unusual punishments—seemingly restricted by the eighth amendment—have become commonplace. Judge Constance Baker Motley has attempted to offset the Rockefeller Drug Law—e.g., six years to life for the sale of 3/8 of an ounce of cocaine—and undoubtedly there is a reasonable chance that she will be reversed by the Second Circuit as she has so many times in the past.[1]

There is a myth and reality to all of this. For some strange reason, neither the bar, the faculties of law schools, nor the judiciary itself have seen fit to point out what is happening to the Bill of Rights. We are left to lay writers such as Richard Harris in *The New Yorker* who, in a brilliant series of articles, now encompassed in a book,[2] touched on much of the destruction of the Bill of Rights to which I am referring. The myth and reality is that the Constitution has a mythological aspect which, in general terms, is glowing and full-blown. In reality, many of these do not exist for all of the population. I have been reminded of Karl Marx's observations about the Eighteenth Brumaire Constitution of Louis Napoleon where he said that each paragraph of the Constitution contained in itself its own antithesis, its own upper and lower house: namely liberty in the general phrase and suspension of liberty in the marginal note. So long, therefore, as the name of freedom was respected, and only its actual realization prevented (of course in a legal way), the constitutional existence of liberty remained intact and inviolate, however mortal the blows dealt to its everyday existence.

*Attorney, New York, New York.

My colleagues, Professors Bice[3] and Goldberg[4] have discussed, essentially in somewhat legalistic terms, the restriction of access to the federal courts, which, theoretically at least, are supposed to be the bulwark against constitutional intrusions by everyone—individuals, states, the national government. But the political realities all too often are ignored. The particular political reality that I have in mind is a restless alienated group of minorities whose members pick the fruit and the cotton, pump the gas, pave the streets, collect the garbage, and furnish the perpetual cheap labor supply that must always be available to twentieth century capitalism and the industrial state. Moreover, political dissidents may someday catalyze the energies of these groups in a way that the status quo fears. One of the control mechanisms of all this, of course, is restricting access to the courts.

Recently, after the termination of the great criminal conspiracy trials of the last ten years (those of Dr. Spock, the Chicago Seven, the Wounded Knee defendants, Daniel Ellsberg and Anthony Russo, the Harrisburg trial of the Berrigans, and many others), the Justice Department wrote a memo indicating to its infrastructure that there was some rationale for all of this. That is, access to the courts and the lawyers who had that access had to be curbed or the government would continue to lose its politically motivated cases.

I will confine myself to criminal cases, although access to civil courts for political reasons has been so restricted and so diminished that it would be unrecognizable to, say Alexis de Tocqueville, who reminded his international reading audience that in America all problems— at least all political problems—eventually end up in the courts. The Board of Governors of the Society of American Law Teachers, in October of 1976, said the following about what we call the Burger court:[5]

> Although the pattern in not uniform it is clear enough; the Supreme Court is making it harder and harder to get a federal court to vindicate federal constitutional and other rights. In some cases prior decisions have been overruled, either explicitly or silently. In other contexts, restrictive implications and prior cases have been taken up and expanded. In still other situations, new approaches developed by the lower courts have been repudiated.[6]

In calling this pattern an insidious one, the Board of Governors went on to say that the Supreme Court had sharply restricted the federal courts' power to protect basic rights. But why is this so? What is the rationale behind it? Is it just the idiosyncracies of the Nixon appointees, or of Justice White, or is there something more to it? Is this part of the status quo's defense mechanism against those it fears the most? Is it part of its long range defense against those who may someday, like Markham's man with the hoe, stand up and disrupt and destroy in wholly justified retaliation for past and present injustices? I think it is and I think the political reality must be understood. Otherwise, we talk in law school terms and only to each other at the expense of ignoring the rest of the world.[7]

Let us look at what the court has done, keeping in mind that I see its action as politically motivated and not just as intellectual exercises by nine justices or a majority thereof.

In 1965, I had the thrill and the pleasure of writing a complaint in the back seat of a diesel automobile going from New Orleans to Hattiesburg, Mississippi in which a lawyer who was driving the car, Benjamin Smith, was the defendant in a state criminal prosecution brought under the Louisiana Communist Control and Subversive Activities Act. Smith, another lawyer, and James Dombrowski, then the director of the Southern Conference Educational Fund, had been accused by the State of Louisiana of violating those two acts. A complaint was drawn by myself and my colleagues—Arthur Kinoy and others—in the back seat of that car. We completed it by the time we reached Hattiesburg. We claimed that overbroad statutes that chilled the first amendment right of expression should be enjoined by the federal courts. Eventually, in 1965, we won.[8] In a five to two decision, written by Mr. Justice Brennan, the court said yes, there should be an injunctive process against overbroad state criminal statutes that threatened free expression.

Just five years later, by an eight to one majority in *Younger v. Harris,*[9] the Supreme Court destroyed this principle by upholding the California Criminal Syndicalism Act which was being applied against people who were distributing leaflets on the streets and byways of that state seeking a change in industrial ownership through political action. The Court said that first amendment overbreadth and chilling effect problems were not enough. You must show a bad faith prosecution or an intention to harass—something virtually impossible to prove.

Three years later, in *Steffel v. Thompson,*[10] a unanimous Court seemed to say that declaratory judgments were all right when coupled with imminently threatened state prosecutions which were claimed to be under overbroad statutes restrictive of free expression. That lasted exactly one year because in *Hicks v. Miranda*[11] (a *Miranda* case that is not as well known as John P. Frank's *Miranda v. Arizona,*[12] which of course has been destroyed as well in effect), the Court held that a federal action under *Steffel* could be placed beyond federal jurisdiction if the prosecution was commenced after the federal suit was filed. Consequently, the moment a 1983 action[13] was filed asking for a declaratory judgment, no injunctive relief was possible unless there existed these extraordinary circumstances which are impossible to have. All the state had to do was to prosecute immediately, then the civil rights action would be dismissed. The Supreme Court held that until proceedings of substance are begun in the civil rights action, the state may indict and prosecute, thereby destroying the civil rights action.

The same path was followed in *Doran v. Salem Inn*[14] in the same year. So now we have nothing left of *Dombrowski* despite Mr. Justice Blackmun's agonized cries in the *Bates v. State Bar of Arizona* case where Mr. Frank was not as successful as he was in *Miranda*—I'm referring to the legal advertising case in which the right of lawyers to advertise was sustained.[15] Mr. Justice Blackmun maintained that, in the usual case involving restraint on speech, a showing that the challenged rule served unconstitutionally to suppress speech would end the constitutional inquiry. In the first amendment context, the Court thus has permitted attacks on overbroad statutes without requiring any demonstration that the specific conduct was constitutionally protected. For that proposition, he had the audacity to cite *Dombrowski* as an example[16]—the dead *Dombrowski* doctrine.

This is mythology without meaning. After *Hicks v. Miranda* you have a whole variety of cases, all of which do much the same thing. In *Huffman v. Pursue,*[17] the *Younger* doctrine was extended even to civil proceedings of a quasi-criminal nature. An abatement action brought by the state against theater owners on antiobscenity grounds is now sufficient to prevent the injured parties from going into court under the normal civil rights action to attempt to declare the statute unconstitutional. In *Kugler v. Helfant,*[18] a 1975 case from New Jersey again, an ex-judge who was being prosecuted for perjury claimed that he had been coerced into appearing before the federal grand jury by members of the Supreme Court of New Jersey and the Deputy Attorney General. The Court held that *Younger v. Harris* prohibited the *Dombrowski v. Pfister* remedy.

In yet two more lower court cases the *Younger* rule prevailed. For example, in *New Jersey v. Chesimard,*[19] a case which I argued before the *en banc* Third Circuit, the court held that *Younger* prevented the court from considering claims that it held were valid: namely, that a Black Muslim defendant should not have to be tried on her sabbath, Juma, or Friday. The court found that the defendant had a constitutional right not to be tried, but that it could not consider the issue because *Younger* prevents any injunction against a state court prosecution on that or any other grounds, including any declaratory judgment relief.

Bedrosian v. Mintz[20] involved Attica defendants, inmates who sought to have out-of-state counsel appointed. The reason was not only because of the unwillingness of many local attorneys to represent them, but also because of their feared incompetence or relationship to the prosecution. The court rejected the claims: we could not enjoin the prosecution so that the defendants could have the counsel of their choice because the Supreme Court has ruled that the courts can no longer handle these cases. This thinking has gone so far as to prevent an injunction against a military trial in which the defendant alleges that the matter is being brought in bad faith to suppress his first amendment rights to organize GI servicemen.[21]

In any event, *Dombrowski v. Pfister,* which was one method of enjoining state court prosecutions by criminal defendants, is now dead-letter law, not because there is an intellectual difference, but because the political realities apparently demand it. Likewise, habeas corpus has been virtually destroyed by the Burger Court—I'm referring to federal habeas. Three recent cases will indicate to you what the court has done—the petitioners in these cases are interesting to note as far as their color, race, and degree of poverty are concerned.

Francis v. Henderson[22] last term, six to two: a seventeen year old Black youth indicted in Louisiana (1960) for felony murder. Because he was indigent, he was given a lawyer. The nonpaid attorney was in failing health and died shortly after the trial—he had no criminal experience during the last eighteen years of his life. This man's defense counsel did absolutely no work on the case. There was a one-day trial and Francis was sentenced to life imprisonment. His lawyer never challenged the composition of the grand jury as to its racial makeup. Francis' accomplices all pleaded guilty and were sentenced to eight years. The federal district court in Louisiana held that the exclusion of Blacks from the grand jury was unconstitutional. The Supreme Court reversed, denying federal habeas corpus relief since the lawyer neglected to raise the claim in the first instance. So Mr. Francis will serve out the rest of his life in prison because his incompetent attorney failed to raise a fundamental constitutional challenge. But all of this flies in the face of *Fay v. Noia,*[23] the leading habeas corpus case, in which the Court held in its majestic pronouncement—which, again, is more myth than reality—relief will be denied only if a plaintiff had deliberately sought to subvert or evade the orderly administration of his federal defense in the state court. A choice made by counsel, not participated in by the petitioner, does not bar relief. Now how do you interpret that? Francis had no choice in the attack on the grand jury. He was seventeen years old. What did he know about attacks on the grand jury?

Stone v. Powell,[24] another vindictive case, six to three: a conviction based on illegally seized evidence. Here the Court held that no habeas corpus review will be available in the federal courts if the state court found that the challenged search was legal. So what is the purpose of a federal judiciary? If the state decides, the federal judiciary is excluded. Here was a seizure made pursuant to an arrest under a vagrancy statute later found to be unconstitutional.

Estelle v. Williams,[25] Texas state prosecution: a man forced to stand trial in prison garb. Here there was a clear violation of a constitutional right, no question about that, no one would disagree. The Court held that, since the defendant's lawyer made no timely objection in the state court, no relief in the federal court was therefore available.

So habeas corpus relief is being destroyed as a federal remedy along with federal injunctive relief. Next let's consider the removal statutes.[26] One great shining accomplishment of the Reconstruction Congress was that newly freed slaves and others could remove their cases to the federal courts if there was no relief possible or probable in the state courts.

It seems that the '60s in every age became our great periods, at least for the last three centuries. Even though the Civil Rights Act of 1964 expressly provided an appellate remedy for the denial of removal, the prosecutors always had their way—*City of Greenwood v. Peacock*,[27] permitting removal in only the most limited of circumstances. When the Fifth Circuit attempted to revitalize removal in *Johnson v. Mississippi*,[28] the Court overturned it. This was an economic boycott case, which later resulted in the enormous money judgment against the NAACP. The demonstrators were trying to sustain that boycott. State criminal conspiracy charges were brought against them whereupon they attempted to remove their prosecutions from the state to the federal court. The Supreme Court held: "We reaffirm *Greenwood v. Peacock*."

The immunity doctrines—immunity that prosecutors and judges now enjoy—are yet another example of denying any needed relief so that judges and prosecutors are free to do what they will do. In *United States v. Brown*[29] a federal district judge, Lansing Mitchell in Louisiana, was found to have said prior to the trial, "I am going to keep my health because I am going to try the H. Rap Brown case and I want to get that nigger." That is a finding of fact by a federal district court! And yet there is no recourse against Judge Mitchell who still sits—presumably still violating his oath of office and all morality and decency—as a federal district judge in the United States District Court for the Eastern District of Louisiana.

There has been much talk about *Trafficante v. Metropolitan Life Insurance Co.*[30] and *Warth v. Seldin*[31] which involved essentially middle class white plaintiffs. But what about *Rizzo v. Goode*,[32] where black plaintiffs brought an action against the mayor of Philadelphia claiming that there was a practice of permitting police officers to run amok in black neighborhoods? The district court found that such practice had occurred; it worked out, with the approval of the Philadelphia Police Department and the State of Pennsylvania, a civilian complaint procedure. This was reversed by the Supreme Court on the grounds not only of no injury—specific injury—to the Black plaintiffs, but also because there is supposedly no duty under the Constitution for public officials to control their subordinates. Thus disappears *Monroe v. Pape*,[33] *Hague v. CIO*,[34] and even the statute under which the action was brought (42 U.S.C. 1983). Yet, the Civil Rights Act of 1866 provided that neglect is just as much a cause of action as actual injury itself.

Lastly, to wind this up, the Court in 1975 took away attorney fees in all public interest cases so that plaintiffs cannot even get the wherewithal to get competent counsel to go into court for them.[35] Even though Congress has restored attorney public interest fees, it has restored them for Civil Rights Act cases alone.[36]

By brief conclusion, this erosion of constitutional rights and privileges is not all by happenstance. It is not simply a result of intellectual differences of opinion between lawyers and courts. This is the system's reaction to the use of the courts to redress fundamental constitutional violations and to achieve equality of treatment. When the courts are closed to legal actions, other alternatives will surely be sought. And if those other alternatives do arise, it will be largely because of the inaction of lawyers, judges, and professors. Put aside the general public because you cannot talk to it in these terms, for they are far too esoteric, essentially, to raise issues around which people can rally. But it will be mainly *our* fault, because we have a solemn obligation, if we believe half of what we say about the Constitution, to attack and oppose any Supreme Court decision, and indeed any court decision, which resorts to indecency, deprivation, and violation of rights to achieve political purposes which go far beyond the litigation before the tribunal in question. If our respective oaths of office have any meaning at all, they surely must mean at least this.

Notes

1. Carmona v. Ward, 436 F. Supp. 1153 (S.D.N.Y. 1977). (Ed's. Note: The case subsequently was reversed, 576 F.2d 405 (2d Cir. 1978)).

2. R. Harris, Freedom Spent (1976).

3. *See* Bice, *Congress' Power to Confer Standing in the Federal Courts, supra.*

4. *See* Goldberg, *Finding the Outer Limits of Federal Jurisdiction, infra.*

5. It is hardly confined to the Burger Court and to talk of it as of an entity unto itself without a past, or perhaps a future, is I think a mistake.

6. Statement released by Board of Governors, Society of American Law Teachers (Oct. 1976).

7. I would say that if there ever were a sufficient reason for overturning *Bakke,* it was the make-up of this Conference as I watched it on the first day. It was living proof of the necessity that the program of Davis University's Medical School must be sustained, as it probably will not, despite Judge Wyzanski's feelings, which I share wholly, that it should be. (The *Bakke* reference is to the lower court opinion.)

8. Dombrowski v. Pfister, 380 U.S. 479 (1965).

9. 401 U.S. 37 (1971).

10. 415 U.S. 452 (1974).

11. 422 U.S. 332 (1975).

12. 384 U.S. 436 (1966).

13. 42 U.S.C. § 1983.

14. 422 U.S. 922 (1975).

15. Bates v. State Bar of Ariz., 433 U.S. 350 (1977).

16. *Id.* at 380.

17. 420 U.S. 592 (1975).

18. 421 U.S. 117 (1975).

19. 555 F.2d 63 (3d Cir. 1977) (en banc).

20. 518 F.2d 396 (2d Cir. 1975).

21. *Id.*

22. 425 U.S. 501 (1976).

23. 372 U.S. 391 (1963).

24. 428 U.S. 465 (1976).

25. 425 U.S. 501 (1976).

26. 28 U.S.C. §§ 1441–1448.

27. 384 U.S 808 (1966).

28. 421 U.S. 213 (1975), *aff'd.* 488 F.2d 284 (5th Cir. 1974).

29. 321 F. Supp. 681 (E.D. La. 1971).

30. 409 U.S. 205 (1972).

31. 422 U.S. 490 (1975).

32. 357 F. Supp. 1289 (E.D. Pa. 1973), *aff'd.* 506 F.2d 542 (3d Cir. 1974), *rev'd,* 423 U.S. 362 (1976).

33. 365 U.S. 167 (1961).

34. 307 U.S. 496 (1939).

35. Alyeska Pipeline Co. v. Wilderness Society, 421 U.S. 240 (1975).

36. Civil Rights Attorneys Fees Awards Act of 1976, Pub. L. No. 94-559, 90 Stat. 2641.

Access to the Federal Courts in Constitutional Cases

By Carole E. Goldberg-Ambrose*

Questions of access to the federal courts involve constitutional law in two different but related ways. First, access itself is regulated by constitutional language. Article III of the Constitution limits the kinds of litigation federal courts may entertain and gives Congress some power to place even further limits on federal subject matter jurisdiction. Article III also limits the federal courts to deciding what are known as "cases" or "controversies"— lawsuits that present issues in a form suitable for judicial resolution. Finally, the Eleventh Amendment restricts federal judicial power to entertain certain suits against states. Thus a constitutional issue is raised when someone argues that federal courts are adjudicating cases that fall outside the Article III definition of federal subject matter jurisdiction, that a federal court is being asked to entertain a suit that does not present a case or controversy, or that a federal court is attempting to decide a suit against a state in violation of the Eleventh Amendment.

Issues of access to the federal courts intersect with constitutional law in yet another way. A person's ability to enforce constitutional rights of all sorts is affected by ease of access to federal courts. Imagine, for example, an individual who wants to leaflet against an unpopular war in a shopping center, but who fears prosecution under a state criminal trespass law that he thinks is overbroad and vague in violation of the First Amendment. If Congress exercises its powers to restrict federal subject matter jurisdiction in such a way that all First Amendment claims are excluded, people will be forced to rely on state courts to protect their federal constitutional rights. In fact, while there are exceptional states, most state courts will not be as sympathetic to federal constitutional claims or as efficient in resolving them as federal courts, especially when the constitutional claims challenge the conduct of state officers.[1] To the extent that individuals lack confidence in the capacity or willingness of state courts to vindicate their federal rights, or to do so expeditiously, these individuals may decline to engage in the protected activity. Similarly, if the Supreme Court interprets the constitutional limits on federal jurisdiction and the congressional statutes regulating federal jurisdiction so as to exclude large numbers of constitutional claims from federal courts, then constitutional rights may not be tested or vindicated.

It is precisely this last sort of problem that I am interested in. In particular, how has the United States Supreme Court been interpreting the constitutional limits on federal jurisdiction when individuals come into court claiming their constitutional rights have been violated? Appropriately enough, the answer to this question implicates constitutional law in both the ways I identified. It entails analysis of the meaning of Article III of the Constitution and the Eleventh Amendment. At the same time, it bears on the likelihood that constitutional claims will receive a sympathetic hearing in some federal court.

There is an assumption implicit in the way I have posed the problem: that the Supreme Court may treat jurisdictional issues differently depending on whether the substantive claim

*Professor of Law, University of California, Los Angeles.

involved rests on the Constitution alone or on some federal statute. The Supreme Court's decisions over the last five years largely validate this assumption, although they indicate the assumption must be refined. Constitutional claims against state officials rarely rest on the Constitution alone. Usually they can be brought under the post-Civil War general civil rights act, 42 U.S.C. § 1983, together with its companion jurisdictional provision, 28 U.S.C. § 1343(3).[2] For purposes of ascertaining jurisdiction, the Supreme Court has tended to treat such constitutional claims as if they were "purely" constitutional. What seems to be required before the Supreme Court will treat a claim as a statutory claim is some more recent, more specific statute than section 1983 that creates the cause of action, and some congressional act that more or less specifically provides for jurisdiction over such statutory claims. The emerging pattern of Burger Court decisions is that where plaintiffs rest their claims solely on the constitution, or on the constitution plus some older, more general civil rights or other federal statute, constitutional limits on federal jurisdiction will be interpreted restrictively. By contrast, where plaintiffs rely on recent, specific statutes providing claims for relief and authorizing federal jurisdiction, the Supreme Court will take a more lenient view of those same constitutional limits on federal jurisdiction. In sum, the Court has been rejecting constitutional claims on grounds that there is no federal jurisdiction as a matter of constitutional law, and simultaneously accepting similar claims simply because Congress has authorized them to be heard in federal court.

This practice poses problems of several sorts. First, it suggests that the meaning of constitutional limits on federal jurisdiction may vary depending on congressional action. Such a suggestion deserves close scrutiny in light of *Marbury v. Madison's*[3] holding that Congress may not expand the Supreme Court's original jurisdiction beyond the categories prescribed in Article III. Implicit in the Supreme Court's recent decisions may be a sense that the Court should defer to congressional judgments in construing the outer limits of the judicial power. The justifications for such deference ought to be examined. Second, to the extent that the Court is denying federal jurisdiction to hear constitutional claims because they do not rest on specific, recent statutory enactments, the rationales for such treatment ought to be considered. Is there some reason why federal courts should be less available when a litigant relies on the constitution or the older, more general civil rights statutes that authorize suits against state officers to enforce constitutional rights? Or to the contrary, is adjudicating constitutional claims something federal courts should be especially willing to do? Third, has the Supreme Court's unwillingness to hear constitutional claims, coupled with its willingness to hear congressionally sanctioned claims, produced unsound doctrine interpreting Article III and the Eleventh Amendment? In other words, has the Court been producing overly restrictive interpretations of constitutional limitations on federal jurisdiction because it is able to relax those restrictions whenever it identifies a congressional action dictating that result?

This paper will describe the situations in which constitutional claims have been less welcome in federal court than similar claims backed by recent, specific federal statutes. Then it will address the problems the Supreme Court's double standard poses.

I. THE DOUBLE STANDARD FOR FEDERAL JURISDICTION
A. Standing

The Supreme Court has been developing a double standard for ascertaining standing to sue in federal court. Constitutional claims resting on nothing more than 42 U.S.C. § 1983 have been rejected for lack of standing where similar statutory claims have been accepted.

This development has taken place after decades of vague, confusing Supreme Court decisions on the subject of standing.[4] Only recently has the Supreme Court begun clarifying the doctrine. In the course of doing so the Court has articulated a distinction between constitutionally based standing requirements and standing requirements that are merely "prudential."[5] The constitutional requirement seems to be that the plaintiff actually be harmed by the acts complained of.[6] The prudential requirements seem to be that the plaintiff be harmed in some way that sets him or her apart from the general public, and that the plaintiff be asserting his or her own rights.[7]

My concern is with Supreme Court decisions that articulate and apply Article III limits on standing when constitutional claims are brought, but not when similar statutory claims are brought. It is difficult to quarrel with Congress's power to supercede a prudential rule.[8] But Congress's power to stretch the Article III requirement for standing requires more elaborate justification. This requirement derives from the limitation of the federal judicial power in Article III to "cases or controversies." The constitutional language itself is imprecise and poorly illuminated by constitutional history.[9] Several commentators have argued persuasively that this language imposes no standing requirements at all;[10] but the Supreme Court never has adopted that view. What the Court seems to have done instead is to enforce Article III limits on standing when a constitutional claim comes without recent, specific statutory support, and to ignore those limits when the congressional support is present.

This practice may be traceable to the time when prudential standing rules were more elaborate and restrictive than they are now. When prudential standing rules required that plaintiffs assert rights analogous to traditional common law rights (in Justice Harlan's language, that they be "Hohfeldian" plaintiffs), even Justice Harlan conceded that Congress could confer standing on some individuals who failed to satisfy this requirement.[11] He suggested that Congress could authorize such non-Hohfeldian plaintiffs to sue as representatives of the public interest, but declined to consider what, if any, constitutional limits there were on this congressional power. The reason for this omission, I believe, was his failure to examine the component of standing derived from Article III itself. All the cases he cited of Congress conferring standing on non-Hohfeldian plaintiffs involved plaintiffs who clearly were "injured in fact."[12]

Once the Court identified the requirement of "actual harm" or "injury in fact" as the only Article III component of standing, the thorny question of Congress's power to exceed that limit emerged. In *Sierra Club v. Morton*,[13] the Supreme Court denied standing under the Administrative Procedure Act[14] to an environmental group challenging government approval of a skiing development in a national forest. The group had failed to allege that any of its members had been or would be injured by the approval. While the decision purported to be a statutory interpretation, Justice Stewart added that "where a dispute is otherwise justiciable, the question whether the litigant is a 'proper party to request an adjudication of a particular issue,' . . . is one within Congress's power to determine."[15]

This suggestion that standing is wholly within Congress's control gained credibility in a case decided eight months later, *Trafficante v. Metropolitan Life Insurance Co.*[16] There the Court upheld the standing of white tenants to sue under the 1968 Civil Rights Act[17] to redress housing discrimination against blacks who wanted to rent units in their building. Plaintiffs had alleged harm based on lost social benefits of integrated living, missed business and professional advantages from contact with minorities, and stigmatization as residents of a "white ghetto." The Court noted that the Act authorized suit by "[a]ny person who claims to have been injured by a discriminatory housing practice," and that the legislative history of the Act included a finding that the whole community suffered because of housing discrimination against minorities. Furthermore, the federal agency charged with responsibility for administering the Act had found plaintiffs qualified to make an administrative complaint. Having found that Congress had intended to go as far as Article III allowed in conferring standing, the Court found sufficient "injury in fact" to satisfy the constitutional as well as the statutory standing requirement.

Three Justices led by Justice White concurred,[18] voicing their own doubts that sufficient "injury in fact" had been alleged to satisfy Article III, but also their willingness to set aside their doubts because Congress had been satisfied. The clear implication, based on precedents cited,[19] was that Congress could confer Article III standing where it otherwise would not exist.

Three years later, this implication was confirmed in *Warth v. Seldin*.[20] There white, high-income residents of a town were denied standing to challenge the town's zoning laws for excluding low and moderate income as well as minority group people. Plaintiffs' claim was based on the equal protection clause of the Fourteenth Amendment and 42 U.S.C. § 1983. They alleged they were injured for purposes of Article III's standing requirement because they were deprived of the benefits of living in a racially and ethnically integrated community. In rejecting standing, the Court relied in part on prudential standing rules that made it difficult to assert the legal rights of another. But the Court went further to note that these white plaintiffs had not alleged "harm . . . sufficiently direct and personal to satisfy the case or controversy requirement of Art. III,"[21] and that the existence of a federal statute conferring standing could have overcome this deficiency. According to the Court, "Congress may create a statutory right or entitlement the alleged deprivation of which can confer standing to sue even where the plaintiff would have suffered no judicially cognizable injury in the absence of statute."[22]

There are other cases in which the lower courts have ignored Article III standing requirements imposed in constitutional cases because the claims were based on recent, statutory enactments including provisions for standing. For example, the Clean Air Act provides that "any person may commence a civil action on his own behalf—(1) against any person . . . who is alleged to be in violation of (a) an emission standard or limitation under this Act or (b) an order issued by the Administrator [of the Environmental Protection Agency] or a State with respect to such a standard or limitation, or (2) against the Administrator where there is alleged a failure of the Administrator to perform any act or duty under this Act which is not discretionary with the Administrator."[23] While it is possible to argue that any person anywhere in the world may be harmed by pollution anywhere because of the total interdependence of the ecosystem, it is hard to imagine that every violation of every emission standard in Nevada alters the air breathed in Maine. Yet according to the Clean Air Act, any resident of Maine could sue any polluter in Nevada. The District of Columbia Court of Appeals upheld the citizen suit provision of the Act, denying that "injury in fact" had to be established at all.[24] The Court's reasoning and conclusion rested on Supreme Court language espousing congressional expansion of standing, and ignored other language insisting that Article III limits remained.[25] By contrast the Tenth Circuit went out of its way to construe another provision of the Clean Air Act to require actual harm before an individual could initiate suit.[26] The court construed the statute as it did for fear that any less restrictive construction would run afoul of Article III's case or controversy requirement.

Another statute in which Congress seemingly has conferred standing on individuals who suffered no preexisting distress is the Truth-in-Lending Act.[27] Under this Act, any "aggrieved debtor" may sue to enforce the requirement that lenders give as part of each billing statement "a brief identification . . . of the goods or services purchased."[28] Statutory minimum penalties are provided. The Fourth Circuit has interpreted "any aggrieved debtor" to include credit card holders who have never incurred finance charges and who have never suffered because they were not provided an adequate identification.[29] The Court accepted the notion that once Congress creates the right to disclosure, failure to disclose necessarily produces harm. Under the Fourth Circuit's reasoning, Congress could have conferred disclosure rights on any citizen, regardless whether he or she was a cardholder with the defendant creditor.

It has not always been easy for the lower courts to ascertain when a congressional act is sufficiently recent, specific, or sufficiently explicit in authorizing jurisdiction to warrant relaxation of the Article III standing requirements imposed in constitutional cases. In *Trafficante*[30] the Court could rely on some legislative history as well as administrative interpretation to sustain its holding. But courts have found statutorily conferred standing in situations where one or both of these were missing. For example, in *Waters v. Hublein, Inc.*,[31] the Ninth Circuit found a white woman had standing to sue an employer under Title VII of the Civil Rights Act of 1964[32] for employment discrimination against minorities. Like the Civil Rights Act of 1968 construed in *Trafficante*, Title VII has a broad standing provision.[33] The Ninth Circuit analogized a white worker's interest in an integrated work environment to a white tenant's interest in an integrated living place. There was no legislative history for Title VII confirming the existence of this interest as there was legislative history confirming the white tenant's interest in *Trafficante*.[34] However, the agency charged with administering Title VII had determined that the white woman had standing to complain of racial discrimination under the Act.

In other cases, courts have disagreed about whether statutory language expanded the Article III limits on standing. The problem has arisen most often where there is no specific statutory language referring to standing, but there is evidence of legislative policy favoring vigorous enforcement of rights. For example, in *TOPIC v. Circle Realty*[35] and *Fair Housing Council of Bergen County v. Multiple Listing Service*,[36] plaintiffs who resided in segregated communites claimed standing under section 3612 of the Civil Rights Act of 1968[37] to challenge racial steering by real estate brokers. Their alleged harm was similar to the harm alleged in *Trafficante*. The statutory language they relied on was different from the provision involved in *Trafficante*, however. In *Trafficante*, plaintiffs rested on language in section 3610 allowing suit by "any person who claims to have been injured by a discriminatory housing practice. . . ." By contrast, section 3612 provides that rights "may be enforced by civil actions, in federal or state courts." In addition, administrative remedies are provided prior to suit under section 3610, while no such remedies have to be exhausted under section 3612. The Ninth Circuit found these differences sufficient to warrant denying standing to the plaintiffs in *TOPIC*. According to the court, the disparities of language and procedure were more important than the unity of policy. The District Court in New Jersey concluded to the contrary, relying on "the congressional policy reflected in the Fair Housing Act of 1968 of protecting not only those at whom discrimination is directed, but also those who are affected by such discrimination."[38] Both decisions relied on *Trafficante*.

The question whether to look to statutory language or congressional policy to extend standing beyond judge-made limits has arisen with claims under statutes more general than the Civil Rights Act of 1968. One commentator has argued that section 1983, the general civil rights statute, "should be read to confer broader standing rights than heretofore have been acknowledged. In the field of housing it could be contended that there is congressional intent under section 1983 to allow a broad range of persons to bring actions to challenge unfair housing practices and policies as evidenced by Sections 3601 and 3610 (a) of the 1968 Civil Rights Act."[39] This approach was not followed, however, in *Cornelius v. City of Parma*.[40] There plaintiffs were residents of an almost all-white community who wanted to challenge ordinances that made it difficult to construct housing for low and moderate income people. Plaintiffs' claim was that these ordinances were designed to exclude minorities. The suit was based in part on 42 U.S.C. §1982, another general post-Civil War civil rights statute that provides:

"All citizens of the United States shall have the same right . . . as is enjoyed by white citizens . . . to . . . purchase, lease, sell, hold, and convey real and personal property." The District Court held that this general statute did not confer the rights to "interracial associations" granted by the Civil Rights Act of 1968, and that no injury existed in the absence of such conferred rights. While the court acknowledged similarities in the purposes of the Civil Rights Act of 1968 and section 1982, the difference in generality and comprehensiveness of the two statutes was dispositive. The newly created right of "interracial association," springing as it did from a detailed, comprehensive statute, could not be read into the more general nineteenth century counterpart.

It is the general civil rights statutes that suffer by contrast when the Court begins focusing on recent, specific statutes to support standing. In the standing cases, the Supreme Court is leaving lower courts with the impression that constitutional rights claimed under general civil rights statutes are less important than statutory rights. While the lower courts have become willing to infer broad rights of standing from statutes that do not even mention standing, the courts have been unwilling to do so where constitutional provisions are relied on via the older, more general civil rights statutes.

It is not clear why the general civil rights statutes should be treated differently. As one commentator noted, "Whether a claim under 42 U.S.C. §§1981, 1982, and 1983 should be categorized as statutory or non-statutory review is not clear. . . . Since section 1983 creates a statutory cause of action to enforce constitutional rights, it is not clear exactly where on the continuum between statutory and non-statutory review it lies."[41] Yet the lower courts have been much less hospitable to constitutional claims based on general statutes. For example, in *City of Hartford v. Hills*,[42] the city challenged HUD grants to certain communities with extremely low percentages of minority residents. Allegations were made that these grants violated the general civil rights statutes, the Civil Rights Act of 1964 and 1968, and the Housing and Community Development Act of 1974.[43] Asserting jurisdiction under the Administrative Procedure Act[44] and the general federal question statute,[45] the city based its standing on the fact that it would be eligible to receive any funds the communities were denied. The court upheld standing, even though the city had not yet applied for the disputed funds. Defendants argued that under *Warth v. Seldin*,[46] the injury was too speculative and indirect. The court rejected this argument, finding *Warth* distinguishable because "that case involved constitutional, not statutory claims."[47] Since Congress had created a statutory right to participate in a reallocation of funds denied the defendant communities, injury could be found where none previously would have existed. Interestingly, there was no language referring to standing in the provision concerned with reallocation of funds. In another case, where the plaintiffs relied on general civil rights statutes to challenge HUD's allocation of funds to communities that discriminate on the basis of race, no standing was found within the meaning of Article III because it was too speculative whether housing opportunities for low and moderate income persons would increase if HUD withdrew the funds.[48]

The implications of these standing decisions are relatively clear: anyone with a constitutional claim should find some corresponding federal statutory claim as well. A statute that specifically offers standing is best. One that grants specific rights and attacks a policy problem comprehensively is second best. One that simply creates a cause of action in general terms is third best. In this hierarchy of standing claims, a constitutional case under a general civil rights statute is least likely to succeed.

B. Ripeness

Ripeness, like standing, is a requirement that stems from Article III's insistence that federal courts decide only cases or controversies. Unlike standing requirements, ripeness requirements have some firm basis in constitutional legislative history. The Framers were especially concerned that the Supreme Court not inject itself too early into the process of evaluating federal legislative or executive action. This concern stemmed from fear that the Court would acquire a vested interest in these early evaluations, that would bias its judgment of specific applications of the legislation in individual cases.[49]

Beyond that, the ripeness component of the case or controversy requirement reflects the desirability in all cases—whether or not they involve challenges to federal legislation—of a specific focus for judicial evaluation of facts and law. If the harm plaintiff will suffer is too remote or speculative, the courts will not be able to observe the full impact of the challenged action, and the parties may not litigate vigorously.

Perhaps because the constitutional origins of the ripeness doctrine are easier to identify than those of standing, the Supreme Court has never articulated elaborate prudential rules of ripeness comparable to those of standing. There is precedent for rejection of appeals to the Supreme Court from state courts if the case "fails to tender the underlying constitutional issues in cleancut and concrete form."[50] But only recently[51] has the Supreme Court suggested that "ripeness" per se may be a nonconstitutional requirement, in federal district courts as well as in the Supreme Court, and that a case may be "unripe" but still present a case or controversy within the meaning of Article III. Whether this suggestion signals the development of prudential rules of ripeness comparable to the prudential rules of standing is uncertain.

Significantly, however, the Burger Court made its suggestion in a case in which Congress had authorized suit despite the apparent lack of ripeness. As in the standing cases, what the Court may be indicating is that its interpretation of the Ariticle III ripeness requirement in constitutional cases is subject to congressional expansion.

The case in question was *Buckley v. Valeo,*[52] a suit by a Presidential candidate, a United States Senator running for reelection, a potential contributor and a number of political organizations challenging the constitutionality of the 1974 amendments to the Federal Election Campaign Act of 1971.[53] The portions of the suit that raised ripeness questions involved challenges to the power of the Federal Election Commission that was created in 1974 to administer the Act. This Commission was given power to receive, index, disclose and investigate reports required to be filed under the Act, to make rules and give advisory opinions interpreting the Act, to authorize convention expenditures in excess of limits set by the Act, and to enforce the Act civilly through adjudicative procedures leading to fines and candidate disqualification. Plaintiffs claimed that given the Commission's extensive powers, the method of choosing its members ran afoul of the separation of powers embedded in the Constitution. Leaders of the House and Senate each appointed two members to the Commission.

This challenge to the method of selecting Commission members was brought at a time when the Commission had not yet exercised many of its powers. None of the plaintiffs had been thwarted because of any particular action the Commission had taken. Ordinarily, the Supreme Court would find such a case unripe unless the plaintiff could show some way in which the Commission's very existence constituted a threat.[54] Indeed, the District of Columbia Circuit had held the case unripe because no such finding was possible.[55]

In *Buckley*, however, plaintiffs were invoking federal jurisdiction under a statute that revealed Congess's eagerness to obtain an early ruling on the Act's constitutionality. The statute provided, "The Commission, the national committee of any political party, or any individual eligible to vote in any election for the office of President of the United States may institute such actions in the appropriate district court of the United States, including actions for declaratory judgment, as may be appropriate to construe the constitutionality of the provisions of this Act. . . ."[56] Additional language provided for expedited hearing of such cases in the Courts of Appeal and the Supreme Court. Without offering any other analysis, the Supreme Court found the case ripe because "Congress was understandably most concerned with obtaining a final adjudication of as many issues as possible litigated pursuant to [the above-mentioned provision]."[57] Here Congress appears to have ripened an otherwise unripe case.

In arriving at its result, the Court relied on another case that found ripeness despite the existence of contingencies that might avert or minimize plaintiffs' harm. In that case as well, effectuation of congressional policy was at stake, although there was no statute specifically authorizing early suit. The case[58] involved a challenge to the constitutionality of the Regional Rail Reorganization Act of 1973,[59] that directed transfer of certain railroad properties to a federal corporation in exchange for its stock and bonds. Plaintiff railroads argued that this form of exchange constituted a "taking;" but at the time they sued, the terms of the transfer had not been determined, and the entire transfer could have been voided by judicical proceedings mandated under the Act. Nevertheless, the Court found the case ripe, and upheld the Act's constitutionality.

These cases are even more troubling than the standing cases because they extend federal jurisdiction precisely in the situation where the Framers were most fearful of it—where a federal statute's effects have not really been felt. It is more or less true that in all these cases the challenge to the statute was on its face, and the application of the challenged law was inevitable. But the Supreme Court has denied jurisdiction on grounds of ripeness in other cases where those circumstances existed, only there was no indication that Congress wanted early adjudication of the constitutional claim.

For example, in *Socialist Labor Party v. Gilligan*,[60] plaintiffs were challenging various Ohio laws restricting minority party access to the ballot. During the course of the litigation much of the challenged legislation was repealed or altered significantly. One challenged provision remained unamended, however—the state's requirement that a political party, other than the two major political parties, file an affidavit under oath stating in substance that the party is not engaged in an attempt to overthrow the government by force or violence, is not associated with a group making such an attempt, and does not carry on a program of sedition or treason as defined by the criminal law. Plaintiffs challenged this provision on grounds that it violated the equal protection clause as well as the First Amendment, that its affidavit requirement was impermissibly vague, and that its enforcement procedures failed to comport with due process. Justice Rehnquist denied jurisdiction, relying on the party's past compliance with the oath requirement, the state's failure to prosecute the party's officers for perjury, and the "skimpiness" of the factual allegations. At the same time, he admitted that plaintiffs "may be parties to a case or controversy" and that jurisdiction may be "technically present."[61] Justices Douglas, Brennan, and Marshall dissented,[62] noting that all the prerequisites for a ripe action were met. Without question the oath requirement had been applied to plaintiffs, and the plaintiffs would seek to nominate candidates for political office in Ohio in the future. They already had suffered harm and would suffer harm in the future from the invidious distinction between the two major political parties and all others, and from the allegedly facially unconstitutional oath. Nevertheless, ripeness was not found.

Similarly, in *California Bankers Association v. Shultz*,[63] plaintiffs challenged the constitutionality of the federal Bank Secrecy Act,[64] which requires banks to keep records of financial transactions with their customers and to report to the government domestic financial transactions exceeding $10,000 in currency or its equivalent. The Act also requires persons to report the transportation of monetary instruments into or out of the United States, or receipts of such instruments in the United States from places outside the United States if the amount exceeds $5,000. Plaintiffs' principal contention was that these provisions violated the guarantees of the First, Fourth, Fifth, Ninth, Tenth, and Fourteenth Amdendments. The Court refused to entertain certain of these claims on the basis that they were unripe or premature. In particular it declined to hear plaintiff ACLU's claim that the recordkeeping requirements violated First and Fourth Amendment rights. The First Amendment claim rested on the fact that the identities of ACLU members and contributors could be ascertained through government examination of the organization's bank records. The Fourth Amendment claim rested on the fact that banks in the past had voluntarily allowed law enforcement officials to inspect bank records without the issuance of a summons. That no government process had yet issued, requiring disclosure of records, was irrelevant to each claim on the merits. Plaintiffs alleged the very existence of records would chill exercise of First Amendment rights and would threaten personal privacy. Yet the Court chose to deny jurisdiction even to consider these claims on grounds of lack of ripeness.[65]

Justice Marshall, dissenting,[66] pointed out that because of the acknowledged bank practice of voluntarily allowing law enforcement officials to inspect bank records, the Fourth Amendment claims could not be raised at all if they could not be raised now. Once recorded, the checks would be readily accessible, without judicial process and without any showing of probable cause, to any of the several agencies that presently have informal access to bank records. In view of the ACLU's related First Amendment claims, there was surely as great a need for prompt adjudication as in *Buckley v. Valeo.*

The only real difference between *California Bankers Association v. Shultz* and *Buckley v. Valeo* is the absence of congressional interest in early consideration of the constitutional issues in the former case and the presence of such interest in the latter. As in the standing cases, however, this reliance on congressional action to determine ripeness is prejudicing constitutional claims brought under the post-Civil War general civil rights statutes.[67]

C. Eleventh Amendment

The Supreme Court has interpreted the Eleventh Amendment to be a broad charter for state immunity from suit in federal court. A recent decision[68] has raised the intriguing possibility that this constitutional immunity may be abrogated by congressional action. It suggests that immunity that might exist in the absence of a federal statute would disappear if Congress so prescribed. Thus, like the standing and ripeness cases previously discussed, this Eleventh Amendment case hints that Congress may be able to alter constitutional jurisdictional boundaries previously established by the Court in purely constitutional cases.

State immunity from suit under the Eleventh Amendment became a real obstacle to constitutional litigation following the Supreme Court's 1974 decision in *Edelman v. Jordan.*[69] *Edelman* involved a challenge to state welfare department regulations on grounds that they conflicted with provisions of the Social Security Act and the equal protection clause of the Fourteenth Amendment. Plaintiffs' Social Security Act claim was based on section 1983 and the statute that authorizes denial of federal funds to noncomplying states.[70] The federal trial court sustained the Social Security Act claim, and ordered payment of unlawfully withheld back benefits as well as cessation of unlawful practices. The Supreme Court reversed the award of back benefits on the ground that it constituted a money award against the state, something a federal court had no jurisdiction to enter under the Eleventh Amendment. The Court did not consider whether it would have interpreted the Eleventh Amendment differently had plaintiffs pressed their Fourteenth Amendment equal protection claim, since that claim was extremely weak on the merits.[71]

The Supreme Court addressed part of the problem of interaction between the Eleventh and Fourteenth Amendments in *Fitzpatrick v. Bitzer.*[72] *Fitzpatrick* was an employment discrimination suit brought under Title VII of the Civil Rights Act of 1964 as amended in

1972 to cover state and local employers.[73] The claim was against the State Employees' Retirement Commission, and sought monetary relief in the form of back pay and attorneys' fees. To the extent that *Edelman* seemed to deny federal jurisdiction to award money damages against a state, the claim seemed impermissible.

The Supreme Court upheld the claim nevertheless. It distinguished *Edelman* because the claim in *Edelman* had not been based on a federal statute enacted pursuant to the Fourteenth Amendment and expressly authorizing suits for money against states in federal court. By contrast, *Fitzpatrick* was based on a federal statute enacted pursuant to Congress's Fourteenth Amendment power to enforce the restrictions on state action embodied in that amendment. According to the Court, the Fourteenth Amendment authorized limited "intrusions by Congress into the judicial, executive, and legislative spheres of autonomy previously reserved to the States."[74] Thus the principle of state sovereignty embodied in the Eleventh Amendment was limited by the enforcement provisions of the Fourteenth Amendment; and congressional acts authorizing suits against states in an exercise of that enforcement power "may provide for private suits against States or state officials which are constitutionally impermissible in other contexts."[75]

The decision to allow Congress, in exercising its Fourteenth Amendment powers, to supesede the Eleventh Amendment, seems a straightforward interpretation of constitutional intent. The more perplexing question, left unanswered in *Fitzpatrick*, is whether congressional legislation should be necessary to override the Eleventh Amendment if suit is brought to enforce Fourteenth Amendment rights. This situation typically arises when suit is brought against a state officer under the general civil rights statute, 42 U.S.C. §1983, or against the state on a cause of action implied directly from a constitutional prohibition.[76] Section 1983 authorizes actions against state officers who are alleged to have violated the plaintiff's constitutional rights. Unlike the provision of Title VII involved in *Fitzpatrick*, however, section 1983 does not authorize suits against states themselves.[77] Nevertheless, since *Ex Parte Young*,[78] it has been interpreted to permit injunctions against state officers when the only way to comply is by expending state funds.[79]

When a claim is brought for damages for violation of constitutional rights under section 1983 or directly under the Fourteenth Amendment, and it appears that the judgment in fact will be borne by the state rather than the state officer, should the case be treated more like *Edelman* or like *Fitzpatrick*? Assuming, arguendo, that section 1983 is not the kind of legislation referred to in *Fitzpatrick*, should the existence of Eleventh Amendment immunity depend on whether Congress has sought to abrogate it pursuant to the Fourteenth Amendment? Should the Fourteenth Amendment's restrictions on state action be interpreted instead to eliminate immunity whether or not Congress acts? If congressional abrogation is deemed necessary, and sufficient to deny immunity, the same constitutional claim will be allowed or disallowed depending on whether Congress has authorized it.

There is some indication the Supreme Court will allow damages actions to enforce Fourteenth Amendment rights even without an authorizing federal statute. In *Fitzpatrick*, for example, the Court emphasized that the substantive portions of the Fourteenth Amendment "themselves embody significant limitations on state authority."[80] Thus "When Congress acts pursuant to §5, not only is it exercising legislative authority that is plenary within the terms of the constitutional grant, it is exercising that authority under one section of a constitutional amendment whose other sections *by their own terms* embody limitations on state authority."[81] This language, no doubt, implies that the substantive portions of the Fourteenth Amendment may be effective by themselves to override state immunity. However, other language in the opinion hints that congressional exercise of enforcement powers may be required as well. For example, the Court stated that Congress may provide for private suits against states or state officials "which are constitutionally impermissible in other contexts."[82]

Lower courts that have considered the question since *Fitzpatrick* was decided have refused to find that "the Eleventh Amendment has been devitalized by the Fourteenth."[83] In *Jagnandan v. Giles,*[84] plaintiffs sued under section 1983 to recover tuition paid for a state university education. They claimed that the state residency requirement for in-state tuition charges unconstitutionally discriminated against aliens. The Fifth Circuit denied their claim for monetary damages, holding that "the Fourteenth Amendment, though ratified last, does not preempt the operation of the Eleventh Amendment's bar against recovery of the excess tuition payments from the state in a federal court."[85] The court distinguished *Fitzpatrick* because of the congressional legislation present there. It refused to equate section 1983 with Title VII because section 1983 was not "specifically directed against a state or states."[86]

The court failed to explain why congressional authorization of suit should affect the interpretation of the scope of state immunity under the Eleventh Amendment in constitutional suits against state officers. All the court could say was that its holding "is in keeping with the historical balance placed upon a coterminous recognition of the Eleventh and Fourteenth Amendments."[87]

Judge Goldberg, concurring,[88] was troubled by the result, but felt compelled by *Fitzpatrick* to join in the majority opinion. He noted that section one of the Fourteenth Amendment was intended to serve as a sword against state action even in the absence of congressional legislation. However, Judge Goldberg perceived that the existence of enforcement legislation under section five of the Fourteenth Amendment was critical to the abrogation of immunity in *Fitzpatrick*. He did not seriously consider that section 1983 might satisfy this requirement, even though *Fitzpatrick* stated that "Congress may, in determining what is 'appropriate legislation' for the purpose of enforcing the provisions of the Fourteenth Amendment, provide for private suits against States *or state officials* which are constitutionally impermissible in other contexts."[89]

These Eleventh Amendment cases suggest that Congress, acting pursuant to the Fourteenth Amendment, may have powers to abrogate Eleventh Amendment immunity which otherwise would exist in constitutional cases. They also reflect the tendency in the standing and ripeness cases to devalue purely constitutional claims and constitutional claims that rest on the venerable but general civil rights statute, section 1983.

II. PROBLEMS POSED BY THE DOUBLE STANDARD FOR JURISDICTION OVER CONSTITUTIONAL AND OTHER CLAIMS

A. Should the Supreme Court Defer to Congress in Construing the Judicial Power?

Implicit in the standing, ripeness, and Eleventh Amendment cases discussed above is an idea that the Supreme Court should allow Congress to expand the judicial power beyond constitutional limits the Court previously has established. At the outset this is a startling proposition. While Article III expressly acknowledges Congress's power to restrict the judicial power of the lower federal courts,[90] Article III also sets outer limits on the federal judicial power.

The only potential sources of congressional power to expand jurisdiction are the Article I power to establish lower federal courts,[91] and the necessary and proper clause.[92] Notwithstanding these provisions, since *Heyburn's Case*[93] and *Marbury v. Madison,*[94] the Supreme Court has taken special pains to protect federal jurisdiction from congressional enlargement. It is one thing to acknowledge Congress's general authority to exercise its constitutionally granted powers according to its own interpretation rather than the Supreme Court's.[95] Separation of powers may dictate that result. It is quite another thing to say the Supreme

Court should be bound by congressional determinations in deciding the outer boundaries of the federal courts' own jurisdiction. Separation of powers may dictate judicial independence most clearly when the Supreme Court is defining the outer boundaries of federal jurisdiction.[96]

For example, the case or controversy requirement was designed at least in part to insulate the Court from involvement in and the appearance of involvement in the legislative process. This policy may be violated when the Court rules early that a statute is constitutional on its face, for then it must rule in future cases on the constitutionality of the applications of the approved statute. Congressional power to determine ripeness might result in constitutional decisions being advanced precisely where the appearance of partnership with the legislature is most damaging to the judiciary. Similarly, the Court's elaborate prudential rules of standing[97] bespeak the Court's longstanding concern with protecting its image and functions from excessive political involvement. While it may be true that congressional expansion of federal jurisdiction may indicate public satisfaction with a more active judicial role, it also may indicate inappropriate congressional desires to have the courts absorb political controversy.

These separation of powers problems have provoked scholarly concern in discussion of the standing cases. "How," Professor Currie asks, "can a statute affect the requirements of the Constitution?"[98] Professors Bator, Mishkin, Shapiro, and Wechsler have echoed Professor Currie's question, but are less concerned about the answer. They query, "Can or cannot Congress confer standing on someone who is not personally injured (or threatened with injury) in fact in some meaningful sense? At the same time, if a matter is important enough to be dealt with by an Act of Congress, how difficult should it be to identify persons meeting such a requirement?"[99]

The Court has suggested that in the standing cases, it is not really permitting Congress to expand the Article III limits on jurisdiction. Rather, Congress is creating new rights, the violation of which produces injury in fact that did not exist before.[100] This suggestion is intuitively appealing. An impoverished person, for example, cannot claim actual harm at the hands of the government if the government simply fails to enact a system of welfare and fails to pay him money to live or eat decently. However, once the government establishes a welfare system with certain eligibility requirements, the individual may claim actual harm if he alleges he is eligible and has been denied benefits. It seems that the establishment of a statutory right has created "actual harm" where none before existed.

That is not the only way to view the situation, however. One could say that the "injury in fact" was the individual's inadequate income and diet, wholly apart from the government's inaction or action. The government's establishment of a welfare system therefore created a cause of action on the merits, not the harm itself. The statute simply recognized and tried to remedy a preexisting situation by allowing the needy person to sue. This usually will be the case where Congress passes a law, and therefore Professors Bator, Mishkin, Shapiro, and Wechsler are correct in suggesting that Congress rarely will confer standing where no actual harm exists.[101]

It is possible, however, to imagine situations where Congress might confer a right of action and standing on a person who is not experiencing any preexisting harm or injury. In such situations, it would be sheer bootstrapping to suggest that Congress's creating a cause of action has produced injury where none existed before. For example, Congress could announce that everyone has a right to work in an economy in which people are paid a minimum wage. Accordingly, any person may sue employers who pay less than the minimum wage, and may collect minimum damages set by statute. A person who works for more than the minimum wage in an industry where everyone is paid the minimum wage (for example, a first-year lawyer) has not been perceptibly harmed by some employer in the garment industry paying less than the minimum wage. A congressional enactment of the sort described above would not alter his situation in any way that would cause an outside observer to say he was harmed when he otherwise would not have been. Rarely, of course, does Congress confer a right and standing on an individual of this sort; but the situation is not wholly unheard of. The Clean Air Act and Truth-in-Lending Act cases discussed above are two instances of Congress doing exactly that.[102] In both cases Congress seems to have provided jurisdiction where otherwise none would exist.

Congress's power to expand jurisdiction in the ripeness and Eleventh Amendment as well as the standing cases could be defended on several grounds. One frequently invoked ground is that it is preferable to rely on Congress rather than the courts to make inroads into state power and state interests.[103] Since Congress is structured to represent states as well as people, a congressional act extending jurisdiction is some indication that the states acquiesce in that extension.[104] This justification is particularly strong where the jurisdictional limit involved applies to jurisdiction over state defendants. The Eleventh Amendment cases invariably present this situation. Indeed, Professor Tribe has argued that regardless whether a suit against a state raises constitutional issues, the Eleventh Amendment ought to be understood to restrict federal judicial power only, not congressional power to regulate the states.[105]

In the standing and ripeness cases, congressional expansion of jurisdiction would make most sense according to this rationale where suits against states or state officers are involved. The ripeness cases have tended to involve congressional expansion of jurisdiction to hear suits against federal officers, however;[106] and the standing cases have tended to involve expansion of jurisdiction to hear suits against private parties.[107]

In all three types of cases, however, there are reasons to insist that the courts, not Congress, make the determination whether federal jurisdiction exists to hear a constitutional claim against the state or a state officer. Deference to Congress is most justified where the only significant competing interests are state and national.[108] But in constitutional cases, there are important individual rights at stake as well. To let Congress determine whether there shall be federal jurisdiction to vindicate these rights may result in the rights going unfulfilled. As Judge Goldberg noted in his concurrence in *Jagnandan v. Giles,* "The Congress cannot realistically be expected to provide fully adequate remedies for every fourteenth amendment violation, because such violations often reflect the type of overreaching that tempts all governments."[109] In other words, it is unwise to rely on Congress to authorize suits against states that Congress might be unwilling to authorize against the federal government.[110]

Thus, while Congress may be entitled ordinarily to some greater freedom than the Court in authorizing incursions into state judicial power and state sovereign immunity, the Court should feel free to define federal jurisdiction expansively in cases where Fourteenth Amendment rights are at issue. Yet these are precisely the cases in which the Court has insisted on recent, specific federal legislation before authorizing jurisdiction. In the standing and Eleventh Amendment cases, even the existence of *some* congressional authorization for suit, in 42 U.S.C. §1983 and 28 U.S.C. §1343 (3), has been deemed insufficient to invoke federal jurisdiction.

Another potential justification for Congress's power to expand federal jurisdiction rests on Congress's perceived superiority in finding facts underlying jurisdictional decisions. This justification resembles the basis on which the Court sustained Congress's power under section five of the Fourteenth Amendment, to prohibit state action that would not independently violate the equal protection or due process clauses of section one.[111] In the standing cases, for example, the Court may be allowing jurisdiction where Congress has authorized it, despite apparent Article III restrictions, because the Article III standing requirement it has carved out is not always easy to apply. Just because a person alleges "injury in fact," it does not mean that the person actually was injured in any meaningful way. Some injuries are more indirect and subjective than others, and it is difficult to establish standards by which to separate injuries that are too indirect and subjective from those that are not. Congress, with its more flexible fact-finding techniques, may be better able to sort out the meaningful injuries from others. Hence a congressional act conferring standing would be strong evidence that the constitutional requirement has been met. Similarly, in ripeness cases, it may be difficult and time-consuming for the Court to distinguish cases where the rights are sufficiently "definite" and the governmental interferences sufficiently "prejudicial" for purposes of Article III. The Court may prefer to apply simple rules of thumb that result in rejecting some cases that in fact are appropriate for judicial resolution. That is, the Court may utilize general principles of ripeness that speak in terms of Article III but operate short of the real constitutional limits; then it may let Congress select the individual cases that would be rejected under these principles, but nevertheless are suitable for early adjudication.

This justification for congressional power to expand federal jurisdiction cannot withstand scrutiny, however. In the standing cases, for example, there is no reason to expect that Congress would be better than the courts at determining the existence of actual harm or injury. Standing under Article III depends on tracing plaintiff's actual or threatened harm to the actions of the defendant. Courts are quite accustomed to taking evidence of damages and deciding which damages are caused by a particular action. In fact, they are probably better able to contend with an individual plaintiff's claim of harm than would a legislative body. All that a legislative finding of harm might do is spare the courts the necessity of making factual findings of harm in every individual case. However, such factual findings would have to be made anyway in the course of determining the relief to which any plaintiff—even one with statutory standing—could receive.[112] In the ripeness cases, the same judicial ability to assess relevant facts exists. By contrast, in the cases construing Congress's powers to enforce the equal protection clause, it was apparent that Congress was better able than courts to assess whether state practices had fostered inequality.

Finally, another potential justification for letting Congress interpret federal jurisdiction more expansively than the courts may be the desirability of having Congress decide when judicial caseloads should be increased beyond their current size. In a time when caseloads have become burdensome,[113] the Court may want some recent, specific indication from Congress that the litigation is important enough to warrant the additional burdens.

This argument presupposes that Congress undertakes some process similar to the "Judicial Impact Statement" Chief Justice Burger has advocated.[114] Yet the Chief Justice made his recommendation precisely because Congress was not anticipating and weighing the potential impact on the courts when it enacted new legislation.

More important, however, this argument presupposes that in the absence of congressional action, the Court itself should make jurisdictional interpretations on the basis of caseload considerations. This assumption may have some merit outside the realm of constitutional claims,[115] although even for nonconstitutional claims, it is questionable whether general jurisdictional statutes should be read narrowly because of caseload concerns.[116] Where constitutional claims are involved, however, the Court has no business assigning cases a low priority because of caseload. The primacy of the constitution is axiomatic. If federal jurisdiction to hear such claims is authorized generally by congressional act, the Court should accept such cases without regard to the burden they impose.[117]

Deference to Congress's definitions of outer limits of federal jurisdiction cannot be justified in suits to enforce constitutional rights. The Court should not wait for congressional permission to be generous with federal jurisdiction. In any event, as the standing cases demonstrate, there usually is room for interpreting whether Congress has authorized federal courts to hear a category of claims. Deferring to Congress can result in courts accepting and rejecting cases depending on whether they favor the plaintiff's claim or the decision below.[118]

B. Should the Older, More General Civil Rights Statutes Receive Less Weight than Newer, More Specific Statutes?

Treating suits under 42 U.S.C. § 1983 as less entitled to federal jurisdiction than suits under more recent, specific statutes makes sense if congressional approval is viewed as a precondition to expansive jurisdictional decisions. A specific, recent enactment might reflect knowing state acquiescence in federal jurisdiction where such jurisdiction affects state interests. It might indicate congressional factfinding that bears on particular jurisdictional problems. And it might suggest congressional willingness to increase the federal caseload in view of current burdens. Speaking more cynically, it also produces more friction if the Court denies jurisdiction where Congress has provided for it recently and specifically.

By contrast, an older, more general civil rights statute reveals nothing except a congressional interest in providing a federal forum for vindication of federal rights. It provides no directions for resolving difficult standing, ripeness, or Eleventh Amendment problems. Thus, the Court does not appear to be contravening legislative policy so clearly when it denies jurisdiction over a case brought under such a statute. And what friction is produced is with a long since dead Congress. Accordingly, the Supreme Court has been treating both section 1983 and the general habeas corpus statutes as no more than starting places for a kind of common law of federal jurisdiction. Even where these statutes call for a federal forum, that forum has been denied.[119]

As I have tried to demonstrate, however, the arguments for congressinal power to expand federal jurisdiction are not strong, particularly in constitutional cases. In constitutional cases, the courts ought to feel free to create expansive jurisdictional doctrine, regardless what Congress prefers. Especially when there is a broad charter of federal jurisdiction to hear constitutional claims, as there is in 42 U.S.C. § 1983 and 28 U.S.C. § 1343 (3), the federal courts ought to seize the opportunity. Vindicating individual rights enshrined in the Constitution is a task for which the lifetime tenured federal judiciary is specially suited. There are policies that dictate narrow or expansive interpretations of jurisdictional doctrines, such as ripeness, standing, and Eleventh Amendment immunity; but their articulation ought not to be influenced, at least in constitutional cases, by the presence or absence of recent federal legislation specifically authorizing suit.

C. Has Deference to Congress Produced Overly Restrictive Jurisdictional Decisions?

The Supreme Court unquestionably has created a double standard for federal jurisdiction; and the presence or absence of recent, specific congressional authorization for suit determines which standard shall be applied. If, as I have argued, this dichotomy is inappropriate in constitutional cases, then the question remains which standard to use—the more expansive one that has been used where statutory authorization exists, or the more restrictive one that has been used in purely constitutional cases?

On the whole, I think that the double standard has served as an excuse for overly restrictive jurisdictional decisions. The Court has been able to dampen criticism of its standing decisions in particular by leaving the "escape hatch" of congressional authorization of jurisdiction.

In the law of standing, for example, the core consideration is insuring effective adversarial presentation of facts and legal issues.[120] But it is not at all clear that the current "injury in fact" requirement, as interpreted by the Supreme Court in cases such as *Warth v. Seldin*, is necessary to insure such presentation. People who are uninterested in vigorously pursuing a case rarely undertake the expensive rigors of litigation. Mere outrage, apart from any injury whatsover, rarely is sufficient motivation for commencing litigation. Perhaps lawyers' economic interests may motivate litigation in cases where Congress has authorized recovery of attorneys' fees by victorious plaintiffs. But in these cases, effective adversarial presentation is especially likely so long as settlement of class actions is supervised. Furthermore, in these cases it is difficult to distinguish private litigation from suits by attorneys on the government payroll to enforce the public interest.

What this suggests to me is that any allegation of harm, no matter how indirect, ought to be sufficient to satisfy constitutional concerns. *Warth's* requirement of a "direct" connection between plaintiff's harm and defendant's conduct is unnecessarily restrictive. Most often the constitutional cases in which standing is at issue are class actions. If a court is concerned about effective adversarial presentation, it usually has at its disposal the provisions of Rule 23 of the Federal Rules of Civil Procedure, that govern class actions. In such actions, the court must be satisfied that the named plaintiff will adequately represent the class.[121] Among the facts the court must consider are lead counsel's expertise and resources (both time and money). By this means, the courts may be able to weed out the less suitable cases.

The ripeness cases present a more complex problem. The constitutional component of ripeness has been articulated less clearly by the Court than the constitutional component of standing. Thus, it is difficult to know what standards the Court is applying, regardless whether Congress has intervened. If there is any pattern at all, it is that the Court considers the merits of plaintiffs' claims in deciding whether there is sufficient harm to trigger judicial intervention. Only congressional action seems to be sufficient to provoke a finding of ripeness for a disfavored claim.

The practice of considering the merits at the jurisdictional stage—condemned in other contexts by the very Justices who invoke it to determine ripeness[122]—is inappropriate and subject to abuse. Regardless whether Congress has authorized jurisdiction, a plaintiff's good faith allegation of harm as a result of enactment of legislation, coupled with supporting allegations, ought to be accepted, especially when plaintiff alleges violation of First Amendment rights. Yet the Court's most restrictive decisions have been in cases that raise First Amendment claims but lack specific, recent congressional authorization.[123]

In the Eleventh Amendment area, the Supreme Court has yet to decide whether a constitutional claim brought under section 1983 abrogates states' immunity from suit for monetary relief. However, the lower courts have interpreted the precedent to deny such claims.[124] To the extent the Supreme Court has been communicating that interpretation, it has been reading the Eleventh Amendment too restrictively. Whether or not Congress authorizes suits against states, the Fourteenth Amendment should be understood to override states' Eleventh Amendment immunity from suit. If section 1983 provides a constitutional claim to individuals who want to recover state funds by means of suits against state officers, the Eleventh Amendment should serve as no obstacle. If such claims are available against the state by direct implication from the Fourteenth Amendment, the Eleventh Amendment likewise should be no barrier. The nature of Fourteenth Amendment rights suggests that their enforcement should not be entrusted exclusively to Congress.[125]

III. CONCLUSION

The Supreme Court has been applying more stringent jurisdictional requirements to purely constitutional claims than to similar claims resting on recent, specific statutes authorizing jurisdiction. This practice cannot be justified on any theory of congressional superiority to make jurisdictional determinations in constitutional cases. Furthermore, it has produced overly restrictive interpretations of jurisdictional doctrine where congressional authorization for suit is lacking.

If the Supreme Court continues to follow this practice, the responsibility will fall on Congress to insure effective enforcement of constitutional claims. Bills already have been introduced to expand jurisdiction in section 1983 and habeas corpus cases.[126] For people who fear erosion of constitutional rights, support for such bills is imperative.

Notes

1. *See* Neuborne, *The Myth of Parity*, 90 HARV. L. REV. 1105 (1977).

2. Constitutional claims against federal officers and the federal government may be implied from the Constitution at least in some circumstances. Bivens v. Six Unknown Named Agents of the Federal Bureau of Narcotics, 403 U.S. 388 (1971). Jurisdiction is invoked in such cases under 28 U.S.C. §1331.

3. 5 U.S. (1 Cranch) 137 (1803).

4. "Standing has been called one of 'the most amorphous [concepts] in the entire domain of public law.'" Flast v. Cohen, 392 U.S. 83, 99 (1968), quoting Hearings on S. 2097 before the Subcommittee on Constitutional Rights of the Senate Judiciary Committee, 89th Cong., 2d Sess. 498 (statement of Prof. Paul A. Freund).

5. *See* 422 U.S. 490 (1975).

6. *Id.* at 498-99. In Village of Arlington Heights v. Metropolitan Housing Development Corp., 97 S. Ct. 555, 561 (1977), the Supreme Court elaborated on this requirement by announcing that "[t]he injury may be indirect, . . . but the complaint must indicate that the injury is indeed fairly traceable to the defendants' acts or omissions."

7. Warth v. Seldin, 422 U.S. 490, 499 (1975).

8. Indeed, the more difficult question is whether courts have the power to fashion such prudential rules at all. *See* Gunther, *The Subtle Vices of the "Passive Virtues"—A Comment on Principle and Expediency in Judicial Review*, 64 COLUM. L. REV. 1, 16 (1964).

9. The best discussion of English practice with respect to standing at the time the Constitution was drafted is Berger, *Standing to Sue in Public Actions: Is It a Constitutional Requirement?*, 78 YALE L.J. 816 (1969).

10. *See, e.g.*, Berger, *supra* note 9; Monaghan, *Constitutional Adjudication: The Who and When*, 82 YALE L.J. 1363 (1973).

11. Flast v. Cohen, 392 U.S. 83, 131-33 (1968) (Harlan, J., dissenting).

12. 392 U.S. at 131-32. The cited cases were Oklahoma v. Civil Service Comm'n, 330 U.S. 127, 137-39 (1947) and Scripps-Howard Radio v. Comm'n, 316 U.S. 4, 21 (1942).

13. 405 U.S. 727 (1972).

14. 5 U.S.C. §702 (1970).

15. 405 U.S. at 732 n.3.

16. 409 U.S. 205 (1972).

17. 42 U.S.C. §3610 (a) (1970).

18. 409 U.S. at 212 (White, Powell, & Blackmun, concurring).

19. The precedents were cases where the Court had permitted Congress to interpret the Fourteenth Amendment more broadly than the Court itself had interpreted it. *See, e.g.*, Katzenbach v. Morgan, 384 U.S. 641 (1966).

20. 422 U.S. 490 (1975).

21. *Id.* at 514.

22. *Id.*

23. 42 U.S.C. §1857h-2 (a) (1970).

24. Metropolitan Washington Coalition for Clean Air v. District of Columbia, 511 F. 2d 809, 814 n. 26 (D.C. Cir. 1975).

25. Even Justice White, who favors congressional power to expand federal jurisdiction, has insisted that

"[plaintiffs] still must show actual or threatened injury of some kind to establish standing in the constitutional sense." O'Shea v. Littleton, 414 U.S. 488, 493 n. 2 (1974).

26. Natural Resources Defense Council Inc. v. United States Environmental Protection Agency, 481 F. 2d 116, 120-21 (1973).

27. 15 U.S.C. §1601 *et seq.* (1970).

28. 15 U.S.C. § § 1637 (b) (2), 1640 (a) (1970); *see* (1968) *U.S.C.C.A.N.* 1962.

29. White v. Arlen Realty and Development Corp., 540 F. 2d 645 (4th Cir. 1975).

30. *See* notes 16-19 & accompanying text *supra*.

31. 547 F. 2d 466 (9th Cir. 1976).

32. 42 U.S.C. §2000e *et seq.* (1970).

33. 42 U.S.C. §2000e-5 (f) (1970).

34. *See* text accompanying note 16 *supra*.

35. 532 F. 2d 1273 (9th Cir. 1976).

36. 422 F. Supp. 1071 (D.N.J. 1976).

37. 42 U.S.C. §3612 (1970).

38. 422 F. Supp. at 1083.

39. Comment, *Standing to Challenge Exclusionary Land Use Devices in Federal Courts After* Warth v. Seldin, 29 STAN. L. REV. 323, 358 (1977).

40. 374 F. Supp. 730 (N.D. Ohio 1974), *aff'd*, 521 F. 2d 1401 (6th Cir. 1975).

41. Comment, *Standing to Challenge Exclusionary Land Use Devices in Federal Courts After* Warth v. Seldin, 29 STAN. L. REV. 323, 358 n. 214 (1975).

42. 408 F. Supp. 879 (D. Conn. 1975).

43. 42 U.S.C. §§5301 et. seq. (Supp. 1974).

44. 5 U.S.C. §702 (1970).

45. 28 U.S.C. §1331 (1970).

46. 422 U.S. 490 (1975).

47. 408 F. Supp. at 886.

48. Evans v. Lynn, 537 F. 2d 571, 589 (2d Cir. 1976) (on rehearing en banc).

49. P. BATOR, P. MISHKIN, D. SHAPIRO, & H. WECHSLER, HART AND WECHSLER'S THE FEDERAL COURTS AND THE FEDERAL SYSTEM 7-11 (2d ed. 1973) [hereinafter HART AND WECHSLER 2d].

50. Rescue Army v. Municipal Court, 331 U.S. 549, 584 (1947).

51. *See* Buckley v. Valeo, 96 S. Ct. 612, 681 (1976).

52. 96 S. Ct. 612 (1976).

53. 2 U.S.C. §§431 et. seq (Supp. 1974).

54. *Compare* Toilet Goods Ass'n v. Gardner, 387 U.S. 158 (1967) *with* Gardner v. Toilet Goods Ass'n, 387 U.S. 167 (1967).

55. Buckley v. Valeo, 519 F. 2d 821, 893 (D.C. Cir. 1975).

56. 2 U.S.C. §437h (Supp. 1974).

57. Buckley v. Valeo, 96 S. Ct. 612, 681 (1976).

58. Regional Rail Reorganization Act Cases, 419 U.S. 102 (1974).

59. 45 U.S.C. §§701 *et. seq.* (Supp. 1974).

60. 406 U.S. 583 (1972).

61. *Id.* at 588.

62. *Id.* at 589 (Douglas, Brennan, & Marshall, J.J., dissenting).

63. 416 U.S. 21 (1974).

64. 12 U.S.C. §§1730d, 1929b, 1951-1959 and 31 U.S.C. §§1051-1062, 1081-1083, 1101-1105, 1221-1222 (1970).

65. 416 U.S. at 68, 75-76.

66. 416 U.S. at 96-97 (Marshall, J., dissenting).

67. *See, e.g.,* O'Shea v. Littleton, 414 U.S. 488 (1974); Rizzo v. Goode, 96 S. Ct. 598 (1976). In the Regional Rail Reorganization Act Cases, 419 U.S. 102, 143 n. 29 (1974), the Court specifically distinguished ripeness issues in suits challenging the constitutionality of state criminal laws. *See* notes 58-59 *supra* & accompanying text.

68. Fitzpatrick v. Bitzer, 96 S. Ct. 2666 (1976). For a general discussion of Supreme Court interpretation of the Eleventh Amendment, see Tribe, *Intergovernmental Immunities in Litigation, Taxation, and Regulation: Separation of Powers Issues in Controversies About Federalism*, 89 HARV. L. REV. 682, 684-85 (1976) [hereinafter Tribe].

69. 415 U.S. 651 (1974).

70. 42 U.S.C. §1384 (1970), now 42 U.S.C. §804 (Supp. 1973).

71. 415 U.S. at 694 n. 2 (Marshall, J., dissenting).

72. 96 S. Ct. 2666 (1976).

73. 42 U.S.C. §§20003 et. seq. (1970). The 1972 amendment was Pub. L. 92-261, §2(1).

74. 96 S. Ct. at 2671.

75. *Id.*

76. Whether the Supreme Court will permit such actions to be implied is yet to be decided. *See* Mt. Healthy City School District v. Doyle, 97 S. Ct. 568, 571 (1977).

77. In a recent decision, *Monell v. Department of Social Services of New York,* 98 S. Ct. 2018 (1978), the Supreme Court overruled an earlier holding that municipal corporations were not "persons" within the meaning of 42 U.S.C. § 1983.

78. 209 U.S. 123 (1908).

79. *See, e.g.,* Brown v. Board of Education, 347 U.S. 483 (1954).

80. Fitzpatrick v. Bitzer, 96 S. Ct. 2666, 2671 (1976).

81. *Id* (emphasis added).

82. *Id.* At one point it appeared that the Supreme Court might resolve this issue during the 1976 Term. 45 U.S.L.W. 3007 (U.S. July 13, 1976). However, the Court resolved the case that raised this question without ever addressing it. *See* Maucelet v. Nyquist, 406 F. Supp. 1233 (W.D.N.Y. and E.D.N.Y. 1976), *aff'd sub. nom.,* Nyquist v. Maucelet, 97 S. Ct. 2120 (1977).

83. Summers v. Civis, 420 F. Supp. 993, 997 (W.D. Okla. 1976).

84. 538 F. 2d 1166 (5th Cir. 1976).

85. *Id.* at 1184.

86. *Id.* at 1183.

87. *Id.* at 1185.

88. *Id.* at 1186 (Goldberg, J., concurring).

89. Fitzpatrick v. Bitzer, 96 S. Ct. 2666, 2671 (1976) (emphasis added).

90. Sheldon v. Sill, 49 U.S. (8 How.) 440 (U.S. 1850).

91. U.S. Const. Art. I, §8, cl. 9.

92. U.S. Const. Art. I., §8, cl. 18.

93. 2 U.S. (2 Dall.) 409 (U.S. 1792). Congress had attempted to recruit the federal courts to participate in the administration of the legislation authorizing benefits for disabled war veterans. The courts would determine the existence and extent of disability; but the War Department would have the final say on whether the veterans' war records entitled them to benefits. The Justices refused to participate in their capacities as Supreme Court Justices.

94. 5 U.S. (1 Cranch) 137 (U.S. 1803). *See* text accompanying note 3 *supra.*

95. This understanding of congressional power is presented in L. Tribe, Constitutional Law §3.4 (1977). On this understanding, Congress may interpret its powers more broadly than would the states.

96. *See* Strong, *Judicial Review: A Tri-Dimensional Concept of Administrative-Constitutional Law,* 69 W. Va. L. Rev. 111, 118-20 (1976).

97. *See* note 7 *supra* & accompanying text.

98. D. Currie, Federal Courts: Cases and Materials 47 n. 2 (2d ed. 1975).

99. Hart and Weschsler 2d 45.

100. *See* text accompanying note 22, *supra.*

101. *See* text accompanying note 99, *supra.*

102. *See* notes 23-29 *supra* and accompanying text.

103. *See, e.g.,* Tribe, *supra* note 68, at 695.

104. This analysis is criticized heavily in Baker, *Federalism and the Eleventh Amendment,* 48 U. Col. L. Rev. 139, 182-85 (1977). Baker argues that it is unrealistic today to expect Congress to reflect state interests over national interests. He notes that even scholars who rely on this analysis of Congress's power to represent state interests question their own analysis.

105. Tribe, *supra* note 68.

106. *See* text accompanying notes 52-59, *supra.*

107. *See* text accompanying notes 16-29, *supra.*

108. *See* Wechsler, *The Political Safeguards of Federalism,* 54 Colum. L. Rev. 543, 559 (1954).

109. 538 F. 2d at 1188 (Goldberg, J., concurring).

110. Baker argues in addition that insistence on congressional action to abrogate state immunity calls into question the result in *Ex Parte Young.* Furthermore, he points out that a legislative check on judicial activism is always available in Congress's power to restrict the jurisdiction of the lower federal courts. Baker, *Federalism and the Eleventh Amendment,* 48 U. Colo. L. Rev. 139, 186-87 (1977).

111. *See* Katzenbach v. Morgan, 384 U.S. 641, 652-58 (1966). The Court found that Congress was better able to determine which government practices affected equality among citizens.

112. *See* Trafficante v. Metropolitan Life Ins. Co., 409 U.S. 205, 209-10 (1972). Where minimum damages are set by statute, as in the Truth-in-Lending Act, proof of harm often will be unnecessary to support recovery. If the courts had to find actual harm in order to establish standing in these cases, the courts' burden would be increased.

113. *See* H. FRIENDLY, FEDERAL JURISDICTION: A GENERAL VIEW 15-54 (1973).

114. Such a statement would assess the impact on the federal caseload of litigation brought under newly enacted legislation.

115. *See* Cohen, *The Broken Compass: The Requirement that A Case Arise "Directly" Under Federal Law*, 115 U. PA. L. REV. 890, 906 (1967) (federal question cases).

116. Goldberg, *The Influence of Procedural Rules on Federal Jurisdiction,* 28 STAN. L. REV. 395, 456-58 (1976).

117. *See, e.g.,* 151 Cong. Rec. 17848 (1976) (statement of Sen. Gaylord Nelson):

> In my view, the assertion of constitutional rights—and the existence of a Federal forum to review those claims—is vitally important for the society, as well as for the petitioner. Our willingness to use scarce judicial resources in this way reflects again the high priority this society places on constitutional liberties and individual freedom. If this society no longer values constitutional rights to the same degree, that judgment should be reflected by the representatives of the people—Congress—through a decision to restrict the habeas jurisdiction of the Federal courts. Congress is also the only body which can address the rising caseload in the Federal courts in a systematic way and make some basic judgments about how scarce judicial resources should be allocated.

118. In fact, it is the poor and the politically unpopular who have been unable to show enough congressional support to gain admittance to federal court. *See, e.g.,* Warth v. Seldin, 422 U.S. 490 (1975); Linda R. S. v. Richard D., 410 U.S. 614 (1973) (mother of illegitimate child lacks standing to challenge state court interpretation that criminal child support law applies only to fathers of legitimate children).

119. *See, e.g.,* Trainor v. Hernandez, 97 S. Ct. 1911 (1977) (federal courts lack power to enjoin state attachment proceedings challenged under due process clause); Wainwright v. Sykes, 97 S. Ct. 2497 (1977) (federal courts lack power to entertain habeas corpus petitions where an independent and adequate state ground would bar direct review and petitioner cannot show "cause" or "prejudice").

120. Baker v. Carr, 369 U.S. 186, 204 (1962). Professor Scott has suggested that standing rules also may serve to allocate scarce judicial resources to those most in need of them. Scott, *Standing in the Supreme Court—A Functional Analysis*, 86 HARV. L. REV. 645, 670-83 (1973).

121. Fed. R. Civ. P. Rule 23 (a).

122. *Compare* California Bankers Ass'n v. Shultz, 416 U.S. 21 (1974) (Rehnquist, J.) *with* Cox Broadcasting Corp. v. Cohn, 420 U.S. 469-502 (1975) (Rehnquist, J., dissenting).

123. *See* notes 60-66 *supra* & accompanying text.

124. *See* notes 83-87 *supra* & accompanying text.

125. *See* text accompanying note 109, *supra.*

126. S. 35, 95th Cong., 1st Sess. (1976) (amendments to section 1983); S. 3886, 94th Cong; 2d Sess. (1975) (amendments to 28 U.S.C. §2254).

The Origins of the Tenth Amendment:
History, Sovereignty, and the Problem of Constitutional Intention
By Charles A. Lofgren*

I. Fire Amidst Constitutional Ashes: The Search for Historical Meaning

Why examine the Tenth Amendment? An authoritative survey of Supreme Court decisions through 1972 found no practical force to the Amendment's guarantee that "[t]he powers not delegated to the United States by the Constitution, nor prohibited by it to the States, are reserved to the States respectively, or to the people."[1] The Amendment tellingly received only eight pages in the massive volume, against 140 for the commerce clause and 255 for the Fourteenth Amendment, each of which has had obvious constitutional importance in limiting state discretion.[2]

More recently, however, stirrings have been visible. In 1975, *Fry v. United States* announced by way of dictum that the Tenth Amendment "is not without significance. . . . [It] expressly declares the constitutional policy that Congress may not exercise power in a fashion that impairs the States' integrity or their ability to function effectively in a federal system."[3] The next year, speaking for the Court in *National League of Cities v. Usery*, Justice William H. Rehnquist relied on the Amendment, as well as on limits which arise from "our federal system of government" and to which Amendment gives "an express declaration," to overturn federal wages and hours legislation as applied to state and municipal employees.[4] Some sense of the controversial quality of the close decision in *Usery* emerges from Justice William J. Brennan's dissent, which found in Rehnquist's opinion a "portent . . . so ominous for our constitutional jurisprudence as to leave one incredulous."[5]

Coming after forty years of desuetude for the Tenth Amendment, *Usery* reaffirms the Amendment's constitutional potential. In broader historical terms, of course, this potential is readily apparent. From the Taney Court through the heyday of the "Four Horsemen" in the 1930s, the Amendment was associated with "Dual Federalism." This restrictive doctrine rested on the propositions that the Constitution had not vested the federal government with sovereign powers of internal police, and that by the overall constitutional scheme—a scheme "made absolutely certain by the Tenth Amendment"—those sovereign powers were retained by the states and thus positively prohibited to the central government.[6] By 1950, to be sure, Edward S. Corwin proclaimed "the passing of dual federalism" and wrote, with considerable accuracy, that "what was once vaunted as a Constitution of Rights, both State and private, has been replaced by a Constitution of Powers."[7] During its dormancy in the four decades following *National Labor Relations Board v. Jones and Laughlin Steel Corporation*,[8] the Amendment nevertheless found an unlikely champion. In fact, Justice William O. Douglas's occasional arguments for state sovereignty, which he claimed was "attested by the Tenth Amendment," anticipated those advanced by the Court in *Usery*.[9] Finally, even Justice

*Crocker Professor of American History, Claremont Men's College.

Brennan's dissent in the case allowed that the Amendment supported some role for the individual states within the constitutional system.[10]

For Justice Brennan, though, the Amendment's function was far more symbolic than substantive; he appropriated—and challenged the majority with—the historical gloss put on the Amendment in *United States v. Darby*:

> The amendment states but a truism that all is retained which has not been surrendered. There is nothing in the history of its adoption to suggest that it was more than declaratory of the relationship between the national and state governments as it had been established by the Constitution before the amendment or that its purpose was other than to allay fears that the new national government might seek to exercise powers not granted, and that the states might not be able to exercise fully their reserved powers.[11]

Justice Rehnquist, who contrarily saw the Amendment as having independent force, neither quoted it nor explored its history in *Usery,* but he could not have quarreled with having recourse to its original understanding. Dissenting in *Fry v. United States*, he had written: "Surely there can be no more important fundamental constitutional question than that of the intention of the Framers of the Constitution as to how authority should be allocated between the National and State Governments."[12]

In short, an issue with deep historical roots has been joined in a modern setting. It is accordingly worthwhile to attempt to clarify the ambiguities surrounding the Amendment so far as they are susceptible to clarification through a reconstruction of its origins and "original understanding." Such an effort may also clarify why ambiguities almost necessarily remain—that is, why resolving certain historical issues only opens other questions. And it seems appropriate in this context to make a few preliminary and somewhat theoretical remarks about the kind of historical-constitutional enterprise I am undertaking.

Let me be both as unabashed and as clear as I can: the historical issues herein pursued do take on *added* interest because they have figured in a recent constitutional dispute of some significance. But a caveat is in order; this added interest remains in a sense a *secondary* interest for the historian. The issues are primarily interesting because they are there. They offer the historian puzzles about people who acted as if, and evidently thought, that they were up to important things, and who, for reasons which could be adduced, in retrospect seem really to have been engaged in critical activities. This line of comment, I realize, could be unfolded and developed at length into an area different in emphasis from the topic of the papers in this collection, for it easily leads into fundamental questions about the nature, purposes, and limitations of the historical enterprise. I have no intention here of pursuing these questions,[13] except to mention a difference, at least in degree, between the historian's goal and what I take to be the lawyer's. As a historian, I feel no obligation to produce *an* answer to the question of what the Tenth Amendment originally meant. A comment by C.H. McIlwain is apposite: "No single fault has been the source of so much bad history as the reading back of later and sharper distinctions into earlier periods where they have no place."[14]

I imagine there are few today anyway who would look exclusively to the 1780s to determine the present significance and meaning of the Constitution or any of its early amendments. As Justice Holmes reminded us, "when we are dealing with words that are also a constituent act, . . . we must realize that they have called into life a being the development of which could not have been foreseen completely by the most gifted of its begetters." "Our whole experience," he cautioned, needs consideration and "not merely" what was said during the founding period.[15] Still, Holmes's choice of the phrase "not merely" is worth pondering. It suggests that one should at least take account of accurate history in fashioning constitutional arguments, even if that history itself is not fully dispositive of the issues in question. So the lawyer and the historian share a common interest. Certainly Justice Robert Jackson's remark in another context is not *always* true: we are not invariably forced to divine what our forefathers envisioned "from materials almost as enigmatic as the dreams Joseph was called upon to interpret for Pharaoh."[16]

What sort of meaning, then, do I seek? The term "constitutional intention," used in my title, should not obscure the fact that a constitution itself can intend nothing. Rather, people give it meaning in the course of drafting, ratifying, and later interpreting it. Beyond that, because what is at issue herein is the original meaning of an amendment which became part of America's prescriptive framework of government, the understandings of greatest interest are those of the Americans who gave the Tenth Amendment its legal status.[17] Unfortunately, direct documentation for the state legislative debates over its ratification in 1789–1791 is almost non-existent.[18] At the same time, however, warranted conclusions are possible about how Americans in 1789–1791 likely understood the Amendment. After all, the Federal Convention of 1787, the state ratification debates and conventions of 1787–1788, and the discussion in Congress of James Madison's proposed bill of rights in the summer of 1789 culminated over a decade of political controversy. An exploration of pertinent aspects of this period reveals the major concerns which underlay the Amendment Congress sent to the states in September 1789 and which undoubtedly guided deliberations in the states.

II. EARLY CONFRONTATIONS WITH SOVEREIGNTY AND FEDERALISM

The problem of dividing authority between two levels of government was hardly new to the late 1780s. The earlier struggle with Great Britain gave rise to the issue in pressing form and provides a useful starting point for developing the ideas which eventually shaped the Tenth Amendment.

In 1773, John Adams called the dispute with England over the proper locus of sovereignty "the greatest Question ever yet agitated."[19] William Blackstone, whose American readership was substantial, had already advanced what was the orthodox view of sovereignty in both England and America on the eve of the War for Independence. In every state, he argued, "there is and must be . . . a supreme, irresistible, absolute, uncontrolled authority, in which the *jura summi imperii*, or rights of sovereignty, reside." In England these rights rested with the Crown in Parliament. "Sovereignty and legislature," he said, "are indeed controvertible terms."[20] Despite the assertion in the Declaration of Independence that governments "deriv[e] their just powers from the consent of the governed" and similar statements in early state declarations of rights,[21] Americans of the mid-1770s generally followed Blackstone in assigning sovereignty to the tangible organs of government, but not without displaying some confusion. Governmental power justly derived *from* the people, but the people had no means of exercising it without in the process dissolving existing governments (which Americans of course did in 1776).[22] The Massachusetts General Court stated the principle—and evidenced the confusion—in this way: "It is a maxim that in every *government* there must exist somewhere a supreme sovereign, absolute and uncontrolled power; but this power resides always in the body of the people, and it can never be delegated to one man or to a few . . . ."[23]

This conception of sovereignty influenced the break with England; it denied that Parliament and local legislatures could coexist in any but the hierarchical relationship which increasingly became anathema to Americans.[24] Because it provided no basis for the existence of an effective central government *in* America, so long as state authority persisted, the orthodox view also influenced the Articles of Confederation.

Once Independence was declared, Congress turned its attention in July 1776 to framing a plan of union.[25] On July 12, John Dickinson offered a draft which provided that "Each Colony . . . reserves to itself the sole and exclusive Regulation and Government of its internal police, in all matters that shall not interfere with the Articles of this Confederation."[26] This was the only guarantee in favor of the states in the long and detailed document, and it was a highly qualified one at that. Positive grants to Congress were admittedly limited, and most evident in the areas of war and foreign relations, but the complexities of the plan could have led to expansion through interpretation.[27] The sole explicit restriction on Congress's internal authority—a prohibition on levying taxes except for support of the post office—was eliminated in the second draft in August.[28]

Attacks on the Dickinson draft initially focused on three characteristics of the plan: equal representation of the states, apportionment of expenses on the basis of total population, and congressional control over western lands. As debate progressed, equal representation was retained, the basis for apportionment of expenses was changed to total land value, and congressional power over the west was substantially reduced.[29] But the plan's fundamental feature—the restriction of state authority to those "matters that shall not interfere with the Articles of this Confederation"—did not come in for attack until Thomas Burke of North Carolina arrived in Congress in early 1777.[30]

Just after Burke's arrival, James Wilson made several attempts on other issues to establish the principle that Congress already possessed a general authority over the states; these efforts may have sensitized Burke to the question of sovereignty.[31] Wishing in any event "that the Power of Congress [be] accurately defined" in view of "the Delusive Intoxication which Power Naturally imposes on the human Mind," Burke offered an amendment to Dickinson's plan: "all sovereign power [would be] in the States separately, and . . . particular acts of it [Congress], which should be expressly enumerated, would be exercised in conjunction, and not otherwise; but . . . in all things else each State would exercise all the rights and powers of sovereignty uncontrolled." Wilson opposed the change, but Burke's amendment prevailed by an eleven-to-one vote.[32] The resulting Article II of the Articles of Confederation confirmed the rejection of a national government of broad and potentially elastic powers; it read: "Each state retains its sovereignty, freedom and independence, and every power, jurisdiction and right which is not by this confederation expressly delegated to the united states in Congress assembled."[33]

Although a clear victory for the proponents of state sovereignty, passage and ratification of the Articles failed to end confusion over the locus of sovereignty in America.[34] Continuing disagreement on the issue, combined with obvious limitations placed on Congress by the Articles, produced further controversies.

One of these involved the Bank of North America. James Wilson, who remained the leading exponent of congressional sovereignty,[35] defended the congressionally chartered bank when it came under attack in Pennsylvania in 1783-1785.[36] Undeterred by Article II of the Confederation, the future Associate Justice held that since the states severally had never held the power to charter a bank commensurate with the needs of the whole of the United States, they could never have retained such a power. "[T]he United States," he held, "have general rights, general powers, and general obligations, not derived from particular states, nor from all the particular states, taken separately, but resulting from the Union of the Whole . . . ." Wilson also pointed to the section of Article V "that for the more convenient management of the *general interests* of the United States, delegates shall be annually appointed to meet in Congress." Moreover, the Declaration of Independence had brought into being one nation, with all the powers of an independent nation.[37]

No single proponent of state sovereignty matched Wilson, but the bank episode shows state autonomy was a fact which the nationalists of the period had to reckon with. When Robert Morris, the Superintendent of Finance under the Confederation and no friend of state sovereignty, had proposed the Bank of North America in 1781, he questioned "whether it may not be necessary and proper that Congress should make immediate application to the several States to invest them with the power of incorporating a bank . . . ."[38] Because some delegates evidently believed Congress held the power of incorporation and others thought previous pledges bound Congress to grant the charter, the bank resolution passed, but it revealingly requested the individual states to approve the bank.[39] Noting this request, James Madison hardly anticipated his later support for a national government when he wrote: "As this is a tacit admission of a defect of power I hope it will be an antidote against the poisonous tendency of precedents of usurpation."[40]

Several attempts to amend the Articles to give Congress authority over commerce and an independent power of taxation similarly evidenced recognition of the Confederation's limits. Relatedly, opposition to the proposals involved both an ever-lurking fear of consolidated government and an orthodox understanding of sovereignty.[41] As a Georgian described the reaction to a suggested commerce amendment, "The high sounding terms of sovereignty and independence have caught and inflamed the minds of some, and the dread of losing our liberty, by giving power to Congress, has intoxicated and alarmed those of others."[42] An impost amendment would give Congress the financial base which, said Abraham Yates, Jr., "is the first, nay, I say the only object of tyrants. . . . This power is the center of gravity, for it will eventually draw into its vortex all other powers."[43] It would lead to the centralized government which the wisdom of the period taught was impossible over an extended territory without loss of liberty, and which, as the Virginia legislature resolved in 1782, would be "injurious to its [the state's] sovereignty, may prove destructive of the rights and liberty of the people, and . . . is contravening the spirit of the confederation."[44]

These disputes preceding and during the Confederation period lead to several interrelated conclusions bearing on the future Tenth Amendment. First, at a theoretical level, the Blackstonian conception of sovereignty demonstrated a "staying power" making likely its continued potency in the face of a new understanding that obviated the need for explicit reservations on behalf of the states and people. Second, at a constitutional level, Americans constantly confronted Article II of the Articles of Confederation with its guarantee to the states of all powers not *expressly* delegated. Third, at a political level, controversy over the Articles themselves, the Bank of North America, a congressional commerce power, and the impost must have heightened actual awareness of the meaning, for local autonomy, of an express guarantee in favor of the states. Most immediately, these conclusions provide a backdrop for the Philadelphia Convention.

III. THE FEDERAL CONVENTION OF 1787

The importance of the Philadelphia Convention to an understanding of the origins of the Tenth Amendment lies primarily in two areas. First, and most obviously, the Convention produced the Constitution which was debated in the states. This document had elements which predictably evoked opposition and counterproposals from Americans committed to the principles of the Articles of Confederation. Second, the discussions in Philadelphia, though kept secret at the time,[45] aid us today in further understanding then-current views about sovereignty which soon figured in the state ratification debates.

A. James Madison's "Middle Ground" and Its Fate

By the time the Convention met, James Madison had sketched requirements for an adequate national government. Writing George Washington, he claimed to "have sought for a middle ground, which may at once support a due supremacy of the national authority, and not exclude the local authorities wherever they can be subordinately useful." But his "middle ground" was in fact a scheme for national supremacy. Besides holding authority in all matters requiring national uniformity, his proposed central government could veto state laws *"in all cases whatsoever"* and could militarily coerce the states. Also, "[t]o give [his] new System its proper validity and energy," he called for "a ratification . . . from the people, and not merely from the ordinary authority of the Legislatures."[46] As he explained to Jefferson, "such a ratification by the people themselves of the several States . . . will render it [the new government] clearly paramount to their Legislative authorities."[47]

When the convention met in late May 1787, Governor Edmund Randolph of Virginia introduced a plan of government embodying Madison's views.[48] Defending it, Madison, James Wilson, and others reiterated their commitments to national supremacy.[49] On one occasion Madison himself evidently went so far as to use a highly impolitic comparison: "The states ought to be placed under the control of the general government—at least as much so as they formerly were under the king and British parliament."[50] It may be a measure of the nationalists' zeal that in their despondency over defeat of proportional representation in the Senate they apparently overlooked what they had gained in the Supremacy Clause.[51]

Proposing a broad national plan was one thing; securing its adoption was another. As John Roche has aptly observed of the framers, "For over three months, in what must have seemed to the faithful participants an endless process of give-and-take, they reasoned, cajoled, threatened, and bargained amongst themselves."[52] In the end, Congress had no general power of legislation, no veto over state laws, and no power of coercion.

Still, once state equality in the Senate was secure, little opposition remained to a strong national government.[53] After defeating the veto on state legislation, the delegates approved what would become the Supremacy Clause in Article VI of the final Constitution.[54] The Committee of Detail, meeting in late July and early August, declined to include a general grant of legislative power, but inserted the necessary and proper clause at the end of Congress's enumerated powers.[55] Another effort in late August to include a general grant of legislative power also failed, but the Convention now gave Congress "power to lay and collect taxes duties & excises, to pay the debts and provide for the common defence & general welfare."[56] Finally, the delegates accepted ratification by conventions drawn from the people, concluding this would give the new government a legal base independent of the state governments, just as Madison had explained to his correspondents prior to the convention.[57]

B. The Problem of Sovereignty

Besides approving novel nationalistic features which would soon require defense at the state level, the delegates were true to the concerns of the 1780s in puzzling over sovereignty. This occurred particularly in the course of describing the relationship of state and central governments within the new system.

In an early discussion of the Virginia plan, Madison recorded Gouverneur Morris as "explain[ing] the distinction between a *federal* and *national*, *supreme*, Govt.; the former being a mere compact resting on the good faith of the parties; the latter having a compleat and *compulsive* operation. He contended that in all communities there must be one supreme power, and one only."[58] Later, Hamilton was blunter: "The general power whatever be its form if it preserves itself, must swallow up the State powers. [O]therwise it will be swallowed by them. . . . Two Sovereignties can not co-exist within the same limits."[59] When William Johnson argued that the states had a dual nature—"in some respects the States are to be considered in their political capacity, and in others as districts of individual citizens"[60]— Madison denied it. "Some contend that states are sovereign," he charged, "when in fact they are only political societies. There is a gradation of power in all societies, from the lowest corporation to the highest sovereign. The states never possessed the essential rights of sovereignty. These were always vested in Congress."[61] Madison thereby sought to play down the contrast between the Articles of Confederation and the Virginia Plan. Yet in the process of doing so, he revealed his commitment to the premise of Morris, Hamilton, and, as later became apparent, Johnson: sovereignty was by nature indivisible, or very close to it.[62]

Especially telling with respect to the pervasiveness of this premise is an exchange between William Paterson and James Wilson. "A confederacy supposes sovereignty in the members composing it & sovereignty supposes equality," argued Paterson, adding: "If we are to be considered a nation, all State distinctions must be abolished, [and] the whole must be thrown into a hotchpot . . . ." Rejecting Paterson's conclusion, Wilson nevertheless adhered to the same understanding of sovereignty: "If N.J. will not part with her Sovereignty it is vain to talk of Govt." They agreed: the states individually might be sovereign, or the nation, but not both.[63]

Further insight comes from the debate over the treason clause.[64] Here one concern was whether or not the wording of the clause should allow treason as a crime against individual states as well as against the United States. Treason being a breach of allegiance to the sovereign, the delegates were quite aware of the clause's implications for the question of the locus and nature of sovereignty. To the initial wording allowing treason against both individual states and the United States, William Johnson protested "that Treason could not be both agst. the U. States—and individual states; being an offense agst the Sovereignty which can be but one in the same community[.]"[65] The meaning of subsequent debate on the clause becomes clouded because of another concern: the possibility that double jeopardy would arise if states could punish treason.[66] Nonetheless, Johnson twice reiterated that the indivisibility of sovereignty meant treason could be committed only against the United States.[67] The record strongly hints Wilson took the same position.[68]

On the other hand, two members—George Mason of Virginia and Oliver Ellsworth of Connecticut—seemingly admitted the divisibility of sovereignty while discussing treason.[69] But it was also Ellsworth who explained what perhaps made acceptable the final wording which retained the possibility of state treasons. "There can," he noted, "be no danger to the Genl authority from this; as the laws of the U. States are to be paramount."[70]

These various exchanges suggest most of the delegates were highly conventional in their convictions about sovereignty's indivisibility. A few evidently disagreed, but failed to develop their views in much detail. In this regard, then, the Convention did not transcend existing conceptions. Significantly, however, the method adopted for the Constitution's ratification laid a basis for preserving the orthodox notion of indivisibility while departing from the Blackstonian view of sovereignty's locus.

Debate over the ratification process showed a substantial consensus for approval by the people.[71] Legislatures had no power to ratify the Constitution, explained Mason. "They are the mere creatures of the State Constitutions, and cannot be greater than their creators."[72] Only if the new system rested on the people, Madison added, would it be a constitution rather than a treaty and thereby require judges to overturn conflicting state legislation.[73] And even those accepting legislative ratification argued on balance that practice had established this procedure as the equivalent of popular ratification.[74] In short, they too allowed that the new system needed a popular base.

One of those who defended legislative ratification in these terms alluded to a significant trend. Oliver Ellsworth "observed that a new sett of ideas seemed to have crept in since the articles of Confederation were established. Conventions of the people, or with power derived expressly from the people, were not then thought of."[75] By 1787, however, the people themselves had ratified state constitutions.[76] Moreover, opponents of particular policies within individual states had argued that state legislatures could not transgress established constitutional limits precisely because those limits reflected the *continually* binding command of the sovereign people.[77]

By 1787, that is, some Americans came to regard the people as holding, albeit in a hard-to-describe fashion, not only what can be called ultimate political sovereignty but also legal sovereignty. Blackstone's denial to the people of the latter, short of a return to the state of nature, would perhaps have made sense to Luther Martin, who "conceived . . . that the people of the States[,] having already vested powers in their respective Legislatures, could not resume them without a dissolution of their Governments."[78] But Martin's view did not prevail in Philadelphia. Some there feared and others hoped the new government would legally overshadow or even absorb the states; but they did not follow Martin in holding that the act of ratification by the people of the states would *destroy* the state governments. Instead, they apparently concluded that by and through an appropriate expression, the people might control government on an ongoing basis, as well as establish or destroy it.[79]

As it finally emerged from Philadelphia, the Constitution contemplated a "general government partly federal and partly national," to borrow Ellsworth's characterization during the Convention.[80] It thereby lay open to the charge of dooming the states through embodying the solecism of *imperium in imperio*. Yet its provisions soon turned out to allow explanations, grounded in new insights, which denied both that any such solecism inhered in the document and that any further guarding of the states was necessary in order to preserve them.

IV. The Ratification Debates, 1787-1788

Once the contest shifted to the states, its terms changed greatly. In a real sense the measure of the nationalists' strength in the Federal Convention was William Paterson's New Jersey Plan. Although commonly contrasted to Randolph's nationalistic Virginia Plan, Paterson's proposal contained a supremacy clause similar to that of Article VI of the final document; it thereby anticipated a strong central government.[81] This meant the Convention could work for compromise within a framework of commitment to strengthened central authority. The hard core opposition comprised perhaps a half dozen delegates out of the fifty-five who attended at one time or another.[82] In the states, on the other hand, the stakes were all or nothing, at least for the moment. Because the Federalists contended conditional ratification was no ratification, the state conventions had to accept or reject the document outright. Moreover, although the Antifederalists suffered defeat in the end, they had substantial strength in key states and included some articulate spokesmen.[83]

Opposition in the states had important consequences. It forced the Federalists to innovation in their arguments which exceeded, at least in its explicitness, the inventiveness they had displayed in the Philadelphia Convention. Their arguments nevertheless failed to convince the opposition, so they turned to strategic innovation by promising subsequent amendments to the Constitution, including a reserved powers amendment. But, while insufficient in itself, the Federalists' argumentative inventiveness had the effects of contributing an increased acuity to contemporary understandings of the Constitution and the issues surrounding it, and thus also of affecting how Americans soon understood the Tenth Amendment.

A. The Antifederalist Challenge

Assessing the proposed Constitution, Samuel Adams wrote Richard Henry Lee: "I stumble at the Threshold. I meet with a National Government, instead of a Federal Union of Sovereign States."[84] In the Virginia convention, Patrick Henry charged: "The question turns . . . on that poor little thing—the expression, We, the *people*, instead of the *states*, of America." This phrasing had produced an "alarming transition, from a confederacy to a consolidated government."[85] The charge of consolidation was, in fact, the most frequent Antifederalist objection to the Constitution.[86]

Many features of the document warranted the charge in Antifederalist eyes, but especially frightening were the undefined powers implied by terms like "necessary and proper," "general welfare," and "supreme law of the land." As Merrill Jensen has commented, nothing in the Articles of Confederation "remotely resembled such phrases."[87] The Constitution's enumeration meant little in the face of this unguarded wording.[88] One of Samuel Adams' correspondents was "more & more persuaded, that it is a Plan, that the common People can never understand—That if adopted—The Scribes & Pharisees only will be able to interpret, & give it a Meaning."[89] A Maine Antifederalist pursued the same thought: "There is a certain darkness, duplicity and studied ambiguity of expression running through the whole Constitution. . . . As it now stands but very few individuals do or ever will understand it, consequently Congress will be its own interpreter."[90] The object could only be the destruction of the states; and not only did the wording of the document point in that direction. Enough about the nationalists' original designs in Philadelphia had leaked out to give the charge additional credence.[91]

The Constitution met added difficulty because the Antifederalists by and large still viewed sovereignty in orthodox terms, stressing not only its supreme, uncontrolled, and indivisible nature, but also its locus in the tangible organs of government, especially the legislature with its power of taxation.[92] "As to direct taxation—give up this, and you give up everything," warned William Grayson in Virginia, "as it is the highest act of sovereignty." "How are two legislatures to coincide," he asked, "with powers transcendent, supreme, and omnipotent? for such is the definition of a legislature."[93] In a careful and widely circulated analysis of the Constitution, the minority members of the Pennsylvania convention gave the objection full expression:

> We apprehend that two coordinate sovereignties would be a solecism in politics. That therefore as there is no line of distinction drawn between the general and state governments; as the sphere of their jurisdiction is undefined, it would be contrary to the nature of things, that both should exist together, one or the other would necessarily triumph in the fullness of dominion. However, the contest could not be of long continuance as the state governments are divested of every means of defense, and will be obliged by 'the supreme law of the land' *to yield at discretion*. . . . [Moreover, the] legislative power vested in Congress by the foregoing recited sections is so unlimited in its nature; may be so comprehensive, and boundless [in] its exercise, that this alone would be amply

sufficient to annihilate the state governments, and swallow them up in the grand vortex of general empire.[94]

As Gordon Wood has summarized the Antifederalist attack, the doctrine of legislative sovereignty which had so influenced the coming of war with Britain "was now relentlessly thrown back at the Federalists by the opponents of the Constitution. . . . The logic of the doctrine of sovereignty required either the state legislatures or the national Congress to predominate."[95]

B. The Federalist Response

Federalist responses to charges of consolidation and congressional sovereignty sometimes skirted the issues, denied the problems, or charged the Antifederalists themselves with inconsistency. Madison, for example, held that the American Revolution had been fought to secure the happiness of the American people, not to guarantee state sovereignty.[96] He and Hamilton explained that, contrary to the Antifederalist fears, the attachment of citizens to their local governments would jeopardize the central government.[97] Hamilton ridiculed the Antifederalists' inconsistency in conceding the need for a strengthened federal union, yet at the same time demanding a "complete independence in the members." It was they who "seem[ed] to cherish with blind devotion the political monster of an *imperium in imperio*."[98]

Federalists met the attack directly, as well. Because the Constitution carefully enumerated the powers of Congress, no further safeguards were necessary. Unlike the state governments, the new central government could exercise only those powers delegated it. However, explaining this view led the Federalists off in various directions.

1. Divisible Sovereignty

After 1789, the *Federalist* papers of "Publius" quickly became the authoritative exposition of the new system. In fact, of course, the Constitution's proponents produced numerous other tracts, together exceeding the *Federalist* in volume, and this literature probably offers a better guide to how most Federalists viewed the Constitution *during* the ratification fight. Reviewing this material, Herbert Storing found the Constitution's advocates "usually . . . conceded the historical and legal priority of the states."[99] Roger Sherman of Connecticut offered what Storing calls a "rather typical description": "The Powers vested in the federal government are clearly defined, so that each state will retain its sovereignty in what concerns its own internal government, and a right to exercise every power of a sovereign state not particularly delegated to the government of the United States."[100]

Sherman's view implies the *divisibility* of sovereignty. Certain language in the *Federalist* itself arguably carries the same implication. "[A]s the plan of the Convention aims only at a partial union or consolidation," wrote Hamilton, "the State Governments would clearly retain all the rights of sovereignty which they had and which were not by that act *exclusively* delegated to the United States."[101] Madison claimed that "the States will retain . . . a very extensive portion of active sovereignty,"[102] and that state equality in the Senate "is at once a constitutional recognition of the portion of sovereignty remaining in the individual states, and an instrument for preserving that residuary sovereignty."[103]

What to make of language of this sort is problematic. Almost a half century later in his *Commentaries on the Constitution of the United States*, Joseph Story carefully and clearly distinguished sovereignty in its ultimate sense—that is, as the source of, and final control on, government— from the *powers* of sovereignty.[104] Because sovereignty in either of these senses may loosely be labeled "sovereignty," not all language suggesting a division of sovereignty necessarily indicates a division of sovereignty in its ultimate sense. Yet Sherman's remark seems clearly to refer to a division of sovereignty in this ultimate sense, not to a division between different governments of different *powers* of sovereignty. Anyone viewing sovereignty as that power which was supreme and uncontrolled, *and* which inhered *in government*, would likely also interpret the quoted comments from Madison and Hamilton as attempting a division of what was by nature indivisible. In short, these Federalist defenses against charges of consolidation probably carried little weight with the unconverted, whatever their authors themselves meant by them.

2. A Changed Locus of Sovereignty

A few Federalists, most notably Wilson in Pennsylvania and Madison elsewhere in the *Federalist* and the Virginia convention, offered more careful explanations. These differed in complexity, however, and to some extent in content.

In a sense Wilson began his defense in Philadelphia. During the debate over equal representation in the Senate he had explained: "The Genl. Govt. is not an assemblage of States, but of individuals for certain political purposes—it is not meant for the States but for the individuals composing them . . . ."[105] "The truth is," he elaborated in the Pennsylvania convention in November 1787, "that, in our governments, the supreme, absolute, and uncontrollable power *remains* in the people." The central government was "founded on a representation of the *whole* Union; whereas the government of any particular state [was] founded only on a representation of the part . . . ."[106] Or, as he put it later, "the power[s] both of the general government, and the state governments, under this system are acknowledged to be so many emanations of power from the people."[107] As for the charge that the Constitution transferred sovereignty from the state governments to the central government, "the sovereignty [was] not in the possession of the state governments, therefore it cannot be transferred from these to the general government."[108] The Constitution accordingly neither divided the indivisible nor transferred it.

A practical problem remained. Easy as it was "to discover a proper and satisfactory principle on the subject," Wilson admitted that in dividing the *powers* of sovereignty, to use Story's later terminology, the line between the state and central authorities could not be drawn with "mathematical precision." Yet he flattered himself "that upon the strictest investigation, the enumeration will be found to be safe and unexceptionable; and accurate too in as great a degree as accuracy can be expected in a subject of this nature."[109]

This "safe and unexceptionable" enumeration posed no threat to the state governments; indeed, the system was "founded on their existence."[110] But whatever role the existing states played in forming the new government, Wilson's defense of it stressed the sovereignty of the people of the *United* States and, concomitantly, an attack on state sovereignty. Fittingly, his last major address to the Pennsylvania convention proclaimed that "by adopting this system, we become a NATION . . . ."[111]

Far more complex, Madison's defense came close to denying that a single principle informed the relations between the state and general governments under the Constitution. Certainly no principle could be found *in* the Constitution.[112] Concerning the different bases of representation in the Senate and House of Representatives, he advised that "[i]t is superfluous to try by standards of theory a part of the constitution which is allowed on all hands to be the result not of theory, but 'of a spirit of amity, and that mutual deference and concession which the peculiarity of our political situation rendered indispensable.'"[113]

When he sought to describe the Constitution, Madison elaborated a characterization advanced earlier by others in the Philadelphia Convention.[114] Defining the *"federal* form . . . as a *confederacy* of sovereign states" and a *"national* government . . . as a *consolidation* of the States,"[115] he found that "[t]he proposed Constitution . . . [was] in strictness neither a national nor a federal constitution; but a composition of both." Giving the system a national character were the House of Representatives and the operation of the government directly on individuals; giving it a federal character were the Senate and the limitation on the government's operation "to certain enumerated objects only."[116]

In these regards, the complexity of Madison's defense as compared to Wilson's begins to appear, but the differences between the two became more pronounced. Describing the source of the central government's power, Madison did not claim—and could not, in view of the Constitution itself—that the Constitution rested on acts by the states as sovereign units in the sense that the Antifederalists regarded them as sovereign. The new system, that is, did not rest on acts of the existing legislatures of the states. Instead, it rested "on the assent and ratification of the people of America," but not, as Wilson would have it, on the people of the United States collectively. Rather, its source was the people within the individual states acting as the supreme power within each state. Also, the new system would go into operation not by a majority vote of the people of America as a whole, nor upon the vote of a majority of the states, but only upon "the *unanimous* assent of the several States that are parties to it . . . ."[117] And regarding the amendment process, the system was "neither wholly *national,* nor wholly *federal.*" A majority of the people could not amend it by virtue of being a majority; voting on amendments was by states; yet a state could be bound against its will.[118]

Neither Wilson's nor Madison's elaboration convinced the Antifederalists. Wilson denied any theoretical base for state sovereignty. Madison omitted quite such a blatantly heretical discussion of sovereignty, but was just as unpersuasive. Patrick Henry, leading the Virginia opposition, offered ridicule in reply to Madison: "We may be amused, if we please, by a treatise of political anatomy. In the brain it is national; the stamina are federal; some limbs are federal, others national." He was not fooled by this "most curious anatomical description," for "[t]o all common purposes of legislation, it is a great consolidation of government."[119] Nor should Henry's conclusion be attributed too readily to perversity (not that Henry was incapable of it). Seeing sovereignty as indivisible, John Adams, too, thought that the new government was "wholly national," for to conclude otherwise ran head on into what he saw as the "solecism" of "imperium in imperio."[120]

C. Demands for a Reserved Powers Clause

Whether emphasizing a division of sovereignty between the states and the proposed general government, or the absolute sovereignty of the American people, or the partly federal-partly national character of the Constitution, the Federalists concluded that the actual powers of the new government would be limited to those enumerated in the Constitution. Unconvinced by any of these explanations, the Antifederalists were likewise unconvinced by the Federalists' accompanying denials of the need for a bill of rights, in favor either of individuals or of the states, and demands for one quickly surfaced.

1. Background in Philadelphia

Earlier, the subject of explicitly limiting central power over the states had arisen on at least four occasions during the Philadelphia convention. The first proposal came in Charles

Pinckney's plan of government, introduced on May 29, the same day as the Virginia Plan. This provided: "Each State retains its rights not expressly delegated."[121] So far as the records indicate, the restriction received no further hearing. The second occasion came a month later while the basis of representation in the Senate was before the Convention. Rufus King unsuccessfully urged including a statement of "the Rights of States" in the Constitution, but the record is vague regarding what he intended.[122]

As the Convention was about to adjourn, two further suggestions appeared. One came on September 12 when the issue arose of including a guarantee of jury trials in civil cases. Rather than writing an overly specific guarantee into the Constitution itself, George Mason argued that "[a] general principle laid down on this and some other points would be sufficient." Prefacing the Constitution with a bill of rights "would give a great quiet to the people," and by consulting the existing state constitutions one could quickly be drawn. When Roger Sherman protested that the existing state declarations provided adequate guarantees and would remain in force under the Constitution, Mason answered that laws of the general government would be paramount over the states. His pleas unavailing, Mason's motion was unanimously rejected.[123]

Precisely what rights the Convention would have included, had it accepted Mason's motion, is speculative but worth consideration. Mason's own involvement in drafting Virginia's wide ranging declaration of rights in 1776 hints he minimally had in mind a guarantee of individual rights.[124] But judging from his remarks on September 12, he also recognized the need for a limitation on central power to override state guarantees. Moreover, by 1787 each of six states had some kind of general reservation of power in favor of the people or the state, either in the state constitution or in a separate bill of rights. Dating from 1776, the Pennsylvania declaration provided that the people of the state had "the sole, exclusive and inherent right of governing and regulating the internal police of the same."[125] The Maryland and North Carolina declarations of the same year contained sections practically identical to Pennsylvania's.[126] The New York constitution of 1777 forbade exercise of any authority over the people "but such as shall be derived from and granted by them."[127] Showing the influence of Article II of the Confederation, the Massachusetts bill of rights of 1780, which New Hampshire copied almost verbatim in 1784, asserted: "The people of this commonwealth have the sole and exclusive right of governing themselves, as a free, sovereign, and independent State, and do, and forever hereafter shall, exercise and enjoy every power, jurisdiction, and right, which is not, or may not hereafter be, by them expressly delegated to the United States of America, in Congress assembled."[128]

These state provisions, plus the existence of Article II, suggest that in drafting a bill of rights the Convention would have included a reserved powers clause. But the conclusion is less certain in view of what happened three days later when Sherman, despite his earlier reply to Mason, made the fourth suggestion for an explicit limitation in favor of the states. With Article V describing the amendment process under review, Sherman "expressed his fears that three fourths of the States might be brought to do things fatal to particular States . . . ." He therefore moved that under Article V "no State shall without its consent be affected in its internal police, or deprived of its equal suffrage in the Senate."[129] The motion failed on an eight-to-three vote,[130] yet Gouverneur Morris's subsequent motion simply to forbid any deprivation of state equality in the Senate passed without opposition.[131] Perhaps, consistent with the later Federalist defenses of the Constitution, the framers in Philadelphia indeed thought a reserved powers clause either unnecessary or perhaps even unwise. Speculation aside, omission of such a clause had a clear impact on the coming ratification struggle.

2. Maneuvering in the States

Debate in Pennsylvania, the first state to hold its convention, anticipated much of what followed.[132] Even before the state's convention met, Samuel Bryan published a widely reprinted tract scoring the Constitution for its lack of a guarantee of liberty like the one in Pennsylvania's own constitution. The next day, October 6, James Wilson replied in a speech which similarly received wide circulation and contained what became the standard Federalist explanation for the absence of a bill of rights.[133]

The example of state declarations of rights was irrelevant, Wilson explained, for the state legislatures had "every power and authority" which the people had not explicitly reserved; "[b]ut in delegating federal powers, another criterion was necessarily introduced, and the congressional authority [was] to be collected, not from tacit implication, but from the positive grant expressed in the instrument of union." It was evident, he said, that with the states "everything which is not reserved is given," but in the new Constitution "the reverse of the proposition prevails, and everything which is not given is reserved." Thus the new government had no power over the press, for example, so "it would have been merely nugatory to have introduced a formal declaration upon the subject"; it might even have implied that some authority did exist in the area.[134] Further, as he later developed the point, many powers and rights could not be "particularly enumerated," yet "an imperfect enumeration would throw all implied power into the hands of the government; and the rights of the people would be rendered incomplete."[135]

The Pennsylvania Antifederalists remained unconvinced. Robert Whitehill observed that the Constitution in fact contained a rudimentary bill of rights in its provisions regarding habeas corpus and jury trial in criminal cases. This, by Wilson's own logic, threatened the great body of *other* rights. Because the Constitution's consolidating features would destroy "the powers and sovereignty of the several states," the people would ultimately have no protection against their rulers.[136]

This line of attack became common as the ratification process continued, but it proved no match in the Pennsylvania convention for the Federalists' two-to-one voting edge. Accordingly, the Antifederalists failed in their last minute effort to postpone action in order to consider amendments to the Constitution.[137] Significantly, though, the amendments offered by Whitehill included a close paraphrase of the Confederation's Article II, and this was repeated in the separate statement subsequently issued by the Pennsylvania minority. The omission of such a guarantee, charged the dissenters, fitted in with "the plan of consolidation" underlying the Constitution.[138]

But defeat of amendments in Pennsylvania marked only the beginning. Failing otherwise to develop a unified critique of the Constitution, the Antifederalists agreed on the need for a bill of rights,[139] and their insistence produced results. As elaborated, for example, by Wilson in Pennsylvania, Hamilton in *Federalist 84*, and Madison in the Virginia convention,[140] the Federalist argument that the people needed no guarantee of rights against the sovereign, because the people themselves were sovereign, could not overcome widespread suspicion of government. An obvious corollary to the notion of state legislative sovereignty, the old view persisted of a constitution as a "compact between the Governors and the Governed."[141] At a less theoretical level, the locus of sovereignty made little difference, for the new government would hold broad powers anyway, and these, if unguarded, might serve as bases for attacks on individuals and states under the necessary and proper clause. Then, too, the existence of a few guarantees raised questions about whether the Constitution compromised other rights. Finally, the supremacy clause invalidated state guarantees.[142] "The victory in the argument clearly lay with the Antifederalists," concludes Cecilia Kenyon, "for the reasoning of their opponents was muddled, inconsistent, contradictory, and thoroughly unpersuasive."[143]

Convening on January 9, 1788, the Massachusetts convention proved pivotal. Five states had already ratified, but the Massachusetts Antifederalists held an initial majority of perhaps twenty out of the 310 delegates.[144] By late January the issue appeared in such doubt to the Federalist leaders that they developed a new tactic. Rufus King wrote to Madison: "We are now thinking of amendments to be submitted not as a condition of our assent & Ratification, but as the opinion of the Convention subjoined to Ratification."[145] Playing on Governor John Hancock's vanity with the prospect of the Vice-Presidency—there was even a chance at the Presidency if Washington declined or Virginia did not join the Union—the Federalists persuaded him to introduce recommendatory amendments. With these, the state's ratification would be unconditional, but Antifederalist fears could still be quelled. The amendments passed and the tactic succeeded: the final majority for ratification was 187 to 168.[146]

Massachusetts set the pattern for the remaining states. Of the additional five which ratified before the new government went into operation,[147] four adopted recommendatory amendments, including geographically vital New York and Virginia. In the fifth, Maryland, recommendatory amendments at least gained committee support.[148] Federalist acceptance of recommendatory amendments was, says Robert Rutland, "the master stroke of the ratification campaign."[149]

3. The Problem of "Expressly"

The sets of amendments offered by Massachusetts, New Hampshire, New York, South Carolina, and Virginia each contained a provision reserving to the states those powers not delegated to the central government; and all but Virginia's would have reserved all powers not "expressly" or, as New York put it, "clearly" delegated.[150] The significance of such wording was well recognized. In North Carolina, which initially declined to ratify, Antifederalist Samuel Spencer held that a clause like the Confederation's Article II "would render a bill of rights unnecessary."[151] In the same vein in Massachusetts, Samuel Adams, now maneuvered into supporting the Constitution,[152] praised the reservation of all powers not expressly delegated as a summary of a bill of rights.[153] Federalist Charles Jarvis agreed that "by positively securing what is not expressly delegated, it leaves nothing to the uncertainty of conjecture, or to the refinements of implication, but is an explicit reservation of every right and privilege which is nearest and most agreeable to the people."[154] Their descriptions of the difficulties Article II caused the Confederation government disclose other Federalists knew the importance of "expressly." Scouting Patrick Henry's proposal in Virginia for this kind of restrictive amendment,[155] Governor Randolph provided an example when he asked if "these gentlemen [are] zealous friends to the Union, who profess to be so here, and yet insist on a repetition of measures which have been found destructive of it?"[156]

In these ways, the ratification controversy indicates a contemporary understanding that absent "expressly" or "clearly," a reserved powers clause would have little meaning. There is more direct evidence, too. By the time George Wythe introduced into the Virginia convention a resolution of ratification which provided, among other things, that "every power not granted remains with the people,"[157] Madison had already attacked the inclusion of "expressly" in the Articles of Confederation.[158] He accordingly found unexceptionable Wythe's formulation omitting the term. "There cannot be a more positive and unequivocal declaration of the principle of the adoption—that every thing not granted is reserved. This is obviously and self-evidently the case, without the declaration."[159] Despite the importance assigned "expressly" by Henry and George Mason,[160] the Virginia convention deleted the term from its recommendatory amendments.[161]

The New York debate showed the same awareness. When the convention there turned to the necessary and proper clause, Robert Lansing introduced an amendment "[t]hat no power shall be exercised by Congress, but such as is expressly given by this Constitution; and all others, not expressly given, shall be reserved to the respective states, to be by them exercised."[162] Sometime before the state's final ratification, this was changed from a recommendatory amendment to an explanation "that every power, jurisdiction and right which is not by the said Constitution *clearly* delegated to the Congress of the United States, or the departments of government thereof, remains to the people of the several states, or to their respective state governments, to whom they may have delegated the same . . . ."[163] When the change occurred is uncertain,[164] but Gilbert Livingston's sketchy notes offer a clue to why it was made. For the debate over the amendment, which still contained "expressly," Livingston recorded:

> explanitory amendt . . .
>
> 2d—No power to be exercised—but what is expressly given.
>
> Ham[ilton]—combats the propriety of the word "expressly"—congress one [are?] to regulate trade—now they must do a thousand things not expressly given —Virginia say not given
>
> Harper—the Committee may correct this.
>
> Yates—agrees—that in grantg genl powers—the powers to execute are implied.
>
> questn on the paragraph—agreed.[165]

That the change to "clearly" occurred at this time seems unlikely, for shortly afterwards Hamilton again mentioned the difficulty that "expressly" posed.[166] But the exchange once more indicates an understanding of the term's importance. (It reveals, too, that Virginia's omission of it drew notice.) By subsequently substituting "clearly" for "expressly," the convention likely intended to lessen the restrictive force of its "explanation."[167]

V. Framing the Tenth Amendment

Although endorsing Virginia's recommendatory amendments, Madison emerged from his state's convention at best as a lukewarm supporter of a bill of rights. He conceded, though, that a declaration of "political truths . . . in that solemn manner" could help "counteract the impulses of interest and passion," as well as provide the basis "for an appeal to the sense of the community" against the occasional usurpations by government.[168]

Once a member of Congress, Madison overcame his misgivings and quickly responded to President Washington's inaugural reminder to consider amendments.[169] Correspondence with Jefferson may have helped him appreciate the barrier a bill of rights would provide against usurpation.[170] Then, too, in five states a Federalist commitment to seek consideration of amendments had accompanied ratification and was probably crucial to it.[171] In Virginia itself, Madison's promise to support amendments helped him win a seat in the new House of Representatives.[172] On the ominous side, although ratifying unconditionally, New York had circularized the other states with a call for a second convention to consider revisions to the Constitution.[173] Sensing the diverse dangers such a convention would pose after the open airing of dissent in the state ratifying conventions, and perhaps overestimating support for a second convention, Madison saw the New York move as an added reason to act quickly in the new Congress on specific and limited amendments.[174]

In spite of opposition—other business should take priority, said the footdraggers[175]—Madison introduced amendments on June 8, 1789. His proposal for what became the core of the Tenth Amendment read: "The powers not delegated by this constitution, nor prohibited by it to the States, are reserved to the States respectively."[176] Attempts to add "or to the people" came on August 18 and August 21. The latter move may have succeeded. The *Annals of Congress*, based on contemporary newspaper reports of the debates, shows it did, but the official journal neither reported the action nor included the phrase in its version of the amendment.[177] In any event, the Senate approved the Amendment in its final form, including "or to the people," on September 7, and a conference of the two Houses accepted it as the Twelfth Amendment on September 24.[178] The first two amendments failed to receive the required state ratifications, so the reserved powers amendment became the Tenth Amendment to the Constitution with Virginia's approval in December 1791 and the Secretary of States's official proclamation on March 1, 1792.[179]

Congressional debate on the Amendment allows fairly firm conclusions about its meaning to its framers. In his introductory speech, Madison explained that he found, "from looking into the amendments proposed by the State conventions, that several are particularly anxious that it should be declared in the constitution, that the powers not therein delegated should be reserved to the several States."[180] Yet, as already discussed, three of the states (or five, counting the unofficial Pennsylvania and Maryland recommendations) had included "expressly" in their proposals; one had included "clearly"; and only one—Madison's own Virginia—had recommended an amendment in the form Madison adopted, without either "expressly" or "clearly" to strengthen its restrictive force. Accordingly, if he meant to suggest that his amendment should entirely calm state anxieties, then he was misleading; but it seems unlikely that many were misled. His next comment was revealing: "Perhaps words which may define this [reservation of power] more precisely than the whole of the instrument now does, may be considered superfluous. I admit that they may be deemed unnecessary; but there can be no harm in making such a declaration, if the gentlemen will allow that fact is as stated. I am sure I understand it so, and I do therefore propose it."[181] In sum, Madison viewed the Amendment as adding nothing to the existing Constitution.

Subsequent unsuccessful attempts to insert "expressly" reveal that Madison's colleagues shared his understanding. The first was on a motion by Thomas Tucker of South Carolina on August 18. Madison "objected to this amendment, because it was impossible to confine a Government to the exercise of express powers; there must necessarily be admitted powers by implication, unless the constitution descended to recount every minutia." Roger Sherman agreed with Madison, but Tucker protested he was being misunderstood. He "did not view the word 'expressly' in the same light with the gentlemen who opposed him; he thought every power to be expressly given that could be clearly comprehended within any accurate definition of the general power."[182] Differing understandings of "expressly" aside, Tucker obviously thought that without the term in the Amendment, the Constitution would allow exercise of implied powers and not very clearly implied powers at that.

The records of the other two abortive attempts to insert "expressly," in the House on August 21 and in the Senate on September 7, are more sketchy, with only the notation that when Elbridge Gerry moved the change in the House, he regarded it "of great importance."[183]

The alteration in Madison's wording which met success—that is, the inclusion of "or to the people" at the end of the Amendment—likewise had primarily a declaratory meaning to those in Congress. The addition evidently had its origin in the first of the amendments Madison proposed on June 8. This, probably based on suggestions from Virginia, New

York, and North Carolina,[184] was "[t]hat there be prefixed to the constitution a declaration that all power is originally vested in, and consequently derived from, the people."[185] The words "We the People" in the existing preamble, combined with the fact of ratification by conventions drawn from the people, made the prefix nugatory in the eyes of some. Madison replied that although self-evident, the words would have a calming effect, and that one would "be puzzled to find a better place" for them.[186] However, once the House voted to arrange the amendments in a separate and subsequent section rather than incorporate them into the body of the Constitution as Madison had originally contemplated,[187] his first proposal was dropped.[188] Thomas Tucker had already moved unsuccessfully to preface the reserved powers amendment with the wording "all powers being derived from the people," holding that this was "a better place to make this assertion than the introductory clause of the constitution . . . ."[189] Now that Madison's amendment to the preamble had been discarded, a comparable declaration in the reserved powers amendment did not create redundancy in wording, and so Congress added "or to the people."[190]

Although primarily declaratory, the final phrase of the Amendment may have had the further purpose of clarifying and qualifying the reservation of power to the states. The conclusion here is speculative, but seems plausible despite scanty records. As already described, the ratification debates in the states disclosed many still accepted the notion of legislative or governmental sovereignty. These people could have easily equated a reservation to the "states" with a reservation to the "state governments." Inserting "or to the people" guarded against this meaning.

VI. The Original Understanding of the Tenth Amendment

The course of the Tenth Amendment prior to its submission to the states constituted an essential step in the causal chain which led to its inclusion in the Constitution. For this reason, if no other, its evolution to September 1789 needs attention in relating its origins. But the pre-ratification history also gives insight into the Amendment's likely meaning to the state legislators who ratified it; and this insight is invaluable in the absence of other evidence.

The Amendment as sent to the states contrasted sharply with the Confederation's Article II and all but one of the state recommendations. It omitted reference to state sovereignty, and it failed to restrict the general government's powers to those "expressly" or "clearly" delegated. Against the background of 1787-1788, these silences must have caught the attention of contemporaries. Arguments for the sovereignty of the people surely sensitized politically aware Americans to the Constitution's claim to a base independent of the existing state governments. Similarly, debates over its specific provisions—especially the general welfare, necessary and proper, and supremacy clauses—surely sensitized Americans to the potential for a central government under the Constitution with an expansive reach, whatever the locus of sovereignty. Probably many shared the reaction of Virginia's two Senators to the amendments Congress sent to the states: "It is impossible," they wrote, "for us not to see the necessary tendency to consolidated Empire in the natural operation of the Constitution, if no further Amended than as now proposed."[191]

In particular, omission of "expressly" must have loomed as ominous to those who still looked to the states for their political salvation as it appeared hopeful to those who doubted the states' capacity to provide stable yet energetic government. Madison, it will be recalled, had argued in Congress that its *inclusion* would require the Constitution "to recount every minutia." By this reading of the term, its *exclusion* meant that the central government's powers needed no detailed base in the Constitution. Thomas Tucker had, of course, disagreed with Madison, holding that the term's inclusion would only require specification of powers in a clear and unambiguous fashion, but not in full detail. By this less restrictive reading of the word, exclusion of "expressly" was yet more significant. For central powers to exist, not only need the Constitution not describe them in full detail; the document need not even state them with great clarity. Moreover, each definition had eighteenth century currency.[192]

The preamble Congress attached to the twelve amendments sent to the states noted the desire in a number of the state conventions of 1787-1788 "that further declaratory and restrictive clauses should be added."[193] Contemporaries who knew of Article II of the Confederation and who had witnessed the earlier state and congressional debates certainly did not find the Tenth Amendment restrictive; it was instead declaratory of the Constitution's overall scheme. Indeed, in historical context, it probably reaffirmed the centralizing tendencies of the new system.

Still, it does not follow that the Amendment provided a constitutional warrant for limitless central authority: the constitutional scheme it attested was not one of unrestricted power. However much the nationalists in the Philadelphia Convention may have desired a consolidated government, they and their cohorts in the states subsequently denied that the Constitution established one. On its face, in fact, the document recognized the states. George Sutherland was doubtlessly correct when he argued that had Americans in 1787–1788 believed the Constitution would "reduce them [the states] to little more than geographical subdivisions of the national domain, . . .it would never have been ratified."[194] Ultimately the supporters of the Constitution had to defend it as partly federal and partly national, whether or not they used that precise formulation; and if, as seems the case, the Tenth Amendment is declaratory rather than restrictive, then it is declaratory of that proposition.

VII. CONCLUSION: SOME PRESENT CHALLENGES

How, then, does the "original" Tenth Amendment square with Justice Rehnquist's recent glosses upon our so-called "federal" system—that is, upon what Americans in the late eighteenth century described as a mixed federal and national system? Beyond that, are the origins of the Amendment of any "use" to the present?

Read together, Rehnquist's dissenting opinion in *Fry v. United States* and his majority opinion in *National League of Cities v. Usery* show him arguing that the commerce clause provides no constitutional base for congressional action in instances where the action "transgresses an affirmative limitation on the exercise of its power . . . ."[195] One such affirmative limitation for Rehnquist is the Tenth Amendment, which "expressly declares" the Constitution's commitment to state freedom from impermissible congressional regulations.[196] A less explicit limitation derives from the American constitutional structure—in other words, from the relationship of the states and central government within the system erected by the Constitution. In *Fry*, Rehnquist spoke of the "concept of constitutional federalism."[197] In *Usery*, he relied on two 1869 cases in which the Court had held that "the Constitution, in all its provisions, looks to an indestructible Union, composed of indestructible states,"[198] and that "in many Articles of the Constitution the necessary existence of the States, and, within their proper spheres, the independent authority of the States, is distinctly recognized."[199] The Court had "repeatedly recognized," he found, "that there are attributes of sovereignty attaching to every state government which may not be impaired by Congress, not because Congress may lack an affirmative grant of legislative authority to reach the matter, but because the Constitution prohibits it from exercising the authority in that manner." Congress cannot control those decisions of a state which are "functions essential to [the state's] separate and independent existence." Regarding such decisions, state authority is "plenary."[200]

The Tenth Amendment argument is easily disposed of—at least superficially. By the historical evidence, the Court was correct in 1941 in labeling the Amendment a "truism."[201] Declaratory of the overall constitutional scheme, it had no independent force as originally understood. Yet the overall constitutional scheme did entail essential roles for the states. Accordingly, although merely declaratory, the Amendment militates at a deeper level against the central government's compromising the states' constitutional roles. As a beginning in this regard, one could do worse than to recall the rule of constitutional interpretation suggested by the Antifederalist "Brutus" (who, however, feared its application would lead to consolidated government): ambiguities in the Constitution are to be resolved in light of the general constitutional design.[202]

Such a rule of interpretation clearly has present-day ramifications: the states remain pretty much essential to today's constitution of government, which is to say that American government and politics would be significantly different without them. As an English scholar has observed, the states may not be sovereign in an ultimate sense, but even in the face of growing central authority they still exercise actual powers which "are of a different order from those of English local government authorities. Indeed, many of the powers they exercise *are* ones which the Englishman does automatically connect with sovereign legislative bodies; they are essentially 'central' powers—powers even of life and death."[203] And not only do the states have significant powers in law which are *separate from* those of the central government; they also figure as states *in* the central government and the politics associated with it. The Senate, the electoral college (and, within it, the practice of unit voting), and the "national" party system all contain elements that Madison and his contemporaries would have termed "federal." Put differently, "federalism" in its eighteenth century sense—which is what Justice Rehnquist seemed intent on defending, albeit without retaining the more precise (and perhaps more analytically useful) eighteenth century terminology—persists as both a legal and a political force.[204] Given this legacy, the states deserve constitutional recognition in areas where the explicit constitutional warrant for central power is obscure.

All of this, however, does not redeem Rehnquist's *application* of his structural argument in *Usery*. Neither the Tenth Amendment nor the constitutional system produces that "invisible radiation" Justice Holmes asked about in *Missouri v. Holland*.[205] Once an activity is conceded to affect interstate commerce, it is hard to get around Professor Corwin's observation that "the supremacy clause [does not] recognize any distinction between laws of a State which must yield and those which need not yield to a conflicting exercise by Congress of its delegated powers."[206]

What a review of the origins of the Tenth Amendment does suggest is that reconciling central authority with state autonomy has roots as deep as the Constitution. Untangling these roots reveals a willingness on the part of at least some late eighteenth-century Americans to set aside preconceived theories in order to gain acceptable government and to develop corresponding new theoretical formulations. If new distinctions and limits need to be developed and observed today (rethinking the constitutional meaning of "commerce" comes readily to mind),[207] then the innovations in constitutional thought during the 1780s provide a standing challenge.

Notes

1. See CONGRESSIONAL REFERENCE SERVICE, LIBRARY OF CONGRESS, THE CONSTITUTION OF THE UNITED STATES OF AMERICA: ANALYSIS AND INTERPRETATION 1263–71 (1973).

2. See *id.*, *passim.*

3. Fry v. United States, 421 U.S. 542, 547 n. 7 (1975) [hereinafter *Fry*].

4. National League of Cities v. Usery, 426 U.S. 833, esp. 842–44 (1976) [hereinafter *Usery*].

5. *Id.* at 875. See generally, *e.g.*, Barber, *National League of Cities v. Usery: New Meaning for the Tenth Amendment?* 1976 SUP. CT. REVIEW 161; Lofgren, *National League of Cities v. Usery: Dual Federalism Reborn*, 4 CLAREMONT J. OF PUBLIC AFFAIRS 19 (Spring 1977).

6. See *e.g.*, E. CORWIN, THE COMMERCE POWER VERSUS STATES RIGHTS, *passim* (1936), which excerpts the leading cases. The quotation in the text is from Kansas v. Colorado, 206 U.S. 46, 89 (1907).

7. Corwin, *The Passing of Dual Federalism*, 36 VA. L. REV. 1, 2 (1950).

8. 301 U.S. 1 (1937).

9. See New York v. United States, 326 U.S. 572, 590 (1946); Case v. Bowles, 327 U.S. 92, 103 (1946); Maryland v. Wirtz, 392 U.S. 183, 201 (1968) (the quotation in the text is at 205) (all dissenting opinions).

10. See *Usery* at 861 n. 4.

11. United States v. Darby, 312 U.S. 100, 124 (1941), quoted by Brennan in *Usery* at 862 (Brennan's italics omitted).

12. *Fry* at 559.

13. The literature on the subject is of course enormous; see, *e.g.*, E. CARR, WHAT IS HISTORY? (1961); D. FISCHER, HISTORIANS' FALLACIES: TOWARD A LOGIC OF HISTORICAL THOUGHT (1970); A. MARWICK, THE NATURE OF HISTORY (1970).

14. C. MCILWAIN, THE AMERICAN REVOLUTION: A CONSTITUTIONAL INTERPRETATION 64 (1923).

15. Missouri v. Holland, 252 U.S 416, 433 (1920).

16. Youngstown Sheet and Tube Co. v. Sawyer, 343 U.S. 579, 634 (1952) (concurring).

17. Cf. James Madison's remark in 1796 about the Constitution itself:

> "As the instrument came from them [the framers in Philadelphia] it was nothing more than the draft of a plan, nothing but a dead letter, until life and validity were breathed into it by the voice of the people, speaking through the several State Conventions. If we were to look, therefore, for the meaning of the instrument beyond the face of the instrument, we must look for it, not in the General Convention, which proposed, but in the State Conventions, which accepted and ratified the Constitution."

Quoted in 3 THE RECORDS OF THE FEDERAL CONVENTION OF 1787 at 374 (M. Farrand ed., rev. ed., 1937) [hereinafter cited as FARRAND, RECORDS]. See THE FEDERALIST, No. 40 at 263–64 (Cooke ed.) [all further citations to *The Federalist* are to the Cooke edition]; C. MILLER, THE SUPREME COURT AND THE USES OF HISTORY 159 n. 23 (1969). On the problems of determining constitutional intent generally, see *id.*, *passim*; Anderson, *The Intention of the Framers: A Note on Constitutional Interpretation*, 49 AM. POL. SCI. REV. 340 (1955).

18. See THE BILL OF RIGHTS: A DOCUMENTARY HISTORY 1171 (B. Schwartz ed. 1971) (editor's note).

19. Quoted in G. WOOD, THE CREATION OF THE AMERICAN REPUBLIC, 1776–1787 at 345 (1969) [hereinafter cited as WOOD, CREATION]. Wood describes the doctrine of sovereignty as "the single most important abstraction of politics in the entire Revolutionary era," *id.*, and as "the ultimate abstract principle to which nearly all arguments were sooner or later reduced." *Id.* at 354.

20. 1 W. BLACKSTONE, COMMENTARIES ON THE LAWS OF ENGLAND *46, *49–51, *160–62.

21. *E.g.*, THE FEDERAL AND STATE CONSTITUTIONS, COLONIAL CHARTERS, AND OTHER ORGANIC LAWS OF THE UNITED STATES 958 (Massachusetts 1780, Art. V), 1541 (Pennsylvania 1776, Art. IV), 1908 (Virginia 1776, Sec. 2) (B. Poore, comp. 1878) [hereinafter cited as FEDERAL AND STATE CONSTITUTIONS].

22. See WOOD, CREATION 344–63; R. ADAMS, POLITICAL IDEAS OF THE AMERICAN REVOLUTION 153–81 (1922). Blackstone himself accepted John Locke's claim that the people possessed "*a Supream Power* to remove or *alter the Legislative*," but he also followed Locke in holding that "however just this conclusion may be in theory, we cannot practically adopt it, nor take any *legal* steps for carrying it into execution. . . ." J. LOCKE, TWO TREATISES OF GOVERNMENT, Book II, secs. 149–50, 212, 227 (P. Laslett ed. 1960); BLACKSTONE, COMMENTARIES *52, *161–62.

23. Quoted in ADAMS, *supra* note 22, at 173.

24. See, e.g., B. BAILYN, THE IDEOLOGICAL ORIGINS OF THE AMERICAN REVOLUTION 198–229 (1967).

25. For the standard account, see M. JENSEN, THE ARTICLES OF CONFEDERATION: AN INTERPRETATION OF

THE SOCIAL-CONSTITUTIONAL HISTORY OF THE AMERICAN REVOLUTION, 1774–1781 esp. chs. 4–13 (1940) [hereinafter cited as JENSEN, ARTICLES].

26. 5 JOURNALS OF THE CONTINTENTAL CONGRESS 546–54 (1906) (the quoted provision appears at 547).

27. See JENSEN, ARTICLES 129–37, 241–42.

28. Compare 5 JOURNALS OF THE CONTINENTAL CONGRESS 552 with *id.* at 685.

29. JENSEN, ARTICLES 140–60.

30. *Id.* at 169–70.

31. *Id.* at 170–74. The apparently catalytic issues included the permissibility of regional meetings of states without congressional approval, control over desertion from the army, the basis of voting on congressional adjournments, and the nature of citizenship.

32. Letter from Thomas Burke to the Governor of North Carolina, March 11, 1777, in 2 LETTERS OF MEMBERS OF THE CONTINENTAL CONGRESS 294 (E. Burnett ed. 1923); letter from same to same, April 29, 1777, in *id.* at 345–46.

33. Art. of Confed., Art. II., in 9 JOURNALS OF THE CONTINENTAL CONGRESS 908 (1907).

34. See F. MCDONALD, THE FORMATION OF THE AMERICAN REPUBLIC, 1776–1790 at 190–91 & n. † (1967), for a summary of the positions [hereinafter cited as MCDONALD, FORMATION]. The debate over the locus of sovereignty in America in the 1770s and 1780s has continued into the twentieth century; compare Van Tyne, *Sovereignty in the American Revolution: An Historical Study*, 12 AM. HIST. REV. 529 (1907), and D. BOORSTIN, THE AMERICANS: THE NATIONAL EXPERIENCE 400–05 (1965) (both arguing state sovereignty and the priority of the states over the nation), with Nettels, *The Origins of the Union and of the States*, 58 PROC. OF MASS. HIST. SOC. 68 (1957–60), and Morris, *"We the People of the United States": The Bicentennial of a People's Revolution*, 82 AMER. HIST. REV. 1, 10–14 (1977) (both taking the opposing positions). Justice George Sutherland had it both ways, depending on whether he was discussing "internal" or "external" sovereignty. See G. SUTHERLAND, CONSTITUTIONAL POWER AND WORLD AFFAIRS 24–47 (1919); Carter v. Carter Coal Co., 298 U.S. 238 (1936); United States v. Curtiss-Wright Export Corp., 299 U.S. 307 (1936). Although the question of the devolution of sovereignty in America in the 1770s and 1780s prior to the adoption of the Constitution has thus had judicial significance, "legal" resolution of the issue is not, I think, vital to understanding the meaning of the Tenth Amendment. The issue is instead important because of the debates over it in the 1770s and 1780s and the insights into the understandings of that period which those debates provide. But see Professor Jaffa's comment: "[T]he meaning of the Tenth Amendment turns decisively upon the question of whether the states are conceived to have this prior and independent existence." Jaffa, *"Partly Federal, Partly National": On the Political Theory of the Civil War*, in A NATION OF STATES 109, 114–15 (R. Goldwin ed., 2d ed., 1974). However, if the Amendment is declaratory of the overall constitutional scheme (and Professor Jaffa apparently agrees with me that it is; see *id.* at 117–18), then the crucial question would seem to be the status of the states *under* the Constitution. But whether or not resolution of their status prior to the Constitution entails a particular answer to the question of their status under the Constitution is, in turn, a question requiring resolution of other issues (and those other issues were, roughly speaking, those debated by the people discussed in this paper). The Constitution may have formed "a more perfect Union," to take a point Professor Jaffa raises (see *id.* at 120), but even if great importance is assigned these several words, I question whether the framers and ratifiers would necessarily have accepted the proposition that the Union of the Constitution was *only* a "more perfect" (that is, in modern usage, a "more complete") version of the same *kind* of union as that in existence under the Confederation. See *infra, passim.*

35. See MCDONALD, FORMATION 191 n. †.

36. See C. SMITH, JAMES WILSON: FOUNDING FATHER, 1742–1798 at 140–68.

37. Wilson, *Considerations on the Bank of North America*, 1785, in THE WORKS OF JAMES WILSON 824, 828–31 (R. McCloskey ed. 1967) (Wilson's emphasis). I believe Professor Smith is incorrect in finding in Wilson's bank defense "the first expression of the doctrine of dual sovereignty which Wilson was to develop most eloquently two years later in the Federal Convention" (see Smith, *supra* note 36, at 152), because Wilson did not develop a doctrine of *dual* sovereignty in the Federal Convention (or in the ratification debates). See *infra*, text accompanying nn. 49, 63, 68, 105–11.

38. Letter from Robert Morris to the President of Congress, May 27, 1781, in 4 THE REVOLUTIONARY DIPLOMATIC CORRESPONDENCE OF THE UNITED STATES 421 (F. Wharton ed. 1889).

39. Letter from the Virginia Delegates to the Governor of Virginia, January 8, 1782, in 6 LETTERS OF MEMBERS OF THE CONTINENTAL CONGRESS 288 (E. Burnett ed. 1933); Resolve of December 31, 1781, in 21 JOURNALS OF THE CONTINTENTAL CONGRESS 1187–90 (1912). See Resolve of May 26, 1781, in 20 *id.* at 546–48 (1912); letter from Morris to the Governors of the States, January 8, 1782, in 5 REVOLUTIONARY DIPLOMATIC CORRESPONDENCE, *supra* note 38, at 94.

40. Letter from Madison to Edmund Pendleton, January 8, 1782, in 6 LETTERS OF MEMBERS OF THE CONTINENTAL CONGRESS, *supra* note 39, at 289, 290. Madison's future collaborator, Alexander Hamilton, also doubted congressional authority in this regard. See Letter from Hamilton to Robert Morris, April 30, 1781, in 2 THE PAPERS OF ALEXANDER HAMILTON 604, 629–30 (H. Syrett and J. Cooke eds. 1961).

41. See MCDONALD, FORMATION 133–42; M. JENSEN, THE NEW NATION: A HISTORY OF THE UNITED STATES DURING THE CONFEDERATION, 1781–1789 at 399–421 (1962); J. MAIN, THE ANTIFEDERALISTS: CRITICS OF THE CONSTITUTION, 1781–1788 at 72–102, 110–15 (1964) [hereinafter cited as MAIN, ANTIFEDERALISTS].

42. Quoted in MAIN, ANTIFEDERALISTS 110.

43. Quoted in *id*. at 79.

44. Quoted in *id*. at 80.

45. 1 FARRAND, RECORDS xi–xii. During the ratification controversy, however, some of the framers discussed their work in Philadelphia; see esp. Luther Martin's "Genuine Information . . . ," November 29, 1787, in 3 *id*. at 172–232.

46. Letter from Madison to Washington, April 16, 1787, in 2 THE WRITINGS OF JAMES MADISON 344, 344–49 (G. Hunt, ed. 1901). Accord, letter from Madison to Edmund Randolph, April 8, 1787, in *id*. at 336–40. Also revealing are notes Madison made on the defects of the Confederation, and on ancient and modern confederacies, in *id*. at 361–412.

47. Letter from Madison to Thomas Jefferson, March 18, 1787, in *id*. at 324, 326.

48. 1 FARRAND, RECORDS 18–23 (Madison's notes, May 29).

49. See, *e.g.*, *id*. at 36–37, 136, 282–93, 323, 492; 2 *id*. at 390–92 (all Madison's notes, May 30, June 6, 18, 19, 30, August 23).

50. 1 *id*. at 471 (Yates's notes, 29 June). In his old age, Madison tried to explain away this comment and his accompanying remarks about sovereignty quoted *infra*, text accompanying n. 61, but his own notes indicate he probably made the comments. See letters from Madison to N.P. Trist, December [?], 1831, and to W.C. Rives, October 21, 1833 in 3 *id*. at 516, 521; 1 *id*. at 463–64.

51. See A. MASON, THE STATES RIGHTS DEBATE: ANTIFEDERALISM AND THE CONSTITUTION 49–52 (2d ed. 1972). Even after the Convention, Madison continued to defend a congressional veto on state legislation. See letter from Madison to Jefferson, October 24, 1787, in 12 THE PAPERS OF THOMAS JEFFERSON 274 (J. Boyd ed. 1955).

52. Roche, *The Founding Fathers: A Reform Caucus in Action*, in AMERICAN CONSTITUTIONAL LAW: HISTORICAL ESSAYS 12, 45 (L. Levy ed. 1966).

53. See, *e.g.*, the evidence reviewed in 3 I. BRANT, JAMES MADISON 101–05 (1950). See also MCDONALD, FORMATION 167–70.

54. 2 FARRAND, RECORDS 27–29 (Madison's notes, July 17).

55. Compare *id*. at 131–32 (proceedings referred to the Committee of Detail) with *id*. at 182 (Madison's notes of report of Committee of Detail, August 6). For speculation that the change occurred during discussion within the Committee, see 3 BRANT, *supra* note 53, at 117.

56. 2 FARRAND, RECORDS 367, 473 (Journal, August 22, 31), 497, 499 (Madison's notes, September 4). See 3 BRANT, *supra* note 53, at 132–34, 139.

57. To trace this provision, see index entries under "Ratification" in 4 FARRAND, RECORDS 203–04; for the major debates, see 1 *id*. at 122–23; 2 *id*. at 88–94 (Madison's notes, June 5, July 23).

58. 1 *id*. at 34 (Madison's notes, May 30).

59. *Id*. at 287 (Madison's notes, June 18).

60. *Id*. at 461 (Madison's notes, June 29).

61. *Id*. at 471 (Yates's notes, June 29). Accord, *id*. at 463–64 (Madison's notes, June 29). See also *supra* n. 50 and accompanying text.

62. Cf. letter from Madison to Jefferson, October 24, 1787, *supra* note 51, at 273–74: "Without such a check in the whole over the parts, our system involves the evil of imperia in imperio. If a compleat supremacy some where is not necessary in every Society, a controuling power at least is so. . . ."

63. 1 FARRAND, RECORDS 178, 180 (Madison's notes, June 9). Paterson later repeated his comment; see *id*. at 251 (Madison's notes, June 16).

64. See 2 *id*. at 345–50 (Madison's notes, August 20). See also B. CHAPIN, THE AMERICAN LAW OF TREASON: REVOLUTIONARY AND EARLY NATIONAL ORIGINS *passim* and esp. 81–84 (1964); A. MCLAUGHLIN, A CONSTITUTIONAL HISTORY OF THE UNITED STATES 178 & n. 36 (1935).

65. 2 FARRAND, RECORDS 346.

66. See esp. Madison's comments, *id*. at 346, 349.

67. *Id*. at 347.

68. See *id*. at 348.

69. See *id*. at 347, 349.

70. *Id*. at 347.

71. See 1 *id*. at 122–23; 2 *id*. at 88–94 (Madison's notes, June 5, July 23).

72. *Id*. at 88.

73. *Id*. at 93.

74. See comments of Ellsworth and King, *id*. at 91, 92. Although willing to accept legislative ratification as

the equivalent of ratification by conventions drawn from the people, King preferred the latter; see *id.* 92. But see Luther Martin's comments, *id.* at 89–90, 476.

75. 2 FARRAND, RECORDS 91.

76. In Massachusetts (1780) and New Hampshire (1784). See FEDERAL AND STATE CONSTITUTIONS 956, 1280.

77. See WOOD, CREATION 369–89. See also *id.* at 430–67.

78. 1 FARRAND, RECORDS 341 (Madison's notes, June 20). Accord, *id.* at 437 (Madison's notes, June 27): " . . . to resort to the Citizens at large for their sanction to a new Governt. will be throwing them back into a State of Nature: . . . the dissolution of the State Govts. is involved in the nature of the process: . . . the people have no right to do this without the consent of those to whom they have delegated their power for State purposes; through their tongue only they can speak, through their ears, only, can hear. . . ." Cf. Martin's comments cited in note 74 *supra.*

79. See generally 3 BRANT, *supra* note 53, at 155.

80. 1 FARRAND, RECORDS 474 (Yates's notes, June 29).

81. See *id.* at 242–45 (Madison's notes, June 15); MCDONALD, FORMATION 167–70; Diamond, *What the Framers Meant by Federalism,* in A NATION OF STATES 25, 38 (R. Goldwin ed. 1974).

82. See MCDONALD, FORMATION 187–88; 3 BRANT, *supra* note 53, at 154–60; Roche, *supra* note 52, *passim.*

83. See, *e.g.,* R. RUTLAND, THE ORDEAL OF THE CONSTITUTION: THE ANTIFEDERALISTS AND THE RATIFICATION STRUGGLE OF 1787–1788, *passim* [hereinafter cited as RUTLAND, ORDEAL]; MAIN, ANTIFEDERALISTS 119–248.

84. Quoted in RUTLAND, ORDEAL 81.

85. 3 THE DEBATES IN THE SEVERAL STATE CONVENTIONS ON THE ADOPTION OF THE FEDERAL CONSTITUTION 44 (J. Elliot ed., 2d ed. 1888) (June 5, 1788) [hereinafter cited as ELLIOT, DEBATES].

86. For a sampling of other Antifederalist remarks to this end, see WOOD, CREATION, 526–27; MAIN, ANTIFEDERALISTS 120–26. For additional citations, see Ranney, *The Bases of American Federalism,* 3 WM. AND MARY Q. 1, 25 n. 97 (3rd ser. 1946).

87. MAIN, ARTICLES 242.

88. See MAIN, ANTIFEDERALISTS 122–23, 153–55; THE ANTIFEDERALISTS lxii–lxxiv (C. Kenyon ed. 1966) [hereinafter cited as KENYON, ANTIFEDERALISTS]. Hamilton commented that the necessary and proper clause and the supremacy clause "have been the sources of much virulent invective and petulant declamation against the proposed constitution, they have been held up to the people, in all the exaggerated colours of misrepresentation, as the pernicious engines by which their local governments were to be destroyed and their liberties exterminated. . . ." THE FEDERALIST, No. 33 at 204. For one of the best developed Antifederalist statements, see Robert Yates, *The Letters of Brutus,* 1788, excerpted in MASON, *supra* note 51, at 107–13.

89. Quoted in RUTLAND, ORDEAL 96–97.

90. Quoted in MAIN, ANTIFEDERALISTS 153.

91. See, *e.g.,* Luther Martin, *Genuine Information, supra* note 45.

92. See MAIN, ANTIFEDERALISTS 123–24; WOOD, CREATION 526–29. Cf. RUTLAND, ORDEAL 56–57, 81, 202, 212. See also Professor Corwin's discussion of Luther Martin's assimulating "state" and "government" in Corwin, *National Power and State Interposition, 1787–1861,* 3 SELECTED ESSAYS ON CONSTITUTIONAL LAW 1171, 1175 (Assoc. Am L. Schools ed. 1938).

93. 3 ELLIOT, DEBATES 280–81 (June 11, 1788). Accord, 2 *id.* at 403 (Thomas Tredwell, N.Y. convention, July 1, 1788).

94. 2 THE DOCUMENTARY HISTORY OF THE RATIFICATION OF THE CONSTITUTION (*Ratification of the Constitution by the States: Pennsylvania*) 628–29 (M. Jensen ed. 1976) [hereinafter cited as *Pa. Ratification Debates*].

95. WOOD, CREATION 527.

96. THE FEDERALIST No. 45 at 309.

97. *Id.,* Nos. 17 (Hamilton) and 45 (Madison).

98. *Id.,* No. 15 at 93.

99. Storing, *The "Other" Federalist Papers: A Preliminary Sketch,* 6 POL. SCI. REVIEWER 215, 220 (1976).

100. Quoted in *id.* at 222.

101. THE FEDERALIST No. 32 at 200.

102. *Id.,* No. 45 at 310.

103. *Id.,* No. 62 at 417. The conclusion that sovereignty is divisible can also be read into the letter from Gen. Washington, September 17, 1787, officially transmitting the Constitution to the President of Congress; see 2 FARRAND, RECORDS 666.

104. See 1 J. STORY, COMMENTARIES ON THE CONSTITUTION OF THE UNITED STATES 191–94 (secs. 207–08) (1833).

105. 1 FARRAND, RECORDS 406 (Madison's notes, June 25, 1787).

106. *Pa. Ratification Debates* 361, 355–56. Accord, *id.* at 471–74, 555–56.

107. *Id.* at 559.

108. *Id.* at 560.

109. *Id.* at 355, 496.

110. *Id.* at 560. Wilson did not here explain how the general government was founded on the existence of the states, but he had earlier described the role of the state legislatures in electing the new Senate. See *id.* at 170.

111. *Id.* at 581.

112. Note should be taken of Professor Jaffa's explication of *Federalist 43* (see Jaffa, supra *note* 34 at 136–37), in which he shows that Madison held the central government's authority rested ultimately on the *extra*-constitutional principle of self-preservation.

113. THE FEDERALIST, No. 62 at 416.

114. 1 FARRAND, RECORDS 331 (King's notes, June 19), 468 (Madison's notes, June 29).

115. THE FEDERALIST No. 39 at 253. See the comparable definition offered by Gouverneur Morris in Philadelphia, 1 FARRAND, RECORDS 34. Madison defined the terms in this way in the course of summarizing the Antifederalist case against the Constitution, but his definitions have general applicability for the 1780s. See Diamond, *supra* note 81 at 27–28.

116. THE FEDERALIST No. 39 at 254–57. Accord, 3 ELLIOT, DEBATES 93–95 (Virginia convention, June 6, 1788).

117. THE FEDERALIST No. 39 at 254.

118. *Id.* at 257.

119. 3 ELLIOT, DEBATES 171 (June 9, 1788). See letter of Luther Martin, *Maryland Journal*, March 21, 1788, in ESSAYS ON THE CONSTITUTION OF THE UNITED STATES . . . 1787–1788 at 360, 366–68 (P. Ford ed. 1892).

120. Quoted in WOOD, CREATION 580–81.

121. 3 FARRAND, RECORDS 607 (italics omitted) (Farrand's reconstruction of Pinckney's plan).

122. See 1 *id.* at 493 (Madison's notes, June 30).

123. 2 *id.* at 587–88 (Madison's notes, September 12).

124. See FEDERAL AND STATE CONSTITUTIONS 1908–09; R. RUTLAND, THE BIRTH OF THE BILL OF RIGHTS, 1776–1791 at 32–40 (1955) [hereinafter cited as RUTLAND, BILL OF RIGHTS]. See also *id.* at 106–25.

125. FEDERAL AND STATE CONSTITUTIONS 1540.

126. See *id.* at 817, 1409.

127. *Id.* at 1332.

128. *Id.* at 958, 1281.

129. 2 FARRAND, RECORDS 629–30 (Madison's notes, September 15).

130. *Id.* at 630.

131. *Id.* at 631.

132. See generally RUTLAND, BILL OF RIGHTS 126–89.

133. See *Pa. Ratification Debates* 128, 158–59, 166, 167–72.

134. *Id.* at 167–68.

135. *Id.* at 388.

136. *Id.* at 397–98, 427.

137. See MAIN, ANTIFEDERALISTS 288; RUTLAND, ORDEAL 55–58; *Pa. Ratification Debates* 589–91, 597–600.

138. *Id.* at 599, 624, 629.

139. See RUTLAND, ORDEAL 313; KENYON, ANTIFEDERALISTS, editor's introduction, *passim*.

140. See text accompanying notes 134–35 *supra*; THE FEDERALIST No. 84 at 578; 3 ELLIOT, DEBATES 620 (June 24, 1788).

141. *Letters of "John DeWitt,"* in KENYON, ANTIFEDERALISTS 98. See WOOD, CREATION 540–43.

142. See KENYON, ANTIFEDERALISTS lxx–lxxi; RUTLAND, ORDEAL *passim*; and esp. the common sense view of the "Federal Farmer": "The truth is, . . . it is mere matter of opinion, and men usually take either side of the argument, as will best answer their purposes: But the general presumption being, that men who govern, will in doubtful cases, construe laws and constitutions most favourably for increasing their own powers; all wise and prudent people, in forming constitutions, have drawn the line, and carefully described the powers parted with and the powers reserved." . . . *Letters from the Federal Farmer to the Republican,* 1787, in PAMPHLETS ON THE CONSTITUTION OF THE UNITED STATES . . . 1787–1788 at 277, 313 (P. Ford ed. 1888).

143. KENYON, ANTIFEDERALISTS lxxi.

144. MAIN, ANTIFEDERALISTS 203, 288.

145. Quoted in RUTLAND, ORDEAL 105.

146. See *id.* at 104–09; MAIN, ANTIFEDERALISTS 288.

147. North Carolina and Rhode Island failed to ratify.

148. For a summary of this sequence of events and of the amendments proposed, see E. DUMBAULD, THE BILL OF RIGHTS AND WHAT IT MEANS TODAY 14–30 (1957).

149. RUTLAND, ORDEAL 301. See *id.* at 33, 160–62, 197.

150. See 1 ELLIOT, DEBATES 322 (Massachusetts), 325 (South Carolina), 326 (New Hampshire), 327 (New York); 3 *id.* at 659 (Virginia). The unofficial Maryland and Pennsylvania recommendations also included reserved powers proposals using "expressly." See 2 *id.* at 550 (Maryland); *Pa. Ratification Debates* 624. Strictly speaking, the New York and South Carolina reserved powers proposals constituted each convention's "understanding" of the Constitution, but were put forward in the context of recommendations for amendment. In addition to its recommendation for a reserved powers amendment, Virginia included a reserved powers "understanding." See 3 ELLIOT, DEBATES 656.

151. 4 *id.* at 163 (July 29, 1788).

152. See MCDONALD, FORMATION 216 for the details of the maneuver.

153. 2 ELLIOT, DEBATES 131 (February 1, 1788).

154. *Id.* at 153 (February 2, 1788).

155. Elliot does not include the text of Henry's amendments, but Randolph's remarks, Henry's stated views, and other evidence, when taken together, indicate that Henry included "expressly" in his amendments. See 3 *id.* at 445–46, 593, 600–601, 622–23; THE BILL OF RIGHTS: A DOCUMENTARY HISTORY 1118 (B. Schwartz ed. 1971) (*Annals of Congress,* August 28, 1789) [hereinafter cited as DOC. HIST. OF BILL OF RTS.]

156. 3 ELLIOT, DEBATES 601 (June 24, 1788). See, *e.g.,* THE FEDERALIST No. 21 at 129–30, No. 44 at 302–05, for other Federalist critiques of the inclusion of "expressly" in the Articles.

157. 3 ELLIOT, DEBATES 587, 653 (June 24, 1788).

158. See THE FEDERALIST No. 44 at 302–05.

159. 3 ELLIOT, DEBATES 620 (June 24, 1788).

160. See *id.* at 441–42, 445–46, 622–23 (June 16, 24, 1788).

161. Elliot does not include the actual decision to delete, but Madison subsequently referred to it in Congress in 1789, and his recollection is consistent with other evidence herein reviewed. See citations in note 155 *supra.*

162. 2 ELLIOT, DEBATES 406 (July 2, 1788).

163. 1 *id.* at 327 (italics added).

164. From the material discussed in the text accompanying notes 165–66 *infra,* Professor Schwartz concludes the change occurred on July 19, 1788 (see DOC. HIST. OF BILL OF RTS. 854), but as I read it, the evidence is not as clear.

165. Gilbert Livingston Papers, New York Public Library, July 19, 1788, in DOC. HIST. OF BILL OF RTS. 898.

166. *Id.* at 899.

167. See text accompanying note 192 *infra.*

168. Letter from Madison to Jefferson, October 17, 1787, excerpted in MASON, *supra* note 51, at 176, 177. See *id.* at 176–78; A. KOCH, JEFFERSON AND MADISON: THE GREAT COLLABORATION 52 (1964). For this entire section (*i.e.,* text accompanying notes 168–90), see generally RUTLAND, BILL OF RIGHTS 190–215.

169. 1 MESSAGES AND PAPERS OF THE PRESIDENTS 45 (J. Richardson, comp. 1897) (April 30, 1789); DOC. HIST. OF BILL OF RTS. 1012 (*Annals of Cong.,* May 4, 1789).

170. See letters from Jefferson to Madison, December 20, 1787, and March 15, 1789, excerpted in MASON, *supra* note 51, at 170–72, 180–82. See also KOCH, *supra* note 168, at 51–59.

171. See text accompanying notes 139–49 *supra.*

172. See 3 BRANT, *supra* note 53, at 240–42; RUTLAND, ORDEAL 297; letter from Madison to George Eve, January 2, 1789, in DOC. HIST. OF BILL OF RTS. 996–97.

173. Letter from George Clinton to the Several Governors, July 28, 1788, in 2 ELLIOT, DEBATES 413–14.

174. See letters from Madison to Jefferson, April 22, September 21, December 8, 1788, excerpted in MASON, *supra* note 51, at 173–74, 175–76, 178–79; RUTLAND, ORDEAL 279–300; 3 BRANT, *supra* note 53, at 264.

175. See DOC. HIST. OF BILL OF RTS. 1017–23 (*Annals of Cong.,* June 8, 1789).

176. *Id.* at 1028 (*Annals of Cong.,* June 8, 1789). Madison initially proposed incorporating his amendments in the text of the Constitution. The House eventually voted instead to append the amendments as a separate and supplementary section, some members arguing that this form was more convenient, and others that it was inappropriate to use the amendment process of Article V to change the body of a document which had been approved by conventions drawn from the people. See *id.* at 1066–75, 1126 (*Annals of Cong.,* August 13, 19, 1789).

177. See *id.* at 1118, 1127–28 (*Annals of Cong.,* August 18, 21, 1789), 1124–25 (*House Journal,* August 21, 1789).

178. See *id.* at 1150–51, 1164, 1165 (*Senate Journal,* September 7, 24, 26, 1789) 1160–61 (*House Journal,* September 24, 1789).

179. See documents and editor's notes in *id.* at 1201–03.

180. *Id.* at 1033 (*Annals of Cong.,* June 8, 1789).

181. *Id.*

182. *Id.* at 1118 (*Annals of Cong.*, August 18, 1789).

183. *Id.* at 1127 (*Annals of Cong.*, August 21, 1789), 1150–51 (*Senate Journal*, September 7, 1789).

184. See remarks of William Smith in *id.* at 1076 (*Annals of Cong.* August 14, 1789). Although not ratifying the Constitution, North Carolina's first convention had proposed amendments to it. See 4 ELLIOT, DEBATES 242–47, 251 (August 1, 2, 1788).

185. DOC. HIST. OF BILL OF RTS. 1026 (*Annals of Cong.*, June 8, 1789).

186. *Id.* at 1076–77 (*Annals of Cong.*, August 14, 1789).

187. See note 176 *supra*.

188. DOC. HIST. OF BILL OF RTS. 1126 (*Annals of Cong.*, August 19, 1789).

189. *Id.* at 1118 (*Annals of Cong.*, August 18, 1789).

190. See notes 177–78 *supra* and accompanying text.

191. Letter from Richard Henry Lee and William Grayson to the Speaker of the Virginia House of Representatives, September 28, 1789, in 2 THE LETTERS OF RICHARD HENRY LEE 507, 508 (J. Ballagh ed. 1914).

192. See 3 OXFORD ENGLISH DICTIONARY 448. W. CROSSKEY, POLITICS AND THE CONSTITUTION IN THE HISTORY OF THE UNITED STATES 680–84 (1953) contains a valuable discussion of the exchange between Tucker and Madison and of the eighteenth century meaning of "expressly." Crosskey's general discussion of the Tenth Amendment (see *id.* at 675–708) is useful on the Amendment's legislative history but otherwise is subservient to the author's overall thesis that the Constitution grants Congress a general power of legislation. Among other things, in contrast to his discussion of "expressly," Crosskey assigns overly narrow meanings to key words of the Amendment when the occasion demands. A crucial example is his treatment of "reserved." Contrasting it to "retained," Crosskey reads it in the narrow legalistic sense of creating a new right in the course of conveying other rights (as in reserving an easement through property being conveyed to another). By this reading, the Tenth Amendment arguably makes all state authority dependent on the Constitution. See *id.* at 701–02. This was *one* definition of the term in the eighteenth century, but not the only one (see 8 OXFORD ENGLISH DICTIONARY 513–14), and the disputants in the ratification debates—even the Antifederalists, who of course sought to preserve the states—commonly used the term interchangeably with "retained." See, *e.g.*, THE FEDERALIST No. 45; *Pa. Ratification Debates* 629 (dissent of the Pennsylvania minority).

193. DOC. HIST. OF BILL OF RTS. 1164 (Senate Journal, September 26, 1789).

194. Carter v. Carter Coal Co., 298 U.S. 238, 296 (1936).

195. *Usery* at 841. See *id.* at 842; *Fry* at 552–54. In this final section I am drawing freely on Lofgren, *National League of Cities v. Usery: Dual Federalism Reborn*, 4 CLAREMONT J. OF PUBLIC AFFAIRS 19 (1977).

196. *Usery* at 843 (quoting *Fry* at 547 n. 7). See *id.* at 842–43; *Fry* at 550. See also Maryland v. Wirtz, 392 U.S. 183, 205 (1968) (Douglas, J., dissenting).

197. *Fry* at 554. See also Maryland v. Wirtz, 392 U.S. 183, 204 (1968) (Douglas, J., dissenting) ("constitutional principles of federalism").

198. Texas v. White, 7 Wall. 700, 725 (1869), quoted in *Usery* at 844.

199. Lane County v. Oregon, 7 Wall. 71, 76 (1869), quoted in *Usery* at 844.

200. *Usery* at 845–46, in part quoting Coyle v. Smith, 221 U.S. 559, 580 (1911), in turn quoting Lane County v. Oregon, 7 Wall. 71, 76 (1869). See also Trimble v. Gordon, 97 S. Ct. 1459, 1469 (1977) (Rehnquist, J., dissenting), in which Rehnquist offers a short summary of his view of the federal system.

201. United States v. Darby, 312 U.S. 100, 124 (1941), quoted in text accompanying note 11 *supra*. See generally Berns, *The Meaning of the Tenth Amendment* in A NATION OF STATES 139, *passim* and esp. 144–51 (R. Goldwin, ed. 2d ed. 1974).

202. Robert Yates, *Letters of Brutus*, No. XI, January 31, 1788, excerpted in MASON, *supra* note 51, at 107, 108–09.

203. M. VILE, THE STRUCTURE OF AMERICAN FEDERALISM 4 (1961).

204. See Diamond, *The Federalist on Federalism: "Neither a National Nor a Federal Constitution, But a Composition of Both,"* 86 YALE L.J. 1273, esp. 1281–85 (1977); Wechsler, *The Political Safeguards of Federalism: The Role of the States in the Composition and Selection of the National Government*, 54 COLUM. L. REV. 543 (1954) (but note that some "political safeguards" have disappeared or diminished in effectiveness since Professor Wechsler published this essay and that his terminology is less precise than Madison's).

205. 252 U.S. 416, 433–34 (1920). See generally Lofgren, *Missouri v. Holland in Historical Perspective*, 1975 SUPREME COURT REVIEW 77.

206. CORWIN, *supra* note 6, at 257. See *id.* at 255–57. But cf. Tribe, *Unraveling National League of Cities: The New Federalism and Affirmative Rights to Essential Governmental Services*, 90 HARV. L. REV. 1065 (1977) (arguing that whatever were Rehnquist's and the Court's "motives," *Usery* gives recognition to affirmative individual rights which the central government may not infringe when such rights are furthered by the activities of states).

207. See generally BARBER, *supra* note 5, at 171–73 (questioning congressional use of the commerce power for "pretextual" purposes).

American Federalism
By Martin Shapiro*

Any discussion of federalism in a legal context must begin with the absurdity of federalism as a legal concept. While we know of ancient and medieval leagues of cities, federalism is an invention of the 16th, the 17th and the 18th centuries which witnessed the rise of the Dutch and American federations.[1] Yet these are the very centuries in which the nation state became the dominant political form of the Western World. Indeed the Dutch and Swiss federations arose out of the turmoil created by the breakup of the previously dominant political institution of Europe, the Holy Roman Empire, into such nation states. The key feature of the nation state was the rejection of the medieval system of multiple, overlapping and fragmented fedual obligations and its replacement by a single political authority to whom all those living within a defined national territory owed exclusive obligation. The nation state reduces political complexity and diversity to political simplicity and unity within its territorial boundaries.

Sovereignty was necessarily the dominant legal concept of the nation state builders. While one wing of political theorists insisted that every sovereign state was equal to every other,[2] another developed the claim that within each nation state there must be some ultimate authority who had the last word in every political decision and held a monopoly of legitimate, coercive power.[3]

In the 19th century too this notion of sovereignty dominated both the positivism of Bentham and Austin and the negativism of Hegel.[4] Whatever their allegiance to natural law, American and British lawyers knew the positive law as the command of the sovereign.

As we have noted, unity was a key feature of sovereignty. Kings sought to express this unity in theories of absolute monarchy—that sovereignty must be wielded by the sovereign.[5] Others, however, while insisting that sovereignty was unified and absolute, held that such sovereignty might be wielded by some sort of collectivity. The English attributed sovereignty to the King in Parliament. Rousseau and others, including our founding fathers, dealt in popular sovereignty. Nevertheless both England and France ultimately rejected separations of powers as a contradiction to the unitary nature of sovereignty.

France is, of course, the home of Montesquieu, a firm believer in national sovereignty and yet a proponent of separation of powers.[7] Locke is sufficiently a proponent of sovereignty to assign its foreign aspects to a separate branch of government,[7] but nonetheless espouses three branches. For at least one school of thought then, while sovereignty might be unitary, the government that wielded it might be composed of several persons or parts.

This kind of deviation from unity, which we customarily call separation of powers, is, however, very different from the division of powers of federalism. Holding to the strictest notions of unity of sovereignty, it is not difficult to envision sovereignty being wielded by a committee or an assembly or even the whole people, in which a majority vote of the

* Professor of Law, University of California at Berkeley, School of Law.

governing body becomes the unified command of the sovereign. Federalism is quite a different matter. For it specifies that two sovereigns shall rule over the same national territory, and conversely that each citizen shall owe political loyalty to two sovereigns. Within the intellectual framework of sovereignty, federalism is an absurdity, a contradiction in terms. For the interlocking notions of sovereignty and nation state demand that there be one people, one territory, one ultimate political authority.

The course of the Supreme Court's federalism decisions is the history of its struggle to deal with this absurdity. Perhaps the low point of that struggle is the self-incrimination cases in which the Court actually tried to pretend that there were two sovereigns.[7] But there are no high points because within a legal framework that accepts the notion of sovereignty, there is no logical, principled place for federalism. Two cannot be made to equal one so long as we accept the premises of sovereign arithmatic.

The conventional solution to this problem is the assertion that federalism is simply the interjection of a second set of functional boundaries within the territorial boundaries of the nation state. Each sovereign shall be supreme within the functional spheres assigned to it. Thus no absurdity occurs because each citizen is confronted by only one sovereign at a time as he moves from one sphere of socio-political economic life to another.

In the first place, the Founding Fathers did not always do this neat kind of bounding job. There is a substantial list of "concurrent powers", the best known of which is taxation, in which the citizen is indeed, and much to his regret, confronted by two sovereigns at once. What is sometimes forgotten is that the Framers intially allocated even military affairs concurrently to both the states and the federal government. The War of 1812 would seem to have demonstrated conclusively not only the logical but the practical absurdity of that arrangement. In fact, however, it continued into the Civil War where it hampered the Confederacy even more than the Union.[8]

More importantly, even where the Framers seemed to be seeking a relatively neat boundary, none has actually proved available or defensible. The most famous example is, of course, commerce. Those most famous pronouncements of Marshall: "Commerce is . . . intercourse" "to regulate . . . is to prescribe the rule" and "more states than one"[9] are, from the point of view of drawing boundaries between sovereigns, vapid judicial posturings. If we pair *Gibbons v. Ogden* with *Willson v. Blackbird Creek Marsh Company*[10] and then go on to the *Cooley* rule, with its rigamarole silences of Congress doctrine, and to the diverse opinions in the *License and Passenger Cases*,[11] it is clear that neither the Marshall nor Taney Courts could find the neat boundaries that would have avoided the absurdity of two sovereignty federalism.[12]

The Corwin style commentary of New Deal debunking of the "dual federalism"[13] decisions of the Supreme Court need not be repeated here to show how absurd the boundary problem was. Instead the same point may be demonstrated by debunking the debunkers. It is sometimes forgotten that most of the doctrinal content of the despised *E.C. Knight* Case, which ruled that manufacturing was not in interstate commerce, was drawn from *Paul v. Virginia*[14] in which the Court had attempted to strengthen the power of the states against foreign corporations. Similarly the much maligned direct-indirect test employed by the four old men to the end of their days,[15] began in an attempt to legitimate federal intervention in what was admittedly intrastate commerce.[16]

The New Deal experience itself is enlightening. One way to attempt some kind of functionally realistic boundary drawing under the commerce clause is to envision a kind of prototype that runs:

State		Federal		State
Raw materials (agriculture and mining)	Manufacturing	Transportation	Wholesaling	Retailing and consumption

In this "chain" of commerce the farmer in the field and the miner down a hole in the ground are literally as rooted to the local scene and as far away from the interstate link of transportation as it is possible to be. And just as locally rooted and as far from the central, interstate link is the retailer and consumer. If any line is to be drawn between interstate and intra-state commerce, then these two extremes must be placed in intra-state. Is it purely a coincidence that the leading anti-New Deal commerce cases involved farmers, miners and ultimate retailers literally one step from the consumer's cook pot?[17]

Of course it can be argued that this chain of commerce is itself unrealistic and unworkable. In the first place it does not settle the manufacturing problem. Why should the Knight Company, which imported its raw sugar from abroad, processed it in Philadelphia and then shipped the finished product on to other states, be considered over toward the left end of the chain while the meat packers, who got their steers from mid western states processed them into dressed beef in Kansas City or Chicago, and shipped the beef to other states, be considered a pause in the midst of the transportation link?[18] Why should the fact that the coal miner never leaves home be more relevant than the fact that at the time 90% of the locomotives transporting goods in interstate commerce burned coal? In short wouldn't the truly functional approach to the problem be to drop "artificial" tests such as the chain or stream of commerce and the direct-indirect test and go to a really economic test of whether the effect on interstate commerce was substantial. That is what the Court did in 1937 and after.

There is, indeed, a moral to be drawn from the "switch in time" in which Roosevelt's Court ended the vicious practices of its predecessors. That moral is *Wickard v. Filburn*.[19] Once the "artificiality" of the chain of commerce view and the direct-indirect test are replaced by economic realities, no boundary between inter and intra state commerce can be drawn and the interstate commerce clause is deleted from the Constitution. In short if the Court seeks to escape the absurdity of two sovereigns by drawing boundaries between their sovereign spheres in the national territory they share, it will simply involve itself in other absurdities. By 1942 in the commerce area we must either take the Court as having exposed the basic absurdity of federalism or as having abolished the federal system. As we shall see shortly, what it had actually done was in reality the former and in constitutional theory the latter.

Having briefly reviewed what every student of constitutional law knows, that federalism cannot be reduced to sense in the crucial realm of commerce, I need hardly go through the same story again in half a dozen other realms. The ultimate intellectual dynamic is clear. Within the framework of sovereignty, the drive toward consistency in law must lead from the absurdity of federalism to the logic of a single, ultimate political authority. Given the economy and technology of modern America the only way that logic can be accommodated to reality is to assign that single ultimate political authority to the central government. The pursuit of a principled, logical, consistent legal and constitutional theory of federalism can lead, and for the most part has lead, only to the abolition of the constitutional provisions guaranteeing federalism.[20]

Politics, however, works fairly well without a consistent constitutional theory. This fact has been somewhat obscured in the study of federalism because it seemed self evident that federalism depended upon written constitutional provisions. No nation to which we would even be tempted to attribute the label federal operates without such provisions. The early scholarship in the field was dominated by K.D. Wheare who defined federalism very rigorously in terms of key constitutional provisions guaranteeing two sovereignties.[21] Even the most recent and self-consciously social scientific study of federalism deliberately maintains a jural element.[22] Nevertheless the whole tendency of political science studies of federalism has been to shift from emphasis on key constitutional guarantees of sovereignty to emphasis on federalism as a style or process embedded in the historical political practices and ideologies of certain nation states.[23] Most political scientists would eschew any one sentence definition of federalism.[24]

There is a certain level of consensus on the origins of federalism. The necessary conditions of federalism appear to be (1) an exterior threat and/or opportunity for aggression; (2) the perception of the elites of the potential constituent units that banding together to oppose that threat or attack others enjoys a higher probability of success than does individual action; (3) a willingness on the part of these elites to suffer some diminution of their particular political authority in exchange for greater security in external relations. Perhaps as an independant cause and perhaps only as a further elaboration of (3), it is observed that at least some shared backround of political, social and cultural values is likely to be a prerequisite to successful federalisms.[25] Most of the worlds federalisms seem to be responses to the breaking up of empires in which the former colonies seek to create some larger structure that will provide a measure of economic and military security formerly provided by the imperial power.

Political scientists have not been very tempted to construct basic propositions about the nature of federalism from this knowledge of origins. No doubt their hesitancy stems in part from their awareness that the most successful of federalisms, our own, has witnessed so many changes of environment that the link between its origins and is present conditions is tenuous at best. Many of the constitutional provisions that were designed by the originators of our federalism to insure its successful operation have been midified or abandoned or reduced to facades. The actual patterns of intergovernmental relations in the United States have changed a number of times as have the beneficiaries of those patterns. Any attempt to set out a definition of federalism composed of a number of detailed prerequisites would inevitably founder because one or another of those prerequisites would not be fully met by every one of the nations we wish to call federal or even by every one of the various federalisms that the U.S. has experienced over the past two hundred years.

Aside from origin the one point of consensus is that a federal system is one in which many governmental units participate in decision making. The principal problem encountered by political scientists here is defferentiating between federalism and administrative decentralization. Federalism is a species of areal division of power.[26] The areal division of power may be seen as a continuum running:

Confederation	Federation	Centralized Government with a decentralized administration	Centralized Government Centralized Administration

In a confederation nearly all final decisions on nearly all policy issues are made by the constituent local units. At the opposite extreme all decisions are made at the center. In the two intermediate forms, some decisions are made centrally and some are made by local units. It has become a truism of modern administrative theory that even the devolution to local administrative agencies of what are explicitly subordinate and "purely administrative" decisions results in substantial amounts of local policy making no matter how strict the hierarchical controls or how great the purported concentration of policy making authority in the capital. Even a government that purports to centralize policy-making may have many governmental units participating decisively in decision-making if it depends heavily on local administration.

On the other hand what purport to be federal systems may so subordinate local government units to hierarchical controls that the local units virtually become administrative subordinates of the central government sovereign even while they maintain the legal status of units of the second sovereign. Precisely this phenomenon has occurred in many spheres of American policy-making. During the 1930s the central government greatly expanded Federal categorical grant in aid programs in what was often called the New Federalism.[27] Typically such programs promised federal money to state governments if they would provide specific services such as vocational education under federal rules or guidelines. The states could not resist the money. The federal guide lines often became so detailed, and federal administrative supervision so intrusive, that the state government agency administering the program became virtually the local field office of the Washington department that dispersed the Federal funds. This tendency has accelerated in the post World War II period.[28]

Today a host of federal programs require that agencies of state government submit detailed plans as a prerequisite for obtaining federal money. The principal activity of thousands of state officials is filling out the federal forms in ways that will get the federal money. While their monthly pay checks are drawn on the state treasury, they and their "state" agencies survive only if they properly anticipate exactly what federal agencies want them to say and then slavishly say it. This is not to say that they may not exercise a considerable amount of policy-making discretion, for instance in choosing what project to do their federal song and dance about and which to ignore. But it is not clear that there is anything distinctively federal as opposed to administratively decentralized about what they do. Nor has revenue sharing markedly changed this picture. In spite of the facade remarkably little federal money gets to the states without the strings of a great deal of Washington supervision.

Derthick has pointed out a considerably subtler undermining of federalism that has resulted from federal grant policy.[29] One of the principal impacts of federal programs has been the "professionalization" of many spheres of public service. Washington money, administered by professional public health or forestry or education specialists, is often first available to "upgrade" the staffs of state services, and frequently more money will not be available unless and until the upgrading is done. The state hires professional foresters to talk the federal professional foresters out of more money. Since all the professional foresters subscribe to the same professional view of what is good for forests, a uniform national policy emerges. And it emerges behind what appears to be a truely non-coercive, non-hierarchical federal facade.

It is for these reasons no doubt that Riker wishes to maintain a "jural" element in his definition of federal which requires that some *"final* decisions"[30] remain in the hands of the constituent units. In that word "final" rests the latent shade of sovereignty and the means of distinguishing a federal system from one that merely practices administrative decentralization. There are many contemporary American instances in which this line between federalism and administrative decentralization has been crossed and state agencies have become merely the field units of Washington departments.

Thus the mere fact that state governments exist and make some decisions is not dispositive of the question of whether we have a federal system in the United States at least under Riker's or other sovereignty based definitions of federalism. The issue has been rendered more obscure by the absolute growth of government in the 20th century. The governmental pie has been growing so fast that even if the states have been a smaller and smaller slice of government in terms of significance or ultimate power, they nevertheless get larger and larger. It is pretty hard to deny that the states of New York and California exist when each employs more people and disposes of more money than most of the nation states of the world. The debate over the existence of federalism in the U.S. is largely waged between those who emphasize the devices by which a growing central government subordinates the states to its will and those who point to the growing size and range of activities of state governments.

Their basic positions emerge concerning the evolution of federalism in the United States. The first concentrates on the growth of centralized government here and throughout the world. It depicts American history as a gradual and then accelerating tendency toward centralization. It particularly emphasizes the growing power of the Presidency as a nationally force, the increased importance of international relations and national security, the role of the Supreme Court in constructing and implement uniform national rules, the growth of the Washington bureaucracy and the fact that the voters seem to know more about and care more about national than state and local politics. It concludes that we have slipped or are slipping from federalism to administrative decentralization. It must be said that no serious scholar of federalism subscribes wholeheartedly to this position. But in part that is because scholars make their living by denying the obvious.

The second school argues that there has been a basic continuity in American federalism. Riker focuses on the extent to which state and federal governments have been in the hands of the same or different political parties. Since he finds that the party not controlling the national government has controlled a substantial number of state governments about the same proportion of the time in all eras of American history, he argues that the U.S. has always enjoyed the same degree of federalism. As to increased central government dominance over key areas of policy, he dismisses all matters of which government controls how much of what policy area as mere "accidents" of federalism that are not to be taken into account in determining the federalism of a political system.[31]

One of the most prominent schools of federalism scholarship has been that of Grodzins and Elazar.[32] They and a number of other commentators argue that American federalism has never been characterized, as the Supreme Court persists in doing, by two sovereigns each of which operates independently within the functional boundaries set for it by the constitution. Instead they find that state and national government decision making has always been intermixed in most areas of public policy. Since that intermixing continues today as it always has in the past, federalism continues.

Elazar has argued that every era of American history witnesses a brief period of central government innovation and activism preceded and/or followed by periods of relative quiescence on the part of the central government. During these quiescent periods, the extent to which the state governments dominate policy making depends on their own will to innovate and skill in doing so.[33]

This school of commentary also tends to focus heavily on the extent to which Congress and interest groups continue to vigorously represent state, regional and local interests in national politics. For instance, quite aside from the representation of the states constitutionally built into the Senate, the state delegations in the House typically form bipartisan blocks to push the pork barrel and other interests of their own states. Weak party discipline in Congress, itself partially a product of the dependency of Congressmen and Senators on local financing, local support and local identification to secure their re-elections, is seen as an important factor in federalism. In short it is argued that in assessing the balance between state and national governments, it must be remembered that a great many state enclaves and points of subversion exist within the national government itself.

In general this school argues that American politicians have always turned to whatever government offers them the best promise of achieving whatever they are trying to achieve, and that they continue to choose sometimes the states and sometimes the national government without regard to which government is the constitutionally appropriate one and without regard to consistency over time. Any port in a storm. Thus even while some observers were proclaiming the death of federalism, state governments have flourished, expanded and offered a wider range of services than they ever had before. Since the political proclivity to use every kind of government continues, federalism continues.

Essentially this school of thought begs the question of the degree of central government dominance over the states. It keeps repeating that there has always been a messy, unrationalized mix of state and national political decision making in the United States and there continues to be. Therefore federalism was and is. Its definitions of federalism are built on the criterion that there be *some* final or independent decision making by the states, not any particular amount or in any particular policy areas. And it stresses the difficulty of measuring just exactly the proportion of national to state political power. It tends to brush aside dire warnings of national domination, particularly of the sort that can be constructed from tracing the demise of most of the constitutional doctrines of states rights, by constantly reasserting that the real political world is a messy mixture of state and federal power, that the states continue to be living political entities and that, therefore, the political system can continue to be about as federal as it wants to be.

A third school of scholarly commentators professes to see stages of American federalism and usually stages along a line to greater and greater centralization. My colleague at U.C.S.D. Harry Scheiber has been a principal spokesman for the view that pre Civil War American federalism was marked by a kind of state mercantilism in which state governments fostered the growth of their own economies. The post Civil War period is marked by the tendency of the then rapidly nationalizing business sector to break this state mold and play state and federal governments off against one another.[34]

Perhaps the most ambitious of these stages arguments is made by Beer.[35] Adopting some of the notions of contemporary political economy, he substantially agrees with Scheiber and company by labelling the pre Civil War Period as one of pork-barrel coalitions and the post Civil War era as one of spillover coalitions. By this he means that before the Civil War, economic interests and benefits tended to be segmented by state, and elites tended to act so as to maximise the cut to their own state of whatever national benefits were available. After the War, as some economic interests and activities took on national aspects, political elites played a mixed game. They moved on to national level politics where spillovers into the national scene of what had earlier been essentially local economic activities occurred. At the same time they used the states to innovate pilot programs that might move on to national acceptance. Beer then moves beyond the time period covered by Scheiber to characterize the New Deal as one of nation wide class coalitions and the replacement of dual federalism by "cooperative federalism", which may be only a polite way of saying central government domination. Beer goes on to speculate about the current stage as one of "technocratic politics," which may be a polite phrase for the total centralization of political leadership. At this stage he sees the functions of the states as "planning and control" and "mobilization of consent." The former really comes down to a shift from federalism to administrative decentralization with the states becoming local coordinators of federal programs. The latter is the most polite way of proclaiming the demise of federalism. Since the autonomy of state political apparatuses cannot be totally overcome, they are to be turned into transmission belts for engineering local popular approval of central government policies.

Elazar and other proponents of federalism sometimes offer an alternate version to the next or contemporary stage proposed by Beer. It is one based on the current disillusion with bigness for its own sake and the pessimism about central planning that we shall return to in a moment. Given current sentiments, one might envision the next stage as one in which more and more decisions were brought back from central to local levels. In such a situation the states might increase their role in policy-making.[36] Beer may have these developments in mind when he speaks of state "planning and control" functions. As usual the line between federalism and decentralized administration may depend on nuances of just how "final" or "independent" state decisions would be even during a stage of reaction against big government.

These three schools of descriptive commentary do not, of course, exist in a normative vacuum. While there are gradients of evaluation, and many mixed evaluations, it is possible to discern fairly well defined pro and con positions on federalism.

Whether using the new language of externalities or the older vocabulary of national versus local interests or majorities versus minorities, most commentators have noted that the principal political impact of federalism is the furtherance of local political values and interests particularly where they stand in opposition to nationally dominant political interests. Thus federalism is identified with the triumph of minorities over majorities.[37] And in the context of U.S. history the most prominent, long term minority beneficiary has been the southern white minority seeking to preserve slavery and its post-Civil War surrogates.

While one principal strain of anti-federalism is majoritarian, a second strain is that of rational planning. Those who have considerable confidence in the ability of government to rationally plan economic, political and social development are wont to argue that the states cannot provide such planning because most of the key phenomena to be planned are national in scope. Only the central government has a planning jurisdiction coterminus with what needs planning.

The proponents of federalism are likely to speak of local majorities versus national majorities to avoid the stigma of minoritarianism in a polity that favor democracy. They are also likely to point to the whole body of modern voting, public opinion and legislative behavior literature which indicates that a unified, national, majority opinion or even a simple congressional majority on an issue of public policy rarely exists anyway. They tend to emphasize the advantages that multiple channels and agencies of government may yield in experimenting on a limited scale and providing the kind of redundancy that allows one agency to pick up the ball dropped by another with parallel responsibilities.[38]

Indeed among the principle defenders of federalism must be counted those who are not particularly concerned about the strain of majoritarianism in anti-federalist thinking but challenge the faith of the anti-federalists in rational central planning. Here the debate over federalism gets subsumed under the general debate about rational planning versus incremental decision-making.[39] One of the leading proponents of incrementalism, Wildavsky, has recently written a paper which collects a great deal of literature on the central government's failures to adequately plan and implement policies designed to have their principal impact at local levels. The moral of his story is that federalism provides the opportunity for multiple, limited, pragmatic and experimental programs that seem to have a better chance of success than the technological rationality which Beer feels will dominate future politics and inevitably favors central government.[40]

The incremental defenders of federalism need not, however, specify exactly what they mean by federalsm. They tend to view political decision making as a continuous process of interdependent decision. So the very notions of final or independent decision-making which are the basic building blocks of many definitions of federalism are to them mere fictions. So long as there are many participating decision makers, there are the prerequisites of redundancy and incrementalism they desire.

What emerges from this variety of definitional, descriptive and evaluative perspectives on federalism that might be useful to those interested in framing or criticising constitutional doctrine?

First there is not, and there will not be, a single, satisfactory definition of federalism that bridges the fundamental absurdity of two sovereigns operating in the same territory and on the same persons. Secondly, this absurdity cannot be bridged by constructing precise functional boundaries between the two sovereigns that will allow each to operate unhindered in its own sphere. No such boundaries can be realistically articulated nor have such boundaries historically existed in the United States. Thirdly, there is not substantial agreement on whether we now have as much federalism as we used to nor on how much we should have. Fourthly there is substantial agreement that many areas of government policy making will be characterized by the participation of many government agencies, among them state agencies. To what extent this participation should be denominated administrative decentralization and to what extent federalism is unclear.

With these points in mind we might turn briefly to what appear to have been the two most prominent recent attempts by the Supreme Court to reassert the federal nature of our constitution. The first of these is *Oregon v. Mitchell*[41] a decision in which the Court held that a Congressional statute lowering the voting age to 18 was unconstitutional insofar as it sought to regulate state as opposed to national elections. By the time of *Mitchell* the Supreme Court had approved a great deal of Congressional regulation of state election processes,[42] and the Court had done a great deal of regulation of its own, much of it in the name of the equal protection clause.[43] It had long been conceded that, whatever federalism was at the time of the founding, it had been somehow modified by the Civil War Amendments in the direction of greater access by the central government to the control of local behavior. The Warren Court's very active equal protection jurisprudence had pushed the amendments far beyond any notion that they had authorized more extensive central government action than the founder's intended only in the area of racial discrimination.

Justice Black's opinion for the Court in *Mitchell* tries valiantly to show that the preservation of some state electoral autonomy can be squared with the election jurisprudence of the Warren Court. Justice Harlan is more frank and openly admits that the two can not be squared.[44] He opts to reject the recent opinions in favor of what he views as more fundamental truths of federalism.

Short of this downright rejection of a well established line of cases, a rejection in which the majority upholding the states was not willing to engage, the Court could not really find a neat, clear or fixed boundary between state and national authority over elections. While it did not say no explicitly, its decision implicitly accepts the vision of the Grodzin's school of federalism watchers, a vision in which national and state authority intermixes even over such matters as state elections. Justice Black's opinion finally rests on a lingering remembrance of sovereignty. In an elective, representative democracy, if the states do not even control their own elective processes, in what sense are they sovereign at all? Justice Black draws no boundaries. He simply says that if the logic of the equal protection clause is pushed too far then the federalism envisioned by "the whole Constitution" will be destroyed and the states reduced to "impotent figureheads."[45]

In a curious sense Justice Black is returning to the often misunderstood root of the "political questions" doctrine, a point which Justice Harlan makes clear in his opinion's explicit distinction between civil rights and the "distribution of political power."[46] For the root of that doctrine was really the Court's reluctance to tamper with basic questions of sovereignty as opposed to more limited questions of the constitutionality of particular statutes.[47]

The controlling opinions in *Oregon v. Mitchell* are pretty much in accord with the contemporary understanding of federalism. They do not really draw functional boundaries between exclusive spheres of federal and state authority. To do so would be to deny a body of experience and judicial decision that the Court is unwilling to deny. So the Court cannot even say that the state has exclusive authority over what it clearly ought to have exclusive control over if it had exclusive control over anything, namely its own election processes. On the other hand the majority wish to somehow say that unless some reserve of final or independent decision is left to the states then you have not federalism but administrative decentralization. They cannot say how much reserve is enough. In *Mitchell* about all they say is "too much national control is too much" and the "too much" occurs when the central government tampers with the very mechanism that gives the states their being as governments.[48]

It is sufficient to say here that *National League of Cities v. Usery*[49] is a perfect example of the absurdity that necessarily follows from the two sovereignties notions that underlies federalism. Justice Rehnquist for the majority repeatedly focuses on "integral governmental functions" in areas of "government services which the states and their political subdivisions have traditionally afforded their citizens," and on "activities . . . typical of those performed by state . . . government" such as "fire prevention, policy protection, sanitation, public health, and parks and recreation." He hold that the power to determine the wages and hours of those employed in these areas in "one undoubted attribute of state sovereignty . . . essential to separate and independent existence" of the states. Since the states are sovereign in their own sphere, it follows that the central government may not regulate state decisions about the wages and hours of those of its employees performing in areas of traditional state services.

Justice Brennan's dissent has an even simpler sovereignty argument. The statute which the majority struck down and Brennan wishes to uphold was enacted under Congress's commerce powers. Justice Brennan need only go through the Marshallian canon to conclude that the central government is sovereign in the sphere of interstate commerce. So in regulating commerce the central government is not constrained by the existence of the states even where it uses its commerce power to regulate the wages of state employees.

Both Rehnquist and Brennan are eminently correct. The central government is sovereign in the sphere of interstate commerce. The states are sovereign in the appropriate sphere of their own operations. When the Congress declares that the governor's body guard, who is undoubtedly an arm of the state's sovereignty, is also engaged in interstate commerce, we have that classic absurdity of one citizen with two sovereigns that no amount of judicial line drawing will rectify.

Like the decision in *Mitchell,* that in *Usery* rests on no more elegant logic than "too much is too much." Just as pushing the equal protection clause to its logical extreme can destroy all independent state decision-making, so pushing the commerce power to that extreme could do so. Aside from using the words "integral" and "traditionally" over and over again, Justice Rehnquist does not, and cannot, draw the boundaries of state sovereignty. All he can say is that if federalism is to mean anything, it must mean that state governments must have power over their own employees. Here again, as in *Mitchell,* we get down to the basic existence of government itself as an irreducible minimum of sovereignty. Where a government is elective, it surely is not sovereign unless it controls its own election. Where a government is one of civil servants, it surely is not sovereign unless it controls the employment of those civil servants.

Justice Rehnquist's opinion is attuned to that aspect of contemporary federalism studies that clings to the notion that federalism can only be distinguished from administrative decentralization if the constituent units render some final decisions. For Rehnquist, however, it is not just any final decisions but particularly those which he sees as related to the state governments as governments. Justice Brennan's opinion is, in spite of its naive talk of exclusive spheres of sovereignty, actually attuned to that aspect of contemporary federalist studies that emphasizes the intermingling and overlapping of state and federal authority. After all, given all the other overlaps, why shouldn't federal and state authority overlap even on the question of how much state employees should be paid.

Along another dimension, and here again *Mitchell* and *Usery* are similar, Rehnquist rests on common sense and Brennan on precedent. Rehnquist joins that school of observers who perceive, and decry, a long term trend of creeping centralization that gradually turns the states into administrative sub-divisions. He would like to call a halt to that trend by refusing to take the next step and indeed by rolling back the precedents a bit. Brennan, either because he is unconcerned about federalism or because he belongs to the school that sees the states as alive and thriving, with their destinies in their own hands no matter what the current stage of constitutional nuance, is content to build upon what he sees as an unbroken line of pro-commerce power, pro central government decisions. Indeed Brennan explicitly says that the states are capable to protecting their own interests in the political process.

Justice Brennan notes that the majority approach the case in something of the spirit of the pre 1937 court instead of that of the 1937 and after majority. No doubt he is correct. But that may only be to say that the New Deal majority and the subsequent Warren majority did not care about federalism and that the current majority does.

Justice Stevens' brief dissent signals what may be the crucial issue for both judges and social scientific observers of federalism. In effect he says that since the central government now has and uses the ultimate power to control nearly every aspect of state policy, he can't see how in logic it could be denied the power to set state employees' wages as well. This same point must be made to those who define federalism as a system in which the constituent units have a final or independent say over some decisions and who persist in seeing no fundamental change in federalism so long as the units continue to make some independent decisions. Under such a mode of analysis, the observer will continue to see federalism day by day until the last day, when the central government has taken away the very last independent decision making power of the states. Then he will say: "oh yes — on Thursday we had federalism, but on Friday, we had a centralized government." Perhaps, with some regret, Justice Stevens is telling us it is Friday. Or perhaps he is only saying what the most optimistic school of federal observers is saying, that whether or not legal protections of state sovereignty remain in the Constitution and the opinions of the Supreme Court, federalism will continue as long as the states are significant focuses of political activity.

Notes

1. On the Dutch federation see W. TEMPLE, OBSERVATIONS UPON THE UNITED PROVINCES OF THE NETHERLANDS (1972).

2. See H. GROTIUS, THE LAW OF WAR AND PEACE.

3. See J. BODIN, SIX BOOKS CONCERNING THE STATE; T. HOBBS, LEVIATHAN; J. ROUSSEAU, THE SOCIAL CONTRACT.

4. See J. AUSTIN, LECTURES ON JURISPRUDENCE (4th ed., 1876); See F. HEGEL, THE PHILOSOPHY OF RIGHT AND LAW (Modern Library ed. 1953). The utopian and Marxist socialists and the anarchists of course, denied the legitimacy of national sovereignty.

5. See THE POLITICAL WORKS OF JAMES I (C. McIlwain ed., 1918). This is, of course, the origin of the comment attributed to Louis XIV, "L'Etat, C'est moi."

6. See SPIRIT OF THE LAWS (1748).

7. See Murphy v. Waterfront Commn., 378 U.S. 52 (1964) for a critique of the earlier cases.

8. See W. RIKER, SOLDIERS OF THE STATES (1958).

9. Gibbons v. Odgen, 9 Wheat. 1 (1824).

10. 2 Pets. 245 (1829).

11. Cooley v. Board of Wardens, 12 How. 299 (1852); License Cases, 5 How. 504 (1847); Passenger Cases, How. 283 (1849).

12. Marshall's one great success was Brown v. Maryland, 12 Wheat 419 (1827), where in the original package doctrine he was lucky enough to find an instance in which actual commercial practice roughly yielded a functional boundary between the two sovereigns.

13. See E. CORWIN, COURT OVER CONSTITUTION (1938).

14. U.S. v. E.C. Knight Co., 156 U.S. 1 (1895); Paul v. Virginia, 8 Wall. 168 (1869).

15. See McReynolds dissenting in N.L.R.B. v. Jones & Laughlin Steel Corp. 301 U.S. 1 (1937).

16. The Shreveport Case, 234 U.S. 342 (1914).

17. United States v. Butler, 297 U.S. 1 (1936); Carter v. Carter Coal Company, 298 U.S. 238 (1936); A.L.A. Schechter Poultry Corp. v. U.S., 295 U.S. 495 (1935).

18. Swift and Co. vs. U.S., 196 U.S. 375 (1905); Stafford v. Wallace, 258 U.S. 495 (1922).

19. 317 U.S. 111 (1942).

20. This is the true meaning of the famous announcement that the 10th Amendment had no constitutional force. See U.S. v. Darby, 312 U.S. 100, 124 (1941).

21. See K. WHEARE, FEDERAL GOVERNMENT (3rd ed. 1956.

22. Riker, *Federalism*, in 5 HANDBOOK OF POLITICAL SCIENCE 93, 106 (F. Greenstein and N. Polsby, eds., 1975).

23. See *id.* at 144; C. FRIEDRICH, TRENDS OF FEDERATION IN THEORY AND PRACTICE 7 (1968).

24. *A Bias Toward Federalism; Confronting the Conventional Wisdom on the Delivery of Governmental Services,* 6 PUBLIUS 95 (1976).

25. See RIKER, *supra* note 22, at 113–128.

26. See AREA AND POWER: A THEORY OF LOCAL GOVERNMENT (A. Maass, ed., 1959).

27. See J. Clark, *The Rise of a New Federalism* (1938).

28. See J. Sundquist and D. Davis, *Making Federalism Work* (1969).

29. THE INFLUENCE OF FEDERAL GRANTS (1970).

30. Riker, *supra* note 22, at 101 (emphasis added).

31. *Id.* at 131–141.

32. See M. Grodzins, *The Federal System,* in Presidents' Commission National Goals, GOALS FOR AMERICANS (1960); THE AMERICAN SYSTEM (1966); D. ELAZAR, AMERICAN FEDERALISM: A VIEW FROM THE STATES (1966).

33. See *The States as Keystones; A Reassessment in the Mid-1970's,* 6 PUBLIUS 3 (1976).

34. See Scheiber, *Federalism and the American Economic Order, 1789–1910,* 10 LAW & SOC. REV. 57 (1975).

35. *Modernization of American Federalism,* 3 PUBLIUS 49 (1973).

36. ELAZAR, *supra* note 32, at 13–19.

37. See Riker, *supra* note 22, at 153.

38. See Landau, *Federalism, Redundancy and System Reliability,* 3 PUBLIUS 173 (1973).

39. The general debate is summarized and related to judicial behavior in M. SHAPIRO, SUPREME COURT AND ADMINISTRATIVE AGENCIES 73–91 (1968).

40. *A Bias Toward Federalism, supra* note 24.

41. 400 U.S. 112 (1970).

42. See particularly Katzenback v. Morgan, 384 U.S. 641 (1966).

43. See particularly Baker v. Carr, 369 U.S. 186 (1962); Reynolds v. Sims, 377 U.S. 533 (1964); Carrington v. Rash, 380 U.S. 89 (1965); Harper v. Virginia State Board of Elections, 383 U.S. 663 (1966).

44. Oregon v. Mitchell, 400 U.S. 112, 217–18 (concurring in part, dissenting in part).

45. *Id.* at 125–6.

46. *Id.* at 303.

47. See M. SHAPIRO, LAW AND POLITICS IN THE SUPREME COURT 174–253 (1964).

48. It should be noted that in his opinion Justice Harlan subscribes to the theory that the colonies inherited their sovereignty from the British crown and then passed some of it on to the central government through ratification of the Constitution. This theory is currently less in favor among historians and social scientists than the theory that at the ratification of the Constitution both the states and the federal government received their sovereignty simultaneously by delegation from the people.

49. 426 U.S. 833 (1976) (Involving a federal statute declaring state employees to be involved in interstate commerce and bringing them under federal wages and hours regulations). See L. TRIBE, AMERICAN CONSTITUTIONAL LAW § 5–22 at 308–18 (1978).

Federalism
By Jesse H. Choper*

In addressing the problem of constitutional federalism, I would like to begin with a personal anecdote. About three years ago I received a telephone call from a city official in Southern California. He said that a federal environment agency was proposing to order that the city change all its downtown parking meters from taking nickels and dimes to taking nothing smaller than quarters. The rationale was to discourage automobile traffic, thus resulting in fewer air pollutants. The city official asked me, "Can they do that?" Based on what I then believed to be the existing state of the law as articulated in the decision of *United States v. California*,[1] I responded that, if the broad language used by the Court in that opinion were to be taken seriously, then, yes, Congress had the authority to authorize the federal agency to require municipalities or states to do this.

The city official was quite convinced, at least when he began talking to me, that the federal government had no such power. Well, I am not sure that I then gave him the wrong advice, but it is certainly true that, since talking to him several years ago, considerable doubt has been cast on the accuracy of my advice.

Last year, a group of cases—from three federal courts of appeals—reached the Supreme Court concerning the constitutional authority of the federal government, acting through the Environmental Protection Agency, to impose certain requirements on state governments.[2] The cases involved regulations of the EPA which obliged states "(1) to develop an inspection and maintenance program pertaining to the vehicles registered in the affected Air Quality Control Regions, and to submit to the Administrator, by fixed deadlines, both a schedule of compliance and the operative regulations by which the program was to run; (2) to develop various retrofit programs pertaining to several classes of older vehicles, in order to minimize several different types of emissions; (3) to designate and enforce preferential bus and carpool lanes, on streets sometimes specifically identified in the regulations and sometimes left to be chosen by the State; (4) to develop a program to monitor actual emissions as affected by the foregoing programs; and to adopt certain other programs which varied from State to State."[3] If state officials refused to comply with these regulations, the Clean Air Act could be read to authorize the imposition of both civil and criminal penalties on them for failing to abide by federal law.

The federal courts of appeals which had previously reviewed challenges to the validity of these regulations had gone off on various grounds. Most had held, as a matter of statutory interpretation, that the EPA's regulations were not authorized by Congress, although cautioning that serious constitutional problems concerning state sovereignty protected by the tenth amendment would be presented if the statute were read otherwise.[4] Two courts of appeals upheld the constitutionality of at least some of the regulations.[5] The cases were argued in the Supreme Court in January. In May, the Court avoided decision because it was

*Professor of Law, University of California, Berkeley. This article is an edited transcription of remarks made at the September 17-18 Constitutional Law Conference.

informed in the course of its consideration of the cases that the Environmental Protection Agency was in the process of modifying its regulations. Therefore, the Court said it was not going to pass on the validity of regulations which were no longer going to be in existence.

Obviously, the decision that was argued to the Supreme Court as calling for the unconstitutionality of the EPA regulations was *National League of Cities v. Usery*[6]—the only opinion of the United States Supreme Court in forty years that has held an act of Congress, promulgated pursuant to the Commerce Clause, to be invalid because it exceeded Congress's power vis-a-vis the states.

I would like to talk for a few minutes about the *Usery* decision. The essence of its rationale appears to be that the challenged provisions of the Fair Labor Standards Act— which extended federal wage and hour regulations to virtually all state and municipal employees—were beyond Congress's power under the Commerce Clause because they operated "to directly displace the States' freedom to structure integral operations in areas of traditional governmental functions,"[7] and thus interfered with "'functions essential to [the] separate and independent existence'"[8] of the states. The Court, in an opinion by Justice Rehnquist, focused most pointedly on the application of the minimum wage and maximum hour regulations to police and fire personnel, indicating that these were functions traditionally within the province of state and local government.

The Court emphasized several times that these federal regulations operated on "the States *qua* states."[9] It went out of its way to affirm Congress's extraordinarily broad power under the Commerce Clause to regulate the conduct of private persons or businesses within the states, but stressed that the law before it was invalid because it regulated state and local governments as such.

I would like to quote what is perhaps the broadest statement by the Supreme Court of Congress's power under the Commerce Clause to regulate individuals within the states and throughout the country. In *Usery*, Justice Rehnquist wrote, "'Even activity that is purely intrastate in character may be regulated by Congress, where the activity, combined with like conduct by others similarly situated,"—and here, I think, is the key phrase—"affects commerce among the States or with foreign nations."[10] Note that Justice Rehnquist did not say that the intrastate activity had to have a "substantial" effect on interstate commerce. Nor did he say that Congress has to be shown to have some reason for believing that the intrastate activity has a substantial effect on interstate commerce. Rather his description of Congress's power was most unqualified.

Now this is not terribly revolutionary. A long line of decisions, beginning with *Gibbons v. Odgen*[11] in the early part of the nineteenth century, used similar language. But, as I shall amplify shortly, there is a certain irony that, in a decision striking down an act of Congress as being beyond its power because the statute operated on "the States *qua* States," the Court underlines the gargantuan power of Congress to regulate people and businesses within the states.

Having set forth the *Usery* decision as background, I would like to make a few observations on the papers presented by Mr. Lofgren and Mr. Shapiro, both of which I commend to you.

In examining the original intention of the Tenth Amendment, I was most interested to note that at no point did Mr. Lofgren indicate that there was significant reliance on judicial review to secure whatever sovereignty of the states was sought to be preserved by the Tenth Amendment. Yet, just a little over a year ago, we see the Court exercising its momentous power of judicial review as a way of satisfying the original intent of the Tenth Amendment's preservation of state soveignty.

The point that Mr. Lofgren made in his paper that I found of greatest interest, however, was that the purpose of the Tenth Amendment was not to preserve the sovereignty of the state governments *as such*, but rather to preserve the sovereignty of the people within the states. This indicates that the historic concern for states' rights was that decentralized decision-making units within the states would assure greater individual participation in the political process and would result in the selection of officials whose views were sympathetic to those of their constituents. The notion was that the lower the level of government, the closer to the people, the greater the control that each individual would have over his own destiny. Especially because of the wide religious, political and cultural diversity of the people who were spread over the large territory of the colonies, the feeling was that small groups of like-minded persons would be more disposed, than would be a distant national government, to impose laws that were in harmony with local values. Further, it was thought that having these decisions made in smaller units would promote government efficiency. The view existed, I believe the historical record will indicate, that a remote national government in Washington would possess neither the knowledge of local conditions nor the flexibility required for wise administration, whereas heterogeneous state governments would be more manageable and would encourage experimentation and innovative response to social needs. Indeed, in modern times many political theorists—Buchanan and Tullock, for example[12]— continue to urge the greater efficiency of having collective decisions made in the smallest feasible political units. (And this may well be an idea whose time, if it hasn't fully come yet, is indeed forging ahead more strongly.) They stress the opportunity for those political parties out of power nationally to have laboratories for testing their policies locally.

I think it is important to note that the *Usery* decision does not seek to preserve this local decision-making ability of people. Rather it is addressed to only a very limited and relatively insignificant aspect of small collective decision-making units. It seeks only to protect their judgments about what "the States *qua* States" may do, but not their policies concerning what the people within the states may do.

Mr. Shapiro's paper was of particular interest to me because he demonstrated the virtual impossibility—and I quote what he said—of drawing "a principled, logical, legal and constitutional theory of federalism." Well, it is a "principled, logical, legal and constitutional theory" that we ordinarily expect from the Supreme Court, which is an antimajoritarian agency, when it overturns the acts of popularly elected representatives. Indeed, the notion that the Court acts in a principled, logical and consistent fashion is often advanced as the major justificaton for judicial review in our system of government. Rather, Mr. Shapiro tells us that politics works well, without any consistent constitutional theory, in defining and redefining just what federalism means in modern America. At the same time, he points out that the *Usery* decision seeks in some way to set limits on the principles that the Court has laid down on the scope of Congress's power under the Commerce Clause; it attempts to cut these principles off before they are pushed to the extreme of destroying state sovereignty as originally conceived and as we know it. Most important, however, I think, is Mr. Shapiro's conclusion that the Court's effort in *Usery* is quite unsuccessful in achieving its goal.

Let me now return directly to the *Usery* case. I feel its emphasis on preserving the ability of "the States *qua* States" to function is not only out of line with what I believe to be the dominant historical intention for preserving local sovereignty, but it is misdirected as a practical matter as well. As I earlier suggested, I think that the truly important element of state sovereignty is not the state's ability to determine, for example, how much it can pay its employees, but rather it is the extent to which states can regulate the enormous variety of private activities that take place within their particular borders. Governance of these matters, the Court in the *Usery* case has conceded to Congress, affirming that the states have virtually no sovereign power in respect to them. It seems to me, for example, that it is a much deeper wound to local sovereignty for Congress's Civil Rights Act of 1964 to promulgate a national policy in respect to racial discrimination[13] than for the national government to require that local police and firemen receive the minimum wage. This point may be illustrated even at the level of financial matters, which the Court stressed very strongly in the *Usery* case by showing the additional funds that would be required for state and local governments to satisfy the Fair Labor Standards Act for various state and local employees. I suggest that many national economic policies which are plainly within Congress's power—for example, regulating the amount of profits or income that people within the states can generate—have a much more substantial impact on a state's ability to finance its programs than does the requirement that they pay \$.40 or \$.50 more an hour to state employees. Indeed, the level of federal taxation is probably one of the most significant, if not the greatest, determinants—the economic principle, I guess, being that there is only so much juice in the orange. Given Congress's virtually unlimited constitutional power to increase or decrease federal taxes, that has a tremendous impact on how much is left for the state to finance its activities.

Beyond the fact that *Usery* does very little to preserve the authentic force of state and local sovereignty, the reach of the *Usery* decision is highly ambiguous and, indeed, it may well be irrelevant. First of all, *Usery* was a 5-4 decision. One of the five, Justice Blackmun, although joining the opinion of the Court, also wrote separately where, I believe, he effectively disclaimed much of what the Court said, expressing his own view that the Court had really adopted a "balancing approach,"[14] and indicating that even if Congress were to seek to regulate "the States *qua* States" under the Commerce Clause, that there may well be important enough national interests to justify such regulation. He did not find a sufficient federal interest in the Fair Labor Standards Act wage and hour provisions, but he quite clearly suggested that he might well find it "in areas such as environment protection. . . ."[15] Ironically, such regulation might have a much greater impact on "the States *qua* States," as I will indicate in a moment, than would the wage and hour legislation.

Secondly, the Court's emphasis on the broad power that Congress has under the Commerce Clause over individuals, it seems to me, pretty much gives the national government the ability to do what it wants. For example, suppose it were held that Congress has no power to use the Clean Air Act to require states to set up exhaust emission control agencies. (And, although Justice Blackmun's concurrence must give one pause, I think that after *Usery* there is a powerful argument to that effect since the law would operate on "the States *qua* States" in that Congress would be saying that states officials must set up these agencies.) Nonetheless, Congress plainly has the power to set up such agencies itself within the states and to establish a national system of controlling automobile exhaust emission. I can't believe for a minute that there would be one justice on the Supreme Court who would hold that Congress has no authority under the Commerce Clause to regulate this matter which affects both energy and the environment.

Similarly, suppose the Court had ruled in the *Fry* case,[16] as Justice Rehnquist in dissent urged that it hold, that Congress had no power under the Commerce Clause to set maximum wages that state and local governments should pay their employees. Nonetheless, it would then be easy enough for Congress to turn to its taxing power and say, "all right, we will not regulate the amounts that can be paid to employees—private, state or local; but what we will do is tax any amount that exceeds what we believe to be proper."

It must be remembered that the Court, in *Usery*, was very careful to say that it was dealing only with the scope of Congress's power under the Commerce Clause. But that is not the only grant of power to Congress whose exercise may have a substantial impact on federalism. For example, the Court specifically stated that it passed no judgment on the scope of Congress's power to spend.[17] There was a case in the mid 1940s, *Oklahoma v. United States Civil Service Commission*,[18] which was cited in *Usery* and bears importantly on our consideration of *Usery's* potential impact. Congress had passed a statute denying federal funds to any state agency with officials who were too active politically. The Oklahoma Highway Commission, which received federal highway money, had as one of its members a person who was chairman of the state Democratic Party. The U.S. Civil Service Commission said either the official must be removed or the federal funds will be cut off. Oklahoma challenged this as being beyond the authority of Congress, but the Court had no difficulty in sustaining Congress's power to condition the disbursement of funds in this way.

On the basis of the *Oklahoma* decision, could not Congress also control the wages of state and local police? We are all familiar with federal Law Enforcement Assistance grants which funnel substantial sums of money to states in order to improve their police departments. Could not Congress simply say, and I think quite rationally in connection with its program, that if states want continued Law Enforcement Assistance grants from the federal government, then they must pay their police the minimum wage?

Further, suppose Congress were to want the states to set up automobile exhaust emission control agencies. Could not Congress—through its spending power—tell the states that if they wish continued federal anti-pollution funds, then as a condition for their receipt, they must set up state agencies to regulate the amount of pollution from automobiles? Indeed, could not Congress, pursuant to its spending power, actually control state property taxation on the ground that if they wish to receive continued federal revenue sharing funds then they must grant relief to local property taxpayers?

Finally, I should like to refer to one other provision of the Constitution that bears on this question—Section 5 of the Fourteenth Amendment—which Justice Rehnquist also said in the *Usery* case was not at issue in regard to Congress's power to affect "the States *qua* States."[19] Within a week of the *Usery* decision, in a unanimous opinion—interestingly enough, written by Justice Rehnquist—the Court was presented with the question of whether Congress had power under Section 5 of the Fourteenth Amendment to regulate state and municipal employees.[20] The case involved state employees in Connecticut who claimed that they had been discriminated against on the basis of sex in violation of the Civil Rights Act of 1964 and who sought money damages against the State of Connecticut. In holding that the Eleventh Amendment did not forbid the suit to be brought in federal court, Justice Rehnquist assumed that Congress had power under Section 5 to regulate the hiring practices of state and local governments.

This brings us to what I think is a somewhat neglected opinion in the *Usery* case— Justice Stevens' very short dissent. I would like to refer to a few sentences from that opinion. Justice Stevens says, "The Federal Government may, I believe, require the State to act impartially when it hires or fires the janitor. . . ."[21] Justice Stevens had the benefit at the time he wrote of knowing how the Court had decided *Fitzpatrick v. Bitzer*, although the decision had not yet been handed down. But now the Court has confirmed his view. He also says that "the Federal Government may . . . require the States . . . to withhold taxes from . . . [the janitor's] pay check. . . ."[22] May it? Is that consistent with the *Usery* case? Does that interfere with the integral operations of the state governments? Is *Usery* distinguishable because here Congress would be acting under its taxing power rather than pursuant to the Commerce Clause? In any event, Justice Stevens, without any reaction by the majority, assumes Congress has this power.

Justice Stevens goes on to say that Congress can require a state to have its janitor "observe safety regulations when he is performing his job. . . ."[23] That certainly can be an expensive interference with the functioning of state and local governments—and Congress would be acting, as it did in *Usery*, through the commerce power. Justice Stevens further writes that the national government can "forbid . . . [the janitor] from burning too much soft coal in the capitol furnace, from dumping untreated refuse in an adjacent waterway, from overloading a state-owned garbage truck, or from driving either the truck or the governor's limousine over 55 miles an hour."[24] All of these federal regulations—probably also based on the Commerce Clause—would appear to burden state and local governments in a way similar to the Fair Labor Standards Act.

I think that Justice Stevens was pointing out again and again, without meaningful disagreement from the Court majority, that the thrust of the *Usery* rationale would seem to cover these situations, yet he suggests that the Court is quite unprepared to hold that Congress doesn't have the power in these instances. I think that the *Usery* decision is not only highly ambiguous but, as I indicated, it may well amount to very, very little—except an opinion that's going to confuse and concern lower courts and teachers and students of Constitutional Law who will be trying to discern just what the Court had in mind.

My position is to agree with Professors Lofgren and Shapiro that the Court should not play a significant role in determining when the national government has exceeded the bounds of federalism. But then one might fairly ask who is going to preserve this aspect of American federalism? Is it going to be, in Mr. Shapiro's phraseology, "Friday very, very quickly," so far as our federalism is concerned? I don't think so. In an article soon to be published,[25] I contend that state and local interests that are sought to be protected by our precept of divided sovereignty are very well represented in the national political process—in the Congress and in the Presidency—and that, as Mr. Shapiro indicates, politics works well, has worked well, and will continue to work so far as preserving these values of American federalism.

I would like to take a few more minutes and talk about the *Usery* case in this particular context. *Usery* is of special interest because the attorneys general of 22 states argued to the Supreme Court that the federal law was unconstitutional. Only four states had their attorneys general file amicus curiae briefs seeking to support the provision of the Fair Labor Standards Act extending maximum hour and minimum wage regulation to state and local employees.

From this data, one could conclude that state interests were not very well represented in Congress. After all, Congress passed the statute and here we have the states acting through their attorneys general, opposing it by 22-4. The provision of the Fair Labor Standards Act that was before the Court in the *Usery* case was voted on by only one house of Congress. There had been a proposed amendment to the bill in the Senate which sought to exempt police and firemen from the coverage of the Act. The Senate defeated the amendment, 29 to 65, despite the fact that the amendment had the support of the Nixon administration. There was no specific vote taken in the House of Representatives on this particular issue. The bill went to conference and the Conference Committee adopted a modified Senate version which extended coverage to most state and local government employees, including police and fire personnel. Then the House, by a resounding vote, approved the whole bill.

While I do not want to rely on the House vote enacting the complete bill, the Senate did vote specifically on the issue—65 to 29 in favor of extending the wage and hour regulation to state and local police and firemen. Here we have a great majority of the Senate—composed of two Senators from every state, you recall—supporting the bill, and a great majority of the state attorneys general opposing its constitutionality.

Was the bill approved by representatives of the majority of the separate states? That is the crucial question. Well, it is informative to note the position of the Senators of the 22 states whose attorneys general contested the constitutionality of the provision before the Supreme Court. Both Senators from 7 of those 22 states voted to regulate wages and hours of police and firemen. These included Democrats such as Alan Cranston of California, Republicans such as Jacob Javits of New York, liberals such as George McGovern of South Dakota and conservatives such as James Buckley of New York—quite a broad spread of views supporting this position. In one additional state—Missouri—only one senator voted. The Attorney General of Missouri opposed the statute before the Supreme Court. The Missouri Senator was in favor of it. The Senators from 10 of the other states split on the proposed Senate amendment. The one senator from Arizona who was recorded cast his vote in accordance with the position of his state's attorney general—against the amendment. But from only three of the 22 states whose attorneys general challenged the constitutionality of the law before the Supreme Court, did both Senators vote against police and fire coverage.[26]

Now, at a formalistic level, it is tempting to equate a state's interest with the position voiced by state and local officials rather than with that taken by the state's representatives in the Senate. It is often heard that once Congressmen get to Washington they shed their regional bonds and adopt a broader, national perspective. I suggest to you that the available data indicate otherwise. And even if it can be assumed that an argument before the United States Surpeme Court by a state attorney general describes the view of that state's governor or of its legislature—and this is an extremely fragile presumption in the many states where the attorneys general are elected independently (certainly those from California know that what Mr. Younger contends does not necessarily represent the position of Governor Brown)—nonetheless, it does not follow that that position better resembles the opinion of the state than that articulated by the state's representatives in Congress. That state and local officials may, because of budgetary problems, oppose a federal minimum wage for state and local employees does not necessarily mean that the "state" is opposed. In support of this view, I return to Mr. Lofgren's paper which indicates that it was not the purpose of the Tenth Amendment to protect the sovereignty of state governments as such—and perhaps (at least in some states) state governments are represented by the attorney general—but to represent the interest of the people within the states to act as a collective unit. As to this, I suggest that the judgment of the state's congressional representatives, who are politically responsible to the electorate of the entire state (just as is the attorney general and the governor), may fairly be relied upon. Thus, the political process does and will continue to work well in protecting the state sovereignty element of American federalism.

Notes

1. 297 U.S. 175 (1936).
2. *See* Environmental Protection Agency v. Brown, 431 U.S. 99 (1977).
3. *Id.* at 101.
4. Brown v. EPA, 521 F. 2d 827 (9th Cir. 1975); Arizona v. EPA, 521 F. 2d 825 (9th Cir. 1975); District of Columbia v. Train, 521 F. 2d 971 (D.C. Cir. 1975); Maryland v. EPA, 530 F. 2d 215 (4th Cir. 1975).
5. Pennsylvania v. EPA, 500 F. 2d 246 (3d Cir. 1974); District of Columbia v. Train, 521 F. 2d 971 (D. C. Cir. 1975).
6. 426 U.S. 833 (1976).
7. *Id.* at 852.
8. *Id.* at 845.

9. *See, e.g., id.* at 847.

10. *Id.* at 840 (quoting from Fry v. United States, 421 U.S. 542, 547 (1975)).

11. 22 U.S. (9 Wheat.) 1 (1824).

12. See J. BUCHANAN & G. TULLOCK, THE CALCULUS OF CONSENT 113-15 (1962).

13. See Heart of Atlanta Motel, Inc. v. United States, 379 U.S. 241 (1964); Katzenbach v. McClung, 379 U.S. 294 (1964).

14. 426 U.S. at 856 (Blackmun, J., concurring).

15. Id.

16. Fry v. United States, 421 U.S. 542 (1975).

17. 426 U.S. at 852 n. 17.

18. 330 U.S. 127 (1947).

19. 426 U.S. at 852 n. 17.

20. Fitzpatrick v. Bitzer, 427 U.S. 445, 451-56 & n. 11 (1976).

21. 426 U.S. at 880 (Stevens, J., dissenting).

22. Id.

23. Id.

24. Id.

25. Choper, *The Scope of National Power Vis-a-Vis the States: The Dispensability of Judicial Review*, 86 YALE L.J. 1552 (1977).

26. For details of the voting, see id. at 1565-66.

The Constitutional Limits on Land Use Controls

By R. Marlin Smith*

This is another zoning case. Black, J., in *Double I*
Development Company v. Township of Taylor.[1]

The judicial sigh with which Justice Eugene Black began yet one more zoning opinion is understandable. Disputes over zoning controls on the use of land became a staple in the state case reports not long after the U.S. Supreme Court decided that while zoning restrictions were a constitutionally permissible exercise of the police power, such restrictions, in their application to particular parcels of property, might fail to measure up to federal constitutional equal protection or substantive due process standards.[2]

Despite the constitutional trappings that have traditionally accompanied the average zoning dispute, it has been only rarely that the issues have transcended such mundane questions as whether it was reasonable to prohibit a gas station at Oak and Main or to refuse to allow a three-flat across the street from the houses in the Home Run Subdivision.[3] In some instances decisions have consisted largely of a detailed judicial inventory of all the land uses in a vicinity and have required a high degree of tolerance for tedium.[4] The volume of zoning litigation has been prodigious—by 1969 there were at least 10,000 reported decisions.[5]

The Role of Change

This stupendous volume of litigation is largely attributable to the fact that, unlike almost any other form of police power regulation, the opportunity for individuals to secure a change in the zoning regulations that apply to their property is a central feature of zoning ordinances and enabling statutes. Provision is made for amendments to the zoning ordinance so as to change the text of the regulations or so as to change the regulations applicable to a particular piece of property by reclassifying the property in a different zone. In the case of demonstrated hardship, variances excusing compliance with the strict terms of the ordinances may be secured if the standards set in the statute or ordinance are met. In this respect zoning is nearly unique. Apart from an occasional variance provision, public health regulations, traffic ordinances, building codes, and other police power regulations do not contemplate such a constant succession of requests for change. This distinctive feature of zoning regulations was recognized very early by Ernst Freund who observed:

> Legally, all zoning enabling acts contemplate the possibility of dezoning, the power to amend zoning ordinances serving that purpose. The provisions do not show on their face whether they are intended to remedy particular errors or hardships or whether they contemplate readjustments called for by the changing character of neighborhoods; undoubtedly, however, they may be made available for either purpose.[6]

The necessity of providing mechanisms for change in zoning ordinances has occasionally been recognized explicitly by a court. For example, Justice Levin of the Michigan Supreme Court, concurring in *Kropf v. City of Sterling Heights*,[7] observed:

---

* Partner, Ross, Hardies, O'Keefe, Babcock & Parsons, Chicago, Illinois.

For most communities, zoning as long range planning based on generalized legislative facts without regard to the individual facts has proved to be a theoretician's dream, soon dissolved in a series of zoning map amendments, exceptions and variances—reflecting, generally, decisions made on individual grounds—brought about by unanticipated and often unforeseeable events: social and political changes, ecological necessity, location and availability of roads and utilities, economic facts (especially costs of construction and financing), governmental needs, and, as important as any, market and consumer choice.[8]

Making an opportunity for change central to the zoning process has ensured that requests for change will occur constantly. Inevitably zoning restrictions will prevent the use and development of land for purposes for which there would otherwise be a market. It is equally inevitable that requests for rezonings will often generate intense controversy between the landowner and his neighbors. When the battle is lost before the local authorities, the disappointed party turns to the judicial system to seek a reversal of the adverse local decision.[9] As a result the courts have been asked to arbitrate land use disputes mindful of the admonition in *Euclid* that:

> We [the courts] have nothing to do with the question of the wisdom or good policy of municipal ordinances.[10]

For a zoning restriction to be found unconstitutional it must be

> . . . clearly arbitrary and unreasonable, having no substantial relation to the public health, safety, morals or general welfare.[11]

The Rule of Reasonableness

In general, the courts have decided the question of whether a zoning ordinance is unreasonable by determining whether there is any reasonable use to which the property can be devoted under the zoning restrictions. Zoning restrictions do not become invalid just because the landowner cannot devote his property to its most profitable use.[12] A typical exposition of the reasonable use rule appears in *Arverne Bay Construction Company v. Thatcher*:

> The rule established . . . is this: To sustain an attack upon the validity of the ordinance an aggrieved property owner must show that if the ordinance is enforced the consequent restrictions upon his property preclude its use for any purpose to which it is reasonably adapted.[13]

Under the reasonable use rule, a mere diminution in land value or profits, or an increase in the cost of doing business, does not make a zoning restriction unconstitutional.[14]

Some decisions, the bulk of which come from Illinois, have attempted to balance the burden imposed on the landowner against the public benefit secured by the regulations. *Weitling v. County of Du Page*[15] contains a typical formulation of the balancing test.

> The rule is well established that if the gain to the public is small when compared with the hardship imposed upon individual property owners, no valid basis for an exercise of the police power exists. It is not the owner's loss of value alone that is significant but the fact that the public welfare does not require the restriction and the resulting loss. Where, as here, it is shown that no reasonable basis of public welfare requires the restriction and resulting loss, the ordinance must fall and in determining whether a sufficient hardship on the individual has been shown the law does not require that his property be totally unsuitable for the purpose classified. It is sufficient that a substantial decrease in value results from a classification bearing no substantial relation to the public welfare.[16]

In applying the balancing test, the Illinois courts have evolved a rather elaborate formula for testing the reasonableness of zoning regulations in which "paramount importance" is assigned to the use and zoning of nearby land.[17] The specific factors considered in Illinois zoning disputes have become a litany that is recited in nearly every decision. They include examination of the impact on property values, a balancing of public and private interests, and a consideration of whether the property can be used as zoned.[18]

One state, Maryland, has devised a distinctive test for determining the reasonableness of zoning changes that operates independently of questions of reasonable use or a balancing of public and private interests. The Maryland courts require strong evidence of a mistake in the original zoning restrictions or of a substantial change in conditions for a rezoning of a particular tract of land to be valid.[19] The Maryland rule applies whether the change involves a relaxation or a tightening of the regulations.[20]

Neither the reasonable use rule nor the balancing test is wholly satisfactory. Reasonable use may be employed to sustain very restrictive rezonings that destroy a significant percentage of the market value of real estate.[21] On the other hand, unless the courts steadfastly sustain local zoning regulations in all but the most flagrantly arbitrary situations, the balancing test will encourage disgruntled landowners or neighbors to importune the judiciary to pass judgment on the wisdom of local land use decisions. The temptation to intervene when a decision is patently foolish can be a persuasive incentive for a judicial finding that a local zoning restriction is so arbitrary that it is not constitutionally sustainable. That temptation is encouraged by a conviction on the part of some judges, perhaps based on their own experience, that the decisions of local councils and boards are not really entitled to the same presumption of reasonableness that is accorded to the acts of the state legislature.[22]

Planning as a Warrant of Reasonableness

The pressure for change that is inherent in zoning restrictions creates the risk that decisions with respect to particular parcels of land will be made in response to the oratory and colored architectural renderings offered by the land owner, the shouts and political threats of the neighbors, or a simple desire to get the combatants out of the room so that the routine but necessary business of local government can be conducted. The ad hoc land use decision is suspect and the only way to remove the suspicion is to demonstrate that the guidelines and principles for making that particular decision have engaged the attention of the council at a time when battle had yet to be joined before it. The planners call such prudence a "comprehensive planning process." More simply, it is nothing more than evidence of forethought, a point that was stressed by Justice Keating of the New York Court of Appeals in *Udell v. Haas*[23]—a perceptive and thoughtful discussion of the relationship between planning and zoning. In *Udell*, the local governing body had amended the zoning map so as to reclassify a parcel of land on the edge of the Village from a business zone to a residential zone. In ruling that the rezoning was invalid, the court tested the particular question against the long-established community policies of the municipality. The court explained:

> Zoning is not just an expression of the common law of nuisance. It seeks to achieve much more than the removal of obnoxious gases and unsightly uses. Underlying the entire concept of zoning is the assumption that zoning can be a vital tool for maintaining a civilized form of existence only if we employ the insights and the learning of the philosopher, the city planner, the economist, the sociologist, the public health expert and all the other professions concerned with urban problems.
>
> This fundamental conception of zoning has been present from its inception. The almost universal statutory requirement that zoning conform to a 'well-considered plan' or a 'comprehensive plan' is a reflection of that view. . . . In exercising their zoning powers the local authorities must act for the benefit of the community as a whole

following a calm and deliberate consideration of the alternatives and not because of the whims of either an articulate minority or even a majority of the community. *DeSena v. Gulde*, 24 A.D. 2d 165, 265 N.Y.S 2d 239 [2d Dept., 1965]. Thus the mandate of the Village law (§ 177) is not a mere technicality which serves only as an obstacle course for public officials to overcome in carrying out their duties. Rather the comprehensive plan is the essence of zoning. Without it, there can be no rational allocation of land use. It is the assurance that the public welfare is being served and that zoning does not become nothing more than just a Gallup poll. . . .

Moreover, the 'comprehensive plan' protects the landowner from arbitrary restrictions on the use of his property which can result from the pressures which outraged voters can bring to bear on public officials.[24]

The court added a criticism of ad hoc, poorly informed decisions:

In recent years, many experts on land use problems have expressed the pessimistic views that the task of bringing about a rational allocation of land use in an evermore urbanized America will prove impossible. But of one thing, we all may be certain. The difficulties involved in developing rational schemes of land use controls become insuperable when zoning or changes in zoning are followed rather than preceded by study and consideration. By this statement, we do not mean to imply that the courts should examine the motives of local officials. What we do mean is that the courts must satisfy themselves that the rezoning meets the statutory requirement that zoning be 'in accordance with [the] comprehensive plan' of the community.[25]

Nor would a show of hands in the community justify the decision:

These vague desires of a segment of the public were not a proper reason to interfere with the appellant's right to use his property in a manner which for some 20 odd years was considered perfectly proper. If there is to be any justification for this interference with the appellant's use of his property, it must be found in the needs and goals of the community as articulated in a rational statement of land use control policies known as the "comprehensive plan."[26]

Five years later, the Court of Appeals reaffirmed its views in *Udell*:

We have held that zoning changes must indeed be consonant with a total planning strategy, reflecting consideration of the needs of the community (*Udell v. Haas*, 21 N.Y. 2d 463, 288 N.Y.S. 2d 888, 235 N.E. 2d 897). What is mandated is that there be comprehensiveness of planning, rather than special interest, irrational *ad hocery*. The obligation is support of comprehensive planning, not slavish servitude to any particular comprehensive plan. Indeed, sound planning inherently calls for recognition of the dynamics of change.[27]

Decisions in both Michigan and Illinois have emphasized the importance of comprehensive planning by refusing to extend the usual presumption of validity to local zoning decisions that were not the product of comprehensive planning.

In *Raabe v. City of Walker*,[28] homeowners challenged the validity of a zoning amendment which reclassified neighboring property from agriculture to industrial. In ruling that the amendment was invalid, the Michigan court said:

The absence of a formally adopted municipal plan, whether mandated by statute or not, does not of course invalidate municipal zoning or rezoning. But it does, as in *Biske*, [*Biske v. City of Troy*, 381 Mich. 611, 166 N.W. 3d 453 (1969)], weaken substantially the well-known presumption, which, ordinarily attends any regular-on-its-face municipal zoning ordinance or amendment thereof. This is particularly true of an ordinance purposed toward contradictory rezoning, after years of original zoning upon which concerned persons have come to depend.[29]

In *Forestview Homeowners Ass'n, Inc. v. County of Cook*,[30] there was evidence that not only was there no comprehensive plan, but the County had not even availed itself of the planning assistance and recommendations that were available to it. Finding that the reclassification of 96 acres to intense multiple family use was invalid, the Appellate Court said:

> There is recurring recognition that a comprehensive plan is a factor to be considered in determining the validity of an amendatory ordinance adopted by the zoning authorities of a county. . . . A comprehensive zoning plan is a scheme or formula of zoning that reasonably relates to the regulation and restriction of land uses including establishment of districts therefore, to the health, safety and welfare of the public, and thus to the police power. . . . It is a plan relevant in determining whether a zoning change is in harmony with the orderly utilization of property in a locality.
>
> "Zoning necessarily involves a consideration of the community as a whole and a comprehensive view of its needs." . . . This being so, we are constrained to agree that the failure of Cook County to plan comprehensively for the use and development of land in its unincorporated areas, and its failure to relate its rezoning decisions to data files and plans of other related county agencies, weakens the presumption of validity which otherwise would attach to a county zoning ordinance.[31]

This judicial insistence on evidence of planning is no more than a requirement that advance reflection on land use concerns be the warrant of reasonableness when the regulations applicable to a particular piece of land are in question.

The use of a comprehensive plan or planning process is not without its own risks. The requirement that individual land use decisions be consistent with the comprehensive plan can work to transform the plan from a statement of policy into a regulatory tool that dominates the zoning ordinance. The experience of the Oregon courts since the decision in *Fasano v. Board of County Commissioners of Washington County*[32] gives some cause for concern. The Oregon Supreme Court has already decided that the local governing body must bring zoning regulations into conformity with the plan when the plan is more restrictive.[33] More recently, an intermediate California court decided that the statutory requirement that zoning ordinances be amended "within a reasonable time" so as to be consistent with the general plan mandated by the statute[34] transforms what had been a legislative decision into a ministerial act:

> We conclude the duty to amend to conform the zoning ordinances becomes mandatory. The element of discretion by the Board has been eliminated.[35]

Accordingly, and before the state Supreme Court took the case, the lower court noted:

> The sole question remaining is whether the Board of Supervisors has acted within a 'reasonable time as required by the terms of the statute.' This is a question of fact for the trial court to ascertain from examination of the totality of the circumstances.
>
> If the Board has not, does not, rezone to conform the Rancho del Dios area to the San Dieguito General Plan as amended within a reasonable time, the writ of mandamus may issue to compel its action.[36]

And why not? If the legislative decision with respect to appropriate land use has been made, and the local governing body simply declines to implement its own decision, it is fair to characterize the refusal as arbitrary. The decision should stand as a warning to municipal officials who are tempted to slight the planning process by producing a plan and enshrining it in a cubbyhole in the planning department so that they can more speedily be about the really important business of adopting zoning regulations. A plan has to be more than maps, charts, and vague goals. It must contain a carefully articulated and detailed set of governmental policies and an exposition of how, when and where those policies will be transformed into regulation. It must serve to inform rather than surprise the citizen and landowner.

Exclusionary Effects as Proof of Unconstitutionality

Zoning was designed to permit some uses and exclude others. Until the mid-1950's, it had not occurred to anyone that there was anything pernicious about that result. Charles Haar and Norman Williams, Jr., deserve the credit for first calling attention to the social and economic consequences of zoning patterns and practices.[37] Perhaps the first judicial recognition that zoning ordinances may be used unlawfully to wall off some segments of the population from access to better living conditions came in the prophetic dissent of Justice Frederick Hall in *Vickers v. Township Committee of Gloucester Township,*[38] in which the majority of the New Jersey Supreme Court upheld the exclusion of trailer parks from a township. Justice Hall argued that the interest of a community must be weighed against the interests of potential residents of that community, and of nearby communities, in securing a fair allocation of socially necessary development. He rejected the idea that the exclusion of trailers was merely in aid of achieving the purposes contained in the enabling legislation:

> I submit that [the statutory purposes of zoning] are perverted from their intended application when used to justify Chinese walls of exclusion on the borders of roomy or developing municipalities for the actual purpose of keeping out all but the 'right kind' of people or those who will live in a certain kind and cost of dwelling. What restrictions like minimum house size requirements, overly large lot area regulations and complete limitation of dwellings to single family units really do is bring about community-wide economic segregation.[39]

It was a lone voice, however. At that time, Robert Anderson expressed the conventional wisdom:

> The cases are rare which expressly require that the zoning municipality consider the extra-territorial effect of a zoning restriction. . . . Most courts have respected the power of each municipality to seek its own solutions, to fashion its own character, and to prescribe its own exclusions, without regard (or with very small regard) to the needs of its neighbors or its larger community.[40]

The socially and economically exclusionary effects were there for all to see. Indeed, some suburban residents had understood the parochially beneficial effects of zoning ordinances all too well and kept smugly quiet about the discovery. Richard Babcock, having surveyed the suburban Chicago North Shore, reported:

> Winnetka, Illinois is a leafy, lakeside suburb north of Chicago where the median income per family is around $20,000, the vote is better than 2 to 1 Republican, and a well-deserved reputation for civic virtue is relished without much reflection on the insignificance of the municipal temptations that goodness must resist. Although there are rare aberrations, it is fair to say that the inhabitant of Winnetka is conservative in every sense of the word—and that he regards the zoning ordinance as an essential weapon in his battle with the forces of darkness. He is right. Zoning and its companion, the subdivision ordinance, have been major factors in preserving the character of the community: the integrity, if you will, of the large lot, detached single-family residence. If Winnetka is troubled today by pressures for varied dwelling types it is reassured by the knowledge that most of its land area is built upon; and it can feel that it is dealing with the problem by debating the risks of providing multiple-family dwellings for elderly Presbyterians. Zoning in Winnetka is respectable. Anyone that challenges it is, if not a money-grubbing parvenu, obviously a wild-eyed dreamer intent upon foisting his ideas of social mobility upon the few remaining enclaves of gracious living.[41]

One may suppose that Justice Hall was not the only observant state supreme court judge, but the judiciary had decided themselves into a corner where local land use decisions were concerned. Years of incantations about reasonable use, fairly debatable restrictions, abstaining from substituting judicial judgment for that of local officials, and non-interference with the wisdom of municipal policy had created an inconvenient body of precedent. Those precedents would have to be ignored or reversed if zoning ordinances were to be prevented from perpetuating social and economic segregation in a time of rapid growth in population and household formation. But even if the courts were willing to innovate, how could they do so without changing the ground rules and unleashing an avalanche of gas stations, drive-ins, kiddie carnivals, and other commercial delights upon the unsuspecting residents of reasonably quiet neighborhoods? The dilemma was acute. The state judiciary had been, as the old saying goes, "hoist by its own petard."

Escape from the dead weight of the orthodox rules required a new approach to zoning litigation, at least where housing was concerned. Initially, it seemed that aid might be had from the familiar constitutional rule that classifications by state governments (or their instrumentalities) that differentiate among citizens on the basis of race are suspect and affect the citizen's fundamental right to be free of racial discrimination. Consequently, the equal protection doctrine subjects governments employing such classifications to the burden of demonstrating that they are justified by some compelling state interest.[42] Where zoning ordinances were concerned, this reversal of the burden of proof produced some victories over restrictive ordinances. In both *Dailey v. City of Lawton*[43] and *Kennedy Park Homes v. City of Lackawanna*,[44] proof of a racially discriminatory effect and evidence of white hostility resulted in the invalidation of zoning restrictions. Traditional zoning defenses grounded in the need to prevent traffic congestion, overcrowded schools, and the devaluation of adjacent single family homes were swept away when subjected to strict scrutiny for some compelling state interest.[45]

The message that zoning restrictions that discriminated overtly on racial grounds would be invalidated did not, to no one's great surprise, effect an immediate reform of local government officials who preferred to preserve the status quo. It just encouraged them to find more sophisticated exclusionary techniques. Actually, the task was not difficult because the main thrust of exclusionary zoning restrictions had always been primarily economic,[46] and it soon developed that the new interest of the federal courts in land use restrictions did not extend to economic discrimination.

In *James v. Valtierra*,[47] the Supreme Court upheld the validity of a California requirement that public housing projects receive voter approval at a referendum. The court found no unconsitutional discrimination in the differing treatment accorded public and private housing. Then, in a landlord-tenant case, the Court pursued the theme of *James* by ruling that housing is not a fundamental constitutional right.[48] In the lower federal courts, claims that a challenged restriction was economically discriminatory or that the land use restrictions of a community ignored the housing needs of the region failed to ignite interest in fashioning a federal constitutional remedy.[49] *Village of Belle Terre v. Boraas*,[50] employing language that recalled the 1920's, put an end to any hope that the Supreme Court might be persuaded to attempt to cope with social or economic discrimination in housing with murmurs about the "blessings of quiet seclusion" and a reaffirmation of the traditional judicial deference to local police power decisions.[51]

The already discouraging climate for land use litigants in the federal court grew gloomier with the Court's decision in *Village of Arlington Heights v. Metropolitan Housing Development Corp.*[52] There the Court rejected evidence of a racially discriminatory effect or a disproportionate impact as sufficient proof of racial discrimination. More would now be required:

Our decision last Term in *Washington v. Davis*, 426 U.S. 229 (1976), made it clear that official action will not be held unconstitutional solely because it results in a racially disproportionate impact. 'Disproportionate impact is not irrelevant, but it is not the sole touchstone of an invidious racial discrimination.' *Id.*, at 242. Proof of racial discriminatory intent or purpose is required to show a violation of the Equal Protection Clause. Although some contrary indications may be drawn from some of our cases, the holding in *Davis* reaffirmed a principle well-established in a variety of contexts.

Davis does not require a plaintiff to prove that the challenged action rested solely on racially discriminatory purposes. Rarely can it be said that a legislature or administrative body operating under a broad mandate made a decision motivated solely by a single concern, or even that a particular purpose was the 'dominant' or 'primary' one. In fact, it is because legislators and administrators are properly concerned with balancing numerous competing considerations that courts refrain from reviewing the merits of their decisions, absent a showing of arbitrariness or irrationality. But racial discrimination is not just another competing consideration. When there is proof that a discriminatory purpose has been a motivating factor in the decision, this judicial deference is no longer justified.

Determining whether invidious discriminatory purpose was a motivating factor demands a sensitive inquiry into such circumstantial and direct evidence of intent as may be available. The impact of the official action—whether it 'bears more heavily on one race than another,' may provide an important starting point. Sometimes a clear pattern, unexplainable on grounds other than race, emerges from the effect of the state action even when the governing legislation appears neutral on its face. . . . The evidentiary inquiry is then relatively easy. But such cases are rare. Absent a pattern as stark as the one in *Gomillion* or *Yick Wo*, impact alone is not determinative, and the Court must look to other evidence.[53]

One question remained. Was the refusal of Arlington Heights to permit Lincoln Green to be built a violation of the Fair Housing Act?[54] The Seventh Circuit has held that the Act imposed on the Village a statutory obligation to refrain from zoning policies that have a racially discriminatory effect by effectively foreclosing the construction of any low cost housing within its boundaries and has remanded the case to the district court to determine whether the Village has done just that.[55]

In 1974 there was a brief moment when it appeared that employment of the "right to travel" rationale of the durational residency cases might be the way to create a fundamental federal right that would require justification of local land use restrictions with a compelling state interest.[56] In emulation of the growth control restrictions successfully defended in *Golden v. Planning Board of the Town of Ramapo*,[57] Petaluma, California, imposed an absolute limit of 500 on the number of building permits that could be issued in any one year.[58] The federal district court for the Northern District of California sustained an attack on the ordinance on the ground it violated a fundamental federal constitutional right to travel and settle freely.[59] The new doctrine was short-lived, however. In *Construction Industry Assoc. of Sonoma County v. City of Petaluma*,[60] the Ninth Circuit held that neither the Association nor the landowner involved had standing to challenge the ordinance because it was not *their* right to travel that had been frustrated. With this issue gone, the presumption of validity was sufficient to sustain the ordinance. There may be a right to travel that can upset local land use controls if infringed, but plaintiffs in such a case may be hard to come by.

By this time the conclusion was obvious. The federal courts were not likely to provide an effective forum for relief from economically exclusionary land use restrictions.

The Rise of State Constitutional Remedies

The flurry of land use disputes filed in the federal courts in the late 1960's and early 1970's was an exception to the customary practice. Despite the fact that federal due process and equal protection were the foundation for challenges to the reasonableness of zoning restrictions, almost all of the zoning litigation had been conducted in the state courts.[61] It was not uncommon for zoning challenges in the state courts to be based on both federal and state constitutional grounds,[62] with little or no recognition in the reported decisions that the state courts were free to impose stricter state constitutional due process standards than those imposed by the federal courts interpreting federal due process.[63] Years of litigation over motels, gas stations, apartments, shopping centers, and sanitary landfills on "constitutional" grounds had obscured the independent importance of state constitutional law. The issue of *whose* constitution had been violated by the zoning restrictions in question was usually blurred with a description of the complaint as one attacking the "constitutionality of the zoning restrictions."[64]

Notwithstanding the attitude of the federal courts toward economically exclusionary zoning restrictions, in the state courts the results have been dramatically different. Starting with a series of cases in Pennsylvania, state courts in New York, New Jersey and most recently California have moved onto the field left vacant by the federal courts. In 1970 the Pennsylvania Supreme Court, in *National Land and Investment v. Kohn,*[65] held a four acre minimum lot requirement unconstitutional, rejecting character of the area, greenbelt policy, protection of historic sites, and preservation of rural character as rationales. The Pennsylvania court was quite explicit:

> A zoning ordinance whose primary purpose is to prevent the entrance of newcomers in order to avoid future burdens, economic and otherwise, upon the administration of public services and facilities cannot be held valid.[66]

In New Jersey, Justice Hall was finally vindicated. In *Southern Burlington County NAACP v. Township of Mount Laurel* (the *"Mount Laurel"* case)[67] the New Jersey Supreme Court imposed on every "developing" municipality an obligation to take the general welfare of the region into account in its zoning regulations:

> We conclude that every such [developing] municipality must, by its land use regulations, presumptively make realistically possible an appropriate variety and choice of housing. More specifically, presumptively it cannot foreclose the opportunity of the classes of people mentioned for low and moderate income housing and in its regulations must affirmatively afford that opportunity, at least to the extent of the municipality's fair share of the present and prospective regional need therefor. These obligations must be met unless the particular municipality can sustain the heavy burden of demonstrating peculiar circumstances which dictate that it should not be required to do so. . . . However, it is fundamental and not to be forgotten that the zoning power is a police power of the state and the local authority is acting only as a delegate of that power and is restricted in the same manner as is the state. So, when regulation does have a substantial external impact, the welfare of the state's citizens beyond the borders of the particular municipality cannot be disregarded and must be recognized and served.[68]

The consequence is that for every developing municipality

> . . . the presumptive obligation arises for each such municipality affirmatively to plan and provide, by its land use regulations, the reasonable opportunity for an appropriate

variety and choice of housing, including, of course, low and moderate cost housing, to meet the needs, desires and resources of all categories of people who may desire to live within its boundaries. Negatively, it may not adopt regulations or polices which thwart or preclude that opportunity.[69]

Decades of deciding gas station cases with the judicial mind only half on the tedious task had taken their toll, however. At a time when the federal bench was making it quite plain that economically exclusionary land use restrictions did not offend the federal constitution, the state courts were deciding "exclusion" cases without specifying whether the transgressions involved the state or federal constitutions or both. Justice Hall was one of the few judges to whom it had occurred that it might matter. Thus, the most significant feature of the *Mount Laurel* opinion was that Justice Hall perceived the risk in relying on federal constitutional standards. Instead he cut loose from the federal constitution and, with one short but critical logical leap, he rested the decision solely on a state equal protection requirement that he deduced from the New Jersey Constitution. It took an innovative turn of mind to find a guarantee of equal protection in the New Jersey Constitution because, unlike the provisions in some state constitutions, the New Jersey Constitution contained no express guarantee of equal protection. Justice Hall was equal to the task, however, and he provided the constitutional rationale early in the *Mount Laurel* decision:

> It is elementary theory that all police power enactments, no matter at what level of government, must conform to the basic state constitutional requirements of substantive due process and equal protection of the laws. These are inherent in Art. I, par. 1 of our Constitution, the requirements of which may be more demanding than those of the federal Constitution.[70]

Once the matter had been confined to one of New Jersey constitutional law, the substantive rule followed:

> We have spoken of this obligation of such municipalities as 'presumptive.' The term has two aspects, procedural and substantive. Procedurally, we think the basic importance of appropriate housing for all dictates that, when it is shown that a developing municipality in its land use regulations has not made realistically possible a variety and choice of housing, including adequate provision to afford the opportunity for low and moderate income housing or has expressly prescribed requirements or restrictions which preclude or substantially hinder it, a facial showing of violation of substantive due process or equal protection *under the state constitution* has been made out and the burden, and it is a heavy one, shifts to the municipality to establish a valid basis for its action or non-action. The substantive aspect of 'presumptive' relates to the specifics, on the one hand, of what municipal land use regulation provisions, or the absence thereof, will evidence invalidity and shift the burden of proof and, on the other hand, of what bases and considerations will carry the municipality's burden and sustain what it has done or failed to do. Both kinds of specifics may well vary between municipalities according to peculiar circumstances.[71]

This tour de force effectively insulated the decision from U.S. Supreme Court review.[72] At the same time it shifted the burden of proof to the municipal defendant.

The *Mount Laurel* decision provided the prospect that the courts might become actively involved in supervising the rewriting of local ordinances. However, it was not to be. After hearing reargument, with Justice Hall gone from the court, the New Jersey Supreme Court retrenched in *Oakwood at Madison, Inc. v. Township of Madison.*[73] Madison Township (now Old Bridge Township) was held to be subject to the *Mount Laurel* rule, but the court declined to attempt to devise a formula to determine what a fair share of lower income housing needs would be. The court simply held the ordinance exclusionary, gave the land-owners permission to build their development, and remanded with an order for the municipality to present a revised ordinance in 90 days. Subsequent New Jersey decisions have held, as expected, that the *Mount Laurel* rule does not apply to developed municipalities.[74]

In New York, the Court of Appeals in *Berenson v. Town of New Castle*[75] stopped short of the same result as that reached by the *Mount Laurel* court. The New York court accepted the concept that local land use restrictions must take into account the welfare of the region, but it will be satisfied if the "appropriate range" of housing opportunities can be found within the region. In California, the Supreme Court has remanded *Associated Home Builders v. City of Livermore*[76] to determine:

> The more difficult question whether the measure is one which reasonably relates to the welfare of the region affected by its exclusionary impact, and thus falls within the police power of the city, cannot be decided on the limited record here. That issue can only be resolved by a trial at which evidence is presented to document the probable impact of the ordinance upon the municipality and the surrounding region.[77]

Incredibly, however, neither the New York nor the California courts specified whether their decision rested on federal or state constitutional grounds.

The lesson was taught by the *Mount Laurel* decision, but there is some question as to whether it has been absorbed by other courts. The Pennsylvania Supreme Court was able to rely on the *Mount Laurel* decision in *Township of Williston v. Chesterdale Farms* without indicating whether it was applying state or federal constitutional doctrines.[78] On remand, in *Forest City Enterprises v. City of Eastlake*,[79] the Ohio Supreme Court passed up the opportunity to apply stricter state constitutional due process standards than the United States Supreme Court was willing to perceive in the federal Constitution.

Notwithstanding some blurring of constitutional rationales, *Mount Laurel* and its companion New York and Pennsylvania decisions have broken through the barrier of traditional zoning doctrines that insulated local zoning ordinances from attack because they excluded people and a variety of housing types from the suburbs. The response of local government has not usually been to revise the zoning ordinances so as to reflect the teachings of the recent decisions. Instead, a second generation of ever more sophisticated growth control ordinances have sprung up, one of which has already been invalidated in a Florida trial court decision.[80] These new ordinances which are not, on the surface, overtly exclusionary may, to the extent they seek to turn development into the city and prevent further development on the periphery, produce the same exclusionary results. It remains to be seen whether the courts will be willing to apply the same regional welfare, acceptance of burdens, and fair share requirements to this new class of restrictions.

The Requirement of Compensation as a Limitation

If regulation may become a "taking," will it ever justify compensation for the loss of value inflicted by regulation? Until recently, the answer was, almost uniformly, "no."[81] However, a judicial system that is disposed to sustain municipal zoning regulations in almost all circumstances can succeed in creating a municipal attitude that there is virtually no land use restriction that the courts will not sustain. Thus, it should come as no surprise that it was a California municipality that finally overreached and found out that it had bought the property it thought it had only zoned. The City of Palo Alto, after long negotiations to acquire property in the foothills, abandoned their acquisition attempts and zoned the property of the Arastra Limited Partnership in the Open Space District. In that zone agriculture, botanical conservatories, and single family homes on 10 acre lots were permitted. In *Arastra Limited Partnership v. City of Palo Alto*,[82] a federal district court held that the land had been taken for public use and that compensation must be paid.[83]

The result in *Arastra* may well be an anomaly. The New York Court of Appeals has declined to reach the same result in *Fred French Investing Co. v. City of New York*,[84] in which open space in Tudor City was zoned for a public park with the landowner permitted to transfer the number of dwelling units that could otherwise be built on the site to other property even if it meant selling those development rights on the market. The market for such development rights being entirely speculative, the court found that the zoning deprived the owner of substantially all of the value of its property. The proper remedy, however, was not compensation as the landowner urged, but simply invalidation of the regulation.[85]

Estoppel and Vested Rights as a Limitation

There is one final problem that presents acute constitutional issues. That is the question of the circumstances under which land use regulations may be changed after the landowner has begun to expend money or change his position in the belief that he will be permitted to complete his development. The traditional rule has been that reliance may only be predicated upon a lawfully issued building permit.[86] A minority view has been that rights may vest or the municipality may be estopped if money is expended, or a change of position made, in reliance either upon a building permit, or upon a good faith belief that a permit will issue.[87] The recent Florida decision in *Town of Largo v. Imperial Homes*[88] adopted what can best be described as the fair play, or "welcome mat" standard:

> Stripped of the legal jargon which lawyers and judges have obfuscated it with, the theory of estoppel amounts to nothing more than an application of the rules of fair play. One party will not be permitted to invite another onto a welcome mat and then be permitted to snatch the mat away to the detriment of the party induced or permitted to stand thereon. A citizen is entitled to rely on the assurances and commitments of a zoning authority and if he does, the zoning authority is bound by its representations, whether they be in the form of words or deeds. . . .[89]

The problem can be simply stated, but for the land developer there are no easy solutions. No development of any size is built all at once. Developments, whether residential or commercial, frequently extend over a period of years with substantial early investments in grading, water and sewer mains, roadways and other development costs. If the land use regulations can be changed in the middle of that process, large sums of money expended in the course of development can be irretrievably lost. In the current development and building industry, the building permit is practically the last permit secured, not one of the first.[90] In the long succession of permits and authorizations required for any development today, the building permit may be the least significant. It is no more than a "certificate of probable non-collapse."[91]

Earlier approvals such as the issuance of planned development approval or a special use permit, the approval of a site plan, or the approval of final land improvement plans and engineering are much more significant. In some states there have been decisions recognizing that the current development process bears little resemblance to that which was prevalent in the formative years of the vested rights rule.[92]

In California, however, the rigid enforcement of the outdated building permit standard has produced what must be economic disasters for some developers. In *Avco Community Developers v. South Coast Regional Commission*,[93] the supreme court refused to find that Avco's rights had vested in the regulations that were in force before the Coastal Commission regulations took effect. Avco had secured approval for a final subdivision map and had commenced rough grading but had not completed grading or secured any building permits on the date the Coastal Commission acquired jurisdiction of its land. Avco had, however, spent over two million dollars, had liabilities of $740,000, and was losing $7,113.46 every day. Despite the heavy expenditures in reliance on the former restrictions the California Supreme Court declined "to carve out an exception to [the vested rights] rule for planned unit zoning."[94]

In *Oceanic California, Inc. v. North Central Coast Regional Commission* (the *"Sea Ranch"* case),[95] the facts were even more dramatic. Briefly, the landowner had 5,200 acres of land on the northern Sonoma County coast for which a planned development had been approved by the County in 1964. During an eight year period, the County had granted zoning and development approvals, subdivision map approvals, other infrastructure permits, as well as building permits for some structures. Prior to the adoption of the coastal initiative on November 7, 1972, Oceanic had spent $26,900,000 in direct project expenditures, $9,250,000 of which represented hard development costs. To no avail. The court held, following *Avco*, that Oceanic's right to complete the Sea Ranch as originally approved had not vested as to any portion of the acreage for which building permits had not been secured. There was no right to rely on any zoning or other development approvals preparatory to the construction of buildings. A planned unit development, despite the fact that it commits the developer to build a specific project on a specific piece of property, "merely imposes a special zoning on the property."[96] Quite plainly, the California court did not or could not understand the difference between a general zoning classification and the approval of a specific development plan.

Recognition of the harshness of the California rule has begun to dawn. In *Raley v. California Tahoe Regional Planning Agency*,[97] the court applied its usual rules with respect to vesting and estoppel and permitted an administrative "change of mind" to send the plaintiff back into the administrative process to secure again the approvals he had secured once before. But the court was not happy with the result:

> Nevertheless, the denouement of this lawsuit leaves the members of this court, as appellate chancellors in equity, with a dissatisfied sense of justice. In hard fact, Raley spent $150,000 in reliance upon a landuse permit lawfully granted by a state instrumentality which was then repudiated by a related state instrumentality. The two agencies had overlapping membership and occupied a relationship of mutual awareness and privity. . . .
>
> Raley is the victim of maladroitly engineered environmental controls. California's current need for 200,000 new jobs each year can be met only by a flow of venture capital. The protection of the state's remaining environmental amenities unavoidably constricts this flow. . . .
>
> The mechanisms at work here combined to 'protect' the environment by protracted and undependable administrative procedures followed by years of litigation. Only the most hardy and well-heeled can run so harsh a gauntlet. Burdened by land costs, loan interest, architectural, engineering and attorney fees, many entrepreneurs run out of money or heart or both long before the finish line. . . .
>
> Handmaiden of prevailing administrative anarchy is the vested rights rule, as voiced by the authoritative decisions cited earlier. The vested rights rule gives a green light to administrative vacillation virtually up to the moment the builder starts pouring concrete. The rule has been described as a 'common law' rule and as a 'constitutional common law principle.' It is neither. The rule, as we have observed, is a manifestation of equitable estoppel.[98]

But in the end the court concluded nothing could be done short of legislation:

When and if the rigidities of the vested rights rule are tempered by heightened concern for the citizen-entrepreneur, the California legislature may be prodded into an acutely needed redesign of environmental control mechanisms. As an intermediate appellate court, we take the statutes and the binding decisional doctrines as we find them. In their present condition, they permit Raley no judicial relief.[99]

The court was simply wrong. The vested rights and equitable estoppel rules arise from precedent, not statute. The California courts have it in their power to ameliorate the harshness of those rules if they so choose. Other courts have done so and the path is clearly marked.[100]

There is more at stake than a "dissatisfied sense of justice." The development industry reads the case reports and understands the implications of them. If the courts will not protect the investments they make in land development, they will do so themselves by never committing themselves to more development than they can secure approvals and building permits for before the ordinances or the municipal minds change. The result will be a proliferation of small, "build it and run" developments because no developer will be able to afford the risk of an *Avco* or *Sea Ranch* disaster.

Careful planning, with the attention to environmental protection, preservation of open space, and the provision of the visual and recreational amenities that communities profess to want, requires developments that are planned in detail and in which extensive investments in site development and physical improvements are made long before the first building permit is issued. In short, they require precisely the kind of long range development commitment that the California courts hold is not available. Under those circumstances no one should look surprised when entrepreneurs decline to assume the risks that strict application of the vested rights rule imposes.

Conclusion

On other fronts the interest may be focused on federal constitutional doctrines, but in land use matters the most significant issues center on the state constitutions. The principles that have been urged unsuccessfully as federal constitutional norms are gaining acceptance as state constitutional laws. It is none too soon. We are likely to see marked changes in both the type and source of land use controls in the immediately coming years.[101] The state courts appear far more disposed to attempt to preserve a sensible balance among competing public interests than are the federal courts. To do so, however, they will need to articulate more useful standards of state constitutional doctrine than have been devised to date. Decisions like *Mount Laurel* and its progeny give some reason to hope that the state courts are equal to the task.

Notes

1. 372 Mich. 264, 125 N.W. 2d 862 (1964).

2. *Village of Euclid v. Ambler Realty*, 272 U.S. 365 (1926); *Nectow v. City of Cambridge*, 277 U.S. 183 (1928). Although neither *Euclid* nor *Nectow* mention the decision in *Pennsylvania Coal Co. v. Mahon*, 260 U.S. 393 (1922), both decisions impliedly accept the view expressed by Justice Holmes that the difference between regulation and "taking" is merely a difference of degree and that if regulation becomes a "taking," then either compensation must be paid or the regulation declared invalid (260 U.S. at 413). The history and background of the *Pennsylvania Coal* decision is traced in BOSSELMAN, CALLIES & BANTA, THE TAKING ISSUE 124–38 (U.S.

Government Printing Office) (1973). The Illinois Supreme Court has expressed the view that even if zoning disputes raise constitutional issues, they do not raise "substantial" constitutional issues. *First National Bank & Trust Co. v. City of Evanston*, 30 Ill. 2d 479, 197 N.E. 2d 705 (1964).

3. A real subdivision in Bolingbrook, Illinois. The streets are named after famous baseball players.

4. Two especially bad examples are *Offner Electronics, Inc. v. Gerhart*, 398 Ill. 265, 76 N.E.2d 27 (1947) and *Krom v. City of Elmhurst*, 8 Ill. 2d 104, 133 N.E.2d 1 (1956).

5. The count was made by Norman Williams, Jr. who reported that it took four years just to read them all. 1 N. WILLIAMS, AMERICAN LAND PLANNING LAW vii.

6. Freund, Ernest, *Some Inadequately Discussed Problems of the Law of City Planning and Zoning*, 24 ILL. L. REV. 135, at 145 (1929).

7. 391 Mich. 139, 215 N.W.2d 179 (1974).

8. *Id.* at 168 and 191–92.

9 A Georgia court described one such contretemps in *Pendley v. Lake Harbin Civic Association*, 230 Ga. 631, 633–634, 198 S.E.2d 503, at 505 (1973):

> The evidence in this complaint for injunctive relief shows 36 zoning petitions were scheduled to be heard before the Commissioners of Clayton County on October 11, 1972, at 7:30 o'clock p.m.; that the hearings continued until 3:30 o'clock a.m., October 12, 1972; that from 1,200 to 1,500 people were present to attend the public meeting; that the hearings were held in the commissioners' hearing room, which accommodates approximately fifty people; that there were three other larger rooms in the courthouse where the hearings could have been legally held; that people were packed so closely in the entire corridor outside the hearing room that those interested in various petitions could not get close to the door, much less inside the hearing room.

10. *Euclid* 272 U.S., at 393.

11. *Id.* at 395.

12. *Arverne Bay Construction Co. v. Thatcher*, 278 N.Y. 222, 15 N.E.2d 587 (1938); *McCarthy v. City of Manhattan Beach*, 41 Cal.2d 879, 264 P.2d 932 (1953); *Trever v. City of Sterling Heights*, 53 Mich. App. 144, 218 N.W.2d 810 (1974); *Guaclides v. Borough of Englewood Cliffs*, 11 N.J. Super. 405, 78 A.2d 435 (1951); *Dusi v. Wilhelm*, 25 Ohio Misc. 111, 266 N.E.2d 280 (1970). Occasionally, limitations on the use of land that really do not permit any reasonable use have been sustained. See, *Consolidated Rock Products v. City of Los Angeles*, 57 Cal.2d 515, 20 Cal.Rptr. 638, 370 P.2d 342 (1962).

13. *Arverne Bay Construction v. Thatcher*, op cit., 278 N.Y.2d at 226, 15 N.E.2d at 589.

14. For a collection of decisions from 22 states see 1 RATHKOPF, THE LAW OF ZONING AND PLANNING 6.10–6.11 (4th Ed.). The Rathkopf text is one of the most comprehensive and valuable sources in the field. Courts rely on it frequently.

15. 26 Ill.2d 196, 186 N.E.2d 291 (1962).

16. *Id.* at 199 and 292. See also, *Miller Bros. Lumber Co. v. City of Chicago*, 414 Ill. 162, 111 N.E.2d 149 (1953); *La Salle National Bank v. City of Chicago*, 5 Ill.2d 344, 124 N.E.2d 609 (1955); *White v. City of Twin Falls*, 81 Ida. 176, 338 P.2d 778 (1959); *Janesick v. City of Detroit*, 337 Mich. 549, 60 N.W.2d 452 (1953); and *Chusud Realty Corp. v. Village of Kensington*, 40 Misc.2d 259, 243 N.Y.S.2d 149 (1963), aff'd. 22 A.D.2d 895, 255 N.Y.S.2d 411 (1964). The balancing test is discussed in BOSSELMAN, (et al.), THE TAKING ISSUE, *supra* note 2, at 195–211. It has also been criticized by one eminent commentator. See, 5 WILLIAMS, AMERICAN LAND PLANNING LAWS 438–39.

17. *River Forest State Bank & Trust Co. v. Village of Maywood*, 23 Ill.2d 560, 179 N.E.2d 671 (1962); *La Salle National Bank v. Village of Palatine*, 92 Ill.App.2d 327, 236 N.E.2d 1 (1968).

18. In *La Salle National Bank v. County of Cook*, 12 Ill.2d 40, 145 N.E.2d 65 (1957), the supreme court identified the factors as follows:

> (1) The existing uses and zoning of nearby property, (2) the extent to which property values are diminished by the particular zoning restrictions, (3) the extent to which the destruction of property values of plaintiff promotes the health, safety, morals or general welfare of the public, (4) the relative gain to the public as compared to the hardship imposed upon the individual property owner, (5) the suitability of the subject property for the zoned purposes, and (6) the length of time the property has been vacant as zoned considered in the context of land development in the area in the vicinity of the subject property.

To these considerations the supreme court has added an additional factor: the care with which a community has undertaken to plan for the use of land. *Sinclair Pipeline v. Village of Richton Park*, 19 Ill.2d 370, 167 N.E.2d 406 (1960).

19. *Board of County Commissioners for Prince George's County v. Edmonds*, 240 Md. 680, 215 A.2d 209 (1965); *MacDonald v. Board of Commissioners for Prince George's County*, 238 Md. 549, 210 A.2d 325 (1965).

20. *Board of Zoning Appeals of Baltimore County v. Bailey*, 216 Md. 536, 141 A.2d 502 (1958). Virginia has utilized a modified form of the "change or mistake" rule in a piecemeal downzoning case. See, *Board of Supervisors of Fairfax County v. Snell Construction*, 214 Va. 655, 202 S.E.2d 889 (1974).

21. California represents one extreme. See *Ensign Bickford Realty Corp. v. City Council of the City of Livermore*, 68 Cal. App. 3d 467, 137 Cal. Rptr. 304 (1977), where the court found it was not arbitrary of the Council to refuse a rezoning that conformed to the City's General Plan. At the other pole are the Illinois courts in which one appellate district can uphold single family zoning of property that faces into a restaurant, the back of an automobile agency, a gas station, and other commercial uses while another district finds single family zoning to be arbitrary and confiscatory when the immediate area contains nothing but houses, soybean fields and a school with the nearest commercial uses a mile away. Compare *Zenith Radio v. Village of Mount Prospect*, 15 Ill. App. 3d 587, 304 N.E. 2d 754 (1973) with *Beaver v. Village of Bolingbrook*, 12 Ill. App. 3d 923, 298 N.E. 2d 761 (1973).

22. See, R. BABCOCK, THE ZONING GAME 105 (1966). Babcock reports that a "state supreme court justice told me he decided at least one well-noted case against the municipality because he simply could not accept the view that officials of a small governmental unit were capable of exercising fairness where decisions on land use matters required considerable discretion." In *Ward v. Village of Skokie*, 26 Ill. 2d 415, 424, 186 N.E. 2d 529, 533 (1962), Justice Klingbiel, concurring, observed:

> It is not part of the legislative function to grant permits, make special exceptions, or decide particular cases. Such activities are not legislative but administrative, quasi-judicial or judicial in character. To place them in the hands of legislative bodies, whose acts as such are not judicially reviewable, is to open the door completely to arbitrary government. I need not dwell at length on the obvious opportunity this affords for special privilege, for the granting of favors to political or financial benefactors, for the withholding of permits from those not in the good graces of the authorities, and so on.

23. 21 N.Y. 2d 463, 288 N.Y.S. 2d 888, 235 N.E. 2d 897 (1968). The requirement that zoning be "in accordance with a comprehensive plan" has long been mandated by many state enabling acts. It derives from the Standard Zoning Enabling Act published by the U.S. Dept. of Commerce in 1928. See, Haar, *In Accordance With a Comprehensive Plan*, 68 HARV. L. REV. 1154 (1955); Sullivan and Kressel, *Twenty Years After - Renewed Significance of the Comprehensive Plan Requirement*, 9 URBAN LAW ANNUAL 33 (1975).

24. 21 N.Y. 2d at 469, 288 N.Y.S. 2d at 893–94, 235 N.E. 2d at 900–901.

25. *Id.* at 471 and 895, 901.

26. *Id.* at 476 and 899, 905.

27. *Town of Bedford v. Village of Mount Kisco*, 33 N.Y. 2d 178, at 188, 351 N.Y.S. 2d 129, 306 N.E. 2d 155, at 159 (1973).

28. 383 Mich. 165, 174 N.W. 2d 789 (1970).

29. *Id.* at 178 and 796.

30. 18 Ill. App. 3d 230, 309 N.E. 2d 763, *lv. to app. den.* 56 Ill. 2d 582 (1974). See also *Fleming v. City of Tacoma*, 81 Wash. 2d 292, at 295, 502 P. 2d 327, at 329 (1972); *Board of Supervisors of Fairfax County v. Snell Construction Co.*, 214 Va. 655, at 658, 202 S.E. 2d 889 at 894 (1974); *Grant v. Washington Township*, 1 Ohio App. 2d 84, at 87, 203 N.E. 2d 859, at 861–62 (1963); and, *Daviess County v. Snyder*, 556 S.W. 2d 688 (Ky., 1977).

31. *Forestview Homeowners v. Cook County*, 18 Ill. App. 3d at 240, 242, 243, 309 N.E. 2d at 771, 773. The "plan" need not be an adopted document, however. *First National Bank of Highland Park v. Village of Vernon Hills*, 55 Ill. App. 3d 985, 371 N.E. 2d 659 (1977).

32. 264 Ore. 574, 507 P. 2d 23 (1973).

33. *Baker v. City of Milwaukie*, 271 Ore. 500, 533 P. 2d 772 (1975). The subsequent history can be found in *Green v. Hayward*, 275 Ore. 693, 552 P. 2d 815 (1976); *South of Sunnyside Neighborhood League v. Board of Commissioners of Clackamas County*, 280 Ore. 3, 569 P. 2d 1063 (1977); *Peterson v. Mayor & Council of City of Klamath Falls*, 279 Ore. 249, 566 P. 2d 1193 (1977); and *1000 Friends of Oregon v. Benton County Commissioners*, 320 Ore. 413, 575 P. 2d 651 (1978).

34. Cal. Gov't Code § § 65860(a) and 65860(c).

35. *Youngblood v. Board of Supervisors of San Diego County*, 71 Cal. App. 3d 655, (modified on appeal, 72 Cal. App. 3d 763), 139 Cal. Rptr. 741 (1977). Since this paper was prepared the California Supreme Court has affirmed, vacating the intermediate appellate decision. The question of whether the city could be compelled to conform its zoning ordinance to the general plan had been made moot because the city had done so. Nevertheless, the California Supreme Court held that the city was required to approve the subdivision map because it had received tentative approval prior to the change in the plan. *Youngblood v. Board of Supervisors of San Diego County*, 22 Cal. 3d 644, 150 Cal. Rptr. 242, 586 P. 2d 556 (1978).

36. 71 Cal. App. 3d at 671, 139 Cal. Rptr. at 750.

37. Haar, *Zoning for Minimum Standards: The Wayne Township Case*, 66 HARV. L. REV. 1051 (1953); Williams, *Planning Law and Democratic Living*, 20 LAW & CONTEMP. PROB. 317 (1955). These seminal articles were followed by Babcock and Bosselman, *Suburban Zoning and the Apartment Boom*, 111 U. PA. L. REV. 1040 (1963).

38. 37 N.J. 232, 181 A. 2d 129 (1962) app. dismd. 371 U.S. 233 (1963).

39. *Id.* at 252 and 140.

40. Anderson, *Provincialism and the Public Interest in* FEDERALISM PLANNING INFORMATION REPORT 405 (N.J. Federation of Planning Officials 1970).

41. BABCOCK, THE ZONING GAME 20–21.

42. See, e.g. *Reitman v. Mulkey*, 387 U.S. 369 (1967); *Jones v. Alfred H. Mayer Co.*, 392 U.S. 409 (1968).

43. 425 F.2d 1037 (CA 10, 1970).

44. 318 F.Supp. 669 (W.D.N.Y. 1970) aff'd 436 F.2d 108 (CA 2, 1970), cert. den. 401 U.S. 1010 (1971).

45. *United States v. City of Black Jack*, 508 F.2d 1179 (CA 8, 1974). See also, *Park View Heights Corp. v. City of Black Jack*, 467 F.2d 1208 (CA 8, 1972); *United Farmworkers v. City of Delray Beach*, 493 F.2d 799 (CA 5, 1974); and, *Sisters of Providence of St. Mary's of the Woods v. City of Evanston*, 335 F.Supp. 396 (N.D. Ill. 1971). Whether the proposed housing in these cases is ever built often remains unreported. In *Sisters of Providence* nothing more ever happened. The prospective developer was unable to renew its option. Ultimately, the City bought the property and now uses the old high school building (since remodeled) as a city hall. On remand of the *Park View Heights* case, the district court held it would not require the city to take affirmative steps to ensure construction of a low income housing project. *Park View Heights v. City of Black Jack*, 30 Zoning Digest 552 (E.D. Mo., 1978, No. 71–15 c (A)).

46. For a discussion of the economic factors affecting housing costs, see BABCOCK & BOSSELMAN, EXCLUSIONARY ZONING 3–17 (Praeger/ASPO, 1973).

47. 402 U.S. 137 (1971).

48. *Lindsey v. Normet*, 405 U.S. 56 (1972).

49. *Acevedo v. Nassau County*, 500 F.2d 1078 (CA 2, 1974); *Mahaley v. Cuyahoga Metropolitan Housing Authority*, 500 F.2d 1087 (CA 6, 1974); *Ybarra v. Town of Los Altos Hills*, 503 F.2d 250 (CA 9, 1974).

50. 416 U.S. 1 (1974).

51. The Court's more recent decision in *Moore v. City of East Cleveland*, 431 U.S. 494, 97 S.Ct. 1932 (1977), was not, in its view, out of step. Having justified *Belle Terre* because the ordinance promoted "family needs" and "family values," the Court found no difficulty in overturning an ordinance that attempted to regulate housing "by slicing deeply into the family itself." The inconsistency of the Court's assertion that it "has long recognized that freedom of personal choice in matters of marriage and family life is one of the liberties protected by the Due Process clause of the Fourteenth Amendment" (97 S.Ct. at 1934), with the *Belle Terre* decision does not seem to have occurred to the Court. Apparently local governmental interference with the personal choice of some individuals to establish unconventional households will continue to remain outside the orbit of Fourteenth Amendment protection. But on this issue, see, *Holy Name Hospital v. Montroy*, 153 N.J. Super. 181, 379 A.2d 299 (1977).

52. 429 U.S. 252, 97 S.Ct. 555 (1977).

53. *Id.* at 264–266, 563–64. See also *Joseph Skillken & Co. v. City of Toledo*, 528 F.2d 867, at 881 (CA 6, 1975), vacated and remanded, 429 U.S. 1068, 97 S.Ct. 800, (1977), re-affirmed on remand, 558 F.2d 350 (CA 6, 1977), which held that the refusal of the City to approve three scattered site public housing developments was not racially discriminatory, explaining:

> We live in a free society. The time has not yet arrived for the courts to strike down state zoning laws which are neutral on their face and valid when passed, in order to permit the construction at public expense of large numbers of low cost public housing units in a neighborhood where they do not belong, and where the property owners, relying on the zoning laws, have spent large sums of money to build fine homes for the enjoyment of their families.

54. 42 U.S.C. §§ 3601 *et seq.*

55. *Metropolitan Housing Development Corp. v. Village of Arlington Heights*, 558 F.2d 1283 (CA 7, 1977). After remand to the district court the parties negotiated a proposed consent decree which would have required the Village to annex a different tract of land presently outside of, but contiguous to, the Village and permit the development of subsidized family and elderly housing on twelve acres of that tract with commercial zoning and two restaurant special use permits on the remaining fourteen acres of the tract. Under the proposed decree the owners of the commercial property would get a five year veto over any land use changes. A neighboring municipality and three property owners associations were granted leave to intervene to object to the entry of the proposed consent decree. *Metropolitan Housing Development Corp. v. Village of Arlington Heights*, (N.D. Ill.) (No. 72 C 1453, August 21, 1978). At this writing a decision on the objections is pending.

56. See, e.g., *Memorial Hospital v. Maricopa County*, 415 U.S. 250 (1974); *Dunn v. Blumstein*, 405 U.S. 330 (1972); and *Shapiro v. Thompson*, 394 U.S. 618 (1969).

57. 30 N.Y.2d 359, 334 N.Y.S.2d 165, 285 N.E.2d 291 (1972), appeal dismissed 409 U.S. 1003 (1972). The *Ramapo* phased growth ordinance rested on a master plan, a zoning ordinance that implemented the plan, and an eighteen year program for constructing public improvements. No permit for residential development during those eighteen years would be issued unless the proposed development accumulated fifteen points on a sliding scale of values assigned to the presence and proximity of five types of public facilities or services: (1) public

sanitary sewers or an approved substitute; (2) drainage facilities; (3) public parks or other recreational facilities, including public schools; (4) roads and highways; and, (5) firehoues. The New York Court of Appeals was uneasy about the Ramapo ordinances:

> There is, then, something inherently suspect in a scheme which, apart from its professed purposes, effects a restriction upon the free mobility of a people until sometime in the future when projected facilities are available to meet increased demands. Although zoning must include schemes designed to allow municipalities to more effectively contend with the increased demands of evolving and growing communities, under its guise, townships have been wont to try their hand at an array of exclusionary devices in the hope of avoiding the very burden which growth must inevitably bring. (30 N.Y.2d at 375, 285 N.E.2d at 300).

The court's uneasiness was well-founded. *Ramapo* was decided on cross motions for summary judgment. The bona fides of the Ramapo plan and planning process were never subjected to litigation on the merits. See Bosselman, Fred, *Can the Town of Ramapo Pass a Law to Bind the Rights of the Whole World?*, 1 FLA. ST. U.L. REV. 234 (1973).

58. For a description of the Petaluma Plan, see Smith, *Does Petaluma Lie at the End of the Road from Ramapo?*, 19 VILL. L. REV. 739, at 745–46 (1974) or Hart, *The Petaluma Case*, 9 CRY CALIFORNIA 6–9 (Spring, 1974).

59. *Construction Industry Assoc. of Sonoma County v. City of Petaluma*, 375 F.Supp. 574 (N.D. Calif. 1974).

60. 522 F.2d 897 (CA 9, 1975). See also, *Rasmussen v. City of Lake Forest*, 404 F.Supp. 148 (N.D. Ill., 1975) in which a right to travel rationale was rejected in an attack on large lot zoning restrictions.

The principal limitation on access to the federal courts in land use matters is *Warth v. Seldin,* 422 U.S. 490 (1975), wherein the Court insisted that nonresident plaintiffs must allege "specific, concrete facts demonstrating the challenged practices harm him," that is, that plaintiff has sustained an injury in fact; and, that the remedy sought will redress the injury. See Sager, *Insular Majorities Unabated,* 91 Harv. L. Rev. 1373, 1376–1402 (1978).

61. There have been occasional exceptions. See, e.g., *Lerner v. Town of Islip*, 272 F.Supp. 664 (E.D.N.Y. 1967).

62. See, *Reschke v. Village of Winnetka*, 363 Ill. 478, 2 N.E.2d 718 (1936); *Wolverine Sign Works v. City of Bloomfield Hills*, 279 Mich. 205, 271 N.W. 823 (1937).

63. In *State v. Johnson*, 68 N.J. 349, 346 A.2d 66 (1975), Justice Sullivan of the New Jersey Supreme Court said:

> [W]e have the right to construe our State constitutional provisions in accordance with what we conceive to be its plain meaning.

See also, *People v. Disbrow*, 16 Cal.3d 101, 127 Cal.Rptr. 360, 545 P.2d 272 (1976); *State v. Sklan*, 317 A.2d 160 (1974); *People v. Jackson*, 391 Mich. 323, 217 N.W.2d 501 (1974); *Parkham v. Municipal Court*, 86 S.D. 531, 199 N.W.2d 501 (1972). And compare *Burrows v. Superior Court*, 13 Cal.3d 283, 118 Cal.Rptr. 166, 529 P.2d 590 (1974) with *United States v. Miller*, 425 U.S. 435, 96 S.Ct. 1619 (1976). See also, Brennan, *Developments in Constitutional Law*, 99 N.J.L.J. 473, 482–83.

64. *Consolidated Rock Products v. City of Los Angeles*, 57 Cal. 2d 515, 20 Cal.Rptr. 638, 370 P.2d 342 (1962); *City of Miami v. Silver*, 257 S.2d 563 (Fla. 1972); *La Salle National Bank v. County of Cook*, 12 Ill.2d 40, 145 N.E.2d 65 (1957); *Pearce v. Village of Edina*, 263 Minn. 553, 118 N.W.2d 659 (1962); *Church v. Town of Islip*, 8 N.Y.2d 254, 203 N.Y.S.2d 866, 168 N.E.2d 680 (1960); and *Mobil Oil Corp. v. City of Rocky River*, 38 Ohio St.2d 23, 309 N.E.2d 900 (1974).

65. 419 Pa. 504, 215 A.2d 597 (1966).

66. *Id.* at 532 and 612. In four subsequent cases the Pennsylvania court has elaborated on the *National Land* rule. See *Appeal of Kit-Mar Builders, Inc.*, 439 Pa. 466, 268 A.2d 765 (1970) (two and three acre minimum lot sizes) and *Appeal of Girsh*, 437 Pa. 237, 263 A.2d 395 (1970) (exclusion of apartments from a 4.64 square mile township); and *Township of Willistown v. Chesterdale Farms* (exclusion of nearly all apartments), 462 Pa. 445, 341 A.2d 466 (1975); and *Surrick v. Zoning Hearing Board of the Township of Upper Providence*, 476 Pa. 182, 382 A.2d 105 (1977) (in which the court debates the wisdom of the *Mt. Laurel* "fair share" approach). See also, *Berenson v. Town of New Castle*, 38 N.Y.2d 102, 341 N.E.2d 236 (1975); *Suffolk Housing Services v. Town of Brookhaven*, 91 Misc. 80, 397 N.Y.S.2d 302 (1977), mod. & aff'd., 405 N.Y.S.2d 302 (1978); and *Associated Home Builders v. City of Livermore*, 18 Cal.3d 582, 135 Cal.Rptr. 41, 557 P.2d 473 (1976).

67. 67 N.J. 151, 336 A.2d 713 (1975).

68. *Id.* at 174, 177, and 724–25, 726.

69. *Id.* at 179–180 and 728.

70. Footnote 11 to the opinion provides the constitutional text:

> All persons are by nature free and independent, and have certain natural and unalienable rights, among which are those of enjoying and defending life and liberty, of acquiring, possessing, and protecting property, and of pursuing and obtaining safety and happiness.

71. 67 N.J. 180–181, 336 A.2d at 728 (emphasis added).

72. It also produced what the court itself later modestly described as "extensive discussion in the literature," *Oakwood at Madison, Inc. v. Township of Madison*, 72 N.J. 481, 371 A.2d 1192 (1977), footnote 3, at page 1198. The note contains as complete a list of law review articles and comments as anyone could ever desire.

73. 72 N.J. 481, 371 A.2d 1192 (1975).

74. *Pascack Assoc. Ltd. v. Mayor and Council of Washington Township*, 74 N.J. 470, 379 A.2d 6 (1977); *Windmill Estates v. Zoning Board of Adjustment*, 147 N.J. Super. 65, 370 A.2d 541 (1976). The *Mount Laurel* rule has recently been held inapplicable to proposals to build housing that will be affordable only by middle or upper-income owners or tenants. *Castroll v. Township of Franklin*, 161 N.J. Super. 190, 391 A.2d 544 (1978); and, *Swiss Village Associates v. Township of Wayne*, 162 N.J. Super. 138, 392 A.2d 596 (1978).

75. 38 N.Y.2d 102, 341 N.E.2d 236 (1975). The *Berenson* case has now been tried and the *Mt. Laurel* "fair share" rule was applied with what passes for mathematical certainty. The trial court found with respect to housing needs in New Castle: 1) in 1977 there was an "unmet housing need in and for the Town of New Castle" of 800 to 900 dwelling units; 2) the unmet housing need was primarily for persons whose families have a gross income of $15,000 or less; 3) average house sales in new Castle in 1976 were $89,750 and 80% of such sales were in one and two acre zones and had an average sales price of $109,000; 4) New Castle's housing inventory consists "exclusively of single family residences and a very few old non-conforming, multi-family structures"; 5) 89.2% of the Town is zoned for one or two acre residential lots, 8.1% is zoned for one-half and one-quarter acre lots, and the remaining 2.7% is commercial, industrial and public uses; and 6) New Castle has not adequately met its housing needs and new construction will be necessary to meet present and future housing needs, and the zoning and planning policies that preclude such development must be changed. The court also evaluated the regional need for lower income housing and the question of whether other "accessible areas in the community at large" could supply the sub-regional share of unmet housing need. The Court determined that in New Castle and 12 surrounding communities the *1970 need* for housing for households having an annual income of less than $10,000 was 6,000 units. The court further found that for at least 25 years New Castle's planning and zoning policies were predicated upon the ability of four nearby communities to meet New Castle's need for multi-family housing. The court found that these four communities were unable to meet their own present or future housing needs, that regional housing needs are not being met by New Castle's neighbors, and that if New Castle's and *"other now undeveloped communities"* zoning policies "are permitted to continue without change, it will be impossible to supply the housing needs of the county during the next decade." The court specifically determined that New Castle's share of the regional need for multi-family housing was 3500 dwelling units over the next ten years. The court granted specific relief to the plaintiff by finding the existing zoning restrictions invalid as they affected plaintiff's land and ordered rezoning within six months at a density "in the middle" of the Westchester County recommended density of one to sixteen units per acre. In an attempt to avoid subsequent trials to establish the rights of other developers to construct housing to meet the housing need found to exist, the court held that New Castle must "affirmatively afford the opportunity to meet such needs" and that the planning and zoning policies of New Castle, to the extent that they frustrate that objective, were invalid. Therefore, the court held that the Town would have the "heavy burden of showing compelling reasons to justify the exclusion of future proposals of multi-family housing up to 3,500 units of such housing over the next ten years." If the Town does not "adopt adequate changes in its zoning, planning and land use regulatory policies," then any disappointed applicants for multi-family rezoning could secure judicial relief by showing that the proposed development would contribute to meeting New Castle's housing need and that the Town had "frustrated that objective for less than compelling reasons." This declaratory relief was labeled "interim relief pending the revision of the Town's planning and zoning policies to accommodate the needed housing." The court retained jurisdiction to determine when the interim relief "should be lifted because of the Town's adoption of a satisfactory zoning, planning and land use regulatory policy in regard to needed housing." The effective date of the interim relief was deferred for six months and the court provided the Town with guidelines for what it called an "inclusionary policy statement" with respect to housing. *Berenson v. Town of New Castle*, Supreme Court, Westchester County, December 6, 1977 (emphasis added). The decision has not, at this writing, been reported. A summary may be found in the LAND USE LAW AND ZONING DIGEST, 30 ZD 61 (1978). On appeal the Appellate Division held the New Castle ordinance unconstitutional, affirmed the site specific relief awarded by the trial court to the developer, but reversed the portion of the trial court decree that mandated relief in the form of affirmative action by the Town of New Castle. *Berenson v. Town of New Castle*, 415 N.Y.S.2d 669 (1979). The same court also held a five acre minimum lot requirement invalid because of its exclusionary purpose and effect. *Kurzius v. Incorporated Village of Upper Brookville*, 414 N.Y.S.2d 573 (1979).

76. 18 Cal.3d 582, 135 Ca.Rptr. 41, 557 P.2d 473 (1976).

77. *Id.* at 610–611, 54–58, 489–490.

78. 462 Pa. 445, 341 A.2d 466 (1975).

79. 48 Ohio St. 47, 356 NE.2d 499 (1976); *City of Eastlake v. Forest City Enterprises*, 226 U.S. 668, 96 S.Ct. 2358 (1976), reversing *Forest City Enterprises v. City of Eastlake*, 41 Ohio St. 2d 187, 324 N.E.2d 740 (1975). See Sager, *Insular Majorities Unabated*, 91 Harv. L. Rev. 1373, 1402–24 (1978). Two subsequent state court decisions have held referendums to be unavailable. *San Pedro North Ltd. v. City of San Antonio*, 562 S.W.2d 260

(Tex.Civ.App., 1978); and, *Leonard v. Bothell,* 87 Wash.2d 847, 557 P.2d 1306 (1976).

80. The Boca Raton population "cap." See *Boca Villas Corp. v. Pence,* 45 Fla.Supp. 65 (1976), *aff'd sub. nom. City of Boca Raton v. Boca Villas Corp,* Case #76-2322, April 18, 1979. For extensive discussion see *Management & Control of Growth,* (3 Vols.) (Urban Land Institute, Washington, D.C. 1975). A shorter treatment is GODSCHALK, BROWER, MCBENNETT & VESTAL, CONSTITUTIONAL ISSUES OF GROWTH MANAGEMENT (The ASPO Press, Chicago, Illinois, 1977). A survey of growth management techniques is contained in *Urban Growth Managment Systems.* (Planning Advisory Service Reports, Nos. 309 and 310, American Society of Planning Officials, Chicago, Illinois, 1975). See also, Bosselman, *Growth Management and Constitutional Rights, Part I: The Blessings of Quiet Seclusion,* 8 URBAN L. ANN. 3 (1974), and *Part II: The States Search for a Growth Policy,* 11 URBAN L. ANN. 3 (1976); Deutsch, *Land Use Controls, A Case Study of San Jose and Livermore, California,* 15 SANTA CLARA L. REV. (1974); and Urban Land Institute and Gruen, Gruen & Associates, EFFECTS OF REGULATION ON HOUSING CODES: TWO CASE STUDIES, (Washington Urban Land Institute, 1977). Two very recent New Hampshire decisions have invalidated "slow growth" ordinances. *Beck v. Town of Raymond,* 394 A.2d 847 (1978) (limit on residential building permits in each 12 month period from April 1 to March 31—four permits for owners of 50 or more acres, three permits for owners of 25 to 50 acres, two for owners of 10 to 25 acres, and one for owners of 10 or fewer acres; and, *Stoney-Brook Development Corp. v. Town of Pembroke,* 394 A.2d 85 (1978) (prohibition on subdivision of land into any more than five building lots in any one calendar year).

81. *HFH, Ltd. v. Superior Court of Los Angeles County,* 15 Cal.3d 508, 125 Cal.Rptr. 365, 425 P.2d 237 (1975); *Mailman Development Corp. v. City of Hollywood,* 286 S.2d 614 (DCA Fla., 1973); *Gold Run Ltd. v. Board of County Com'rs., 544 P.2d 317, (Colo.App., 1976); and, Maple Leaf Investors v. State Dept. of Ecology,* 88 Wash.2d 726, 565 P.2d 1162 (1977).

82. 401 F.Supp. 962 (N.D. Cal. 1975).

83. Liability having been determined, a trial on damages was set for May of 1976. The author understands that the question of compensation was settled with a purchase of the property for $7 million prior to the second trial. The *Arastra* opinion has since been vacated by stipulation presumably in connection with the settlement. 417 F.Supp. 1125 (N.D. Cal., 1976) The next best thing to prevailing is to get the embarrassingly inconvenient precedent erased. A second case was filed and reached the California court of appeals from a judgment dismissing the complaint. The reviewing court reversed. *Eldridge v. City of Palo Alto,* 129 Cal.Rptr. 575, 57 Cal. App.3d 613 (1976). See also, *Brown v. Tahoe Regional Planning Agency,* 385 F.Supp. 1128 (D.Nev. 1973) reh. den. 387 F. Supp. 429 (D.Nev., 1975) (In denying rehearing the court retreated from its initial view and said that only declaratory or injunctive relief was available.); and, *Benensen v. U.S.,* 548 F.2d 939 (U.S. Ct. of Claims, 1977) (holding that restrictions on the old Willard Hotel were a taking that required compensation). In *Agins v. City of Tiburon,* 23 Cal.3d 742, 591 P.2d 514 (1979), the California Supreme Court has now held that an "excessive use of the police power" will not support an inverse condemnation action for compensation, but that the only remedy available is invalidation of the ordinance. An additional case is pending before the California Supreme Court in which an action in inverse condemnation was held to be available by the District Court of Appeal. See, *San Diego Gas & Electric v. City of San Diego,* 80 Cal.App.3d 1026, 146 Cal.Rptr. 103 (1978) lv. to app. granted, see 151 Cal.Rptr. iv. Cf. *City of Austin v. Teaque,* 556 S.W.2d 400 (Tex.Civ.App., 1977) (arbitrary delay of permits while city attempted to acquire scenic easements held to permit an action in inverse condemnation). See also Hagman, *Planning and Regulatory Acquisition,* 1 Urban Law and Policy (1978).

84. 39 N.Y.2d 587, 385 N.Y.S.2d 5, 350 N.E.2d 381 (1976). But see, *Spears v. Berle,* 407 N.Y.S.2d 590 (1978), holding that the restrictions imposed under the authority of the New York Freshwater Wetlands Act (ECL § §24-0301 *et seq.*) precluded the plaintiff from realizing any economic return on his land and that the Department of Environmental Conservation must either issue the permit to mine peat as the plaintiff sought or else purchase the land.

85. A similar result was reached in *Horizon Adirondack Corp. v. State of New York,* 88 Misc.2d 619, 388 N.Y.S.2d 235 (Ct. of Claims of N.Y., 1976), and *Charles v. Diamond,* 41 N.Y.2d 288, 392 N.Y.S.2d 594, 360 N.E.2d 1295 (1977). See also, *Penn Central Transportation Co. v. City of New York,* 42 N.Y.2d 324, 397 N.Y.S.2d 914, aff'd. 98 S.Ct. 2646 (1978).

86. *City of Omaha v. Glissman,* 151 Neb. 895, 39 N.W.2d 828 (1949); *City of Ann Arbor v. Northwest Park Construction Corp.,* 280 F.2d 212 (CA 6, 1960); *Russian Hill Improvement Ass'n. v. Board of Permit Appeals,* 66 Cal.2d 34, 56 Cal.Rptr. 672, 423 P.2d 824 (1967).

87. *Fifteen Fifty North State Bldg. Corp. v. City of Chicago,* 15 Ill.2d 408, 155 N.E.2d 97 (1958); *Bregar v. Britton,* 75 So.2d 753 (Fla. 1954).

88. 390 So.2d 571 (DCA Fla. 1975).

89. *Id.* at 573.

90. For a discussion of the multiple permit problem, see BOSSELMAN, FEURER & SIEMON, THE PERMIT EXPLOSION, (ULI, Washington, D.C. (1976)).

91. The phrase is Howard Ellman's, a member of the California bar, and can be found at page 95 of Mr. Ellman's brief on behalf of the plaintiff in the California Court of Apeals, in the *Sea Ranch* case, see *infra* note 95.

92. *Parkridge v. City of Seattle,* 89 Wash. 2d 454, 573 P.2d 359 (1978); *Allen v. City and County of Honolulu,* 571 P.2d 328 (Haw., 1977); Boise City v. Blaser,* 98 Ida. 789 , 572 P.2d 893 (1977); *Board of Supervisors of Fairfax County v. Medical Structures, Inc.*, 213 Va. 355, 192 S.E.2d 799 (1972); *Board of Supervisors of Fairfax County v. Cities Service Oil Co.*, 213 Va. 359, 193 S.E.2d 1 (1972); *Telimar Homes v. Miller, 218 N.Y.S.2d 175, 14 A.D.2d 586 (1961); Gruber v. Mayor and Township Committee,* 30 N.J. 1, 186 A.2d 489 (1962).

93. 17 Cal.3d 785, 132 Cal.Rptr. 386, 553 P.2d 546 (1976).

94. *Id.* at 796, 393, 553.

95. 63 Cal.App.3d 57, 133 Cal.Rptr. 664 (1976).

96. *Id.* at 70 and 671.

97. 68 Cal.App.3d 965, 137 Cal.Rptr. 669 (1977).

98. *Id.* at 984–86 and 711–712.

99. *Id.* at 986 and 712.

100. See cases in note 92, *supra*, and *Nott v. Wolff,* 18 Ill.2d 362, 163 N.E.2d 809 (1960); *Cos Corporation v. City of Evanston,* 27 Ill.2d 570, 190 N.E.2d 364 (1963).

101. The ALI Model Land Development Code is a storehouse of innovative ideas. (AMER. LAW INST., A MODEL LAND DEVELOPMENT CODE, Washington, D.C., 1975). A survey of the increasing involvement of state government appears in BOSSELMAN & CALLIES, THE QUIET REVOLUTION IN LAND USE CONTROLS, (Council of Environmental Quality, GPO, December, 1971). For a useful, recent and exhaustive survey of the state of land use law, see *Developments in the Law—Zoning,* 91 Harv. L. Rev. 1427 (1978).

The Idea of Revolution in the Declaration of Independence and the Constitution

By Daniel Sisson*

There are few, if any, scholars in the twentieth century who have argued that the period 1761 to 1800, the politically active years of the revolutionary generation, ought to be seen as one *continuous* and *uninterrupted* experiment in revolution. Nor has a historian proposed that in order to understand the complexity of the idea of revolution in American history it is necessary, even essential, to consider the period from James Otis' resistance against the Writs of Assistance to Thomas Jefferson's Revolution of 1800.

Rather the opposite is true. The average American citizen's idea of revolution is limited to the structure that has been imposed upon him by the academic establishment. An overview of the period 1761 to 1800 does not exist in any college catalogue or university bulletin. According to traditional historical studies the American Revolution is viewed as a separate and distinct period of study. Its origins usually begin in 1759 or 1761 or 1775 at Lexington and last until 1781 or at most 1783 with the ratification of the Treaty of Paris.

Next is the "Critical Period," or Articles of Confederation, characterized by eleven difficult years of turbulence and uncertainty. Following the Critical Period is the establishment of the Federal Constitution, an era which most Americans, until recently, have interpreted as the period of Thermadorian Reaction. These two periods still are perceived as distinct, unrelated and for most of our history opposed to one another. Finally, there are the years 1789 to 1800, usually described as the Early National Period.

For generations this has been the accepted way of viewing the late eighteenth century in American history and it has enabled professors and students alike to conveniently categorize, pigeon-hole and otherwise segment the lives of the Founding Fathers.

This article, however, will argue from a different perspective. In order to fully comprehend the relationship between revolution, the Declaration of Independence and the Constitution, the period 1761 to 1789 must be seen as a whole.[1] As much as possible, 'the idea of revolution' will be used as the lens by which we can focus upon that whole. For through that revolutionary lens the differences between academic periods disappear and the decades stretch out not in terms of periods, but in a way that grapples with the problems of establishing governments in the midst of revolution. Implicitly, then, by recounting the struggles of the Founding generation maturing in power, it is possible for us to view America as a nation which, from the beginning, possessed a permanent, peaceful, democratic, constitutional revolutionary tradition.

The Declaration of Independence provides, by its very words, the first clues. In its most celebrated paragraph that begins, "We hold these truths to be self-evident, that all men are created equal, that they are endowed by their Creator with certain unalienable rights. . .," there is the recognition of the right to revolution as something inherent in man. The Declaration continues, "whenever any Form of Government becomes destructive of these

*PhD., Claremont Graduate School. Author, THE AMERICAN REVOLUTION OF 1800 (1974).

ends, it is the Right of the People to alter or to abolish it, and to institute new Government, laying its foundation on such principles and organizing its powers in such form, as to them shall seem most likely to effect their Safety and Happiness." An even stronger assertion follows. It is not only the people's "right, it is their duty, to throw off . . . Government, and to provide new Guards for their future." Finally, a third reference to revolution is made which appeals to necessity: "such is now the necessity which constrains them to alter their former Systems of Government."

These references to the idea of revolution, mentioned more frequently than any others in the substantive paragraphs of the Declaration, are inescapably to permanent and unalienable rights—beyond the power of any government in history to deny or abridge.[2] But more important is their implication for a theory of revolution that is permanent, democratic and constitutional. By examining those words more closely we might agree that using the pronoun "We," meaning the people, and joining that with the idea of equality, in "all men are created equal," the Founders were recognizing the importance of democracy. That their emphasis upon "instituting new governments, laying its foundations on such principles and organizing its powers in such form" clearly implies a regard for constitutions and constitution making as it was known in the eighteenth century. Finally, to "provide new Guards for their future" implies a deep concern for constitutional rights, without which no happiness or safety can be achieved.

While there was no explicit mention in the Declaration of achieving these ends peacefully, it is also true that the *means* the Founders chose to realize their revolutionary ideals were peaceful. The burden of initiating violence rested upon their opponents. They were content, as we shall see, to convene, reason, declare and print their objections without resorting to violence. Indeed, for fifteen years they avoided bloodshed and ultimately it came against their will. Yet, before their generational experience with revolution was complete, they would also have found a way to guarantee that their permanent, democratic, constitutional revolution was peaceful too.

The Declaration's references to revolution imply that it was a fully human act, that men resorted to it only after long and careful deliberation, that it recognized the laws of nature and was, most importantly, consistent with political reality. Abraham Lincoln, who once stated, "I have never had a feeling politically that did not spring from the . . . Declaration of Independence,"[3] made the last point most explicitly: "Any people anywhere, being inclined and having the power, have the *right* to rise up, and shake off the existing government, and form a new one that suits them better. This is a most valuable—a most sacred right—. . . which we hope and believe, is to liberate the world."[4] What Jefferson, his colleagues and those who followed were insisting upon in the Declaration was simply the basic right of men everywhere to act according to their own self-conscience.

It is this view of a permanent revolutionary right to "dissolve political bands" that is most compelling about the Declaration for it implies a view of revolution that seems to have been lost in twentieth century America. For most of this century the tone has been set by a still acknowledged master of the period 1783 to 1789. Andrew C. McLaughlin wrote, "the men of those days could not quite see that if the[ir] Revolutionary principles were made complete . . ." they would lead "not [to] imperial organization; not [to] law and systems, but [to] personal assertion, [to] *confusions that might threaten the foundation of all reasonable order.*" "Even a man like Jefferson," wrote McLaughlin, "was ready to talk *nonsense* about fertilizing the tree of liberty with the blood of tyrants, and about the advisability of occasional rebellions, which ought not to be too much discouraged."[5]

But the men who initiated the American Revolution were not wild-eyed radicals who threatened all order or subscribed to an "ideology" of revolution for its own sake. The word had not yet been invented. Nor were the Founders motivated by an egotistical desire for mere action. This would imply they committed themselves to revolution unaware of the consequences of their acts; or, that they made decisions based upon more than they could know. To the contrary, the signers of the Declaration took elaborate pains to document the reasons why they took the course they did and then presented those reasons as proof to a "candid world."

The Founders, in their search for a legitimizing constitutional theory, grounded their revolution in the English Constitution. The influence of Locke upon the Engish Revolution of 1688 and upon Jefferson is an old story. In short, Locke assumed a compact between the ruler, or chief magistrate, and his subjects. If the magistrate violated the compact and acted unlawfully he "ceases in that to be a magistrate, and acting without Authority, may be opposed. . . ."[6] As Carl Becker pointed out, however, it hardly matters that "Jefferson copied Locke and Locke quoted Hooker. In political theory and in political practice the American Revolution drew its inspiration from the parliamentary struggle of the seventeenth century. The philosophy of the Declaration [was taken from] good old English doctrine newly formulated to meet a present emergency."[7]

Jefferson and the committee that wrote the Declaration were committed to a constitutional tradition that was accepted throughout the colonies. More than a year and a half before the Declaration was written, James Wilson, then the outstanding lawyer in the colonies, summarized the lessons of the idea of revolution in English constitutionalism:

> If . . . it is true, that all force employed for the purposes so often mentioned, is force unwarranted by any act of parliament; unsupported by any principle of the common law; unauthorized by any commission from the crown—that, instead of being employed for the support of the constitution and his majesty's government, it must be employed for the support of oppression and ministerial tyranny—if all this is true—and I flatter myself it appears to be true—can anyone hesitate to say, that to resist such force is lawful: and that both the letter and the spirit of the British constitution justify such resistance?
>
> Resistance, both by the letter and the spirit of the British constitution, may be carried farther, when necessity requires it, than I have carried it. Many examples in the Engish history might be adduced, and many authorities of the greatest weight might be brought to show, that when the king, forgetting his character and dignity, has stepped forth, and openly avowed and taken a part in such iniquitous conduct as has been described; in such cases, indeed, the distinction above mentioned, wisely made by the constitution for the security of the crown, could not be applied; because the crown had unconstitutionally rendered the application of it impossible. What has been the consequence? The distinction between him and his ministers has been lost: but they have not been raised to his situation: he has sunk to theirs.[8]

Because of this deep concern for constitutionalism, the Founders have been justifiably described as conservative. Indeed, most of them were men of property, aware of the dangers to social stability that always follow the wake of revolutions. They were understandably hostile to any suggestion that their efforts would result in a small cadre seizing power and then ruling as tyrants. As Jefferson so well put it, "[o]ne hundred and seventy-three despots would surely be as oppressive as one."[9] Thus whatever differences Paine, Wilson, Gadsden, Jefferson, Henry, Franklin, the Adamses, Lees, etc. may have had regarding the form of government that would follow, they were essentially agreed upon one point: revolution was itself only a *means* to an end and the end was constitutional government. No one, as a deluded writer put it in the 1960's, believed in "revolution for the hell of it."[10]

Compared to our modern conception of what a revolutionary mentality or psychological profile might suggest, the Founders were indeed conservative. Their choice of revolution as the means to "institute new government" did not mean they had been seriously alienated from institutions, or society, or their constitutions or even reason. To the contrary, they were trying to protect them. Until the day violence broke out upon Lexington Green there was disagreement on whether or not the only way the above could be preserved was through an act of revolution. Despite the King, his ministers and Parliament's determination to destroy colonial assemblies, usurp charters and disrupt trade, there had still been offered, as late as August 1775, an Olive Branch Petition. A majority of delegates at the Continental Congress of 1774 had voted for a peaceful settlement. Finally, the colonists were given no choice when the King and his Ministers declared them in a "state of rebellion" and ordered them to be crushed with no quarter given.[11]

From this seemingly contradictory situation there emerged, if it had not already existed, a concrete idea of revolution. The deliberations of the Continental Congress from 1774 had centered on questions of the constitutional power and authority of Parliament, legislative authority at home, individual rights and methods of resistance. But in the judgment of John Adams even these discussions were anticlimactic: the revolution was already accomplished. Reflecting on these discussions in Congress more than forty years later, Adams noted:

> What do we mean by the Revolution? The War? That was no part of the Revolution. It was only an Effect and Consequence of it. The Revolution was in the Minds of the People, and this was effected, from 1760 to 1775, in the course of fifteen years before a drop of blood was drawn at Lexington. The records of thirteen Legislatures, the Pamp[h]lets, Newspapers in all the Colonies ought [to] be consulted, during the Period, to ascertain the Steps by which the Public Opinion was enlightened and informed concerning the authority of Parliament over the colonies.[12]

Implicit here are two elements of the idea of revolution that merit discussion. One, "before a drop of blood was drawn," indicates the revolution took place peacefully, before violence broke out. Hence the emphasis in the Declaration upon "necessity." Adams was saying that the colonists were forced into armed resistance a full year after the most profound discussion had taken place on the nature of government in America. The emphasis upon reason and education of the public reveals that, for the colonists at least, revolution took place primarily in the minds of the people and was regarded separate from war. The second element is the concern over constitutional questions in an assembly that was representative of "the people."

That the Declaration of Independence was produced in a duly elected representative body, charged with discussing the critical questions of the British Constitution was more than appropriate. It was a novel contribution by Americans to the idea of making a revolution: a group of wise men, representatives of "the people," gathered in the midst of crisis, rationally discussing the records of legislatures, Parliaments and constitutions and ensuring through pamphlets and newspapers that the people were informed. More than a link between the idea of revolution and constitutions had been forged: the two were seen as inseparable, a part of the same revolutionary process.

John Adams clarified, years later, what most Americans believed was the proper relationship between the two: "the last twenty-five years of the last century and the first fifteen years of this, may be called the age of revolutions and constitutions. We began the dance, and have produced eighteen or twenty models of constitutions, the excellences and defects of which you probably know better than I do."[13] Thus Adams was observing what the American revolutionaries already knew: the secret of making a successful revolution was ensuring that whenever changes of power occurred or rights were gained, they proceeded on a firm and orderly constitutional basis. At the full tide of independence on April 22, 1776 he had written James Warren, "there is one thing . . . that must be . . . sacredly observed, or we are all undone. There must be decency and respect and veneration introduced for persons in authority, of every rank, or we are undone. In a popular government this is the only way of supporting order. . . ."[14]

Experience had shown that if the connection between radical change and the idea of a fundamental law was destroyed, not only would the purpose of the revolution be lost, a vacuum of power would be created and the entire effort would be plunged into a chaotic and violent struggle for lawless power. At that point the rights and freedoms which had been gained by all previous generations would disappear. One European observer, writing after the Revolution of 1776 but from the perspective of the French Revolution of 1789, noted: "the Revolution in the United States was caused by a mature and thoughtful taste for freedom, not by some vague, undefined instinct for independence. No disorderly passions drove it on; on the contrary, it proceeded hand in hand with a love of order and legality."[15]

This obsession with constitutionalism was deeply embedded in the American experience and extended backward in time nearly a century and a half to the earliest colonial settlements in Massachusetts Bay. The first act of those who journeyed to the New World in 1620 was a constitutional one: "We, whose names are underwritten . . . hereof, do enact, constitute, and frame such just and equal laws, ordinances, acts, constitutions, and officers, from time to time, as shall be thought most meet and convenient for the general good of the colony, unto which we promise all due submission and obedience."[16]

When the Puritans followed in 1630 it had also been their intention to maintain physical possession of their charter of government. They viewed it as their constitution, to be implemented, interpreted, and revised as they saw fit and to meet the conditions of the New World. Indeed, they went to great lengths, even deception, to convince the King's administrators that it was unnecessary to return the Charter to England.[17] What was discreet in Massachusetts Bay's Puritan Colony was accomplished overtly by Connecticut in 1639, by Rhode Island in 1641 and by Pennsylvania in 1682.[18]

Less than four generations later in 1764, Thomas Hutchinson, Lt. Governor of Massachusetts Bay, complained that the colonists "thought themselves at full liberty . . . to establish such sort of governments as they thought proper, and to form a new state as full to all intents and purposes as if they had been in a state of nature, and were making their first entrance into civil society."[19] The pattern, then, of beginning new systems of governments, was an old one. By May of 1775, if he had been so inclined, Hutchinson could have reported that the fever of forming new governments was sweeping the colonies. A resolution of the Continental Congress "recommended to the respective Assemblies and Conventions of the United Colonies, where no Government sufficient to the exigencies of their affairs has been hitherto established to adopt such Governments as shall . . . best conduce to the happiness and safety of their constituents. . . ."[20]

Hutchinson's observations that the colonists were ready to form a new government in 1764 and the resolution of the Congress to do so reveals an attitude about *political change* that underlay the Founding Father's approach to revolution. As the Declaration clearly points out, governments were not viewed as permanent institutions, but were themselves subject to change in their "forms," "principles," "powers" and "foundations." Hence the Founders were committed to *a permanent idea of change,* that was ongoing and not limited to a generation or the establishment of a specific constitution.

The Founder's understanding of the nature of change, or revolution, as the primary constant in nature reflected a classical view of politics. And for a document that is often characterized as "inflammatory," "rhetorical" and "expedient," the Declaration was curiously in that tradition. It is recognized the brutal nature of politics over centuries: governments come and go. Specific forms of government are neither sacred nor immortal; they are instrumental and serve only for limited terms as vehicles to provide public happiness. Thus the Declaration implictly recognized that no monarchy could remain enlightened; ultimately it became a tyranny. No aristocracy was wise forever; at some point it became an oligarchy. And no republic could remain virtuous for it too would degenerate into a democracy.

Paradoxically, this last form only appeared to contradict the intentions of the revolutionary generation. Democracy had been the forcing bed of change in the Revolution: it was rooted in the character of a highly individualistic people and as such would play a major role in the formation of their institutions. Despite pejorative references to democracy during the Constitutional Convention, most delegates to the Continental Congress and the Articles of Confederation recognized the necessity of appealing to the sentiments of the people. Without them they possessed no claim to legitimacy. As Tocqueville was the first to observe:

> The American Revolution broke out. The dogma of the sovereignty of the people came out from the township and took possession of the government: every class enlisted in its cause; the war was fought and victory obtained in its name; it became the law of laws. . . . Just when all could see this effect of the laws and the Revolution, democracy's victory had already been irrevocably pronounced. Circumstances put power in its hands. It was not even permissible to struggle against it any longer. So the upper classes submitted without complaint or resistance to an evil which had by then become inevitable. . . . The people reign over the American political world as God rules over the universe. It is the cause and the end of all things; everything arises out of it and is absorbed back into it.[21]

We must always remember that the Declaration was, above all, a revolutionary manifesto, a call to the people to enlist their immediate efforts in a struggle for independence. In its fervor the Declaration proclaimed "that all men are created equal," thus unleashing the forces of egalitarian democracy upon the new nation for all time. Joined with the proposition that legitimate governments derive their "just powers from the consent of the governed," these two phrases framed for the United States a permanent revolutionary ideal.

From July 4, 1776 until the American people should choose to relinquish their sovereignty, a tension had been introduced into society that was impossible to ignore: any discrepancy between the constitutional laws of the country and the political-revolutionary ideals of the Declaration would work—perhaps slowly at times—but inexorably to force the laws to conform to the latter as closely as the political conditions of the time would allow. The Declaration recognized a valuable principle implicitly: no form of government would or could be perfect in its inception. Perfection was something to strive for over time. Indeed, the revolutionary generation knew they had begun a "great experiment," one that would require viewing their efforts at establishing constitutions and governments as a permanent revolutionary process. Jefferson, for example, described the Virginia Constitution of 1776 thusly: "This constitution was formed when we were new and unexperienced in the science of government. It was the first, too, which was formed in the whole United States. No wonder then that time and trial have discovered very capital defects in it."[22] John Adams had similar sentiments: "Nay, I go further, and say, that from the constitution of human nature, and the constant course of human affairs, it is certain that our constitution will be subverted, if not amended. . . ."[23]

It was with this expectation of change in constitutions that the Declaration established a revolutionary dialectic in the body politic at the birth of the nation. Its philosophy of goverment could not be repealed because its unanimous approval was an accepted historical fact. It could not be ignored because its universal appeal to common sense—even its style—commanded respect from liberty loving people all over the world. No single man was responsible for its authorship who could later be discredited and his work repudiated. It was the work of a committee, a Congress, and ultimately, the "sentiments were of all America. . . ."[24] What Jefferson and his colleagues had done was lay the groundwork for an ideal that could never be completely attained, but would spur successive generations to expand the rights of mankind and resist any backsliding toward tyranny.

It has often been argued that there is absolutely no connection between the Declaration of Independence, the Articles of Confederation and the Constitution; that these documents stand apart and must be considered separately. In a strictly legal sense there can be no question that this is true. Yet to the generation of the Founders this was not a closed case. James Wilson noted in the Convention that "The declaration of independence preceded the state constitutions. What does this declare? In the name of the people of these states, we are declared to be free and independent. The power of war, peace, alliances and trade, are declared to be vested in congress."[25] Obviously for Wilson the connection between a revolutionary declaration and the government necessary to achieve its goals had been present from the beginning. James Madison made the connection between the Revolution, Confederation and new Constitution even more complete when he wrote "all debts contracted and engagements entered into by or under the authority of . . . the Revolutionary Congress shall be as valid under this Constitution as under the Confederation."[26]

This raises the question of legitimacy, largely ignored in the twentieth century but nevertheless a point of heated debate in the era of the Founders. The problem of legitimacy has to do with the distinction that was made between a legitimate constitutional convention whose members were elected specifically to ratify or reject a constitutional document and a general legislative body whose functions are viewed as limited to upholding laws and passing legislation within the context of the existing fundamental law. But what happens when the constitution suddenly, as in the case of the Revolution, ceased to exist? Or what would happen if a legislature, as in the case of the Continental Congress in 1786, found it structurally impossible to agree to "amend" the constitution satisfactorily?[27] The debate that centered around the legitimacy of the state constitutions in 1781 gives us some idea of how a compromise was reached in 1787.

Jefferson addressed this issue by describing how Virginia dealt with the problem of transition in a revolutionary government, i.e., establishing a republican constitution in the place of a monarchical one. He allowed that the Assemblies, formerly the House of Burgesses, as well as the delegates to the Continental Congress were "ordinary legislatures." Conventions formed in 1774 had called the latter into being for a limited term (1774 to 1775) and the authority of the conventions themselves had also been limited. "But in March, 1775," said Jefferson, "they recommended to the people to choose a convention, which should continue in office a year." That convention elected delegates to the Continental Congress in April of 1775. However, Jefferson noted, "It is well known, that in July 1775, a separation from Great Britain and establishment of republican government, had never yet entered into any person's mind. A convention, therefore, chosen under that ordinance, cannot be said to have been chosen for the purposes which certainly did not exist in the minds of those who passed it. . . . So that the electors of April 1776, no more than the legislators of July 1775, not thinking of independence and a permanent republic, could not mean to vest in these delegates powers of establishing them, or any authorities other than those of the ordinary legislature. So far as a temporary organization of government was necessary to render our opposition energetic, so far their organization was valid. But they received in their creation no powers but what were given to every legislature before and since. . . . I am safe, therefore, in the position that the constitution itself is alterable by the ordinary legislature."[28]

Thus in Jefferson's mind, at least, the references in the Declaration to "instituting new governments" were not accidental. In his contemporaries' experience the revolutionary legislatures and the revolutionary conventions were "convertible terms." The Assembly in Virginia and the Continental Congress of 1774, and, by implication, the Convention of 1787, were within their rights to create a new revolutionary government whether it be the republican constitution of the State of Virginia or the Federal Constitution of the American States.

The manner in which these transition governments were brought about contributed greatly to the avoidance of what Hannah Arendt has called the problem of "absolute power" in revolution. It is this, she claims, which has destroyed all modern revolutions.[29] Jefferson gave us some insight into this problem by recalling that in December of 1776 and later in June of 1781, "it was proposed in the house of delegates to create a *dictator,* invested with every power legislative, executive, and judiciary, civil and military, of life and of death, over our persons and over our properties. . . ." The measure was defeated, albeit narrowly, and the arguments opposed to a dictatorship reveal why the choice of a republican form of government and the calling of successive "constitutional conventions" were instrumental in preventing the collapse of a constitutional revolution. As recorded in his *Notes on the State of Virginia,* Jefferson's response to the call for a dictator went straight to Virginia's new Constitution:

> Every lineament expressed or implied, is in full opposition to it. Its fundamental principle is, that the State shall be governed as a commonwealth. It provides a republican organization, proscribes under the name of *prerogative* the exercise of all powers undefined by the laws; places on this basis the whole system of our laws; and by consolidating them together, chooses that they should be left to stand or fall together, never providing for any circumstances, nor admitting that such could arise, wherein either should be suspended; no, not for a moment. . . .[30]

An interesting observation by Jefferson is his projection of what would have happened if the vote for a dictator had gone the other way. He noted, "if our assemblies supposed such a recognition in the people [to choose a dictator] . . . I am of opinion, that the government . . . would have been thrown back upon the bungling machinery of county committees for administration, till a convention could have been called, and its wheels again set into regular motion."[31]

The expectations of many colonists were such that following the Declaration a new form of government was envisioned that would completely level the distinctions of wealth, property and influence in the new nation. Democracy was viewed as a leveling idea poised against the elitism of the aristocracy. This has been the wellspring of class struggle which, since 1913, has dominated scholarship about the years 1776 to 1789. That extreme democrats, as well as extreme loyalists, were unable to seize total power separates the American Revolution from almost every revolution that has occurred in the nineteenth and twentieth centuries. Because no single extreme faction was successful, they did not exercise real influence on the theory and practice of the revolution.

This was due not only to the circumstances surrounding the selection of delegates to the various assemblies and congresses that composed the leadership of the revolution, but to the nature of those republican governments which sprang up in all of the thirteen colonies. The delegates elected in April 1776 were not given any mandate to establish a new form of government, as Jefferson pointed out. Nevertheless, they were the established leaders whose knowledge and experience were deemed most valuable in protesting the colonists' violations of rights. Thus only men already considered responsible or, at minimum, acquainted through experience with power and its dangers were in positions of elected or delgated authority. They were dependent on their constituencies for their election and indeed, many of them had been for decades. This fact alone made it unlikely, though it did not guarantee, they would attempt to usurp power.[32]

Jefferson's statement in 1781 that "[a]n *elective despotism* was not the government we fought for, but one which should not only be founded on free principles, but in which the powers of government should be so divided and balanced . . . as that no one could transcend their legal limits. . . ,"[33] was echoed in other states. Pennsylvania's Demophilus argued "no country can be called *free* which is governed by an absolute power or an absolute legislative power, as the consequences will be the same to the people." In South Carolina, when the Assembly attempted to repeal portions of the state constitution eight years after its adoption in 1778, the *Charleston Gazette* complained: "If any over-grown influence should be ever permitted to encroach so far as to sap the foundation of Public Freedom, and by that means dethrone the Majesty of the People; the usurpers will then have it in their power to subjugate both Civil and Religious Liberty, to the arbitrary, whimsical and capricious edicts, of a few domineering tyrants. . . ."[34]

Out of this fear of absolute power arose a revolutionary contribution to the idea of establishing constitutions, i.e. from 1776 on constitutions were to be written. Departing from the English tradition of viewing a constitution as merely an "assemblage of laws, institutions and customs derived from certain fixed principles of reason . . .," the Americans were determined to achieve a more exact definition. This had been a definition offered by Viscount Bolingbroke in 1733. It was an ideal, as stated. But the evolution of the British Constitution had been away from its prescriptions by the 1760's. As an incentive toward finding a better definition the colonists had only to recall Lord Chancellor Northington's statement of 1776 that "Every *government* can *arbitrarily* impose laws on all its subjects. . . . And all the subjects of each state are bound by the laws made by the government."[35] Most Americans, then, agreed with Tom Paine, who summed up his thoughts in the 1970's: "the continual use of the word 'constitution' in the English Parliament shows there is none; and that the whole is merely a form of government without a constitution, and constituting itself with what power it pleases."[36]

This reflected a concern that had arisen as early as 1768 in Massachusetts. Sam Adams noted then "that in all free States the Constitution is fixed; and as the supreme Legislative derives its Power and Authority from the Constitution, it cannot overleap the Bounds of it without destroying its own foundation." By 1775 Tom Paine cried out in exasperation "something must exist in a free state, which no part of it can be authorised to alter or destroy, otherwise the idea of a constitution cannot subsist."[37] That something became one of the most important revolutionary achievements: a series of written constitutions in each of the thirteen states. By 1784 a South Carolinian arrived at a definition of a constitution that captured the American spirit: "The constitution should be the avowed act of the people at large. It should be the first and fundamental law of the State, and should prescribe the limits of all delegated power. It should be declared to be paramount to all acts of the Legislature, and irrepealable and unalterable by any authority but the express consent of a majority of the citizens collected by such regular mode as may be therein provided."[38]

This emphasis upon written and limited constitutions indicates that the colonists had taken their bearings, very early, from a group of writers called Whigs. These writers had been the political philosophers and politicians who triumphed in the Glorious Revolution of 1688. This, however, was not the perspective of those in London, especially in the Colonial Office. The rebellious colonists were considered hopelessly old-fashioned by the administrators of the British Empire in the 1760's and 1770's. Those self-satisfied men, conscious of major shifts of power in the British Constitution after the era of Robert Walpole, found it difficult to even comprehend what the colonists were protesting about.

Not only were ministers like Bute, North, Grenville and Townshend attempting to arrogate all power to the executive and corrupt the House of Commons by buying the favors of legislators to obtain a permanent majority, they were, in fact, producing a counter-revolution that threatened to destroy the delicate balance of power in the British Constitution established by the Glorious Revolution of 1688. Successive administrators viewed the problems of empire solely in pragmatic terms. They did not see themselves necessarily bound by a constitutional theory that was formulated nearly eighty years before. They were "crisis managers," concerned with manipulating power and conducting the affairs of a vast empire of which the British North American Colonies were only a small part. In any contest between the ministers and the colonists there was little question as to who would prevail. The latter's frame of reference being a mystery, it was totally ignored.

But the heroes of the colonists, i.e. those who had formulated their ideas on revolution, were men who advocated rebellion, even revolution, against Kings and Parliaments whenever they acted tyranically or against right reason. Algernon Sydney, on the scaffold for treason, made his last address state, "God has left nations the liberty of setting up such governments as best please themselves. . . ."[39] The colonists also knew that Sydney had stated magistrates who violate their oaths, which had the force of contracts, could not do so without destroying the entire social fabric. John Locke stated essentially the same proposition. Also in that tradition were James Harrington, Marchmont Nedham, John Milton and Edward Ludlow, seventeenth century philosophers who were known intimately by the colonists in America.[40] Add to them the eighteenth century writers Thomas Gordon, John Trenchard, Robert Molesworth, James Burgh, Bolingbroke and Hoadley and a full blown revolutionary philosophy emerges.[41] These men's works were read avidly by the American revolutionary generation and provided the intellectual underpinning for their idea of revolution.

Nothing illustrates this perspective more clearly than James Otis' argument against the Crown in the Writs of Assistance case of 1761. Reaching back to a precedent established in 1610 by Lord Coke, Otis claimed that a fundamental law existed, that it was limited and that if Parliament acted contrary to natural law and right reason their acts were void.[42]

The significance of this old-fashioned Whig idea of a King in Parliament, limited and controlled by a fundamental and natural law, was this: the right to revolution was the legitimate expression of a people, the only way in which political liberty could be maintained if and when an administration began to act in an oppressive manner. In sum, the constitutional order could only be preserved by making resistance and revolution an integral part of the political process. The fact that Otis' interpretation of Dr. Bonham's Case and Judge Coke's intentions regarding judicial review may have been confused is beside the point. What mattered was that most Americans believed Otis had struck the right chord for resistance. Indeed, fifty years later, John Adams all but confirmed how his contemporaries felt when he wrote, on that "day . . . the child Independence was born."[43]

Within the next fifteen years this Whig idea of revolution would emerge full blown along with the necessity to institute governments. After independence had been declared and the colonists had converted the right to assemble into an organizational technique for revolution, "the royal governors stood helpless as they watched paragovernments grow up around them, a rapid piecing together from the bottom up of a hierarchy of committees and Congresses that reached from the counties and towns through the provincial conventions to the Continental Congress."[44]

Indeed, the connection between revolution and a Congress had gained such acceptance that Tom Paine, in an attempt to stir those who were discontented in England, could write matter of factly, "Your present king and ministry will be the ruin of you; and you had better risk a revolution and call a Congress. . . . America has set you the example, and you may follow it and be free."[45]

While new governments and new Congresses and conventions were accepted by the people generally, there were many who viewed the new order as critically as they had the old. This period, from 1774 through 1789, was one continual attempt by State governments to legitimate their authority in the eyes of the people and of the Continental Congress attempting to generate power and authority at the expense of the States. Assemblies that claimed to represent "the people" against the interest of the "new governments" multiplied and extra-legal committees, mobs and associations sprang up to put pressure on loyalists and patriots alike. Riots broke out in major cities as "the people" spoke out against the authorities and demanded that special conventions be called whose delegates were not legislators but men who would be independent of the establishment.

By the late 1780's the American people had sufficient experience in making constitutions and calling conventions because though "revolutionary in origin," these acts had become "institutionalized. . . ."[46] John Marshall, writing in January of 1787, implied that the practice might have become too widespread. Daniel Shays' Rebellion appeared to threaten the new order in a way that could become general. "I fear," wrote Marshall, "that those have truth on their side who say that man is incapable of governing himself. I fear we may live to see another revolution."[47] Ironically, Marshall was still in the midst of a revolution; one moreover, that he, after 1801, would play a major role in refining, restructuring and consolidating its principles.

Thus it came as little surprise to most Americans when the Federal Convention was called in 1787. Denounced as a 'rump convention' and an 'illegal gathering' by a number of twentieth century historians, it is interesting to note that among Cecelia Kenyon's wide choice of Antifederalists — from every section of the new nation — not one complained about the illegality of the convention. Those who were most articulate in their opposition to the new government pointed out the theoretical weaknesses in the new republican form, questioned whether liberty could be preserved, wondered what was in store for the States and countless other objections. But none directly attacked the Convention as a means to stabilize the Revolution.

Rawlin Lowndes of South Carolina had reservations about the propriety of the Federal Convention changing the Articles of Confederation. Yet he "recommended that another convention should be called. . . ."[48] An Antifederalist writing from Pennsylvania demanded, "let another Convention be immediately called and let a system of government fitted to the pure principles of the Revolution be framed."[49] Evidently the connection between the right to revolution and the calling of a convention had become accepted among Federalists and Antifederalists alike.[50]

Yet it remained for an arch-conservative, General Henry Knox, to place the relationship between the right to revolution and the calling of a convention to form a new government in a common sense perspective. Knox wrote at the end of January, 1787:

> I have heard all that has been said about legal and illegal conventions. I confess I do not find the objections on this point so weighty as some people do. Should the Convention agree on some continental constitution and propose the great outlines either through Congress or directly to their Constituents the respective Legislatures with a request that State Conventions might be assembled for the sole purchase [purpose] of choosing delegates to a Continental Convention in order to confer and decide upon the articles of confederation and perpetual union, would not this to all intents and purposes be a government derived from the people and assented to by them as much as they assented to the confederation?[51]

By the eve of the Convention in Philadelphia the various factions had claimed, each in their own way, the validity of the right to revolution. James Madison echoed them when addresing the critics of the Convention. "[A] rigid adherence," he claimed, to the Articles of Confederation ". . . would render nominal and nugatory the transcendent and precious right of the people to 'abolish or alter their governments as to them shall seem most likely to effect their safety and happiness.'" Then, after quoting the Declaration, he proceeded to give a complete description of the way constitutions were formed in the midst of revolution

> since it is impossible for the people spontaneously and universally to move in concert towards their object; and it is therefore essential that such changes be instituted by some *informal and unauthorized propositions,* made by some patriotic and respectable citizen or number of citizens. They must have recollected that it was by this irregular and assumed privilege of proposing to the people plans for their safety and happiness that the States were first united against the danger with which they were threatened by their ancient government; that committees and congresses were formed for concentrating their efforts and defending their rights; and that *conventions* were *elected in the several States* for establishing the constitutions under which they are now governed. . . .[52]

From the responses of those living abroad one can also see that the news of the Philadelphia Convention was received in a revolutionary context. Jefferson, covertly mid-wifing a new revolution in France, was kept informed of the progress of the convention by his friend Madison. In his rely to the first draft of the new constitution Jefferson referred specifically to the convention as "our Second Revolution."[53] He pointed with pride to the means and methods which achieved it: "Happy for us . . . that . . . we are able to send our wise and good men together to talk over our form of government, discuss its weaknesses and establish its remedies. . . . The example we have given to the world is single, that of changing the form of government under the authority of reason only, without bloodshed."[54] Like John Adams' earlier assessment of the American Revolution the emphasis was placed upon reason, reflection, constitutional issues and the absence of violence.

But the faith Jefferson had in the means of stabilizing the Revolution was greater than his acceptance of the results of the Convention itself. After listing his chief objections to the new document Jefferson attempted a dialogue between himself, Madison and the American people:

Jefferson to Madison: ". . . after seeing the parts they generally dislike, and those they generally approve, . . . say to them . . . ."

Madison to the people: "We see now what you wish. You are willing to give up to your federal government such and such powers; but you wish, at the same time, to have such and such fundamental rights secured to you, and certain sources of convulsion taken away. Be it so. Send together deputies again. Let them establish your fundamental rights by a . . . declaration, and . . . pass the parts of the Constitution you have approved. . . ."

Jefferson to Madison: "This is what might be said, and would probably produce a speedy, more perfect and more permanent form of government. At all events, I hope you will not be discouraged from making other trials, if the present one should fail."[55]

The constitutional convention then, was the primary means by which the revolutionary generation believed governments made their transition from one stage to the next. The fact that the people generally accepted successive conventions speaks highly of an age when deference in politics may have influenced their opinions.[56] The Framers were, however, consistent in the means used to attain both principles and form. As Madison noted when discussing the nature of republican government, "[i]t is evident that no other form would be reconcilable with the genius of the people of America [or] with the fundamental principles of the Revolution. . . ."[57] Thus a straight line connected the revolutionary aspirations of colonies become states, of states attempting to deal with continental problems and finally, a national Union, that in constitutional theory, at least, reflected their connection with the idea of revolution.

The notion of revolution always assumes that which is novel or innovative has come into existence. And the idea that men could and would "institute new government" was as revolutionary in the eighteenth century as the assertion that "all men are created equal." No one knew precisely what those phrases meant. There were no blueprints to follow and a procedure of trial and error had inevitably to follow. That the formation of the Constitution was seen as a part of that same experiment there can be little doubt. Hamilton stated in the very first paragraph of *The Federalist* what the Declaration had asserted: We are "to decide the important question, whether societies of men are really capable or not of establishing good government from reflection and choice, or whether they are forever destined to depend for their political constitutions on accident and force."[58]

The fact was no one, in the eighteenth century, could know when self-government had been fully achieved. After the treaty of Paris was signed and the unifying pressure of war with Great Britain had been removed, a crisis mentality developed that was, for all practical purposes, a continuation of the revolutionary emergency. Everybody in a position to know realized that unless dramatic change occurred the conclusion of the American revolutionary experiment would be disastrous.

The style of legislative resolutions has always been notoriously arid, but nothing so well characterizes the mood of the delegates to the Philadelphia Convention as the resolution which authorized Virginians to attend yet another constitutional convention in 1786. The gravity of the situation forced Madison to use words that he believed would produce the desired results:

> [We] can no longer doubt that the Crisis is arrived at which the good People of America are to decide the solemn question whether they will by wise . . efforts reap the just fruits of that Independence which they have so gloriously acquired and of that Union which they have cemented with so much of their common Blood, or whether . . . they will renounce the auspicious blessings prepared for them by the Revolution, and furnish to its Enemies an eventual Triumph. . . .[59]

Thus of necessity the Founding Fathers introduced and grafted on to the republican form an array of novel mechanical and theoretical inventions unequalled in modern times: the theory of the enlarged republic, separation of powers, checks and balances, a theory of factions, *application* of a theory on the nature of man, considerations of liberty and happiness, constitutionalism, the amendment process, federalism and judicial review. These last three are especially appropriate because they not only legitimized, but for the first time in history, institutionalized the idea of revolution in constitutional history.

The idea of accommodating revolution by amending the constitution assumed a degree of citizen participation that was characteristic of a revolutionary generation. Knowing from experience that governments tend to consolidate power and reject change, the Framers assumed that some flexibility could be built into the constitutional system without tearing it apart. As George Mason put it in the Convention, "the plan now to be formed will certainly be defective, as the Confederation has been found on trial to be. Amendments therefore will be necessary, and it will be better to provide them, in an easy, regular and Constitutional way than to trust to chance and violence."[60] In 1789, however, thirteen states were not considered overwhelming and it was expected that two thirds of the state legislatures could, and would, if necessary, call a convention.

There can be little doubt that the Founders viewed the amendment process as one intimately connected with revolution. James Madison was the first member of Congress to introduce a series of amendments that were to become essentially the Bill of Rights. He proposed nine separate amendments on June 8, 1789. "Amendments," he said, "which have occurred to me proper to be recommended by Congress to the State Legislatures."[61] The first dealt with the preamble to the Constitution and brought together those ideas which his generation had experienced from the Declaration to the new Constitution:

> First, That there be prefixed to the constitution a declaration, that all power is originally vested in, and consequently derived from, the people.
>
> That Government is instituted and ought to be exercised for the benefit of the people. . . .
>
> That the people have an indubitable, unalienable and indefeasible right to reform or change their Government, whenever it be found adverse or inadequate to the purposes of its institution.[62]

That these sentiments, reinforcing the Declaration of Independence, were not included in the final form of the preamble does not lessen the fact they were introduced by the one man who understood more about the philosophy, meaning and intent of the American system of government than any other. The idea Madison wanted accepted in the preamble was this: "We, the People" shall, by revolution if necessary, determine the future of the government.

Madison considered his amendment proposal an indispensable idea and it was unfortunate that the majority in Congress, perhaps wishing to set a precedent for future ages, mistook substance for form. One twentieth century scholar who, had he lived in the eighteenth century would no doubt have signed both the Declaration and the Constitution, described the logic of Madison's intention as it was reflected in both documents: "All other purposes, whether individual or social, can find their legitimate scope and meaning only as they conform to one basic purpose[:] that the citizens of this nation shall make and . . . obey their own laws, shall be at once their own subjects and their own masters."[63] This implied an ability on the part of the people to alter or abolish government if the amendment or constitutional remedies were exhausted.

Decades later Madison had an opportunity to clarify his position on the idea of revolution and the amendment process. After recounting a large number of provisions in the Federal Constitution designed to safeguard the people as opposed to the government, Madison presented a complete historical and political theory of constitutional revolution. He included within his theory, in language reminiscent of the Declaration, a description of the right to revolution, forms of government that included the Confederation and Constitution and the problems that the States would have with the Federal government. It was an explosive analysis, one which the nation would realize, to its horror, thirty years later. But it was one that was *perfectly consistent* with James Madison's experience as a revolutionary in the 1770's, in the Confederation of the 1780's, in the formation of the Constitution, in the 1790's and in his services rendered throughout the entire National Period as Secretary of State and President up to 1830:

> Should the provisions of the Constitution, as here reviewed, be found not to secure the government and rights of the states against usurpations and abuses on the part of the United States, the final resort within the purview of the Constitution, lies in an amendment of the Constitution, according to a process applicable by the States. And in the event of a failure of every constitutional resort, and an accumulation of usurpations and abuses, rendering passive obedience and non-resistance a greater evil than resistance and revolution, there can remain but one resort, the last of all—an appeal from the cancelled

obligations of the constitutional compact, to original rights and the law of self-preservation. This is the *ultima ratio* under all governments, whether consolidated, confederated, or a compound of both; and it cannot be doubted, that a single member of the Union, in the extremity supposed, but in that only, would have a right, as an extra and ultra-constitutional right, to make the appeal.[64]

Yet under the most hopeful of conditions the amendment process aided the citizenry in maintaining control of their government and specifically their right to revolution. The first amendment guaranteed the freedoms of conscience, speech, press, petition and assembly—all necessary to discuss the policies and actions of a government and put into motion an idea of resistance that, if the government were unresponsive, would lead to revolution.

The second amendment guaranteed the right to bear arms, thereby safeguarding the individual's access to the means of resistance. Indeed, it was no accident that resistance could be directed against local or national authorities as well as foriegn enemies.[65] The third amendment prohibited government from using the time honored method of quartering soldiers in homes to overawe the citizenry. Finally, the ninth amendment reflected the Declaration's idea that there were certain rights that were unalienable and would be retained by the people under all circumstances. The Bill of Rights and, by implication, the amending process were thus esential in keeping alive the right to "alter" the government if the necessity arose.

While most modern political scientists are willing to concede that federalism produced a division of power in the new government and judicial review resulted in a novel way of limiting legislative power, few have been inclined to recognize the revolutionary theory implicit in these inventions. Federalism in particular was seen as a repository of the right to revolution. One political scientist, Harvey Wheeler, has noted: "Initially, federalism was the doctrine that citizens possessed dual citizenship and allegiance. One was to their state and its laws, the other was to the central government. Clearly, this was an effort to institutionalize, inside the new government, protections against the kinds of despotism that the English Parliament had visited on the colonies. States rights, interposition and secession were the ultimate guarantors."[66] Both Madison and Jefferson would have concurred in Wheeler's "constitutional theory of federalism."

Madison in *The Federalist* outlined exactly how those guarantees ought to work: "ambitious encroachments of the federal government on the authority of the State governments would not excite the opposition of a single State, or of a few States only. They would be the signals of general alarm. Every government would espouse the common cause. A correspondence would be opened. Plans of resistance would be concerted. One spirit would animate and conduct the whole. The same combinations, in short, would result from an apprehension of the federal, as was produced by the dread of a foreign, yoke; and unless the projected innovations should be voluntarily renounced, the same appeal to a trial of force would be made in the one case as was made in the other."[67]

Twenty-two years later Jefferson, having collaborated with Madison to act on his theory in the Revolution of 1800, echoed the same sentiments. They seem especially pertinent since his close friend was firmly ensconced in the Presidency and entrusted with continuing the great experiment. Writing to a friend in France who was wondering why the American Revolution had not fallen into the same trap of absolute power that had victimized the French Revolution, Jefferson conluded:

[T]he true barriers of our liberty in this country are the State governments; and the wisest conservative power ever contrived by man, is that of which our Revolution and present government found us possessed. Seventeen distinct States, amalgamated, . . .

regularly organized. . . , and enlightened by a free press, can never be so fascinated by the arts of one man, as to submit voluntarily to his usurpation. Nor can they be constrained to it by any force he can possess. While that may paralyze the single State in which it happens to be encamped, sixteen others . . . rise up on every side, ready organized for deliberation by a constitutional legislature, and for action by their governor, constitutionally the commander of the militia of the State . . . .[68]

Federalism was combined with the doctrine of judicial review, at least where dual allegiance is concerned, to make civil-disobedience an integral part of both constitutional theory and constitutional law. Because the Constitution is not static, a citizen challenging the law by disobeying it can convince a judge that in theory his "so-called acts of civil-disobedience were never really unlawful at all."[69] Thus the citizen owes his dual allegiance to the 'temporal' side and also to the 'emergent' or higher law side. One requires obedience to ordinances, statutes, etc.; the other requires obedience to moral conscience and right reason, those standards the American revolutionaries adhered to in defense of their actions against tyranny. Edwin S. Corwin likewise claimed that judicial review "kept alive, even after the fires of revolution had cooled, the notion that the claim of law to obedience consists of its intrinsic excellence rather than its origin. It made rational the notion of a hierarchy of laws in which the will of merely human legislators might on occasion be required to assume a subordinate space."[70]

Those who signed the Declaration of Independence and the Constitution were not only often the same men, but by their close association in bringing the new republic into maturity, were generally agreed on the main points of human nature, liberty and constitutional government. They recognized that liberty could be won or lost in a single generation; that human beings were fallible, incapable of creating perfect institutions. Hence there would always be a necessity to reform or change the fundamental laws. "Founders," "men of the Revolution," "Patriots," "Framers," "Founding Fathers," call them what we will, they were unanimous when asserting their idea of revolution and the dual claim that the United States was the first nation founded on the right to revolution and the constitutional convention the means by which its spirit would be preserved.

So it was that the "Father of the U.S. Constitution," James Madison, having lived through a continuous and uninterrupted experiment in making revolutions and constitutions from 1774 to 1792 could, only four years after the Federal Constitution was ratified, project its basic principle into the future:

> If there be a principle that ought not to be questioned within the United States, it is that every nation has a right to abolish an old government and establish a new one. This principle is not only recorded in every public archive, written in every American heart, and sealed with the blood of a host of American martyrs, but is the only lawful tenure by which the United States hold their existence as a nation.[71]

Notes

1. For purposes of this article the years 1790 to 1800 have been omitted. See my THE AMERICAN REVOLUTION OF 1800 (1974) for the extension of this thesis. *See also* D. SISSON, THE AMERICAN REVOLUTIONARY TRADITION (forthcoming).

2. Tom Paine wrote in the beginning of the American Revolution that "the Natural Right of the Continent [America] to independence, is a point which never yet was called in question. It will not even admit of a debate." T. PAINE, THE AMERICAN CRISIS, # II, p. 25 (London, 1835).

3. Abraham Lincoln, *Speech in Independence Hall,* Philadelphia, 22 February 1861, in 4 THE COLLECTED WORKS OF ABRAHAM LINCOLN 240 (R.P. Basler, ed., 1953).

4. I *id.* at 438.

5. A. MCLAUGHLIN, THE CONFEDERATION AND THE CONSTITUTION 1783–1789, 39–40 (New York, 1905).

6. JOHN LOCKE, TWO TREATISES OF GOVERNMENT 446–77 (P. Laslett ed., 1960).

7. CARL BECKER, THE DECLARATION OF INDEPENDENCE 79 (1922).

8. JAMES WILSON, THE WORKS OF JAMES WILSON 758 (R.G. McCloskey ed., New York, 1967).

9. THOMAS JEFFERSON, THE LIFE & SELECTED WRITINGS OF THOMAS JEFFERSON 237 (A. Koch & W. Peden eds., 1944).

10. FEE, REVOLUTION FOR THE HELL OF IT (1968).

11. THE AMERICAN CRISIS # III, *supra* note 2, at 239.

12. John Adams to Jefferson, 24 August 1815, in 2 THE ADAMS-JEFFERSON LETTERS 455 (L.J. Cappon ed., 1971).

13. John Adams to James Lloyd, 29 March 1815, in 10 THE WORKS OF JOHN ADAMS 148–49 (C.F. Adams ed., Boston, 1856).

14. John Adams to James Warren, 22 April 1776, in SOURCES AND DOCUMENTS OF THE AMERICAN REVOLUTION 147 (S.E. Morison ed., Oxford, 1923).

15. ALEXIS DE TOCQUEVILLE, DEMOCRACY IN AMERICA 64 (G. Lawerence, trans. 1966).

16. P. MILLER, ORTHODOXY IN MASSACHUSETTS 32 (New York, 1933).

17. *Id.; see* Ch. V, *The Body Politick.*

18. TOCQUEVILLE, *supra* note 15, at 32.

19. Quoted in B. SCHWARTZ, THE GREAT RIGHTS OF MANKIND 50 (1977).

20. P. FORCE, AMERICAN ARCHIVES 466 (4th series).

21. TOCQUEVILLE, *supra* note 15, at 52–53.

22. SELECTED WRITINGS, *supra* note 9, at 236.

23. John Adams to Roger Sherman, 17 July 1789, 6 WORKS, *supra* note 13, at 432.

24. Jefferson to Joseph Delaplaine, 12 April 1817, THE LIFE & SELECTED WRITINGS OF THOMAS JEFFERSON 680 (1944).

25. James Wilson in the Federal Convention, 19 June 1787, in 1 THE RECORDS OF THE FEDERAL CONVENTION 329 (M. Farrand ed., New Haven, Conn., 1911).

26. James Madison to Andrew Stevenson, 17 November 1830. Quoted from his *Notes on the Convention,* in 3 RECORDS OF THE FEDERAL CONVENTION, *supra* note 25, at 485.

27. JAMES MADISON, THE FEDERALIST PAPERS # 40, at 251 (C. Rossiter ed., 1961).

28. SELECTED WRITINGS, *supra* note 9, at 239–40.

29. H. ARENDT, ON REVOLUTION 139–78 (1963).

30. SELECTED WRITINGS, *supra* note 9, at 245.

31. *Id.* at 246.

32. See C. SYDNOR, AMERICAN REVOLUTIONARIES IN THE MAKING (1952).

33. SELECTED WRITINGS, *supra* note 9, at 237.

34. Quoted in WOOD, THE CREATION OF THE AMERICAN REPUBLIC 279 (1969).

35. MCILWAIN, CONSTITUTIONALISM: ANCIENT AND MODERN 5 (1947).

36. *Id.* at 2.

37. Quoted in WOOD, *supra* note 34, at 266.

38. Quoted in *id.* at 281.

39. C. ROBBINS, THE EIGHTEENTH CENTURY COMMONWEALTHMAN 44 (1959).

40. *Id.* at 22–55.

41. BERNARD BAILYN, THE IDEOLOGICAL ORIGINS OF THE AMERICAN REVOLUTION (1967), Ch. II, *Sources and Traditions.*

42. B. BAILYN, PAMPHLETS OF THE AMERICAN REVOLUTION 1750–1776, 411–12 (1965).

43. 10 JOHN ADAMS, WORKS, *supra* note 13, at 244–45.

44. WOOD, *supra* note 34, at 314.

45. THE AMERICAN CRISIS, # VII, *supra* note 2, at 86.

46. R. PALMER, THE AGE OF THE DEMOCRATIC REVOLUTION 214 (1959).

47. John Marshall to James Wilkinson, 5 January 1787, 12 AMER. HIST. REV. 348 (1907).

48. M. KENYON, THE ANTIFEDERALISTS 182 (1966).

49. *Id.* at 87.

50. The expectation that a convention was essential can be seen in Horatio Gates' comment in November, 1787: "everything I hear, everything I know, convinces me, that unless we have as Speedily as possible a Firm Efficient, Federal Constitution established, all must go to Ruin, and . . . blast every Hope that so Glorious a

Revolution entitled us to Expect." General Horatio Gates to James Madison, 26 November 1787, 10 THE PAPERS OF JAMES MADISON 272–73 (R. Rutland ed., 1977).

51. General Henry Knox to Stephen Higginson, 28 January 1787, Knox Papers, Vol. XIX, quoted in THE ERA OF THE AMERICAN REVOLUTION 387–88 (R.B. Morris ed., 1939).

52. THE FEDERALIST # 40, *supra* note 27, at 253.

53. Jefferson to St. John de Crevecoeur, 9 August 1788, 13 PAPERS OF THOMAS JEFFERSON 485–86 (J.P. Boyd ed., 1950).

54. Jefferson to Ralph Izard, 17 July 1788, 13 PAPERS, *supra* note 53, at 373.

55. Jefferson to James Madison, 20 December 1787, 13 PAPERS, *supra* note 53, at 439.

56. Acceptance of the convention idea, however, was not unanimous. In the Constitutional Convention Oliver Ellsworth stated, "if the plan [i.e. the Constitution] goes forth to the people for ratification several succeeding Conventions within the States would be unavoidable. He did not like these conventions. They were better fitted to pull down than to build up the Constitutions." Recorded in Madison's Journal, 20 June 1787, 1 THE RECORDS OF THE FEDERAL CONVENTION, *supra* note 25, at 355.

57. THE FEDERALIST # 39, *supra* note 27, at 240.

58. *Id.* # 1, at 33.

59. The Virginia Resolution of 16 October 1786, quoted in THE FEDERAL CONVENTION AND THE FORMATION OF THE UNION OF THE AMERICAN STATES, 60–61 (W.U. Solberg, ed., New York, 1958). Following the Convention Madison had become so frustrated at one point that he seemed to equate opposition to the Convention with opposition to the American Revolution. Writing at the time when he was composing the numbers of *The Federalist,* he criticized the rebels who "in [western] Massts. [sic] are known to aim at confusion, and are suspected of wishing a reversal of the Revolution." James Madison to Edmund Randolph, 10 January 1788, PAPER OF JAMES MADISON, *supra* note 50, at 355.

60. JOURNAL OF THE FEDERAL CONVENTION KEPT BY JAMES MADISON 149 (E.H. Scott, ed., N.Y 1840).

61. Madison to Samuel Johnston 21 June 1789, 5 THE WRITINGS OF JAMES MADISION 409 (G. Hunt ed., 1950–60).

62. 1 THE DEBATES AND PROCEEDINGS IN THE CONGRESS OF THE UNITED STATES 450–51 (compiled from authentic materials by Joseph Gales, Sr., Wash., D.C., 1834).

63. A. MEIKLEJOHN, FREE SPEECH AND ITS RELATION TO SELF-GOVERNMENT 15 (1948).

64. James Madison to Edward Everett, August 1830, quoted in THE COMPLETE MADISON 156–57 (S. Padover ed., 1953).

65. James Madison had stated flatly, in Convention, that "there might be a rebellion against the United States!" Quoted in J. BUTZNER, CONSTITUTIONAL CHAFF 130 (1941).

66. Wheeler, *The Foundations of Constitutionalism,* 8 LOY. L.A.L. REV. 507, 554 (1975).

67. THE FEDERALIST # 46, *supra* note 27, at 298.

68. Jefferson to M. Destutt De Tracy, 26 January 1811, 19 THE WRITINGS OF THOMAS JEFFERSON 20–21 (A. Lipscomb ed., 1905).

69. Wheeler, *supra* note 66, at 577–80.

70. Corwin, *The Progress of Constitutional Theory Between the Declaration of Independence and the Meeting of the Philadelphia Convention,* 30 AMER. HIST. REV. 523 (April, 1925).

71. In answer to "Pacificus," April 22, 1793, quoted in THE COMPLETE MADISON, *supra* note 64, at 48. *See also* Henry Steele Commager's *Our Declaration is Still a Rallying Cry,* in FREEDOM AND ORDER 173 (1966).

Abraham Lincoln's Emancipation Proclamation*
By George Anastaplo†

*A word fitly spoken
is like apples of gold
in pictures of silver.*

Proverbs 25: 11

I

There are, in responses to men singled out for our attention as Abraham Lincoln is, two tendencies among articulate citizens. One tendency is virtually to deify them as people somehow outside and above the Constitution. The other tendency is to denigrate them, even (as in the case of Lincoln) to dismiss them as "racists" and the like.

Thus, one writer observed, "However admirable the character of the American Constitution, it [is not] the most admirable expression of the regime. The Constitution is the highest American thing, only if one tries to understand the high in the light of the low. It is high because men are not angels, and because we do not have angels to govern us. Its strength lies in its ability to connect the interest of the man with the duty of the place. But the Constitution, in deference to man's nonangelic nature, made certain compromises with slavery. And partly because of those compromises, it dissolved in the presence of a great crisis. The man—or the character of the man—who bore the nation through that crisis, seem[s] to me . . . the highest thing in the American regime. . . ."[1]

Thus, also, another writer (in the *Chicago Tribune*, taking issue with an editorial therein on President Lincoln) observed, "A close look at Lincoln, the Civil War, slavery, and the political, social, and economic movements and moral climate of that era convinces me that Lincoln should not be credited with freeing the slaves. Rather he was clearly forced by his critics and the urgencies of war to end chattel slavery or go down in defeat. No thinking person objects to Lincoln's adept use of the art of compromise. What I, as a black descendant of slaves, cannot escape is the fact that he also used that talent to delay as long as he could the recognition of a black human as something other than a piece of property." And, this columnist went on to say, "His insistence that a slave was a property first and a person second resulted in the great Lincoln plan: the freeing of slaves thru (1) Southern state initiative (slavery forever); (2) government payment for slaves to be freed; (3) gradual

*This commentary has been developed from a talk given on April 14, 1974, K.A.M. Isaiah Israel Congregation, Chicago, Illinois and from papers prepared for the Center for the Study of Democratic Institutions, Santa Barbara, California, June 19, 1974 and for the First West Coast Conference on Constitutional Law, Los Angeles, California, September 17-18, 1977. The reader is urged to begin by reading the text of this commentary without reference to the notes.
†Lecturer in the Liberal Arts, The University of Chicago; Professor of Political Science and of Philosophy, Rosary College; A.B., J.D., Ph.D., The University of Chicago.

emancipation (to be complete around the year 1900); (4) government aid to slave states suffering from loss of slaves (more sympathy for the criminal than for the victim); and (5) colonization of blacks out of the United States. To those unsung heroes who didn't permit Lincoln to 'push thru his program,' this one descendant of slaves belatedly thanks you."[2]

A defense of Lincoln (by the *Tribune*, referred to in the column just quoted) argued that Lincoln's attitudes and policies should not be judged by "today's standards." Such a defense, however, misses the point: it implies (does it not?) that we know better than Lincoln did what should have been done, that our consciences or our understanding or our feelings are somehow superior to his.

It is not only we who believe ourselves in a superior position. Many, perhaps most of Lincoln's fellow citizens believed at one time or another that their judgments and consciences were better than his. (At times, all they would give him credit for was a rough honesty, or sincerity.) Thus, even his Secretary of State could observe in 1862 of Lincoln's policy: "[W]e show our sympathy with slavery by emancipating slaves where we cannot reach them, and holding them in bondage where we can set them free."[3]

But, as I will try to show, a *more* prudent assessment of that policy than may be found in most of the writings of either our contemporaries or Lincoln's is suggested by an oration delivered by Frederick Douglass on April 14, 1876, "on the occasion of the unveiling of the Freedmen's Monument [in Washington, D.C.] in memory of Abraham Lincoln." The distinguished former slave argued, "I have said that President Lincoln was a white man, and shared the prejudices common to his countrymen toward the colored race. Looking back to his times and to the condition of his country, we are compelled to admit that this unfriendly feeling on his part may be safely set down as one element of his wonderful success in organizing the loyal American people for the tremendous conflict before them, and bringing them safely through that conflict. His great mission was to accomplish two things: first, to save his country from dismemberment and ruin; and, second, to free his country from the great crime of slavery. To do one or the other, or both, he must have the earnest sympathy and the powerful co-operation of his loyal fellow-countrymen. Without this primary and essential condition to success his efforts must have been vain and utterly fruitless. *Had he put the abolition of slavery before the salvation of the Union, he would have inevitably driven from him a powerful class of the American people and rendered resistance to rebellion impossible.* Viewed from the genuine abolition ground, Mr. Lincoln seemed tardy, cold, dull, and indifferent; but measuring him by the sentiment of his country, a sentiment he was bound as a statesman to consult, he was swift, zealous, radical, and determined. Though Mr. Lincoln shared the prejudices of his white fellow-countrymen against the negro, it is hardly necessary to say that in his heart of hearts he loathed and hated slavery."[4] Douglass quotes at this point Lincoln's letter of April 4, 1864, "I am naturally anti-slavery. If slavery is not wrong, nothing is wrong. I cannot remember when I did not so think and feel." Whether Lincoln was, in fact, "prejudiced" would depend, first, on what one means by this term; second, on what all the causes were of African slavery; and, third, on what the effects were on the slaves of their bondage.

Earlier in his oration, Douglass made an observation about his immediate response to the Emancipation Proclamation, an observation which can provide our point of departure both in considering that Presidential decree and in assessing Lincoln's political judgment: "Can any colored man, or any white man friendly to the freedom of all men, ever forget the night which followed the first day of January, 1863, when the world was to see if Abraham Lincoln would prove to be as good as his word [pledged the preceding September 22]? I shall never forget that memorable night, when in a distant city I waited and watched at a public meeting, with three thousand others not less anxious than myself, for the word of deliverance which we have heard read today. Nor shall I ever forget the outburst of joy and thanksgiving that rent the air when the lightning [the telegraph] brought to us the emancipation proclamation. In that happy hour we forgot all delay, and forgot all tardiness, forgot that the President had bribed the rebels to lay down their arms by a promise to withhold the bolt which would smite the slave-system with destruction; and we were thenceforward willing to allow the President all the latitude of time, phraseology, *and every honorable device that statesmanship might require* for the achievement of a great and beneficent measure of liberty and progress."[5]

II

It is the statesmanship of Lincoln, as reflected in the Emancipation Proclamation, with which we will be concerned on this occasion. In order to understand what happened and why, we must remind ourselves of the circumstances in which the proclamation was issued. The first part, the Preliminary Proclamation, was issued September 22, 1862; the second part, the Final Proclamation, was issued January 1, 1863.

The general setting was, of course, the Civil War, that war the prosecution of which President Lincoln understood as primarily an effort, in accordance with his constitutional duty, to save the Union from dismemberment. Thus, he observed (in a statement of August 22, 1862, just one month before his issuance of the Preliminary Proclamation—a statement which continues to anger his critics): "I would save the Union. I would save it the shortest way under the Constitution. The sooner the national authority can be restored; the nearer the Union will be 'the Union as it was.' If there be those who would not save the Union, unless they could at the same time *save* slavery, I do not agree with them. If there be those who would not save the Union unless they could at the same time *destroy* slavery, I do not agree with them. My paramount object in this struggle *is* to save the Union, and is *not* either to save or to destroy slavery. If I could save the Union without freeing *any* slave I would do it, and if I could save it by freeing *all* the slaves I would do it; and if I could save it by freeing some and leaving others alone I would also do that. What I do about slavery, and the colored race, I do because I believe it helps to save the Union; and what I forbear, I forbear because I do *not* believe it would help to save the Union. I shall do *less* whenever I shall believe what I am doing hurts the cause, and I shall do *more* whenever I shall believe doing more will help the cause."

Lincoln concluded this statement—an open letter to Horace Greeley—with the assurance, ". . . I intend no modification of my oft-expressed *personal* wish that all men every where could be free." It should be noticed that Lincoln's flexibility, in his effort to save the Union, did not include a willingness to *enslave* anyone for that end. Indeed, he observed on December 6, 1864, "I repeat the declaration made a year ago, that 'while I remain in my present position I shall not attempt to retract or modify the emancipation proclamation, nor shall I return to slavery any person who is free by the terms of that proclamation, or by any of the Acts of Congress.' If the people should, by whatever mode or means, make it an Executive duty to re-enslave such persons, another, and not I, must be their instrument to perform it."[6] This suggests the limits of what he was willing to do or say in the service of "statesmanship."

That is, he was not willing to enslave or to reenslave anyone, even though he was willing to live with slavery. But we should be clear what "living with slavery" meant for him. It meant that the Union would be preserved, a Union in which slavery would be permitted to continue in those Southern States where it happened to exist at the time he became President. He did not mean to touch it there but neither did he mean to let it expand into any new territory. Thus, he was a "Free-Soil Man," not an "Abolitionist." But, he also believed, if slavery *could* be contained, it would wither away—and in such a way as to leave both former slaves and former masters in the best possible condition for living with one another as free men. In the meantime, a South which continued to remain part of the Union could not help but be moderated by Northern opinion and Federal power in what it did to its slaves, both at home and abroad.

The abolitionists insisted, of course, "No union with slaveholders." It has been noticed that "[t]he extreme abolitionists, in the supposed purity of their principles, would have abandoned the four million slaves to their fate."[7] The alternative for them, of preserving the Union but destroying slavery, depended, of course, on a successful war effort—and that, it was generally believed, depended on a united effort on the part of the diverse factions loyal to the Union. Among those factions were not only the abolitionists—Lincoln figured, no doubt, that they had nowhere else to go—, but also Northerners who did not have strong opinions about slavery (but who did care about the Constitution and the Union) and Middle State men who retained both slaves and loyalty to the Constitution. These men of the Middle States were not, despite their slavery institutions, simply bad men; nor for that matter were the Southerners. Lincoln recognized that slavery was essentially a national affliction, that (for the most part) those who were burdened by it would have gotten rid of it if they could have seen a way to do so—a way both economically and socially feasible.

In this respect, Lincoln appreciated the long past of the country and looked ahead to an even longer future. That is, he realized why one section of the country was slave and why another was free. He had long hoped so to contain and thereby begin to ease out slavery as to make it possible for the two races (both emancipated from the curse of slavery) to live thereafter, whether together or separated, in the best possible way. What was called for, he saw, was neither sentimental indifference nor bitter recrimination. He was obliged, in any event, so to conduct the war as not to lose the support of the many men in both the Northern and the Middle States who were, at best, indifferent about slavery. He believed that the goal for which the maximum support could be gathered was that of preserving the Union. Thus, "[f]ighting the war was always secondary to keeping alive the political coalition willing to fight the war."[8]

Once great sacrifices had been made, however, more could be ventured. Once, that is, considerable Northern and Middle States blood had been shed on behalf of the Union, it was possible to direct the attention of the country to slavery itself. "Slavery was what the rebel states were fighting for, and slavery enabled them to fight for slavery."[9] It had long been recognized by the laws of war that one could deprive an enemy of whatever property helped keep him in the field—and, indeed, one could appropriate such property for one's own use. The slaves were for the South such useful, perhaps even essential, property. It was on this basis that Lincoln could then direct Union men to move against Southern slavery, to unite themselves (in effect) with the slaves held by the rebels.

The Emancipation Proclamation was, thus, a military realization of a prophecy Lincoln had made in his famous "House Divided" speech of June 16, 1858: "'A house divided against itself cannot stand.' I believe this government cannot endure, permanently half *slave* and half *free*. I do not expect the Union to be *dissolved*—I do not expect the house to *fall*—but I *do* expect it will cease to be divided. It will become *all* one thing or *all* the other. Either the *opponents* of slavery, will arrest the further spread of it, and place it where the public mind shall rest in the belief that it is in course of ultimate extinction; or its *advocates* will push it forward, till it shall become alike lawful in *all* the States, *old* as well as *new—North* as well as *South*."

III

Much of what I have said thus far should be generally familiar. Indeed, too much originality in such matters should be suspect. No doubt some may be inclined to question the assessment I have been tacitly making about Lincoln's judgment. That assessment is, to state it plainly, that Lincoln seems to me most impressive in his sure-footedness: he never seemed to step wrong in the major moves he made once he assumed the Presidency. The mistakes he did make were due not to faulty judgment but to mistaken information, and in circumstances where he had to rely on what was told him. Thus, throughout the war, he was remarkably adept, knowing both what he wanted and what he was doing. He was, in short, a model of prudential judgment, or at least as fine a practitioner of such judgment as we have had in the Presidency.

I can best illustrate what I mean—what prudence means in action, and especially in war circumstances (and a civil war, at that, where passions are particularly apt to run wild)—by examining the terms of the two documents which comprise the Emancipation Proclamation. By so doing, we can see as well what the Civil War meant and how it progressed, for the entire history of that war seems to me distilled in these documents. But even more important, we can see how first-class practical reason works.

The Emancipation Proclamation, unlike the Declaration of Indepedence and the Constitution, was in a sense the work of one man—and hence of one mind. It was carefully thought out by Lincoln, with only a few suggestions by his Cabinet added after he revealed to them what he proposed to do. It is, we will see, both bold in its conception and disciplined in its execution, the lawyer's art in its perfection. It is, I should add, more American than either the Declaration or the Constitution, in that *its* author had been fully shaped by the regime established after 1776.

There are, in our effort to grasp what Lincoln did, both a challenge and an opportunity. There is the opportunity of fully asserting ourselves as citizens, in that we can, at least for the moment, walk with someone who thought as deeply as any American statesman has about the character, aspirations and deficiencies of our regime. There is also a challenge in that we are obliged to strive for a degree of seriousness to which we are not accustomed. That is, we have become accustomed in our discussions of political things to the exposes and the superficialities of journalism or to the abnormalities and irrationalities of psychology—so much so that it is difficult to avoid sentimentality and sensationalism. We have to make an effort, then, to understand the Emancipation Proclamation. But then, the Proclamation *was* issued for the likes of us.

Thus, Lincoln challenges us to think: he challenges us to reconstruct the thinking he devoted to the problems he faced. We know that he devoted many hours to the text of the Emancipation Proclamation, especially the preliminary statement of September 22, 1862. If we should be able to work out what he took into account, and why, we can then we assured that we begin to understand the Civil War as an eminently political man can and did.

To take seriously another's carefully expressed thought is, after all, the best tribute we can pay to him. That is, indeed, the most noble imitation and worthy of our greatest efforts if we are to understand who we are and what we aspire to.

IV

It is said that Lincoln issued no statement or argument to support the Emancipation Proclamation. "He let the paper go forth for whatever it might do . . ."[10] But this is not to say that he never discussed it, for in a preparatory cabinet meeting, he "proceeded to read his Emancipation Proclamation, making remarks on the several parts as he went on, and showing that he had fully considered the whole subject, in all the lights under which it has been presented to him." The discussion of the Proclamation on that occasion, we are told, included "the constitutional question, the war power, the expediency, and the effect of the movement."[11]

It is that discussion in Lincoln's Cabinet which we can, in effect, recreate if we are so minded. We turn first to an examination of the Preliminary Proclamation of September 22, 1862.

i.

> I, Abraham Lincoln, President of the United States of America, and Commander-in-chief of the Army and Navy thereof, do hereby proclaim and declare that hereafter, as heretofore, the war will be prossecuted for the object of practically restoring the constitutional relation between the United States, and each of the states, and the people thereof, in which states that relation is, or may be suspended, or disturbed.

This is the first of Lincoln's proclamations as President which opens with his name and titles.[12] It is as if he intends to assert from the outset that this statement is especially his doing, that it emanates from his very being—and, insofar as he is a thinking being and this is well thought out, that is so.

This is only the second of his proclamations in which the title as Commander-in-Chief is invoked. Such invocation was not customary in Presidential proclamations.[13] (We notice in passing the precision in his language, "proclaim and declare that hereafter, as heretofore." Such precision encourages us to expect that what he says throughout may profitably be read with care.)

The insistence at the outset upon his status as Commander-in-Chief anticipates his insistence throughout upon this action as a legitimate war measure. No doubt he thought then what he was to say a year later (August 26, 1863) to a critic of the Proclamation, "I think the constitution invests its commander-in-chief, with the law of war, in time of war. The most that can be said, if so much, is, that slaves are property. Is there—has there ever been—any question that by the law of war, property, both of enemies and friends, may be taken when needed? And is it not needed whenever taking it, helps us, or hurts the enemy? Armies, the world over, destroy enemies' property when they can not use it; and even destroy their own to keep it from the enemy. Civilized belligerents do all in their power to help themselves or hurt the enemy, except a few things regarded as barbarous or cruel. Among the exceptions are the massacre of vanquished foes, and non-combatants, male and female."

We see in this opening paragraph of the Preliminary Proclamation an insistence as well upon the purpose of this war, that of restoring the constitutional relations among the States. An anti-slavery crusade would have been far more questionable than an effort to save the Union—and that was, in many quarters, questionable enough. (We should remember that even today more citizens are in favor of "law and order" than are in favor of "racial justice" or military justice or "class justice.") For most men, justice is what the law prescribes: they cannot be depended upon to habitually accept much more than that or even to want much more than that. Would "much more than that" be for them an unwelcome freedom? Does not Lincoln's approach recognize the limits of public opinion? Does it not recognize that respect for law is more "knowable" than respect for justice?

But, one is obliged to ask, are there not various kinds of constitutions (or master-laws)? Should this one have been established in the first place? That is, should the bargain have been made in the first place, that "constitutional relation" which permitted the States to retain jurisdiction over slaves? Was that bargain so immoral that it should never have been expected to hold? Still, what would have happened if the Slave States had been allowed to depart, whether in 1787 or 1861? Had not the Union by 1861 served better the Free States, permitting them to grow to a stronger position in relation to the Slave States than they had been in the beginning?

Granted that the Union is to be preserved, upon what terms can it best be defended? Cannot people more readily be led to see that their interest is served by a constitutional regime (by orderly government, a continent-wide market, an absence of threatening neighbors) than it is served by a free regime (especially when the freedom yet to be fought for is that of others, not obviously their own)? On the other hand, once the crusade for freedom *is* launched, it is much more difficult to control: passions are much more likely to rage unchecked, whereas constitutionalism has a sense of restraint built right into it. [14]

Besides, to blatantly attack slavery *is* to attack property rights and perhaps even the principle of property. Where is the stopping point once one starts down that road? Today, slaveholders; tomorrow, the wealthy? And the day after, anyone of talent or distinction? Is it not sensed by men of affairs that property does depend on the arbitrary, on the accidental, on peculiarly local circumstances? Does it not depend on the bargains which happen to be made from time to time? Lincoln must insist upon the object of restoration of the constitutional relation as critical, especially in light of what he is about to do. Indeed, cannot he effectively do what he is about to do partly because he *has* insisted heretofore on the proper constitutional relation, on constitutional technicalities and niceties? (We should remember that he has even annulled decrees of emancipation issued by various of his generals in the field.) Does one adhere scrupulously to a constitution and the law (as generally understood) in order to be able to step above them at the propitious moment, thereby leading one's people to a higher or more solid constitutional plateau than they are yet accustomed to?

However that may be, we notice the emphasis on *restoration*. Things will go back to what they were—except for the opinion which some had held that secession was proper. But, of course, full restoration will be impossible once that opinion is disavowed, for the status of slavery will never be the same again. Still, the closest the South can come to having the original constitutional relation restored is by quickly acceding to the terms of the Preliminary Proclamation, thereby not "permitting" Lincoln to declare *any* slaves emancipated.

We should notice as well that it is not only the South which threatens the constitutional regime. Thaddeus Stevens, one of the radical abolitionist leaders in Congress, had proclaimed that there was no longer any Constitution and reported that he was weary of hearing the "never-ending gabble about the sacredness of the Constitution." [15]

Finally, we notice that the "constitutional relation" has not been destroyed; rather, it has been "suspended, or disturbed" in certain States—and it is there that restoration is called for. Self-preservation calls for such restoration—that self-preservation which we shall later on see to be so critical a guide for human action.

Much more can be said about this first paragraph. But we must pass on to the subsequent paragraphs, about which far less than this must be said if we are to canvass the entire document on this occasion.

ii.

That it is my purpose, upon the next meeting of Congress to again recommend the adoption of a practical measure tendering pecuniary aid to the free acceptance or rejection of all slave-states, so called, the people whereof may not then be in rebellion against the United States, and which states, may then have voluntarily adopted, or thereafter may voluntarily adopt, immediate, or gradual abolishment of slavery within their respective limits; and that the effort to colonize persons of African descent, with their consent, upon this continent, or elsewhere, with the previously obtained consent of the Governments existing there, will be continued.

Having laid the groundwork—that is, "We are out to restore the authoritative constitutional relation"—, Lincoln can then indicate what would be an improvement consistent with such restored constitutional relation: compensated emancipation by non-rebellious slaveholders. This offer is extended, it seems, to all Slave States, "so called," those now in rebellion and those which had never been in rebellion against the United States. It was unlikely that the rebellious States would be won over, but what about the other Slave States, the Middle States? They would not be affected by the impending proclamation, but was there not for them the suggestion here, as there had been the preceding March, that they would do better to sell their slaves now to the United States than to be deprived of them later?

Is not at least a useful appearance of fairness achieved by Lincoln's offer to pay for what he considered himself empowered and even obliged to take? Does not this reinforce the Lincolnian position that it is not the slaveholder, but slavery, which is the problem, that it is not punishment but union which he is after? And it is to be a Union in which the traditional role of the States is respected: that is, it is up to the States "voluntarily" to adopt a program of abolishment of slavery.

Does he use "abolishment" rather than "abolition" in order to soften what he is asking for? That is, *abolition* may still have been seen as far too radical, even by many anti-slavery Northerners. However that may be, Lincoln cannot abolish slavery in any State: he can only emancipate certain people in a certain place at a certain time. Abolition requires a more comprehensive change, of a permanent legislative character, than he is constitutionally capable of.

The reference to "gradual abolishment" recognizes not only concerns among the public at large about the danger of precipitate action but those of Lincoln as well. What *was* to be done with the millions of people "of African descent" if they should be cut loose from their accustomed moorings? Would they thereafter be exploited even more than they had been? Would they constitute a danger to the community? Could they be expected to know what to do with themselves? Was time needed to effect the transition? Or, failing that, should their removal from the country be planned, for their good as well as that of the Caucasians? Did Lincoln have to explore alternatives in this way, if only to indicate that he understood what many of his countrymen, North and South, were concerned about? By so indicating, did he not make it more likely that the public would eventually accept whatever *he* decided upon and ordered as the least objectionable way of achieving the desired end? If he had failed to appreciate alternative positions, he would not have been trusted the way he came to be.

But to "appreciate" is not to agree: it is rather to understand why another should make the mistake he is making. And slavery was, to say the least, a mistake, not only a moral mistake but (perhaps even more important for the future of the regime) a constitutional mistake. That is, was not our constitutionalism (with its rule of law and its dependence upon an essential equality) bound eventually to undermine slavery or to be undermined by it? Was not slavery somehow antithetical to the principles of the regime? Thus, the Slave States depended on the law-abidingness of the Free States—on the respect of Free States for constitutional arrangements—, in order to be protected in an institution which was (in a sense) lawless.

Finally, we notice the double emphasis on the necessity for consent: (1) the consent of those to *be* colonized, (2) the consent of those governments which would receive the colonists. This, along with the deference to voluntariness on the part of the Slave States, points up the vulnerability of slavery in any regime where consent of the governed is made as much of as it is in ours.[16]

iii.

> That on the first day of January in the year of our Lord, one thousand eight hundred
> and sixty-three, all persons held as slaves within any state, or designated part of a state,
> the people whereof shall then be in rebellion against the United States shall be then,
> thenceforward, and forever free; and the executive government of the United States,
> including the military and naval authority thereof, will recognize and maintain the
> freedom of such persons, and will do no act or acts to repress such persons, or any of
> them, in any efforts they may make for their actual freedom.

One offer has just been made, that of compensated emancipation. Now comes another:
"You can keep your slaves, if you wish, so long as you return to your allegiance." This once
again emphasizes that it is the Union which he seeks to preserve, not Slavery which he seeks
to destroy. One hundred days are provided in which to take advantage of this offer. No
doubt many of the North needed to be assured that Southern property and the American
Constitution were being dealt with fairly.

"[A]ll persons held as slaves": does not this formulation imply that they are not really
slaves? One who is called a slave may be no more than someone held as a slave, perhaps as a
prisoner of war. May he merely be regarded as a slave? Is not slavery as practiced in North
America at that time only conventional slavery, with its convention based primarily on
force? Yet, even if slavery originated in injustice, it may have compounded the original
injustice to have freed all the slaves at once or to have freed them one way rather than
another.

Notice that Lincoln can command only the response of the "executive government of
the United States." The courts and Congress act independently. (We can see in the second
paragraph of the Preliminary Proclamation that it is Congress, not the Executive, which can
provide the "pecuniary aid" Lincoln speaks of there.)

Notice also that freedom comes in two stages, so to speak: recognized freedom and
actual freedom. Recognized freedom is what comes to someone from the sayings and doings
of others; actual freedom depends more on one's own efforts. It should go without saying
that not everyone who is recognized to be free is actually free. Men who have lived for
generations in slavery may need generations of purgation and training before they become
actually free—as the "forty years in the desert" suggest.

iv.

> That the executive will, on the first day of January aforesaid, by proclamation,
> designate the States, and parts of states, if any, in which the people thereof respectively,
> shall then be in rebellion against the United States; and the fact that any state, or the
> people thereof shall, on that day be, in good faith represented in the Congress of the
> United States, by members chosen thereto, at elections wherein a majority of the qualified
> voters of such state shall have participated, shall, in the absence of strong countervailing
> testimony, be deemed conclusive evidence that such state and the people thereof, are not
> then in rebellion against the United States.

A promise is made as to what Lincoln will do on January 1st: to wit, *designate* the
States, or parts of States, if any, in which the people thereof shall then be in rebellion. Is not
that to be the principal purpose of that January 1st proclamation? That is, what *follows* from
such designation will have already been indicated in this September 22nd proclamation.
Little more needs to be added on January 1st: in fact, the emancipation then will even have
the effect of a promise fulfilled. That is, that revolutionary step will then be living up to a
bargain already struck. There is about this sequence a psychological master-stroke.

By thus pointing ahead, Lincoln succeeded in shifting attention to an occasion which was itself "expected" and even "demanded" by a kind of contract. (The designation required for that day was, for the most part, perfunctory: most of the States designated could have been designated by anyone; as we shall see, they in effect designated themselves.) Lincoln succeeded so well in shifting attention to the expected measure (on January 1) from the extraordinary measure (of September 22) that the later statement (which is, except for its concluding language, more pedestrian) has become the one which is remembered and reproduced in anthologies, not the earlier one which had truly been decisive. (Does not this, by the way, again point up the limits of public opinion and remind us of the problems responsible statesmen must deal with in both acting justly and appearing to act justly?)

Notice his precise use of "if any"—"the States, and parts of states, *if any*." After all, an offer has been made; it must not be assumed in advance that it will be rejected by anyone. To do so would be virtually to admit that it is a mere form. It would, besides, deny the rationality and hence the humanity of those in rebellion: they must be considered as, in principle, open to argument. They, too, are American citizens.

Notice, also, that the decisive indication that a State is *not* in rebellion is that of good-faith representation in the Congress. He says, in effect, "If you wish to avoid the effects of a military measure, exercise your rights as free men; send men of your choice to Congress; return to your seats in the national legislature and resume the duty and power you have always had there to help run the country." Is there not something generous in this approach? Does it not acknowledge the fundamentally republican character of the country, a character to which the military power is ultimately subservient? (We need not concern ourselves here with whether Congress would have immediately accepted such representatives from the States which had been in rebellion. It suffices to notice that republican standards were apparently relied upon, even in those trying times.)

Notice, finally, that Lincoln in effect cedes to the rebellious States the power to decide themselves whether they are again to be in good standing. "[I]n the absence of strong countervailing testimony," their recourse to Congressional elections will "be deemed conclusive evidence" that they "are not then in rebellion against the United States." Is there not something generous about this also? Indeed, does not generosity pervade the Proclamation, the generosity of a truly magnanimous man who can at the same time be shrewd and knowing about the usefulness of generosity?

v.

That attention is hereby called to an act of Congress entitled "An act to make an additional Article of War" approved March 13, 1862, and which act is in the words and figure following:

"*Be it enacted by the Senate and House of Representatives of the United States of America in Congress assembled*, That hereafter the following shall be promulgated as an additional article of war for the government of the army of the United States, and shall be obeyed and observed as such:

"Article—. All officers or persons in the military or naval service of the United States are prohibited from employing any of the forces under their respective commands for the purpose of returning fugitives from service or labor, who may have escaped from any persons to whom such service or labor is claimed to be due, and any officer who shall be found guilty by a court-martial of violating this article shall be dismissed from the service.

"Sec. 2. *And be it further enacted*, That this act shall take effect from and after its passage."

Also to the ninth and tenth sections of an act entitled "An Act to suppress Insurrection, to punish Treason and Rebellion, to seize and confiscate property of rebels, and for other purposes," approved July 17, 1862, and which sections are in the words and figures following:

"Sec. 9. *And be it further enacted*, That all slaves of persons who shall hereafter be engaged in rebellion against the government of the United States, or who shall in any way give aid or comfort thereto, escaping from such persons and taking refuge within the lines of the army; and all slaves captured from such persons or deserted by them and coming under the control of the government of the United States; and all slaves of such persons found on [or] being within any place occupied by rebel forces and afterwards occupied by the forces of the United States, shall be deemed captives of war, and shall be forever free of their servitude and not again held as slaves.

"Sec. 10. *And be it further enacted*, That no slave escaping into any State, Territory, or the District of Columbia, from any other State, shall be delivered up, or in any way impeded or hindered of his liberty, except for crime, or some offence against the laws, unless the person claiming said fugitive shall first make oath that the person to whom the labor or service of such fugitive is alleged to be due is his lawful owner, and has not borne arms against the United States in the present rebellion, nor in any way given aid and comfort thereto; and no person engaged in the military or naval service of the United States shall, under any pretence whatever, assume to decide on the validity of the claim of any person to the service or labor of any other person, or surrender up any such person to the claimant, on pain of being dismissed from the service."

And I do hereby enjoin upon and order all persons engaged in the military and naval service of the United States to observe, obey, and enforce, within their respective spheres of service, the act, and sections above recited.

This extended "paragraph" (if it can be called that) draws attention to two acts of Congress: one prohibits military officers from returning certain fugitive slaves, and the other (in the sections quoted from it) declares certain fugitive slaves free and places restrictions on the return of certain other fugitive slaves to their masters. The passage thereafter orders "all persons engaged in the military and naval service of the United States to observe, obey, and enforce, within their respective spheres of service, the act, and sections above recited."

What is all this doing in here? Perhaps it is partly to suggest that what Lincoln is now doing is not without Congressional precedent. This passage may address itself to the more conservative Unionists. That is, they are assured, all this is not simply executive usurpation on the President's part. Perhaps, also, it is partly to counter the hostility of abolitionists who would not like an emancipation decree framed in so qualified and so partial a manner as this one is. That is, such singleminded critics are reminded that at least the hated Fugitive Slave Clause (of the Constitution) has been in effect suspended.

In addition, there are other hints. The first act he calls attention to is reproduced in its entirety, including the superfluous enacting clause (the title of the act, also given, would have sufficed) and the "immediate effect" clause. But only two sections of the second act are called to our attention, in marked (and intended?) contrast to what was done with the first act. Does Lincoln thereby tacitly repudiate the other sections of the second act? We cannot, on this occasion, explore this question: it suffices to notice that several of the sections of the second act which he does *not* mention here are quite harsh, authorizing death sentences and comprehensive confiscation of all property. That harsh spirit is against what he is interested in establishing in the Proclamation: slave property *is* to be "confiscated," so to speak; but, after all, free men will thereby come into being.

In any event, the emphasis here is on fugitive slaves. Does not this suggest who may be able to take advantage at once of the Proclamation—those who flee from rebel territory? Is not an implicit invitation issued? This anticipates and to some extent deals with the complaint that the Proclamation emancipates only where the Union army is *not*.

Finally, we cannot help but notice—are we intended to notice?—that the language of Congress is less precise, less carefully thought out, than that of Lincoln. Does this show the reader that Lincoln is really more responsible, more worthy of being taken seriously?

vi.

> And the executive will in due time recommend that all citizens of the United States who shall have remained loyal thereto throughout the rebellion, shall (upon the restoration of the constitutional relation between the United States, and their respective states, and people, if that relation shall have been suspended or disturbed) be compensated for all losses by acts of the United States, including the loss of slaves.

Once again, we see that the demands of war are not to be permitted to obscure permanently either the desire or the duty to see justice done. Certainly, loyalty must be recognized and compensated. And, it has to be said, the United States should recognize that there has existed up to now a legitimate property interest in slaves which must still be taken account of. Does this remark (the closing one among the substantive paragraphs of the Preliminary Proclamation) appeal to the apprehensive Middle State Unionists (just as the preceding passage incorporating the acts of Congress appealed in large part to disappointed Abolitionists)? Do we once again see, that is, that Lincoln must keep quite divergent, but vitally necessary, horses yoked together if the war chariot is to advance?

vii.

> In witness whereof, I have hereunto set my hand, and caused the seal of the United States to be affixed.

This is the standard testamentary statement for such proclamations. We will return to it at the end of the Final Proclamation.

viii.

> Done at the City of Washington, this twenty second day of September, in the year of our Lord, one thousand eight hundred and sixty two, and of the Independence of the United States, the eighty seventh.

The 87th year hearkens back to 1776 and the Declaration of Independence. It is that 87 which Lincoln will transform into "four score and seven" when he speaks in November of 1863 at Gettysburg. (That is, they were, on September 22, 1862, *in* the 87th year; there would be 87 years past by the time of the Gettysburg Address.)

Why September 22nd? Lincoln had planned to issue this Preliminary Proclamation some weeks earlier (in fact, in July). But he had been dissuaded by Secretary Seward's argument that he should at least wait until the Union forces won another victory rather than make the proclamation seem an act of desperation—for it *had* been a time of one defeat after another. Then there came the victory of Antietan, in the middle of September 1862—and a few days later, the Emancipation Proclamation.[17]

Did Lincoln choose an interval of one hundred days so that the final proclamation would fall on New Year's Day, a day of rebirth and rededication?

ix.

There is, in the handwritten original of the Preliminary Proclamation of September 22, 1862, the repetition of "sixty two," in this fashion, "in the year of our Lord, one thousand, eight hundred and sixty two, and sixty two, and of the Independence of the United States the eighty seventh." This passage is in the hands of a clerk.[18]

Here, for the first time in this commentary, I move from what Lincoln thought and intended, to what may have been "unconscious" (and hence "inspired"?). This inadvertent repetition by a clerk of "sixty two" suggests that he, at least, made much of the date—as if to emphasize, "It is late 1862, not early 1861. We loyalists *have* tried for a year and a half to put down this dreadful rebellion with conventional measures. We *can* now proceed in good faith to a measure which we have had to be cautious in using, not only because it challenges certain longstanding constitutional arrangements (after all, it *is* a constitution we are defending) but also because it conforms to and gratifies the deepest desires of those of us who have always hated slavery. It *is* 1862!"

I must leave further poetic probings of the unconscious (or of the providential) to others.

We turn now to the Final Proclamation of (January 1, 1863). Much of what might be said about the parts of this proclamation has already been said in my review of the Preliminary Proclamation. We can be brief.

x.

Whereas, on the twentysecond day of September, in the year of our Lord one thousand eight hundred and sixty two, a proclamation was issued by the President of the United States, containing, among other things, the following, towit:

"That on the first day of January, in the year of our Lord one thousand eight hundred and sixty-three, all persons held as slaves within any State or designated part of a State, the people whereof shall then be in rebellion against the United States, shall be then, thenceforward, and forever free; and the Executive Government of the United States, including the military and naval authority thereof, will recognize and maintain the freedom of such persons, and will do no act or acts to repress such persons, or any of them, in any efforts they may make for their actual freedom.

"That the Executive will, on the first day of January aforesaid, by proclamation, designate the States and parts of States, if any, in which the people thereof, respectively, shall then be in rebellion against the United States; and the fact that any State, or the people thereof, shall on that day be, in good faith, represented in the Congress of the United States by members chosen thereto at elections wherein a majority of the qualified voters of such State shall have participated, shall, in the absence of strong countervailing testimony, be deemed conclusive evidence that such State, and the people thereof, are not then in rebellion against the United States."

A solemn version of the date of the Preliminary Proclamation is given, that version used in the final paragraph of that proclamation. We recall that when the dates were given for Acts of Congress in that first proclamation, simpler versions of their dates were given (that is "March 13, 1862," "July 17, 1862"). Is a proclamation somehow of greater dignity than an Act of Congress? Indeed, does the Presidency, properly employed, have a greater dignity than the Congress? Is this one reason why a Presidential proclamation about Southern slaves means more, has a greater effect, than Congressional enactments? Is the Commander-in-Chief, in time of war, somehow the decisive ruler of a country, especially when the war is a civil war—for that makes war comprehensive?

These questions lead us to notice that there is nothing said about Congress in this proclamation. Whereas before Lincoln had quoted at length from Congress, here he quotes only from himself. Both Congress and the States take second place in the constitutional drama now being enacted. They have served their purpose, they have had their chance—and now he must get on with conducting the war to save the Union.

We also notice that nothing is said of compensation for voluntary emancipation; nothing is said of compensation for loss of slaves by loyal slaveowners. (Both of these had been proposed, as promised, to Congress. But nothing substantial had come from the proposals.) The emphasis is now upon emancipation and its consequences.

A new stage has been reached in the war—but a stage which, it can be argued, developed constitutionally from the preceding stage. This proclamation "gets right down to business": there are no "frills" or offers or alternatives—but rather a judgment set forth in prosaic yet somehow solemn terms.

xi.

Now, therefore I, Abraham Lincoln, President of the United States, by virtue of the power in me vested as Commander-in-Chief, of the Army and Navy of the United States in time of actual armed rebellion against authority and government of the United States, and as a fit and necessary war measure for suppressing said rebellion, do, on this first day of January, in the year of our Lord one thousand eight hundred and sixty three, and in accordance with my purpose so to do publicly proclaimed for the full period of one hundred days, from the day first above mentioned, order and designate as the States and parts of States wherein the people thereof respectively, are this day in rebellion against the United States, the following, towit:

Arkansas, Texas, Louisiana, (except the Parishes of St. Bernard, Plaquemines, Jefferson, St. Johns, St. Charles, St. James, Ascension, Assumption, Terrebonne, Lafourche, St. Mary, St. Martin, and Orleans, including the city of New Orleans) Mississippi, Alabama, Florida, Georgia, South-Carolina, North-Carolina, and Virginia, (except the fortyeight counties designated as West Virginia, and also the counties of Berkley, Accomac, Northampton, Elizabeth-City, York, Princess Ann, and Norfolk, including the cities of Norfolk & Portsmouth); and which excepted parts are, for the present, left precisely as if this proclamation were not issued.

Lincoln's status of Commander-in-Chief is again emphasized, and reinforced further by the references to "time of actual armed rebellion" and "fit and necessary war measure." A solemn version of the date is again relied upon as he draws in this decree upon the full majesty of the language as well as upon the full force of the war power.

But the war power is properly to be employed for a certain purpose. It must be used discriminatingly, if constitutional government is truly to be defended. This is recognized by the exceptions Lincoln insisted upon making, in the application of his proclamation, for certain parishes in Louisiana and for certain counties in Virginia where Union forces were already in control. Might not Lincoln also have thought that such exceptions made his policy *seem* discriminating and hence contributed to its effectiveness?

The Secretary of the Treasury argued against such exceptions and kept after the President thereafter to extend the Emancipation Proclamation to all of Virginia and Louisiana. Lincoln replied on September 2, 1863: "Knowing your great anxiety that the emancipation proclamation shall now be applied to certain parts of Virginia and Louisiana which were exempted from it last January, I state briefly what appear to me to be difficulties in the way of such a step. The original proclamation has no constitutional or legal justification, except as a military measure. The exemptions were made because the military necessity did not apply to the exempted localities. Nor does that necessity apply to them now any more than it did then. If I take the step must I not do so, without the argument of military necessity, and so, without any argument, except the one that I think the measure politically expedient, and morally right? Would I not thus give up all footing upon constitution or law? Would I not thus be in the boundless field of absolutism? Could this pass unnoticed or unresisted? Could it fail to be perceived that without any further stretch, I might do the same in Delaware,

Maryland, Kentucky, Tennessee, and Missouri; and even change any law in any State?"[19] Notice the words, "Could this pass unnoticed", "Could it fail to be perceived." It *is* important for constitutional government what the people of the country understand their officers to be doing and on what authority. And it is important that the people be trained to expect authority to be evident, especially when extraordinary measures are resorted to.

Yet, we might ask, in what sense *are* the "excepted parts" "left precisely as if this proclamation were not issued"? Should not it have been evident to all—was it not evident to (and perhaps even intended by) Lincoln—that if the proclamation was effective with respect to the States and parts of States listed, then slavery was finished not only in the rebellious States but also in the loyal Middle States and in the "excepted" counties and parishes? That is, the emancipation of so massive a body of slaves made slavery itself quite vulnerable in the country at large. Such slavery as then existed in North America could find intelligent defenders only if virtually all members of the slaves' race were subjected to slavery. If a significant number were free, and could develop themselves as free and responsible citizens, the supposed natural basis for slavery would no longer be tenable. Slavery could not survive, in a regime such as ours, if it clearly rested as much as it would have had to (after the Emancipation Proclamation) upon the obvious accident of geography. That is, the moral basis of slavery would have been undermined, insofar as everyday morality rests in large part upon the customary and the uniform.

Consider, finally, in this paragraph, how the States are listed: they are not alphabetical; nor in the order of admission to the Union; nor in order of secession. Rather, Lincoln begins with the only landlocked state (Arkansas), and then moves along the coast, starting with the State farthest away from him (Texas) and coming closer and closer to Washington (ending with Virginia). It is as if he sweeps them all in to himself. (States are listed differently in other proclamations.) Lincoln displays here a methodical turn of mind. In this way, too, we should be reassured to notice, he avoids "the boundless field of absolutism"—and this means we can safely think about what he is doing, for then we are thinking about thinking rather than trying to think about that which is irrational or accidental and hence essentially unknowable.

xii.

> And by virtue of the power, and for the purpose aforesaid, I do order and declare that all persons held as slaves within said designated States, and parts of States, are, and henceforward shall be free; and that the Executive government of the United States, including the military and naval authorities thereof, will recognize and maintain the freedom of said persons.

We see here brought to completion what had been promised on September 22. We again see that Lincoln's formal control is limited to the Executive government of the United States. Most of what one might say about this paragraph has been anticipated in this commentary.

But what about the "order and declare"? Perhaps *he* realizes that he can order only some things; that he can merely express a strong preference or hope with respect to other things. Consider another pair of terms in this paragraph: "are, and henceforward shall be free"; "recognize and maintain the freedom of said persons." Does he *order* said persons to be free *now?* Does he *order* said freedom to be recognized *now?* He can do that, perhaps. But he cannot order that such freedom be "henceforward" or that it be maintained. Will not that depend on future governments and future circumstances?

I note in passing that "maintain" had been put into the Preliminary Proclamation at the suggestion of a cabinet member; but Lincoln had misgivings about it. He was reluctant, he indicated, to promise something he did not know he could perform. He has retained "maintain" here but perhaps not without hinting at his reservations.

xiii.
And I hereby enjoin upon the people so declared to be free to abstain from all violence, unless in necessary self-defence; and I recommend to them that, in all cases when allowed, they labor faithfully for reasonable wages.

We see here one great problem of the future, a problem which continues to this day. In dealing with the freed people, Lincoln recognizes what he can and cannot say. He can, as President, *enjoin* them to "abstain from all violence": that is what the law ordains. But he cannot *enjoin* them to work: if they are truly free men, they must decide *that* on their own. Here he can recommend only: they can be urged to work faithfully; their prospective employers are implicitly instructed to pay them reasonable wages. Thus, emancipation is one thing; humanization is quite another—for *that* takes time, and such willingness as Lincoln had to face up to the facts and to restrain himself. What can be proclaimed, therefore, is neither virtue nor genuine freedom but, at best, the removal of chains and a provision of opportunities. Education and training must thereafter do their part. Is not the problem with immediate, massive abolition reflected in the virtually complete silence about what is to become of the emancipated slaves? Is it sensible to expect them to manage on their own like other free men? Is not this why Lincoln had argued again and again for gradual, compensated emancipation, a mode of emancipation which would both motivate and empower masters to provide a proper transition for their slaves into a free life? Such a mode would have had the minimum of bitterness and of general poverty (due to the passions and ravages of war) to contend with.

Violence on the part of freed slaves is forbidden. Lincoln is speaking here to longstanding fears among slave owners of bloody slave rebellions, fears which Middle State unionists as well as Northern humanitarians shared. Should such violence have broken out on a large scale, the Union cause might have been discredited: the old concerns, and repression in the South, might have then appeared justified. Still, violence is understood to be permitted for "necessary self-defense." Is this a law of nature? Would it be self-defense to use force against the master who wants to retain his emancipated slave?

We see in this "necessary self-defense" an echo of the "necessary war measure" Lincoln had declared himself obliged to resort to in defense of the Union. Indeed, self-defense had promoted and permitted the original compromise with slavery in 1787—that is, the defense of the several States, threatened by European powers and by continual war among themselves.

xiv.
And I further declare and make known, that such persons of suitable condition, will be received into the armed service of the United States to garrison forts, positions, stations, and other places, and to man vessels of all sorts in said service.

This sentence is quietly stated: the use of "declare and make known" almost suggests he is reporting something rather than ordering something—reporting something that is happening, that is bound to happen. The military uses to which freed slaves may be put are *not* immediately, or obviously, combative. He has to think of Southern fears and Northern prejudices, both of which can lead to actions harmful either to the slaves or to Lincoln's government. There would be something shocking, perhaps even unnatural, many must have thought, in former slaves fighting against their former masters. This was a development which took some time to get used to—but it eventually came about, on a significant scale.

Southerners themselves were finally reduced to freeing slaves who would serve in *their* army—thereby vindicating Lincoln's policy as a genuine war measure, a war measure which made African slavery thereafter untenable among Americans.

xv.
> And upon this act, sincerely believed to be an act of justice, warranted by the Constitution, upon military necessity, I invoke the considerate judgment of mankind, and the gracious favor of Almighty God.

This is perhaps the most complicated sentence in the two proclamations. We must settle on this occasion for a few preliminary observations about it. Interpretation is made even more difficult when one understands it to have been supplied (in large part?) by a member of the Cabinet, not by Lincoln himself. If that should be so, what appears to be complexity may only be confusion.

Still, a few questions may be in order: "this act" is considered to be "warranted by the Constitution upon military necessity." Is it done because it is warranted? Or it is done for some other reason, and the power (but not the purpose) in so doing is provided by "military necessity"? An "act of justice" is pointed to as somehow involved here. Is this the true purpose? Or is it understood that a respect for justice is itself good military strategy? Notice that it is regarded as certainly a "military necessity" but that it is only "sincerely believed" to be an "act of justice." Is the truth about justice far harder to arrive at than truth about military strategy? The President had delayed a long time doing this: he had had to decide what the right thing to do was—and that depended not only on military strategy and natural right, but also on his Constitutional powers, duties and limitations.

The "considerate judgment of mankind" reminds of the language of the Declaration of Independence's "opinions of mankind." Mankind has judgment; Almighty God has "gracious favor." It is not for man to evaluate what moves God or, indeed, whether God moves at all. Man, it seems, must do what he thinks right—and then hope for the best. The references to both mankind and God serve to remind the reader that immediate, personal concerns should not be permitted to usurp in us the proper, one might even say the constitutional, role of the truly human, the justly divine.

xvi.
> In witness whereof, I have hereunto set my hand and caused the seal of the United States to be affixed.

It is said that the issuance of the Emancipation Proclamation was delayed on January 1st because when it came to be signed in the morning, another formal testamentary paragraph, one appropriate for another kind of proclamation, had been inadvertently used in the place of this one in the official copy. It had had to be sent back to the State Department to be redone. (It is this, along with a reception Lincoln had had to be at much of the day, which contributed to the delay indicated in the passage I have quoted from Frederick Douglass.)

We can see even here, in constitutional matters as in worship, the importance of forms, of appearance, as well as (perhaps) of chance.

xvii.
> Done at the City of Washington, this first day of January, in the year of our Lord one thousand eight hundred and sixty three, and of the Independence of the United States of America the eighty-seventh.

Nothing more (in addition to what has been said about the conclusion of the Preliminary Proclamation) needs to be said about this concluding sentence—except perhaps to notice that it *is* in the City of Washington that the decisive declaration against slavery was issued, that slavery which even the slaveholders of Washington's generation, including Washington himself, can be said to have looked forward to ending in a responsible manner as the republic matured.

That is, has not this commentary argued that if Lincoln, as Washington's legitimate successor, could have constitutionally "save[d] the Union" *either* by "sav[ing] slavery" *or* by "destroy[ing] slavery," he would have preferred to do so by taking advantage of this opportunity to destroy slavery? Indeed, to preserve the Union on his terms *was*, even without the Emancipation Proclamation, to destroy slavery?

V

Three topics remain to be discussed—but not on this occasion. I will indicate them briefly, suggesting the sorts of things which need to be considered.

There is needed, first, a consideration of the effects of the Emancipation Proclamation. One should note first and foremost that it did "work," that it promoted the flight of slaves from the South, that it undermined both the economy and the moral standing of the South both at home and in Europe, that it contributed to the North a significant military force of freed slaves. We can see that, in order for such a policy to work, timing was critical. Also critical was that the President should have had a clear notion of goals and standards—which means that the ultimate considerations drew upon prudence and justice more than upon liberty and equality (as these are generally understood).

As the Union army moved South, thereafter, it "naturally" left freed slaves in its wake. This had, it seems, a great moral effect on what the North was doing and what it was seen to be doing. Thus, for example, the Proclamation emancipated Lincoln himself and people like him, as well as the Constitution itself and the very idea of republican government, from the burden of slavery.

We can see as well that ideas do matter in political life. In a sense, one might even say that *only* ideas matter. That which we call "symbolic" can be very important. One should begin, in considering such matters, with the fact that the Proclamation was at once regarded as important. Only the Thirteenth Amendment, abolishing all slavery in the United States (adopted by Congress early in 1865 for ratification by the States), produced as tumultuous a response from the antislavery people as the Proclamation had done. To be regarded as important *is*, in political matters, to be at least somewhat important.

It should be evident to us, upon thinking about the Proclamation and its effect, how critical opinion is for law and, in turn, how critical law is for morality and for civilization. And above all, it should be evident to us how critical it is to know what one is doing.

But it should also be evident to us that the Proclamation and the war it served have had bad effects as well: the ascendancy of Executive power in the United States can be understood to have started here; the separation of powers was undermined as were the States; the war power was magnified; the notion of "total war" was made respectable. Should not a political man of Lincoln's understanding and temperament now devote himself to redefining, for *our* changed circumstances, what is appropriate in our constitutional relations? Would not Lincoln himself insist today that practical reforms, some of a far reaching character, should be made if we are to address ourselves sensibly and safely to the new challenges which confront us?

VI

That is one topic which should be developed. I have already touched upon my second remaining topic—that which addresses itself to what we can learn, of a more general nature, from our study of the Emancipation Proclamation.

We see, of course, what prudence can mean in a particular situation—and hence what prudence itself means. One must adjust to one's materials, including the prejudices and limitations of one's community. Such adjustment often includes settling for less than the best. But the most useful adjustment is not possible unless one *does* know what the very best would be. We can also sense, upon the study of the doings of prudent men, how important chance is in human affairs—and hence how limited we often are in what we can do, even when we know what should be done.

We should notice as well, and guard against, that fashionable opinion which dismisses what is reasonable and deliberate as cold-blooded and calculating. It is also important, however, if one is to be most effective as a reasonable, deliberate and deliberating human being, to seem other than cold-blooded and calculating—that is, it is important to be a good politician. Once again we are reminded of the importance in political things of appearances, of a healthy respect for the opinions (and hence the errors as well as the sound intuition) of mankind.

Certainly, self-righteousness should always be held in check, but not always a show of indignation. Still, indignation even in a good cause should be carefully watched. Consider, for example, the famous Abolitionist William Lloyd Garrison's 1831 promise, "I *will* be as harsh as truth, and as uncompromising as justice. On this subject I do not wish to think, or to speak, or write, with moderation." Such passion may be useful, even necessary, if great evils are to be corrected, but only if a Lincoln should become available to supervise what finally happens and to deal prudently with others (zealous friends and sincere enemies alike) with a remarkable, even godlike, magnanimity.[20]

VII

Now, to my final topic for the future, which I preface with three quotations which can serve to illuminate as well this entire commentary on the Emancipation Proclamation.

The first quotation is from the New Testament. "Behold, I send you forth as sheep in the midst of wolves: be ye therefore wise as serpents, and harmless as doves."[21]

The second is from Stephen A. Douglas who said of Lincoln, in the course of their celebrated Illinois debates, that Lincoln "has a fertile genius in devising language to conceal his thoughts."[22]

The third is from Lincoln himself who once observed, "I am very little inclined on any occasion to say anything unless I hope to produce some good by it."[23]

Artemus Ward was evidently Lincoln's favorite humorist during the Civil War. "The President's reading of the humorist's story, 'High-Handed Outrage at Utica' to his cabinet before presenting them with the Emancipation Proclamation [on September 22, 1862] is well known. 'With the fearful strain that is upon me night and day,' said Lincoln, 'if I did not laugh I should die, and you need this medicine as much as I do.'"[24]

But, I suggest, there may be even more to this famous episode than is recognized. Why was that particular story selected by Lincoln for that occasion? The story Lincoln read to his cabinet *is* amusing. But notice, also, that it is about a great traitor, perhaps indeed the greatest traitor who has ever lived. This traitor is dealt with soundly, if irrationally, in the story.[25]

Consider the title: "High-Handed Outrage at Utica." Utica was the famous African city which allied itself to republican Rome in the mighty struggle against Carthage. Did not Lincoln intend to gather to the cause of the American Republic an African power (those men of "African descent") against the threatening Carthage represented by the South?

But, perhaps he recognized, there was in his own action something questionable, something dubious, even high-handed and outrageous—at least, there would be, in appearance or if he did not handle it properly. Thus, he saw himself as others saw him, *or as others might see him*—and laughed at himself.

This would be, of course, most subtle—and far higher humor than anything Artemus Ward was ever capable of. But if he should have been so subtle, so detached, should not that really make us take notice? It points up the deliberateness, the self-conscious artistry, the coolness of Lincoln. This is, indeed, startling self-criticism, which he would share with his most perceptive observers. Or should what I am now drawing upon be dismissed as mere chance and hence unsound speculation? So be it—for those who would have it so.

In any event, we are obliged to emphasize, even more than we have already, that Lincoln must have known what he was doing, including what impression he needed to make. This man is truly a remarkable child (indeed, a prodigy) of the American constitutional regime. Should not these observations induce us to return to the Emancipation Proclamation and to take it even more seriously than we have? We have merely examined its surface—but in doing so, have we not also learned that the surface, the appearance of things, is critical for responsible political action?

The words one uses—and the words one suppresses—very much contribute to the appearance of things and hence to one's effect. In this sense, indeed, a word fitly spoken is like apples of gold in settings of silver.[26]

Notes

1. H. JAFFA, THE CONDITIONS OF FREEDOM 8 (1975). *See American Constitutionalism and the Virtue of Prudence* in ABRAHAM LINCOLN, THE GETTYSBURG ADDRESS AND AMERICAN CONSTITUTIONALISM 165-68 n. 64 (L. deAlvarez ed., 1976) (essay reprinted, with additions, from 8 LOY. L.A.L. REV. 1 (1975)). *See also*, note 20, *infra*.

Does not Lord Charnwood's biography, ABRAHAM LINCOLN (1917), remain the best one-volume account of Lincoln's character and career?

See F· NIETZSCHE, THE USE AND ABUSE OF HISTORY 9-10 (1957).

2. Vernon Jarrett, "Why we must re-evaluate heroes of past," *Chicago Tribune*, February 20, 1974, § 1, at 14, col. 2. The rather sensible editorial to which Mr. Jarrett responded may be found in the *Chicago Tribune*, February 15, 1974, § 1, at 12, col. 1 (and was itself a response to the column of February 13, 1974, by Mr. Jarrett in the *Chicago Tribune*). (The paragraphing of various authors quoted in the text has *not* been preserved. This is related to the practice in this commentary of indenting, in the text of this commentary, *only* the Emancipation Proclamation.)

It should be remembered that Lincoln always had to contend with the anti-Negro prejudices of Unionists in the North and in the Middle States. *See e·g.*, 2 J.G. RANDALL, LINCOLN THE PRESIDENT 133 (1945) (hereinafter cited as RANDALL I) ("the Africanization of our Society"), *id.* at 172; 2 J. T. MORSE, Jr., ABRAHAM LINCOLN 126-27 (American Statesman Series; Boston: Houghton, Mifflin & Co., 1896). See, for Lincoln's periodic and deliberate recourse to talk about "colonization of blacks" as his way of lulling the racial fears of white Unionists, S. OATES, WITH MALICE TOWARD NONE 268, 297-99, 307, 312-13, 322, 325-26, 330-31, 339-42 (1977); RANDALL I, *supra* at 138f. 151, 172. Compare ROBERT DALE OWEN, THE WRONG OF SLAVERY, THE RIGHT OF EMANCIPATION 228-29 (Philadelphia: J.B. Lippincott & Co., 1864). How these matters could be seen, whether or not correctly, is indicated by the account of Karl Marx (in November 1862), "Of Lincoln's emancipation [proclamation, of September 1862,] one sees no effect up to the present, save that from fear of a Negro inundation the Northwest [what we today know as the Midwest] has voted Democratic [that is, against Lincoln's party]." J. FRANKLIN, THE EMANCIPATION PROCLAMATION 85 (1963).

See, on slavery in antiquity, 1 GIBBON, THE DECLINE AND FALL OF THE ROMAN EMPIRE 35f (New York: Modern Library, no date).

3. C. SANDBURG, 2 ABRAHAM LINCOLN: THE WAR YEARS 21-22 (1939). (The Secretary of State was William H. Seward. He had just said, "I mean that the Emancipation Proclamation was uttered in the first gun fired at Fort Sumter, and we have been the last to hear it.") *See also,* J.G. RANDALL, CONSTITUTIONAL PROBLEMS UNDER LINCOLN 379-80 (New York: D. Appleton and Co., 1926). See as well, notes 23, 26 *infra.*

4. WHAT COUNTRY HAVE I? POLITICAL WRITINGS BY BLACK AMERICANS 52-53 (H. Storing ed., 1970) (emphasis added).

5. *Id* at 51-52 (emphasis added). *See also,* 2 RANDALL I, *supra* note 2, at 201, 202-03; Krug, *Lincoln, the Republican Party, and the Emancipation Proclamation,* 7 HIST. TEACHER 48 (November 1973).

6. 8 THE COLLECTED WORKS OF ABRAHAM LINCOLN 152 (R. Basler, ed., 1953) (Annual Message to Congress). (By this time "a proposed amendment of the Constitution abolishing slavery throughout the United States" had passed the Senate. *Id.* at 149.) Lincoln had expressed similar sentiments in his Annual Message to Congress of December 1863. 7 *id.* at 51. *See also,* 6 *id.* at 411; 7 *id.* at 81. (The references by dates to Lincoln's speeches and letters, in the text, are sufficient to guide the reader to the Basler edition of Lincoln's *Works.*)

See, for Lincoln's comments on his letter to Greeley, 7 *id.* at 499-501. This letter was in response to Greeley's published criticism of "the policy [Lincoln seemed] to be pursuing with regard to the slaves of Rebels." This criticism had included the complaint, "We think you are unduly influenced by the counsels . . . of certain fossil politicians hailing from the Border Slave States." 5 *id.* at 389 (Consider what is implied in Lincoln's salutary preference for "Middle States" over "Border States." A rare exception may be found at 7 *id.* at 282.)

See notes 8, 26, *infra.*

7. H. JAFFA, EQUALITY AND LIBERTY 157 (1965). See note 20, *infra.*

Students today of Lincoln and the Civil War are most fortunate to have available to them the pioneering work of Mr. Jaffa, particularly his CRISIS OF THE HOUSE DIVIDED (1959). My own considerable debt to him is particularly evident in Sections I and II of this commentary.

I have, on various occasions, developed some of the points touched upon in this commentary: (1) NOTES ON THE FIRST AMENDMENT TO THE CONSTITUTION OF THE UNITED STATES (Ph.D dissertation, The University of Chicago, 1964) (e.g., the lecture, "Neither Black nor White: The Negro in America"); (2) *The Declaration of Independence,* 9 ST. L.U.L.J. 390 (1965); (3) THE CONSTITUTIONALIST: NOTES ON THE FIRST AMENDMENT (1971) (corrections are collected in notes 3 and 4 of the next item listed); (4) *American Constitutionalism and the Virtue of Prudence: Philadelphia, Paris, Washington, Gettysburg,* in ABRAHAM LINCOLN, THE GETTYSBURG ADDRESS AND AMERICAN CONSTITUTIONALISM 77-170 (L. de Alvarez, ed. 1976) (reprinted, with additions, from 8 LOY. L.A.L. REV. 1 (1975)); (5) HUMAN BEING AND CITIZEN: ESSAYS ON VIRTUE, FREEDOM AND THE COMMON GOOD (1975) (e.g., the essays, "Natural Right and the American Lawyer," "Race, Law and Civilization," and "Citizen and Human Being: Thoreau, Socrates and Civil Disobedience"); (6) Review of Howard Brotz, *The Politics of South Africa: Democracy and Racial Diversity,* Chicago Sun-Times, Book Week, August 14, 1977, p. 8, col. 1 (abridged) (reprinted, in its entirety, in *University of Chicago Maroon,* April 11, 1978, p. 8); (7) *The Public Interest in Privacy: On Becoming and Being Human,* 26 DEPAUL L. REV. 767 (1977) (e.g., pp. 802-05, "Martin Luther King and the Soul of America"). See also, M.E. Bradford and G. Anastaplo, *Slavery and the Constitution: A Conversation,* The Newsletter, Politics Department, The University of Dallas, Spring 1977, p. 1. See, as well, note 26, *infra.*

8. EQUALITY AND LIBERTY, *supra* note 7, at 158. See note 19, *infra.*

Lincoln's "historical" view of slavery, and of what was to be done about it in the American constitutional system, had been set forth in this manner on October 13, 1858 (in the course of the Lincoln-Douglas Debates):

> . . . When Judge Douglas undertakes to say that as a matter of choice the fathers of the government made this nation part slave and part free, *he assumes what is historically a falsehood.* More than that; when the fathers of the government cut off the source of slavery by the abolition of the slave trade, and adopted a system of restricting it from the new Territories where it had not existed, I maintain that they placed it where they understood, and all sensible men understood, it was in the course of ultimate extinction; and when Judge Douglas asks me why it cannot continue as our fathers made it, I ask him why he and his friends could not let it remain as our fathers made it?

> It is precisely all I ask of him in relation to the institution of slavery, that it shall be placed upon the basis that our fathers placed it upon. Mr. Brooks, of South Carolina, once said, and truly said, that when this government was established, no one expected the institution of slavery to last until this day; and that the men who formed this government were wiser and better men than the men of these days; but the men of these days had experience which the fathers had not, and that experience had taught them the invention of of the cotton gin, and this had made the perpetuation of the institution of slavery a necessity in this country. Judge Douglas could not let it stand upon the basis upon which our fathers placed it, but removed it and *put it upon the cotton gin basis.* It is a question, therefore, for him and his friends to answer—why they could not let it remain where the fathers of the Government originally placed it.

I hope nobody has understood me as trying to sustain the doctrine that we have a right to quarrel with Kentucky, or Virginia, or any of the slave States, about the institution of slavery—thus giving the Judge an opportunity to make himself eloquent and valiant against us in fighting for their rights. I expressly declared in my opening speech, that I had neither the inclination to exercise, nor the belief in the existence of the right to interfere with the States of Kentucky or Virginia in doing as they pleased with slavery or any other existing institution. Then what becomes of all his eloquence in behalf of the rights of States, which are assailed by no living man?

3 THE COLLECTED WORKS *supra* note 6, at 276-77. See notes 23, 26 *infra*.

See, for a brilliant use of the "created equal" language of The Declaration of Independence, Harry V. Jaffa, *Equality, Justice, and the American Revolution: In Reply to Bradford's "The Heresy of Equality,"* 21 MODERN AGE 114 (Spring 1977). See also, Anastaplo *Mr. Justice Black, His Generous Common Sense and the Bar Admissions Cases,* SW.U.L. REV. 977, 1042 (1977). "The other part of our freedom consists in the civil rights and advancements of every person according to his merit: the enjoyment of those never more certain, and the access to these never more open, than in a free commonwealth." J. MILTON, *The Ready and Easy Way to Establish a Free Commonwealth,* in COMPLETE POEMS AND MAJOR PROSE OF JOHN MILTON, 896 (Merritt Y. Hughes ed. 1957).

9. EQUALITY AND LIBERTY, *supra* note 7, at 163. Consider the suggested recourse by the Confederates themselves to the slaves as fighting man:

> [I]n the autumn and winter of 1864, the cause of the South was already lost and the collapse of the Confederate Government plainly foreshadowed to all except the leaders, whose infatuation and wounded vanity made them unwilling to acknowledge and accept defeat. Yet this effort to avoid confession of error in one direction compelled them to admit it in another. They had seceded for slavery, had made it the corner-stone of their government, had anathematized President Lincoln for his decrees of emancipation, had pronounced the ban of outlawry, and had prescribed the sentence of death against every white officer who might dare to command negro troops; but now, in their extremity, some of them proposed to throw consistency to the winds and themselves commit the acts upon which they had invoked the reprobation of mankind, and for which they had ordained extreme punishment.

> It would be difficult to estimate the benefit they had derived from the direct military labor of the slave, especially in building fortifications. They now proposed not only to put arms in his hands, but also, as a final step, to emancipate him for the service. Even the flexible political conscience of Jefferson Davis, however, winced a little at the bold abandonment of principle which the policy involved, and in his message of November 7, 1864, to the Confederate Congress he argued the question with the reluctance of a man preparing to walk over live coals. . . .

> . . . Mr. Davis's hesitating and tentative recommendation was seed sown on barren ground. If the dose was unpalatable to him it appears to have been yet more bitter to the Members of the Confederate Congress, who doubtless felt, as has been pithily expressed by a Confederate writer, that it was an admission of the inherent injustice of slavery; that "if the negro was fit to be a soldier he was not fit to be a slave"; and that "by a few strokes of the pen the Confederate Government had subscribed to the main tenet of the abolition party in the North and all its consequences, standing exposed and stultified before the world." As the fall of the Confederacy drew nigh the stress of disaster compelled his acceptance of the distasteful alternative, though even then he could not refrain from expressing the hope that the grim necessity would somehow be averted . . .

> They debated the unwelcome subject with qualms and grimaces through November, December, January, and most of February. On the 11th of January [1865], and again on the 18th of February, the proposal received a notable support in letters from General Lee, in which he declared the measure of employing negro soldiers "not only expedient but necessary," and recommended that the Confederate President be empowered "to call upon individuals or States for such as they are willing to contribute, with the condition of emancipation to all enrolled."

JOHN G. NICOLAY AND JOHN HAY, 6 ABRAHAM LINCOLN: A HISTORY 484-87 (New York: Century Co., 1914). See IV, xiv, *infra*. See, also, ELLEN G. WILSON, THE LOYAL BLACKS (1976) (on promises of emancipation of soldier-slaves by the British during the American Revolution).

Transformation of the burdens of slavery can take different forms. See, for example, THUCYDIDES, PELOPONNESIAN WAR, IV, 80; W. FAULKNER, THE SOUND AND THE FURY & AS I LAY DYING 18 (1946) (Jason Compson's "emancipation").

10. 2 ABRAHAM LINCOLN: THE WAR YEARS, *supra* note 3, at 20.

11. 6 NICOLAY AND HAY, *supra* note 9, at 161-62. See, for Lincoln's public discussion of emancipation prior to his issuance of the Proclamation, 5 COLLECTED WORKS, *supra* note 6, at 419-425. See, for his comments upon and reviews of the effects of the Proclamation, 6 *id.* at 192, 407-409, 423; 7 *id.* at 49-52, 281-82, 499-501, 506-507.

See, on emancipation generally and its legal consequences as well as on the Emancipation Proclamation itself, *Constitutional Problems Under Lincoln, supra* note 3, at chapters 15 and 16. "Back in Washington, meanwhile, Hay brought Lincoln a sampling of editorial opinion from the leading papers [on the Emancipation Proclamation], but Lincoln wasn't too interested in their comments. He'd studied the emancipation problem so long, he said, that he knew more about it than the papers did." OATES, *supra* note 2, at 321. See notes 16, 26, *infra.*

12. There are collected in the Appendix to the *United States Statutes* thirteen of Lincoln's proclamations prior to this one. I take my texts of the Preliminary Proclamation (of September 22, 1862) and of the Final Proclamation (of January 1, 1863), which together constitute the Emancipation Proclamation, from the Basler edition of 5 THE COLLECTED WORKS OF ABRAHAM LINCOLN, *supra* note 6, at 433-36; 6 *id.* at 28-30.

Both documents bear the superscription, "By the President of the United States: A Proclamation" (and their respective dates); both bear the signatures, "By the President: Abraham Lincoln/William H. Seward, Secretary of State."

The complete texts of the two documents are set forth, in order, in this commentary. These documents are the only quotations which are indented in the text of this commentary.

Earlier drafts of these two documents may be found in 5 *id.* at 336-37 (July 22, 1862); 6 *id.* at 23-26 (December 30, 1862). Lincoln usually referred to these documents, as I have in this commentary, as "the preliminary Emancipation Proclamation" and "the final Emancipation Proclamation." See, e.g., 6 *id.* at 186; 7 *id.* at 49. But, on one occasion at least, he referred to the Preliminary Proclamation as "the Summer Proclamation." 6 *id.* at 186.

13. 2 RANDALL, I, *supra* note 2, at 162. Cannot it be said that Lincoln skillfully marshalled all his forces, political as well as military, to put an effective yet just end to slavery (a "golden" objective) within the conventional ("silver") setting provided by the Constitution (and *its* underpinning, the Declaration of Independence)? See note 26, *infra.*

Consider the tribute paid the martyred President by two of his younger associates, "Fame is due Mr. Lincoln, not alone because he decreed emancipation, but because events so shaped themselves under his guidance as to render the conception practical and the decree successful. Among the agencies he employed none proved more admirable or more powerful than this two-edged sword of the final proclamation, blending sentiment with force, leaguing liberty with Union, filling the voting armies at home and the fighting armies in the field. In the light of history we can see that by this edict Mr. Lincoln gave slavery its vital thrust, its mortal wound." 6 NICOLAY AND HAY, *supra* note 9, at 437.

14. One need only read the youthful Lincoln's Temperance Speech to sense his lifelong concern about moral passion. 1 THE COLLECTED WORKS, *supra* note 6, at 271 (1842). See CRISIS OF THE HOUSE DIVIDED, *supra* note 7, at 233f. See also, the text at note 20, *infra.*

15. 2 MORSE, *supra* note 2, at 109.

16. The two "consent" qualifications are said to have been inserted in the Preliminary Proclamation at the suggestion of Seward. 5 COLLECTED WORKS, *supra* note 6, at 434n. "As the pro-slavery extremists utterly disregarded the humanity of the Negro, so did the abolitionists disregard utterly the element of consent required for the just acts of government. . . . What both disregarded was at bottom the same thing—the principle of equality." EQUALITY AND LIBERTY, *supra* note 7, at 167.

Consider, also, the element of consent, or "voluntarism," in Lincoln's efforts to persuade non-rebellious slavehodlers in the Middle States to sell their slaves to the United States before they were deprived of them. See 2 MORSE, *supra* note 2, at 22; EQUALITY AND LIBERTY, *supra* note 7, at 166. (On the Middle States, see the text at note 19, *infra.*) "In a sense, it is true that Lincoln never intended to emancipate the Negro: what he intended was to emancipate the American republic from the curse of slavery, a curse which lay upon both races and which, in different ways, enslaved them both." *Id.*

17. See RANDALL I, *supra* note 2, at 156-57, 159; FRANKLIN, *supra* note 2, x, 43-44, 46-47; OATES, *supra* note 2, at 311, 317-20.

It should be noticed, however, that Lincoln had issued, on July 25, 1862, a proclamation based on the Act of Congress (approved July 17, 1862), "An act to suppress insurrection, and to punish treason and rebellion, to seize and confiscate property of rebels, and for other purposes." 5 COLLECTED WORKS, *supra* note 6, at 341. (Parts of that act were later incorporated in the Preliminary Proclamation. See IV, v. *supra.*) Lincoln's proclamation of July 25, 1862 drew upon the first paragraph of his first draft, of July 22, 1862, of the Preliminary Emancipation Proclamation. 5 COLLECTED WORKS, *supra* note 6, at 336-37. The section of the Act of Congress relied upon by Lincoln in his Proclamation of July 25, 1862, "provided that property of persons in States in rebellion, who did not cease to give aid to the rebellion within sixty days after proclamation by the president, would be liable to seizure." 5 *id.* at 337. The Emancipation Proclamation of September 22, 1862 went much further than did either the draft proclamation of July 22, 1862 or the proclamation of July 25, 1862. (Thus, under the Emancipation Proclamation, all slaves in the areas designated were immediately affected, not just the "property of persons . . . who did not cease to give aid to the rebellion" and not just the property actually seized.) The issuance of the more sweeping Emancipation Proclamation may well have waited upon a Union victory to prepare the way for it.

But the sixtieth day from July 25 does happen to be September 22 (counting both days). Did Lincoln settle upon the September 22 date, once the victory of Antietan of September 17 had become available, in order to tie his Preliminary Proclamation (if that should later become necessary) to the sixty day interval provided by Congress in its Act of July 17 and keyed to his proclamation of July 25? See OWEN, *supra* note 2, at 157. See the quotation from Senator Douglas in the text at note 22, *infra*. See, also, 2 RANDALL I, *supra* note 2, at 186-87.

See, on the Confiscation Acts, 6 NICOLAY AND HAY, *supra* note 9, at 97-104, 151; 2 MORSE, *supra* note 2, at 14-15; CONSTITUTIONAL PROBLEMS UNDER LINCOLN, *supra* note 3, at 357-365; 2 RANDALL I¿ *supra* note 2, at 131; EQUALITY AND LIBERTY, *supra* note 7, at 142, 164-65; OATES, *supra* note 2, at 309-310.

18. The clerk had written in everything at the end of what is otherwise Lincoln's handwritten original of the Preliminary Proclamation (beginning at "In witness whereof"). 5 COLLECTED WORKS *supra* note 6, at 433, 436; FRANKLIN, *supra* note 2, at 56.

19. See 6 NICOLAY AND HAY, *supra* note 9, at 405, 416f; 2 MORSE, *supra* note 2 at 99-100.

Lincoln's letter of September 2, 1863 to the Secretary of the Treasury (Salmon P. Chase) continues, "Would not many of our friends shrink away appalled? Would it not lose us the elections, and with them, the very cause we seek to advance?" 6 COLLECTED WORKS, *supra* note 6, at 429. See the text at note 8, *supra*. See also, FRANKLIN, *supra* note 2, at 85-86; OATES, *supra* note 2, at 323. (A respect for the Constitution may be seen, we have noticed, in Lincoln's provision that the decisive indication that a State is not in rebellion is that it is properly represented in Congress. The republican form of government is thereby deferred to. See IV, iv, *infra*. See, also, Basler, ed., 6 COLLECTED WORKS, *supra* note 6, at 440; 7 *id.* at 50-52, 66, 476-77. Is not such deference to be seen as well in the uses throughout the Emancipation Proclamation of "people"?)

See, on the critical Middle States, 6 NICOLAY AND HAY, *supra* note 9, at 108f, 163, 167; 2 MORSE, *supra* note 2, at 3, 125-126; 2 RANDALL I, *supra* note 2, at 153.

20. See, for Garrison's "extremist" promise, DOCUMENTS OF UPHEAVAL: SELECTIONS FROM WILLIAM LLOYD GARRISON'S THE LIBERATOR, 1831-1865 at xiii, 1. (T. Nelson ed., 1966). Compare Ralph Waldo Emerson's November 1862 address, "The Emancipation," which includes these sentiments, "The extreme moderation with which the President advanced to his design—his long-avowed expectant policy, as if he chose to be strictly the executive of the best public sentiment of the country, waiting only till it should be unmistakably pronounced—so fair a mind that none ever listened so patiently to such extreme varieties of opinion—so reticent that his decision has taken all parties by surprise, whilst yet it is just the sequel of his prior acts—the firm tone in which he announces it, without inflation or suplasage—all these have bespoken such favor to the act that, great as the popularity of the President has been, we are beginning to think that we have underestimated the capacity and virtue which the Divine Providence has made an instrument of benefit so vast. He has been permitted to do more for America than any other American man. . . ." B. ATKINSON, THE SELECTED WRITINGS OF RALPH WALDO EMERSON 886 (1950). See the text at note 1, *supra*. See also, HUMAN BEING AND CITIZEN *supra* note 7, at 260, n. 3.

21. MATTHEWS 10: 16. "The law of nations is naturally founded on this principle, that different nations ought in time of peace to do one another all the good they can, and in time of war as little injury as possible, without prejudicing their real interests." MONTESQUIEU, THE SPIRIT OF LAWS, I, iii.

22. 3 COLLECTED WORKS, *supra* note 6, at 261. Compare, 3 *id.* at 249-250, 277, 279-281. See, on salutary concealments, PLATO, REPUBLIC 414E; THUCYDIDES, PELOPONNESIAN WAR, II, 65; 2 MORSE, *supra* note 2 at 209 ("Temporarily the great Republic was under a 'strong government,' and Mr. Lincoln was the strength. Though somewhat cloaked by forms, there was for a while in the United States a condition of 'one-man power,' and the people instinctively recognized it, though they would on no account admit it in plain words.")

23. 5 COLLECTED WORKS, *supra* note 6, at 358. "I never did ask more, nor ever was willing to accept less, than for all the States, and the people thereof, to take and hold their places, and their rights, in the Union, under the Constitution of the United States. For this alone have I felt authorized to struggle; and I seek neither more nor less now . . . After the commencement of hostilities I struggled nearly a year and a half to get along without touching the 'institution' [of slavery]; and when finally I conditionally determined to touch it, I gave a hundred days fair notice of my purpose, to all the States and people, within which time they could have turned it wholly aside, by simply again becoming good citizens of the United States. They chose to disregard it [the Preliminary Proclamation], and I made the peremptory proclamation [the Final Proclamation] on what appeared to me to be a military necessity. And being made, it must stand. . . ." 6 *id.* at 48-49 (January 8, 1863). See note 8, *supra*, note 26, *infra*.

24. AUSTIN, ARTEMUS WARD 107-08 (1964); See also, OATES, *supra* note 2, at 318-19; FRANKLIN, *supra* note 2, at ix, 47; 1 ABRAHAM LINCOLN, THE WAR YEARS, *supra* note 3, at 583; CHARNWOOD, *supra* note 1, at 324.

25. I take the complete text of "High-Handed Outrage at Utica" from THE COMPLETE WORKS OF ARTEMUS WARD (CHARLES FARRAR BROWNE) 36-37 (New York: G.W. Dillingham Co., 1898):

> In the Faul of 1856, I showed my show in Utiky, a trooly grate sitty in the State of New York.
>
> The people gave me a cordyal recepshun. The press was loud in her prases.
>
> 1 day as I was givin a descripshun of my Beests and Snaiks in my usual flowry stile what was my skorn disgust to see a big burly feller walk up to the cage containin my wax figgers of the Lord's Last Supper, and cease Judas Iscarrot by the feet and drag him out on the ground. He then commenced fur to pound him as hard as he cood.
>
> "What under the son are you abowt?" cried I.
>
> Sez he, "What did you bring this pussylanermus cuss here fur?" and he hit the wax figger another tremenjis blow on the hed.
>
> Sez I, "You egrejus ass, that air's a wax figger—a representashun of the false 'Postle.'"
>
> Sez he, "That's all very well for you to say, but I tell you, old man, that Judas Iscarrot can't show hisself in Utiky with impunerty by a darn site!" with which observashun he kaved in Judassis hed. The young man belonged to 1 of the first famerlies in Utiky. I sood him, and the Joory brawt in a verdick of Arson in the 3d degree.

The Artemus Ward volume includes a number of instructive pieces on slavery, Lincoln and the Civil War.

26. PROVERBS 25: 11. See M. MAIMONIDES, THE GUIDE OF THE PERPLEXED xl, 10-12 (1963). See, on self-conscious artistry (or poetry), IX, ix, *supra*.

The Emancipation Proclamation shows Lincoln as a lawyer able to use his skills in the best tradition of public service. An exhibition of what he does, why and how, is particularly salutary in the wake of the Watergate-induced skepticism about lawyers in public life. See note 22, *supra*. James A. Garfield who was then a Brigadier in the Union Army, wrote upon the issuance of the proclamation that it was a strange moment in world history "when a second-rate Illinois lawyer is the instrument to utter words which shall form an epoch memorable in all future ages." Sandburg, 2 ABRAHAM LINCOLN: THE WAR YEARS, supra *note 3, at 22*. See, on the American bar and especially the Illnois bar, the articles by Irving Dilliard and George Anastaplo in the "Justice Black Symposium," 9 Sw. U.L. REV. 953, 977 (1977). *See, also, Chicago Lawyer,* Feb 1, 1979, p. 7; NATIONAL L.J. 18 (Feb. 19, 1979).

Lincoln, aware that the Emancipation Proclamation was necessarily limited its scope and not without problems as to its authority, encouraged (in due time) the constitutional amendment with respect to slavery that his proclamation can be said to have prepared the way for. Thus, he announced on June 9, 1864, that he approved his party's "declaration in favor of so amending the Constitution as to prohibit slavery throughout the nation":

> When the people in revolt, with a hundred days of explicit notice, that they could, within those days, resume their allegiance, without the overthrow of their institution [of slavery], and that they could not so resume it afterwards, elected to stand out, such an amendment of the Constitution as is now proposed, became a fitting, and necessary conclusion to the final success of the Union cause. Such alone can meet and cover all cavils. Now, the unconditional Union men, North and South, perceive its importance, and embrace it. In the joint names of Liberty and Union, let us labor to give it legal form, and practical effect.

Basler, ed. 7 *Complete Works, supra* note 6, at 380. See, for the party platform on which he is commenting, *id.* at 381-382, 411. See also, notes 8, 11, *supra*.

A newspaper account of February 1, 1865 reports Lincoln's response to a serenade—a response which develops further his opinion on the relation between his great proclamation and what is now the Thirteenth Amendment:

> The President said he supposed the passage through Congress of the Constitutional amendment for the abolishment of Slavery throughout the United States, was the occasion to which he was indebted for the honor of this call. [Applause.] The occasion was one of congratulation to the country and to the whole world. But there is a task yet before us—to go forward and consummate by the votes of the States that which Congress so nobly began yesterday. [Applause and cries— "They will do it," & c.] He had the honor to inform those present that Illinois had already to-day done the work. [Applause.] Maryland was about half through; but he felt proud that Illinois was a

little ahead. He thought this measure was a very fitting if not an indispensable adjunct to the winding up of the great difficulty. He wished the reunion of all the States perfected and so effected as to remove all causes of disturbance in the future; and to attain this end it was necessary that the original disturbing cause should, if possible, be rooted out. He thought all would bear him witness that he never had shrunk from doing all that he could to eradicate Slavery by issuing an emancipation proclamation. [Applause.] But that proclamation falls far short of what the amendment will be when fully consummated. A question might be raised whether the proclamation was legally valid. It might be added that it only aided those who came into our lines and that it was inoperative as to those who did not give themselves up, or that it would have no effect upon the children of the slaves born hereafter. In fact it would be urged that it did not meet the evil. But this amendment is a King's cure for all the evils. [Applause.] It winds the whole thing up. He would repeat that it was the fitting if not indispensable adjunct to the consummation of the great game we are playing. He could not but congratulate all present, *himself*, the country and the whole world upon this great moral victory.

8 *id*. at 254-255 (emphasis added). Notice in Lincoln's response his continued use of "abolishment" (see IV, ii, *supra*) and the echoes from his Gettysburg Address. *See* note 13, *supra*. *See also* text at note 22, *supra*.

Change on the Supreme Court: An Instance Appraised
By Irving Dilliard[*]

Every change in the membership of the Supreme Court of the United States means inevitably that its future is certain to be at least somewhat different from its past. The extent of that difference will vary depending on who leaves our highest bench and who arrives as the replacement.

The departure from the Court of Justice William Orville Douglas[1] beyond any question closed an era. It took away the last survivor among President Franklin D. Roosevelt's nine appointees. Also, and of greater significance, it removed the jurist who had served longer[2] and more staunchly as exponent and defender of the people's constitutional liberties than any of his predecessors in the entire history of the Supreme Court.

Whatever the role that Justice John Paul Stevens (who was President Gerald R. Ford's only Supreme Court appointee) comes in time to fill, the Stevens contribution necessarily will be different from that of Justice Douglas. In the several terms since being sworn in,[3] Justice Stevens has given repeated indications that he does his own deliberating.[4] Even though the junior Justice may be strongly attached to the Bill of Rights, his affirmation will vary in one way or another from the historic place permanently identified with the more spirited third of a century of service to human liberty of Justice Douglas. Yet, the newest opportunity belongs to the newest Justice. Countless of his fellow citizens are reading his opinions and noting his position in the hope that he will make the fullest possible use of that opportunity. The need is clear.[5]

In view of the watershed that came with the retirement of Justice Douglas, now is an appropriate time to inform ourselves on how much of a change the filling of a vacancy can produce on the Supreme Court—on its outlook, its procedures, and its law. Although this has gone largely unmeasured, a striking double-instance is provided for us in relatively recent Supreme Court experience. Let us examine the facts and, in so far as we can, calculate some of the consequences.

The year is 1949. The Court is in summer recess. A full bench rose in June but that same bench of nine will not reconvene for a new term in October. For on July 19 comes the sad word that Justice Frank Murphy, a Roosevelt appointee from Michigan, has died suddenly. He is only fifty-nine years old and he has been a member of the Supreme Court barely more than nine years, beginning in 1940, as a successor to Justice Pierce Butler.[6]

This unexpected loss is hardly comprehended before there is the distressing news on September 10, 1949, of the death of Justice Wiley Blount Rutledge.[7] And Justice Rutledge *is* relatively young, a little more than fifty-five. He too is a Roosevelt choice, elevated from the United States Court of Appeals in Washington after law school service in Colorado, St. Louis, and Iowa. He has held for barely six years the seat vacated by Justice James Francis Byrnes in 1943.

*Ferris Professor Emeritus, Princeton University.

President Harry S. Truman loses little time in filling the two seats. For the place of Justice Murphy he nominates, from his Cabinet, Attorney General Thomas Campbell Clark of Texas. To the chair of Justice Rutledge the President elevates an old friend of the Senate years, Sherman Minton of Indiana. For Justice Minton it is a promotion from the United States Court of Appeals for the seventh circuit in Chicago.

The only way to begin to understand what the replacement of Justices Murphy and Rutledge by Justices Clark and Minton could mean is to look at the records that were being made by Justices Murphy and Rutledge when death closed their tenures so abruptly.

Since it is obviously impossible to canvass for this purpose the whole range of legal issues that confronted the Court in the 1940s, let us consider only cases in the Bill of Rights field. These come in an area that affords opportunity for disagreement arising from conflicting constitutional interpretations. They deal with the heart and soul of American democracy—free thought and free speech, free religion and free press, freedom to assemble and freedom to petition, due process and fair trial, right to counsel and right to remain silent, right to be secure in person and effects, protection against double jeopardy, and the right to the equal protection of the laws. The list of constitutional protections for the individual could be extended longer still.

The record shows that Justices Murphy and Rutledge were two of the most consistent supporters of human rights ever to serve on the Supreme Court. Had their tenures been two to three times longer this would have been made impressively plain.

We focus first on the *1946–47 term*.[8] This is the term in which President Truman's first and second appointees, Justice Harold Hitz Burton of Ohio and Chief Justice Frederick Moore Vinson of Kentucky,[9] sit together initially. Here is how the nine Justices in effect rank themselves by their stands in nonunanimous decisions arising from Bill of Rights issues:

TABLE I

Justice	For Right Invoked	Against Right Invoked
Rutledge	11	1
Murphy	10	1
Douglas	8	4
Black	8	4
Burton	3	9
Jackson	2	9
Frankfurter	2	10
Reed	2	10
Vinson	0	12

The positions of Justices Rutledge and Murphy are strikingly evident at the top of the table of bare statistics. But they take on far more meaning when we remember that the twelve cases include the *Harris* search and seizure case from Oklahoma,[10] the New Jersey school transportation case,[11] the Corpus Christi newspaper contempt case,[12] right-to-counsel cases from Illinois[13] and the *Adamson* case which upheld a California prosecuting attorney in his comment to a jury that the defendant had not taken the witness stand in his own defense[14]—a decision later expressly overruled.[15]

Now we turn to the *1947–48 term*. Outstanding in this term is the Vashti McCollum case involving a question of separation of church and state.[16] The term also brings racial discrimination cases[17] and still others in the Bill of Rights area that are arising in increasing numbers. This is the way the Justices in effect ranked themselves in the nonunanimous human liberties decisions for that term:

TABLE II

Justice	For Right Invoked	Against Right Invoked
Rutledge	26	1
Murphy	25	2
Douglas	23	4
Black	19	7
Frankfurter	12	15
Jackson	7	20
Burton	6	21
Vinson	6	21
Reed	4	23

Almost every time in a total of 27 nonunanimous decisions involving Bill of Rights claims, Justices Rutledge and Murphy were on the side of the citizen who invoked a constitutional guarantee against a unit of government or an official. Only two others came even close to them—Justices Douglas and Black. The five others took their stands against the claimed right, substantially more times than not.

This brings us to the last term in which Justices Murphy and Rutledge sat. It is the term that decides the highly controversial *Terminiello* free speech case by the narrow margin of 5 to 4.[18] Here is how the Justices stood in nonunanimous Bill of Rights cases in the *1948—49 term:*

TABLE III

Justice	For Right Invoked	Against Right Invoked
Murphy	18	0
Douglas	16	2
Rutledge	15	2
Black	12	6
Frankfurter	9	9
Jackson	5	12
Reed	2	16
Vinson	2	16
Burton	1	17

Although the rankings of the nine Justices vary little from term to term, their positions are established in a firm pattern when we merge the statistics for the three terms. Now we have a total of 57 cases in a three-year span. The result places Justices Murphy and Rutledge as preeminent in their concern for challenges under the Bill of Rights during the *1946—49 terms* combined:

TABLE IV

Justice	For Right Invoked	Against Right Invoked
Murphy	53	3
Rutledge	52	4
Douglas	47	10
Black	39	17
Frankfurter	23	34
Jackson	14	41
Burton	10	47
Reed	8	49
Vinson	8	49

With this the tenures of Justice Rutledge and Murphy are closed. Justices Clark and Minton join the two earlier Truman appointees, Burton and Vinson who are, as we do well to note, at the bottom of the rankings. The question for us is: How much of a change in the work of the Supreme Court in the Bill of Rights area did these changes among the Justices bring to constitutional interpretation and application? Necessarily, there is speculation here. Yet, as I view it, this speculation is without substantial risk.

Before we take up representative cases in the 1950s whose outcome turned on the substitution of Justices Clark and Minton for Justices Murphy and Rutledge, let us remind ourselves as to what the Murphy-Rutledge period was like in terms of the times and their directions, political and constitutional.[19] As we know, Truman was in the White House. By the mid-1940s World War II had ended, but under the impetus of the Man from Independence, the Cold War got off to a running start. The political climate lost little time in readying itself for Joseph R. McCarthy. The ex-Marine — misplaced in the La Follette Senate seat from Wisconsin in the same 1946 election that first sent Richard M. Nixon to the House of Representatives from California — had not yet come across the "Communist menace" which became his means to personal fame and national misfortune. Indeed, both Justices Rutledge and Murphy were gone from the scene when McCarthy began his 1950 Lincoln Day speaking trip at Wheeling, West Virginia, with a preview of what was to come.[20]

The fact is that McCarthy was a Joey-come-lately. He allowed much time to pass while others pressed along the line that he would later take over. By 1948, so much repressive legislation had been enacted and so many dubious investigations undertaken and wide-ranging blacklists promulgated, that John Lord O'Brian was moved to sound a clear warning. The warning was in the form of a *Harvard Law Review* article, "Loyalty Tests and Guilt by Association."[21] But warning it was nonetheless. The questions this most distinguished member of the bar of Washington put were sharp and challenging. And he put them not only to his profession with its special concern but to the whole of the country and its ultimate responsibility:

> How far, if at all, should we tolerate a policy of having our government officials build up, through secret investigations, these enormous numbers of secret dossiers dealing with the private lives of the people? For sound historical reasons the founding fathers dreaded above everything else secret activities in government operation. Must we take a different view? Is this aberration from the principles guaranteeing the privacy of the individual justified by any substantial proved facts? May not all of this agitation turn

out, as after the first World War, to be an unreasonable and unworthy result of emotional instability?[22]

The immediate post-World War II period was characterized by the patently political indictment of the twelve Communist leaders under the Smith Act in the Truman-Dewey election year of 1948. Above it all stood the Supreme Court; above and apart, because the Supreme Court in the 1940s was holding the line for constitutional liberties. For if the House Un-American Activities Committee was gaining the headlines, the Supreme Court did not hesitate to discipline that Committee in words no one could mistake. To cite by name one noteworthy adherence to historic constitutional principle, the Supreme Court, with Justices Murphy and Rutledge participating, declared a congressional act invalid as a bill of attainder in its application to proscribed government employees, Robert Morss Lovett, Goodwin B. Watson, and William E. Dodd, Jr. (*U.S. v. Lovett,* 1946).

This in essence suggests the highest judicial outlook through the 1940s cases involving the liberties and rights of the American people. Sometimes the Supreme Court was unanimous; sometimes it was divided. On the whole the Bill of Rights fared exceedingly well. And Justices Murphy and Rutledge, as our tables showed, led all their colleagues in devotion to the basic guarantees of the First Ten Amendments. When the highest bench assembled for its 1949–50 term, an era had closed; another had begun. It would not take long for that to be demonstrated. For my findings lead me to the conclusion, for what it may be worth, that many important cases in the 1950s that were decided against the invocation of the Bill of Rights would have gone the other way, that is, in support of constitutional protections, had Justices Murphy and Rutledge continued in their seats through those years.

Let us begin with the unusually interesting case of *United States v. Alpers* (1950).[23] Alexander Alpers was convicted in a Federal District Court in California for the interstate shipment of phonograph records "of indecent character." The case raised the question whether Congress meant to include phonograph records when it banned interstate shipment of "indecent books, pictures and films." The Supreme Court in effect answered "yes" and upheld the conviction, 5 to 3. The majority consisted of Minton, Vinson, Reed, Burton, and Clark. The minority took the position that courts should exert utmost care in construing an act of Congress when censorship resulted. Holding to this view and opposing the conviction were Black, Frankfurter, and Jackson. Had Murphy and Rutledge been on the bench and voted with the three dissenters—as they most surely would have done—the censorship decision would have been reversed, 5 to 3. It then would have been the responsibility of Congress to clarify the uncertain point.

One such case follows closely on another in the 1950s. All bear the fuller attention that resort to the *Supreme Court Reports* makes readily possible. Here are a few in summary form:

Breard v. Alexandria (1951).[24] Jack H. Breard was convicted in Louisiana of violating an ordinance prohibiting house-to-house canvassing without having been invited to make the call. He contended that his due process and freedom of the press rights were violated. Conviction upheld, 6 to 3. Majority: Reed, Frankfurter, Jackson, Burton, Clark, and Minton. Minority: Vinson, Black, and Douglas. Had Murphy and Rutledge participated the Bill of Rights invocation would have been upheld, 5 to 4.

Garner v. Board of Public Works (1951).[25] Ray H. Garner asked reinstatement after discharge by the City of Los Angeles for objecting to a loyalty oath as a condition to public employment. He contended that a series of basic rights were violated. Relief denied, 5 to 4. Majority: Clark, Vinson, Reed, Jackson, and Minton. Minority: Black, Frankfurter, Douglas, and Burton. Participation of Rutledge and Murphy would have sustained the constitutional rights of the discharged employee, 6 to 3.

Adler v. Board of Education (1952).[26] Irving Adler and fellow teachers challenged the Feinberg Act which disqualified from the New York schools any person teaching or advocating the overthrow of the government. The argument against the law was not in support of violent overthrow, but in behalf of freedom of speech. Statute upheld, 6 to 3. Majority: Minton, Vinson, Reed, Jackson, Burton, and Clark. Minority: Black, Frankfurter, and Douglas. Participation of Murphy and Rutledge would have supported the protesting school employees in their First Amendment stand, 5 to 4.

Sacher v. United States (1952).[27] Harry Sacher and other lawyers who defended the eleven Communist leaders in the *Dennis*[28] case were held in criminal contempt by Federal District Court Judge Medina in New York. The contempt order and jail terms were upheld, 5 to 3. Majority: Jackson, Vinson, Reed, Burton, and Minton. Minority: Black, Frankfurter, and Douglas. Participation of Murphy and Rutledge would have called for a fuller measure of fairness for the cited counsel, 5 to 4.

Beauharnais v. Illinois (1952).[29] Joseph Beauharnais was convicted in Chicago for passing out racist leaflets. Although it was argued that there was "no present danger," that the statute was ambiguous and that his right of free speech was violated, the conviction was upheld, 5 to 4. Majority: Frankfurter, Vinson, Burton, Clark, and Minton. Minority: Black, Reed, Douglas, and Jackson. Participation of Murphy and Rutledge would have upheld the Bill of Rights, 6 to 3.

Shaughnessy v. United States (1953).[30] Ignatz Mezei, resident alien, was the victim of one of the worst injustices in American history. Because he left the United States to visit a sick mother in Romania, he became a near permanent resident of Ellis Island, kept from his home and wife in Buffalo, New York. Lower Federal Courts supported Mezei's application for a writ of habeas corpus, but were reversed, 5 to 4. Majority: Clark, Vinson, Reed, Burton, and Minton. Minority: Black, Frankfurter, Douglas, and Jackson. The facts in the *Mezei* case would have angered Murphy and Rutledge. Their participation would have guaranteed due process of law, 6 to 3.

Irvine v. California (1954).[31] Because Patrick E. Irvine was suspected of illegal bookmaking, police broke into his Long Beach, California home. They rigged the hall with a listening device that transmitted to a neighbor's garage. On a second entry the microphone was moved to a concealed place in the bedroom, and on a third invasion to a closet where it stayed until its mission was "accomplished." This shocking police misconduct, though severely criticized, was upheld, 5 to 4. Majority: Jackson, Warren, Reed, Minton, and Clark. Minority: Black, Frankfurter, Douglas, and Burton. Murphy and Rutledge would have been outraged by such lawlessness by police. Their participation would have rejected any part of it, 6 to 3.

Barenblatt v. United States (1959).[32] Lloyd Barenblatt, Vassar College psychology teacher, refused on First Amendment privacy grounds to answer political questions put to him by the House Un-American Activities Committee. He expressly disclaimed reliance on the Fifth Amendment. His conviction was upheld, 5 to 4. Majority: Harlan, Frankfurter, Clark, Whittaker, and Stewart. Minority: Black, Warren, Douglas, and Brennan. With Justice Brennan now in the seat of Minton by appointment of President Eisenhower in 1956, the Bill of Rights stand of Justice Rutledge is in effect restored. Thus had Murphy been in his seat instead of Clark when *Barenblatt* was decided, Barenblatt's invocation of the First Amendment would have been sustained, 5 to 4. The so-called "balancing" precedent that Justice Harlan advocated with respect to constitutional rights would not have been written into our Supreme Court law in *Barenblatt*.

Uphaus v. Wyman (1960).[33] Dr. Willard Uphaus spent his seventieth year in jail because, though he answered questions about himself, he would not give up the guest list of his World Fellowship camp in New Hampshire. He said that he would not "bear false witness against his neighbor," since the hidden purpose was to harass and embarrass those who had registered at the camp. State Attorney General Louis C. Wyman found Uphaus in contempt of an authorized investigation. The conviction was upheld, 5 to 4. Majority: Clark, Frankfurter, Harlan, Whittaker, and Stewart. Minority: Brennan, Warren, Black, and Douglas. With Brennan in effect casting the Rutledge vote, participation by Murphy in place of Clark would have made the decision 5 to 4 against sending that kindly, moral teacher to jail for a year. Thus our constitutional law would have been spared one of its least excusable blows.

Wilkinson v. United States (1961)[34] and *Braden v. United States* (1961).[35] Frank Wilkinson and Carl Braden were declared in contempt of the House Un-American Activities Committee for refusing to answer questions about their political views and personal associations. Notwithstanding their reliance on the Supreme Court's decision in *Watkins v. United States* (1957),[36] the contempt citations were upheld, 5 to 4. Majority: Stewart, Frankfurter, Clark, Harlan, and Whittaker. Minority: Black, Warren, Douglas, and Brennan. Participation by Murphy would have produced 5 to 4 decisions for the constitutional rights of Frank Wilkinson and Carl Braden.

In re Anastaplo (1961).[37] George Anastaplo, a World War II army air corps navigator, passed the examination for admission to the Illinois bar even before he was graduated from the University of Chicago law school. But he was not certified by the Bar's Committee on Character and Fitness. He had declined to say whether he believed in "a Supreme Being" and to answer questions about his political views, "the right of revolution," and so-called subversive organizations. His position was that such questions violated the Constitution; he therefore refused to compromise. He appealed to the Illinois Supreme Court and was rejected, 4 to 3. He lost in the United States Supreme Court, 5 to 4. Majority: Harlan, Frankfurter, Clark, Whittaker, and Stewart. Minority: Black, Warren, Douglas, and Brennan. Participation of Murphy would have produced a 5 to 4 decision for the Bill of Rights and George Anastaplo would have been an ennobling member of the bar for the last quarter century.

These dozen cases easily could be increased. The larger number would only underscore what the cited ones show—that the presence of Clark and Minton where Murphy and Rutledge had been, changed the course of our constitutional law, at high cost to the Bill of Rights. But someone asks: How do you know that Murphy and Rutledge always would have voted as you say? How do you know that one or the other might not have been concerned with a procedural point upon occasion and so not have reached the question of a basic liberty?[38]

The answer is: I do not know—for a certainty. But look again at Table IV which merges the statistics for the final three terms during which Murphy and Rutledge sat. It shows them leading Black and Douglas by generous margins in support of invoked Bill of Rights guarantees. If that was their record in the 1940s there is no plausible reason whatever to believe that their support for constitutional freedoms would have been any the less through the 1950s and the 1960s.

Yet another asks: Are you not being unfair to Justices Clark and Minton? Are you not ignoring the times when they were on the side of the Bill of Rights? What about Justice Clark's opinion for the Court in the New York City censorship case concerning "The Miracle," which extended the First Amendment's protection of freedom to motion pictures for the first time.[39] What about his opinion for the Court in *Mapp v. Ohio*[40] that reversed the search precedent of *Wolf v. Colorado*?[41] What about Justice Minton's majority opinion invalidating racially restricted covenants in California?[42] What about a series of decisions in the early 1950s in which Justices Clark and Minton joined in upholding constitutional rights?[43]

My answer is simple; and, so I think, wholly in order. I distinguish between unanimous decisions and those in which the Justices split narrowly 5 to 4 or 6 to 3. The Court was unanimous in the moving picture censorship case. It was unanimous in many of the cases just cited, including *Sweatt v. Painter*,[44] and *Niemotko v. Maryland*.[56] For Justices Clark and Minton to support Chief Justice Vinson in these cases when all the other Justices were with him was an easy thing to do. For them to have broken from the stand of fellow Truman appointees Vinson and Burton in nonunanimous Bill of Rights cases, to join Black and Douglas to make a narrow 5 to 4 or possibly a close majority for an invoked constitutional right, would have been something far different. Thus it is not enough to know where Justices Clark and Minton were. We need to know *with whom* they were.

Had Justices Murphy and Rutledge continued in their places, the momentous decision in *Dennis v. United States* (1951)[46] might well have gone the other way. *Dennis* was the case in which the conviction of eleven Communist leaders was upheld, 6 to 2—Justice Clark not participating since he had been Attorney General at the time of the arrests. Justices Black and Douglas comprised the small but strongly vocal minority. The votes of Justices Rutledge and Murphy would have made the division 5 to 4 and that would have seriously undercut the force of the ruling. The narrow majority would have been Vinson, Reed, Frankfurter, Jackson, and Burton. It is not at all unthinkable that some one among those five would have joined Black, Douglas, Murphy, and Rutledge to produce a 5 to 4 majority for the freedoms of thought, speech and press, involved in *Dennis*. When the scales are closely balanced in numbers, they may tip either way.

There was still another undermining of the Bill of Rights, and though almost unseen perhaps it was even greater than that which was seen. As long as Justices Murphy and Rutledge were with Justices Black and Douglas, the four of them, under Supreme Court procedure, could require the Court to take for argument and probable decision, on certiorari, cases that the four believed important. With the loss of Murphy and Rutledge in 1949, that phalanx of four no longer existed.[47] A necessary consequence was that many cases carried to the Supreme Court were rejected and hence never heard. That situation cut heavily into the work of the Supreme Court as a tribunal of last resort for citizens who held that their constitutional rights had been violated. It remained largely so until the appointments of Chief Justice Warren and Justice Brennan again brought support to Justices Black and Douglas.

What it cost Bill of Rights' advocates to lose Justices Rutledge and Murphy becomes more evident when we look at the succeeding Justices in the 1950s and 1960s. For then we note that Justice Minton was succeeded by Justice William J. Brennan of New Jersey[48] in 1956 and that Justice Clark was succeeded by Justice Thurgood Marshall of New York in 1967.[49] Since Justices Brennan and Marshall have stood firmly for basic rights provisions throughout their respective services, the Clark-Minton tenures appear almost as gaps between the tenures of Justices Murphy and Rutledge in the 1940s and those of Justices Brennan and Marshall that continue to this day.

And so now three decades after that double blow in 1949, let us join in grateful remembrance of Frank Murphy and Wiley Rutledge. If ever Supreme Court deaths were untimely, theirs were!

One final word. Since Justice Douglas has retired and has been replaced, and that not long after the retirement and death in 1971 of his liberty-loving colleague of three decades plus, Justice Hugo LaFayette Black,[50] we can only wonder what later changes will bring in constitutional trends. Wonder, yes, and work and pray that our precious liberties will not be further eroded as the United States of America moves into our third century.

Notes

1. November 12, 1975.
2. Justice Douglas' total service was 36 years 6 months and 25 days.
3. December 19, 1975.
4. *See, e.g.,* Young v. American Mini Theaters, 427 U.S. 50 (1976); Gardner v. Florida, 430 U.S. 349 (1977).
5. *See, e.g.,* Paul v. Davis, 424 U.S. 693 (1976); Andresen v. Maryland, 427 U.S. 463 (1976); Stone v. Powell, 428 U.S. 465 (1976).
6. For a more current review of Justice Murphy's service, *see* Kerr, *The Neglected Opinions of Mr. Justice Murphy,* 1977 DET. C. L. REV. 1.
7. THE DICTIONARY OF AMERICAN BIOGRAPHY 712 (Supp. 4, 1974) contains an excellent summary of the service of Justice Rutledge by Ralph F. Fuchs. There is a similar appraisal of Justice Murphy in the same volume by Sidney Fine, *id.* at 610.
8. *Compare* my "Truman Reshapes the Supreme Court," 184 *Atlantic Monthly* 30 (Dec. 1949), with Mark DeWolfe Howe's "Justice in a Democracy," *id.* at 34. "Box score" tables in this article were developed from statistics compiled by John P. Frank in successive annual articles on the work of the United States Supreme Court in the *University of Chicago Law Review,* as follows, beginning with the 1946–47 term: 15 U. CHI. L. REV. 1; 16 U. CHI. L. REV. 1 (1948); 17 U. CHI. L. REV. 1 (1949). Frank's Table No. 3 in the third of these articles, 17 U. CHI. L. REV. at 36, assembles the positions of the nine Justices in the nonunanimous civil rights and liberties cases in the three terms preceding the deaths of Justices Murphy and Rutledge.
9. THE DICTIONARY OF AMERICAN BIOGRAPHY 711 (Supp. 5. 1977) presents a fair, well-balanced article on Chief Justice Vinson by Paul L. Murphy and James McCarthy.
10. Harris v. U.S., 331 U.S. 145 (1947).
11. Everson v. Bd. of Educ., 330 U.S. 1 (1947).
12. Craig v. Harney, 331 U.S. 367 (1947).
13. Foster and Payne v. Illinois, 332 U.S. 134 (1947).
14. Adamson v. California, 332 U.S. 46 (1947).
15. *See* Malloy v. Hogan, 378 U.S. 1 (1964).
16. McCollum v. Bd. of Educ., 333 U.S. 203 (1948).
17. Barrows v. Jackson, 346 U.S. 249 (1953).
18. Terminiello v. Chicago, 337 U.S. 1 (1949).
19. For the role of the White House in the political climate of the 1940s, *see* B. COCHRAN, HARRY TRUMAN AND THE CRISIS PRESIDENCY (1973); A. Westin & T. Hayden, *Presidents and Civil Liberties from FDR to Ford: A Rating by 64 Experts,* THE CIVIL LIBERTIES REVIEW, Oct.–Nov., 1976, at 9.
20. *See* D. CAUTE, THE GREAT FEAR: THE ANTI-COMMUNIST PURGE UNDER TRUMAN AND EISENHOWER (1978); FRED J. COOK, THE NIGHTMARE DECADE: THE LIFE AND TIMES OF SENATOR JOE MCCARTHY (1971); JACK ANDERSON AND RONALD W. MAY, MCCARTHY: THE MAN, THE SENATOR, THE "ISM" (1952); WISCONSIN CITIZENS COMMITTEE ON MCCARTHY'S RECORD, THE MCCARTHY RECORD (1952).
21. O'Brian, *Loyalty Tests and Guilt by Association,* 61 HARV. L. REV. 592 (1948).
22. *Id.* at 610.
23. 338 U.S. 680 (1950).
24. 341 U.S. 622 (1951).
25. 341 U.S. 716 (1951).
26. 342 U.S. 485 (1952).
27. 343 U.S. 1 (1952).
28. Dennis v. United States, 341 U.S. 494 (1951).
29. 343 U.S. 250 (1952).
30. 345 U.S. 206 (1953).
31. 347 U.S. 128 (1954).
32. 360 U.S. 109 (1959).
33. 364 U.S. 388 (1960).
34. 365 U.S. 399 (1961).
35. 365 U.S. 431 (1961).
36. 354 U.S. 178 (1957).
37. 366 U.S. 82 (1961). The Illinois Supreme Court decision, with its blistering dissent by Justice George Washington Bristow appears in 18 Ill. 2d 182 (1959). *See also* ANASTAPLO, THE CONSTITUTIONALIST: NOTES ON THE FIRST AMENDMENT (1971); ANASTAPLO, HUMAN BEING AND CITIZEN: ESSAYS ON VIRTUE, FREEDOM AND THE COMMON GOOD (1975); Dilliard, *Mr. Justice Black and In re Anastaplo,* 9 SW. U.L. REV. 953 (1977). Of course, much of the same holds true for the 5–4 decision in Konigsberg v. State Bar of California, 366

U.S. (1961); *see* Collins, *Battling the Bar: Victory after Twenty-five Years*, L.A. Times, May 15, 1978, Pt. 2, p. 7, col. 1.

38. John P. Frank provides a sound caution when he notes that the placing of a case on one side or the other "is not an expression of the wisdom or legal rightness of the position." It may be, as he says, without regard to the preoccupation of a particular Justice with a procedural matter, as for example, Chief Justice Vinson in *Terminiello*. Frank, *The United States Supreme Court: 1946–47*, 15 U. CHI. L. REV. (1947).

39. *See* Burstyn v. Wilson, 343 U.S. 495 (1952).

40. 367 U.S. 643 (1961).

41. 338 U.S. 25 (1949).

42. *See* Barrows v. Jackson, 346 U.S. 249 (1953).

43. *See* Cassell v. Texas, 339 U.S. 282 (1950); Sweatt v. Painter, 339 U.S. 629 (1950); McLaurin v. Oklahoma, 339 U.S. 637 (1950); Niemotko v. Maryland, 340 U.S. 268 (1951); Rochin v. California, 342 U.S. 165 (1952); Day Brite Co. v. Missouri, 342 U.S. 421 (1952); Weiman v. Updegraff, 344 U.S. 183 (1952); Avery v. Georgia, 345 U.S. 559 (1953); Barrows v. Jackson, 346 U.S. 249 (1953).

44. 339 U.S. 629 (1950).

45. 340 U.S. 268 (1951).

46. 341 U.S. 494 (1951).

47. The *St. Louis Post-Dispatch* in an editorial entitled, "Something to Watch," (Oct. 23, 1949), called attention to this development and its probable consequences. A year later Fowler V. Harper and Alan S. Rosenthal of the Yale Law School documented the results in their article, *What the Supreme Court Did Not Do in the 1949 Term*, 99 U. PA. L. REV. 293 (1950). They gave chapter and verse on appeals declined by the Supreme Court.

48. Justice Brennan was appointed by President Eisenhower.

49. Justice Marshall was appointed by President Johnson.

50. For some more recent and worthwhile commentaries on the life and philosophy of Justice Black, *see* G. DUNNE, HUGO BLACK AND THE JUDICIAL REVOLUTION (1977); Frank, *Hugo L. Black: Free Speech and the Declaration of Independence*, 1977 U. ILL. L. FOR. 577; *Justice Hugo L. Black: A Symposium*, 9 SW. U.L. REV. 845–1155 (1977).

Four Ways of Looking at the Court—
And a Fifth
BY MAX LERNER*

Speaking to a class of law students at Brown University, Justice Holmes said, "your business as thinkers is to . . . show the rational connection between your fact and the frame of the universe."[1] That is still our business as thinkers. However, in talking of the perspectives of constitutional law, it is not the Holmesian global frame I have in mind but the frame of American civilization.

There have been a number of models for our perception of the Constitution and Court in history. One is the *determinist* model. It sees constitutional history as moving in stages which are determined by—and in turn determine—the changes occurring in society. It tries to explain the problems these changes present to the Court, and the ways by which the Court copes with them, by a developmental model of the economy and society.[2]

In the late 1920s and through the '30s and early '40s my approach to constitutional history was an effort to adapt a largely determinist historical model to my own vision both of law and of history and society. I called my first sustained study of the history of constitutional decisions, "The Supreme Court and American Capitalism."[3] While I wouldn't write it the same way now, I feel it was useful as well as provocative for its time. The model itself has some value, provided it doesn't become reductionist and mechanical but is used with some sense of complexity. Its strength lies in compelling us to probe deeply into the dynamics of historical change and the relations between law, class, and power. Its dangers lie in simplifying and distorting the flow of relationship and causality in history and society.

When I wrote my essay I was even more deeply under the influence of Thorstein Veblen and Charles A. Beard than of Marx and his successors, and I owed much also to Frederick W. Maitland's capacious view of English legal history and his insight that it was largely a gloss on the history of property relations. Their influence kept me from stumbling more than I did and saved me from much of the stultifying dogma and jargon that Marxist determinism usually carries with it.

I must add that any developmental scheme, whether Marxist or any other, is best when it is used as macromethod rather than micromethod. Its value lies in leading to novel relationships and periodizations in the Court's history, and thus in shedding a hard and fresh light on the power context tying together sequences of cases. It is better there than it is in explaining a particular case or doctrine or the delicate fabric of interactions between the minds of the Justices in any given Court.[4]

The second model of the perception theme is broadly the *behavioral,* or *structural-functional* model. It considers the lawmakers who make laws, the judges who sit on cases, the lawyers who argue them, the Presidents who appoint the judges, and the rest of us who respond to all this, as human animals whose functions and behavior—within a structural frame of institutional and social change—can be studied with some precision.

Actually, this is a sprawling model which has gone through several successive phases, under shifting names of schools, without being subjected to an adequately exacting critical

* Distinguished Professor of Human Behavior, Graduate School of Human Behavior, U.S. International University, San Diego, California; Columnist, New York Post.

analysis. At the start of the century it was broadly called "sociological" when sociology was a convenient umbrella term for all the approaches that were not narrowly legal. It got much of its strength less from its own merits than from the pervasive "revolt against formalism" which hit every social discipline in the early decades of the century.

As legal thinkers began to explore psychology, anthropology, and politics there emerged a school of "legal realism," notably with the work of Karl Llewellyn, Jerome Frank, and Thurman Arnold, which prided itself on being antinormative and antimoralist, and on seeing through the myths and obfuscations with which law had been invested. The legal realists also set themselves against the mystical elements in both "natural law" and the idea of a "higher law."

This was a trend in legal thinking better defined by what it was *against* than by what it was *for,* and the vigor of its champions was thus largely critical, getting much of its impetus from British and American empirical philosophy. As it developed into the middle decades of the century it picked up strains from two other directions: (1) from *structural-functional* theory which asked where the legal cases and decisions fitted into the structure of the society and what functions the legal disciplines and doctrines performed, and (2) from *social-interest* and *conflict-and-equilibrium* theory, which tried to locate the cases and decisions in the conflict and balancing of social interests. It was also deeply influenced by the attitude studies and statistical models of the social psychology of the 1940s-1960s, and by the "behavioral" school of political theory—from Charles Merriam and Harold Lasswell to Robert Dahl and David Easton.

My third model is the *psychological* model which has come down largely from the Freudian model—through Jerome Frank, Harold Lasswell and their followers—and which will inevitably emerge in the psycho-biographical and psycho-historical approach to judicial decision-making.

It goes back of course to those weekly evening meetings of Freud and his "Vienna Circle"[5] at which they tried to develop a method of studying creative leaders, especially great writers and artists. Freud applied it first to Leonardo da Vinci and Dostoevsky, then to a great lawgiver, Moses, and late in his life (and wretchedly) to Woodrow Wilson.[6] While there have been a number of recent psycho-historical studies of American Presidents,[7] there have thus far been none of Supreme Court Justices. It is not that they possess an unusual degree of psychological normality, or offer fewer difficulties in the relation between their developmental life-course and their work, but that they have come less into the area of controversy than the Presidents. Yet in any contextual study of judicial decision-making, and in the very pragmatic tasks of brief-writing and Court argument, the psychological and psycho-historical model is bound to take on importance.

In a system of case law, with a Supreme Court perched at the tip of a pyramidal judicial structure, the real intellectual storms are bound to swirl around the screening and selective processes in the minds of the Justices. Thus my fourth model—actually a pair—must be the *positivist-activist* model of those who feel that judges do (and should) play an active role in projecting their own values toward positive social goals, and the *neutralist-restraint* model of those who feel that judicial neutrality and values restraint are best and should be earnestly striven for.

The positivist-activist model goes back historically to the sociological school of the 1910s when it was fighting a rearguard action against a deeply conservative Court majority entrenched behind the doctrinal fortress of judicial review, sanctity of contracts, freedom of contract, due process, and the "higher law." The school became "Realist" when it sought to strip away the formal rhetoric which masked the Court's interventionism in the policy-making process.

The Realists, however, failed to recognize that the vanguard of liberal Justices—Brandeis, Black, Douglas, Murphy, Rutledge, Fortas, Goldberg, Warren—were as deeply interventionist as the conservative majority had been, although in a different direction and with a different animus. They were also positivist in their values approach to the cases. "Positivist" is a treacherous term with multiple meanings, including the stern emphasis on law as proceeding from a single sovereignty, from Thomas Hobbes and John Austin to their modern followers. I use it here in a different sense—that of August Comte and his social engineering school, at once meliorist, scientific, empiricist, and perfectionist. The liberal jurists have believed broadly in law as a way of human betterment, in progress through the intervention of the sovereign judicial authority, and in the essential perfectibility both of man and society.

The neutralist-restraint model is at once Jeffersonian and Burkean. It is Jeffersonian in terms of his scepticism of the judicial and his preference for the legislative role in social change. It is Burkean in terms of Burke's concern for historical continuities in society, and his sense of the fragile and vulnerable nature of the social organism.

Justice Holmes had this combination in him of Jefferson and Burke, and of the neutralist and restraint elements, and (along with his sense of life as risk and gamble) it explains more of his thought than other approaches. So did Justice Frankfurter, who tended toward the positivist-activist in his early Brandeisian phase but shifted with the Holmes influence and with the later impact of Hitler's advent to power and World War II. Justice Jackson had it, and also the younger Justice Harlan. Among constitutional scholars one finds it in the writings of Herbert Wechsler, Philip Kurland, Alexander Bickel, and Raoul Berger.

The war between these two viewpoints intersects with a broader war raging through all the human sciences, between a values-free and a values-bound discipline. I shall be commenting below on how both approaches have operated in recent constitutional history, especially in the periods of the Roosevelt and Warren Courts.

In this confrontation about values the activists tend to see law as values-bound, since it expresses the changing values of the society and therefore of judges as members of it. Some, like Justices Douglas and Warren, were largely willing to accept their own values orientation as a factor in their decisions. Others, notably Justice Black, refused to admit it, perhaps even to themselves. Black insisted that the literal language of the Constitution, especially the Bill of Rights, was a clear enough guide to decision-making. His literalism was on a level with his Populism, with a quality of the one-dimensional and reductionist. But both were only the integument of a passionate critical intelligence which in turn was at the service of his values.

The neutralists may themselves tend toward varying political philosophies—liberal, conservative, centrist—but they agree on trying to squeeze values as far as possible out of the law as an operative discipline. Unlike the "values-free" movement in most of the other human sciences, their allegiance is not toward some vision of law as approaching the precision of the "hard" sciences. They feel instead that the law, basically concerned with *ordering* a society, needs therefore to be free of the arbitrary element of the judge's own personal values, admirable though they may be as an expression of his vision of life.

Thus, behind the differences in rhetoric and method between the two schools, there are real differences about the nature of the polity and the role of judges. They are the difference between stressing change and stressing continuity in the polity, and the difference between seeing judges as agents of social change and seeing them as arbiters who must subordinate their own all-too-human values to the values-free imperative imbedded in the very heart of the judicial process.

In my own view no judge can be wholly values-free in his decision-making since absolute detachment is unattainable. But each of us—whether judge or commentator—would do well to make a heroic effort at being aware of his values bias, taking account of it, and striving to minimize it.[8]

This personal note will serve to introduce a fifth and final model—one that has not yet emerged but about which I feel strongly, and which expresses my own approaches and embodies a number of the currents of thought and feeling of our time. I call it once *contextual, organismic,* and *integrative.*

Constitutional history is in large part institutional history, but even more it is intellectual history—the history of concepts, doctrines, ideas, attitudes, and myths, social and intellectual environments, and above all, of soils and *climates.* Every case worth intensive study contextually is imbedded in—and gets its nourishment from—the *soil of the culture* and the *climate of the society.* The cultural soil contains the roots of belief and the ways of life of everyone involved in a case, from the original principals to the Supreme Court Justices. The social climate, whether that of institutions or of thought and opinion, conditions the ways in which a new constitutional doctrine emerges, and an old one grows obsolescent and is replaced, the ways in which a case is presented to the courts, is accepted, is argued and decided, is fought over in the law journals and the popular media, and becomes part of the life of institutions and the thinking of people.

Just as Chief Justice Marshall and Justice Story lived and worked and had their being in the Enlightenment climate that Professor Commager (among others) has charted to us,[9] so too there were those extraordinary two decades at the turn of the 20th century which we must count as a second American intellectual renaissance.[10] Much of the intellectual history of those decades may be summed up as an effort to break out of the straitjacket of mechanical thinking.

This was true of each of the three great Justices—Holmes, Brandeis, and Cardozo— whose thinking was for most of us "touched with fire."[11] I venture some personal memories of all three and trust they will not be out of place here. I was a freshman at Yale when Judge Benjamin Cardozo delivered his historic lectures there on "The Nature of the Judicial Process."[12] I was impressed, moved, baffled—but never got over it. I had watched an episode in a play whose plot I was ignorant of, and it would be at least another decade before I caught up with it, and came to understand what Cardozo was talking about when he spoke so elegantly of the delicate ways in which a judge had to discriminate between the inner and outer urgencies of the task he was engaged in, in order to balance continuity of legal experience and doctrine with the need for change in the society.

In the mid-1920s, when I was a graduate student in Washington, Justice Brandeis would invite several of us to his Sunday afternoons at home. It was not the Brandeis of the "Brandeis briefs" who talked to us, and of the opinions heavily documented with statistics about social actuality. It was the Brandeis who spoke of Pericles and the Greek city-state, of Palestine and the Hebrew prophets, of Jefferson and the early compassable American Republic, and of the conditions that made for creativity in each. I got a hint of the personal and social passion which—if you knew how to recognize it—somehow broke through the screen of detachment and statistics he had built against it.[13]

Adjoining our graduate school was Justice Holmes' house. I used to wait, often toward noon, until he emerged on the arm of his law secretary for his daily "constitutional." Since then both buildings have been torn down, but much in Holmes' thought has endured. We miss a good deal about him by stressing only the anti-formalist theme—that "the life of the law is not logic; it is experience." That made him speak of the "felt needs" of the time, and made him cut the knot of the activist-neutralist problem by saying that it was not unreasonable for a legislator to take account of those needs.[14]

But what counted for him even more was struggle and risk. He saw struggle in the whole evolutionary process, in war itself, in the competition of ideas. He saw risk-taking in all social experiments, not only in the "insulated chambers of the states" but in the Constitution itself which—he said—"is an experiment, as all life is an experiment." He saw law less as contract than as wager, in which a potential infringer bets on what will or won't happen to him—the "hypostasis of a prophecy." It was a mixture of Darwin, William James, his own "can't helps" of belief, and a considerable mystique about what was enduring and prevailing in the Constitution and the Nation, as in human life as a whole.

After the arid 1920s the New Deal period was one of intense constitutional crisis when, as in the Civil War, there was a real question of whether the polity itself could survive. Franklin Roosevelt had great success in carrying the people with him in an eco-political crusade against the "economic royalists" and the "money-changers in the Temple," and hoped to have the same success in a judicial crusade against the "Nine Old Men" who were blocking the constitutional acceptance of necessary social legislation.

But he miscalculated with his "Court-packing" plan. What he didn't understand was the difference between his economic reforms and his constitutional proposal. The people saw the first as a necessary change of the machinery. They saw the Constitution and Court not as a mechanism but as an organismic entity. But there was a saving sense of this inside the Court—at least, in the timely "switch" of Justice Roberts—and also inside the legal intellectual community. Thus Roosevelt lost his battle but won his war, and the people could retain their sense of the organism even as the organism itself changed.

We deal here with a crisis approach to constitutional history that stretches from the *Federalist Papers* and the decisions of the Marshall Court, through the slavery crisis and the Civil War, through the New Deal and the Roosevelt Court, to the Warren and Burger Courts and to Richard Nixon and Watergate. The pace and frequency of these constitutional crises have quickened, and the time-gap between them has narrowed. Even more the popular reaction to them has changed. There was an élan about the New Deal crisis, even at its seamier points, which didn't exist in the crisis of the Pentagon Papers and the Nixon Watergate cases. But in the large I am suggesting that the crisis approach is neither complete nor intelligible unless we see it as an approach to the wounds and resilience of a society which is an organismic web.

Consider here a sentence from Holmes' brief but elegant 1901 talk commemorating John Marshall: "A great man represents a great ganglion in the nerves of society, or, to vary the figure, a strategic point in the campaign of history, and part of his greatness consists in his being *there*." What struck me when I first came upon this was the phrase "campaign of history."[15] What strikes me now is another phrase—"a great ganglion in the nerves of society." Holmes speaks casually of varying the metaphor, but a metaphor may be the skin of a paradigm. The metaphor of a campaign on a battlefield is very different from that of a neural ganglion in an organism. If a society does indeed have a nervous system—and it is useful to assume it does—then it is an organism and not a battlefield, and from that a number of consequences can flow. As I have suggested above, Roosevelt would have fared better in his efforts to change the Supreme Court if he had seen the Court less as a battlefield and more as an organism.

In his Presidential address to the American Historical Association, Carl Becker used the phrase "everyman his own historian," to describe the historical memory of ordinary people. It comes out of their prides and discontents, their conscience and guilts, their sense of their ideal mission as a people. This conditions the screen-memories of the past that stay in their minds. In them history becomes a living faith.

Better even than the Roosevelt Court, the Warren Court illustrates the truth of Becker's theme. If it operated, as I think it did, on the assumption of the need to bridge the gap between a too slowly changing Court and a rapidly changing society, then it was a delayed session of the Roosevelt Court. The fact that its two prime activist Justices—Hugo Black and William O. Douglas—were carry-overs from the Roosevelt Court is emblematic of the continuum.

On that score the Warren Court—and indeed the whole decade of the 1960s of which it formed part—illustrated the need to counter rigidity in a civilization. "When the leaders of a people," said Harold J. Laski, "ask their followers to die for a dream they have a right to know in whose behalf the dream is being dreamt." Great civilizations have died of a failure of belief among those who wondered whether the dream was being dreamt in their behalf.

In long-range terms the Warren Court decisions bolstered two themes in America's history—the idea of equal access to equal life chances (not equality of result but of opportunity), and the ideal of equal justice before the law—that no one is too helpless to be beyond the protection of the laws or too rich and powerful to be beyond their reach. To that extent the Warren Court, in fending off some of the rigidifying forces, gave the civilization a base in belief.

Yet some queries remain. The Warren Court moved from a Bill of Rights seen as freedoms to one seen as equalities, and finally to one seen as entitlements. Daniel Bell's quip about "a revolution of rising entitlements"[16] has a sharpness of edge here. The social-cultural revolutions of the 1960s raised claims and expectations among classes that had in effect become wards both of public employment and of public subsidies. By doing away with the Hohfeldian distinction between "rights" and "privileges" the Court turned the privileges into rights and thus brought into being "the new property."[17]

The criminal law decisions of the Warren Court presented another area of popular disaffection that cannot be brushed aside as a stamping ground for reactionary yahoos. True, it formed part of the collective fantasy of killing the evil king which ended with the exhaustion of the crackpot movement to "impeach Earl Warren." But its meaning didn't stop there. It was the expression of one phase of the democratic dilemma—how to be large-minded enough to protect the procedural rights of every accused person, including the most technical of procedures, but also how to be rigorous enough to insure domestic tranquillity and keep the Hobbesian fear from unsettling the social contract, which is as necessary in latter-day America as it was in the 17th century England of Hobbes.

The Warren Court, no less than the pre-Roosevelt Court, presented the Nation with a constitutional crisis, although of a very different sort. Both crises came out of the excessive activism of the Court. In the pre-Roosevelt Court it was an activism from the traditionalist Right in striking down necessary social legislation, while in the Warren Court it was an activism from the positivist Left in breaking established precedents in order to safeguard the procedural rights of the accused, thus seeming to leave the rights of potential victims unguarded. The popular recoil, which has left a residual deposit in the culture, expressed a double-bind sense of the conflicting pair of messages the Court sent out to the people. Thus the same Court which produced a general liberating sense among a large section of the population also produced a "self-inflicted wound" in the estimate of an even larger section— a wound inflicted not only by the Court on itself but one inflicted on the social organism by the social organism.

These two areas, I take it, form the frame of the criticisms of the Warren Court expressed, archetypically, by Alexander Bickel. They reached to the Court's role in the acceleration of social change. Elsewhere I have called this the "Tocqueville effect"—that in a situation of rapid change the passion for change feeds on itself, that to legitimize it by law doesn't moderate the passion but excites it farther.[18] Bickel had a Burkean sense of the fragility of the social organism and the danger of discontinuities in history and of absolutisms in doctrine. His *Supreme Court and the Idea of Progress* is straight out of Carl Becker, and depicts a heavenly city of the Warren Court that goes back to Becker's heavenly city of the 18th century philosophers with its revolutionary fervors spurred by Utopian symbolism. Nor does the force of this rest on the French example alone. In American intellectual history too there is the strain of Calvinism as redemptive history, with the "journey of the elect" to salvation beyond history, and a "covenant of salvation" which sees the society as redeemable if its people are perfectable.[19]

There remains, as the most recent of the crisis periods, the crisis of Presidential power and authority in the later Nixon years—the sharpest crisis of the constitutional polity of our time. Here one must grasp the consequences of the power element within the democratic imperium. It started with Theodore Roosevelt's sense of America as a world power and Woodrow Wilson's grand manner in his domestic reforms as well as his moralism in war policy. It reached its height in the period since Franklin Roosevelt, when America has operated as an imperium (a power mass) in a world of power and ideological struggle. I use the term "democratic imperium" to comprise several elements: a major if not dominant role in world rivalries, a liberal welfare society, a polity of pressure groups, a frame of national security needs and of Intelligence policy within this frame, and a centralized and augmenting presidential power.[20]

Although Nixon brought the constitutional crisis phase of the democratic imperium to its sharpest point, he didn't create the entity itself. It grew out of the needs and realities, but also out of the imagination, of the past half-century and more. It is not an outgrowth of reactionary trends in the society but of the liberal image of the conditions of the good life for all, and of Jefferson's historic sense of "an empire for liberty." Nixon himself was a conservative, but his five predecessors—starting with FDR and including liberal Republican Dwight Eisenhower—were in the liberal tradition, and the basic idea of affirming the need for an "active-positive" President is part of the liberal intellectual tradition.[21]

Nixon was aware of this and used it to the hilt. In his *apologia pro vita sua,* both in his David Frost interviews and in his *Memoirs,* he defended his conduct in part by the plea that his presidential role made the liberties he took with the Constitution legal, and in part by appealing to Lincoln's precedent in the constitutional struggle which marked the Civil War. In the 1864 presidential campaign, when the issue of his enrollment of black soldiers was under attack, Lincoln wrote a letter saying he had to take extraordinary measures because only by saving the Union could he save the Constitution.

Even with Lincoln this was a tortured syllogism. With Nixon a similar one loses force because the parallel doesn't work. Under Nixon the civilization was not caught in a civil war for sheer survival. The question of the survival of the Nation was not at stake, however much Nixon inflated his sense of the Nation's need for the continuance of his policies. What was at stake was the survival of his own power. This made him forget the distinction between political opponents of the regime and enemies of the Republic. It was the ultimate corruption of political language.

If I have traced this succession of constitutional crises and of social-cultural climates too rapidly I trust I have not omitted the crux of it, which is the need for a *contextual* approach to these aspects of constitutional history. I have also several times referred to the *organismic* character of the polity, society and culture in which law is imbedded.

With Thomas Kuhn's seminal work on paradigm shifts in the history of scientific revolutions[22] there is no longer any excuse for continuing to think of constitutional law in terms of a mechanistic model. Man is not a machine but an organism. So are his institutions, his societies, his cosmos. Nowhere is the unsatisfactoriness of the machine model more evident than in judicial decisions and constitutional history.

Actually there was a mechanistic element even in those models which purported to recoil from mechanical jurisprudence. I find this element in economic determinism which puts both history and society into chains where human will and initiative become helpless. I find it among the legal realists who were so bent on unmasking all forms of "myths," play-acting and institutions, including capitalism, government, and law, that they left only "realism" itself unmasked. I find it in the psychoanalytic approaches which strip away everything except repression and the unconscious mechanisms. The mechanism and rigidity remain in the very instruments that reject the mechanism and rigidity of mechanical jurisprudence. "When me they fly I am the wings."

The time is ripe for an *organismic model* which sees constitutional law—as it sees human beings, institutions, and societies—as a living matrix of change, growth, illness, homeostasis, decay, and the eternal recurrence of death and rebirth.

If my final model is *contextual* and *organismic* it is also an *integrative* model. The reality we must all address is actually very complex. It has an eco-political objective aspect in the power of the great economic aggregates, in the pressures of a pressure group polity, and in the power of the courts themselves. It has an environmental aspect not only in the physical and technological environments, but in the climates of ideas and opinions within which court decisions are reached. It has a social aspect in the context of class, status, and ethnicity, and in the institutional structures of kin groups, age groups, and all the associative clusters that make up a society.

It has a bio-psychic aspect in the basic human drives and propensities, in the individual life journey, and in the personal strategies that operate within it. Finally, it has a subjective aspect in the ways in which we perceive reality, in the meanings we attach to it, in the values and belief systems we commit ourselves to, in the symbols and myths by which we live—all of which condition our attitudes toward the Constitution, the courts, and the living reality of the law.

Obviously this calls for a multi-disciplinary approach from which none of the life sciences or human sciences can be excluded. One might call this a *holistic* view, using the term from Jan Smuts, which is making headway in medical theory and practice, as it is in psychology. Or one might call it a *total systems* approach, taking over the model of systems analysis.

Either of these would be useful, but each also runs the danger of being question-begging if it doesn't attempt to answer the question of what is the *constitutive* or *integrating principle* in the assemblage of elements gathered under the roof-top. Hence my preference for an integrative model by which we study the legal case, decision, doctrine, principle not only in all its embedded contexts, but with the intent to find the organismic interrelationships that make it a living entity, not a dead and reductionist abstraction.

If I end with the role of the symbolic and mythic it is because they are more powerful than anything else in shaping what I have called the constitutive and integrative principle in the approach to law. Long ago I wrote a law review article—"Constitution and Court as Symbols"—exploring the hold that both institutions still retain on the popular mind.[23] If I were writing it today I would only strengthen it. All through the Watergate crisis, when presidential authority was eroded and congressional authority impaired, the authority of the Constitution and its interpreters held steady. Despite the fact that four of the members of the Supreme Court, including the Chief Justice, were Nixon appointees, the Court's response to the challenge of the Watergate cases was above political partisanship, and the people's response in turn to the Court was supportive.

In the end this comes down to myth and the symbols of faith. We tend to use the Calvinist ethos as a frame for our thinking about the American national character, which leads us sometimes to explain away the use of religion in social interpretation by linking it with the economic. But the mythic and sacral don't need the economic to validate them. They represent the deepest level of human experience. *Imaginatio facit casum:* the imagination creates the event.

In constitutional concerns, as in much else, the stuff of our imaginings which is larger than life and thus gives meaning to our daily experience—the symbolic and mythic—represents the ultimate reality because it comes closest to the ways by which we create the meanings of our existence. It is the source of many of our collective fantasies, and can therefore be dangerous and destructive, but it is also the source of constitutional strength and viability.

This then is my own way of looking at the Court—contextual, organismic, integrative, even mythic. I have dwelt on the contextual because it serves best to illumine the Court's recent history from the Roosevelt to the Burger era, seen as institutional, intellectual, and crisis history. To speak of a contextual approach is to speak of climates of opinion and the whole cluster of environments within which an institution functions.[24]

I have also stressed the need for an awareness of the paradigmatic character of whatever approach we use. My own paradigm is at once organismic and integrative, seeing the Court, the society, and the culture as organisms, and seeing each of them as interrelated wholes, with the Court inside the culture and the society. The mythic element is not to be seen apart from the organismic but as an integral phase of it, operating as a crucial phase of the imaginative and symbolic interaction between the Constitution, Court, culture, and people.

Notes

1. THE MIND AND FAITH OF JUSTICE HOLMES 31-32 (M. Lerner ed. 1943).

2. In one sense the "mechanical jurisprudence" of the Court conservatives, so fiercely attacked by Dean Roscoe Pound and the "sociological jurisprudence" of the Harvard Law School in the early decades of the century, was also determinist. It operated on a kind of slot-machine theory: you put a case like a coin into the machine of the Constitution, and out comes the appropriate decision, defined inevitably by the constitutional text.

3. Lerner, *The Supreme Court and American Capitalism,* 42 YALE L.J. 668 (1933) *reprinted in* ESSAYS IN CONSTITUTIONAL LAW 107 (R. McCloskey ed. 1957).

4. *See also* Lerner, *Minority Rule and the Constitutional Tradition, in* M. LERNER, IDEAS ARE WEAPONS 461 (1939). The most ambitious single work regarding a Marxist interpretation of the history of the Supreme Court is Louis Boudin's GOVERNMENT BY JUDICIARY (2 vols. 1932). Charles Beard wrote that he was more indebted to James Madison and Michael Harrington than to Karl Marx for his economic interpretation of history, but he could not have written either his ECONOMIC INTERPRETATION OF THE CONSTITUTION (1935) or his ECONOMIC ORIGINS OF JEFFERSONIAN DEMOCRACY (1943) if Marx had not cleared the path. For a sharp criticism of my legal essays in this vein, *see* L. HARTZ, THE LIBERAL TRADITION IN AMERICA (1955) and more recently P. SMITH, THE CONSTITUTION (1978). A criticism of Beard's thesis—and incidentally of my own sympathetic treatment of Beard in my IDEAS ARE WEAPONS (1939)—is presented in R. BROWN, CHARLES BEARD AND THE CONSTITUTION (1956). It is noteworthy that while the Marxist school has achieved a strong toehold in the disciplines of economics, politics, history, sociology, and anthropology, there is no comparable "radical" faction or school today in constitutional law. Not unexpectedly, the closest approach to it is in the area of civil liberties and civil rights.

5. *See* V. BROME, FREUD AND HIS EARLY CIRCLE (1967).

6. *See* S. FREUD & W. BULLITT, THOMAS WOODROW WILSON (1966), which threw consternation into the psycho-historical discipline.

7. Studies have been made of Jefferson, Wilson, Harding, Franklin Roosevelt, Kennedy, Johnson, and Nixon.

8. I draw heavily here upon the work of Max Weber and his formulation of the debate between the values-free and values-bound approaches. The best concise treatment of the views of Weber and others on this score is H.S. HUGHES, CONSCIOUSNESS AND SOCIETY (1958).

For a view of Justice Black's constitutional positions which differs from mine on the degree of his activism, see the closely reasoned analysis of Yarbrough, *Justice Black and Equal Protection,* 9 S.W.U.L. REV. 899 (1977).

9. *See* H. COMMAGER, THE EMPIRE OF REASON (1977).

10. For the first see F.O. MATTHIESSEN, AMERICAN RENAISSANCE (1941). For both, see M. LERNER, AMERICA AS A CIVILIZATION (1957).

11. For the phrase and the whole ambiance of Holmes' thought which it describes, *see* M. HOWE, TOUCHED WITH FIRE (1946).

12. B. CARDOZO, THE NATURE OF THE JUDICIAL PROCESS (1921).

13. *See* M. LERNER, *The Social Thought of Mr. Justice Brandeis* in IDEAS ARE WEAPONS (1939).

14. *See* M. LERNER, THE MIND AND FAITH OF JUSTICE HOLMES 90 *passim* (1943).

15. *See* Lerner, *John Marshall and the Campaign of History,* 39 COLUM. L. REV. 396 (1939).

16. Originally used in an article in *Fortune. See also* D. BELL, THE CULTURAL CONTRADICTIONS OF CAPITALISM (1976).

17. *See* Reich, *The New Property,* 73 YALE L.J. 733 (1964).

18. *See* M. LERNER, TOCQUEVILLE AND AMERICAN CIVILIZATION (1966).

19. On this theme see A. Schlesinger, Jr., *America: Experiment or Destiny?,* 82 AM. HISTORICAL REV. 505 (1977).

20. *See generally* Lerner, *America Agonistes,* 52 FOREIGN AFFAIRS 287 (Jan. 1974).

21. For the typology of which "active-positive" is part, see J. BARBER, PRESIDENTIAL CHARACTER (2nd ed. 1977).

22. T. KUHN, THE STRUCTURE OF SCIENTIFIC REVOLUTIONS (2nd ed. 1970).

23. *See* M. LERNER, IDEAS FOR THE ICE AGE 232 (1941).

24. Professor Laurence Tribe's treatise, AMERICAN CONSTITUTIONAL LAW (1978), is important for the models, or paradigms, that he uses in giving a frame to American constitutional history. It may also be seen as a massive challenge to Alexander Bickel's work and influence, and as a sharp and powerful assertion that values-bound judicial decision-making is a creative duty. It is likely to become the Bible of the liberal positivist-action school of constitutional thought.

Equal Protection As An Instrument of Revolution
By Henry Steele Commager*

The Fourteenth Amendment is the King Charles' head of American constitutional law and history. It is not without interest that the latest edition of the semi-official *Constitution Annotated* devotes some 250 pages to that amendment and another 250 or so to annotations on decisions which embrace those rights and privileges subsumed into the guarantees of the Amendment.

It was the Due Process Clause of that Amendment which for almost a generation dominated constitutional interpretation by way of a broad spectrum of challenges to state action or inaction. What we are witnessing now is a shift, not as yet decisive but significant, of the center of gravity from the Due Process Clause to the Equal Protection Clause of that Amendment.[1] It is highly probable that to the next generation the Equal Protection Clause will be, in constitutional and political interpretation, what the Due Process Clause was in the past. If this does indeed eventuate, it will present in more urgent form than before a number of difficult and challenging problems, not alone of American law, but of American democracy. The first of these is the problem of the extent to which the Equal Protection Clause can be given that substantive meaning which the Due Process Clause once enjoyed but which it can no longer claim—or command. Closely connected with this is a second problem: the extent to which what we may call the admonitory (or negative) phrases of the Equal Protection Clause can be infused with what we may call mandatory authority—as has happened with due process in the realms of civil rights and liberties. The third problem is larger and philosophically even more challenging: it is a new form of the ancient problem of the authority, or merely the responsibility, of the courts to impose their views of "equal protection" on the political processes of the states. Fourth, and closely related to the third, is the problem of the extent to which equal protection will emerge as a federalizing or centralizing instrument in the broad realm of public welfare, as the Due Process Clause has served in the broad realm of fundamental rights and liberties. There is a final consideration: if the Powell interpretation[2] of equal protection triumphs—the argument rejected by a unanimous Court in *Pacific States Telephone and Telegraph Co. v. Oregon*[3]—the applicability of the Guarantee Clause[4] of the Constitution may yet become the cornerstone of a new structure of equalitarianism.

Beginning in the decade of the fifties, the problem of the application of the Equal Protection Clause emerged on a score of fronts, raising questions more difficult even than those which had been raised by due process, and by deprivations of liberty and property. Since the abandonment of the judicial search for reasonableness and of the concept of liberty of contract in legislation addressed to larger economic and labor regulations,[5] due process

* Woodruff Simpson Lecturer, Amherst College, Massachusetts.

had been confined increasingly to the arena of racial discrimination, and of classifications that involve, even if they do not wholly hinge on, wealth, poverty, and gender. More and more it is equal protection that promises—or threatens (depending on your point of view)—to embrace the broadest spectrum of political, social and economic rights.

The issue of the reach and the implications of equal protection has come to a head in the realm of education. Not surprisingly, this, for education is a kind of catch-all which, in one way or another, embraces almost all rights and interests of society. It is also undeniable that education, whether itself a fundamental right or not, has close relations to a number of rights which are accepted as fundamental even by the most rigid interpretation, and to others that have some claim to be fundamental by more latitudinarian standards. Certainly education has been assumed to be fundamental to the intelligent exercise of the political rights of voting and office holding, and to effective service in the armed forces and therefore connected with the security of the Nation.

The issue is crucial. For this was really the nub of the matter in the now historic debate between Mr. Justice Powell and Mr. Justice Marshall in the case of *San Antonio Independent School District v. Rodriguez,*[6] which may come to rank, in the history of our constitutional law, with *Plessy v. Ferguson*[7] in the persuasiveness with which it invites reversal.

I need not here recite the issues which faced the Court—analogous as they are to those which confronted the California Supreme Court in the parallel case of *Serrano v. Priest.*[8] Suffice it to note that confronted with palpable inequalities in the financing of education in the two neighboring school districts of San Antonio—the impoverished Edgewood and the affluent Alamo Heights—the Supreme Court rejected the allegation that the Texas educational financing laws constituted a denial of equal protection for children of Edgewood (and all other children in Texas similarly situated) and ruled 5–4 that education was not, in any event, one of those fundamental rights embraced in the Fourteenth Amendment. Furthermore, notwithstanding the palpable nexus between education and freedom of speech or education and voting, the Court, said Justice Powell, cannot be presumed to possess either the ability or the authority to guarantee to school children (or others) "the most *effective* speech or the most *informed* electoral choice. . . . These", he added, "are indeed goals to be pursued, but they are not values to be implemented by judicial intrusion into otherwise legitimate state activities."[9]

Permit me a few brief observations on these two assertions. First, the question is not, as Mr. Justice Powell later acknowledged, whether the Court thinks education a fundamental right; it is rather whether the political branches of the government, federal and state, so assume it to be one. This is not the place for a review of federal and state legislation on this subject, but a word is relevant. As for the federal government, it is sufficient to recall the recognition of education in the Northwest Ordinance which was reenacted by the First Congress, which has been incorporated into the constitutions of most American states, and which has, therefore, over the years, taken on an almost constitutional authority:

> Religion, morality, and knowledge, being necessary to good government and the happiness of mankind, schools and the means of education shall forever be encouraged.[10]

This was originally addressed to the people of the Northwest Territory. But it was, quite clearly, a statement of national policy, first written into the land ordinance of 1785, reenacted in subsequent land laws passed by the Congress, given larger significance by the Morrill Land Grant Act of 1862, and then by massive legislative programs in the past quarter century. Either by deductive or by inductive standards, e.g., by solemn declarations of principle or by voluminous legislative commitments, the Congress has made it inescapably clear that it considers education to be one of the most fundamental rights of Americans.

Certainly, as *Brown v. Board of Education*[11] made clear, it was an "equal" right and one therefore to be protected against discrimination by the states. Nor should we overlook the forceful statement by Justice Frankfurter in *McCollum v. Board of Education*,[12] that public schools are "the most powerful agency for promoting cohesion among a heterogeneous democratic people . . . at once the symbol of our democracy and the most pervasive means for promoting our common destiny."[13] Perhaps no less relevant is the fact that the constitution of Texas clearly recognizes public education as fundamental, and that few states (if any) have made more generous contribution to the support of public education than has Texas.

As for Justice Powell's aphorism that though education may be related to both speech and voting the Court is under no obligation to require states to provide for the most effective speech or the most informed voting, Justice Marshall's dissenting observation is in order: that the question before the Court was not that of either effective or informed education, but simply of "equal" education.[14]

The question of the degree of freedom or of education raised by Justice Powell does not differ greatly from those raised in so many of the due process cases of the past. The Court sustains the principle of a fair jury though it cannot require of juries that they achieve a just verdict. It requires a fair trial though it cannot require that judges will always make the same punishment for the same crime, or that penal sentences achieve their presumed objective or rehabilitation. So with a dozen other fundamental rights; the ultimate objective cannot be guaranteed but the process is to be protected. All that the Court can do, it must do. That is, it must require that the processes of justice be equally fair whether black or white, poor or rich, and —wherever there are no natural impediments—it must guarantee women and men equal access to courts, to counsel, to an impartial jury, to due process of law, to equal compensation for equal work, to equal opportunity for jobs, and so forth.[15]

To these objections to Justice Powell's aphorism on the somewhat nebulous effectiveness of the application of equal protection to education, we may add yet another of a more substantial character: that while the connection between education and voting may not be clear, the connection between education and the national defense is. During World War II it was found that approximately fifty per cent of young men subject to the draft in two southern states were rejected as ineligible on grounds of educational and health deficiencies, while the rate of rejection on these grounds in such states as Iowa and Minnesota was about two per cent. If, as the Supreme Court has asserted, the power to wage war is the power to wage it successfully, does any state have the right to deprive the Nation of the services of a large proportion of potential members of the armed services by an almost contumacious neglect of education and health, thus imposing on states with more enlightened educational and health services an unequal burden? That no state may affirmatively deprive the Nation of the services of its otherwise eligible citizens in time of war was settled by the Court in 1827 in the case of *Martin v. Mott*.[16] May the state by inaction or neglect do what it may not do by direct intervention, imperil the ability of the Nation to defend itself?

In disposing of the *San Antonio School District* case, Justice Powell took refuge in another argument, plausible enough but potentially risky: the argument that if we accept the contention that equal protection extends to the realm of education, where do we stop?

> [T]he logical limitations on appellees' nexus theory [,said Justice Powell,] are difficult to perceive. How . . . is education to be distinguished from the significant personal interests in the basics of decent food and shelter? Empirical examination might well buttress an assumption that the ill-fed, ill-clothed, ill-housed are among the most ineffective participants in the political process, and that they derive the least enjoyment from the benefits of the First Amendment.[17]

This note of alarm was echoed in Mr. Justice Stewart's concurring opinion which referred, in startled accents, to "the uncharted directions of such a departure" from traditional equal protection decisions which had made clear that the Equal Protection Clause "is offended only by . . . classifications that are wholly arbitrary or capricious."[18]

This contingency is a very real one, and I am reminded of Benjamin Franklin's response to the Committee of the House of Commons which asked, "if the colonists reject internal taxes [the Stamp Act etc.] today, what is to prevent them from rejecting external taxes later?" Replied Dr. Franklin, "We have not heretofore so reasoned, but in time you may persuade us."[19]

The fears of Justices Powell and Stewart are legitimate: it is by no means improbable that within this generation we shall see the concept of equal protection extended to the realms of public health, mental care, prison sentences, penal conditions, unemployment, and perhaps even to housing. Outrageous as this prediction may seem, it is, after all, one with which we should by now be familiar. The idea (the principle) and the practice of substantial equality in these areas has in fact been long accepted in four Scandanavian countries and, in part, in other Western countries, without—so far as the record shows—catastrophic consequences. It is possible that even our Republic might survive should it provide substantial equality and justice in health, welfare, and employment, whether through State or Nation or whether through political or judicial intervention. In any event, we ought to respond to this line of argument as Thomas Jefferson did when his critics raised the spectre of the French Revolution: "Shake not your raw heads and bloody bones at me!"

The most famous footnote in American legal history, footnote four of *Carolene Products*,[20] launched a debate, in and outside the courts, whose echoes have not yet wholly died down. I need do no more than remind everyone of the essence of that footnote: that there is a narrower scope for the presumption of legislative constitutionality when legislation appears on its face to be within a specific prohibition of the first ten amendments. This is particularly true of legislation which restricts those political processes which might be expected to bring about repeal of undesirable legislation or to curtail the operation of those political processes which can be relied on to protect minorities. The difficulty of detecting, or determining, with any degree of accuracy, such legislation did not discourage bold members of the Stone and Warren Courts—I have in mind chiefly Douglas, Black and Brennan—who were inclined to assign a preferred position to the guarantees of the First Amendment. The Burger Court has pretty well abandoned any flirtation with a "preferred position," and neither Justices Brennan nor Marshall any longer advance it with any urgency.

Might not the *Carolene Products* standard, not so much rejected as subordinated by the present Court, take on new significance by application to and illumination of the Equal Protection Clause? And might it not be given an affirmative significance? Both of these considerations were implicit in *Brown v. Board of Education*[21] and in *Baker v. Carr*:[22] the readiness to adopt a closer scrutiny of legislation or regulations which might weaken or curtail political processes ordinarily relied on to protect minorities and the obligation to remedy this situation by positive and substantive action. In terms of protection of minority rights, this means not only ending the scandal of segregation but also by implementing positive re-arrangements such as busing. In terms of the political process, this means not only ending the scandal of ignoring constitutional provisions for re-apportionment, but also the implementation of positive provisions for one-person-one vote. Thus by analogy, where states deny equal protection by permitting wide variations in the quantity or the quality of education, or of health and psychiatric care, or of other services which may be presumed to weaken the fulfillment of the obligations of citizenship, might not courts be under an obligation to require states to repair such inequalities and deficiencies? Footnote four of

The Bill of Rights: Physics, Idealism and Pragmatism*
By John P. Frank†

I.

The constitutional law of the twentieth century ought to emerge from the physics of the twentieth century, and it does not. This is the most peculiar element of contemporary constitutionalism. There is a great void, and the generation just closed has sought to fill that void with intellectual concepts post Darwinian or much earlier. The immediately contemporary generation of constitutionalists is, intellectually, isolated from the concepts of matter which now, in fact, dominate our world.

Far reaching constitutional thought, particularly as to the place of the individual in society, comes from philosophy, and the philosophy of a given time comes from the world view of the age in which it is conceived.

Thus, if a society believes that the sun is drawn through the heavens and over the earth in a chariot directed by a god, then the rest of philosophy will fit around this improbable bit of transportation, and so will law; dire results will flow from violating the fancied will of some member of the ethereal pantheon. If Copernicus and Galileo show that the sun isn't going anywhere and that it is the earth which really does move, not merely astronomy but the whole structure of truth is revolutionized. When it becomes nonsensical for Joshua to command the sun to stand still because it wasn't moving anyway, all belief must change and authority must find a new basis.

Until now, law and philosophy have followed science. Professor Morton White speaks of "the most important and most interesting strain in the development of American philosophy" as "its response to the challenge of modern science and scientific method. From Jonathan Edwards to John Dewey, American philosophers have felt obliged" to accomodate to science.[1]

This statement is surely true as far as it goes. Carl Becker's great work on the Declaration of Independence brilliantly develops the manner in which Newton led to Locke, and Locke to the Declaration.[2] The effect of Darwin on all philosophic thought in the latter

---

*These brief remarks are made as a keynote to a meeting of distinguished students of the Constitution. The requisite brevity requires telescoping in every direction. I have developed my thoughts on idealism and pragmatism in relation to the Constitution more fully in the David C. Baum Lecture at the University of Illinois, Frank, *Hugo L. Black: Free Speech and the Declaration of Independence*, 1977 U. ILL. L. FORUM 577. While I have drawn a little from that source, my object here is to put that discussion into a broader context and also to make some tentative resolutions. I am using the terms idealism and pragmatism without careful definition, realizing that each is a many splendored thing; I shall be satisfied if I convey a mood of tension between a priori and a posteriori conceptions of truth, between "self-evident truths" no matter how obtained and truth empirically measured. The distinction I adopt is from James: Pragmatism is "the attitude of looking away from first things, principles, categories, supposed necessities; and of looking toward last things, fruits, consequences, facts." W. JAMES, PRAGMATISM 54-55 (1907).

†Partner, Lewis & Roca, Phoenix, Arizona. Law clerk to Mr. Justice Black, 1942 Term.

half of the nineteenth and the first part of the twentieth century makes him the greatest intellectual force of that era. After Darwin, most disciplines could be looked at in terms of a biologic evolutionary analogy. This set up the contretemps between the absolute values of Locke's idealism and the shifting values of twentieth century philosphy. The consequences in terms of the development of pragmatism, and the interplay of the pragmatism of the post-Darwinian philosophers and of the idealism of Locke will be the second theme of this paper.

This is because the key intellectual forces of contemporary constitutional law are drawn from sources which antedate today's science. The great physicist of this century is Albert Einstein, and Crane Brinton writing in 1950 spoke of him as "a great natural scientist from whose work philosophers and essayists and men of ideas in general could apparently take the kind of lead the eighteenth century took from Newton."[3]

The intervening quarter century demostrates that this, perceptibly at least, is not true. Sir James Jeans, who discusses the consequences on all human thought of Copernicus, Darwin and Newton, suggests that "the philosophy of any period is always interwoven with the science of the period" and then directs this discussion to the revolutions in physics in recent years and its philosphic consequences. Alas, he doesn't find much philosophic consequence and his "new philosphic principles" are extremely thin.[4]

With the decline of public interest in pragmatism after World War II, the field of American philosphy has been largely occupied with logical positivism. I do not mean to minimize the relationship of Einstein to this development. He was a participant in the thinking of the Vienna Circle in the 1920s, which takes us into linguistic analysis and logic in the United States and contributed existentialism in Europe. These are developments effected at one or more removes from Einstein's empiricism. More important for this purpose, in the course of their development, those philosophies are now unrelated to Einstein's salient social values.

As Professor John E. Smith of Yale recently put it, "There is the belief that if one first resolves some 'logical' problems, one can then go on to deal with 'problems of human experience.' But . . . that rarely happens."[5]

The greatest of the new physicists have had a strong impulse to be new philosophers as well; they have been keenly aware of the thin line between physics and metaphysics. Three illustrations of this thought will demonstrate why the revolution in physics is causing no revolution in jurisprudence. A first illustration is the hopeless school, illustrated by Max Born, the Nobel Prize winner of 1954 who set out to develop "philosophical principles derived from science." He concludes gloomily that the "political and ethical judgments of scientists are often primitve and dangerous." Yet he finds that the "lawyers, the theologians, philosophers" and humanists generally have no inkling of scientific thought.[6]

A second approach is to move to some form of logical positivism and particularly linguistics. An illustration is Niels Bohr who sought to develop a philosophy from quantum physics fundamentally in terms of conceptual communications both in language and in mathematics.[7] As with logical positivism generally, this does not easily relate to the problems of law and society. At the present stage of its development, positivism postpones values. With the stress on symbols, language, mathematical and logical modes, meaning is paramount. The chasm is between meaning and "the problem".

Finally there is the writing of the physicists who move directly over into the living room of traditional philosophy and comfortably sit down. These scientists are working in two distinct dimensions—social philosphy and philosophy of science. Great physicists themselves tackle social problems from natural law premises as old as God. Robert Oppenheimer for example, embraces Pope John's encyclical, *Pacem in Terris,* as one of the great events that any of us has seen.[8] Alfred Kastler, Nobel Prize physicist of 1966, in the current issue of the Bulletin of Atomic Scientists, takes his moral convictions on the "Challenge of the Century" from Albert Schweitzer and the Holy See.[9]

A foremost participant in the stream of social thought is Einstein. Einstein recognized that, to use his words, it is "a hopeless undertaking to debate about fundamental value judgments." He was prepared to declare values which were satisfactory to him, and those values as he stated them came very close to the concept of the Four Freedoms. To him "those instrumental goods which should serve to maintain the life and health of all human beings should be produced by the least possible labor of all." To him also, "the satisfaction of physical needs is indeed the indispensable precondition of a satisfactory existence, but in itself it is not enough. In order to be content men must also have the possibility of developing their intellectual and artistic powers to whatever extent accords with their personal characteristics and abilities." He stated his own adherence to a view parallel to First Amendment natural law in its most liberal, Newtonian interpretation: he called for "unrestricted communication of all results and judgments—freedom of expression and instruction in all realms of intellectual endeavor."[10]

Einstein's social commentary is largely a reflection of a sophisticated idealism or natural law. He rejects the "religiosity of the naive man" at the same time that he endorses "a rapturous amazement at the harmony of natural law".[11] In short, when Einstein philosophized, he was not seriously attempting to make a bridge from his own physics to his own philosophy.[12]

From Einsteinian physics, a large scale contemporary philosophy, followed or accompanied by a large scale contemporary jurisprudence, might have developed, but it has not. We live in an age of philosophic obscurity. Saul Kripke, formerly at Rockefeller and now at Princeton, is thought by some to be America's foremost philosopher. He is studying physics, dabbling (we are told) in relativity, and concerning himself with truth, but there is no bridge to jurisprudence yet. As Morton White says with striking accuracy, John Dewey was the leader of a "movement in the direction of making philosophy, law, economics, history and political science relevant." He was, White continues, "the last distinguished American philospher to operate in the grand manner."

This lastness of Dewey brings us to where we are in relating philosophy to contemporary constitutional law. I am not scorning contemporary thought in the slightest, but merely describing it, when I say that if a meeting such as this one had been held 75 years ago, everyone in the room would have known the work of Royce, Santayana, and James; and if 40 years ago, everyone would have known of the contributions of Pound, Llewellyn, and Jerome Frank, Hart and Fuller, or more recently Cahn, to name but a few. Yet in this room today, I believe I would successfully win a wager that a majority of those present could not name either three contemporary philosophers or three contemporary jurisprudents outside the circles at their own universities. John Rawls' *Theory of Justice* is the only major jurisprudential work of recent years to achieve national notice, and it is fundamentally a resurgence of idealism.[13] The leading work of 1977, Ronald Dworkin's *Taking Rights Seriously,* is a shorter, less complex work than Rawls' and makes a strenuous argument against positivism and utilitarianism and in favor of "the old idea of individual human rights."[14]

No matter how my little game of name recognition may come out, no one in this room can seriously connect the theory of relativity with any contemporary body of doctrine in American law or even of American philosophy, except perhaps in a metaphorical sense. No one can seriously connect any post-Deweyian American philosopher with any doctrine of the American Constitution which has as yet emerged in the decisions.

Again, let me stress that this is not in the remotest degree criticism. I suspect that Einstein has left us a legacy too complicated for ready absorption and translation; we are, simply, in *media res* and perhaps by the beginning of the next century we will have digested and moved on. Kripke may be an illustration. Moreover, as I have already suggested, the great physicists have not left us devoid of moral values. Einstein and Fermi and Szilard and Bohr and Oppenheimer have not been wanting in intellectual leadership in the uses and controls of the giant powers which they have unleashed. No one has thought more than the physicists on the ethical consequences of atomic energy.

Nonetheless, the present paucity of philosophy and jurisprudence in relation to the Constitution has highly important practical consequences on contemporary intellectual life. In the absence of contemporary philosophy, we are not presently developing constitutional doctrine with any particular systematic philosophical referrant. From Edwards in the seventeenth century to James and Dewey in the twentieth, the main streams of American philosophy have come from the New England and mid-Atlantic states. I recognize the exceptions, but the simplistic referrent is good enough for this purpose. With the deaths of Holmes, Brandeis, Hand, Stone, Frankfurter, and Harlan, we are left with no one in the highest reach of the judiciary nurtured in this tradition. The departures of Justices Black and Douglas took away another philosophic strand.

No contemporary twentieth century judge or justice of whom I know is systematically philosophizing at all. We have in Chief Justice Warren the elemental force of right come to judgment, and in Chief Justice Burger we witness the application in high place of the needed concepts of the managerial revolution. Other contemporaries give us *ad hoc* rather than systemized responses to contemporary problems; we are left to semantics, history and policy as they make their wavering trails. Perhaps Justice Blackmun, very much a heavy-weight in the present scheme of things, reflects the spirit of the times and of empiricism in some of his decisions, as for example on abortion or on commercialism and the First Amendment. Justice Rehnquist is developing a series of constitutionally conservative positions which, by the time he is done, we may see as illustrations on the structure of an integrated philosophy.[15]

Consequence number one, therefore, of the present obscure state of philosophy is that it has no very apparent relation to constitutional law. Consequence number two is that the main philosophic battles of this century in constitutional law have turned on past philosophic doctrine made contemporary by recent champions. Most fundamental controversies in the field of civil rights between 1920 and 1970 have been over idealism and pragmatism. To this I turn.

II.

The suggestion that philosophy in the sense of including both law and education within its province stops with Dewey does injustice to Alexander Meiklejohn, whose influence is still with us. He epitomizes the idealist tradition in philosophy itself and as applied to both law and education.

Meiklejohn's free speech thinking began with Plato and developed through Kant. For him the solution of the fundamental paradox of the *Apology* and the *Crito*, superficially conflicting Socratic dialogues, was the beginning of contemporary wisdom. In the *Apology*, Socrates defies what Meiklejohn describes as the Un-Athenian Subversive Activities Committee, and he refuses to give up teaching the young those notions to which the Committee objects. Socrates will accept death rather than relinquish a free man's right to teach, think, and speak as his spirit and wisdom demand. In short, he rejects the command of the State to be silent. Yet in the *Crito* Socrates refuses to escape from the unjust death penalty; his philosophy requires him to drink the hemlock. He, as a citizen, has consented all his life to accept the laws of the City of Athens. He must obey the law which governs his actions. The State may control his conduct even to ordering his death, but his beliefs and his speech no man may control but himself.

The belief in inherent rights, one of which is speech, carries over to the American Declaration of Independence and to the Bill of Rights.[16] The bridge, of course, was John Locke, who merged empiricism and intuition, and the early American prophets of this point of view include Thomas Jefferson and James Madison. From the philosophic standpoint, the key words in the Declaration are that certain truths are "self-evident . . . that all men are created equal . . . [with] certain unalienable rights" which include life, liberty and the pursuit of happiness. The concept that a truth is "self-evident" means that it does not have to be proved, that its validity is not to be drawn from some demonstration of experience but rather that it can be intuited or deduced from either a designed grand plan for the universe or from the nature of things. For the contemporary concept that nothing is proved unless it is demonstrated, little could be more antithetical than the concept of a truth which is self-evident. The concept of an "unalienable right" is straight Plato, and Socrates demonstrates it in connection with free speech when he goes to his death for his right to teach that in which he believes.

This conception of fixed and absolute truths is central to the eighteenth century enlightenment. As Professor Anastapolo has pointed out, the Constitution itself contains a whole series of absolutes, such as that "no bill of attainder", "no tax on exports", "no preference" for commerce, and "no title of nobility" are allowed.[17] Many absolute prohibitions went into the Bill of Rights which made explicit those "unalienable rights" which were so "self-evident". Hence the provision for "no law" abridging the freedom of speech or of the press or of the right to assemble or concerning the establishment of religion or prohibiting its free exercise; no infringement on the right of the people to bear arms; no quartering of troops; no warrants but upon probable cause, no criminal trials without a grand jury indictment, no double jeopardy, no self-incrimination; no trial without notice, jury, and confrontation.

As a philosopher Meiklejohn developed a Platonic, Lockian and compact exposition of the Bill of Rights.[18] With particular reference to freedom of speech, Professor Meiklejohn argued that this freedom was "absolute" at least so far as public affairs were concerned. He systematically made the philosophic application that "no law" could limit the right of Socrates to teach, and similarly, that by virtue of the First Amendment "no law" could abridge any American's freedom of speech.[19]

The principal exponent of this systematic position on the Supreme Court has been Mr. Justice Black.[20] Black on the Supreme Court represented the eighteenth century enlightenment. Indeed, in his Senate days in 1929, in a debate on a free speech issue he took his position expressly and by name with "the philosphy of Thomas Jefferson, who borrowed largely from the great English writer, John Locke," which he had been reading only a few days before. Meiklejohn expressly accepted the compact theory of government, treating very seriously the passage of the Declaration of Independence which reads, "We mutually pledge to each other. . . ."

Black had the same compact view. He rejected what in our own time has come to be known as the "balancing approach" to civil liberties. So far as he was concerned, that balance was struck two hundred years ago when those who wrote the Constitution made an agreement that the value of speech outweighs hazards to national security. The eighteenth century philosophy was a spin-off from Newtonian physics, a dual concept that truth could be found from sufficiently close observation of nature, and that mankind had an everlasting capacity for improvement. At the heart of the views Black accepted was the eighteenth century optimism of that little handful of rebels who had to be optimists to carry their concept of truth to the wager of battle. They were young, astonishingly young, energetic, and very optimistic indeed; but they were neither naive nor of short memory as they revolted against English oppression.

That history, so fresh in the eighteenth century, was equally fresh to Black. When he objected to the exercise of power by Congress to require certain oaths of labor union officials concerning their previous beliefs and political affilliations, he spoke of the use of oaths against the Huguenots in France and against the heretics of the Spanish Inquisition and against the many denominations which had been persecuted in England. When Justice Black stated his First Amendment hypothesis with all formality he said:

> [T]he First Amendment sought to leave Congress devoid of . . . power to direct any type of national laws against the freedom of individuals to think what they please, advocate whatever policy they choose, and join with others to bring about the social, religious, political and governmental changes which seem best to them.[21]

This same total view, drawn directly from the idealistic natural law concepts of the eighteenth century, Black applied generally to the absolutes of the Bill of Rights.

One of the most discerning critics of the Locke to Black strain in American constitutional history was the late Professor Alexander Bickel of Yale. He describes this view, perfectly fairly, as the contract model resting "on a vision of individual rights . . . derived from nature." As he says, also with perfect accuracy, "society must bend to these rights," and he adds that this view "is weak on pragmatism, strong on theory. For it, law is not so much a process, and certainly not a process in continual flux, as it is a body of rules binding all, rules that can be changed only by the same formal method by which they were enacted."[22]

Bickel espouses instead what he describes as the pragmatic approach in which the function of government "is to make a peaceable, good, and improving society." As he says, this view "partakes, in substantial measure, of the relativism that pervades Justice Oliver Holmes' theory of the First Amendment, although not to its ultimate logical exaggeration. Lacking a catechism of shared values, such as religious societies may cherish, it has no choice but relativism."

This is the approach of Peirce and James and Dewey, and it is no accident that Justice Holmes has been the foremost exponent of this view in American constitutional history. Holmes came to his intellectual maturity in the world of Peirce and of James and was a member of the Boston Metaphysical Club in which Peirce first developed his hypotheses. The most eloquent expression of pure pragmatism in America's free speech history is the Holmes dissent in *Abram v. United States*, a passage so eloquently written that a reader may be so consumed with the music as to miss the words. What Holmes says here is:

> Persecution for the expression of opinions seems to me perfectly logical. If you have no doubt of your premises or your power and want a certain result with all your heart you naturally express your wishes in law and sweep away all opposition. To allow opposition by speech seems to indicate that you think the speech impotent, as when a man says that he has squared the circle, or that you do not care whole-heartedly for the result, or that you doubt either your power or your premises. But when men have realized that time has upset many fighting faiths, they may come to believe even more than they believe the very foundations of their own conduct that the ultimate good desired is better reached by free trade in ideas—that the best test of truth is the power of the thought to get itself accepted in the competition of the market, and that truth is the only ground upon which their wishes safely can be carried out.[23]

The view expressed is the direct parallel of Mill's. Holmes is saying here that we should not persecute those with whom we disagree because we may be wrong about it; because the persecuted may be right; and because the only way to find out is to leave ideas to the sifting process of the intellectual marketplace. In short, Holmes would let speech be free without regard to moral considerations or historic commitments by a process of balancing, because it is socially useful to do so. We owe to Professor Gerald Gunther of Stanford the availability of the correspondence around 1920 between Hand and Holmes and Hand and Professor Chafee on the World War I development of free speech theory.[24] The exchange clearly demonstrates that none of this trio ever thought at all of Jefferson, or the Declaration of Independence, or the compact theory of government. Their approach was pure pragmatism. As a result Holmes is completely endorsed by Dewey who briskly rejects the idealist philosophy and the theory of natural rights. Dewey says:

> Holmes and Brandeis are notable not only for their sturdy defense of civil liberties but even more for the fact that they based their defense on the indispensable value of free inquiry and free discussion to the normal development of public welfare, not upon anything inherent in the individual as such.[25]

An illustration of this defense is the pragmatic approach to free speech from which emerges the clear and present danger analysis. The Holmes hypothesis put a limit to the right of freedom of speech at the point at which that speech might cause a clear and present danger which would itself upset the process of inquiry. While for Holmes and Brandeis that clear and present danger was remote and unlikely in the extreme, it existed. As this concept was re-worked by Judge Learned Hand and adopted by the Supreme Court in a leading Communist prosecution, "In each case [courts] must ask whether the gravity of the 'evil,' discounted by its improbability, justifies such invasion of free speech as is necessary to avoid the danger."

I cannot be happy over the operation of this standard. The record of application of pragmatism to vital liberties is that the liberties always lose. Applying a utilitarian approach to the review of civil liberties issues in the United States Supreme Court particularly in the heyday of seeming pragmatism, during the Chief Justiceship of Fred Vinson, it is clearly too easy to resolve all balances against liberty. James and Dewey were democratic progressives. Their philosophy is not a doctrine but an approach, so loose that "critics ask whether or not pragmatism can be used to justify any social attitude that an individual or group wishes to call progress."[26]

This conflict between an absolute and a relativist point of view is by no means restricted to First Amendment problems. For example the Black position is that the entire Bill of Rights is rigorously applicable to the states with precisely the same scope as with the Federal Government. Justice Frankfurter on the other hand not merely was prepared to come to different judgments on different rights but also to different conclusions as to a particular right.[27] Justice Black, to the contrary, wanted no part of a shock test of constitutional validity. To him the Fifth Amendment prohibition on self-incrimination is applicable to the states, this was self-incrimination, and therefore the conviction was unconstitutional. In his private correspondence, Justice Black had particular strong concurrence from Professor Meiklejohn, who thought the selectivity of the majority approach was wrong in its underlying philosophy. As he wrote Black, "The philosophy of the majority opinion is, as you say, radically unsound, but it has a very strong appeal to the 'American mind,' as it now functions, and it is dominant and dangerous in every phase of our life."

III.

In terms of a philosophical approach to the Constitution, we are in the year 1977 at a hard time. Our general philosophy does not much gear to our general lives, and really not at all to our jurisprudence. Frankfurter is dead, Bickel is dead, Black is dead, Meiklejohn is dead, and it remains to be seen whether the truths of any of them will go marching on. Rawls' book, the major work of the decade thus far, is a restatement of the compact theory of constitutionalism. It is a lonely as well as a brilliant offering.

As a personal matter, I believe that our philosophy has much to teach us, contains much that is vital for current application. It may be that the new physics and the new logical positivism will give us a new jurisprudence, but not yet. Meanwhile we must fumble toward a stand to live by, and I suggest these problems and positions:

1. Integrity does not require a choice in constitutional law between pragmatism and idealism, whether or not it requires such choice in general living. For me at least the pragmatism of James and Dewey remains a viable philosophy of life; I am left pathetically floundering by the logical positivism or existentialists. At the same time, we are interpreting a Constitution which is a written document and which does, in all integrity, represent a "compact" realistically made and truly inherited. However much one may scoff at an aboriginal natural law compact as little more than a fictitious way of speech, the American constitutional compact in fact actually occurred. Between 1776 and 1790, persons on the earth's surface actually debated, actually made compromises, actually came to conclusions and put them down. It has become positive law in the true sense of positivism.

We have a duty to take into account the basic purposes and objectives of the contract we inherit. This carries with it the freight of the particular philosophy with which the document was written. In my view of it, the pragmatic constitutionalists were derelict in their duty in failing to do this, and in this respect it seems to me that Professor Meiklejohn and Justice Black were exactly right.

2. We are left with practical problems. To a degree an eighteenth century document prepared for the governance of three million people two hundred years ago can not give direct solutions to the vastly different problems of another age. The war power in an age where an ultimate hostile act might be putting an embargo on shipments from the Boston harbor is not the same in its constitutional perspective as the power involved in pushing a button which may end the world.

3. For all the differences, the constitutional provisions are not forms of words which have become obsolete with time. Some of the Constitution is rock hard—two senators to a state for example. Some of it has an imprecision with which we must reckon. In dealing with those imprecise clauses, the goal should be to transfer them to our time with as much of an eye as we can to tackling the modern problem with the philosophic predisposition of those who made the compact in the first place.

Here, particularly in connection with freedom of speech, it is time to go beyond the thinking of Professor Meiklejohn and Justice Black to problems on which they never fully focused. I am quite ready to accept the absolute proposition as to free speech. This leaves me, however, with considerable uncertainty as to just what "abridging" means, in the constitutional sense, and just what "speech" is. For example, as I have acknowledged in more detail elsewhere, I do not personally believe that the grand maxims of the First Amendment were remotely intended, either factually or philosophically, to license a peep show, and I do not believe that a public display of sexual activity is, in the constitutional sense, "speech" at all.

The problem in our time ought to be to think through what really is "speech" and what is "action" and what happens when, to use Justice Douglas' phrase, "Speech is brigaded with action." Of the writers and teachers I know, Professor Emerson has done the most in this direction.[28] Nobody supposes, for example, that the First Amendment is infringed by punishing those who conspire to commit murder, though speech is the means of the conspiracy, and this even though they do not in fact commit the murder. I have no trouble with punishing the publicist who disseminates news of troop movements to the detriment of the Army; he is committing murder or trying to and perhaps treason as well. It would not make the matter any more difficult for me if his heart was pure and his real object was to oppose the Vietnam War.

Yet here we come to hard lines. Solicitor General Erwin Griswold grappled with this for the Government in the Pentagon Papers case where, arguably, the publication might assimilate more to release of troop movements than to political discussion. As another quite unrelated illustration of great difficulty, at the current term of the Supreme Court, the largest single question will be the relation of reverse discrimination to the Equal Protection Clause.

I stake out these commonly accepted problems only to suggest how we come to their solution. I do not believe that we can, with proper faith to the forefathers, answer those questions pragmatically. While we cannot look backward for much help from the founding fathers on the precise issue, we can look backward to the approach they took. The contract we have made commits us to tackle these problems with an idealistic, natural law spirit, a spirit which for all its looseness is considerably harder than pragmatism. Insofar as philosophy can get us over the hard spots, the question is not what would have been the James approach, but what would have been the answer of Socrates if he had thought about the problem at all.

This approach, I trust, will not be regarded as merely devoutly quaint. Transportation may have changed from the ox to the space shuttle, but the instruments of Stuart tyranny are always with us. The free speech which concerned Milton does not exist for most of the population of the world today. Freedom from self-incrimination is not an odd relic of a distant past; torture is rampant all over the world. Free and fair trial with a right of confrontation? Would that every American could read the record of the trial of Daniel and Sinyavsky in Russia. As for equal protection of the laws, we are but an inch on the scale of time removed from Hitler. I began with Einstein; let me end with his observation on this point. "The lessons of history—especially the very latest chapters—are all too plain."[29]

From the pragmatic as well as the idealistic vantage point, we need an absolute adherence to the great values of our inheritance.

Notes

1. M. WHITE, SCIENCE AND SENTIMENT IN AMERICA 3 (1972).
2. C. BECKER, THE DECLARATION OF INDEPENDENCE (1942).
3. C. BRINTON, IDEAS AND MEN 496 (1950).
4. J. JEANS, PHYSICS AND PHILOSOPHY 2 (1958). Hillary Putnam, whose essay, *A Philosopher Looks at Quantum Mechanics*, demonstrates that he sees a good deal of quantum mechanics and no philosophy; the essay is published in BEYOND THE EDGE OF CERTAINTY 75 (R. Colodny ed., 1965).
5. Letter, New York Times Magazine Section, Sept. 11, 1977, p. 32.
6. *Recollections of Max Born* (III. *Reflections*), BULL. ATOM. SCIENTISTS 3 (Nov. 1965).
7. A. Petersen, *The Philosophy of Niels Bohr*, BULL. ATOM. SCIENTISTS 9 (1963).
8. R. Oppenheimer, *A Talk in Chicago*, BULL. ATOM. SCIENTISTS 4, 6 (Oct., 1963).
9. BULL. ATOM. SCIENTISTS 20, 21 (Sept. 1977).

10. The passage is taken from Einstein's *Essay on Freedom* in A. EINSTEIN, OUT OF MY LATER YEARS 18 (1950).

11. A. EINSTEIN, IDEAS AND OPINIONS 40 (1954).

12. While he agrees with this proposition, Professor David Kaye of Arizona State University Law School, a friendly critic, observes, "when Einstein does comment on social matters, it is not clear from the quotation you have selected that he actually espouses an idealist or natural law moral philosophy. His treatment of 'fundamental value judgments' is, for instance, consistent with ethical egoism or with the ethical emotivism of the Vienna Circle. His view of intellectual endeavor sounds more like the perfectionism of Aristotle than the idealism of Plato."

13. Another and distinctly different approach in the social contract tradition is R. NOZICK, ANARCHY, STATE AND UTOPIA (1974).

14. R. DWORKIN, TAKING RIGHTS SERIOUSLY vii (1977).

15. D. Shapiro, *Mr. Justice Rehnquist: A Preliminary Review*, 90 HARV. L. REV. 293 (1976) seems to me too harsh a stricture on a Justice who is attempting to go somewhere.

16. While I find Meiklejohn's analysis helpful here, my critic, Professor Kaye, states his difference well: "I question whether Socrates' stingy theory of civil disobedience is actually reflected in the Declaration of Independence. Admittedly, a social contract theory (Locke's) is, but these two theories may not be identical. Socrates' 'inalienable right' to free speech is not very powerful if it countenances capital punishment for its exercise."

17. G. ANASTAPOLO, THE CONSTITUTIONALIST 39, 44 (1971).

18. This concept of the Bill of Rights includes the propositions of the first section of the Fourteenth Amendment. Due process of course is in both the original Bill of Rights and the later Amendment; the concept of equality is in the Declaration of Independence and in the French Bill of Rights of 1790; and I, at least, have no doubts but that the concept of "privileges and immunities" in 1866 was intended to include the original Bill of Rights in its totality. See Frank & Munro, 50 COLUM. L. REV. 131 and n. 4 (1950), *revised and reprinted* in ONE HUNDRED YEARS OF THE FOURTEENTH AMENDMENT 49 (Gerard, ed., 1973).

19. A. MEIKLEJOHN, POLITICAL FREEDOM (1960).

20. For a good development see Dilliard, *The Individual and the Bill of Absolute Rights*, in HUGO BLACK 97 (S. Strickland, ed., 1967).

21. Barenblatt v. United States, 360 U.S. 109, 151 (1959).

22. A. BICKEL, THE MORALITY OF CONSENT 3 (1975).

23. Abrams v. United States, 250 U.S. 616, 630 (1919) (Holmes, J., dissenting).

24. Gunther, *Learned Hand and the Origins of Modern First Amendment Doctrine*, 27 STAN. L. REV. 719 (1975).

25. J. DEWEY, PROBLEMS OF MEN 118-21 (1946).

26. TITUS, LIVING ISSUES IN PHILOSOPHY 272 (1970).

27. *See* Rochin v. California, 342 U.S. 165 (1952), in which Justice Frankfurther for the Court held invalid a conviction obtained by pumping out the stomach of the defendant on the ground that such conduct "shocked the conscience".

28. T. EMERSON, THE SYSTEM OF FREEDOM OF EXPRESSION (1970).

29. A. EINSTEIN, OUT OF MY LATER YEARS, 170, 171.

Judicial Review in America: Some Reflections

I. Opening Statement

By Charles E. Wyzanski, Jr.*

There is always the risk, particularly in law schools, that persons start with the totally false assumption that the Constitution is the province of the lawyers. After all, as C. H. McIlwain, Corwin and others have reminded us, the term "constitution" was not by any means originally a lawyer's term. I am not referring to the usage of Aristotle, who after all used the word *politeia* not meaning constitution but meaning the organization of the *polis*. The first time, according to the *Oxford English Dictionary*, that the word "constitution" came into the English language was perhaps in the 12th century in connection with the constitutions of Clarendon which, whatever else they are, are not primarily lawyers' documents.

In the 17th century when the word had a little larger vogue, what it contemplated primarily was the establishment or organization or body of the government, looked at not so much in legal as in political terms. Moreover, I think it is quite clear that there is a grave danger that if we think of the Constitution exclusively in terms of constitutional law, we shall lose some of its most important symbolic, as well as practical, values to our society. Now I am fully aware that whether one approaches constitutions from a political and historical or a legal angle, there is an inherent ambiguity or polarity in the subject. Lord Acton, perhaps in one sense the most philosophical of all historians, in a lecture which perhaps he would not choose to have remembered as one of his greatest—one on the Civil War—called attention to the fact that inherently the Constitution of the United States had a fundamental ambiguity because of the contradiction between the powers it granted and the inalienable rights it preserved. In this connection, I cannot forebear to tell a story which perhaps some of you know.

Professor Kurt Gödel, the greatest of living mathematical logicians and for many years an ornament of the Institute for Advanced Study at Princeton, when he arrived in this country was told by his then colleague, Professor Albert Einstein, that it would be a good idea if Gödel, who came from Eastern Europe, followed the example of Einstein and, upon becoming a member of the faculty of the Institute at Princeton, became a citizen of the United States. Gödel, when his petition for naturalization was about to be heard, was aware that he would be examined by naturalization officials who would inquire about his understanding of the Constitution of the United States. So he studied the Constitution. Then he came around to Professor Einstein and said, "Professor Einstein, I'm sorry, I can't take the oath." Professor Einstein replied, "What do you mean Professor Gödel, you can't take the oath?" Professor Gödel said, "You know I am a logician and how can I take the oath to support an internally inconsistent document."

*Senior Federal Judge, United States District Court, Boston, Massachusetts. This is a reporter's transcript of what Judge Wyzanski said without manuscript or notes and does not purport to be a finished product. It obviously was designed to provoke and did provoke discussion from the floor. (Editor's note)

But now it is my duty to address myself not to the Constitution primarily in its political or historical but in its legal aspect. I suppose that everyone would expect that I would begin with some recognition of the historical aspect of the origin of the judicial practice, if not usurpation, of review of statutes and executive action from the point of view of the validity of such action under the Constitution of the United States.

I am not going to undertake to show you that I have read Wechsler and Hart and know a list of the new authorities. Nor do I intend to talk about that greatest of all legal teachers—Chancellor George Wythe who early in the experience he had as a judge in Virginia laid down the proposition that the judges had the power to set aside as invalid, acts of the legislature which were repugnant to the Constitution. I am not going to take you on an excursion to Pennsylvania to visit Judge Gibson, nor am I going to pause over the details of *Marbury v. Madison* to challenge its precise reasoning and to try to show the illogicality, even if the necessity, of the opinion.

What I think you really expect from me is an awareness that following *Marbury v. Madison* there was not until the *Dred Scott* case a single instance in which the Supreme Court of the United States declared unconstitutional an act of Congress. Not for want of opportunity, but maybe in part for want of courage. At any rate, those who will look at the trembling John Marshall, as a witness at the time of a threatened removal of Samuel Chase following his impeachment, will wonder whether the Court felt confident that it could exercise satisfactorily the powers claimed in *Marbury v. Madison.*

There then followed a period, not altogether fortunate, in which the Supreme Court showed, shall I say, greater courage or greater folly. In any event, we all know of *Pollock v. Farmer's Loan & Trust Co.* in which the Federal Income Tax Law was set aside in an opinion by the Supreme Court. Moreover, we are fully aware, of course, of actions taken by the nine men whom we then thought old in the period of Franklin Roosevelt.

But let us not suppose that the doctrines of judicial review declaring statutes unconstitutional did in practice lead to anything like what we today accept as the normal volume of litigation on the Constitution. As a student in the Harvard Law School, I had the man who was surely at the time the greatest teacher of constitutional law, not Felix Frankfurter but Thomas Reed Powell. Powell was the teacher of the great teachers of your generation: Freund, Hart, Bickel, Gunther, Kurland, Nathan Nathanson and others.

Professor Powell said to our class in constitutional law in the year 1929–30, "if any of you in your final examination cite the Equal Protection Clause, you will automatically have 5% deducted from your grade for there is no case of importance in which the decision truly turned on that clause."

When, the next year, I was law clerk for Judge Augustus Hand and the year-and-a-half following, law clerk for Judge Learned Hand in the United States Court of Appeals for the Second Circuit, unless my memory betrays me, there was not one case in which the Court of Appeals for the Second Circuit decided a question of constitutional law—so small was the volume of such litigation a mere half century ago.

Professor Commager has also reminded us, in the published lectures he gave in 1943 at the University of Virginia, of how very reticent the Court once was to declare governmental acts unconstitutional. There he pointed out that there were virtually no cases at that time in which the Supreme Court had ruled on a constitutional basis, with respect to national as distinguished from state law, to support minority rights against majority rule. There was a change and yet, not so rapid as many think.

In 1955, I had the good fortune to be a participant in a conference on constitutional law held by Harvard Law School in order to celebrate an anniversary of John Marshall—a rather contrived conference because the date really did not relate to much in John Marshall's life. It was, nevertheless, a very happy occasion for bringing people together who had a common interest in the Constitution. To show you how early in the Warren administration of the Court this conference occurred, I might tell you that one of the more pleasing photographs in the bound volume shows a happy Chief Justice talking with a happy Justice Frankfurter, both gaily smiling.

It was the year after *Brown v. Board of Education* and long before its progeny could be discerned upon the horizon. It was before *Baker v. Carr.* No one could have foreseen that Frank Johnson, that eminent federal judge, would in *Wyatt v. Stickney* undertake to operate or at least provide regulations for the operation of mental institutions in the state of Alabama. None could have been able to foresee that a truly great judge, Senior Circuit Judge Elbert Tuttle, would write for a panel and receive the approval of, believe it or not, then Circuit Judge Griffin Bell for an opinion in which it was determined that the town of Shaw, at the suit of one Hawkins, was bound to furnish equal facilities with respect to public services in areas in which indigent blacks and affluent whites lived. Who could have guessed that a court as evenly balanced as Judge Friendly in the center, Judge Lumbard on the right and Judge Feinberg on the left, would decide in *Beal v. Lindsey* that there was validity in the doctrine laid down in the Fifth Circuit in *Hawkins v. Shaw?*

Now those of you who suppose that the explanation is as naive as Judge Johnson of Alabama has sought to make it appear in his Sibley lecture at the University of Georgia, ought to have your attention called to a statement of Pascal. Maintained Pascal, "judges and bishops should never tell the truth lest there be no established law and no established religion." There can be very little doubt that Judge Johnson is sophisticated enough to be aware that although he begins his article with pages about John Marshall and the different views of Spencer Roane and other opponents of *Marbury v. Madison,* there is a great difference—practically, politically, and philosophically—between what the Supreme Court of the United States did in 1803 and what has been done in the last two decades. Surely we know that to set aside an act of Congress on the ground that it is unconstitutional may be nothing more than to wipe off the books an *ultra vires* act. But we also know that when one talks about the series of cases following *Brown* or when one talks of *Baker* in its application, or when one deals with *Wyatt,* or when one lays down in regulation form as though they were rules for the nation—the doctrine set forth in *Miranda* —or when one divides into trimesters the abortion period for state legislation, one is *governing* society, one is not merely wiping the slate clean of an *ultra vires* act.

If Judge Johnson was trying to fool the public—which he wasn't—he surely did not fool Professor Alexander Bickel, nor Professor Archibald Cox, nor Professor Philip Kurland, nor Professor Ronald Dworkin, nor the professors of constitutional law. The next to the last of Professor Cox's lectures, the full text of the Holmes lectures of Bickel, and the recently published volume of Dworkin's articles all make it quite transparent that whether the professors approve or do not approve, they see that what we are now faced with is a degree of managerial, administrative, governing authority in the federal courts utilizing a doctrine which may have had its origin—as it no doubt did—in *Marbury v. Madison,* but which means something quite different.

We have here one of the most profound examples of the teaching of Alfred North Whitehead on the subject of symbolism in the 1927 lectures he gave at the University of Virginia. Whitehead reminded us that the way that great societies proceed is by treating sudden necessary important change with a due regard for the emotional and historical values of symbolism. For it is by symbols that we manage to handle those disruptive, creative advances which otherwise would tear apart a society and that those who know how to handle in a great and magnificent way, the problems of the social order, utilize the ancient symbol as a method of introducing what Whitehead calls "the arrow in the hand of the child."

The Constitution is the symbol through which we have operated in a most revolutionary manner. Now I do not want you to think that I suppose this was a revolution of some wicked conspiracy of men in black robes, not for a moment. The forces which brought about the change were far more profound than the thinking of any of even the most gifted of occupants of seats upon the high bench in Washington. No one realized this better than the man who is in my view the greatest lawyer whom I ever knew: John Lord O'Brian. In 1955, at the conference at Harvard to which I have referred, Mr. O'Brian already recognized what was happening. He noted, and I use his words, "the growth of the welfare state." He was fully conscious of the extent to which in the FDR and succeeding administrations we had crossed a great divide. He was keenly aware that the changes in our economic, social and political life — responsive to technical changes in commerce, transportation, communication and the manifold aspects of American civilization — had brought a centralization of power in Washington and laid out a vast number of new regulatory schemes in which it was evident that unless there were an increase in judicial power, there would be a great risk of despotism, tyranny and arbitrariness.

Moreover, at the period of time of which I am now speaking, there was in addition to the economic, social and political change, a fundamental ideological change of world dimensions. When in 1944 Franklin Roosevelt and Winston Churchill announced an Atlantic Charter, they were only a few years ahead of what happened in the United Nations when the Universal Declaration of Human Rights was adopted. Throughout the world as a whole, there came an awareness of new claims of rights. Not only the civic and political rights which could, if you like, be traced back certainly to Locke and if you like to the Stoics and if you are inventive, to the Greeks. There came as well for the first time, perhaps on a world scale, a recognition of the economic, social, and cultural claims called rights, which individuals assert and look to the government to perfect by giving them job security, Social Security, education, housing and the like. So that you have emerging, not only within the United States but everywhere, a set of new demands presenting new constitutional issues. It was then that the Supreme Court, like the rest of us, became aware that one of the three objects of the founders was the maintenance of a balance of power, and as the Court and the rest of us observed — through war and depression and war again — the Chief Executive was increasing in power.

Through the Sixteenth Amendment and its taxing power the Congress of the United States had become the master of the economy, with the subsidiary aid of the Commerce Clause when the taxing power was thought inadequate as a source of strength. The industrial and military complex had suddenly seemed to be an unlisted major power. The corporations operating on a world scale, the labor unions of a size never before contemplated, and pressure groups from ethnic and other sources were becoming factors of a kind that Hamilton and Madison and Jay never described when they talked about factions. And so, the Supreme Court, watching (consciously or unconsciously) all these increasingly powerful groups, found that its own role as a court must be magnified if one were really to keep a true balance of power.

I hope that I have made it clear that I do not think it was nine or ninety black robed gentlemen who are responsible for the new governing, managerial and administrative role of the federal courts. There are much more profound causes. Yet I do not want you to think that I suppose for one moment that the arguments are all in favor of the expansion and that there is nothing to be said to the contrary. I do not find all the arguments of equal weight.

Early on, as a Harvard product, I was told of James Bradley Thayer and his views, perhaps best expressed in his biography of John Marshall, and of the degree to which Thayer's views were shared at least nominally by Holmes, Brandeis, Frankfurter and company. According to this school of thought, it is a derogation of public participation, an interference with the voter and his democracy, for the judges to exercise ultimate power since it weakens and debilitates the citizenry. Nonsense! Does anybody who has really studied the record suppose that the opinions of the Supreme Court have *weakened* the citizenry? On the contrary, the opinions of the Supreme Court are among the great sources of the education of the citizenry. If anything, the total effect of judicial power in constitutional cases is to make the voter more knowlegeable and more responsible.

What about the objection raised again and again by Judge Learned Hand? He warns that if judges are to be given the power to handle constitutional cases with the freedom that has characterized the last decades, judges will be selected, not for their legal merit, but for their political vote. And so, is that a novelty? In the more than 60 years that the Council of the American Law Institute has existed—a body which, by common concession, has among its members some of the ablest judges, professors and lawyers of the country—only one president, Herbert Hoover, has ever named to the Supreme Court a member of the Council of the American Law Institute. Charles Evans Hughes and Justice Lewis Powell were presidents of the American Bar Association, but the truly great justices of the Supreme Court— Holmes, Brandeis, Black, if you like, Brennan, Douglas—would not have been selected, even in the case of Holmes, on the basis of a poll of professional opinion. When Holmes was nominated, the Massachusetts lawyers united to give him a present and the chairman of the committee, Moorfield Storey, suggested that the form of the gift should be a bas-relief because the lawyers didn't like Holmes.

The great judges have been selected because they were great fighters in the political area. Or if they weren't selected for that reason, that is the reason that they were great. Unless one has the love of battle and believes with Heraclitus that strife is the source of all things, he does not belong on the Supreme Court. *Vide* Cardozo, J.—the greatest of state court jurists but surely not the greatest of justices of the Supreme Court.

But then are there no good arguments against the managerial, administrative and like powers of this governing federal judiciary? Circuit Judge Shirley Hufstedler has called to our attention that the judicial forum is not a wholly satisfactory place in which to get all the evidence which sociologists, economists, political theorists and practical people generally would deem approriate. The rules do not really encourage judges to talk with mayors and governors and vice versa. It is not at all clear that a kind of controversy (in which no matter how many *amici curiae* are permitted to intervene) which is fundamentally an adversary proceeding between generally, only two parties, is the best way to deal with complicated questions of public policy. There is much to be said for Judge Hufstedler's skepticism. Those of us who live in Greater Boston might be able to add a few footnotes to Judge Hufstedler's observation.

Moreover, it is quite true that looked at generally, as Professor Commager has put it, the people of the United States have by their silence at least ratified the usurpation, if there were any, of the judiciary's seizure of managerial and like problems in a way never foreseen by Hamilton, Madison or Marshall. There is nonetheless a considerable undercurrent of not as yet joined dissidents. Do not be mistaken because you are academic, at least in part, in your interest that there are not large and important groups in our society who severally, if not collectively, are resistant with respect to the changes of the last two decades. I do not come to praise former president Nixon—that would be well beyond my capacity—but I do not think he was totally ignorant in the degree to which he thought there was a large body of dissatisfaction with the Supreme Court as it was constituted under Chief Justice Warren. We make a mistake, we who pretend to be intellectuals, if we think we are representative of public opinion. Not at all. And we would do very well to take more seriously than we are inclined to the views of Edmund Burke with respect to habit, custom and even inertia in connection with reform and the degree to which it can be effectuated rapidly.

Lord Acton was fond of pointing out what every athlete knows, that success is a matter of timing. One must not think that because one can dart rapidly intellectually, it follows that political bodies move rapidly. Now having stated some of the difficulties, what have I to say more concretely?

Would it not be happy—oh indeed it would—if the Executive and the Legislative would bear their fair share of the responsibility of taking the load. There are uncharted aspects of section 5 of the Fourteenth Amendment which have indicated to some, though not to all, that Congress has a large power to deal with the more perplexing of these problems by exercising its authority to enact legislation to implement that Amendment. So far, I haven't much reason to be hopeful in the light of the Omnibus Crime Bill of 1968—Congress seems not to be in the mood to work out sensible compromises and proposals. Yet, maybe, there is something to be hoped for in that a wide reading of *Katzenbach v. Morgan* would justify us in supposing that there is sufficient legal basis for Congressional action to implement the Fourteenth Amendment.

There is something else. Here I tread on ground which surely is going to invite rejoinder, it is a question of the pace at which a court can move. It was with admiration and emotional agreement that I considered Professor Commager's observations on *Rodriguez v. San Antonio Independent School District*. I likewise shared some of his admiration for Justice Marshall's dissent and some of his dissatisfaction with Justice Powell's majority opinion. But Justice Powell didn't say what I rather think was the dominant thought which lead to that 5 to 4 vote. When the courts are administering with such difficulty problems of desegregation in the various districts, is this just the time to tackle, in addition, the problems of financing schools throughout the Nation? Perhaps the time for this rightful claim had not yet come, lest the load the courts undertook would provoke an even more passionate disapproval than has already manifested itself in so many areas.

Let me hope that if there is a slowing down and a moderation, it is based on a principle—and the highest of principles. It was Lord Acton's belief, it was Toqueville's belief, it seems to me a sound belief, that the greatest contribution politically made by our country has been in its preservation of federalism. In the times of Acton and Toqueville the federal principle was more respected than today. When Holmes and Brandeis spoke of experiments in the insulated chambers of the state, they were pointing not only to the chance of adventure and experiment, but to the importance of local, no less than national, power.

Maybe, in spite of some of the arguments that I have heard, the Supreme Court of the United States will in *Bakke* have the good sense to decide that the Fourteenth Amendment does not stand in the way of local experiments so long as they are not directed with a pernicious motive. Hence, no matter whether there be doubt or not as to whether a measure for affirmative purposes is good policy, there is a reasonable degree of hope that experiments on a local basis will give us information which we do not now possess and which should not be foreclosed and that federalism should encourage those affirmative efforts made to deal with the difficult and impracticable problems.

You will see that in the last few sentences I have been invoking political, sociological or economic considerations apart from history. Those of us who recall when Benjamin Nathan Cardozo delivered the Storrs Lectures on "The Nature of The Judicial Process" will remember that one of his lectures was devoted to the role of history. We live in a generation where unfortunately too many people believe that Henry Ford is right, that history is bunk. There is a general tendency to doubt whether the past has much to tell us—believe it or not.

Judge Walter Hoffman, when head of the Federal Judicial Center, was called upon to prepare a list of books to be supplied to the new judges—over 100 in number—who were shortly to be appointed by the Carter administration. For their libraries, the Judicial Center intends to give them only such reports as have been published since 1950—Marshall, Taney, Holmes, Brandeis and Cardozo wrote no opinions after 1950.

There is a great myth, maybe one of the greatest, in *The Republic* of Plato where we are all, we living persons, said to be in a cave. According to the myth, the eternal ideas are moving behind us and casting shadows ahead. Most of us probably would reject the absolutist ideas in the platonic sense—the supposed principles which are good for all persons and at all places and forever. But is it not true that as we sit in the cave, we have in front of us the shadows of Plato himself, of the Stoics, of Cicero, of those who in the great religious struggles of the Middle Ages and the early Renaissance fought for toleration. Alongside them there are the persons who in England, before there was a Columbus, were responsible for the Magna Carta. What of the following history of the English and of the colonists? What of the work of Marshall, Taney, Holmes, Brandeis, and Black? Are we not ultimately to join the people in the back of the cave and may we not rightly expect that we shall be measured against their great height?

II. Response

By Frank R. Strong*

It takes a courageous soul to agree to serve as a devil's advocate following this great address from a truly great judge of our judicial system. I am not in complete disagreement with Judge Wyzanski. But I do suggest this: That a full understanding of what the Supreme Court of the United States has meant in history and what it ought to mean today requires an appreciation of the different levels at which it has historically operated.

Let me illustrate what I mean by drawing upon the difference to which Judge Wyzanski referred, the difference in time between *Marbury v. Madison* and *Dred Scott*. *Marbury v. Madison* is, I contend, in basic accord with early state court decisions beginning shortly after 1776, where constitutional review was exercised only in a defensive posture to protect the third branch of government from annihilation by inroads on the part of legislatures. When we come to *Dred Scott v. Sandford*—by the time of this unfortunate decision—Chief Justice Taney, in common with state courts, was asserting what I would call affirmative constitutional review. That is review where there is no threat to judicial engagement in traditional judicial functions as the third branch of government. The most outstanding state court precedent for the defensive type of review was the North Carolina case of *Bayard v. Singleton*.

In other words, once constitutional review secured a toe-hold it evolved from a purely defensive stance into one of much different dimension. In this new dimension the Court, and also state courts, proceed to assert that they have the final authority to determine a particular issue although the problem does not concern judicial operations but, rather, lies between the Executive and the Legislative departments, or between Federal and State gov-

*Cary C. Boshamer University Distinguished Professor, University of North Carolina at Chapel Hill. An expansion of the views expressed in this Reply can be found in Strong, *Bicentennial Benchmark: Two Centuries of Evolution of Constitutional Processes,* 55 N.C.L. REV. 1 (1976). (Editor's note)

ernments, or between Government and the Individual. Illustrations of the exercise of affirmative constitutional review are many and familiar.

This trend was initially resisted to some extent. But in time the public came to accept this new dimension of constitutional review, which should be carefully distinguished from judicial review. With the latter, review operates according to the traditional functions that courts exercise in any legal system, at least in any legal system of the western world. But while judicial power is vastly extended by embrasure of affirmative constitutional review, it purports to be exercised in conformance with a written text enunciating the constitutional principles of limitation of governmental power.

What is surfacing today Judge Wyzanski has described as a managerial matter. With due respect, however, that does not adequately identify the development. Rather, the move on the part of the Supreme Court of the United States—not so much the state courts—is openly to exercise this power of review of governmental action for constitutionality to achieve results that it believes are desirable for a given time and circumstance regardless of textual or historical basis in the Constitution. Consider, for example, what Judge Braxton Craven urged shortly before his very tragic death. For him the fact that a right was not provided for in the Constitution was not the end of the inquiry, but only the beginning.

There is major disagreement over the legitimacy of this latest concept of judicial power. As Judge Wyzanski has indicated, most of us are influenced by the great social and political concerns that agitate our times. Perhaps the other branches of government are not going to carry the burdens that they should assume if satisfactory solutions are to be found. But it does trouble me if the third century of our Nation is going to have as one of its major features the exercise of this newest dimension of constitutional review by the Supreme Court to the extent that is beginning to emerge. Judge Wyzanski made reference to Archibald Cox's Oxford Lectures, now in book form. At the very end of that small but powerful book, Professor Cox says that whereas he is willing to trust a town meeting, he has no confidence in what a state legislature does and even less in what the Congress of the United States does. He may be justified in his pessimism, but to find solution in judicial oligarchy is to me unjustified. I do not believe that this new development on the part of the judiciary is prudent or wise. If I can make any contribution to this exchange, it is that, despite the complexities of our time, we ought not to rush in and accept this new dimension without giving it some very, very careful consideration.

III. *Response*
BY HENRY STEELE COMMAGER*

I was delighted with some of Judge Wyzanski's recollections, particularly of that great scholar Thomas Reed Powell. I appeal to the Judge whether it is true that Professor Powell habitually opened his constitutional history lectures by advising the young men not to read the Constitution of the United States as it tended to confuse their minds. That is at least what we heard at Columbia University where he taught for so many years. I sometimes think that the members of the Supreme Court follow that advice. I could single out two or three who are particularly assiduous in their evasion of the Constitution.

*Woodruff Simpson Lecturer, Amherst College, Massachusetts.

There has been mention of the failure to pay attention to section 5 of the Fourteenth Amendment which gives authority to the Congress—indeed something of a mandate—to enforce the terms of the Fourteenth Amendment. By the same token, one of the great forgotten parts of the Constitution is the guarantee by the United States to every state of a republican form of government. This general guarantee assigned only to the Congress may emerge as one of the great sleepers of the Constitution and one which offers, to every student of law, extraordinary attractions. It does so because we do not yet know what a republican form of government is nor do we know what a guarantee is, or how the Congress guarantees. Thus, it opens up a very wide avenue of exploration on the part of the courts.

But, I want to address more seriously, though not at length, some of the many things that Judge Wyzanski discussed. I am reminded of that famous chapter in Lord Bryce's *American Commonwealth,* published in 1888, in which he contrasted the American and British constitutions (in the favor of the British) observing that the American Constitution was rigid and the British Constitution enormously flexible. There may have been some truth in that observation in the 1880's, which was in many ways an era of constitutional rigidity. But, I think, there is no truth to it in the longer historical perspective. What is extraordinary is how flexible the American Constitution has been. We have somehow managed with a rigid Constitution to achieve an important degree of flexibility. For better or worse, we have also managed with the separation of powers to mix all the powers so extricably that it is almost impossible to say where any one power should be exercised. So of course the judiciary is a legislative branch, it has been legislating since John Jay, not just since John Marshall and has always been something of a super constitutional convention. All of its important judgments have legislative features or implications to them. There is no way of preventing this. We can't put the judiciary back in the insulated chamber of simply judging.

The whole notion of separation of powers so rigidly stated in the eighteenth century provides that the Executive can never exercise the legislative and judicial powers; the Judiciary shall never exercise the executive or legislative, and so forth, "to the end that this shall be a government of laws and not of men." But of course, all have intervened in each other's powers from the very beginning and continue to do so.

Today the idea of federalism has grown far beyond what the original Founders intended. It is not that the federal government is usurping the power of the states. It is rather that all government is enlarging. There is further this paradox: so-called conservatives hold that everything possible should be returned to the local authority. Yet, that same conservative thought insists on having the largest military power in the world despite the fact that the greatest single centralizing force in our history has been the military. It is also, on the whole, so called conservative thought that ceaselessly champions the giant corporation and big business, which are the most nationalizing forces in our economy. I think it is true (there may be some exceptions), that federal centralization has almost invariably followed economic centralization, not anticipated it. The central government has been forced to act in order to control larger organizations of military and economic power or other kinds of power, labor, for example.

What is most extraordinary about our system is our ability to maintain the framework of the original Constitution while developing so many other institutions and activities to overcome successive difficulties. The growth of judicial power is not an isolated thing but must be put against that general background. It is not an aberration of American constitutional development, but an integral and normal part of that development. Other branches of the government inevitably accommodate themselves to the enormous changing situation of a national economy, world power, etc. So too the Judiciary must accommodate itself.

I return to a point I elaborated upon in my essay on the Fourteenth Amendment, that the American public—which is not really constitutionally minded, though it reveres the

Constitution without quite knowing what it reveres—wants to get on with the job and is impatient with doctrinaire and theoretical distinctions of one kind or another. It expects the Executive to exercise other than executive powers, takes for granted that the national legislature will intervene in local affairs and also that the states and localities will operate in ways that benefit—and no doubt harm—the national interest and national powers. After all, that Minnesota could not or would not stop the Zenith Mining Company from pouring 60,000 tons of impurities into Lake Superior, affected not only local, but national and international interests.

The ingenuity of our constitutional system is dramatized in its ability to accommodate itself to extraordinary and unforeseen developments that confront us. These unforeseen developments in the three branches of the government, and in a complex federal system, are now even more complicated because our federal system is part of a world of global systems. Today no major problem can be solved by the United States acting alone. We shall have to make concessions to the needs of the rest of the globe. I foresee a continuation of such accommodation if only the public will allow it and not be bemused by doctrinaire considerations.

I am not now so concerned with the growth of judicial review as I was 40 years ago. It has become a normal part of our technique of constitutional accommodation, and I think, on balance, it does less harm than good. The harm it does to the operation of democracy has been exaggerated; (I have myself tended to exaggerate it) just as we exaggerate (with Professor Cox) the virtues of the New England town meeting, and of state legislatures. Generally, I think what we are seeing now is a Congress which is doing rather a better job than any state legislature, certainly in the realm of civil liberties, and a Court which with all its failings, is doing a better job than the Congress and the Executive.

The point I want to make is rather simple: ours is a very mixed up system and we cannot expect it to fit back into its original slots. We cannot expect the twentieth century nor the twenty-first to go back to the Newtonian age of politics. Our constitutional system was initially set up to embody 17th century notions of the nature of the universe and of law. That system was accommodated, somehow, to the relations of men and governments, just at the time when we were entering into the Industrial Age and, later, the Dynamo Age where most of these notions were to prove somewhat irrelevant. Because of the extraordinary success of the Founding Fathers in almost all matters of constitutional law and institutions, we have been able to meet the challenges of our times with unexpected success. The Founding Fathers did not know evolution, but embraced it; they did not use the word "pragmatism" but they embraced a pragmatic philosophy. "Reason may mislead us" said John Dickinson, "experience must be our guide."

IV. Response

BY MAX LERNER*

This evening and this afternoon, I was struck by a paradox. My friend Henry Commager, who is not a judge, has some equanimity about the power of the judges—he *does* want the judges to have power (particularly under the Equal Protection Clause) and to govern. Conversely, my friend Charles Wyzanski, who is a judge, *does not* want the judges to

*Columnist, New York Post; Distinguished Professor of Human Behavior, School of Human Behavior, U.S. International University, San Diego, California.

have power and to govern. I've been trying to resolve the paradox in my mind, and it's not very easy.

I have known Henry and Charles for many years and we've been through the wars together: the New Deal wars and the later ones—the constitutional crises, not only of the "nine old men" and the Roosevelt court plan and Hugo Black's appointment after the plan failed of passage but also after the Court had in effect submitted. Then there was the crisis of FDR's presidential power as he used it both in the New Deal and in the war, and of the presidential power of the later presidents as well. Note that the presidential story is as much a part of our constitutional crises as the story of the judicial power.

Within the past few decades we have witnessed the concentration of power in the Executive and the bureaucracy. Henry described well the framework of social changes which brought it about. But I must add—and I don't think Henry would disagree—that while these social changes brought it about, a number of us including him and myself, did our best to help it along. We were very much on the side of that increasing presidential power. As creatures of our time we are all creatures of the political climate and the social dynamics of the era in which we work, live and have our being.

Henry and I both favored President Roosevelt's court plan. Why? I think it was because we were determined to get certain social programs and certain social results. In my first book, published around that time, I called that program "a democratic collectivism." I was deeply wedded to it, and I think Henry was, although he used different terms for it. We thought that the Court was obstructing the achievement of the result we wanted, that it was an obstructive minority. It was getting in the way of the will of the majority.

The symbol of that majority was a strong President. We wanted to help him overcome the resistance of the little group of old and willful men on the Court, and in one way or another we did. My perception of the Court at that time was one of good guys and bad guys, with the bad guys overwhelmingly swamping the good guys.

There were Holmes and Brandeis, now and then there was Stone, and in a very few cases Hughes joined the others in voting for civil liberties. Mostly it was Holmes and Brandeis against the rest. Our model of reality was that of a moral dualism. As we perceived the Court, that's how we saw it.

What we liked particularly about Holmes and Brandeis was not that they wanted to exercise judicial power; actually it was the others who were exercising judicial power in striking down a whole array of legislative acts for social welfare. The thing we liked about Holmes and Brandeis was their libertarianism. But their libertarianism embraced the doctrine of judicial restraint. They were willing to have the Legislature have its say as the spokesman of majority will. That was the climate of the time. Chief Justice Stone expressed it best when he told his brethren, "the only restraint we have is our self-restraint."

Are we today embracing again the theory that there are no limits to the judicial power unless they are self-imposed limits? I don't want to squeeze Judge Wyzanski's words into my own view that this is a questionable development, but that is how I understand him. It is questionable not only for the society as a whole, but it is a burden that we ought not to place upon the judges themselves.

I look back, as we all do, to that earlier period when we were hot for the legislative power. We were upbeat about it as against the judicial power. We were hot for presidential power as against both legislative and judicial power.

Note that this was before the Roosevelt Court, which became the New Deal Court in its majority. It was before the Warren Court, which (after a break) became an extension of the Roosevelt Court. They changed our views about the judicial power. These were courts we could identify with. I identified strongly with the Roosevelt Court, even though I had been against the previous Court that had obstructed the New Deal legislation. And pretty much the entire liberal community identified with the Warren Court. Note also that this was before the outcry against the "imperial Presidency" that reached its height in the Nixon Administrations.

All this in turn was before the most revolutionary decade in American history—that of the 1960's, with its activisms, its revolts of minority groups, and its women's revolutions.

Now the climate has changed, we are now down on presidential power and are skeptical of legislatures. Our scepticism is the greater because we feel that they often yield to majorities among the people of whose views we disapprove. We fear that they will yield to the popular view on crime, on capital punishment, on school district plans, on prayer in the schools, on abortion. We are upbeat on the courts because they have been using their authority to resist these majorities. Note that I have been tracing the successive climates of opinion within which we have changed our perception of the role of President, legislatures, courts.

I listened to a number of panels today: one on criminal justice, one on the First Amendment and the media, one on privacy, a statement on the Equal Rights Amendment. I profited from all. But running through the current of my mind there was something curious.

A few years ago a number of us were invited to the Centennial celebration at M.I.T. Judge Wyzanski was chairman of the group I was assigned to. Aldous Huxley was also a member. For a week we talked but Huxley never said a word until the last day. Charles then said to him, "Mr. Huxley, every member of this group has been talking but you've been sitting there saying nothing." Huxley unlimbered that long, gangly frame of his, and he said: "That's true Judge Wyzanski. While you've all been talking I've been listening to you. But mostly I've been listening to myself." He spoke of the subcurrents we must attend to, in our own minds, during any group discussion. In a way, I have been doing this a little during this Conference. There was a subcurrent running through my mind and I want to describe it to you.

It had to do with the word "they." As I listened I seemed to hear that "they" are outside, "they" are irrational, "they" are constantly pressuring legislatures, "they" are ignorant, "they" are prejudiced, "they" are boorish, "they" don't care about First Amendment rights, "they" don't much care about the right of the accused nor about privacy, "they" are on the side of intrusions. Some of "them" are yahoos, and they contrast with "we." "We" are rather different: "we" are enlightened, "we" have the right opinions about freedom and equality and privacy and the First Amendment. Oh, there are differences between us, but differences within a frame of consensus.

It is crucial for us not to fall into this "we" and "they" dualism. Large groups of people may be misled by it and they can become dangerous and destructive. We saw it in the time of the Nazis in Germany. "They" may destroy a whole social fabric. "They" may be a temporary majority that can doom a society.

But we must face the fact that there are many people, often majorities, in our society who do have these views. These are not views that "we" agree with. If we are going to be tough minded however, we have to face the reality principle about "them." It means facing the Gorgon head, the coil of serpents so terrible to behold that when you look at them they turn you to stone. But if we are going to be tough minded, we have to face that fact. I have to ask who these people are and what they stand for.

If "culture" means the ways of living, thinking, perceiving by the many—and their belief systems—I think these people are in the culture. Not the "high" culture, but the culture. They have grown into it and it has grown into them. It is their perception and belief systems we must reckon with—how they see crime and punishment, how they see the media, the courts, the Presidency.

We once had the mystique of the people. Lincoln had it, Whitman had it. What has happened to it? Why is it that so many liberal intellectuals seem to have lost that sense of a certain strength in the people over long periods of time? We once had a skepticism about the judicial elite. What has happened to it? We once had a belief in presidential leadership. What has happened to it?

What hit me hardest in Judge Wyzanski's remarks was when he spoke of the aggressive-destructive forces which might tear a society apart. He used Whitehead as his starting point. It sent me back to Freud speaking, in *Civilization and Its Discontents,* about Eros and Thanatos, the god of love, the god of death. The god of love and therefore of life and the life affirming. The god of death and therefore of the life denying. Both these gods, said Freud, are locked within each of us in a deathly embrace. That's true of our civilization as well.

I don't think we can assume that it is inevitably going to come out all right. I agree with Henry when he speaks of the flexibility we have shown up until now. One of the things about the civilization that makes it survive is its flexibility. If it is rigid, it dies. But it does not follow that we will therefore continue to show this kind of flexibility. If the powers of any one of these groups—the Executive, the Legislative, the Judicial—become really swollen, it does not follow that they will be contained and restrained.

The symbols that Whitehead spoke of—the myths, the enduring human experiences which are personified and dramatized in legendary figures and stories—all these are part of us. Within each of us there is the agonized struggle between the life affirming and the life denying forces. The importance of the myths is that they dramatize this struggle.

The health of our society demands that we transcend the destructive elements of this struggle in a dialectic of thesis and antithesis, leading to synthesis. Lewis Thomas, in his remarkable book on *The Lives of a Cell,* called himself a cell-watcher. I suggest that all of us have to become civilization-watchers. Part of the viability of our civilization is very likely to consist of our capacity as members of elite groups—political, judicial, and legislative elites—always to touch the earth again.

I speak here of the Antaeus myth, the giant who was invincible as long as he could touch the earth. If you could lift him up you could crush him. But if he could touch the earth again, he remained invincible.

When we have finished all our discussion about power and law and the power groups, it isn't enough to reject "them" out there in the culture. Rather must we be aware of what "they" are thinking and reckon with it, and face the reality of it. In short, we must touch the earth again.

Index